AMERICAN HISTORY
VOLUME II

Reconstruction
Through the Present

Twelfth Edition

Editor

Robert James Maddox
Pennsylvania State University
University Park

Robert James Maddox, distinguished historian and professor of American history at Pennsylvania State University, received a B.S. from Fairleigh Dickinson University in 1957, an M.S. from the University of Wisconsin in 1958, and a Ph.D. from Rutgers in 1964. He has written, reviewed, and lectured extensively, and is widely respected for his interpretations of presidential character and policy.

A Library of Information from the Public Press

Cover illustration by Mike Eagle

The Dushkin Publishing Group, Inc.
Sluice Dock, Guilford, Connecticut 06437

The Annual Editions Series

Annual Editions is a series of over 55 volumes designed to provide the reader with convenient, low-cost access to a wide range of current, carefully selected articles from some of the most important magazines, newspapers, and journals published today. Annual Editions are updated on an annual basis through a continuous monitoring of over 300 periodical sources. All Annual Editions have a number of features designed to make them particularly useful, including topic guides, annotated tables of contents, unit overviews, and indexes. For the teacher using Annual Editions in the classroom, an Instructor's Resource Guide with test questions is available for each volume.

VOLUMES AVAILABLE

Africa
Aging
American Government
American History, Pre-Civil War
American History, Post-Civil War
Anthropology
Biology
Business Ethics
Canadian Politics
China
Commonwealth of Independent States
Comparative Politics
Computers in Education
Computers in Business
Computers in Society
Criminal Justice
Drugs, Society, and Behavior
Dying, Death, and Bereavement
Early Childhood Education
Economics
Educating Exceptional Children
Education
Educational Psychology
Environment
Geography
Global Issues
Health
Human Development
Human Resources
Human Sexuality
India and South Asia

International Business
Japan and the Pacific Rim
Latin America
Life Management
Macroeconomics
Management
Marketing
Marriage and Family
Microeconomics
Middle East and the Islamic World
Money and Banking
Nutrition
Personal Growth and Behavior
Physical Anthropology
Psychology
Public Administration
Race and Ethnic Relations
Social Problems
Sociology
State and Local Government
Third World
Urban Society
Violence and Terrorism
Western Civilization, Pre-Reformation
Western Civilization, Post-Reformation
Western Europe
World History, Pre-Modern
World History, Modern
World Politics

Library of Congress Cataloging in Publication Data
Main entry under title: Annual editions: American history, volume two.
  1. United States—History—Periodicals. 2. United States—Historiography—Periodicals. 3. United States—Civilization—Periodicals. I. Title: American history, volume two.
ISBN 1-56134-188-6   973'.05   75-20755

Twelfth Edition

Manufactured by The Banta Company, Harrisonburg, Virginia 22801

Printed on Recycled Paper

Editors/ Advisory Board

To the Reader

In publishing ANNUAL EDITIONS we recognize the enormous role played by the magazines, newspapers, and journals of the *public press* in providing current, first-rate educational information in a broad spectrum of interest areas. Within the articles, the best scientists, practitioners, researchers, and commentators draw issues into new perspective as accepted theories and viewpoints are called into account by new events, recent discoveries change old facts, and fresh debate breaks out over important controversies.

Many of the articles resulting from this enormous editorial effort are appropriate for students, researchers, and professionals seeking accurate, current material to help bridge the gap between principles and theories and the real world. These articles, however, become more useful for study when those of lasting value are carefully *collected, organized, indexed,* and *reproduced* in a *low-cost format,* which provides easy and permanent access when the material is needed. That is the role played by *Annual Editions.* Under the direction of each volume's *Editor,* who is an expert in the subject area, and with the guidance of an *Advisory Board,* we seek each year to provide in each ANNUAL EDITION a current, well-balanced, carefully selected collection of the best of the public press for your study and enjoyment. We think you'll find this volume useful, and we hope you'll take a moment to let us know what you think.

Historical controversies among professional scholars have long been the norm. In recent years many such disputes have been aired in newspapers, popular magazines, and on television. The 500th anniversary of Columbus's voyage to the new world provides a case in point. Not so long ago, Columbus was treated in the history books as an intrepid sailor who "discovered" the New World. Columbus Day was the occasion for pupils in primary schools to put on skits and for parades down Main Street. Now Columbus is reviled by some as a villain who paved the way for despoliation of a paradise. Which one was he? Could he have been a combination of both? That is what the study of history can *help* tell us, although ultimate truths can never be known. A decision each of us has to make is whether we want to learn what really happened (as far as we can), or whether we are seeking versions of history that make us feel good about ourselves.

The essays included in *American History* are intended to serve several purposes: to afford fuller treatments of events, people, or issues that can be dealt with only briefly in textbooks, and to cover some areas that may not be mentioned at all in textbooks. The final section, "New Directions for American History," contains articles that attempt to assess what is likely to occur in the future (though based on what already has happened). In those cases where the editor believed it advisable, opposing views have been presented within the same article. It is hoped that students will be able to decide for themselves through critical reading or will be stimulated to seek other sources.

This volume contains a number of features designed to make it "user friendly" for students, researchers, and professionals. These include a *topic guide* to locate articles on specific subjects; the *table of contents extracts* that summarize each essay with key concepts in bold italics; and a comprehensive *index.* Articles are organized into six units. Each unit is preceded by an overview that provides background for informed reading of the articles, emphasizes critical issues, and presents *challenge questions.*

There will be a new edition of *American History* in two years, and more than half the existing essays will be replaced. The number of publications renders it impossible to consider all the articles that might be suitable for inclusion—sometimes they turn up in the most unlikely places. We seek two kinds of help from readers of this edition: We welcome your opinions of the selections included so as to help us judge which should be retained, and we urge you to recommend others (or better yet, send along a copy) of those you think should be included in the next edition. Please complete and mail the postpaid article rating form included in the back of the book. Your suggestions will be carefully considered and appreciated.

Robert James Maddox
Editor

Contents

Unit 1

Reconstruction and the Gilded Age

Five articles examine the development of the United States after the Civil War. Society was changed by expansion, technology, merchandising, and agricultural development.

The concepts in bold italics are developed in the article. For further expansion please refer to the Topic Guide and the Index.

Unit 2

The Emergence of Modern America

Seven articles review the beginnings of modern America. Key issues of this period are examined, including immigration, racial consciousness, and poverty in the early twentieth century.

The concepts in bold italics are developed in the article. For further expansion please refer to the Topic Guide and the Index.

Unit
3

From Progressivism to the 1920s

Seven articles examine American culture in the early twentieth century. The economy began to reap the benefits of technology, women gained the right to vote, Henry Ford ushered in mass production, and the Jazz Age arrived.

The concepts in bold italics are developed in the article. For further expansion please refer to the Topic Guide and the Index.

Unit 4

From the Great Depression to World War II

Six selections discuss the severe economic and social
trials of the Great Depression of the thirties, the slow
recovery process, and the enormous impact of World
War II on America's domestic and foreign social
consciousness.

The concepts in bold italics are developed in the article. For further expansion please refer to the Topic Guide and the Index.

Unit 5

From the Cold War to the 1990s

Nine articles cover the post-World War II period in the United States. The Truman Doctrine influenced America's foreign policy, equality of education became the law of the land, the Vietnam War changed the way America looked at conflict, Nixon's Watergate tested the United States' system of balanced political power, and the poor of America increasingly affected society's conscience.

Unit 6

New Directions for American History

Six articles discuss the current state of American society and the role the United States plays in the world.

The concepts in bold italics are developed in the article. For further expansion please refer to the Topic Guide and the Index.

Topic Guide

This topic guide suggests how the selections in this book relate to topics of traditional concern to American history students and professionals. It is useful for locating articles that relate to each other for reading and research. The guide is arranged alphabetically according to topic. Articles may, of course, treat topics that do not appear in the topic guide. In turn, entries in the topic guide do not necessarily constitute a comprehensive listing of all the contents of each selection.

TOPIC AREA	TREATED IN:	TOPIC AREA	TREATED IN:
African Americans	11. Brownsville Affray 12. George Washington Carver 15. America's Black Press 17. When White Hoods Were in Flower 27. Trumpet of Conscience 36. Disuniting of America *and* Painful Demise of Eurocentrism 38. Black and White in America	**Diplomacy**	8. Our First Southeast Asian War 22. 1941 31. Lessons From a Lost War 34. Hollow Victory 39. America and Russia
		Eisenhower, Dwight D.	28. Ike Age
Anti-Semitism	9. Anti-Semitism in American Culture	**Environment**	40. Cleaning Up the Environment
		Farming	4. Great Oklahoma Land Rush 12. George Washington Carver
Asians	14. Angel Island 23. Racism and Relocation	**Ford, Henry**	18. Citizen Ford
Business	18. Citizen Ford	**Government**	2. "Master Fraud of the Century" 6. Cycle of Reform 13. Woodrow Wilson, Politician 20. 'Give Us Roosevelt' 30. Watergate Redux 33. How the Seventies Changed America
Carver, George	12. George Washington Carver		
Children	1. First Chapter of Children's Rights		
Culture	9. Anti-Semitism in American Culture 15. America's Black Press 16. What We Lost in the Great War 19. Media and Morality in the Twenties 21. Things to Come 27. 'If I'd Stood Up Earlier . . .' 36. Disuniting of America *and* Painful Demise of Eurocentrism 38. Black and White in America	**Hayes, Rutherford B.**	2. "Master Fraud of the Century"
		Hispanics	36. Disuniting of America *and* Painful Demise of Eurocentrism
		Immigrants	7. Ellis Island 9. Anti-Semitism in American Culture 14. Angel Island 17. When White Hoods Were in Flower
		Indians	5. Geronimo
Depression, Great	20. 'Give Us Roosevelt' 21. Things to Come	**King, Martin Luther, Jr.**	29. Trumpet of Conscience
		Korean War	26. Forgotten War

TOPIC AREA	TREATED IN:	TOPIC AREA	TREATED IN:
Labor	20. 'Give Us Roosevelt'	**Roosevelt, Franklin D.**	11. Brownsville Affray 20. 'Give Us Roosevelt' 22. 1941 25. Face of Victory
Movies, The	19. Media and Morality in the Twenties	**Society**	1. First Chapter of Children's Rights 3. *These* Are the Good Old Days 9. Anti-Semitism in American Caricature 10. Fighting Poverty 19. Media and Morality in the Twenties 21. Things to Come 24. 'Since You Went Away' 25. Face of Victory 27. 'If I'd Stood Up Earlier . . .' 29. Trumpet of Conscience 33. How the Seventies Changed America 35. Suburban Century Begins 36. Disuniting of America *and* Painful Demise of Eurocentrism 38. Black and White in America
Multiculturalism	36. Disuniting of America *and* Painful Demise of Eurocentrism		
Native Americans	32. New Indian Politics		
Politics	2. "Master Fraud of the Century" 6. Cycle of Reform 13. Woodrow Wilson, Politician 20. 'Give Us Roosevelt' 30. Watergate Redux 32. New Indian Politics 33. How the Seventies Changed America 35. Suburban Century Begins 37. "Remember the Ladies"		
Progressivism	10. Fighting Poverty 13. Woodrow Wilson, Politician	**Technology**	21. Things to Come 40. Cleaning Up the Environment
Racism	5. Geronimo 8. Our First Southeast Asian War 11. Brownsville Affray 12. George Washington Carver 14. Angel Island 15. America's Black Press 17. When White Hoods Were in Flower 23. Racism and Relocation 29. Trumpet of Conscience 32. New Indian Politics 36. Disuniting of America *and* Painful Demise of Eurocentrism 38. Black and White in America	**Urban Problems**	3. *These* Are the Good Old Days 33. How the Seventies Changed America
		Vietnam War	31. Lessons From a Lost War
		War in the Desert	34. Hollow Victory
		West, The	4. Great Oklahoma Land Rush
		Women	10. Fighting Poverty 24. 'Since You Went Away' 37. "Remember the Ladies"
Reform	1. First Chapter of Children's Rights 6. Cycle of Reform 10. Fighting Poverty 13. Woodrow Wilson, Politician 20. 'Give Us Roosevelt' 29. Trumpet of Conscience	**World War II**	22. 1941 23. Racism and Relocation 24. 'Since You Went Away' 25. Face of Victory

Reconstruction and the Gilded Age

The Civil War was the bloodiest conflict in American history. The union was preserved and slavery abolished. But what lay in store for the millions of black people released from bondage? Some Northerners hoped to gain full equality for freedpeople through what became known as "Radical Reconstruction." Southern whites resisted with every means they had, including violence. In the end they won out, though at a great cost to the region in future decades. As Northern enthusiasm for Reconstruction faded, white Southerners were able to "redeem" their states, by which they meant to restore white domination and to deny civil rights to blacks. By 1877 federal troops were removed from the last three Southern states.

Westward expansion continued after the Civil War until the 1890 census reported that, for all practical purposes, there no longer was any frontier to settle. Miners, cattlemen, sheepherders, and farmers sought better lives for themselves and their families. Some succeeded—a few made huge fortunes—others failed. All these occupations were risky. Mines petered out, cold weather and storms ravaged herds, and a year of exhausting farm work could be destroyed when the locusts came. And successive waves of white settlements pushed Native Americans onto the least desirable lands set aside for them as "reservations." Some went peacefully, some resisted, but the number and firepower of whites proved irresistible.

American industry grew rapidly during the last 25 years of the nineteenth century. Corporations achieved size, wealth, and power that would have been undreamed of earlier. Labor and management clashed frequently over what "rights" workers had to determine working conditions and pay. Cities grew swiftly, usually with little or no planning. Immigrants from southern and eastern Europe crowded into slum areas, often living in cramped and unhealthy tenements without heat·or running water. Their languages, the clothes they wore, and their religious affiliations offended many Americans who wished to limit or close off this new immigration.

The "Gilded Age" produced contrasts of enormous wealth and abject poverty, rampant corruption and dedicated social reform, glitzy popular culture, and real accomplishment in art and literature.

"The First Chapter of Children's Rights" deals with a problem that remains controversial: To what extent are governmental agencies responsible for child abuse within families? In 1874 little Mary Ellen McCormack's eloquent testimony of how she was treated "changed our legal system's view of the rights of the child."

The election of 1876 was one of the most emotional in American history. Bitter memories of the Civil War remained fresh, and 16 years of Republican control appeared likely to end. Controversy over election returns led to a constitutional crisis that was not resolved until shortly before inauguration day. "Master Fraud of the Century: The Disputed Election of 1876" tells how this political mess was settled through compromises, one of them being an end to Radical Reconstruction in the South.

One article in this section deals with the process of settling the West. One of the most widely held interpretations of American history stated that the existence of a frontier had exercised great influence on the way this nation developed. "The Great Oklahoma Land Rush of 1889" provides an account of how part of the Indian Territory was thrown open to white settlers.

Conditions existing in many sections of our larger cities today are appalling. "*These* Are the Good Old Days" describes how the lower classes lived in New York City one hundred years ago, and it concludes that things have not changed all that much.

The section ends with an essay on Geronimo, an Apache leader who sought to save his people from the degrading conditions forced upon them. It provides a single example, among many, of how the westward movement destroyed the Indian way of life.

Looking Ahead: Challenge Questions

What obligations does government have to prevent child abuse within families? Should agencies charged with such responsibilities be liable if they fail to prevent it?

Based on the article about the election of 1876, analyze the way our electoral system works. Could such a near paralysis happen again?

What factors accounted for the way Indians were mistreated? In your opinion, what political pressures existed that prevented more honorable conduct by the U.S. government?

The First Chapter of Children's Rights

*More than a century ago an abused child began a battle
that is still being fought today*

**Peter Stevens
and Marian Eide**

In the quiet New York courtroom, the little girl began to speak. "My name is Mary Ellen McCormack. I don't know how old am. . . . I have never had but one pair of shoes, but can't recollect when that was. I have had no shoes or stockings on this winter. . . . I have never had on a particle of flannel. My bed at night is only a piece of carpet, stretched on the floor underneath a window, and I sleep in my little undergarment, with a quilt over me. I am never allowed to play with any children or have any company whatever. Mamma has been in the habit of whipping and beating me almost every day. She used to whip me with a twisted whip, a raw hide. The whip always left black and blue marks on my body. I have now on my head two black and blue marks which were made by mamma with the whip, and a cut on the left side of my forehead which was made by a pair of scissors in mamma's hand. She struck me with the scissors and cut me. I have no recollection of ever having been kissed, and have never been kissed by mamma. I have never been taken on my mamma's lap, or caressed or petted. I never dared to speak to anybody, because if I did I would get whipped. . . . Whenever mamma went out I was locked up in the bedroom. . . . I have no recollection of ever being in the street in my life."

At the beginning of 1874 there were no legal means in the United States to save a child from abuse. Mary Ellen's eloquent testimony changed that, changed our legal system's view of the rights of the child.

Yet more than a century later the concerns that arose from Mary Ellen's case are still being battled over in the courts. The classic dilemmas of just how deeply into the domestic realm the governmental arm can reach and what the obligations of public government are to the private individual take on particular urgency in considering child abuse.

Early in 1989, in the case of *DeShaney* v. *Winnebago County,* the Supreme Court declared that the government is not obligated to protect its citizens against harm inflicted by private individuals. DeShaney brought the case before the court in a suit against county social service agencies that had failed to intervene when her estranged husband abused their son, Joshua, who, as a result of his father's brutality, suffered permanent brain damage. The father was convicted, but his former wife believes that fault also lies with the agencies, whose failure to intercede violated her son's Fourteenth Amendment right not to be deprived of life or liberty without due process of the law. Chief Justice William H. Rehnquist wrote that intervening officials are often charged with "improperly intruding into the parent-child relationship." Justice William J. Brennan, Jr., dissenting, wrote: "Inaction can be every bit as abusive of power as action, [and] oppression can result when a State undertakes a vital duty and then ignores it."

The difficulty in bringing Mary Ellen McCormack into the New York Supreme Court in 1874 grew from similar controversy over the role of government in family matters, and Mary Ellen's sad history is not so different from Joshua DeShaney's.

When Mary Ellen's mother, Frances Connor, immigrated to the United States from England in 1858, she took a job at the St. Nicholas Hotel in New York City as a laundress. There she met an Irishman named Thomas Wilson who worked in the hotel kitchen shucking oysters. They were married in April 1862, shortly after Wilson had been drafted into the 69th New York, a regiment in the famous Irish Brigade. Early in 1864 she gave birth to their daughter, whom she named Mary after her mother and Ellen after her sister.

The birth of her daughter seems to have heralded the beginning of Frances Wilson's own decline. Her husband was killed that same year in the brutal fighting at Cold Harbor, Virginia, and with a diminished income she found it necessary to look for a job. In May 1864, unable to pay someone to watch the baby while she was at work, she gave Mary Ellen over to the care of a woman named Mary Score for two dollars a week, the whole of her widow's pension. Child farming was a common practice at that time, and many women made a living taking in unwanted children just as others took in laundry. Score lived in a tenement in the infamous warrens of Mulberry Bend, where thousands of immigrants crowded into small, airless rooms, and it is likely that providing foster care was her only means of income.

FINALLY FRANCES WILSON BECAME UN-able to pay for the upkeep of her child; three weeks after the payments ceased, Score turned Mary Ellen over to the Department of Charities. The little girl—whose mother was never to see her

Reprinted with permission from *American Heritage*, Vol. 41, No. 5, July/August 1990, pp. 84-91. Copyright © 1990 by American Heritage, a division of Forbes, Inc.

again—was sent to Blackwells Island in July 1865. Her third home was certainly no more pleasant than Mulberry Bend. Mary Ellen was among a group of sick and hungry foundlings; fully two-thirds of them would die before reaching maturity.

The same slum-bred diseases that ravaged the children on Blackwells Island had also claimed all three children of a couple named Thomas and Mary McCormack. So when Thomas frequently bragged of the three children he had fathered by another woman, his wife was more receptive to the idea of adopting them than she might otherwise have been. Those children, he told her, were still alive, though their mother had turned them over to the care of the city.

The child belonged to the animal kingdom; perhaps the Society for Prevention of Cruelty to Animals could save her.

On January 2, 1866, the McCormacks went to the Department of Charities to reclaim one of the children Thomas's mistress had abandoned. The child they chose as their own was Mary Ellen Wilson. Because the McCormacks were not asked to provide any proof of relation to the child and gave only the reference of their family doctor, there is no evidence that Thomas was in any way related to the child he brought home that day. More than a month later an indenture was filed for Mary Ellen in which the McCormacks promised to report on her condition each year. There were no other requirements.

Shortly after bringing the child home, Thomas McCormack died, and his widow married a man named Francis Connolly. Little more than that is known of the early childhood of Mary Ellen. She came to her new home in a flannel petticoat, and when her clothing was removed from Connolly's home as evidence six years later, there was barely enough to fill a tiny suitcase. She was beaten, set to work, deprived of daylight, and locked in closets for days at a time; she was rarely bathed, never kissed, and never addressed with a gentle word. During the six years she lived with Connolly, only two reports on her progress

were filed with the Commissioners of Charities and Correction.

Late in 1873 Etta Angell Wheeler, a Methodist caseworker serving in the tenements of New York City, received a disturbing report. It came from Margaret Bingham, a landlord in Hell's Kitchen, and told of a terrible case of child abuse. The child's parents had been tenants of Bingham for about four years, and almost immediately after they moved in, Bingham began to observe how cruelly they treated their child, Mary Ellen. They confined her in close quarters during hot weather, kept her severely underdressed in cold, beat her daily, and left her unattended for hours at a time. On several occasions Bingham tried to intervene; each time the child's mother said she would call upon the fullest resources of the law before she would allow any interference in her home. Finally Bingham resorted to threat: The beatings and ill treatment would have to stop, or the family would be evicted. When her plan backfired and the family left, Bingham, in a last-ditch effort, sent for Etta Wheeler. In order to observe Mary Ellen's predicament, Wheeler went to the Connollys' neighbor, an ailing tubercular woman named Mary Smitt. Enlisting Smitt's aid, she proposed that Mary Ellen be sent over each day to check on the patient. Smitt reluctantly agreed, and on the pretext of inquiring about this sick neighbor, Wheeler knocked on Mary Connolly's door.

Inside she saw a "pale, thin child, bare-foot, in a thin, scanty dress so tattered that I could see she wore but one garment besides.

"It was December and the weather bitterly cold. She was a tiny mite, the size of five years, though, as afterward appeared, she was then nine. From a pan set upon a low stool she stood washing dishes, struggling with a frying pan about as heavy as herself. Across the table lay a brutal whip of twisted leather strands and the child's meager arms and legs bore many marks of its use. But the saddest part of her story was written on her face in its look of suppression and misery, the face of a child unloved, of a child that had seen only the fearsome side of life. . . . I never saw her again until the day of her rescue, three months later. . . ."

Though social workers often witnessed scenes of cruelty, poverty, and grief, Wheeler found Mary Ellen's plight especially horrifying. She went first to

the police; they told her she must be able to furnish proof of assault in order for them to act. Charitable institutions she approached offered to care for the child, but first she must be brought to them through legal means. There were none. Every effort Wheeler made proved fruitless. Though there were laws to protect children—laws, in fact, to prevent assault and battery to any person—there were no means available for intervention in a child's home.

Finally Wheeler's niece had an idea. The child, she said, was a member of the animal kingdom; surely Henry Bergh, the founder of the American Society for the Prevention of Cruelty to Animals, who was famous for his dramatic rescue of mistreated horses in the streets of New York, might be willing to intervene. Within the hour Wheeler had arranged a meeting with Bergh. Despite its apparent strangeness, this sort of appeal was not new to Bergh. Once before he had tried to intervene in a case of child abuse and had failed. This time he was more cautious.

"Very definite testimony is needed to warrant interference between a child and those claiming guardianship," Bergh told Wheeler. "Will you not send me a written statement that, at my leisure, I may judge the weight of the evidence and may also have time to consider if this society should interfere? I promise to consider the case carefully."

WHEELER PROVIDED A STATEMENT IMMEdiately, including in it the observations of neighbors to whom she had spoken. Bergh was convinced. "No time is to be lost," he wrote his lawyer, Elbridge T. Gerry. "Instruct me how to proceed."

The next day Wheeler again visited the sick woman in Hell's Kitchen and found in her room a young man who, on hearing Wheeler's name, said, "I was sent to take the census in this house. I have been in every room." Wheeler then knew him to be a detective for Bergh.

On the basis of the detective's observations and the testimony provided by Etta Wheeler, Bergh's lawyers, Gerry and Ambrose Monell, appeared before Judge Abraham R. Lawrence of the New York Supreme Court to present a petition on behalf of Mary Ellen. They showed that Mary Ellen was held illegally by the Connollys, who were neither her natural parents nor her lawful custodians, and went on to describe the physical abuse

Mary Ellen endured, the marks and bruises on her body, and the general state of deprivation that characterized her existence. They offered a list of witnesses willing to testify on behalf of the child and concluded by stating that there was ample evidence to indicate that she was in clear danger of being maimed or even killed. The lawyers requested that a warrant be issued, the child removed from her home and placed in protective custody, and her parents brought to trial.

Bergh testified that his efforts on behalf of the child were in no way connected to his work with abused animals and that they did not make use of the special legal provisions set up for that purpose. Because of Bergh's association with animal rescue, to this day the case is often described as having originated in his conviction that the child was a member of the animal kingdom. Bergh, however, insisted that his actions were merely those of any humane citizen and that he intended to prevent cruelties inflicted on children through any legal means available.

Judge Lawrence issued a warrant under Section 65 of the Habeas Corpus Act as requested. This provision read in part: "Whenever it shall appear by satisfactory proof that any one is held in illegal confinement or custody, and that there is good reason to believe that he will . . . suffer some irreparable injury, before he can be relieved by the issuing of a *habeas corpus* or *certiorari,* any court or officer authorized to issue such writs, may issue a warrant . . . [and] bring him before such court or officer, to be dealt with according to law."

THE PRESS OF THE DAY HAILED GERRY'S use of Section 65 of the Habeas Corpus Act as brilliant. The act was rarely invoked, and the legal means for removing a child from its home were nonexistent. In using the little-known law, Gerry created a new method for intervention.

That same day, April 9, 1874, Mary Ellen was taken from her home and brought into Judge Lawrence's court. Having no adequate clothing of her own, the child had been wrapped in a carriage blanket by the policemen who held her in custody. A reporter on the scene described her as "a bright little girl, with features indicating unusual mental capacity, but with a care-worn, stunted, and prematurely old look. . . . no change of custody or condition could be much for the worse."

The reporter Jacob Riis was present in the court. "I saw a child brought in . . . at the sight of which men wept aloud, and I heard the story of little Mary Ellen told . . . that stirred the soul of a city and roused the conscience of a world that had forgotten, and as I looked, I knew I was where the first chapter of children's rights was being written." Her body and face were terribly bruised; her hands and feet "showed the plain marks of great exposure." And in what almost instantly seemed to condemn Mrs. Connolly before the court, the child's face bore a fresh gash through her eyebrow and across her left cheek that barely missed the eye itself. Mary Ellen was to carry this scar throughout her life.

Jacob Riis "saw a child brought in at the sight of which men wept aloud, and heard the story that roused the conscience of a world."

Interestingly, there is no further mention in the ample reports surrounding Mary Ellen's case of her foster father, Francis Connolly. He was never brought into court, never spoke publicly concerning the child. All her life Mary Ellen exhibited a frightened timidity around men, yet it was against her foster mother that she testified.

On the evening of her detention, Mary Ellen was turned over to the temporary custody of the matron of police headquarters. The next day, April 10, the grand jury read five indictments against Mary Connolly for assault and battery, felonious assault, assault with intent to do bodily harm, assault with intent to kill, and assault with intent to maim. Once the stepmother had been brought into the legal system, there were ample means to punish her.

Mary Ellen herself was brought in to testify against the woman she had called her mother. On her second appearance in court she seemed almost wholly altered. She was clothed in a new suit, and her pale face reflected the kindness that surrounded her. She carried with her a new picture book, probably the first she had ever owned. She acted open and uninhibited with strangers, and interestingly, seemed to show no great fear of her

mother or any apparent enmity toward her.

The lawyers Gerry and Monell gathered several witnesses against Mary Connolly, among them neighbors, Wheeler, and Mary Ellen herself. Margaret Bingham said she had seen the child locked up in a room and had told other neighbors, but they said there was no point in interfering since the police would do nothing. Bingham had tried to open the window of the child's room to let in some air, but it would not lift more than an inch. As a constant presence and reminder, a cowhide whip was locked in the room with the child. Wheeler recounted her first visit to Mary Ellen, during which the child washed dishes that seemed twice her size and was apparently oblivious of the visitor's presence. The whip lay on the table next to her. The next day, when Wheeler came by again, the child was sewing, and the whip lay on a chair near her.

Then it was the mother's turn to testify. On the witness stand Mary Connolly showed herself to be a woman of some spirit. Despite her treatment of the child, there is something compelling in Connolly's strength and humor. At one point the prosecutor asked if she had an occupation beyond housekeeping. "Well," she said, "I sleep with the boss." As the trial wore on, she became enraged at Gerry's prodding questions; finally she accused him of being "ignorant of the difficulties of bringing up and governing children." Yet she admitted that contrary to regulations, in the six years she had Mary Ellen in her custody, she had reported on her condition to the Commissioners of Charities and Correction only twice.

Two indictments were brought against Connolly, the first for her assault on the child with scissors on April 7, the second for the continual assaults inflicted on the child throughout the years 1873 and 1874. After twenty minutes of deliberation the jury returned a verdict of guilty of assault and battery. Connolly was sentenced to one year of hard labor in the city penitentiary, then known as the Tombs. In handing down this sentence, the judge defined it not only as a punishment to Connolly but also as a statement of precedence in child-abuse cases.

Mary Ellen never returned to the Connollys' home. In the ensuing months the publicity that her case received brought in many claims of relation. But on investigating, her guardian, Judge Lawrence, discovered the stories were fictions, and he finally placed the child in the Sheltering Arms, a home for grown girls; soon after, she was moved to the Woman's Aid Society and Home for Friendless Girls. This mirrors another critical problem in the system's treatment of minors. All juveniles were handled by the Department of Charities and Correction, and whether they were orphaned or delinquent, their treatment was the same. And so it was that the ten-year-old Mary Ellen was placed in a home with mostly delinquent adolescents.

Etta Wheeler knew this was wrong for Mary Ellen, and she expressed her hesitations to Judge Lawrence. He, in turn, consulted with Henry Bergh, and eventually they agreed to turn the girl over to Etta Wheeler herself. Unable to imagine giving up her work in the slums of New York City but believing that Mary Ellen deserved a better environment, Wheeler brought the child to her mother in North Chili, New York. Wheeler's mother became ill shortly afterward, and Mary Ellen was raised mostly by Wheeler's sister.

"HERE BEGAN A NEW LIFE," WHEELER wrote. "The child was an interesting study, so long shut within four walls and now in a new world. Woods, fields, 'green things growing,' were all strange to her, she had not known them. She had to learn, as a baby does, to walk upon the ground,—she had walked only upon floors, and her eye told her nothing of uneven surfaces. . . . But in this home there were other children and they taught her as children alone can teach each other. They taught her to play, to be unafraid, to know her rights and to claim them. She shared their happy, busy life from the making of mud pies up to charming birthday parties and was fast becoming a normal child."

The happiness of her years in the upstate New York countryside lies in stark contrast to her early childhood. And indeed, as Wheeler wrote, she learned by example the ways of normal childhood. She grew up strong and well, learning how to read and playing with friends and pet kittens. In 1875 Wheeler reported to Gerry that Mary Ellen was growing up as a normal child. "She has some faults that are of the graver sort. She tells fibs and sticks to them bravely, steals lumps of sugar & cookies and only confesses when the crumbs are found in

her pocket—in short she is very much like other children, loving—responding to kindness & praise, hating a task unless there be a play, or a reward thereof, and inevitably 'forgetting' what she does not wish to remember—what children do not do some or all of these forbidden things! She is a favorite with nearly all the people who have come to know her."

When she was twenty-four, Mary Ellen married a widower named Louis Schutt and with him had two children, Etta—named after the woman who had rescued her—and Florence. She adopted a third, orphaned child, Eunice. She also raised Louis Schutt's three children from his first wife.

In 1911 Wheeler visited her protégé in her home, "finding her well and happy. . . . The family income is small, but Mary Ellen is a prudent housewife & they are comfortable. The two daughters are promising girls." The eldest daughter, Etta, worked industriously through that summer, finished high school, and became a teacher. Florence followed her sister's path, teaching first grade for thirty-eight years. When she retired, the elementary school in North Chili was renamed in her honor. Eunice earned a business degree, married, and raised two sons.

Florence remembers her mother as a solemn woman who came alive whenever she listened to Irish jigs and especially to "The Irish Washerwoman." She was unfailingly generous with her time and her affection. Her years in North Chili had saved her from the vicious cycle abused children often suffer of becoming abusers themselves. According to Florence her mother was capable of sternness and certainly willing to punish her daughters, but the terrible experiences of her early childhood never spilled into her own child rearing. As Etta Wheeler wrote, "To her children, two bright, dutiful daughters, it has been her joy to give a happy childhood in sharp contrast to her own."

ETTA AND FLORENCE OFTEN ASKED THEIR mother about the Connollys, but Mary Ellen was reluctant to speak of her early years. She did show her daughters the scars on her arms where she had been burned with a hot iron, and of course they could see the scissors scar across her face. Florence distinctly recalls that in the few times they spoke of her mother's years in New York City, she

never mentioned a woman inflicting her injuries; it was always a man.

In October of 1913 Mary Ellen Schutt attended a meeting of the American Humane Society in Rochester. She was accompanied by Etta Wheeler, who was there to present a paper entitled "The Finding of Mary Ellen." The paper concluded: "If the memory of her earliest years is sad, there is this comfort that the cry of her wrongs awoke the world to the need of organized relief for neglected and abused children."

Mary Ellen was survived by three daughters—and by a movement that would help avert tragedies like hers.

Mary Ellen died on October 30, 1956, at the age of ninety-two. She was survived by her two daughters, her adopted daughter, three stepchildren, three grandchildren, and five great-grandchildren. More important, she was survived by the beginning of a movement to prevent the repetition of tragedies like her own. On December 15, 1874, Henry Bergh, Elbridge Gerry, and James Wright founded the New York Society for the Prevention of Cruelty to Children (SPCC) with the ample assistance of Cornelius Vanderbilt. It was the first organization of its kind in America. At the outset of their work the founders signed a statement of purpose: "The undersigned, desirous of rescuing the unprotected children of this city and State from the cruelty and demoralization which neglect and abandonment engender, hereby engage to aid, with their sympathy and support, the organization and working of a Children's Protective Society, having in view the realization of so important a purpose."

The SPCC saw its role essentially as a legal one. As an agent or a friend of the court, the society endeavored to intervene on the behalf of children, enforcing the laws that were in existence to prevent cruelty toward them and at the same time introducing new legislation on their behalf.

At the first meeting of the SPCC on December 16, 1874, Gerry stressed the fact that the most crucial role of the society lay in the rescue of children from abusive situations. From there, he pointed out, there were many excellent groups available to care for and shelter children and many state laws to punish abusive parents. He went on to predict that as soon as abusers learned that the law could reach them, there would be few cases like that of Mary Ellen.

Bergh was less optimistic. At the same meeting, he pointed out that neglected and abused children were to become the mothers and fathers of the country and that unless their interests were defended, the interests of society in general would suffer.

In its first year the SPCC investigated more than three hundred cases of child abuse. Many people felt threatened by the intrusion of the government into their private lives; discipline, they believed, was a family issue, and outside influence was not only unwelcome but perhaps even unconstitutional. When, with the aid of a state senator, James W. Booth, Gerry introduced in the New York legislature a law entitled "An Act to Prevent and Punish Wrongs to Children," the proposal was immediately and vigorously attacked. The New York *World* wrote that Bergh was to be authorized to "break into the garrets of the poor and carry off their children upon the suspicion of spanking." According to the *World,* the law would give Bergh "power to discipline all the naughty children of New York. . . . We sincerely hope that it may not be finally kicked out of the legislature, as it richly deserves to be, until the public mind shall have had time to get itself thoroughly enlightened as to the state of things in which it has become possible for such a person as Mr. Bergh to bring the Legislature to the point of seriously entertaining such an impudently senseless measure. This bill is a bill to supersede the common law in

favor of Mr. Bergh, and the established tribunals of justice in favor of an irresponsible private corporation." The bill was passed in 1876, however, and became the foundation upon which the SPCC performed its work.

From its initial concentration on preventing abuse in the home, the society broadened its franchise to battle neglect, abandonment, and the exploitation of children for economic gain. In 1885, after considerable effort by the SPCC and in the face of yet more opposition, Gerry secured passage of a bill that made labor by children under the age of fourteen illegal.

As the explosive story of the death of Lisa Steinberg in the home of her adoptive parents revealed to the nation in 1987, abuse still haunts American society. There are still legal difficulties in removing a child from an abusive situation. In 1987 the House Select Committee on Children, Youth, and Families reported that the incidence of child abuse, particularly sexual abuse and neglect, is rising; in 1985 alone almost two million children were referred to protective agencies. In part, the committee said, this increase was due to a greater awareness of the issue, and there has also been an increased effort to educate children themselves about situations that constitute abuse or molestation and about ways to get help.

Despite a plethora of programs designed to address abuse, the committee concluded that not enough is being done. The most effective programs were found to be those that worked to prevent the occurrence of abuse at the outset through education in parenting techniques, through intervention in high-risk situations, such

as unwanted pregnancies, and through screening for mental and emotional difficulties. However, funding for public welfare programs has fallen far below the demands, and what funding there is must frequently be diverted to intervene in more and more sensational and hopeless cases.

If there is still much hard, sad work ahead, there is also much that has been accomplished. And all of it began when Mary Ellen McCormack spoke and, in speaking, freed herself and thousands of other children from torment.

Peter Stevens, who lives in Quincy, Massachusetts, writes frequently on historical themes. Marian Eide is a graduate student in the Comparative Literature and Critical Theory Program at the University of Pennsylvania. We would like to thank Dr. Stephen Lazoritz for his contributions to the research of this article. Lazoritz, a pediatrician specializing in child-abuse cases, first became interested in Mary Ellen's history when, preparing for a lecture on child abuse, he read "The Great Meddler," Gerald Carson's profile of Henry Bergh in the December 1967 issue of *American Heritage.* Lazoritz was fascinated by the child and traced her history through a trail of documents and newspaper articles. In the story of Mary Ellen's childhood he found the roots of a movement to prevent child abuse in which he is very much involved today. Lazoritz's youngest daughter was born during his pursuit of the case. Her name is Mary Ellen. Thanks, too, to the New York Society for the Prevention of Cruelty to Children, whose archives contain full documentation of the Mary Ellen case.

"Master Fraud of the Century": The Disputed Election of 1876

Democratic candidate Samuel J. Tilden won the popular vote—but Republican Rutherford B. Hayes won the presidency.

Roy Morris Jr.

Roy Morris, Jr., a former newspaper reporter, teaches English at the University of Tennessee at Chattanooga.

An angry gloom settled over the editorial office of the *New York Times* on the night of November 7, 1876. Late returns from across the country seemed to suggest, even to the staunchly Republican *Times,* that Democratic presidential nominee Samuel J. Tilden was heading for a victory over his Republican opponent, Ohio Governor Rutherford B. Hayes. Already the rival *New York Tribune,* another Republican mouthpiece, had hit the streets with the headline, "Tilden Elected." The *Chicago Tribune*'s assessment was more despairing: "Lost. The Country Given Over to Democratic Greed and Plunder."

No one suffered from the news more keenly than *Times* managing editor John C. Reid. A survivor of the Civil War's notorious Libby Prison in Richmond, Virginia, Reid hated all Democrats, particularly Southern Democrats. Earlier that evening, when asked which states the *Times* was conceding to Tilden, Reid had snapped, "None." Now, with all but a few states reporting, the nation seemed to have elected its first Democratic President in twenty years. Tilden had a popular margin of more than 250,000 votes. More important, he seemed likely to win a narrow victory in the electoral college.[*]

But while shuffling through a pile of telegrams, Reid came across one from Democratic headquarters: "PLEASE GIVE YOUR ESTIMATE OF ELECTORAL VOTES FOR TILDEN. ANSWER AT ONCE." The wire specifically requested information on returns from Florida, Louisiana, and South Carolina—the three southern states where Republican Reconstruction governments still remained in control.

As Reid reviewed the *Times*'s figures, he realized that the returns from the three states in question were still too fragmentary to call. Hayes conceivably could have carried—or could at least claim to have carried—all three. And if these states' nineteen electoral votes could be certified for Hayes (a distinct possibility in view of Republican control over the political machinery there), he would triumph in the electoral college, garnering exactly the 185 votes needed for victory. The election was not yet decided.

As the sky above the city began to lighten, Reid hurried to Republican headquarters at the Fifth Avenue Hotel. Inside, he found the rooms deserted. Republican National Committee chairman Zachariah Chandler, thinking he

[*]*According to one count, unofficial returns gave Tilden 4,284,265 popular votes, with 4,033,295 going to Hayes. This tally would have assured Tilden of a 37-vote margin in the electoral college, with 203 votes to Hayes's 166.*

knew a lost cause when he saw one, had retired to his bedroom hours before with a large bottle of whiskey.

In the lobby Reid bumped into a little man wearing, strangely enough, an enormous pair of goggles. William E. Chandler, no relation to Zachariah, was a Republican committeeman from New Hampshire. Recognizing the newsman, Chandler flourished a copy of the morning *Tribune* and swore, "Damn the men who have brought this disaster."

Reid assured him there had not yet been a disaster. "If you will only keep your heads up around here," he said, "there is no question of the election of President Hayes."

With Chandler in tow, Reid raced upstairs to locate the Republican chairman. After managing to rouse him, nightshirt and all, the two men explained Reid's plan for saving the election. Zachariah Chandler, sleepy and confused, told them to do whatever they thought best.

Downstairs, Reid and William Chandler grabbed a carriage and raced to the nearest Western Union office. Along the way Chandler drafted telegrams to Republican leaders in the three states. "HAYES IS ELECTED IF WE HAVE CARRIED SOUTH CAROLINA, FLORIDA, AND LOUISIANA," he advised them. "CAN YOU HOLD YOUR STATE? ANSWER IMMEDIATELY."

Across town in his Gramercy Park mansion, New York Governor Samuel Tilden slept. He had gone to bed at

From *American History Illustrated,* November 1988, pp. 28-33, 48. Reprinted through the courtesy of Cowles Magazines, publishers of *American History Illustrated.*

midnight with a seemingly insurmountable lead, the cheers of supporters ringing in his ears.

In Columbus, Ohio, Tilden's Republican opponent was also sleeping. Hayes's private victory party had ended early, spoiled by returns showing Tilden carrying New York and other doubtful eastern states. His wife, Lucy, ordinarily a vivacious hostess, had preceded him to bed, complaining of a headache.

For both candidates, and for much of the nation, the election of 1876 seemed at an end. But with William E. Chandler's telegrams now clattering across the Western Union wires, the political contest was in fact just beginning.

AMERICANS OF ALL POLITICAL PERSUASIONS had entered the centennial year yearning for relief from the endless string of scandals emanating from Ulysses S. Grant's administration. The Whiskey Ring,* the Belknap case,** and dozens of lesser contretemps had made the term "Grantism" a much reviled insult. Grant, seemingly impervious to criticism, had clung stubbornly to hopes of a third term in office. But the criminal indictment of his personal secretary on charges of corruption and bribery effectively ended Grant's presidential pretensions; he reluctantly announced plans for a lengthy tour of Europe once his second term as president concluded.

With Grant removed from consideration, Republicans had gathered in Cincinnati to nominate a successor. By far the leading candidate had been Maine Congressman James G. Blaine. But Blaine, though undeniably charismatic, was burdened by his own scandals, including charges that while speaker of the house he had profited from the granting of federal railroad subsidies. Liberal Republicans had favored Treasury Secretary Benjamin H. Bristow, the man responsible for cracking the Whiskey Ring.

On the seventh ballot the convention had turned to Hayes, a comparative dark horse. Colorless, loyal, and untainted by scandal, Hayes was acceptable to all fac-

---

*Revenue officers were robbing the Treasury of millions of dollars in internal revenue. Grant's private secretary Orville E. Babcock was among the culprits.

**Grant's Secretary of War William E. Belknap was impeached by the House of Representatives after an investigation revealed that he had accepted bribes for the sale of Indian trading posts.

GRAND NATIONAL DEMOCRATIC BANNER.

1876 DEMOCRATIC STANDARD-BEARERS: NEW YORK GOVERNOR SAMUEL J. TILDEN AND INDIANA GOVERNOR THOMAS A. HENDRICKS
THE BETTMANN ARCHIVE, NEW YORK CITY

tions of the party. A Civil War general who had served with merit, he had subsequently demonstrated, through three terms as governor of the nation's most populous state, vote-getting prowess and an uncanny knack for winning close elections. Still, to many Republicans, Hayes's nomination "fell like a wet blanket on the party." Defeat in November was widely predicted.

The Democrats, by contrast, had confidently looked forward to victory. Not only were the Republicans at a disadvantage because of Grant's sorry record, but the General Amnesty Act of 1872 had returned the vote to thousands of former

Confederates, many of whom were now sitting in Congress as a Democratic majority. Moreover, the Democrats had what they considered the perfect candidate, issue, and slogan for scandal-weary 1876; they would campaign for "Tilden and Reform."

New York governor Tilden, at age sixty-two, was an unlikely subject for passionate support. Intellectually brilliant but personally aloof, he had made his fortune as a corporate lawyer. A confirmed bachelor and hypochondriac, he was nevertheless a tireless worker, possessing one of the best political minds of his generation. Tilden had helped expose the "Boss" Tweed Ring,* and later as governor had successfully crushed the Canal Ring.** His national stature as a two-fisted reformer made his nomination for president a foregone conclusion.

AFTER THE CANDIDATES WERE CHOSEN, the election shaped up as the closest in a generation. For the first time since Abraham Lincoln's election, the Democrats could reasonably hope to regain the White House. The corruption of the Grant years, an ongoing depression, and the voting clout of the "Solid South" gave the party a large advantage.

The Republicans, for their part, had controlled federal government for the past sixteen years, and could rightfully claim to have saved the Union. In the South, the army continued to support carpetbagger regimes in Florida, Louisiana, and South Carolina, and millions of Southern blacks could be expected to offset the Democrats' huge advantage among white voters.

Tilden's personally supervised campaign ran with unprecedented efficiency. Under his directions the party prepared a 750-page *Campaign Text Book* detailing the abuses of the Grant administration. A literary bureau cranked out five million pieces of campaign literature on a private printing press, and a bureau of correspondence kept friendly newspapers well-supplied with weekly newsletters and copies of speeches. A speakers bureau coordinated campaign appearances by prominent Democratic orators.

To counter the well-oiled Democratic machine, the Republicans made ready use of campaign "assessments." By long-standing tradition, federal employees were expected to contribute 2 percent of their yearly salaries to help finance their party's political races. Liberals denounced the questionable practice, and Hayes himself mildly complained, but "voluntary" donations continued to fatten the Republican war chest.

Idealists urged Hayes and Tilden to run campaigns worthy of the centennial year. But American politics in the nineteenth century was partisan and dirty. The 1876 election was worse than most. The Democrats, as expected, hit hard at the discredited Grant administration.

Tilden had headed the prosecution that led to conviction of New York City political machine boss William M. Tweed for bribery, graft, and fraudulent elections.

**New York politicians and contractors had conspired to defraud the state in the course of canal repairs.*

GRAND NATIONAL REPUBLICAN BANNER.

1876 REPUBLICAN STANDARD-BEARERS: OHIO GOVERNOR RUTHERFORD HAYES AND NEW YORK REPRESENTATIVE WILLIAM WHEELER
THE BETTMANN ARCHIVE, NEW YORK CITY

The Republicans struck back by "waving the bloody shirt," painting the Democrats as the party of rebellion. One of the harshest attacks came in October at a rally of the Grand Army of the Republic in Indianapolis. For two hours, Colonel Robert G. Ingersoll lashed the Democrats.

"Every enemy this great republic has had for twenty years has been a Democrat," he thundered. "Every man that shot Union soldiers . . . was a Democrat. Every man that loved slavery better than liberty was a Democrat. The man that assassinated Abraham Lincoln was a Democrat. . . . Every scar you have got on your heroic bodies was given to you

by a Democrat. . . . Every arm that is lacking, every limb that is gone . . . is a souvenir of a Democrat."

The Democrats countered by reviving old charges that Hayes had pocketed money given to him for safekeeping by a soldier in his regiment who died in battle, and that he belonged to the American Alliance, a nationalist organization opposing political rights for foreign-born citizens.

In the South, which was still struggling to recover from the disastrous effects of the war, the presidential campaign was a serious business. Already, eight of the eleven old-line Confederate states had thrown out unpopular Reconstruction regimes and replaced them with freshly minted "Redeemers" dedicated to restoring Southern home rule. To many Northerners, "home rule" was perceived as a code name for white supremacy and the renewed subjugation of blacks. Rumors of violence and intimidation were greatly exaggerated by Republicans, but there were more than enough documented cases to inflame Northern public opinion.

In the three "unredeemed" states, the campaign was particularly nasty. Whites used threats, floggings, and outright murder to keep blacks away from the polls. The success of the so-called "Mississippi Revolution of 1875" emboldened some whites to step up their attacks. In that state a last-minute appeal for aid had been rejected by the Grant administration with the terse reply that the public was "tired of these annual autumnal outbreaks." Federal intervention in Southern elections was widely viewed as a thing of the past.

ELECTION DAY DAWNED COLD AND clear in Hayes's Ohio and drizzly and gray in Tilden's New York. A record turnout thronged the polls. Tilden, uncharacteristically sporting a jaunty red carnation in his lapel, was quietly sure of victory. As state after state tumbled into Tilden's column, congratulatory telegrams flooded the private wire he had installed in his home, and excited Democrats from Texas to New England toasted "President Tilden" and "Centennial Sam."

No such expressions of confidence buoyed Hayes at his rented house in Columbus. Disappointed Republicans across the nation went home to bed.

But the next morning, while Hayes accepted defeat, a worried Tilden huddled with aides. Something, he sensed, was very wrong. Despite his huge lead in popular votes, some Republicans were acting as if the issue were still in doubt. That afternoon, Republican chairman Zachariah Chandler threw the nation into a turmoil by flatly declaring, "Hayes has 185 votes and is elected." The *New York Times* exulted, "The Battle Won!"

Meanwhile, William Chandler was en route to Florida, the first in a long line of "visiting statesmen" dispatched by both parties to the three doubtful Southern states. President Grant, for good measure, ordered Army General William T. Sherman to deploy his troops to ensure a peaceful—and presumably honest—tab-

ulation of votes. Hayes now realized "that with a few Republican states in the South to which we were fairly entitled, we would yet be victors." Tilden, as was his nature, kept his own counsel.

According to unofficial returns, Tilden had carried all three states. The election returns, however, still had to be reviewed by state certification or returning boards, which would investigate allegations of irregularities, disqualify fraudulent returns, and certify the official counts. All three boards in question had Republican majorities. South Carolina's board included three Republicans who were themselves candidates for office. Florida's board was Republican by a two-to-one margin, the swing vote in the hands of a former Confederate deserter. Louisiana's board consisted of an undertaker, a saloonkeeper, and two thoroughly disreputable carpetbaggers—all of whom would be indicted for fraud within the year.

With the visiting statesmen looking on, the boards met to determine the outcome in their states. Evidence of fraud, intimidation, and violence by partisans of both sides was undeniable. In Louisiana, where black voters gave bloodcurdling accounts of election-eve atrocities, Republican Senator John Sherman wrote to Hayes that the testimony "seems more like the history of hell than of civilized communities." In Florida, Republican observer General Lew Wallace, future author of *Ben Hur,* remarked, "It is terrible to see the extent to which all classes go in their determination to win. Conscience offers no restraint." The Democratic member of Florida's board hit one of his colleagues on the head with a cane.

To no one's surprise, the three boards all ruled in favor of Hayes, disallowing just enough Democratic votes to give him a razor-thin margin of victory. Newly elected Democratic governors responded by certifying and submitting minority returns in favor of Tilden.

The electoral college, meeting in December, was unable to declare a definite winner.

THE NATION NOW FACED AN UNPRECE-dented crisis: neither candidate, it appeared, had been elected. Tilden had 184 undisputed electoral votes and Hayes had 165; both sides claimed the nineteen contested Southern electoral votes and one in Oregon.

The people looked to Congress to resolve the dispute. Unfortunately, on the

matter of contested elections the Constitution was vague and subject to conflicting interpretations. It merely stated that the president of the Senate (usually the vice president of the United States) was to open all election certificates in the presence of both houses of Congress, "and the vote shall then be counted."

With the death of Vice President Henry Wilson in 1875, Republican Senator Thomas Ferry of Michigan had become the acting vice president. If Ferry were authorized to count the votes, undoubtedly he would choose the ones for Hayes.* But if neither candidate was allowed the disputed votes, the election would be thrown into the Democratic-controlled House, and Tilden would be elected President. Hayes, understandably, favored the first recourse; Tilden the second.

Congress could reach no decision. Committees were appointed to study the situation.

As the stalemate continued, the country became increasingly restive. The threat of violence, never far from the surface, suddenly seemed especially menacing. In New Orleans, Republican gubernatorial claimant S. B. Packard was shot and wounded by a disgruntled Democrat. In Columbus, a bullet crashed through the window of Hayes's home while the family sat down to dinner. Thoughtful men on both sides worried aloud over the possibility of renewed civil war, this time pitting Republicans against Democrats.

In the capital, rumors ran rampant. Mysterious forces such as the Knights of the Golden Circle and the Sons of Liberty were reputedly planning to march on Washington and place Tilden in the White House by force. Tilden Minutemen sprang up in several midwestern states. The Democratic sergeant-at-arms of the House threatened to deputize 100,000 men and bring them to Washington to insure Tilden's election. The phrase heard most frequently was "Tilden or blood."

President Grant took such mutterings seriously, moving several artillery companies into the capital and letting it be known that he would meet any violence with overwhelming force.

Tilden, to his credit, discouraged such talk. "It will not do to fight," he told

---

Considerable controversy centered on whether the president of the Senate had any discretionary power in counting the disputed votes.

supporters. "We have just emerged from one civil war, and it will never do to engage in another." Southern Democrats, having recently fought and lost such a war, were noticeably lacking in martial spirit. Georgia Senator Benjamin Hill acidly remarked that those advocating violence "had no conception of the conservative influence of a 15-inch shell with the fuse in process of combustion."

Still, Democratic leaders became increasingly concerned about Tilden's reluctance to assert his rights. Throughout the deadlock he consistently rejected advice to take his case before the people. Secretive and reticent by nature, he preferred a policy of "watchful waiting." To supporters who warned that the election was being stolen, he blandly assured them that "it will come out all right." Key legislative leaders came away from meetings "uninformed and uninstructed." One group of callers at Gramercy Park emerged to complain that "Tilden won't do anything; he's cold as a damn clam."

IN THE MEANTIME, WITH HAYES'S TACIT approval, talks had been going on for weeks between his representatives and leading Southern Democrats. The Southerners, while still supporting Tilden, were more concerned with preserving the newly elected Democratic governments in Florida, Louisiana, and South Carolina. In return for "not making trouble," Hayes's men hinted broadly to the Southerners that he would implicitly accept home rule and be more generous with federal aid than the notoriously tight-fisted Tilden. Powerful railroad lobbyists put added pressure on the Southern leaders. Tilden was advised of the talks, but continued to discount the threat they posed.

In January 1877, Congress hammered out a compromise that neither side wanted but neither could avoid. Despite opposition from both presidential claimants, a fifteen-man electoral commission was created with the power to rule on disputed ballots. Five senators, five congressmen, and five Supreme Court justices would serve on the commission. Seven of the members would be Democrats, seven would be Republicans, and one, presumably, would be independent.

The independent member of the commission was expected to be Justice David Davis of Illinois. In the event of a tie, he would cast the deciding vote. But on the day before the commission bill passed, Davis was unexpectedly elected to the Senate by the Democratic-controlled Illinois legislature. His place on the commission was taken by Republican Justice Joseph P. Bradley of New Jersey, the least partisan of the remaining jurists.

On February 1, 1877, the day designated to begin counting the ballots, a huge crowd packed the galleries of Congress. Looking on were the foreign ministers of England, Japan, Germany, and numerous other countries. The count proceeded smoothly until Florida, the first contested state, was called. Its conflicting returns were referred to the electoral commission.

After nine days of hearings, Florida's four electoral votes were awarded to Hayes. Voting followed party lines, Bradley siding with his fellow Republicans. Outraged Democrats openly charged that Bradley had been "reached," but they had no choice but to abide by the commission's ruling.

Tilden stoically received the news, changing the subject to his planned trip to Europe. In his mind, at least, there was no longer any doubt of Hayes's election.

When the commission ruled similarly in Hayes's favor on Louisiana's malodorous returns, all but the most partisan observers realized that Hayes would be the next President.

With Tilden's defeat a foregone conclusion, Southern Democrats prepared to fend for themselves. In return for assurances that Hayes would remove federal troops from the three unredeemed states, they agreed to work with Republicans to complete the electoral count before Inauguration Day. They further agreed to guarantee all civil rights for blacks and to oppose continued violence in the region. In turn, they were assured that Hayes would appoint a Southerner to his cabinet. The informal agreement was ratified on February 26 during a secret meeting of Hayes's representatives and a group of Southerners at Washington's Wormley Hotel. Three days later Hayes boarded a train for nation's capital.

Die-hard Tilden supporters desperately sought to delay proceedings by parliamentary maneuvers and filibustering. The House session on March 1 was one of the stormiest in history. Members roared with disapproval as House Speaker Samuel Randall, a former Tilden supporter, stymied all efforts to stop the vote. Some congressmen waved pistols; one climbed atop his desk, screaming with anger. Adding to the pandemonium was a throng of railroad lobbyists on the House floor. Oaths and insults filled the air.

Finally, after eighteen tumultuous hours, the session ended with a telegram from Tilden graciously requesting that the vote count be completed. He knew he must accept the electoral commission's results or risk the nation erupting into civil war.

At 3:55 A.M. on March 2, 1877, weary senators filed into the House to observe the final tally of votes. A clerk entered carrying two mahogany boxes containing election returns from all thirty-eight states. An armed guard preceded him and then stood in front of the Democratic side of the House.

An exhausted Senator Ferry formally certified the final results: 185 electoral votes for Hayes, 184 for Tilden. "Wherefore," he announced in a shaky voice, "I do declare that Rutherford B. Hayes of Ohio . . . is duly elected President of the United States." Hayes, who had been sleeping aboard a train near Harrisburg, Pennsylvania, was awakened about dawn by exultant supporters. "Boys, boys," he cautioned, "you'll waken the passengers."

The next night the President-elect dined privately with Grant at a tomb-like White House. Whatever joy he may have felt at his hard-won victory was tempered by the bitterness it had provoked among many of his fellow countrymen. A Cincinnati newspaper pronounced his election "the master fraud of the century." Democratic wags suggested he change his name to "Rutherfraud" B. Hayes. Others dubbed him "His Fraudulency."

In 1876 the stipulated inauguration day, March 4, fell on a Sunday, requiring that the formal ceremonies be delayed until Monday. But to forestall any last-second chicanery on the part of disgruntled Tildenites, the president and his advisors agreed that Hayes should be sworn into office immediately. On Saturday evening, with a gloomy-visaged Grant looking on, Hayes took his oath of office in the secrecy of the White House Red Room.

After nearly four months of angry uncertainty, filled with blatant fraud, violence, and fears of renewed civil war, the nation finally had its nineteenth President.

Recommended additional reading: The Politics of Inertia: The Election of 1876 and the End of Reconstruction *by Keith Ian Polakoff (Baton Rouge, Louisiana: Louisiana State University Press, 1973).*

These Are
the Good Old Days

If You Think the City
Is Dirty and Dangerous Now,
It's Eden Compared With
Life in Old New York

Luc Sante

Today's New York shares much with the city of a century ago. In our time, prostitutes walk where prostitutes walked a hundred years ago; the homeless are camped on the sites of nineteenth-century shantytowns; street peddlers pitch their wares in spots that once saw pushcart lineups or thieves' markets. Around Tompkins Square Park, there are flurries of anarchist factions, just as there were in 1887, when the police were engaged in making preemptive arrests in the wake of Chicago's Haymarket Riot. Itinerant swindlers still, amazingly, operate out of decoy storefronts in the former Hell's Hundred Acres, the present SoHo. While New York has adopted as its nickname the Big Apple, that hopeful tag given it by jazz musicians, the city might more truthfully answer to the twin appellations by which tramps knew it: the Big Smear and the Big Onion.

The adolescence and early adulthood of New York covers roughly 80 years: from about 1840, when the city began to be transformed by railroads, tenements, and other accoutrements of the modern city, until 1919, which was not only the year of the Volstead Act and the Red Scare but a portal into a new technological era that would alter the city yet again.

While upper-class life in this period has been well documented—by the likes of Edith Wharton and Henry James, especially—the views and vices of Manhattan's lower class have not. What noises did common folk hear in the street, what did the posters slapped on fences promise them, what were their fears and lures and temptations? What was New York like as circus and jungle, as the realm of danger and pleasure, the wilderness that it must have been then, as it is now?

SALOON CULTURE

Rat-baiting was the premier betting sport of the nineteenth century. Its prestige can be gauged in economic terms, circa 1875: Admission to a then-illegal prizefight between humans cost 50 cents, to dogfights and cockfights $2, while a fight pitting a dog against rats ran anywhere from $1.50, if the dog faced five rats or fewer, up to $5, in proportion to the number of rats. In the eighteenth century, the biggest draw had been bear-baiting, but that sport gradually dissipated as the number of available bears decreased, although matches continued to be held up to the Civil War, notably in McLaughlin's bear pit at First Avenue and 10th Street. For a while, dog-versus-raccoon contests were popular, but rats were so readily available that they came to dominate the scene; boys were paid to catch them, at a rate of 5 to 12 cents a head. The dogs were always fox terriers, and they were trained for six months before being sent out at a year and a half, retaining the status of novice until they reached two. The pits were unscreened boxes, with zinc-lined wooden walls eight feet long and four and a half feet high. Matches typically drew no fewer than 100 betting spectators, from all walks of life, with purses starting at $125—a substantial sum for the time. A good rat dog could kill 100 rats in half an hour to 45 minutes, although the modern record was set by Jack Underhill, a terrier belonging to one Billy Fagan, who slew his 100 in eleven and a half minutes at Secaucus in 1885. Late in the century, it briefly became popular to pit rats against men wearing heavy boots. The ASPCA finally drove the game out of the city in the early 1890s.

At the intersection of Dover and Water Streets stood the Hole-in-the-Wall, a brawling den run by a well-known crook, One-Armed Charley Monell, and his female adjutants, Gallus Mag and Kate Flannery. On Cherry Street, not far away, were the domiciles of the crimps, operators who specialized in drugging and robbing sailors, sometimes arranging for them to be shanghaied aboard tramp boats if they survived. At least one place, the Fourth Ward Hotel, had convenient trapdoors through which corpses could be disposed directly into the East River. This hostelry later became famous as the site of the murder of a local woman of uncertain age but dire condition, who was popularly nicknamed Shakespeare because for the price of a drink she could recite all the speeches of the major female roles in *The Merchant of Venice, Hamlet, Macbeth,* and *King Lear.* This talent naturally led to wild speculations about her origins, with most of the locals maintaining that she was of noble birth, and the newspapers capitalized on such rumors. Likewise, her murder, never solved, was exoticized by being attributed to Jack the Ripper, come to New York on vacation.

THE CRIMPS REFINED THE ART OF THE knockout. They used laudanum at first, but this proved inefficient in the long run. A man named Peter Sawyer came from California in the 1850s and became so proficient an artist that for a while all members of his profession were known as "peter players." He is said to have used snuff at first, odd though that may

---

The concert saloon began springing up after the Civil War, mostly along the Bowery, and in cellars along lower Broadway.

---

sound, and employed morphine for a particularly tough or important hit. Then either he or one of his colleagues introduced chloral hydrate around 1866, and it was to remain the drug of choice for many years. Care had to be employed, because the physical action of chloral hydrate (soon permanently dubbed "knockout drops") was to decelerate the heart, and an overdose would paralyze the heart and lungs. The taste was detectable by anyone of sound mind and body, so the victim needed to be thoroughly drunk before he could be thus clobbered. Then he would be robbed, perhaps stripped as well, and dumped in an obscure alley. Some dives maintained an arrangement with the police whereby knocked-out

customers would be brought to a convenient location so that the cops could remove their lifeless bodies to the precinct house, where they would eventually be charged with public intoxication. Sometime during the nineties, technology finally brought a refinement to the art, in the form of the Mickey Finn. This concoction was named after the proprietor of Chicago's Lone Star and Palm Saloons, who supposedly bought the recipe from New Orleans voodoo operators and then went on to sell it to other saloon keepers around the country. The trouble is that no one can seem to agree on exactly what a Mickey Finn was. Some believe it to have been a complex recipe effective only when mixed with alcohol and water; the effect of cigar ashes in beer has also been cited, a dubious possibility.

After the Civil War, vice came into its own, ascending from the gutter to become an institution. Harry Hill's concert saloon, at Houston and Mulberry Streets, lasted almost two decades. A bar stood at one end, and at the other was a stage. On this stage, John L. Sullivan made his first New York appearance, knocking out Steve Taylor in two and a half minutes on March 31, 1881. On most evenings, however, the stage held an orchestra consisting of piano, violin, and bass viol, and patrons were expected either to dance to it with paid female partners or else to leave. This was the major tourist-trap component of Hill's. Actual prostitution was always present but not alluded to publicly; arrangements were to be made in private and the johns taken elsewhere. Hill was flamboyant in his role of protector of peace: He enjoyed intervening in what seemed to be incidents of rough-housing—usually staged for the rubber-necker trade; he often spent all evening dramatically shouting for quiet and order. His rules were posted in rhyme on the wall, forbidding drunkenness, profanity, lack of chivalry toward women, stinting on drinks. Meanwhile, in the basement was a more conventional dive, featuring crooked games, knockout artists, and the like. By the mid-1880s, Hill's profits were estimated at $50,000 a year. By this time, he was a full member of middle-class society, distinguished from mere businessmen only by the adjective *colorful.*

Hill's was known as a concert saloon, but concert saloons were actually a spe-

cific and distinct phenomenon. These establishments began springing up after the Civil War, mostly along the Bowery, and in cellars along the stretch of Broadway between Spring and 4th Streets. Their modus operandi was a prostitution tease, one that has survived into the present day at topless bars and the like. Outside, the concert saloons displayed painted transparencies of 20 or 30 women, who, it was given to understand, were employees of the place, although the pictures were usually bought at random in job lots from photograph dealers, and often included well-known actresses of the day among the assortment. Inside, women were employed as waiter girls—in the parlance of the time—and other women would be sitting around looking vaguely like customers. The sucker would be strongly encouraged to buy numerous drinks for himself and for a minimum of one female companion, whose drinks would be heavily watered or consist simply of colored water; they would cost twice as much as the man's, which were themselves expensive for the time, from 15 to 25 cents. The women did not receive wages but worked on a percentage basis. Sex did not occur on the premises and, in fact, usually did not occur at all; obstreperous customers were treated to knockout drops. The concert saloons derived their name from the fact that some sort of excuse for music, probably three drunks on strings and piano, could be found somewhere on the premises. These houses also usually maintained a sideline in gambling.

VICE—THAT AMORPHOUS CATCHALL OF the time—was also famously on display at the American Mabille, on Bleecker Street, run by "The." Allen, who was popularly known as the "wickedest man in New York," a fortunate bit of publicity encouraged by Allen himself; Allen was also known for having been raided 113 times without a conviction (he was very well connected politically). Nearby, on Bleecker Street, was the Slide, probably the very first—and until recent times virtually the last—open and undisguised gay bar in New York. It is all but impossible to get an idea of what it was like, unfortunately; the loud distaste of contemporary chroniclers made them incapable of turning in an actual description. Frank Stephenson's Black and Tan, also on Bleecker, differed from the average dive in that all the women were white and all the men were something else: African-Americans as well as American Indians, East Indians, Chinese, Malays, Lascars. Reports of the time suggest that non-whites were just as likely to be cold-cocked and fleeced as visiting farmers from upstate.

By popular accord, the very worst dive on the Bowery in the 1890s was John McGurk's Suicide Hall, just above Houston (the building is still standing), and it did not conduct its business in secrecy, since it possessed one of the first electric signs on the avenue. Entertainment consisted of singing waiters and a small band; the customers were, as ever, mostly sailors. "It was said," noted a contemporary, "that his business card reached every seaport in the world." The waiters, led by Short-Change Charley, were equipped with chloral hydrate, and they were reinforced by a formidable bouncer, a mayhem specialist named Eat-'Em-Up Jack McManus. These enforced the house rules, such as that if women were observed stealing from men, they were subjected to spot searches. McGurk's was nearly the lowest rung for prostitutes; hence the suicide craze that gave it its name and, incidentally, its grisly lure as a tourist attraction. Figures are unreliable or uncertain on the total number of suicides that went on there, but in just one year, 1899, there were at least six, as well as more than seven attempts. In October of that year, for example, Blonde Madge Davenport and her partner, Big Mame, decided to end it all, and so they bought carbolic acid, the elixir of choice, at a drugstore a few doors away. Blonde Madge gulped it down, but Big Mame hesitated and succeeded in spilling most of it on her face, and the disfigurement got her permanently barred from the place. Suicide attempts were so common that the waiters, upon getting an indication of same, would form a flying wedge and hustle the party out before she (or occasionally he) succumbed. After a woman named Tina Gordon killed herself, John McGurk gave a speech over her body: "Most of the women who come to my place have been on the down grade too long to think of reforming. I just want to say that I never pushed a girl downhill any more than I ever refused a helping hand to one who wanted to climb." This

rather chilling bit of equivocation overlooks the fact that by then his business depended on the suicides for a good part of its allure. McGurk was shut down in 1902, and he retired to California, supposedly with an estate of $500,000. His last heartbreak came when his daughter was denied admission to convent school after those in charge discovered her father's identity.

PROSTITUTES

In the nineteenth century, a young man born into a poor family, perhaps arrived in New York as an immigrant, might nurse ambitions of wealth and status. If he was sufficiently enterprising, he could practice thrift, save his salary, buy a store, save his earnings, buy another store, keep saving and earning until he had a number of stores or one large store. Or, given that workers' salaries in general were barely enough to live on, let alone save to any appreciable degree, and that acquiring the wherewithal to buy just one store could take decades, he might become a burglar, a footpad, a

After the Civil War, the moral complexion of New York City changed, and prostitution spread all over town. The brothels were identified by the red doorway lights.

shoulder-hitter, a gambling-house shill, a saloon runner, a swindler of immigrants, a poisoner of horses, a mayhem specialist for hire, a river pirate, a crimp, a dip, a ghoul. Then, with sufficient skill, and luck, and drive, and ferocity, he might come to lead his own gang, and from there, if he managed not to get himself killed, he could be launched into politics, or saloonkeeping, or real-estate management, or the business end of the entertainment industry. A poor young woman who harbored similar ambitions generally had only one route open to her: prostitution.

Prostitution went along with careers on the lower levels of the theater; it was

one of the few means for women of the lower class to meet men of a higher station; it gave the appearance of being a way to avoid the drudgery of housework or sweatshop labor; it fostered the illusion of allowing a woman independent enterprise; it dealt in the outward manifestations of a better life, such as fancy clothes and jewelry; it was associated in the popular mind with the realm of leisure, with the pursuit of pleasure. Or if a young woman was solitary—an orphan, for example—that life might be the only possible one for her. Or she might be lured into it by an older sibling already in the profession, or be procured by a lover or a male acquaintance who sought to establish himself as a pimp, or she might be offered money for favors on the street by a stranger who would probably be aware that he was displaying a sum greater than she might otherwise make in a week, or she might, indeed, be sold into the trade by her own parents. After all, no family below the middle class could afford to support children past the age of twelve; few could support them past the age of eight, and many not past infancy. Girls went to work as early as boys, employed as pieceworkers in "light" manufacturing or as shop assistants. In 1888, shop girls were seldom paid more than a dollar and a half per week, not enough to pay for lodging above the flophouse level.

So a young woman not actually seduced or sold into the profession might start by free-lancing. Opportunities were manifold for comely women in their teens and twenties. There were men on the street, at places of amusement, who could spare a dollar or two for a rapid sexual fix. Any woman by herself was fair game, and two together might be thought a team. Any woman out after dark would be assumed to be a whore. Perhaps the young woman could get away with doing this every so often to supplement her income. Too often, however, hazards would intrude. In the nineteenth century, a poor woman who contracted syphilis or gonorrhea, quite apart from the mortal danger posed by the diseases themselves, would find herself barred from conventional society; she could never marry, and any medical treatment would usually be reported to the police and get her branded. Even without this risk, chances are that, in the smaller and more socially claustrophobic order that then prevailed, someone would spot her with a man not of her class, and word would spread. Then she would be ostracized by such relations and acquaintances as thought themselves respectable, and she would be prey to the threats and manipulations of pimps, and the fresh quality that made her attractive to strange men would be spoiled, and she would need to solicit. A young woman who entered a brothel, where her earnings would be taken by the madam, who would pay her only a meager allowance, and where her movements would be as closely monitored as if she were in a nunnery, could nevertheless count herself fortunate, since the alternatives were so much worse.

Before the Civil War, brothels were restricted largely to the waterfront and the slums, to Cherry and Water Streets, to the Bowery and the Five Points (the slum district centered on the intersection of Baxter, Worth, and Park Streets). Immediately after the war, the moral complexion of the city changed, and prostitution spread all over town. Brothels, now identified by their red doorway lights, sprang up in clusters in the side streets west of Broadway in what was then midtown, and soon all through the Tenderloin, the blocks between 24th and 40th Streets and Fifth and Seventh Avenues. In the Broadway district, there was a literal progression in price and quality as one moved uptown, from the houses near and on Canal Street that catered mostly to sailors to the luxurious establishments around Clinton Place (now called 8th Street). All of them, regardless of tone or price, were essentially the same: redbrick residential houses, with names painted in white above their doors—the Gem, the Forget-Me-Not, Sinbad the Sailor, the Black Crook. The fanciest, called parlor houses, featured an atmosphere of considerable decorum in their parlors, where liquor was sold and imbibed with sophisticated restraint, and where a pianist, always called Professor, provided a cultural note. Flora's and Lizzie's were among the most famous and expensive; Josephine Woods's, on Clinton Place between Broadway and University, sold champagne for the then-outrageous sum of $8 a bottle and was celebrated for its annual blindman's-buff party on New Year's Eve and its open house on New Year's Day. Even fancier was Seven Sis-

ters' Row, on 25th Street near Seventh Avenue, where seven adjacent houses were run by seven women said to be sisters from a small New England village. The sisters ran tidy, expensive houses, with parlors in which their young ladies—as well schooled as if they had been convent-reared, which in a sense they were—played the guitar and practiced the art of refined conversation. They attracted customers by sending engraved invitations to important businessmen staying at Fifth Avenue hotels. On certain nights each week, clients were admitted only if they were attired in evening dress and bore bouquets for the girls. The total proceeds from the Christmas Eve trade were donated to charity, a fact given considerable publicity in the press.

In the Tenderloin—sometimes also called Satan's Circus—there clustered an incredible profusion and variety of manifestations of the sex trade, in and among other institutions of vice (by 1885, it was estimated that half the buildings in the district were entirely given over to some kind of immorality). In this area, where turf was carefully divided up between specialties—where 28th Street, for example, was devoted to high-end gambling houses and 27th Street to poolrooms with bookmaking operations—the streets reserved for whorehouses were 24th, 25th, 31st, 32nd, and 35th, and that was not counting the houses of assignation. The brothels ranged in tone from the Sisters' down to places where sex was incidental and robbery uppermost.

There were the panel houses, for example, where, once a john was safely occupied in bed, a male house employee called a creeper would silently push through a detachable panel in the wainscoting and make for the pockets of the pants hung conveniently on a nearby chair. More sophisticated was the badger game. The gangster Shang Draper, for example, ran a saloon on Sixth Avenue and 29th Street where clients were, by fair means or foul, gotten very drunk. When a customer was sufficiently intoxicated, he would be lured by one of the 40 female employees down to a whorehouse on Prince and Wooster Streets. Very near the climactic moment of his encounter with the woman, an angry man would burst in. He was, he would declare, the woman's husband. Enraged by the evidence of adultery, he would threaten to

beat the customer senseless, to kill him, to take him to court. But perhaps, he would hint, he could be mollified, for a significant financial consideration. Identical scenes would meanwhile be taking place in every other room in the joint. Another of Draper's houses employed girls nine to fourteen years of age. In this variation, the "parents" would burst in, the mother would hit the girl in the face so hard her nose would bleed, and the father would shake down the john. It was estimated that 100 men were taken this way every month. Perhaps the all-time champion of the badger game was a Tenderloin operator named Kate Phillips, who one night landed a visiting coffee-and-tea dealer from St. Louis. In the throes of their clinch, a "policeman" appeared, who "arrested" the merchant and took him to "court," where a "judge" fined him $15,000 for adultery: Kate, according to reports, got the money, and the man was never seen again.

CHILD GANGS

The Reverend Lewis Morris Pease, when he opened his Five Points House of Industry in 1850, was among the first to notice the extent of the youthful underworld. Just as the street gangs had female auxiliaries, they also had farm leagues for children. In the Five Points, there were the Forty Little Thieves, the Little Dead Rabbits, and the Little Plug Uglies, and on the waterfront the Little Daybreak Boys.

Considering that the "adult" gang members were often in their early teens themselves, we may speculate on just how young these trainees might be. Their major value to the gangs was their size. They all worked as lookouts and decoys; among the river gangs, they were important for their ability to crawl through portholes. Pease's efforts to arouse the finer instincts among these waifs did produce one apparent success. He boasted of having converted Wild Maggie Carson, who was the leader of the Forty Little Thieves. He claimed to have overseen her first bath, at the age of nine, and subsequently to have gotten her sewing buttons. Eventually he married her off to the scion of a pious family.

Children as young as five or six were enrolled in Fagin schools to learn pocket picking, purse snatching, and cart robbery, tasks at which they might outdo their seniors. In the 1890s, the major Fagin was Monk Eastman's sidekick Crazy Butch, who had begun his own career very young. He first proved his pedagogic ability by teaching his dog, Rabbi, to snatch purses, and then went on to coach preadolescents. He also formed his charges into the improbably named Squab Wheelmen. They were most noted for one trick: A member would hit a pedestrian, preferably an old woman, with his bicycle, and then dismount and begin screaming at the victim. As an interested crowd gathered, the other members would pick their pockets.

There was very little that adult gangsters practiced or enjoyed that child gangsters did not contrive to reproduce on their own scale. There were boys' saloons, with 3-cent whiskeys and little girls in the back rooms, and there were children's gambling houses, in which tots could bilk other tots at the usual menu of games. If it seems that these children must have very early used up the entire stock of adult pleasures—sex, drink, gambling, extortion, racketeering, fraud, intimidation, terrorism—it should be remembered that the life expectancy for kids under those conditions could not have been very high. The whole adult order of high and low sensations had to be experienced in fifteen or twenty years at best before they succumbed to disease, malnutrition, exposure, stab wounds, or gunfire. In an era during which New York produced three or four adolescent crooks called Billy the Kid, all of whom disappeared in some fashion before they were old enough to vote, and all of whom were reported incorrectly to have gone West and become *that* Billy the Kid, it is remarkable that any young person from the slums survived to adulthood at all. Those who did can be assumed to have been the most pious, the most enterprising, or the most murderous—in any case, the least childlike—of children.

TRAMPS

The phenomenon of tramps—the homeless of yesterday—first appeared in the 1870s. Many of them were probably Civil War veterans who hadn't been able to adjust. They were little noticed in the city at first, for one thing because trampdom was generally rural and was thought of as a menace only in farm and range country; for another, because tramps themselves were generally of rural origin and conducted themselves accordingly, remaining mobile and discreet. In the years when Central Park was new, tramps would hide out there, living in its sylvan recesses. They attracted notice as a public nuisance with their penchant for lying prone on the pavement and draining the lees from empty beer kegs set out in front of saloons. For some years, toward the end of the century, a tramp shelter operated quietly in a former hotel at Prince and Marion (Lafayette) Streets. Vagrants were given bed and board, and in return they chopped logs for the firewood business that financed the institution.

After the turn of the century, tramps and hoboes began showing up in the city in greater numbers: adventurers drifting back eastward from the settled West, stragglers from Coxey's Army, men put out of work from suburban factories as a result of the Panic of 1897. New York was a minor way station for tramps and hoboes, and they were perceived in significant numbers in the city only from about 1901 to 1917. Most of the railroad vagrants shunned the city for its expense, its gangs of hoodlums and lush-rollers, its uncertain police force, and also because of its underground rail platforms, which made it difficult to hop trains from anywhere but the stations of the West Side river line. But in the first decade and a half of the twentieth century, there were so many people without fixed abode in the city that flops of all sorts sprang up; the Western tramps must have heard of New York as a storehouse of cheap beds. When they got to the city, though, they found a great deal of competition. In 1909, it was estimated there were 25,000 people on the bum on the Bowery and Park Row alone, in hotels, lodging houses, flophouses, missions, sleeping on chairs, in barrels, on saloon floors, in doorways, in stairwells, on fire escapes.

Tramps and hoboes provided a good deal more fodder for Sunday-supplement human-interest stories than the more typical city vagrants, however. They were usually native English speakers, for one thing, and they were independent, more or less eccentric and colorful, more or less nonviolent and healthy. Among the tramps and bums were enigmatic sorts

and instant legends. There were said to be Oxford graduates and men with dueling scars from German universities. There were remittance men from old families whose month would follow a rigorously determined cycle: Funds would arrive, followed by new clothes and feasting and carousing; then the money would be gone, the clothes would be pawned, and there would follow a week or two of utter destitution, each stage accompanied by a corresponding shift of lodging. One Bowery character, known only as J. Black, would ceremoniously extract a dark suit from hock for a few days each month and disappear to read in the public library. There were the usual legendary rich bums, the authenticity of whose fortunes remains questionable. A man named William Smith, who died in 1913 at the age of 80 after some three decades as a vagrant, was said posthumously to have been playing the stock market all along and to have left some $200,000 in cash and securities. Another man was rumored to have bequeathed $35,000 to two road companions.

The Bowery's term as a magnet for tramps was finally ended by the approach of World War I, especially by the 1917 "Work or Fight" order that conscripted into the armed forces anyone not demonstrably employed, a law that cut a great swath through the area's population and finally killed the street as an entertainment district for anyone but the pathetic derelicts who remained through Prohibition. It provided a handy excuse for the police to make sweeps of the rootless and unprotected in other areas as well, such as Hell's Kitchen and Harlem. The numbers were, of course, to return little more than a decade later, when the Depression struck and shantytowns went up in the parks and Hoovervilles along the waterfront.

CRIMINALS AND LAWYERS

The most famous pirate of the time was a middle-aged crook named Albert E. Hicks, who in 1860 was shanghaied and woke up aboard the sloop *E. A. Johnson*, bound for Virginia to pick up a shipment of oysters. Five days later, the boat was discovered drifting off the coast of New Jersey, empty and with signs of bloodshed. Inquiring policemen found that Hicks had been seen in Manhattan with a great deal of money. He skipped town but was arrested in Providence, Rhode Island, carrying a watch and a daguerreotype that could be traced to the ship's officers. The U.S. Circuit Court found him guilty of murder and piracy on the high seas, and he eventually confessed to having killed all hands with an ax. The case achieved enduring fame when P. T. Barnum acquired a mask of Hicks as well as all his clothes for $25 and two boxes of cigars. Hicks was hanged a mere four months after his deed, to much pomp, on Bedloe's Island (the future site of the Statue of Liberty).

The lawyers in late nineteenth-century New York often represented both sides of the mainstay of their practice; namely, the breach-of-promise blackmail suit. While representing showgirls who had had affairs with society figures and then been dropped, they were often retained by these same playboys as protection against further suits.

The 1860s and 1870s were the grand era of bank robberies. James L. Ford wrote in his memoirs 50 years later, "Such operations as bank burglary were held in much higher esteem [then] than at present, and the most distinguished members of the craft were known by sight and pointed out to strangers." The district gangs of the time were pikers and barroom brawlers compared with such an outfit as that put together by George Leonidas Leslie, also known as Western George and referred to in the press as King of the Bank Robbers. According to George W. Walling, who was police superintendent from 1874 to 1885, the Leslie gang was responsible for 80 percent of the bank robberies in New York between the Civil War and Leslie's death in 1884; estimates of their total take ranged between $7 million and $12 million. Such statistics must be viewed with sus-

picion; one set of devious masterminds, after all, does less to damage police prestige than a whole town full of bank robbers.

Fences in the mid-nineteenth century were powerful enough, and perhaps sufficiently liberal with bribes, to operate with a degree of openness. After the Civil War, Frederika Mandelbaum, an impressive, narrow-eyed figure, secure in her 250-pound bulk, had a three-story building on the corner of Clinton and Rivington Streets where she ran a fencing operation with the assistance of her husband, Wolfe, and their son and two daughters, under the guise of a haberdashery. Her first listing in police records dates to 1862, and she is said to have passed between $5 million and $10 million in goods through her mill over the next twenty years. She was also alleged to have operated a Fagin school on Grand Street, but this very popular allegation was bandied around so carelessly in the decades after the appearance of Dickens's novel that it should be viewed with caution. "Marm" Mandelbaum, whose house was said to be furnished as opulently as any Vanderbilt's—with goods liberated from uptown mansions—was the social leader of the female criminal set. Her friends included such prominent sneak thieves and blackmailers as Big Mary, Ellen Clegg, Queen Liz, Little Annie, Old Mother Hubbard, Kid Glove Rosey, the con woman Sophie Lyons, and Black Lena Kleinschmidt. Black Lena was an uncommonly successful pickpocket and moll-buzzer who was undone by her taste for social climbing. After saving her money for years, she finally moved to the then-fashionable suburb of Hackensack and began entertaining a straight crowd. Legend has it that her end came when, at one of her lunches, a guest recognized a diamond ring Lena was wearing as her own unique piece, stolen years before. Marm Mandelbaum, for her part, was indicted for grand larceny by the district attorney in 1884 but jumped bail and fled to Canada. She had the last laugh, as her bondsmen succeeded in transferring the property pledged for her bail to her possession by means of back-dated documents.

Mandelbaum was represented by the era's paramount criminal lawyers, William Howe and Abraham Hummel, whom she paid a retainer of $5,000 a year. This pair were very nearly a law unto them-

selves, and were so much a part of the New York scene, both high and low, in the latter half of the nineteenth century that they can hardly be discussed without superlatives. In their 40-odd-year career, they were said to have represented more than 1,000 defendants in murder and manslaughter cases alone, with Howe personally pleading more than 650. The firm was established in 1861 by Howe, a corpulent, flashily dressed practitioner noted for his overwhelmingly theatrical manner, in particular much given to weeping in the courtroom. His partner, the canny, diminutive Hummel, joined as an office boy in 1863 and was elevated by Howe to equal status within a few years. They redefined the word *shyster*. Their offices were in a building on Leonard and Centre Streets, directly across from the Tombs, that was ornamented with a 40-foot sign advertising their practice. Their cable address was LENIENT. They sometimes obtained the minutes of successful trials, had them reprinted, and distributed them as publicity. They owned reporters at most of the daily papers and kept a regular stable of professional witnesses. Hummel once got 250 of the little more than 300 prisoners on Blackwell's Island (now Roosevelt Island) released all at once on a technicality. Howe and Hummel kept no records.

The mainstay of their practice was the breach-of-promise blackmail suit, which they effectively worked on both sides, representing showgirls who had had affairs with society figures and then been dropped, and at the same time being kept on retainer by many of these playboys as protection against further suits. Their client list virtually defined the newsworthy part of Manhattan society in the last 30 years of the nineteenth century. In the criminal world they represented entire gangs, such as "General" Abe Greenthal's national pickpocket ring, the Sheeny Mob, the forgers of Chester McLaughlin's Valentine Ring, and the foremost downtown gang of their day, the Whyos. They worked for George Leslie (receiving $90,000 from him in the wake of the 1878 Manhattan Savings fiasco, for many years afterward the largest legal fee on record), the counterfeiter Charles O. Brockway, the major bookmaker Peter De Lacey, the procuresses Hattie Adams and the French Madame, the abortionist Madame Restell, the

Tammany boss Richard Croker, the dive owners Harry Hill and Billy McGlory, and such once-famous murderers as Dr. Jakob Rosenzweig (the Hackensack Mad Monster), Annie Walden the Man-Killing Race-Track Girl, and Ned Stokes, who shot Jim Fisk. In civil cases of various sorts they represented bridge-jumper Steve Brodie, *Police Gazette* publisher Richard K. Fox, exotic dancer Little Egypt, the anarchist Johann Most, and a slew of theatrical figures that included P. T. Barnum, Edwin Booth, John Drew, John Barrymore, and Lillie Langtry. Their industry did not flag until Howe died in 1902 and Hummel was chased from the country by the reform crusader William Travers Jerome, dying in London in 1926.

Some of the flavor of their ambiguous attitude toward the law can be derived from their sole published work, the 1888 *In Danger.* They describe the temptations in mouth-watering detail: " . . . elegant storehouses, crowded with the choicest and most costly goods, great banks whose vaults and safes contain more bullion than could be transported by the largest ships, colossal establishments teeming with diamonds, jewelry, and precious stones . . . all this countless wealth, in some cases so insecurely guarded." Under the guise of alerting the public to the dangers of big-city crime, they offer explicit directions for making burglars' tools and give formulas for rigging cards. The booklet is, in fact, an advertisement for crime, couched in all the subtlety known to the science of publicity at the time.

PEDDLERS

Virtually every kind of inexpensive article was offered for sale on the streets. This trade went on without benefit of advertising, obviously; instead, cries, costumes, locations, and the age or sex or race of the vendor were an indication of what was for sale. There was the clam seller: "Here's clams, here's clams, here's clams today/ They lately came from Rockaway/ They're good to roast, they're good to fry/ They're good to make a clam-pot pie/ Here they go!" There were chimney sweepers ("Sweep o, sweep o") and ragmen ("Rags, rags, any old rags" or "Old clo', old clo', any old clo' "). Most celebrated were the hot-corn vendors ("Hot corn, hot corn, here's your lily-white hot corn/ Hot corn, all hot, just came out of the boiling pot"), who were almost always young girls and sold their wares from baby carriages and children's wagons. The wares sold by street criers gave a fair indication of the range of fast food of the time: oysters, fish, buns, hot spiced gingerbread, strawberries, ice cream, baked pears—a wholesome-sounding list. Competition with the increasing general noise level of the city is presumably what drove the criers out of business, as little is heard from them after about 1860, with the notable exception of newsboys.

Selling became minutely particularized in the middle nineteenth century, as commercial turf lines were drawn up by various groups. As of the 1880s, for example, Irishwomen (popularly identified as smoking pipes) sold apples, "George Washington pie," St.-John's-bread, and flat gingerbread cakes called "bolivars"; Chinese men sold candy and cigars. Men in general sold tobacco, socks, suspenders, hose, yarn, and gloves. Women sold most of the food, although, after the era of the hot-corn girl, roasted ears were almost always sold by black men. Boys sold ties, pocketbooks, pocketbook straps, and photographs. Little girls sold matches, toothpicks, songs, and flowers. After the Civil War, lame soldiers held the monopoly on shoestrings, and they also sold ties and a lesser rank of books and magazines. Italians dispensed ice cream; Germans dealt in sausages.

In residential areas, there were itinerant umbrella menders, tinkers, whitewashers, washtub menders, glaziers, paviors, hod carriers, excrement carriers, odd-job men identifiable by their square paper caps. Ballad vendors and encyclopedia salesmen likewise worked the doors. Orange vendors sold their wares in bundles hung from yokes. Street photographers plied the main arteries with samples of their work mounted on boards. Hackmen waited at stands outside train and ferry stations, calling "Keb, keb, keb." Newsboys were everywhere, fighting for territory, hitching rides on horsecars, yelling "Extra!"

In the Bowery, Chatham Square, and the nearby region, another mercantile style prevailed. Many of the shops were run by "cheap Johns" selling shoddy goods, but even the more respectable merchants behaved with frenzied aggressiveness. In contrast with shopkeepers anywhere else in the city, they displayed the bulk of their stock in stalls and boxes on the sidewalk in front, and they were constantly putting on fire sales that had not been occasioned by fire and going-out-of-business sales that might go on for years at a stretch.

Everything on the Bowery was loaded and short-counted. Even the pushcarts sold bad fruit, cutlery made of scrap that broke at first use, used ink bottles filled with water. There were also businesses that could hardly be found anywhere else: tattoo parlors, for instance, which flourished around Chatham Square until the 1950s, and black-eye fixers, who were essentially makeup artists and whose ability to maintain sufficient trade to set themselves up in storefronts—while only occasionally keeping a second line in something more workaday like barbering—is a testament to the continuous violence of the neighborhood.

DIME MUSEUMS

The peculiar institution of the dime museum probably had its origin in the back rooms of eighteenth-century taverns, where curiosities, anatomical anomalies, and the like were exhibited on an irregular basis. The man who made it into an institution was P. T. Barnum, who started in 1835 by exhibiting an ancient black woman named Joice Heth, who, he alleged, was 161 years old and had been George Washington's wet nurse. Barnum showed her in daily sessions in a coffeehouse at Bowery and Division to great popular acclaim, until she died several months after her debut. Barnum next staged diverse attractions at the Vauxhall Saloon, near Astor Place, from 1840 until 1842, when he had accumulated the capital to purchase the old American Museum, a staid exhibition hall of elegant white marble, at Broadway and Ann Street. There he showed wax figures, "human wonders," a menagerie, dioramas, edifying dramas, mechanical contrivances, panoramic views, and sundry frauds, and was legendarily successful at it. He continued throughout the century, even after his museums succumbed to fire—first the one on Ann Street in 1865, then the one on Broadway between Prince and Spring in 1868—

after which he left for the theatrical nexus of 14th Street and later became a partner in the grand hall called Gilbert's Garden, eventually renamed Madison Square Garden.

The museum format, which Barnum did not invent but which he broadened in appeal, was widely imitated. In 1867, the moniker was established when, as a result of a price war, admissions were reduced to a dime. The first to reach this mark was Bunnell's Museum on the Bowery, which boasted besides its tattooed man, its "double-brained" child, and the like—a "Dante's Inferno" that featured wax figures of widely despised living figures (Boss Tweed, Henry Ward Beecher, Jay Gould, Victoria Woodhull) writhing in eternal torment. Nevertheless, Bunnell's major attraction for the year 1879 was a grand poultry show. Around the Bowery there were scores of emulators, each with its waxworks, its "moral dramas," its mechanical wonders, its panoramas. Slightly risque tableaux and set pieces began showing up in abundance. Everywhere, the museums whispered of "spicy French sensations," "secrets of artists' models," "secrets of the seraglio," "beautiful minuet dancers from the Jardin Mabille," "bewitching female bathers in real water."

On the Bowery, dense as it was with such diversions as nickel shooting galleries featuring animated, noisemaking figures, such lures hardly stood out, but by the 1880s they were creeping uptown. The Eden Musée, on 23rd Street diagonally across from McCreery's Department Store, featured the usual retinue of freaks, midgets, fire eaters, sword swallowers, waxworks, a Chamber of Horrors, and "Ajeeb, the chess mystery," a pseudo-automaton consisting of a hollow figurine inhabited by a child dwarf. At Huber's Dime Museum on East 14th Street, patrons would be regaled by the spiel of the barker, a formidable gentleman in evening dress, with pomaded hair and waxed mustache, who intoned, "Ladies and gents/ For only 10 cents/ You can see all the sights/ And there on your right/ Is the great fat lady./ She's a healthy baby/ Weighing 300 pounds./ She's six feet around./ Her husband is the living/ Skeleton—see him shivering./ The dog-faced boy/ Will give you all joy/ And the tattooed man/ Does the best he can. The human horse/ Is wonderful of course./ And I'll show to you/ The baby

kangaroo," and so on. This worthy is said later to have killed himself "when his muse ceased to be appreciated."

Bowery museums were the true underworld of entertainment and often included so-called freak shows. Twelve to fifteen shows went on daily in these shoddy operations.

Elsewhere, there were mermaids (usually, dead manatees in a tank), two-headed calves, four-legged chickens, calculating horses, dwarves, giants, bearded ladies, armless wonders, wild men of Borneo, "Circassian princesses" possessing incredibly long hair and usually surrounded by snakes, snake charmers, Indian rubber men, glass eaters, mental marvels, ossified girls, legless ladies, men-fish, "iron-skulled" men, men "who will not smile," men "who cannot stop walking," geeks, living half-men, human pincushions, human claw hammers, human anvils, egg cranks (who could eat something like 120 of them at a sitting), idiot-savant calculators, tattooed marvels ("ninety thousand stabs and for every stab a tear," at Barnum's Museum). Inarticulate minor celebrities were also displayed, such as Bob and Charlie Ford, after they had killed Jesse James.

Bowery museums were the true underworld of entertainment and could include anything too shoddy, too risqué, too vile, too sad, too marginal, too disgusting, too pointless to be displayed elsewhere. For the inmates, life in the museums was no doubt rather boring and workaday. At Bunnell's, renamed the Globe, George the Turtle Boy played cards between shows with Laloo the East Indian Enigma, who had a small head growing out of his side. An extra nickel would allow one downstairs for the melodrama or variety (Al Jolson, for one, got his start this way). Twelve or 15 shows went on daily, during which the freaks had to stand around and assume typical poses, although when the immortal Jo-Jo the Dog-Faced Boy hit the Bowery, his

draw was so great that the schedule was expanded to 23 shows daily.

Mostly the museums were desperately cheap and small-time. A great number lacked even the resources to put on shows or hire human oddities, and so instead displayed any rag end they could get their hands on and elevate in stature through imaginative labeling: old coins, old musical instruments, old furniture, spearheads, Civil War rifles. Worth's Museum claimed to display the pickled head of Guiteau, President Garfield's assassin; three separate Bowery museums insisted they possessed the club with which Captain Cook was killed in the South Pacific. Museums would be plastered with signs warning FOR MEN ONLY; NO MINORS ADMITTED and then turn out to contain a scattering of old newspapers, yellowed envelopes, peepholes with views of ordinary chromolithographs. One such establishment was destroyed in 1899 by a group of soldiers returning from the Spanish-American War, enraged at finding no actual sex or depravity.

Depravity was there to be had, of course, at places like the Grand Museum, which featured tableaux vivants by women clad only in flesh-colored tights. There were joints that promised "nude women" and delivered (after the sucker had paid two or three separate admissions to sanctums within sanctums within the museum) a single unadorned showroom dummy, or possibly an embryo in a jar. There were "anatomical museums," which displayed wax models of organs and vaguely obscene charts detailing the "secrets of a successful marriage," and where "professors" who claimed to have lately come from Berlin or Paris droned on while showing lantern slides of horrifying venereal deformities in the faces of victims of tertiary syphilis.

CON GAMES

The dazzling variety of short con games in the late nineteenth century ranged from such acting exercises as the Spanish-prisoner swindle (a grieving wife and children would be toured, pleading for funds to release a prisoner of conscience from foreign confinement) to vaudeville routines like the pedigreed-dog swindle.

This con would begin with a man entering a saloon, accompanied by a dog. Over a drink, he would explain to the bartender that the mutt was a prize-winner, an extremely valuable specimen of some mythical breed. Then he would ask the bartender to watch the dog for half an hour while he attended to a crucial matter of business, possibly sweetening the deal by giving the bartender a small tip. While the dog owner was away, another man would come in, spot the dog, exclaim over it, and then ask the bartender if he was willing to sell. When the bartender refused, the man would pretend that the bartender was simply being canny, and he would offer greater and greater sums. Finally, just as the bartender was beginning to weaken, the man would give up and leave, adding as an afterthought that he might come back later in case the bartender had changed his mind.

Soon after that, the dog's owner would return, looking distraught, announcing that he had been ruined. After accepting the bartender's sympathy, he might allow himself to think of selling the dog, and the bartender, not wanting to seem too eager, would name a smallish but still sizable figure. The dog owner would look both stricken and relieved, accept the money, and leave with tears in his eyes. The accomplice, needless to say, would never return.

The Great Oklahoma Land Rush of 1889

White men had long coveted the lands of the Indian Territory, and on April 22, 1889 they got their chance to occupy part of it in a wild, chaotic dash for 160-acre homesteads.

Stan Hoig

Stan Hoig, professor emeritus at Central State University in Oklahoma, is the author of numerous articles and several books in the fields of Indian and western history. His 1984 book, The Oklahoma Land Rush of 1889, *is available for $14.95 postpaid from the Oklahoma Historical Society, Wiley Post Historical Building, Oklahoma City, Oklahoma, 73105.*

Edna Helm was twenty-one, unmarried, and knew that her chances for a husband and a happy future in Logan County, Kentucky were not the brightest. For weeks she had been reading in the newspapers about the new country in Oklahoma—an area of some two million acres known officially as the Unassigned Lands of the Indian Territory—that was about to be opened for settlement. The more she read about it, the more "pepped up" she became.

So what if it was the wild West? So what if she was a woman? This was 1889, and Helm was as eligible as anyone to make a claim. There was no reason, she felt, why she could not "make the run" for a homestead and begin a new life.

So Helm packed her bags and caught a train west to Arkansas City, Kansas, which bordered the Indian Territory. She found the town overflowing with rough-looking men carrying Winchesters, slick gamblers, real estate brokers, lawyers, and hawkers on every corner. Not a hotel, house, tent, or shack had extra room. Helm walked the hot, dusty streets

with her heavy valises until she finally sat down beneath a tree to rest.

A man walked up to her and said that his name was Martin Ahrens. He was a widower and badly needed someone to care for his three children while he made the run into Oklahoma. Helm said she had hoped to make the run, too, but now realized how slim were her chances. She didn't even have a horse.

Ahrens made a proposition. If Helm would take care of his children, he would make the run and stake a claim. Then, if she were willing, they could get married and share the new homestead.

Helm agreed, and Ahrens took her to a friend's house. Within days he made the run, succeeded in obtaining a homestead, and returned for her. They were married by a justice of the peace and set out in a covered wagon for their new home.

FOR MORE THAN A MONTH, FROM LATE March to late April 1889, the major story in American newspapers was the opening of the Unassigned Lands to white settlement. Also known as the "Oklahoma District" or simply the "Oklahoma lands," this thirty-five by fifty-mile tract near the center of the Indian Territory* had not been assigned to any specific tribe in government treaties with the Indians who occupied the reserve during the 1860s.

*Encompassing much of present-day Oklahoma, the Indian Territory was a vast reserve to which dozens of Indian tribes had been relocated from their ancestral homelands over the course of the previous seventy years.

The Unassigned Lands had been the focus of public interest and controversy for nearly ten years. Kansan David L. Payne and his Oklahoma "boomers" had made numerous illegal forays into the District in attempts to colonize it, and he and others had persistently agitated in the press and lobbied in Congress to secure the opening of the Oklahoma lands.

The government had resisted these pressures, and pro-settlement legislation had repeatedly failed. But in February 1889 congressional supporters shrewdly attached an amendment to the annual Indian Appropriation Bill. This legislation funded the opening of the Unassigned Lands, subject to a proclamation by the president.

On March 22, newly elected President Benjamin Harrison signed the proclamation. The general public would be permitted to line up on the borders of the Oklahoma District at high noon on April 22 and make a run for 160-acre homesteads or lots in the towns to be built there. Potential settlers were prohibited from entering the District early, even to select a site.

Land! To the multitude of desperately poor agrarians of the day, the word was magic. The prospect of obtaining Oklahoma land fostered a mania similar to the California and Colorado gold rushes. With land a man could be his own master, possess his own home, make his own destiny.

"It is an astonishing thing," observed the *New York Herald*, "that men will fight harder for $500 worth of land than they will for $10,000 in money."

The excitement was by no means limited to farmers. Tradesmen, professional

From *American History Illustrated*, March 1989, pp. 40-50. Reprinted through the courtesy of Cowles Magazines, publishers of *American History Illustrated*.

men, common laborers, and capitalists alike looked to the cornucopia of opportunity the opening provided. Groups of Oklahoma colonists formed in almost every major city from New York to California. Prospective settlers and townspeople hitched teams to wagons loaded with their worldly goods, saddled their fastest horses, or caught trains bound for advantageous entry points.

Principal among the entry sites were the south-Kansas border towns of Arkansas City and Caldwell, located some seventy miles north of the District, and the Indian Territory cow town of Purcell, just across the line from the south end of the soon-to-be occupied region. Each town was jammed with land-seekers—farmers from the Midwest, miners from the East, loggers from the North, and merchants, clerks, lawyers, gamblers, and land promoters from all points.

On the outskirts of these and other border towns accumulated a vast army of luckless families who lived in rickety old wagons drawn by emaciated horses and oxen. Many of them belonged to the legion of "old boomers" who had suffered for months and even years in anticipation of moving into Oklahoma.

LAND-SEEKERS ALONG THE KANSAS LINE were restrained by the military until April 18, when they were permitted to move south across the Cherokee Outlet (a sixty-mile-wide strip of land claimed by the Cherokee nation) to the northern border of the District. On that day, long, snaking caravans of covered wagons began their three-day journey.

From Caldwell a procession of cavalry, wagons, and horsemen moved down the old Chisholm Cattle Trail. A Kansan living near the trail counted 1,153 wagons the first day. When the exodus went into camp at Buffalo Springs three days later on Easter Sunday, it included an estimated ten thousand farmers, laborers, cowboys from Cherokee Outlet ranches, old soldiers proudly wearing Grand Army of the Republic badges, women, children, teamsters, and cavalrymen. During the day, religious services, foot and horse racing, wrestling, baseball, and shooting contests occupied the exuberant crowd.

An even larger caravan of wagons and riders moved south from Arkansas City, following the Ponca Trail and the right-of-way for the Atchison, Topeka and Santa Fe Railroad. This rail line, com-

pleted in the spring of 1887, ran from Arkansas City to Gainesville, Texas, and cut straight through the District.

To cross the flooded Salt Fork of the Arkansas River, the Arkansas City emigrants had to tear up a shed and lay planks on the railroad bridge. A double line of wagons backed up for miles waiting to cross. More than seven thousand people and two thousand teams of horses crossed the bridge that day. When the border was finally reached, the settlers fired volley after volley in celebration. Many set up camp near where the railroad crossed the line; others fanned out to the east and west.

At Purcell, about fifty miles to the south, hundreds of impoverished families had gathered. They hailed mostly from the South, Texas, and eastern Indian Territory. Some waited in wagon camps or dugouts along Walnut Creek. Others spread northwestward along the meandering Canadian River, which formed the southern border of the District. Clusters of land-seekers gathered at various wagon crossings as far west as the cattle trail town of Silver City.

A large number of the Purcell crowd headed north along the Indian Meridian line, which marked the eastern boundary of the Unassigned Lands, separating Oklahoma from the Pottawatomie, Kickapoo, and Iowa reservations. Unlike the north and west borders of the District, the south and east sides were not monitored by cavalry troops. As a result, many people entered the rush area early, earning themselves the then-unsavory title of "moonlighters" or later, "sooners."

These "sooners" concealed themselves in gullies, thickets, and box cars. Some lathered their horses with soap to give the appearance of a hard run; others tried to get away with early entry by dressing as Indians and dying their hair and beards.

A bevy of "legal insiders," were already in the District—railroad men, carpenters sent in to build the land offices, woodcutters, teamsters, soldiers, and federal officials—many of whom would make illegal claims. Even some U.S. marshals who were assigned the task of keeping law and order would succumb to land fever and grab claims.

WHEN APRIL TWENTY-SECOND DAWNED AS a beautifully clear spring day, the Oklahoma country was a land surrounded. All around its borders the smoke of campfires swirled skyward as nervous,

grim-faced claim-seekers, perhaps fifty thousand strong, prepared to make their great dash. The largest group gathered on the line at a point north of the Santa Fe's Guthrie Station. Another large crowd toed the line north of the old Kingfisher stage station, and others massed on the western border near Fort Reno. These groups were held in check by troops, as was another sizeable invasion force at Purcell. Some smaller companies and loners broke off from the main caravans and made their way to the unguarded south and east lines.

In the rail-line towns of Arkansas City and Purcell, mobs pushed forward to board trains that would take them to prospective townsites in the District. Claimseekers jammed in the doors, hung from the windows, clutched at the boarding rails, clung to the car tops. The first Arkansas City special, which would have to cross the Cherokee Outlet to reach the District, pulled out from the depot at 8:47 A.M. Among its cargo was a freight car loaded with reporters. Seven other specials would follow in turn, leaving trails of smoke across the blue sky of the Outlet.

At Purcell, the regular northbound passenger train passed through at around 11 A.M., but its engineer refused to stop for the howling crowd. Shortly thereafter a twelve-car train pulled in; within minutes a thousand or more land-seekers crowded aboard. A second train was also loaded and then joined with the first behind double engines. This "Boomer Train" moved up the tracks to the Canadian River bridge, where it waited for Army Lieutenant Sam Adair, whose cavalry troops had arrived at Purcell the previous day, to give the signal to enter the District.

All around the rim of the Oklahoma lands, horses pranced and whinnied nervously, men gripped their reins with iron determination and threw anxious glances at their watches, bonneted women and barefoot children watched in anticipation from camps under blackjack clumps, and blue-jacketed cavalry troops moved into position facing the straining line. The signal to enter would be given by a bugle call, a rifle or pistol shot, or, as was the case at Fort Reno, the firing of a cannon. Unfairly, along the unguarded south and east boundaries each man was free to choose his own moment.

AT THE STROKE OF NOON, PURE CHAOS erupted. The sounds of gunfire, cracking

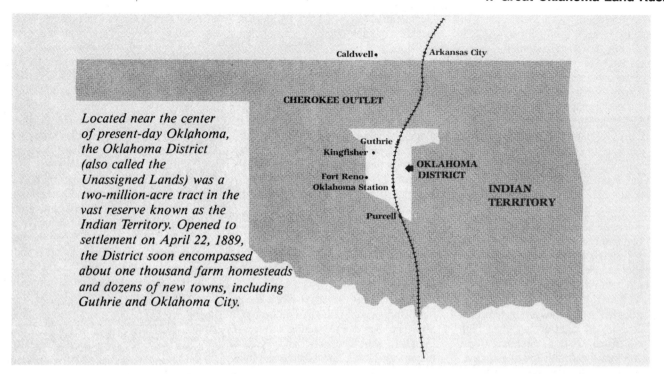

Located near the center of present-day Oklahoma, the Oklahoma District (also called the Unassigned Lands) was a two-million-acre tract in the vast reserve known as the Indian Territory. Opened to settlement on April 22, 1889, the District soon encompassed about one thousand farm homesteads and dozens of new towns, including Guthrie and Oklahoma City.

whips, snapping reins, cursing drivers, whooping horsemen, and cheering spectators all melded into the thunder of hundreds of animals and wagons lurching forward simultaneously. The great land rush of 1889 was on!

Most of those making the run wanted one of the ten thousand farm homesteads available at $1.25 per acre,* but there were many others just as eager to obtain a lot in a promising townsite. The Santa Fe stations that had been lonely outposts in the Unassigned Lands for the past two years were the most favored locations. Guthrie Station, the site of one of the two land offices in the District and the anticipated location for the territorial capital, was the first choice for many of the newcomers. Old-time "boomers"—led by William L. Couch after Payne's death in 1884—had a strong preference for Oklahoma Station. Other settlers liked Kingfisher, site of the second land office. But the majority of the land-seekers, who had never set foot inside Oklahoma, made the rush blindly, hoping for the best.

The goal of most homesteaders was to locate good, rich bottom land without many trees to clear. But what most of them found, often to their surprise and

*Settlers making prescribed improvements on their homesteads and living there for five years gained title to the land without cost; the $1.25-per-acre fee applied if one wished to obtain title to the land before fulfilling the required span of residency.

chagrin, was hard-packed ocher soil covered with scrub oak or buffalo grass. Many would spend this first night by their campfires under the stars wondering if they had done the right thing.

"Are you going to stay?" discouraged Pat McGinty later asked of his neighbor William Fry.

"I've got to stay," Fry answered. "I haven't any place else to go."

Many stuck it out, building their first dugout or log cabin, putting up fences for their stock, breaking the sod for gardens and crops, digging wells, toughing out those first difficult years. Others left in disgust, gaining the title of "goners" to match the Oklahoma nicknames of "boomer" and "sooner."

A few blacks joined the April 22 dash for homesteads, but not many. Blacks were still restrained from such public participation by the racial mores of the day. Still, a number of them followed behind the initial rush and obtained good homesteads passed over by earlier land-seekers. Black colonists from Kansas settled north of the Cimarron River above Kingfisher, naming their town Lincoln.

THE MANIA TO BUILD NEW TOWNS WAS almost as strong as the homesteading fever. Never before had so many towns come into being in such a brief time. Almost overnight, scores of sites were staked out, and tents and frame buildings sprang up on the prairie. Hotels, restau-

rants, saloons, mercantile and grocery stores, banks, real estate agencies, law offices, newspapers, stables, lumberyards, laundries, and undertaking parlors suddenly sprouted on what had been Indian hunting grounds where great herds of buffalo once grazed.

Officials of the Santa Fe line, who had long since learned that good profits lay in town development, had formed a private company called the Seminole Townsite and Improvement Company. Surveyors were sent in to station locations before the run to lay out townsite plans. Then, on the day of the run, they were permitted to return ahead of the rush and stake out the townsites. Lots were sold based on these surveys. But many settlers made their own surveys and plans, and much confusion and conflict ensued in places such as Oklahoma City (formerly Oklahoma Station), Edmond, and Guthrie before matters were eventually resolved.

An estimated ten to fifteen thousand "eighty-niners" inhabited Guthrie during its first days of existence, and nearly ten thousand more populated Oklahoma City. Some of the new Oklahoma settlements thrived; others were "bubble towns" that just didn't take and eventually faded away, usually for want of a railroad.

There had been considerable concern about possible violence during the run. Most men were armed with either a rifle or six-gun. Yet strangely, little conflict took place during the rush itself. That would come later as claimants fought one another in court, where thousands of "sooner" cases from the run of 1889 would clog the legal system for years. Arbitration began at the land office level, where the registrar of deeds and receiver of moneys rendered initial decisions. Some cases went all the way to the United States Supreme Court.

Often, while their cases dragged on for years, bitter enemies lived side-by-side on the same claim. Such was the case of "boomer" leader William Couch, whose claim in the heart of Oklahoma City was acrimoniously contested by J.C. Adams. The rancor grew until Adams eventually shot Couch in the knee, leading to Couch's death from gangrene. In the end, neither man's claim was accepted, both having been "sooners."

Couch had claimed that legally he was not in Oklahoma early, having remained on the railroad right-of-way until high noon on April 22. But a Supreme Court decision on the Smith-Townsend case, which involved land claims in the city of Edmond, ruled that such a pretext was

illegal entry. Most of the old "boomers" lost their choice claims because of this decision.

Perjury was rampant in the "sooner" contests. Men who had entered illegally formed "combinations" to lie for one another. This practice was abetted by lawyers who told their clients it was not illegal to lie before the land office officials. In some cases, witnesses were bribed or bailed out of jail to give false support. The term "sooner" became so derogatory that Ira Terrill of Stillwater shot and killed a man who accused him of being one.

AS THE INDIANS KNEW IT WOULD BE, THE opening of the Oklahoma District was only the first of the great giveaways of Indian territory. Block-by-block the Indian lands would fall: the Pottawatomie, Shawnee, Sac & Fox, and Iowa reserves in 1891; the Cheyenne and Arapaho country in 1892; the Cherokee Outlet, plus lands of the Tonkawas and Pawnees in 1893; the Kickapoo reserves in 1895;

the Kiowa-Comanche-Apache-Wichita-Caddo reserve in 1901; the Ponca Otto Missouri holdings in 1904; and in 1906, the Osage and Kaw lands and the Big Pasture country.

All of these, plus the "No-Man's Land" of the Panhandle and Greer County, would comprise the Territory of Oklahoma, which in 1907 was joined with the remaining Indian Territory as Oklahoma, the forty-sixth state.

For the Indians, the run of 1889 was fatal to tribal identity and autonomy. But to whites it was a grand and glorious event, a historic moment in the lives of those who came and found homes, a triumph of American enterprise and opportunism—with more than a little chicanery and some outright larceny.

Recommended additional reading: *The Oklahoma Land Rush of 1889* by Stan Hoig (Oklahoma Historical Society, 1984) and *David L. Payne, the Oklahoma Boomer* by Stan Hoig (Western Heritage Books, 1980).

GERONIMO

Dee Brown

Geronimo had been only a few months in the Sierra Madre when he decided that all the Chiricahuas should be rescued from the semi-starvation and sickness of the reservation and brought to Mexico. Consequently, in April 1882, after careful planning, Geronimo and his warriors stealthily invaded San Carlos, cut the telegraph lines, and sought out all the Chiricahuas they could find for a flight to Mexico. Not all wanted to leave. According to Jason Betzinez, a cousin of Geronimo who was living on the reservation, they were given no time to find their horses and had to flee on foot. "We weren't allowed to snatch up anything but a handful of clothing and other belongings. There was no chance to eat breakfast. Geronimo . . . was out in front guiding us east along the foot of the hills north of the Gila River."

On their way out of the reservation they encountered a patrol of Apache police and killed the white leader, Albert Sterling. With about 100 warriors and 400 women and children, Geronimo now faced the difficult task of avoiding or outrunning several pursuing Army forces. Lieutenant Colonel George A. Forsyth of Beecher Island fame tried to intercept them with cavalry along the recently completed Southern Pacific Railroad, and came close enough for a sharp fight at Horseshoe Canyon on April 23, but he could not stop them.

"After we had crossed into Mexico," Jason Betzinez recalled, "we began to feel safe from attack by U.S. troops, not knowing that the troop commander, hot on our trail, intended to cross the border with or without permission of higher authorities."

Although Forsyth did pursue Geronimo's escaping band across the border, it was not the U.S. cavalry but that of Mexican Army that was to deal them a deadly blow. In a dry stream bed within view of the Sierra Madre, the Mexicans struck the flank of the relaxed two-mile-long column of Apaches, shooting down men, women, and children. "As we ran," Betzinez said, "my mother and I heard Geronimo behind us, calling to the men to gather around him and make a stand to protect the women and children."

According to Geronimo's own account, told years afterward, the Mexican commander recognized him and ordered his soldiers to exterminate him and his band at any cost. "From all along the ditches arose the fierce war cry of my people," he said. "The columns wavered an instant and then swept on; they did not retreat until our fire had destroyed the front ranks. . . . That night before the firing had ceased a dozen Indians had crawled out of the ditches and set fire to the long prairie grass behind the Mexican troops. During the confusion that followed we escaped to the mountains." Geronimo failed to mention the severe losses suffered by his people—seventy-eight dead, thirty-three women and children made captive, and many wounded. One-fourth of his fighting force of warriors was gone.

To obtain food supplies and horses, the Chiricahuas made lightning raids upon Mexican villages, taking cattle, horses, and mules, and capturing pack trains of supplies. Because they were unable to obtain ammunition that would fit their American-made rifles, Geronimo risked a foray into Arizona. He succeeded in bringing out large quantities of ammunition as well as saddles, bridles, and blankets. But at the same time his action generated headlines and lurid tales for the voracious American press. From that time until his final surrender, Geronimo would be blamed for almost every major or minor raid by Apaches anywhere in Arizona and New Mexico. This added to his notoriety, gave him a far more blood-thirsty image than he deserved, and made his capture or destruction the main objective of General George Crook when he returned to Arizona in September 1882.

In preparation for his campaign against Geronimo, Crook put San Carlos under military control and transformed the Apache police into scouts for tracking. He placed Captain Emmet Crawford in charge of the reservation and gave Lieutenant Britton Davis command of the scouts.

To stop the Apache raids Crook devised a plan for striking at Geronimo's base, the location of which he obtained from a Chiricahua who returned to the reservation. In order to avoid violating international law, he had to obtain permission from Mexican authorities to take his soldiers across the border. The slow process of completing these arrangements as well as making preparations for the expedition delayed the start until the spring of 1883.

With a force of 320, which included 76 civilian packers to handle the pack mules, 193 Apache scouts, and a journalist-photographer, Crook crossed into Mexico early in May. When the mountainous country slowed the column's progress, he sent Captain Crawford with 150 scouts ahead of the pack train. On May 15, Crawford surrounded one of Geronimo's *rancherías* and captured the women and children. In a few days several warriors surrendered in order to join their families.

By this time Crook and his pack train had come up, and he learned from the warriors that Geronimo wanted to talk with him. Captain John Bourke, who was with Crook during the meetings that followed, described Geronimo and his warriors as a "fine-looking lot of pirates" all well-armed with breech-loading Winchesters. Geronimo told Crook that he had always wanted to be at peace, but

From *American History Illustrated*, July 1980. Reprinted through the courtesy of Cowles Magazines, publishers of *American History Illustrated*.

that he had been ill-treated at San Carlos and driven away. He promised the general that if he would be allowed to go back to the reservation and guaranteed just treatment, he would gladly work for his living and follow the path of peace. Crook kept Geronimo in suspense for a few days, then consented to let him round up his scattered band for the long march back to San Carlos.

THE COLUMN MOVED SLOWLY NORTHward, small groups of Chiricahuas joining it daily until there were more than 300 who had to be fed from the dwindling rations of the pack train. "All the old Chiricahuas were piled on mules, donkeys and ponies," Captain Bourke said. "So were the weak little children and feeble women. The great majority streamed along on foot, nearly all wearing garlands of cottonwood foliage to screen them from the sun." For most of the march Geronimo kept far to the rear, trying to convince reluctant members of his band to join the procession or searching for those who might have been away on hunts or on private raids.

Soon after the column crossed into Arizona on June 10, the territorial newspapers began clamoring for the heads of Geronimo and his warriors, demanding that they be executed and their women and children exiled to Indian Territory. Somehow the Chiricahuas learned of these threats—probably from officers who obtained the newspapers, repeated the stories within hearing of the Apache scouts who then told the Chiricahuas—and Geronimo and his lieutenants vanished again into the mountains.

The main column moved on to San Carlos, however, with the women and children, and months passed before the cautious warriors began coming in to join them. Crook sent Lieutenant Britton Davis with the Apache scouts down to the border to make searches for Geronimo and assure him that he would be safe at San Carlos. Not until late in February 1884 did Geronimo suddenly appear at the border crossing. He was riding on a white pony at the head of a herd of 350 beef cattle that he had stolen from Mexican ranchers for the purpose of starting livestock raising on the reservation.

To avoid difficulties with the Mexican Government, Crook ordered the cattle seized as soon as they reached San Carlos, and authorized payment of com-

pensation to the Mexican ranchers from whom the animals had been stolen. Although Geronimo's anger was aroused by the seizure, in the end his people obtained their share of the beef, which was later issued to them as agency rations. But there was no longer a breeding herd.

As soon as he had settled down again at San Carlos, Geronimo petitioned Crook for a better location for his people, a place where there was plenty of grass and water for ranching and farming. He particularly wanted to move to Eagle Creek, but Crook could not help him. The Eagle Creek lands had been withdrawn from the reservation for settlement by whites. Eventually Geronimo was given an area along Turkey Creek that was suitable for small ranches, but Washington bureaucrats in the Indian Office refused to allow them any livestock, insisting that they adopt methods of farming suited to the East but that were impracticable in the arid Southwest. They were given wagons, plows, and harness that was too large for their wiry ponies. "The ponies, unaccustomed to a slow gait, preferred to trot or gallop," observed Lieutenant Davis, "and the plow-points were oftener above ground than in it."

Yet somehow the Chiricahuas managed to grow small crops of corn. Captain Crawford reported that the grain might make it possible to reduce government food allowances, but the Apaches had other plans. They used a considerable amount of their corn to secretly make *tiswin,* an alcoholic drink strictly forbidden by General Crook. The brewing process was fairly simple. After being soaked in moistened grass until it sprouted, the corn was then ground and boiled, the resulting liquid resembling beer that, as Geronimo said, "had the power of intoxication, and was very highly prized."

AFTER ONE OF THE CHIRICAHUA LEADERS named Kayatennae was caught making *tiswin,* he was arrested and sentenced to three years in irons at the federal prison at Alcatraz. Not long after he was taken away rumors began spreading that Kayatennae had been hanged by the Army and that Geronimo was next on the list of victims. This aroused all the old anxieties and fears of betrayal that lingered in Geronimo's mind, and by the late spring of 1885 he was also becoming resentful

over the unfairness of reservation rules. He saw the Army officers relieving the tedium of their lives with whiskey and other forms of alcohol, and could not understand why they forbade his people to make and drink their favorite beverage.

On May 15, Geronimo's discontent came to a head when he joined several other tribal leaders in a demonstration outside Lieutenant Davis' tent. The Chiricahuas told Davis that they had agreed on a peace with the Americans, but that nothing had been said about their conduct among themselves. "They were not children to be taught how to live with their women and what they should eat or drink. All their lives they had eaten and drunk what seemed good to them. . . . They had complied with all they had promised to do when they had their talk with the General in Mexico; had kept the peace and harmed no one. Now they were being punished for things they had a right to do as long as they did no harm to others."

Lieutenant Davis told them that *tiswin* was forbidden because drunken Indians did not know what they were doing. Although Geronimo took little part in the discussion, Davis could see that he was angry and as soon as the Apaches left he sent a warning telegram through channels to Crook. The message was pigeonholed by an inept superior officer, and Crook never received it. Forty-eight hours later Geronimo with 144 followers, including about a hundred women and children, left the reservation. This time Davis could not send a telegram because Geronimo and his warriors had cut the wires in several places, refastening the breaks with thin strips of buckskin so they could not easily be found and repaired.

This last breakaway of Geronimo started one of the longest and most publicized military campaigns of the Indian Wars, involving before it ended thousands of soldiers in pursuit of fewer than fifty warriors, and inspiring a multitude of blood-and-thunder newspaper stories.

"I DID NOT LEAVE OF MY OWN ACCORD," Geronimo was to tell Crook afterward, explaining that he had been informed several times by friends that the Army was planning to arrest and hang him. "I want to know now who it was ordered me to be arrested. I was praying to the light and to the darkness, to God and to the sun, to let me live quietly there with

Geronimo and Natchez at Fort Bowie, Arizona, after surrendering to General Miles in 1886.
Courtesy of the Western History Collections, University of Oklahoma Library.

my family. I don't know what the reason was that people should speak badly of me. . . . Very often there are stories put in the newspapers that I am to be hanged. I don't want that any more. When a man tries to do right, such stories ought not to be put in the newspapers."

With his usual ingenuity, Geronimo eluded pursuit by the cavalry, quickly crossed into Mexico, and reached his old refuge in the Sierra Madre. And once again Crook ordered Captain Crawford to go in pursuit of him. This time Crawford was accompanied by a hardbitten frontiersman, Tom Horn, serving as chief of the Apache scouts. (In an autobiography, which has the veracity of a dime novel, Horn exaggerated his importance in the campaign and added his name to the Geronimo legend.) While Crawford and Horn were tracking into Mexico, an Apache leader named Ulzana conducted bloody raids into New Mexico and Arizona, some of which were credited in the press to Geronimo.

Not until January 9, 1886, did Crawford find Geronimo's *ranchería,* and two days later Geronimo with his characteristic aplomb came in for a conference. After several long discussions he agreed to meet Crook within two moons somewhere near the border. During the inter-

val a large party of Mexican irregular troops in search of bounty scalps attacked the Apache scouts, killing Crawford and slightly wounding Horn. Geronimo nevertheless kept his promise and met with Crook, on March 25.

The meetings just below the Arizona border at El Canon de los Embudos were like scenes from a carefully staged drama. Every word of the rich dialogue of confrontation between Geronimo and Crook was set down by Captain Bourke, and the images of the participants were preserved for history by photographer Camillus S. Fly of Tombstone, Arizona.

In his speeches Geronimo tried to explain his past actions, but Crook responded by calling him a liar. When Geronimo spoke of returning to the reservation, the general bluntly told him that he had only two choices—surrender unconditionally or stay on the warpath, in which case he would be hunted down and killed. By the third day of the meetings, Geronimo knew that Crook meant to make prisoners of him and his warriors, and send them to some distant place. One by one the warriors capitulated, and then Geronimo offered his hand to Crook. "I give myself up to you," he said. "Do with me what you please. Once I moved about like the

wind. . . . That's all I have to say now, except a few words. I should like to have my wife and daughter come to meet me at Fort Bowie."

CROOK PROMISED GERONIMO THAT HIS family would join him in imprisonment, and then left the meeting place to return to Fort Bowie ahead of the column of scouts and the surrendered Chiricahuas. He sent a telegram to the General of the Army, Philip Sheridan, announcing Geronimo's surrender. Three days later he had to send another message informing Sheridan that Geronimo and forty members of his band once again had fled to the Sierra Madre of Mexico. Sheridan was furious, condemning Crook for slackness of command and refusing to accept his explanations. Crook resigned, and on April 2 General Nelson Miles replaced him.

The villain in this last flight of Geronimo was a trader and whiskey runner to the Indians named Bob Tribolett, who had slipped across the border and unknown to the Army officers supplied the Apaches with mescal and other liquors. As soon as the Indians reached a state of intoxication, Tribolett began hinting to them that they would be hanged as soon as the Army got them to Fort Bowie, thus playing upon the suspicions that were always close to the surface in their minds.

"We were not under any guard at this time," Geronimo said afterward. "I feared treachery and decided to remain in Mexico." One of his lieutenants, Natchez, was more direct in his explanation of the flight: "I was afraid I was going to be taken off somewhere I didn't like, to some place I didn't know. I thought all who were taken away would die."

Many Army officers, including General Crook, suspected that Tribolett may have been sent by the "Indian Ring" of Arizona to frighten Geronimo into continuing the fighting. Civilian contractors and traders had profited from the long Apache wars, dealing with both sides, and they had a keen interest in the maintenance of the numerous forts and the continued presence of soldiers in the territories. Whether Tribolett's action was deliberately planned or not, it certainly resulted in a bonanza for the "Indian Ring."

Soon after he took command, the flamboyant and ambitious General Miles quickly put 5,000 soldiers (or about a third of the total combat strength of the U.S. Army) into the field. He also had 500 Apache scouts and many irregular civilian militia. For quick communication he organized an expensive system of heliographs to flash messages back and forth across Arizona and New Mexico. The enemy to be subdued by this powerful force consisted of Geronimo and twenty-four warriors who throughout that summer of 1886 were also under constant pursuit by thousands of Mexican soldiers.

ON AUGUST 23, GERONIMO FINALLY CHOSE to surrender to Lieutenant Charles Gatewood and two Apache scouts who found him in a Sierra Madre canyon. Geronimo laid his rifle down and shook hands with Gatewood, inquiring calmly about his health. He then asked about matters back in the United States. How were the Chiricahuas faring? Gatewood told him that those who had surrendered had already been sent to Florida for imprisonment. If Geronimo would surrender to General Miles, he would be sent to Florida to join them.

Geronimo wanted to know what kind of man General Miles was. Was his voice harsh or agreeable to the ear? Was he cruel or kind-hearted? Did he look you in the eye or down at the ground when he talked? Would he keep his promises? Then he said to Gatewood: "Consider yourself one of us and not a white man . . . as an Apache, what would you advise me to do?"

"I would trust General Miles and take him at his word," Gatewood replied.

And so, for what was to be the last time in his life, Geronimo surrendered. Many Arizonians as well as President Grover Cleveland wanted to hang the old warrior, but Miles kept his promise to send him to Florida, and on September 8 put him on a railroad train at Bowie Station under heavy guard. Two days later Geronimo's enemies in the War Department in Washington ordered him hauled off the train at San Antonio while they debated whether or not he had surrendered or been captured. If it was the latter, they would hang him. While he awaited his fate in San Antonio a photographer posed him against a wall for a poignant portrait of a defeated 60-year-old Apache halfway into the white man's world, clad in a mixed costume of sack coat, hat, and boots over his native breechcloth.

After a month of bureaucratic haggling, the Army sent him on his way to Florida. For some time he was kept in a separate prison from that of his family and friends; at last in May 1888 they were all brought together at Mt. Vernon Barracks north of Mobile, Alabama. There the dying began in that warm humid land so unlike the high dry country of their birth. More than 100 died of a disease diagnosed as consumption, and when the Government took their children away to the Indian school at Carlisle, Pennsylvania, many more died there. Old friends and old enemies interceded for them. General Crook, Captain Bourke, General Howard, Surgeon Walter Reed, and Lieutenant Hugh Scott all came to offer their help, but the people of Arizona refused to permit Geronimo and his Chiricahuas to return to their homeland.

AT LAST IN 1894 THE KIOWAS AND COmanches, after learning of their plight, offered these ancient Apache enemies a part of their reservation near Fort Sill in Oklahoma. There, nearby the fort, Geronimo and the other survivors built houses and plowed small farms. Ger-

onimo began to enjoy life again with his wife and children, taking pride in his watermelon patch, growing enough melons to sell some at the fort. He adapted quickly to the white man's economic system, and because of his fame found it easy to sell his autograph, or bows and arrows, and even old hats to curious visitors. One visitor in 1905 described him as "a smiling, well-kept, well-dressed Indian about five feet nine inches tall . . . dressed in a well-fitting blue cloth suit of citizen's clothes."

It was at about this time that Stephen M. Barrett, a school superintendent in the nearby town of Lawton, asked Geronimo to dictate the story of his life, a task that he willingly undertook when he was assured that he would be paid for it. The result is a unique account of Indian life told from the viewpoint of a warrior-leader.

Although Geronimo was still technically a prisoner of war, the Army permitted him to attend, under guard, international fairs and expositions at Omaha, Buffalo, and St. Louis. He attracted large crowds and profited from the sale of autographs, buttons, hats, and photographs of himself. One Sunday while in Omaha his guard took him out into the country for a buggy ride and they became lost in the fields of tall corn. Darkness fell before they could find their way back to the fairgrounds, and as they were returning through the city streets they could hear the shouts of newsboys selling an extra edition of a local paper with headlines announcing that Geronimo had escaped and was on his way back to Arizona. He would always be a target for the sensational press, but such stories also helped sell more autographs and photos.

When President Theodore Roosevelt invited him to Washington for the inaugural parade, he was sent a check for $171 to cover his travel expenses. Geronimo took the check to his Lawton bank, deposited all but one dollar, and then boarded the train for Washington. At every stop along the way he sold autographs to crowds at the stations. When he rode down Pennsylvania Avenue with five other Indian "chiefs" he practically stole the show from Teddy Roosevelt, and then went home to Oklahoma with a trunkful of new clothes and his pockets full of money. He was no miser, however; he gave freely of his earnings to less fortunate tribespeople and sent needed goods to relatives and friends in Arizona.

IN HIS LAST YEARS GERONIMO BECAME fond of automobiles, although he never owned one. When he was allowed to attend rodeos and local fairs in Oklahoma, he would often ride in one of these new mobile inventions of the white man, preferring the bright red models with shiny brass trimmings. For a stunt at one Wild West show he shot a buffalo from the seat of a racing car. In one of his last public appearances, he was persuaded by a photographer to pose in a black top hat at the wheel of a resplendent open car— the perfect comic image of the American Indian as he was seen in the popular culture of the nation at the beginning of the 20th century.

It was a fall from a horse that finished the old Chiricahua. On a cold February night in 1909 he was returning home from Lawton, where he had sold some bows and arrows and obtained some whiskey. He fell from his saddle beside the bank of a creek, and lay exposed for several hours. Three days later, February 17, he was dead from pneumonia.

His body was scarred with many wounds, but, as he had always boasted, no bullet killed him. At 80, or perhaps a year or two older, he had outlived most of his contemporaries of the Indian wars in the West.

The literature on Geronimo is extensive, but author Dee Brown recommends Geronimo, the Man, His Time, His Place (1976) by Angie Debo as the best documented and most comprehensive biography.

The Emergence of Modern America

The 1890s was a decade of great social ferment. Industrial corporations and "Wall Street" seemed to many to exert ever-greater control over the political and economic life of the nation. The depression of 1893, which resulted in widespread unemployment and falling farm prices, increased discontent and the determination to restructure the society on behalf of farmers and workers. The Populist, or People's Party grew into a formidable challenge to the status quo in western farm areas. Although condemned as radical by conservatives at the time, the Populists espoused many programs that have long since become part of our system. Some legislation aimed at curbing corporate excesses was enacted, but the trend toward ever-larger combinations of capital went on. The return of prosperity and the onset of the Spanish-American War at the end of the decade effectively undermined reform movements.

America's continental expansion had been fulfilled before the Civil War. That terrible conflict sapped energies for further growth for the better part of a decade, although the United States did purchase Alaska in the postwar years. Beginning earlier, but culminating in the 1890s, there developed a mood that was hospitable to overseas expansion. Some claimed that the development of markets abroad would alleviate, if not eliminate, the cycles of boom and bust that seemed to be getting worse. Others stressed the duty of the United States to Christianize and uplift native peoples, particularly in Asia. The Spanish-American War resulted not only in new possessions taken from Spain, such as the Philippines, but paved the way for acquisition of the Hawaiian Islands. Long dominant in the Western Hemisphere, the United States became recognizably a world power and was so considered by other nations.

"The Cycle of Reform" describes the turmoil of the 1890s, from brutal strikes in industry to the last massacre of Indians at Wounded Knee. "Forceful social and political criticism often prepares the way for change," William O'Neill writes, "and did so toward the end of the nineteenth century." He also points out some obvious parallels between that period and the 1990s. "Fighting Poverty the Old-Fashioned Way" explores in depth one reform O'Neill mentions: the settlement house movement that sought to expose the poor to middle-class values. "Ellis Island and the American Immigration Experience" also compares the 1890s with the 1990s. Then, as now, economic and social problems led some people to call for an end to immigration from abroad. Jewish immigrants encountered a particularly virulent form of prejudice through caricatures, according to the article "Anti-Semitism in American Caricature."

The Spanish-American War was short and relatively bloodless, as wars go. Far more destructive in lives and property was the Philippine Insurrection that followed. Philippine nationalists proved how even poorly equipped irregulars could employ guerrilla warfare to stymie a more powerful enemy. "Our First Southeast Asian War" shows the similarities between the Philippine Insurrection and the Vietnam War sixty years later. Both led to widespread atrocities and to an increasingly disenchanted American public.

"The Brownsville Affray" shows how deeply the currents of racism ran, denying to men in uniform even the most elementary standards of justice.

"George Washington Carver: Creative Scientist" tells the struggle of a young black man to gain an education appropriate to his intelligence. "He made no great theoretical breakthroughs," the author writes, "and did not develop a single new commercially successful product." What he did do, through his teaching and research, was to make scientific agricultural techniques available to thousands of struggling farmers.

Looking Ahead: Challenge Questions

A number of people during the 1890s questioned the direction in which the American society was heading. What were the perceived problems? What remedies were put forward? How well did they work?

Analyze the mistaken assumptions that led American policymakers to misjudge the Philippine Insurrection as they would later misjudge the war in Vietnam.

What did people hope to achieve through the settlement house movement? Is such a project feasible today?

Unit 2

The Cycle of Reform

William L. O'Neill

William L. O'Neill is professor of history at Rutgers University. He is the author of, among other books, A Better World *and* Feminism in America, *both published by Transaction.*

1890 has a special meaning to historians of the United States, for the census taken that year revealed a momentous fact. The Census Bureau put it as follows: "Up to and including 1890 the country had a frontier of settlement, but at present the unsettled area has been so broken into by isolated bodies of settlement that there can hardly be said to be a frontier line." A young historian, Frederick Jackson Turner, would soon use this sentence to begin one of the most influential articles ever written about our past. "The Significance of the Frontier in American History," a paper first given by Turner in July l0, 1893 during the World's Columbian Exposition in Chicago, has probably inspired the writing of more books and articles than any other piece of scholarship by an American historian. The central idea, advanced by Turner in this and later works, was that "the existence of an area of free land, its continuous recession, and the advance of American settlement westward explain American development."

What became known as "the frontier thesis" stimulated generations of historians, first to spread Turner's gospel, then to demolish it. Almost every key point that Turner made has since been refuted, and few if any accept today that the existence of free land determined the American character. Yet, like the Columbian Exposition itself—perhaps the greatest world's fair and arguably the most exuberant—Turner's thesis remains a monument to the boldness and optimism of his time. His daring is self-evident. Turner was 31, his Ph.D only three years old, and yet at a meeting of the American Historical Association he informed his seniors that they had contrived to miss the point of the entire national experience. His optimism is less manifest since, if American development was produced by a wilderness that had just disappeared, the future might seem gloomy. But Turner's thesis suggested that the frontier had done its work so well that it was no longer needed. Having triumphed over nature, American democracy was now self-renewing. Americans would go on to greater things, using their pioneer virtues to build a great industrial nation.

The Turnerians were right for the wrong reasons. Turner argued that, in addition to democracy, the "composite nationality" of Americans, our blend of ethnic groups, resulted from the frontier experience. But most historians believe that both the integration of people from many different nations and the extension of democratic rights are products of urbanization. No matter, he had identified many of the most important national traits, and by provoking historians to look at America in a fresh way stimulated lines of inquiry that would later prove more fruitful. Historians still admire Turner, for attacking the hard questions, for his originality, for his eloquence, for the breadth of his learning—he drew upon all the contemporary social sciences—for his love of research, and for his democratic values.

We also envy Turner his optimism, which now seems remarkable given the misery around him. Today many consider the fact that at least 15 percent of all Americans live in poverty to be a national disgrace. Yet in 1890 when Jacob Riis wrote his powerful expose of destitution in New York City he called it *How the Other Half Lives,* and understated the case at that since actually three fifths of the nation fell below the poverty line. Others besides Riis were troubled by the great distance between the few who monopolized America's industrial wealth, and the many who toiled to produce it. Edward Bellamy spoke to the worriers in his utopian novel *Looking Backward* (1888). Set in the year 2000, it described a cooperative social order which had replaced the cutthroat capitalism of America's Gilded Age. Although *Looking Backward* sold a million copies to a population one quarter the size of ours, and prompted the formation of many "Nationalist" clubs devoted to Bellamy's gospel, the tangible results were slight. Most educated Americans were unmoved by the suffering of the poor and did nothing about it.

Yet poverty declined all the same. By 1920 the earlier figure had been reversed, three-fifths of the population now being above, rather than below, the poverty line. And, irregularly to be sure, poverty would go on declining until the 1970s. In a sense, the optimism of Turner's generation has been justified by events. To us that generation often seems complacent beyond belief, quarreling about tariffs and currency questions while ignoring the distress of millions. But they did not view their era as we do, from the vantage point of a century of further development. In 1890 there were men and women still alive who could remember when nine out of ten Americans scratched a bare living from the soil, when the line of settlement was drawn east of the Mississippi, when travel proceeded no faster than a horse could walk or a ship under canvas sail. To Americans the nineteenth century was an age, not just of steam, but of miracles.

CLASS CONFLICT

Even so the basic confidence of the Gilded Age is all the more extraordinary considering that it was a time of savage

From *Society,* Vol. 27, No. 5, July/August 1990, pp. 63-68. Copyright © 1990 by Transaction Publishers. Reprinted by permission.

industrial warfare, labor-management disputes often being settled by those with the greatest firepower. In the summer of 1877 a wave of railroad strikes, together with sympathetic walkouts by factory workers and miners, brought the nation literally to a halt. In Baltimore after nine strikers were killed by state militiamen, riots broke out that took the lives of another 50 persons. In Chicago 19 perished when police and cavalry attacked an unauthorized demonstration. Twenty-six were killed in Pittsburgh during a night of rioting and looting that saw 2,000 railroad cars destroyed and a wall of fire three miles long engulf the center city. Though the death rate was never so high again, shooting strikers remained a management tool as late as 1937, when guards at a Republic Steel plant killed or wounded almost a hundred unarmed people.

To Americans, the nineteenth century was an age, not just of steam, but of miracles

---

Few issues troubled thoughtful men and women in the 1890s so much as class conflict, which involved not only workers but farmers—who were more numerous than workingmen and more political. In 1892 many of them organized as the People's, or Populist Party, and subsequently gained control of a handful of western states. With a platform calling for nationalization of the railroad and telegraph companies, extensive government aid to agriculture, and soft money, they threw a fright into the middle classes. Predictions of a bloody apocalypse more often involved workers than farmers, but some alarmists managed to include both. During the presidential campaign of 1896, when William Jennings Bryan inherited the Populists' following—though, except for soft money, not their program—young Theodore Roosevelt compared prominent Democrats and union heads to the leaders of the Paris Commune. They would try to make a revolution, he was sure, and he expected to meet them on the field of battle. Alternatively, or perhaps afterward, he favored "taking ten or a dozen of their leaders out, standing them against a wall, and shooting them dead."

Of course Roosevelt was excitable, others beside Mark Hanna regarding him

as a "madman." But fantasies of revolution aside, the 1890s were a remarkably turbulent decade, marred by a series of brutal strikes, notably against Carnegie Steel and the Pullman Sleeping Car Company, the Populist uprising, and a market panic in 1893 followed by the worst depression Americans had yet experienced. The last massacre of the Indian wars took place at a creek known as Wounded Knee in South Dakota, where, on December 28, 1890, almost 200 Sioux, men, women, and children alike, were shot by troopers of the 7th U.S. Cavalry. There were more lynchings by far during the 1890s than in any subsequent decade, 230 during one year alone. The level of collective domestic violence was higher than it ever would be again, including even the riot-plagued 1960s.

GREAT EVENTS HAVE ANTECEDENTS

What does this mean as we look to the end of our own century? One thing it fails to suggest is that rioting will become popular again. The bloody strikes of the 1890s resembled previous ones, while lynchings and urban mob actions had an even longer tradition. The Populists too were foreshadowed by earlier agrarian movements. Conversely, little has happened in recent years to indicate that the 1990s will be a stormy decade. Anything is possible, and we remember that much of the violence of the 1960s seemed to come out of nowhere. But it remains a rule of thumb that great events have antecedents, which, though easier to recognize after the fact, are usually visible before it. If such exist today they have escaped attention.

On the other hand, the fallow years we have been passing through must end sooner or later. Long ago Arthur M. Schlesinger, Sr. observed that there was a cycle in American political life which produced waves of reform every few decades. Today the pattern seems less regular than he supposed, but that it exists is hard to dispute. In the 1860s Republicans abolished slavery, passed the Homestead Act, and introduced other important measures, before taking the position Andrew Carnegie expressed in 1886: "If asked what important law I should change I must perforce say none; the laws are perfect." The ideology behind his remark was that of laissez-faire, which had created a great body of litera-

ture to the effect that government meddling in social and economic affairs always made things worse. In practice advocates of laissez-faire found exceptions to the rule, as when manufacturers secured tariffs to preserve "infant" industries long after they had become giants. Its imperfections notwithstanding, middle class people seemed thoroughly committed to laissez-faire in 1890, and yet, before very long, they would turn their backs upon it.

Knowing this does not help us determine what the prospects are for reforms in the 1990s, but history suggests the kind of indicators we ought to be looking for. Forceful social and political criticism often prepares the way for change, and did so toward the end of the nineteenth century. Edward Bellamy was one such critic, and so also was Henry George, whose great tract *Progress and Poverty* (1879), identified the "unearned increment" owners derived from rising land values as the curse of the laboring classes. Though his proposal for a "single tax" on real estate failed, George, like Bellamy, made people think about the sources of inequality. So too did Henry Demarest Lloyd, whose *Wealth Against Commonwealth* (1894) brilliantly attacked monopolies as a whole and Standard Oil in particular. It, and Lloyd's personal efforts, led the Populist convention that year to call for public ownership of all monopolies.

The Social Gospel movement was another precursor to the age of reform. Under laissez-faire Protestant clergymen saw inequality as part of the divine order. Henry Ward Beecher, the most famous minister of his day, announced that "God has intended the great to be great and the little to be little." Poverty was thus predestined, and yet at the same time deserved, for Beecher also said "no man suffers from poverty unless it be more than his fault—unless it also be his sin." This had to change if the leading denominations were not to remain obstacles to reform, and change it did, thanks to Walter Rauschenbusch and other progressive church leaders. Rauschenbusch—then a Baptist preacher in New York, later a theologian—was inspired by Henry George and the English Fabians to believe that it was not the church's role simply to interpret poverty and injustice, but actively to combat them. In 1892 he helped found the Brotherhood of the Kingdom as a means of doing so. Though fundamentalists were beyond reach,

Rauschenbusch and his allies would in time win over the mainstream denominations, making them engines of reform instead of barriers to it.

The social settlement movement would also contribute much to the coming struggle, though few could have guessed this in 1890, when there were only a handful of settlements and Hull House was just a year old. Social settlements enabled middle class men and women, usually recent college graduates, to live in slums and mingle with the local population. In time settlements would provide many social services, but the original intent was for residents to be helpful neighbors rather than case workers, to teach by example and establish rapport between the social classes. For many, including Jane Addams, living with the urban poor was a radicalizing experience. The need was so great, their resources so meager, that residents usually came to believe government alone could provide solutions. Settlements were training camps for young men and women who would become officers in the reform army when it finally mustered.

Most educated Americans were unmoved by the suffering of the poor and did nothing about it

---

George, Bellamy, and Lloyd were journalists and best selling authors, but the seeds of reform were being sown by professors, too. The end of the last century was a time of enormous intellectual vitality in a broad range of disciplines. The Ph.D., today often regarded as stultifying, had just been introduced and the first generation of scholars to possess it was notable both for ability and intellectual courage. William James and John Dewey in philosophy, Richard T. Ely, John Commons, Thorstein Veblen, and Simon Patten in economics, Lester Ward, E.A. Ross, and Albion Small in sociology, Turner, Charles Beard and James Harvey Robinson in history, among many others, destroyed the assumptions upon which laissez-faire depended.

Oliver Wendell Holmes, Jr. argued that legal principles were based on history and experience, not logic. The law is made by judges, he insisted, and can be unmade by them as well when circum-stances warrant. Veblen struck out against orthodox economics for being static, abstract, and preoccupied with discovering non-existent natural laws. His economics was an evolutionary science that saw man as much more than simply a producer and consumer of wealth. Morality also, Dewey held, was evolutionary and progressive. He denounced contemporary ethics for being archaic survivals that stood in the way of needed social and political improvements.

Under laissez-faire, Protestant clergymen saw inequality as part of the divine order

---

Together they staged what Morton White called "the revolt against formalism." By formalism White meant traditional logic, classical economics and jurisprudence, deductive reasoning, and all ways of thinking that were not pragmatic, experimental, and inductive. The rebellious scholars were, or tried to be, scientific, not in the sense of establishing new laws in their disciplines to replace old ones, but rather by employing sophisticated methods in their research, and by challenging the received wisdom. Formalists upheld a status quo based, as they saw it, upon immutable truths, unlike the rebels, who believed that truth was whatever worked for the good of society. Many of their students went on to become a new kind of reformer, a social technician equipped with the latest tools for practical problem solving. Some of these were what we would now call technocrats, but the best were imbued with the humane, rational, tolerant, flexible, and democratic spirit of their teachers.

Though the rebels against formalism did not create progressivism all by themselves, they performed several essential functions in addition to destroying the ideology of laissez-faire. Their work supplied a generation of reformers with arguments and ideas. And they fashioned the academic culture as we know it. We too believe that scholarly as well as scientific research ought to be pragmatic, instrumental and deductive, and, many of us still think that ideas should be used to better the human condition. Dewey and Veblen and their colleagues set the standard liberal academicians have measured themselves against ever since.

URBAN REFORM

Besides intellectual excitement, there was another way in which the 1890s were less barren than they seemed at the time. Though frustrated at the national level, reform blossomed in the cities. Eastern urban reformers tended to be businessmen and professionals mobilized against what they saw as corrupt and incompetent political machines. Their ambitions were often confined to making local government honest and business-like. William L. Strong, mayor of New York from 1895 to 1897, was this kind of reformer. Another type, more common in the Midwest, was epitomized by Hazen S. Pingree, mayor of Detroit from 1890 to 1897. Pingree and his colleagues not only wanted good government, but welfare services for the poor, the regulation of utilities and transport companies, and many other changes.

Urban reform was made necessary by the phenomenal growth of cities, especially in the Midwest. In 1880 one out of every five Midwesterners lived in towns over 4,000, a decade later one in three. In only ten years the urban population had doubled, Chicago, for example, growing from 500,000 to a population of about one million. It would have been difficult even for well run urban governments to cope with this breakneck expansion, which put intolerable strains upon even the most basic services. But the cities, far from being efficiently led, were under the control of bosses who, in connivance with dishonest businessmen, ran them for personal profit. The function of urban government, as they saw it, was to generate bribes and graft.

Middle class people resented this system, but, while times were good, not enough to challenge it. Then came the four year business collapse which followed the panic of 1893. Hard times greatly increased demands upon city governments, while their revenue base declined. Public utilities such as trolley systems, telephone companies, and water works, faced with shrinking earnings tended to raise their rates—despite the fact that most of their customers had less money to spend than before. This outrageous behavior, made possible by monopolization and the corrupt public officials who sustained it, aroused widespread anger. Since it affected virtually everyone in their roles as consumers, the arrogance of power had a unifying effect, bringing together small businessmen, professionals, women's organizations, trade union leaders and others who had never joined forces before.

David Thelen has shown in detail how this process worked in Wisconsin. The high levels of unemployment, as much as 50 percent in some cities, and sharp declines in income experienced by the business and professional classes, undermined faith in the status quo. Investigative journalists, discussion clubs, extension lectures by economists and sociologists from the state university, stirred citizens, got them to talking with one another, and helped them define their problems and seek collective solutions. Political organizations were formed to eliminate graft and corruption, place more employees under civil service, and reduce taxes. The discovery that lower taxes meant fewer services at a time when more were needed led to calls for action against wealthy individual and corporate tax evaders. In order to reduce the power of venal or unresponsive officials, reformers fought for instruments of "direct democracy," such as the recall and referendum.

In the nineteenth century, like today, Congress could not lead and the presidents refused to

---

Then came efforts to effectively regulate utilities, and even replace privately owned utilities with cooperative or municipally owned institutions. As many problems could only be solved with the aid or approval of state government, reformers in different communities reached out to one another. Robert M. La Follette was won over to reform in 1897 and elected governor three years later. Under La Follette Wisconsin became the most politically advanced state in the nation, initiating many reforms that were copied elsewhere. In a few more years "progressivism," as the movement came to be called, was a national phenomenon.

Every state had a somewhat different experience, reform did not always pre-

vail, and even when it did the results often fell short of what was expected. Even so, American political life was dramatically altered in the first decade of this century because of what had gone on earlier. The 1890s, and especially the years from 1893 to 1897, which had been a dark period shadowed by economic collapse and abortive farmer and worker uprisings, came in retrospect to assume a larger significance. It turned out to have been the seed time for an age of reform, an overture to greatness. And when the Progressive Era was born its midwife would be none other than Theodore Roosevelt, the onetime conservative having become a liberal in response to changing circumstances.

UNCERTAIN PARALLELS

What this means for us today is uncertain despite some obvious parallels. In 1890, as in 1990, the United States was suffering from decades of feeble government. Then, as now, the major parties were evenly balanced, Republicans winning most presidential elections while Democrats usually controlled the House and sometimes also the Senate. While partisanship was much more intense than today, the parties did not offer strikingly different programs and neither possessed a mandate for change. Unable to cope with poverty or the consequences of growth, politicians fought over the currency question, which, though hardly the nation's most urgent problem, seemed within their power to answer. Like today, Congress could not lead and the presidents refused to.

Our federal system of government requires presidential leadership to solve problems, but in the late nineteenth century chief executives were so retiring that Woodrow Wilson called his study of how the nation conducted its affairs *Congressional Government* (1885). Being locally oriented Congress cannot define the national interest and is always under pressure to service powerful constituents. Congressional government consisted largely of log rolling, pork barreling, and the delivery of favors. In 1890 there had been no strong presidents since Lincoln. We have not had a strong president since Nixon, who was no Lincoln to be sure, yet who made some historic changes.

Ronald Reagan might seem an exception, but though he was politically formi-

dable, he was also the first activist president since Andrew Jackson to weaken the federal government. Reagan destroyed government's ability to solve problems by raising the national debt to paralyzing levels, while at the same time fixing in stone the twin rules that defense spending must not be cut nor new taxes levied. Until the budget is brought under control there can be no new or expanded government programs, but that cannot be accomplished without reducing defense spending or increasing taxes. This fiscal Catch-22 is Reagan's legacy to America and, so long as it lasts, there can only be presidents like Bush—who, weight apart, reminds one of Grover Cleveland.

Yet there remains the hope that a dynamic new leader has arisen who may lead us out of stagnation. That man is, of course, Mikhail Gorbachev. If he brings the cold war to an end, as seems entirely possible, the defense budget will no longer be sacred. And reductions in defense spending can hardly fail to benefit the nation, by reducing the deficit, or funding new programs, or by some combination of both. Most of the traditional harbingers of reform do not now exist. There is no great literature of protest, except against Reaganomics: there are no promising political movements on the state and local level; neither war nor a great depression quickens the pace of change. But if post-cold war America enjoys the kind of affluence this country once knew, that itself might encourage progress. After all, two of the three twentieth-century reform eras came during periods of record abundance. Even now, just off stage, another Roosevelt may be waiting.

READINGS SUGGESTED BY THE AUTHOR:

Billington, R. *Frederick Jackson Turner.* New York: Oxford University Press, 1973.

Davis, A. *Spearheads for Reform: The Social Settlements and the Progressive Movement, 1890-1914.* New York: Oxford University Press, 1967.

Link, A. & R. McCormick. *Progressivism.* Arlington Heights, Ill.: Harlan Davidson, Inc., 1983.

Thelen, D. *The New Citizenship: Origins of Progressivism in Wisconsin, 1885-1900.* Columbia, Mo.: University of Missouri Press, 1972.

White, M. *Social Thought in America: The Revolt Against Formalism.* New York: Viking Press, 1949.

Ellis Island and the American Immigration Experience

The National Immigration Museum pays homage to those who passed through Ellis Island en route to a new life in the land of liberty as well as the unfortunate ones that were turned away.

Robert F. Zeidel

Dr. Zeidel is assistant professor of history, College of St. Thomas, St. Paul, Minn.

On Sept. 9, 1990, the renovated immigration station at Ellis Island, closed since 1954, reopened its doors amidst considerable fanfare as the National Immigration Museum. In the process, descendants of the station's first visitors sought to discover their roots, at perhaps the most tangible remnant of a myriad of journeys from old world to new. A few of the original immigrants also came back, some no doubt hoping to re-experience what must have been a traumatic rite of passage. As these and other invited guests prowled the grounds and toured the renovated Great Hall, America vicariously celebrated its ethnic past.

The site will stand as a monument to the estimated 12,000,000 men, women, and children who passed through on the final leg of their voyage to America, but it also should serve as a reminder of those turned away and to the policy decisions that prompted their exclusion. It is the latter, perhaps the easiest to overlook, which best explains the immigrant's place in American history.

Amid the pomp and circumstance, some commentators have noted that Ellis Island was a place of travail, where immigrants underwent an inspection that determined their admission or rejection. The unlucky went home. In its *Historic Structure Report*, the National Park Service said of the station: "While a 'Portal of Hope and Freedom' for many, it was an 'Island of Tears' for those who were turned away, when they failed to meet the requirements of the immigration laws and regulations." Even those who met the prerequisites could not escape the indignities of physical examinations and character scrutiny. For example, one former immigrant, who attended the dedication ceremony, recalled being "stripped, poked, prodded, and questioned for what seemed like hours."

Such reminiscences adequately convey the personal traumas experienced by those who passed through the immigrant station, but fail to denote properly either the underlying issue—"the immigration question"—or the years of debate it engendered. Ellis Island owed its existence to a policy of selective immigration restriction, whose authors had concluded that the U.S. must stop taking in every European arrival. (Orientals had been barred previously by the Chinese Exclusion Act of 1882.) Americans came to attribute their social ills to immigration; over time, the restrictionist rationale was that large numbers of otherwise acceptable foreigners could be injurious to the nation's institutions.

Traditional interpretations of the decision to exclude certain new arrivals have focused on the immigrants themselves, but closer examination reveals that the calls for restriction stemmed more from developments within the U.S. The so-called new immigrants—Slavs, Poles, southern Italians, and eastern-European Jews of one generation and the Mexicans, Filipinos, and Vietnamese of another—have aroused enmity because of their different ethnic and cultural characteristics. A number of hard-line restrictionists have expressed the fear that these peoples somehow would dilute America's theretofore homogeneous population, thereby destroying the nation's unique, positive qualities. At the time of the first calls for restriction, such pundits harped on the non-Teutonic ethnicity of an ever-increasing number and percentage of the new arrivals. Yet, more than either the "new" immigrants' ethnicity or the converse nativists' xenophobia, it has been indigenous American conditions that have fueled the debate over alien exclusion.

BLAMING NEWCOMERS

Throughout the 20th century, restrictionists have focused either on the nation's inability to assimilate properly its large and growing number of immigrants or the vague threats posed by smaller numbers of specifically destructive aliens, and Congress has sought to alleviate the situation by remedial legislation. Ellis Island, and the bureaucracy it served, came into being as a result of this agenda. The station owed its existence not to xenophobia, defined as fear of those who are different, or even to a benign desire to welcome immigrants in an orderly fashion. Ellis Island represented, and continues to do so, the nation's response to changing social conditions, deteriorating in the eyes of many Americans, to which immigrants were accused of contributing.

By the late 19th century, the problems of an increasingly urban and industrial society—urban squalor, labor unrest, and economic uncertainty—heightened citizens' fears that their democratic nation,

Until it was closed in 1954, Ellis Island was the first experience faced by millions of immigrants to the United States. For all those that were fortunate enough to enter the United States enormous numbers were turned away due to regulations and a policy of selective immigration.

with its high standard of living, was on the verge of collapse. It seemed that each shipload of new arrivals exacerbated the situation, making corrective actions that much more difficult. Photo-journalist Jacob Riis' depictions of the urban ghetto, Pullman and Homestead strikes, and depressions combined to give impetus to the initial restrictionist movement of the 1890s. In addition, allegations of anarchism, such as that associated with the violence at Chicago's Haymarket Square in 1886, convinced some Americans that revolution was at hand.

As these social maladies captured national attention, a citizenry that traditionally had sought to solve its problems at the local level increasingly turned to the Federal government for direction and assistance. The Supreme Court left little alternative in the case of immigration, ruling in 1876 that state regulation vio-

lated Congress' exclusive right to regulate interstate commerce. This mandate followed a trend toward centralization, as an apprehensive public did little to challenge the concentration of power in Washington. Business leaders supported Congress' move to create a commission to monitor railroads, and property holders approved of Pres. Grover Cleveland's decision to use troops to quell labor unrest. In a similar vein, the Supreme Court acted to define the proper status and behavior of large corporations. It was to be expected, then, that immigration would not escape Federal scrutiny, in this case by Congress.

By 1900, statutes excluded convicts, lunatics, criminals, polygamists, and those suffering from loathsome or contagious diseases. Persons coming to America to fulfill prearranged employment, so-called contract laborers, similarly

were barred. Other laws set forth procedures for the steamship lines that transported immigrants, including a provision whereby they had to return excluded persons to their ports of embarkation. To oversee the growing bureaucracy, Congress provided for the appointment of a Superintendent of Immigration, whose duties included preparing an annual report on the workings of the Immigration Service.

The most salient omission from turn-of-the-century immigration policy was a general exclusion law, but its absence was not due to a lack of effort. Starting in 1895, a core group of Congressmen, led by Henry Cabot Lodge (R.-Mass.), had worked assiduously to draft, pass, and secure presidential approval of a literacy test bill, also called the educational qualification, a measure intended to reduce the number of annual arrivals by excluding illiterates. Its proponents admitted that the inability to read and write did not necessarily render an immigrant undesirable, but advocates viewed the measure as a sure and workable means of general exclusion. Those to be prohibited—the illiterates—were described vaguely as qualitatively less welcome because of their difficulty in assimilation, propensity for living in urban slums, and likelihood of falling under venal influences, such as anarchism. Literacy test supporters could not find specific fault with those they wished to exclude, but did agree that a general reduction in the total number of arrivals would help alleviate domestic social problems.

Cleveland's 1897 immigration bill veto temporarily stymied literacy test supporters, but, soon after 1900, they redoubled their efforts. By this time, the educational qualification had become the preferred method of general exclusion, and it remained at the center of immigration policy debate until its enactment in 1917. In the intervening years, Congress did pass several related acts, which tended to follow an established pattern of tailoring legislation to address specific domestic concerns.

The Immigration Act of 1903, for example, barred alien anarchists and extended the time for deporting an already admitted individual found to have such proclivities. The bill passed shortly after the assassination of Pres. William McKinley by native-born anarchist Leon Czolgosz (whose foreign sounding name did not escape notice) in 1901, an event many Americans believed was linked to some nefarious radical conspiracy. Authorities arrested immigrant anarchist Emma Goldman, alleging her complicity in Czolgosz's actions, and tried to find proof that the assassination was part of a larger, clandestine, revolutionary plot. The immense evidence that he acted alone did little to allay public fears and, in 1902–03, at a time when general public concern for immigration restriction had dwindled, Congressmen on both sides of the immigration question readily embraced the prohibition of alien radicals.

Between 1905 and 1910, domestic issues again carried over into immigration policy discussion. The concern centered on white slavery and the paranoid belief among middle-class reformers that well-organized prostitution rings sought to entrap innocent young females and use them for immoral purposes. Newly arrived immigrants, they asserted, were at

particular risk. Therefore, in 1907, Congress acted to prohibit the importation of females for purposes of prostitution, one of a few universally supported sections of an otherwise acrimoniously debated bill. Three years later, the Mann Act gave the Federal government expanded police powers to combat and interdict the interstate movement of immoral women. At the time of its passage, restrictionists hoped the public's call for action on this issue could be converted into demand for general immigration restriction. Exponents sought to attach a literacy test provision to the Mann Act, but their efforts fell short. Still, the transfer of a negative image—that of purveyor of prostitution—to the immigration question follows the pattern of blaming foreign-born arrivals for domestic ills.

In 1917, proponents finally enacted the literacy test. This measure earlier had passed either the House or Senate, and three times had been approved by both chambers. In 1913 and 1915, Presidents William H. Taft and Woodrow Wilson, respectively, had vetoed such bills; Congress failed to override each time. Wilson invoked the veto for a second time in 1917, but this time supporters secured enough votes to override. As they had in the past, arguments centered on the contention that social progress necessitated reducing the number of new arrivals, not on how illiterates undermined America's social or political institutions. As Sen. John F. Kennedy (D.-Mass.) stated in 1958, the literacy test's passage marked "a significant turning point in immigration policy." It signaled a rejection of the notion that America could absorb and assimilate any number of honest, hard-working foreigners. The time had passed when America could (or would) accommodate a limitless number of immigrants. The problem lay not with the immigrants, but with the U.S.

The literacy test's passage paved the way for additional restrictive legislation. During the 1920s, new means of limiting immigration—the use of numerical quotas—were initiated. Ironically, immigration specialists had developed the concept in the 1910s as a more equitable alternative to the literacy test, envisioning a system that would not discriminate against any nationality or ethnic group, including Orientals. The original scheme would have favored recently arriving nationalities by limiting the annual total for each group to a percentage of its number as enumerated in the most recent census.

The proposal received some attention, but preoccupation with the literacy test precluded serious consideration of numerical restrictions for almost a decade.

Congress debated the quota system in a milieu far different from that at the time of its inception. Americans of the 1920s had grown weary of the progressive ethos of the previous decade and, in the words of newly elected Pres. Warren G. Harding, wanted to "return to normalcy." On the immigration question, this meant further repudiation of the belief that the U.S. should attempt to assimilate a host of diverse foreigners or could try to build a heterogeneous and multi-cultural society. As in other areas, Americans' willingness to devote their time, energies, and resources to the cause of reform, often abstract and too often unfulfilled, waned considerably

Concurrently, a wave of conservatism swept the nation. Attorney General A. Mitchell Palmer planned and executed a series of raids against alleged subversive groups. Carried out in November, 1919, and January, 1920, they resulted in the arrest of 6,000 people, some of whom then were deported to Russia. Those deported on the *Buford,* nicknamed the "Red Ark," included Emma Goldman. In this same reactionary vein, Massachusetts tried, convicted, and put to death Nicola Sacco and Bartolomeo Vanzetti, punished as much for their radical political beliefs as for any proof of their connection to a fatal robbery, and the Ku Klux Klan re-emerged, attracting 100,000 members to its campaign of racial violence. Hardly surprising, a new immigration act exhibited little of the reform mentality of its original authors.

In 1921, Congressional opponents embraced the idea of numerical restriction, but wrote the statute so as to discriminate against the newest arrivals. Rather than using the number of each immigrant group as found in the most recent census—in this case, 1920—Congress opted to use the 1910 census. This worked against the so-called new immigrants, who primarily had arrived during the last decade. In 1924, Congress drafted an even more restrictive procedure, using the 1890 census, effectively prohibiting the immigration of those belonging to some recently arrived nationalities or groups. This change, though certainly ethnocentric, nonetheless represented a conservative attempt to militate against domestic unrest or social challenges by taking drastic action against immigration.

THE "RED MENACE"

Cold War conditions of the late 1940s and early 1950s set the stage for yet another immigration controversy. This time, it was not conditions engendered by mass migration that provoked anti-alien reaction; the quota acts effectively had brought such conditions to an end. Instead, Americans returned their attention to an old adversary, imported radicalism, which now had a new name—communism. A small number of subversives, Americans feared, threatened to undermine the U.S.'s democratic government and social values. This concept of "internal security threats" viewed radicalism as being largely of imported origin. Oddly, this occurred at a time when natives, not immigrants, dominated the leadership of the American Communist Party, the most distrusted manifestation of domestic radicalism.

At the height of the Cold War, Congress passed two acts intended to protect America from the imported "red menace." The 1950 McCarran Internal Security Act denied admission to any person who ever had belonged to a communist party or similar "front" organization. The act also called for the deportation of any alien who had belonged to such organizations. The 1952 McCarran-Walter Immigration Act both codified existing legislation and introduced new provisions aimed at interdicting and deporting alien subversives. Like other Cold War policies, the two McCarran acts told more of America's intolerance for political dissent than of the nature of immigration itself.

Pres. Lyndon Johnson's Great Society brought forth a major revision of U.S. immigration laws, and the 1965 Hart-Celler Act ended the use of national origin as the primary determinant of immigrant admission. The total quota was set at 290,000, with the Western Hemisphere having 120,000 places and the Eastern Hemisphere 170,000; the law gave preferential treatment to family members of those living in the U.S. and to refugees. Though long overdue, this revision again represented changing domestic attitudes, as the Johnson Administration took the lead in seeking reform measures in such areas as civil rights and entitlement programs. If not for this liberal spirit, it is doubtful that Congress would have moved to amend the nation's immigration laws.

Autumn, 1990, witnessed another attempt at immigration reform. Though many distinctly immigrant issues warranted action, purely native concerns attracted much of the public attention. In the new measure, Congress intended to facilitate the immigration of the highly skilled, many of whom have been trained at American universities, as well as raise the total annual quota to 700,000. Yet, much of the debate centered not on the bill's provisions, but on the failure of America's educational system to produce individuals capable of filling skill- or knowledge-intensive positions. The entire notion of the U.S. as a refuge has gotten lost in the quagmire of America's inadequate schools, and, once again, immigrants have seen their interests suppressed by a decidedly non-immigrant issue.

On Nov. 11, 1990, Pres. George Bush signed a new immigration act into law, and tourists ferried out to take in the sights of Ellis Island. For those of immigrant ancestry, the National Park Service offered the opportunity to add the names of their forebears to the American Immigrant Wall of Honor for a $100 donation. To complete this historic tableau, another wall should display the names Henry Cabot Lodge, William P. Dillingham, John L. Burnett, Albert Johnson, Pat McCarran, and Alan K. Simpson. Without the work of these men, and the acts that came to bear their names, Ellis Island and the other manifestations of American immigration policy would not have existed. By the same token, this latter wall should contain the words urbanization, industrialization, anarchism, unionism, and communism, without which those men would have had no foundation for their policies.

BATTLES WON AND LOST

Our First Southeast Asian War

America's turn-of-the-century military campaign against Philippine insurgents consumed three years, involved 126,000 troops, and cost 4,000 lives. The lessons we learned could have been used in Vietnam sixty years later.

David R. Kohler and James W. Wensyel

David R. Kohler, Commander, U.S. Navy, is a Naval Special Warfare officer who has served multiple tours in UDT (underwater demolition) and SEAL (sea, air, land) teams. He has a master's degree in national security affairs from the Naval Postgraduate School in Monterey, California.

James W. Wensyel, a retired Army officer, is the author of three published books and numerous articles. His article on the crash of the dirigible Shenandoah *appeared in the February 1989 issue of* American History Illustrated. *He resides with his wife Jean in Newville, Pennsylvania.*

Guerrilla warfare . . . jungle terrain . . . search and destroy missions . . . benevolent pacification . . . strategic hamlets . . . terrorism . . . ambushes . . . free-fire zones booby traps . . . waning support from civilians at home. These words call forth from the national consciousness uncomfortable images of a war Americans fought and died in not long ago in Southeast Asia. But while the phrases may first bring to mind America's painful experience in Vietnam during the 1960s and '70s, they also aptly describe a much earlier conflict—the Philippine Insurrection—that foreshadowed this and other insurgent wars in Asia.

The Philippine-American War of 1898–1902 is one of our nation's most obscure and least-understood campaigns. Sometimes called the "Bolo War" because of the Filipino insurgents' lethally effective use of razor-sharp bolo knives or machetes against the American expeditionary force occupying the islands, it is often viewed as a mere appendage of the one-hundred-day Spanish-American War. But suppressing the guerrilla warfare waged by Philippine nationalists seeking self-rule proved far more difficult, protracted, and costly for American forces than the conventional war with Spain that had preceded it.

America's campaign to smash the Philippine Insurrection was, ironically, a direct consequence of U.S. efforts to secure independence for other *insurrectos* halfway around the world in Cuba. On May 1, 1898, less than a week after Congress declared war against Spain, a naval squadron commanded by Commodore George Dewey steamed into Manila Bay to engage the Spanish warships defending that nation's Pacific possession. In a brief action Dewey achieved a stunning victory, sinking all of the enemy vessels with no significant American losses. Destroying the Spanish fleet, however, did not ensure U.S. possession of the Philippines. An estimated 15,000 Spanish soldiers still occupied Manila and the surrounding region. Those forces would have to be rooted out by infantry.

President William McKinley had already ordered a Philippine Expeditionary Force of volunteer and regular army infantry, artillery, and cavalry units (nearly seven thousand men), under the command of Major General Wesley Merritt, to "reduce Spanish power in that quarter [Philippine Islands] and give order and security to the islands while in the possession of the United States."

Sent to the Philippines in the summer of 1898, this limited force was committed without fully considering the operation's potential length and cost. American military and government leaders also failed to anticipate the consequences of ignoring the Filipino rebels who, under Generalissimo Don Emilio Aguinaldo y Famy, had been waging a war for independence against Spain for the past two years. And when American insensitivity toward Aguinaldo eventually led to open warfare with the rebels, the American leaders grossly underestimated the determination of the seemingly ill-trained and poorly armed insurgents. They additionally failed to perceive the difficulties involved in conducting military operations in a tropical environment and among a hostile native population, and they did not recognize the burden of fighting at the end of a seven-thousand-mile-long logistics trail.

Asian engagements, the Americans learned for the first time, are costly. The enterprise, so modestly begun, eventually saw more than 126,000 American

From *American History Illustrated*, January/February 1990, pp. 19-30. Reprinted through the courtesy of Cowles Magazines, publishers of *American History Illustrated*.

officers and men deployed to the Philippines. Four times as many soldiers served in this undeclared war in the Pacific as had been sent to the Caribbean during the Spanish-American War. During the three-year conflict, American troops and Filipino insurgents fought in more than 2,800 engagements. American casualties ultimately totaled 4,234 killed and 2,818 wounded, and the insurgents lost about 16,000 men. The civilian population suffered even more; as many as 200,000 Filipinos died from famine, pestilence, or the unfortunate happenstance of being too close to the fighting. The Philippine war cost the United States $600 million before the insurgents were subdued.

The costly experience offered valuable and timeless lessons about guerrilla warfare in Asia; unfortunately, those lessons had to be relearned sixty years later in another war that, despite the modern technology involved, bore surprising parallels to America's first Southeast Asian campaign.

ORIGINS

America's war with Spain, formally declared by the United States on April 25, 1898, had been several years in the making. During that time the American "yellow press," led by Joseph Pulitzer's *New York World* and William Randolph Hearst's *New York Journal,* trumpeted reports of heroic Cuban *insurrectos* revolting against their cruel Spanish rulers. Journalists vividly described harsh measures taken by Spanish officials to quell the Cuban revolution. The sensational accounts, often exaggerated, reminded

Americans of their own uphill fight for independence and nourished the feeling that America was destined to intervene so that the Cuban people might also taste freedom.

Furthermore, expansionists suggested that the revolt against a European power, taking place less than one hundred miles from American shores, offered a splendid opportunity to turn the Caribbean into an American sea. Businessmen pointed out that $50 million in American capital was invested in the Cuban sugar and mining industries. Revolutions resulting in burned cane fields jeopardized that investment. As 1898 opened, American relations with Spain quickly declined.

In January 1898 the U.S. battleship *Maine* was sent to Cuba, ostensibly on a courtesy visit. On February 15 the warship was destroyed by a mysterious explosion while at anchor in Havana harbor, killing 262 of her 350-man crew. The navy's formal inquiry, completed on March 28, suggested that the explosion was due to an external force—a mine.

On March 29, the Spanish govern-

ment received an ultimatum from Washington, D.C.: Spain's army in Cuba was to lay down its arms while the United States negotiated between the rebels and the Spaniards. The Spanish forces were also told to abolish all *reconcentrado* camps (tightly controlled areas, similar to the strategic hamlets later tried in Vietnam, where peasants were regrouped to deny food and intelligence to insurgents and to promote tighter security). Spain initially rejected the humiliation of surrendering its arms in the field but then capitulated on all points. The Americans were not satisfied.

On April 11, declaring that Spanish responses were inadequate, President McKinley told a joint session of Congress that "I have exhausted every effort to relieve the intolerable condition . . . at our doors. I now ask the Congress to empower the president to take measures to secure a full and final termination of hostilities in Cuba, to secure . . . the establishment of a stable government, and to use the military and naval forces

Manila-bound soldiers on a troopship pulling away from a San Francisco pier watch as the last man climbs aboard (right). At the height of the Spanish-American War, President William McKinley sent a seven-thousand-man expeditionary force to occupy the Philippines; during the next three years nearly twenty times that number of Americans would become involved in operations against Filipino insurgents.

of the United States . . . for these purposes. . . ."

Congress adopted the proposed resolution on April 19. Learning this, Spain declared war on the 24th. The following day, the United States responded with its own declaration of war.

The bulk of the American navy quickly gathered on the Atlantic coast. McKinley called for 125,000 volunteers to bolster the less than eighty-thousand-man regular army. His call was quickly oversubscribed; volunteers fought to be the first to land on Cuba's beaches.

The first major battle of the war, however, was fought not in Cuba but seven thousand miles to the west—in Manila Bay. Dewey's victory over Spanish Admiral Patricio Montojo y Pasarón (a rather hollow victory as Montojo's fleet consisted of seven unarmored ships, three of which had wooden hulls and one that had to be towed to the battle area) was wildly acclaimed in America.

American leaders, believing that the Philippines would now fall into America's grasp like a ripe plum, had to decide what to do with their prize. They could not return the islands to Spain, nor could they allow them to pass to France or Germany, America's commercial rivals in the Orient. The American press rejected the idea of a British protectorate. And, after four hundred years of despotic Spanish rule in which Filipinos had little or no chance to practice self-government, native leaders seemed unlikely candidates for managing their own affairs. McKinley faced a grand opportunity for imperialistic expansion that could not be ignored.

The debate sharply divided his cabinet—and the country. American public opinion over acquisition of the Philippines divided into two basic factions: imperialists versus anti-imperialists.

The imperialists, mostly Republicans, included such figures as Theodore Roosevelt (then assistant secretary of the navy), Henry Cabot Lodge (Massachusetts senator), and Albert Beveridge (Indiana senator). These individuals were, for the most part, disciples of Alfred Thayer Mahan, a naval strategist who touted theories of national power and prestige through sea power and acquisition of overseas colonies for trade purposes and naval coaling stations.

The anti-imperialists, staunchly against American annexation of the Philippines, were mainly Democrats. Such men as former presidents Grover Cleveland and

Rutherford B. Hayes, steel magnate Andrew Carnegie, William Jennings Bryan, union leader Samuel Gompers, and Mark Twain warned that by taking the Philippines the United States would march the road to ruin earlier traveled by the Roman Empire. Furthermore, they argued, America would be denying Filipinos the right of self-determination guaranteed by our own Constitution. The more practical-minded also pointed out that imperialistic policy would require maintaining an expensive army and navy there.

Racism, though demonstrated in different ways, pervaded the arguments of both sides. Imperialists spoke of the "white man's burden" and moral responsibility to "uplift the child races everywhere" and to provide "orderly development for the unfortunate and less able races." They spoke of America's "civilizing mission" of pacifying Filipinos by "benevolent assimilation" and saw the opening of the overseas frontier much as their forefathers had viewed the western frontier. The "subjugation of the Injun" (wherever he might be found) was a concept grasped by American youth—the war's most enthusiastic supporters (in contrast to young America's opposition to the war in Vietnam many years later).

The anti-imperialists extolled the sacredness of independence and self-determination for the Filipinos. Racism, however, also crept into their argument, for they believed that "protection against race mingling" was a historic American policy that would be reversed by imperialism. To them, annexation of the Philippines would admit "alien, inferior, and mongrel races to our nationality."

As the debate raged, Dewey continued to hold Manila Bay, and the Philippines seemed to await America's pleasure. President McKinley would ultimately cast the deciding vote in determining America's role in that country. McKinley, a genial, rather laid-back, former congressman from Ohio and one-time major in the Union army, remains a rather ambiguous figure during this period. In his Inaugural Address he had affirmed that "We want no wars of conquest; we must avoid the temptation of territorial aggression." Thereafter, however, he made few comments on pacifism, and, fourteen weeks after becoming president, signed the bill annexing Hawaii.

Speaking of Cuba in December 1897, McKinley said, "I speak not of forcible annexation, for that cannot be thought of.

That, by our code of morality, would be criminal aggression." Nevertheless, he constantly pressured Madrid to end Spanish rule in Cuba, leading four months later to America's war with Spain.

McKinley described experiencing extreme turmoil, soul-searching, and prayer over the Philippine annexation issue until, he declared, one night in a dream the Lord revealed to him that "there was nothing left for us to do but to take them all [the Philippine Islands] and to educate the Filipinos, and uplift, and civilize, and Christianize them." He apparently didn't realize that the Philippines had been staunchly Roman Catholic for more than 350 years under Spanish colonialism. Nor could he anticipate the difficulties that, having cast its fortune with the expansionists, America would now face in the Philippines.

PROSECUTING THE WAR

Meanwhile, in the Philippine Islands, Major General Wesley Merritt's Philippine Expeditionary Force went about its job. In late June, General Thomas Anderson led an advance party ashore at Cavite. He then established Camp Merritt, visited General Aguinaldo's rebel forces entrenched around Manila, and made plans for seizing that city once Merritt arrived with the main body of armed forces.

Anderson quickly learned that military operations in the Philippines could be difficult. His soldiers, hastily assembled and dispatched with limited prior training, were poorly disciplined and inadequately equipped. Many still wore woolen uniforms despite the tropical climate. A staff officer described the army's baptism at Manila: " . . . the heat was oppressive and the rain kept falling. At times the trenches were filled with two feet of water, and soon the men's shoes were ruined. Their heavy khaki uniforms were a nuisance; they perspired constantly, the loss of body salts inducing chronic fatigue. Prickly heat broke out, inflamed by scratching and rubbing. Within a week the first cases of dysentery, malaria, cholera, and dengue fever showed up at sick call."

During his first meeting with Dewey, Anderson remarked that some American leaders were considering annexation of the Philippines. "If the United States intends to hold the Philippine Islands," Dewey responded, "it will make things awkward, because just a week ago Aguinaldo proclaimed the independence of the Philippine Islands from Spain and seems intent on establishing his own government."

A Filipino independence movement led by Aguinaldo had been active in the islands since 1896 and, within weeks of Dewey's victory, Aguinaldo's revolutionaries controlled most of the archipelago.

Aguinaldo, twenty-nine years old in 1898, had taken over his father's position as mayor of his hometown of Kawit before becoming a revolutionary. In a minor skirmish with Spanish soldiers, he had rallied the Filipinos to victory. Thereafter, his popularity grew as did his ragtag but determined army. Aguinaldo was slight of build, shy, and soft-spoken, but a strict disciplinarian.

As his rebel force besieged Manila, Aguinaldo declared a formal government for the Philippines with himself as president and generalissimo. He proclaimed his "nation's" independence and called for Filipinos to rally to his army and to the Americans, declaring that "the Americans . . . extend their protecting mantle to our beloved country . . . When you see the American flag flying, assemble in numbers: they are our redeemers!" But his enthusiasm for the United States later waned.

Stymied by the Filipinos' use of guerrilla warfare, the Americans were forced to change their strategy.

Merritt put off Aguinaldo's increasingly strident demands that America recognize his government and guarantee the Filipinos' independence. Aguinaldo perceived the American general's attitude as condescending and demeaning.

On August 13, Merritt's forces occupied Manila almost without firing a shot; in a face-saving maneuver the Spanish defenders had agreed to surrender to the Americans to avoid being captured—and perhaps massacred—by the Filipino insurgents. Merritt's troops physically blocked Aguinaldo's rebels, who had spent weeks in the trenches around the city, from participating in the assault. The Filipino general and his followers felt betrayed at being denied a share in the victory.

Further disenchanted, Aguinaldo would

later find his revolutionary government unrepresented at the Paris peace talks determining his country's fate. He would learn that Spain had ceded the Philippines to the United States for $20 million.

Officers at Merritt's headquarters had little faith in the Filipinos' ability to govern themselves. "Should our power . . . be withdrawn," an early report declared, "the Philippines would speedily lapse into anarchy, which would excuse . . . the intervention of other powers and the division of the islands among them."

Meanwhile, friction between American soldiers and the Filipinos increased. Much of the Americans' conduct betrayed their racial bias. Soldiers referred to the natives as "niggers" and "gugus," epithets whose meanings were clear to the Filipinos. In retaliation, the island inhabitants refused to give way on sidewalks and muscled American officers into the streets. Men of the expeditionary force in turn escalated tensions by stopping Filipinos at gun point, searching them without cause, "confiscating" shopkeepers' goods, and beating those who resisted.

On the night of February 4, 1899 the simmering pot finally boiled over. Private William "Willie" Walter Grayson and several other soldiers of Company D, 1st Nebraska Volunteer Infantry, apprehended a group of armed insurgents within their regimental picket line. Shots were exchanged, and three Filipino *insurrectos* fell dead. Heavy firing erupted between the two camps.

In the bloody battle that followed, the Filipinos suffered tremendous casualties (an estimated two thousand to five thousand dead, contrasted with fifty-nine Americans killed) and were forced to withdraw. The Philippine Insurrection had begun.

GUERRILLA WARFARE

The Americans, hampered by a shortage of troops and the oncoming rainy season, could initially do little more than extend their defensive perimeter beyond Manila and establish a toehold on several islands to the south. By the end of March, however, American forces seized Malolos, the seat of Aguinaldo's revolutionary government. But Aguinaldo escaped, simply melting into the jungle. In the fall, using conventional methods of warfare, the Americans first struck south, then

north of Manila across the central Luzon plain. After hard marching and tough fighting, the expeditionary force occupied northern Luzon, dispersed the rebel army, and barely missed capturing Aguinaldo.

Believing that occupying the remainder of the Philippines would be easy, the Americans wrongly concluded that the war was virtually ended. But when the troops attempted to control the territory they had seized, they found that the Filipino revolutionaries were not defeated but had merely changed strategies. Abandoning western-style conventional warfare, Aguinaldo had decided to adopt guerrilla tactics.

Aguinaldo moved to a secret mountain headquarters at Palanan in northern Luzon, ordering his troops to disperse and avoid pitched battles in favor of hit-and-run operations by small bands. Ambushing parties of Americans and applying terror to coerce support from other Filipinos, the insurrectionists now blended into the countryside, where they enjoyed superior intelligence information, ample supplies, and tight security. The guerrillas moved freely between the scattered American units, cutting telegraph lines, attacking supply trains, and assaulting straggling infantrymen. When the Americans pursued their tormentors, they fell into well planned ambushes. The insurgents' barbarity and ruthlessness during these attacks were notorious.

The guerrilla tactics helped to offset the inequities that existed between the two armies. The American troops were far better armed, for example, carrying .45-caliber Springfield single-shot rifles, Mausers, and then-modern .30-caliber repeating Krag-Jorgensen rifles. They also had field artillery and machine guns. The revolutionaries, on the other hand, were limited to a miscellaneous assortment of handguns, a few Mauser repeating rifles taken from the Spanish, and antique muzzle-loaders. The sharp-edged bolo knife was the revolutionary's primary weapon, and he used it well. Probably more American soldiers were hacked to death by bolos than were killed by Mauser bullets.

As would later be the case in Vietnam, the guerrillas had some clear advantages. They knew the terrain, were inured to the climate, and could generally count on a friendly population. As in Vietnam, villages controlled by the insurgents provided havens from which the guerrillas could attack, then fade back into hiding.

Americans soon began to feel that they

were under siege in a land of enemies, and their fears were heightened because they never could be sure who among the population was hostile. A seemingly friendly peasant might actually be a murderer. Lieutenant Colonel J. T. Wickham, commanding the 26th Infantry Regiment, recorded that "a large flag of truce enticed officers into ambushes . . . Privates Dugan, Hayes, and Tracy were murdered by town authorities . . . Private Nolan [was] tied up by ladies while in a stupor; the insurgents cut his throat . . . The body of Corporal Doneley was dug up, burned, and mutilated . . . Private O'Hearn, captured by apparently friendly people was tied to a tree, burned over a slow fire, and slashed up . . . Lieutenant Max Wagner was assassinated by insurgents disguised in American uniforms."

As in later guerrilla movements, such terrorism became a standard tactic for the insurgents. Both Filipinos and Americans were their victims. In preying on their countrymen, the guerrillas had a dual purpose: to discourage any Filipinos disposed to cooperate with the Americans, and to demonstrate to people in a particular region that they ruled that area and could destroy inhabitants and villages not supporting the revolution. The most favored terroristic weapon was assassination of local leaders, who were usually executed in a manner (such as beheading or burying alive) calculated to horrify everyone.

By the spring of 1900 the war was going badly for the Americans. Their task forces, sent out to search and destroy, found little and destroyed less.

The monsoon rains, jungle terrain, hostile native population, and a determined guerrilla force made the American soldiers' marches long and miserable. One described a five-week-long infantry operation: " . . . our troops had been on half rations for two weeks. Wallowing through hip-deep muck, lugging a ten-pound rifle and a belt . . . with 200 rounds of ammunition, drenched to the skin and with their feet becoming heavier with mud at every step, the infantry became discouraged. Some men simply cried, others slipped down in the mud and refused to rise. Threats and appeals by the officers were of no avail. Only a promise of food in the next town and the threat that if they remained behind they would be butchered by marauding bands of insurgents forced some to their feet to struggle on."

News reports of the army's difficulties began to erode the American public's support for the war. "To chase barefooted insurgents with water buffalo carts as a wagon train may be simply ridiculous," charged one correspondent, "but to load volunteers down with 200 rounds of ammunition and one day's rations, and to put on their heads felt hats used by no other army in the tropics . . . to trot these same soldiers in the boiling sun over a country without roads, is positively criminal. . . . There are over five thousand men in the general hospital."

Another reported that the American outlook "is blacker now than it has been since the beginning of the war . . . the whole population . . . sympathizes with the insurgents. The insurgents came to Pasig [a local area whose government cooperated with the Americans] and their first act was to hang the 'Presidente' for treason in surrendering to Americans. 'Presidentes' do not surrender to us anymore."

U.S. troops found the tropical climate and Southeast Asian terrain almost as deadly as combat. Thousands of soldiers were incapacitated by dysentery, malaria, and other tropical maladies. The first troops sent to the archipelago wore unsuitable woolen uniforms; these men, photographed in 1900, had at least been issued ponchos for use during the rainy season.

NEW STRATEGIES

Early in the war U.S. military commanders had realized that, unlike the American Indians who had been herded onto reservations, eight million Filipinos (many of them hostile) would have to be governed in place. The Americans chose to emphasize pacification through good works rather than by harsh measures, hoping to convince Filipinos that the American colonial government had a sincere interest in their welfare and could be trusted.

As the army expanded its control across the islands, it reorganized local municipal governments and trained Filipinos to take over civil functions in the democratic political structure the Americans planned to establish. American soldiers performed police duties, distributed food, established and taught at schools, and built roads and telegraph lines.

As the war progressed, however, the U.S. commanders saw that the terrorism practiced by Aguinaldo's guerrillas was far more effective in controlling the populace than was their own benevolent approach. Although the Americans did not abandon pacification through good works, it was thereafter subordinated to the "civilize 'em with a Krag" (Krag-Jorgensen rifle) philosophy. From December 1900 onward, captured revolutionaries faced deportation, imprisonment, or execution.

The American army also changed its combat strategy to counter that of its enemy. As in the insurgents' army, the new tactics emphasized mobility and surprise. Breaking into small units—the battalion became the largest maneuver force—the Americans gradually spread over the islands until each of the larger towns was occupied by one or two rifle companies. From these bases American troops began platoon- and company-size operations to pressure local guerrilla bands.

Because of the difficult terrain, limited visibility, and requirement for mobility, artillery now saw limited use except as a defensive weapon. The infantry became the main offensive arm, with mounted riflemen used to pursue the fleeing enemy. Cavalry patrols were so valued for their mobility that American military leaders hired trusted Filipinos as mounted scouts and cavalrymen.

The Americans made other efforts to "Filipinize" the war—letting Asians fight Asians. (A similar tactic had been used in the American Indian campaigns twenty years before; it would resurface in Vietnam sixty years later as "Vietnamization.") In the Philippines the Americans recruited five thousand Macabebes, mercenaries from the central Luzon province of Pampanga, to form the American officered Philippine Scouts. The Macabebes had for centuries fought in native battalions under the Spanish flag—even against their own countrymen when the revolution began in 1896.

Just as a later generation of American soldiers would react to the guerrilla war in Vietnam, American soldiers in the Philippines responded to insurgent terrorism in kind, matching cruelty with cruelty. Such actions vented their frustration at being unable to find and destroy the enemy. An increasing number of Americans viewed all Filipinos as enemies.

"We make everyone get into his house by 7 P.M. and we only tell a man once," Corporal Sam Gillis of the 1st California Volunteer Regiment wrote to his family. "If he refuses, we shoot him. We killed over 300 natives the first night. . . . If they fire a shot from a house, we burn the house and every house near it."

Another infantryman frankly admitted that "with an enemy like this to fight, it is not surprising that the boys should soon adopt 'no quarter' as a motto and fill the blacks full of lead before finding out whether they are friends or enemies."

That attitude should not have been too surprising. The army's campaigns against the Plains Indians were reference points for the generation of Americans that took the Philippines. Many of the senior officers and noncommissioned officers—often veterans of the Indian wars—considered Filipinos to be "as full of treachery as our Arizona Apache." "The country won't be pacified," one soldier told a reporter, "until the niggers are killed off like the Indians." A popular soldiers' refrain, sung to the tune of "Tramp, tramp, tramp, the boys are marching," began, "Damn, damn, damn the Filipinos," and again spoke of "civilizing 'em with a Krag."

Reprisals against civilians by Americans as well as insurgents became common. General Lloyd Wheaton, leading a U.S. offensive southeast of Manila, found his men impaled on the bamboo prongs of booby traps and with throats slit while they slept. After two of his companies were ambushed, Wheaton ordered that every town and village within twelve miles be burned.

The Americans developed their own terrorist methods, many of which would be used in later Southeast Asian wars. One was torturing suspected guerrillas or insurgent sympathizers to force them to reveal locations of other guerrillas and their supplies. An often-utilized form of persuasion was the "water cure," placing a bamboo reed in the victim's mouth and pouring water (some used salt water or dirty water) down his throat, thus painfully distending the victim's stomach. The subject, allowed to void this, would, under threat of repetition, usually talk freely. Another method of torture, the "rope cure," consisted of wrapping a rope around the victim's neck and torso until it formed a sort of girdle. A stick (or Krag rifle), placed between the ropes and twisted, then effectively created a combination of smothering and garroting.

The anti-imperialist press reported such American brutality in lurid detail. As a result, a number of officers and soldiers were court-martialed for torturing and other cruelties. Their punishments, however, seemed remarkably lenient. Of ten officers tried for "looting, torture, and murder," three were acquitted; of the seven convicted, five were reprimanded, one was reprimanded and fined $300, and one lost thirty-five places in the army's seniority list and forfeited half his pay for nine months.

Officers and soldiers, fighting a cruel, determined, and dangerous enemy, could not understand public condemnation of the brutality they felt was necessary to win. They had not experienced such criticism during the Indian wars, where total extermination of the enemy was condoned by the press and the American public, and they failed to grasp the difference now. Press reports, loss of public support, and the soldiers' feeling of betrayal—features of an insurgent war—would resurface decades later during the Vietnam conflict.

SUCCESS

Although U.S. military leaders were frustrated by the guerrillas' determination on one hand and by eroding American support for the war on the other, most believed that the insurgents could be subdued. Especially optimistic was General Arthur MacArthur, who in 1900 assumed command of the seventy thousand American troops in the Philippines. MacArthur adopted a strategy like that successfully used by General Zachary Taylor in the Second Seminole War in 1835; he believed that success depended upon the Americans' ability to isolate the guerrillas from their support in the villages. Thus were born "strategic hamlets," "free-fire zones," and "search and destroy" missions, concepts the American army would revive decades later in Vietnam.

MacArthur strengthened the more than five hundred small strong points held by Americans throughout the Philippine Islands. Each post was garrisoned by at least one company of American infantrymen. The natives around each base were driven from their homes, which were then destroyed. Soldiers herded the displaced natives into *reconcentrado* camps, where they could be "protected" by the nearby garrisons. Crops, food stores, and houses outside the camps were destroyed to deny them to the guerrillas. Surrounding each camp was a "dead line," within which anyone appearing would be shot on sight.

Operating from these small garrisons, the Americans pressured the guerrillas, allowing them no rest. Kept off balance, short of supplies, and constantly pursued by the American army, the Filipino guerrillas, suffering from sickness, hunger, and dwindling popular support, began to lose their will to fight. Many insurgent leaders surrendered, signaling that the tide at last had turned in the Americans' favor.

In March 1901, a group of Macabebe Scouts, commanded by American Colonel Frederick "Fighting Fred" Funston, captured Aguinaldo. Aguinaldo's subsequent proclamation that he would fight no more, and his pledge of loyalty to the United States, sped the collapse of the insurrection.

As in the past, and as would happen again during the Vietnam conflict of the 1960s and '70s, American optimism was premature. Although a civilian commission headed by William H. Taft took control of the colonial government from the American army in July 1901, the army faced more bitter fighting in its "pacification" of the islands.

As the war sputtered, the insurgents' massacre of fifty-nine American soldiers at Balangiga on the island of Samar caused Brigadier General Jacob W. "Hell-Roaring Jake" Smith, veteran of the Wounded Knee massacre of the Sioux in 1890, to order his officers to turn Samar into a "howling wilderness." His orders to a battalion of three hundred Marines headed for Samar were precise: "I want no prisoners. I wish you to kill and burn, the more you kill and burn the better it will please me. I want all per-

sons killed who are capable of bearing arms against the United States." Fortunately, the Marines did not take Smith's orders literally and, later, Smith would be court-martialed.

On July 4, 1902 the Philippine Insurrection officially ended. Although it took the American army another eleven years to crush the fierce Moros of the southern Philippines, the civil government's security force (the Philippine Constabulary), aided by the army's Philippine Scouts, maintained a fitful peace throughout the islands. The army's campaign to secure the Philippines as an American colony had succeeded.

American commanders would have experienced vastly greater difficulties except for two distinct advantages: 1) the enemy had to operate in a restricted area, in isolated islands, and was prevented by the U.S. Navy from importing weapons and other needed supplies; and 2) though the insurgents attempted to enlist help from Japan, no outside power intervened. These conditions would not prevail in some subsequent guerrilla conflicts in Asia.

In addition to the many tactical lessons the army learned from fighting a guerrilla war in a tropical climate, other problems experienced during this campaign validated the need for several military reforms that were subsequently carried out, including improved logistics, tropical medicine, and communications.

The combination of harsh and unrelenting military force against the guerrillas, complemented by the exercise of fair and equitable civil government and civic action toward those who cooperated, proved to be the Americans' most effective tactic for dealing with the insurgency. This probably was the most significant lesson to be learned from the Philippine Insurrection.

LESSONS FOR THE FUTURE

Vietnam veterans reading this account might nod in recollection of a personal, perhaps painful experience from their own war.

Many similarities exist between America's three-year struggle with the Filipino *insurrectos* and the decade-long campaign against the Communists in Vietnam. Both wars, modestly begun, went far beyond what anyone had fore-

seen in time, money, equipment, manpower, casualties, and suffering.

Both wars featured small-unit infantry actions. Young infantrymen, if they had any initial enthusiasm, usually lost it once they saw the war's true nature; they nevertheless learned to endure their allotted time while adopting personal self-survival measures as months "incountry" lengthened and casualty lists grew.

Both wars were harsh, brutal, cruel. Both had their Samar Islands and their My Lais. Human nature being what it is, both conflicts also included acts of great heroism, kindness, compassion, and self-sacrifice.

Both wars saw an increasingly disenchanted American public withdrawing its support (and even disavowing its servicemen) as the campaigns dragged on, casualties mounted, and news accounts vividly described the horror of the battlefields.

Some useful lessons might be gleaned from a comparison of the two conflicts. Human nature really does not change—war will bring out the best and the worst in the tired, wet, hungry, and fearful men who are doing the fighting. Guerrilla campaigns—particularly where local military and civic reforms cannot be effected to separate the guerrilla from his base of popular support—will be long and difficult, and will demand tremendous commitments in resources and national will. Finally, before America commits its armed forces to similar ventures in the future, it would do well to recall the lessons learned from previous campaigns. For, as the Spanish-born American educator, poet, and philosopher George Santayana reminded us, those who do not learn from the past are doomed to repeat it.

Recommended additional reading: Benevolent Assimilation: The American Conquest of the Philippines, 1899–1902 *by Stuart C. Miller (Yale University Press, 1982);* In Our Image: America's Empire in the Philippines *by Stanley Karnow (Random House, 1989);* Little Brown Brother *by Leon Wolff (Doubleday & Co., Inc., 1961);* Muddy Glory *by Russell Roth (Christopher Publishing House, 1981); and* Soldiers in the Sun *by William T. Sexton (Books for Libraries Press, 1971).*

Anti-Semitism in American Caricature

John Appel
and Selma Appel

John Appel and Selma Appel live in East Lansing, Michigan, where John Appel teaches at Michigan State University. They collect, write, and lecture about printed immigrant and ethnic stereotypes of the nineteenth and twentieth centuries. They have been researchers-in-residence at the Smithsonian Institution; and consultants to publishers, television networks, museums, and public agencies concerned with prejudice and stereotyping. This text and images from their collection appeared in the catalog issued in connection with an exhibition, Jews in American Graphic Satire and Humor. The catalog, which the authors are presently expanding, and the exhibition were projects of the American Jewish Archives, of which we thank Director Jacob R. Marcus and Associate Director Abraham J. Peck.

Caricature, R. W. Emerson wrote, often reflects the truest history of a period. This generalization fits popular American caricature of the late nineteenth and early twentieth century. Highly visible graphic racial and ethnic stereotypes, mostly comic and satiric but some clearly scabrous, were commonplace in music, on the vaudeville stages, and in the expanding printed news and entertainment media of a United States fraught with racial, ethnic, religious, and class tensions, and prejudices.

Those who are familiar only with the romanticized version of America as the haven for millions of immigrants, and of Miss Liberty and Uncle Sam emblazoned as the personifications of American ideals on all manner of printed materials from this period, may see these caricatures as unwarrantedly emphasizing the negative features of a nation rightly valued for tolerating ethnic diversity and extending religious and political freedom to all, or nearly all, of its members from earliest times.

As we view the printed ephemera of the era from the end of the Civil War to World War II, chiefly cartoons in humor and satire weeklies, posters, advertising trade cards, product labels, sheet music covers, newspaper comics, and book illustrations, it becomes disturbingly clear that their iconography sanctioned ethnic and racial slurs that may shock today's observer.

In light of history since the 1920s, when America closed its gates on the basis of discriminatory, racially inspired immigration quota laws (repealed only in the 1960s), after the murder of millions of Jews and the indifference of most nations—including the United States—to their plight, and given the still precarious position of the state of Israel among hostile neighbors, it is understandable that the single most frequently asked question about the cartoons and caricatures depicted . . . concerns the extent to which these images contributed to or undergirded anti-Semitic tendencies in American society. The question deserves a succinct answer, although this should not be equated with an authoritative statement about the origins, extent, and significance of American anti-Semitism, a subject still debated by historians, sociologists, and spokesmen for various ideological constituencies.

The personal and commercial motivations underlying American ethnic and racial stereotyping are complex and cannot always be reduced to simple notions of prejudice, status deprivation, personality deficiencies, or xenophobia, whether dealing with anti-Semitism, anti-Catholicism, or discrimination against blacks, Orientals, and Hispanics. Some images clearly were anti-Jewish or anti-Semitic, anti-Irish-Catholic, anti-Chinese, anti-Indian, and anti-Negro in the racial sense of the word associated with German Nazi propaganda. But not every insulting, jabbing, and condescending picture reveals inflexible, murderous hostility; some stereotypes originated in the clash of cultural values, the fear and insecurity of a native, largely middle-class population, often insensitive to the feelings of the groups portrayed stereotypically but not invariably impugning their humanity or denying them rights and enjoyments granted other Americans in a given historical period.

Some social historians speak of a new urban humor which replaced the older, chiefly rural variety of American humor sometime during the last third of the nineteenth century, particularly on the vaudeville stage (customarily dated from 1881) and in the weeklies that began to flourish in the 1880s. They see this new humor—a mixture of native and foreign influences—as more critical of the sometimes inflated promises of American life, a retaliation against the loneliness and alienation engendered by city life. The older, more kindly, folksy, village or frontier oriented, cracker barrel or whimsical variety of humor turned largely on commonly understood conventions and personal relationships. The newer variety thrived on interethnic and racial tensions and the misunderstandings and verbal impasses encountered by people of different ethnic backgrounds in the impersonal city.

Yet this humor, more professional than the older, rural variety, depending on identities linked to occupation, race, or nationality, on timing, tone, and puns brutally indifferent to personal relationships and to the sociological or economic realities that lay behind them, is also seen as establishing urban norms of behavior for largely foreign migrants to the city. It is seen as releasing these men and women temporarily from the pressures of city life and allowing them to laugh about encounters that in reality were not always pleasant or comic. Thus historian Gunter Barth asserts, in his *City People,* that this new, more aggressive humor "bound together heterogeneous people in a movement of harmony that for them justified laughing at the plight of a harassed minority." Their prejudices, Barth thinks, "actually brought some people closer to each other" because the blatant stereotypes paraded on vaudeville stages and in the comic prints contradicted their experiences with members of these ethnic groups, "on the street, in the store, on the job."

Barth and historians who agree with him overstate their case for ethnic caricature as a positive factor in human relations. Did ethnic stereotypes not also reinforce rather than contradict oversimplified notions about foreigners and blacks acquired from superficial encounters with them in the street, on the job, or in the store? Were the veiled aggressive and antagonistic impulses underlying many ethnic jokes, skits, and cartoons always "merely symbolic," having no deleterious, lasting consequences besides the harmless, temporary release of pent up animosities and tensions? To be sure, the dialect comedy which was so pronounced in all ethnic humor—from black to "Dutch" (German), to Irish, to Jewish—was regarded as "deformed language," hence comical, like the speech

of the stammerer, who also was a fixture on the comic stage and in jokes of the period. According to Irving Howe and others who have studied the immigrant Jewish community at the turn of the century, Jews reacted to caricatural treatment on stage and in cartoons "without much excitement or anger." Having a long tradition of laughing at themselves, they knew that in Christian society the arts, high and low, dealt mockingly with them. Only during the first decade of the present century were Jewish ethnic sensibilities institutionalized, and then largely among the established, German Jews who formed local anticaricatural committees, the forerunners of today's national B'nai B'rith Anti-Defamation League. Many comedians, managers, theater owners, and not a few cartoonists were Jewish. Nevertheless, Jews in caricature were usually pictured as profit-hungry, guileful pawnbrokers, loan sharks, and second-hand clothing dealers or tailors and peddlers living on the margins of trade and society, although Jewish comedians often tried to soften and humanize their material.

Stealth and derision dominated the vocabulary describing the caricature Jew of stage and cartoon. He usually lacked the hearty, unselfconscious aggressiveness and pride of Irish comedy or the jovial, jolly nature of "Dutch" (German) comedy acts and cartoons.

All national types were drawn without subtlety, with usually no more than one, or at most a few, facets of character. All were predictable stereotypes acting in clichéd plot situations that depended on well known salient clues to character,

wildly exaggerated to trigger quick, accurate, predictable recognition and response.

The need for instant recognition, for the familiar, leads to the exploitation of stock situations and characters. That is why many, perhaps most, ethnic jokes and cartoons (often merely illustrated jokes) have an internal development that does not always bear much relation to what is happening in the world they purport to represent. Joke and cartoon conventions go on, with as little relation to reality as little men from flying saucers who ask to be taken to our leaders. Cartoonists working on "Jewish" ethnic themes did not need to refer to any concept, true or false or wildly imagined, of their subject beyond what had already been established by conventional usage.

Irving Howe's summary of ethnic humor as it existed at the turn of the century provides the most balanced interpretation for many of these images. He wrote in *World of Our Fathers* that the popular arts served "as a sort of abrasive welcoming committee for the immigrants. Shrewd at mocking incongruities of manners, seldom inclined to venom though quite at home with disdain, they exploited the few fixed traits that history or legend assigned each culture. They arranged an initiation of hazing and caricature that assured the Swedes, the Germans, the Irish and the Jews that to be noticed, even if through the cruel lens of parody, meant to be accepted—up to a point."

Fighting Poverty the Old-Fashioned Way

Howard Husock

Howard Husock, a former Wilson Center Guest Scholar, is director of Case Studies in Public Policy at Harvard's John F. Kennedy School of Government. Born in Cleveland, Ohio, he received a B.S. from Boston University (1972).

It is difficult to exaggerate the dread sense of crisis that the urban poor inspired in most citizens of the United States a century ago. The phenomenally rapid industrialization that had been underway since the Civil War was attracting millions of eastern and southern Europeans to America's sweatshops, steel mills, and railyards. The influx of these "more foreign foreigners," more alien in language, customs, and religion than the Irish and German immigrants who preceded them, was climbing inexorably toward a one-year peak of 1,285,000 in 1907. Middle-class Protestant America recoiled in fear as entire districts of Chicago, Pittsburgh, New York, and Philadelphia were taken over by what one writer in New York called "the dangerous classes." An early history of this new immigration noted that "districts passed in a few years from the Irish, who were typical of the early influx, to the Russian Jews, who, as they landed represented the extreme of all that was in contrast with the American way of life."

The new masses were not only different but wretchedly poor, and poverty soon began to emerge as a political issue. As early as 1888, President Grover Cleveland warned that "oppressed poverty and toil, exasperated by injustice and discontent, attacks with wild disorder the citadel of rule." Jacob Riis, drawing on his years as a police reporter and photographer on New York's Lower East Side,

lent popular urgency to the problem of urban poverty with the publication in 1890 of *How the Other Half Lives*. Riis attracted national attention with his descriptions of "unventilated and fever-breeding structures," of gangs meeting in "dens" to plan "raids," willing to saw a peddler's head off "just for fun." Nor were such accounts isolated. In Philadelphia, another account, sounding much like a late 20th-century description of the ghetto drug culture, described "boys and girls idling away their time on the street, their characters weakened so that they are liable to the contagion of all kinds of vice."

In his classic 1904 treatise, *Poverty*, reformer Robert Hunter estimated that 10 million of America's 82 million people lived in poverty. In an era without unemployment insurance or workers' compensation, even those with jobs were often but a missed paycheck or an industrial accident away from destitution. "Upon the unskilled masses," wrote Hunter, "want is constantly pressing." He warned, furthermore, of an emerging "pauper" class—an underclass of dangerous and demoralized poor people. On Armour Avenue in Chicago, in Cincinnati's Rat Hollow, in Manhattan's Hell's Kitchen, and in dozens of similar neighborhoods around the country, wrote Hunter, there "lives a class of people who have lost all self-respect and ambition, who rarely if ever work, who are aimless and drifting, who like drink, who have no thought for their children and who live on rubbish and alms."

Today, the astounding upward mobility of this generation of immigrants (or at least of their children) and their assimilation into the American middle class is seen as somehow inevitable—the by-product of an expanding economy, strong demand for unskilled labor, and an immigrant work ethic. By implication, middle-class America today is limited in its

ability to deal with the poor and underclass because both labor conditions and the character of the poor have changed. Yet the upward mobility of the poor hardly appeared inevitable to the contemporary observers of a century ago. Bringing the urban poor into the cultural and economic mainstream was viewed as a challenge requiring extraordinary steps.

OUT OF THE REFORM MAELSTROM OF the turn-of-the-century Progressive era emerged a movement that undertook to bring the poor both hope and the tools of advancement. The settlement-house movement unabashedly promoted bourgeois values and habits—instructing the poor in everything from art appreciation and home economics to the importance of establishing savings accounts. To children in poverty, it offered recreation, books, clubs, as well as a sense of the history of American democratic institutions. It approached thousands of the urban poor, particularly children and teenagers, with a message of inclusion in the larger world beyond the slum. It *expected* them to make it. To make good on that promise, relatively well-to-do Americans, inspired both by religious conscience and fear for the American social fabric, "settled" in poor neighborhoods, there to experience the lives of the poor firsthand, to offer guidance to their neighbors and, in time, to be inspired to suggest policy prescriptions to the nation: child labor laws, industrial safety laws, and old age and unemployment insurance.

Settlements developed in the aftermath of a decades-long debate—in many ways reminiscent of that which has engaged the United States since the early 1960s—over how best to provide financial support to the needy without destroying their incentive to work. Not content with any relief system alone, Jane Addams and other settlement-house founders saw a need for a communitarian movement to bring rich and poor together. Their goal was both to broaden the horizons of the poor and to humanize the classes in each other's eyes. The movement, wrote Addams in 1892, rested on three legs. "First, the desire to interpret democracy in social terms; secondly, the impulsive beating at the very source of our lives, urging us to aid in the race progress; and thirdly, the Christian movement toward humanitarianism."

By attending settlement clubs and classes, the poor would be exposed to middle-class values and be given, it was hoped, the tools of self-betterment. The volunteer residents themselves were thought likely to profit as well. Still, the movement indulged neither the personal nor the political whims of youth. Nor did it veer toward wholesale rejection of the American economic system. It sought redistribution not of wealth per se but of "social and educational advantages." Moreover, although it helped put on the public agenda the social insurance programs that were finally passed during the New Deal, it never believed that these could substitute for individual efforts by rich and poor alike.

The American roots of the settlement-house movement date to the practice of "friendly visiting" of the poor, which arose in response to the breakdown of the traditional social-welfare system during the early 19th century. The traditional system, dating to the Elizabethan "poor laws," had provided financial support for community residents (strangers were pointedly excluded) who were sick, widowed, or temporarily down on their luck. By the 1820s, this community-oriented system was growing increasingly unworkable. Cities were becoming too big, workers too transient, and the poor too concentrated in certain urban neighborhoods. Many towns and cities resorted to poorhouses as an economy measure, requiring the poor to live in them in exchange for support.

THESE CHANGED CONDITIONS ALSO INspired new efforts by men such as the Unitarian minister Joseph Tuckerman of Boston. In 1819 he began his ministry to the poor in their own neighborhoods, where, he believed, they were "living as a caste, cut off from those in more favored circumstances." In New York during the 1840s, Robert Hartley, the English-born son of a woolen-mill owner,

Boys at play on a New York street, 1890.

founded the New York Association for Improving the Condition of the Poor. He fought for temperance (alcohol was the drug menace of the day) and began a system of friendly visiting in which male volunteers took responsibility for the poor in a given political precinct, bringing such offerings as copies of Benjamin Franklin's *The Way to Wealth*. ("It depends chiefly on two words: industry and frugality," Franklin declared.)

Among Hartley's successors was Charles Loring Brace, a seminarian first drawn to social action through visits to New York City prisons. Convinced that inmates were often beyond help, he founded the Children's Aid Society in 1853 and concentrated his efforts on the 10,000 orphaned or abandoned children then thought to be living on New York's streets. Like the settlement-house workers who came after him, he was persuaded that "formative" efforts were far more effective than "reformative" ones. In language foreshadowing Jane Addams, he wrote: "These boys and girls will soon form the great lower class of our city. They will influence elections . . . they will assuredly, if unreclaimed, poison society all around them. They will help to form the great multitude of robbers, thieves, vagrants and prostitutes who are now such a burden upon the respecting community." Brace offered reading rooms, vocational training, and

"newsboy lodging houses." He also "placed out" thousands of children with farm families in the Midwest and West.*

It was with the settlement-house movement, however, that the uplift impulse peaked. Notwithstanding the example of Hartley and Brace, settlements were most immediately inspired by ideas and events in Britain. With its head start on industrialization, England had been forced during the mid-18th century to confront the need to create a new social welfare system suited to a capitalist economy. In his history of the settlement-house movement, *Spearheads of Reform* (1967), Allen Davis traces the geneaology of settlements to London. There, in 1854, a Utopian clergyman and academic named Frederick Denison Maurice founded the Working Men's College, aiming to use education to erase class distinctions and mitigate the Dickensian social inequities of the era. His faculty included charismatic fine arts professor John Ruskin, England's leading art critic, and a critic as well of

*This effort was violently opposed by the Catholic Church, which suspected Brace's motives in placing Catholic children with Protestant families in the Midwest. But Miriam Langsam concludes in her history of the effort, *Children West: A History of the Placing-Out System of the New York Children's Aid Society, 1853–90* (1962), that most of the children benefited.

19th-century industrialization. Like the settlement residents he would inspire, Ruskin was reform-minded, calling for a social-security system, minimum wage, and higher housing standards.

His disciples included Arnold Toynbee, an economist (and uncle of the famed historian) who moved to London's East End slums to teach and to learn. He died there at age 32 in what a history of the settlement movement would call an atmosphere of "bad whisky, bad tobacco, bad drainage." In 1884, Toynbee Hall was created in the same neighborhood to honor the memory of the reformer. Its founder, a minister named Samuel Barnett, took some of his inspiration from an 1883 church publication entitled *The Bitter Cry of Outcast London*. It described a "gulf daily widening which separates the lowest classes of the community . . . from all decency and civilization." To bridge that gap, Barnett brought college students to his Toynbee Hall, where they mounted art exhibitions, gave lectures, and lobbied local officials for a public library and for park and playground improvements.

Many of the leaders of the American settlement-house movement were directly inspired by visits to Toynbee Hall; Stanton Coit, an Amherst graduate with a doctorate from the University of Berlin, went on to found the nation's first settlement, New York's Neighborhood Guild, in 1886; Jane Addams, the daughter of a small-town Illinois Quaker banker, became co-founder of Chicago's Hull House in 1889; and Robert Woods, a graduate of the Andover Theological Seminary, served as "head resident" at Boston's South End house, founded in 1891. Smith College graduate Vida Scudder studied with John Ruskin in Britain, and along with a group which included Katherine Lee Bates, a Wellesley College professor (and the author of "America the Beautiful"), founded the College Settlement Association in 1889, with houses in Philadelphia, New York, and Boston.

THE BELIEFS OF THE PEOPLE WHO STARTED the settlement movement cut across many of the divides which have since developed in American social-welfare philosophy. They were religious women and men inspired to a secular mission. They were political crusaders who never forgot the importance of maintaining direct contact with the poor and providing them with personal attention ("mentoring," to

What The Social Classes Owe Each Other

In 1889, Hull House was "soberly opened on the theory that the dependence of classes on each other is reciprocal," Jane Addams later recalled. Yet she was anything but confident that Hull House could encourage the spirit of reciprocity. The dire commentary below, which she reprinted in her memoir, was written when Hull House opened its doors.

The social organization has broken down through large districts of our great cities. Many of the people living here are very poor, the majority of them without leisure or energy for anything but the gain of subsistence.

They live for the moment side by side, many of them without knowledge of each other, without fellowship, without local tradition or public spirit, without social organization of any kind. Practically nothing is done to remedy this. The people who might do it, who have the social tact and training, the large houses, and the traditions and customs of hospitality, live in other parts of the city. The clubhouses, libraries, galleries, and semi-public conveniences for social life are also blocks away. We find workingmen organized into armies of producers because men of executive ability and business sagacity have found it to their interests thus to organize them. But these workingmen are not organized socially; although lodging in crowded tenement houses, they are living without a corresponding social contact. The chaos is as great as it would be were they working in huge factories without foreman or superintendent. Their ideas and resources are cramped, and the desire for higher social pleasure becomes extinct. They have no share in the traditions and social energy which make for progress. Too often their only place for meeting is a saloon, their only host a bartender; a local demagogue forms their public opinion. Men of ability and refinement, of social power and university cultivation, stay away from them. Personally, I believe the men who lose most are those who thus stay away from them. But the paradox is here; when cultivated people do stay away from a certain portion of the population, when all social advantages are persis-

Jane Addams in 1930.

tently withheld, it may be for years, the result is pointed to as a reason and is used as an argument, for the continued withholding.

It is constantly said that because the masses have never had social advantages, they do not want them, that they are heavy and dull, and that it will take political or philanthropic machinery to change them. This divides a city into rich and poor; into the favored, who express their sense of the social obligation by gifts of money, and into the unfavored, who express it by clamoring for a "share"—both of them actuated by a vague sense of justice. This division of the city would be more justifiable, however, if the people who thus isolate themselves on certain streets and use their social ability for each other, gained enough thereby and added sufficiently to the sum total of social progress to justify the withholding of the pleasures and results of that progress, from so many people who ought to have them. But they cannot accomplish this for the social spirit discharges itself in many forms, and no one form is adequate to its total expression.

—from Twenty Years at Hull-House *(1910).*

use today's term). They were youthful (under 30) cultural radicals who rejected middle-class comforts but saw themselves as mediators between the classes rather than simply as critics of the established order. They were social experimenters who nonetheless championed bourgeois values. They were reformers, not revolutionaries. (This earned them the scorn of writers who were further to the left. Socialist Jack London wrote that settlements "do everything for the poor except get off their backs." Upton Sinclair derisively summed up settlement programs as "lectures delivered gratis by earnest advocates of the single tax, troutfishing, exploring Tibet, pacifism, sea shell collecting, the eating of bran and the geography of Charlemagne's empire.")

THE SETTLEMENT HOUSES FOLLOWED THE wake of the so-called "scientific charity" movement. Scientific charity was designed to achieve some of the same ends as the state and federal welfare initiatives of the past two decades. Its advocates, such as Josephine Shaw Lowell (author of *Public Relief and Private Charity*, 1884), sought to centralize both private and public assistance to guard against fraud and to limit support for the able-bodied, lest the incentive to work be diminished. It is important to note that the settlement movement was not a reaction to scientific charity's callous-sounding agenda. It emerged as an organized supplement to the relief system, designed chiefly for the children of poor families, whether they were receiving relief payments or not. Wrote Jacob Riis: "We have substituted for the old charity coal chute that bred resentment . . . the passenger bridge we call settlements, upon which men go over not down to their duty."

Doing their duty was high on the list of these reformers. They used a vocabulary that seems distant from mainstream social-welfare discussion today. "The impulse to share the lives of the poor, the desire to make social service," wrote Jane Addams in 1892, "to express the spirit of Christ, is as old as Christianity itself. . . . Certain it is that spiritual force is found in the Settlement movement, and it is also true that this force must be evoked and must be called into play before the success of any Settlement is assured." The settlement workers were not missionaries in the literal sense.

If anything, they encouraged the kind of nondenominational religion which has come to typify American life. Theirs was the religion of the social gospel, the belief that social conditions, as well as individual beliefs and practices, come properly under the purview of religion.

The movement believed, too, that there was what Jane Addams called a "subjective necessity" for settlements. "We have in America a fast-growing number of cultivated young people," she wrote, "who . . . hear constantly of the great social maladjustment, but no way is provided for them to change it, and their uselessness hangs about them heavily."*

Movement advocates believed that personal contact between the classes was, as Robert Woods wrote, "not merely a means to some worthy end but, with its implications, as the end above all others. . . . This fresh exchange, continuously growing and deepening, stimulated by the surmounting of barriers of race and religion, was more than anything else to give form and body to the human democracy of the settlement."

The nature of relations between the classes varied. Jane Addams was exhilarated by experiences as mundane as informing a neighborhood woman of the existence of a park several blocks away in a direction the woman had never thought to venture. But Cleveland reformer Frederick Howe found his time in a settlement "anything but fruitful." He felt awkward trying to dance with immigrant women, uncomfortable as a friendly visitor to tenements.

In their early years, the settlements' reach was relatively short, their offerings not that extensive. What activities there were, however, were clearly in the uplift tradition. In the 1892 College Settlement

---

*Most volunteers were children of privilege. Annual reports of the College Settlement Association during the early 1890s, for instance, show that most volunteers were students or graduates of the elite women's colleges: Smith, Wellesley, Vassar, Bryn Mawr, and Mount Holyoke. The 1891–92 report of the College Settlement Association's house on New York's Lower East Side notes that "eighty applications have been received during the year. Many of these it has been necessary to refuse, as the house cannot be crowded beyond a certain point." The length of commitment varied. The New York house had 20 residents between September 1, 1891, and September 1, 1892, each staying an average of four months. Other "visitors" stayed less than one month.

Association's New York house, activities included clubs for boys and girls, establishment of children's savings accounts, a choir for neighborhood men, and home economics classes for neighborhood women. On weekdays, activities did not begin until 3:30 in the afternoon and were over by 9:30 or 10 p.m. A day in the life of the house included a surprising array of activities:

College Settlement Association
New York House, 1892

3 to 5 p.m. Library: Two hundred boys and girls, from ten to 14 years old. Exchange of books and games.

3:30 to 5 p.m. Rainbow Club: Two residents. Twenty girls from ten to fourteen years old. Sewing, singing, gymnastics, and games.

7 to 8 p.m. Penny Provident Bank (Savings account deposits): Two residents. From fifty to one hundred children.

7:30 to 9:30 p.m. Hero Club: One resident, one outside worker. Sixteen boys, fourteen to eighteen years old. Business meeting, talks, music and games. (Discussion of life stories of successful people.)

8 to 9 p.m. The Young Keystones: Ten boys, ten to fourteen years old. Talks on history, music.

Descriptions of even simple programs—carpentry for boys, cooking classes for girls—make it clear that the settlement vision was laden with aspiration for the children of the poor. "The goal of a social programme based on personal interest is to help individuals to the highest level of which each is capable," wrote Lillian Wald of New York's Henry Street Settlement, who was second only to Jane Addams as a voice of the movement. The 1892 report of the College Settlement Association's Philadelphia house stressed what we might now call "empowerment": "Here and there a boy has felt the pleasure, unlike all other pleasures, of creating with the mind and hand that which was not before, and that which was goodly to look upon, even though that something was but a loaf of well-baked bread, a well proportioned step-ladder, or a little clay-modeled apple. When once the boy or girl has felt this pleasure, something of that which inspires our great mechanics or poets has become theirs, and the character transformation begins."

By the turn of the century, the number of settlements had increased (from six in 1891 to 74 in 1897), and their activities had expanded. The activities of houses changed as residents took stock of their environs. Driven by powerful idealism, many settlement workers became political advocates for the poor. Hull House, which had introduced itself to Chicago's Halstead Street in 1889 with an art exhibit, soon opened a kindergarten to make up for the shortage of places in the public schools.* Then the settlement residents took demands for a new school to the Chicago school board. Dismayed by the garbage overflowing in the stables and crowded frame buildings of the 19th ward—with its 50,000 residents of 20 nationalities—Jane Addams and Hull House itself bid on the ward's garbage collection contract. A Hull House resident was eventually appointed garbage inspector.

The settlement impulse also led to efforts beyond the ward. Hull House resident Julia Lathrop organized a campaign to clean up the Cook County poorhouse; Addams and others signed on with a wide variety of reform causes. Hull House resident Florence Kelley was hired by a state commission to investigate child labor conditions. The inquiry (inspired by a Hull House encounter with a 13-year-old Jewish girl who committed suicide rather than admit she had borrowed $3 she could not repay from a coworker at a laundry) led to state legislation banning the employment of children under 14. Settlements even too up the drug abuse issue. Hull House pushed for a 1907 state law banning the sale of cocaine after one of its former kindergarteners fell victim to the drug. "When I last saw him," Addams wrote of the boy, in a line that sounds like countless others being written today, "it was impossible to connect that haggard, shriveled body with what I had known before."

The scope of settlement concerns broadened to the point that by 1904, Robert Hunter, the head resident at New York's University Settlement, wrote his book, *Poverty,* to lay out an ambitious national social welfare program: "Make

---

*Settlement leaders were strong believers in public education, but the public school systems of the day were limited both in size and what they taught. When the philosopher John Dewey created his famous "laboratory school" in 1896 to test his theories of progressive education, he did so in association with Hull House. In her devastating critique of the progressive education movement, *The Troubled Crusade* (1983), Diane Ravitch nevertheless praises Dewey (and Jane Addams) for seeking to end student "passivity" and "teachers' excessive reliance on rote memorization and drill."

all tenements and factories sanitary; prohibit entirely child labor; compensate labor for enforced seasons of idleness, old age or lack of work beyond the control of the workman." Such demands were not the mere conceits of a political fringe. By the first decade of the 20th century, leading settlement residents had gained the ear of President Theodore Roosevelt. In 1903, Lillian Wald called for the establishment of a federal children's bureau to monitor and investigate such matters as infant mortality, child labor, and education. Invited to Washington to see the president, her efforts led, though slowly, to the 1909 White House Conference on the Care of Dependent Children. That gathering led to a spread of state-supported mothers' pensions—intended to allow widows and the wives of the disabled to stay at home to raise their children—and to the establishment in April 1912 of the federal Children's Bureau. Its first director, appointed by President William Howard Taft, was Julia Lathrop of Hull House.

HISTORIANS HAVE PORTRAYED THIS AS THE movement's zenith. At last, they say, the settlement residents emerged as advocates for reform during the Progressive era and as harbingers of better things to come. But even as settlement leaders became national figures—Jane Addams regularly appeared on lists of the most admired Americans—they remained committed to helping individual poor people get ahead. Settlement leaders did not become directors of interest advocacy groups with offices in Washington, far from the poor. They were representatives of neighborhood organizations who also happened to have an important voice in the national debate over poverty.

Between 1900 and 1920, even after reaching their supposed peak, settlements continued to grow and diversify. No longer did volunteers come strictly from upper-middle-class backgrounds; some settlements even added paid staff in certain specialized areas, such as nursing. In their 1913 *Handbook of Settlements,* Robert Woods and Albert Kennedy of Boston's South End House listed 413 settlement houses, concentrated in New York, Boston, and Chicago, but present in some form in 32 states and the District of Columbia. It was a network of bourgeois outposts in the American Calcuttas, boasting tenements refurbished as community centers, programs of educa-

tion and recreation, and resident volunteers from the nation's best schools, all directed toward poor children and their parents.

Hull House itself grew to encompass eight buildings, including a music school, theater, and gymnasium. It operated a large day nursery for the children of the neighborhood's many working mothers. Major settlements such as Pittsburgh's Kingsley House developed elaborate programs of "manual training," kindergartens for children of slum families, and a summer "country home" where children and their families could gain a brief respite from the tenements. In a single week in January 1904, the house was attended by 1,680 children and teenagers. The 13 Kingsley House residents were assisted by 80 "non-resident volunteers" who came to the house for one month or more. Typical days ran from nine in the morning to 10:30 at night.

The annual reports of the house paint a picture of an institution thoroughly integrated into its neighborhood. "To many boys," said the 1905 annual report, "Kingsley is a place where they may spend their evenings—their club house. They know the people who live here are always glad to see them—that the books, the magazines, the games, the warmth of the fire place is for them as for us." There can be no doubt that settlements such as this were predicated on the belief that the development of ambition and a work ethic in the children of the poor could not be left to chance. Wrote head resident William Mathews: "We cannot begin too early. Life changes quickly from one of instincts to one of habits. The child should be given fair opportunities to master the difficulties that have in many cases already crushed the parents.

"What means the work to the boy hammering, chiseling, planing away on the bookshelf, the table, the sled? It means the calling into eager and enjoyable activity the whole power of his being, and the consequent crowding out of the lower passions that ever find their root in idleness and inactivity."

AFTER THE TURN OF THE CENTURY, settlements became a high-profile cause, attracting generous donations from the well-to-do. In 1906, Kingsley House boasted not only more than 900 individual financial supporters but its own endowment. Unlike the super-rich of today, who often flatter themselves with glittering gifts to museums, fashionable environmental causes, and the like, many of the wealthy during this earlier era felt a duty to provide the poor with means of advancement: libraries, schools, and settlement houses. One of Kingsley's supporters was Andrew Carnegie, who also endowed, among many other institutions, more than 2,800 libraries to help poor people improve themselves.

At its height, the settlement movement was a center not only of uplift efforts but a range of social services, including "milk stations" and vocational education, many of which have been assumed (with varying degrees of effectiveness) by government and those under contract to it. Jane Addams, for one, anticipated and approved this prospect. She thought of settlements as places where experiments could be tried and then adopted by government.

How deeply did settlement efforts penetrate? What were the results? Can settlements truly be credited with having an effect on the poor?

The numbers of those touched by settlement houses sometimes seem impressive. In 1906, Pittsburgh's Kingsley House claimed weekly contact with some 2,000 children from the neighborhood around its 14-room building at Bedford and Fulton Streets. But it is undoubtedly true that, in general, settlements reached a minority of their neighbors. New York's East Side House, in the city's Yorkville section, described itself in 1914 as "a radiant center of spiritual, moral and intellectual light in a thickly settled neighborhood of 150,000." Its clubs enrolled 1,346 children.

Almost inevitably, the settlement workers found themselves focusing on those with the best chance to get ahead. In New York, Vida Scudder found reaching the Italian "peasant" so difficult—despite her own knowledge of Italian—that she frankly admitted that she would concentrate her work on those she identified as intellectuals. "The primary function of the settlement house," observed sociologist William Whyte in *Street Corner Society* (1943), "is to stimulate social mobility, to hold out middle-class standards and middle-class rewards to lower-class people. Since upward mobility almost always involves movement out of the slum district, the settlement is constantly dealing with people on their way out. . . . The social workers want to deal with 'the better element.' "

One can speculate as to whether reaching the right people can change the tone and social fabric of an entire neighborhood. Settlement workers believed it possible. Wrote Robert Woods: "Interaction of residents, volunteers, and supporters with neighbors has its sure effect on local opinion. As working people come to know men and women of culture and organizing power, they understand the responsible and humanizing use of the resources of life and are less moved by irresponsible and railing criticism." Settlement workers were convinced they had succeeded in changing at least the course of lives they touched directly. Reflecting on more than 30 years at the Henry Street Settlement, Lillian Wald wrote: "Frequent on musical and dramatic programs are the names of girls and boys whom we have known in our clubs and classes. Not a few are listed in the ranks of the literary. Some have been elected to public office, others drafted into the public service." Among those who passed through the houses were Frances Perkins, secretary of labor under President Franklin Roosevelt, union leader Sidney Hillman and comedian George Burns. Benny Goodman received his first clarinet lesson at Hull House. A gymnastics lesson at New York's Union Settlement House inspired Burt Lancaster to seek a career in show business—as an acrobat. Even today, decades after the heyday of the settlement-house movement, it is possible to make a long list of prominent people whose lives were touched by a settlement house: Nate Archibald, a former professional basketball player, novelist Mario Puzo, actress Whoopie Goldberg, and Robert P. Rittereiser, who was president and chief executive officer of the old E. F. Hutton brokerage firm (and one of a trio of extremely successful brothers who acknowledge a large debt to Manhattan's East Side House).

By the early 1920s, settlement houses seemed likely to become a permanent fixture of American life. Although their pacifism cost Jane Addams, Lillian Wald, and some other settlement-house leaders public favor during World War I, Robert Woods and Albert Kennedy could still confidently assert in their 1922 survey, *The Settlement Horizon*, that "the strong claims of so thoroughly an established tradition of leadership, and the breadth and momentum of the cause, furnish ample guarantees for the future."

It was not to be. In part, settlement houses fell victim to their own success.

During the boom years of the 1920s, many of the poor headed up and out of the old neighborhoods. "There are many 'empties' [vacant apartments] in our neighborhood," wrote Lillian Wald, "because, as standards of living have been lifted, the uncrushable desire for a bathroom has increased, and the people have moved away." Meanwhile, restrictive federal legislation in 1924 ended mass immigration, thus limiting the number of newcomers in settlement neighborhoods.

Some settlement houses closed down; many merged and became part of the group of charities served by local United Way and Community Chest drives, losing their financial independence and public profile. By 1963, in *Beyond the Melting Pot*, Nathan Glazer and Daniel Moynihan described the settlements' role in elegiac terms: "The Puerto Rican has entered the city in the age of the welfare state. Here and there are to be found the settlement houses of an earlier period, in which a fuller and richer concern for the individual was manifested by devoted people from the prosperous classes."

THERE ARE REMNANTS OF THE MOVEMENT today in the major settlement cities—Boston, New York, and Chicago, where Hull House celebrated its centennial last year. Although aspects of the original impulse are still to be found—New York's Henry Street Settlement operates youth clubs, Boston's United South End settlement runs a fresh-air camp—settlements today are run mostly by paid professionals, social workers whose training has its roots in psychiatric casework. Many settlements are really little more than health and counseling centers, which, like all manner of other institutions today, simply deliver impersonal social services to the poor. Government reimbursement provides the bulk of funding. It turned out, contrary to the expectations of Jane Addams and others, that government was simply incapable of doing what the settlements did—and was not really interested in trying, either.

The settlement idea also suffered as a result of the Depression, which, more than any other event in American life, made clear the limits of private charity. The incontrovertible importance of the 1935 Social Security Act, which established the form of the national social insurance system, has overshadowed a dubious assumption that accompanied it: that as pension programs grew to cover the elderly, the blind, and the families of maimed or disabled workers, poverty, over time, would "wither away." Nobody anticipated the massive influx of unskilled workers from outside the industrial system after World War II, workers who had not been covered by the new social insurance. Poverty did not disappear. Yet the persistence of the withering away fallacy discouraged volunteer activities. Poverty, it had been decided, would and should be taken care of by government.

The affluence of the postwar era and the expansion of government responsibility for management of the economy made government solutions to the poverty problem seem all the more appropriate. The need for federal intervention to break down the legal barriers to the entry of blacks into the mainstream of society reinforced the focus on Washington. The settlement-house philosophy—which embraced the need both for a social insurance safety net below *and* a helping hand from above—was largely forgotten.

Inaugurating the War on Poverty in 1965, President Lyndon Johnson spoke of a "hand, not a handout," but the new federal antipoverty programs were captured by people who sought to mobilize the poor to effect a redistribution of wealth and power through political activism. Although VISTA workers and New Left activists followed the settlement example of taking up residence among the poor, few were driven by the idea of assisting the poor in self-improvement. Indeed, many of them rejected the very notion that the poor needed improvement; "the system" was the problem. To these latter-day settlement workers, the "hero club" and the summer camp seemed pathetically inadequate next to the class action suit and the sit-in at City Hall.

By far the most important response to the new urban poverty was the growth of the Aid to Families with Dependent Children (AFDC) program—a descendant, ironically, of the "widows' pensions" for which settlement residents had lobbied Teddy Roosevelt in 1909. Never meant as a large-scale welfare program when it was created under the Social Security Act, AFDC was pushed along by the growth of single-parent families until it became the nation's most important relief program. From \$194 million in 1963, annual outlays for AFDC grew to \$2.5 billion in 1972. As welfare payments grew, so did the unease of a society historically loathe simply to provide alms

for the poor. As early as 1962 and as recently as 1988, Congress attempted to build uplift into the AFDC system. Some of these efforts, such as job training programs for welfare recipients in the 1988 Family Support Act, have shown promise. All of these efforts, however, owe more to such antecedents as the scientific charity movement than to the settlement impulse. They are more "reformative" than "formative." They target the "welfare-eligible," those who have a demonstrated difficulty joining the economic mainstream, not those on the margin who might have a better chance of getting ahead with a little help.

IT IS DIFFICULT TO SUGGEST THAT THERE may be ways to go back to a better future for American social-welfare initiatives. Because the United States delayed providing basic social insurance for so long, historians have cast the pre-New Deal era as a Dark Age of Social Darwinism. Surveying this era in his acclaimed book, *In The Shadow of the Poorhouse* (1986), Michael Katz asserted that the 19th-century social-welfare system "reflected the brittle hostility and anger of the respectable classes and their horror at the prospect of a united, militant working class."

Although the American welfare state has never been as generous as such critics might like, times have changed. Having survived the political assault of Ronald Reagan and the intellectual critique of Charles Murray in *Losing Ground* (1984), the American welfare state is in no immediate danger of being rolled back. At the same time, it is clear that there is no political consensus for its expansion. Left and Right seem to agree only that the current social-welfare system is unsatisfactory. A renewed emphasis on the active promotion of upward mobility offers a way out of this paralysis.

The day of the settlement house itself as the major link between the social classes has passed. Too many of its functions have been taken up, however imperfectly, by other institutions, ranging from the public schools to public television. But the need for such a bridge has not been adequately met. Large numbers of Americans cannot find their way into the economic mainstream and are not spurred on to reach "the highest level of which each is capable." Without knowledge of how the world beyond the neighborhood works—that one can become an engineer, that good colleges are eager to

accept black students with potential—the poor will not reach the highest level of their ability. Hard questions must be asked before such bridge building can begin. First, which values are to be taught to the poor? Second, who will teach them? Educators such as Joseph Clark, the controversial black high school principal from Paterson, New Jersey, have come to symbolize a return to an emphasis on bedrock values as part of schooling. People from beyond the neighborhood can help. Potential middle-class volunteers may not feel the tug of religious commitment as strongly as the Jane Addams generation did, but there are still affluent youths whose "uselessness hangs about them heavily."

In poor neighborhoods throughout the nation, thousands of voluntary wars on poverty are already underway. But overall, too few are being won, and most are being waged without much help from middle-class whites. Perhaps the biggest impediment to the growth and success of such efforts is the lingering belief among liberals and others with the means to provide help that they are somehow beside the point, or even dangerous. Today's reformers pay tribute to impulses like those of the settlement workers—as when New York's Governor Mario Cuomo invokes the image of society as family—but only as prelude to calls for expanded social-welfare programs. They dismiss every pre-New Deal response to poverty—and every new proposal reminiscent of such measures—as paltry and mean-spirited. Thus President George Bush's talk of "a thousand points of light" inspires nothing but liberal satire, apparently out of the belief that any private effort to ameliorate poverty is meaningless, intended only to undermine government social-welfare programs. To that, too, the settlement tradition offers an answer.

"The conditions of life forced by our civilization upon the poor in our great cities are undemocratic, unchristian, unrighteous," wrote Vida Scudder of the College Settlement Association in 1900. But efforts to improve them, she said, must be "wholly free from the spirit of social dogmatism and doctrinaire assertion. . . . As we become more practical, we also become better idealists. . . . As we become more useful here and now, we strengthen and deepen all those phases of our common life that vibrate with the demand for a better society to be."

The Brownsville Affray

*It was the largest mass-punishment in U.S. Army history.
In 1906, without trial or hearing, 167 black soldiers were discharged for a crime
none may have committed.*

Richard Young

*Richard Young is a teacher at the Pierce
School in Brookline, Massachusetts. He
is the author of two chapters in* Above
and Beyond, *Boston Publishing Company's history of the Medal of Honor.*

August 13, 1906: It was just past midnight on a sultry summer night. Fred
Combe, the mayor of Brownsville,
Texas, was falling asleep on his back
porch. Army Major Charles Penrose, the
commanding officer of nearby Fort
Brown, was preparing for bed. A late
birthday party was breaking up at the
Cowen residence near the fort. Downtown, players anted up in a poker game
at the Crixell Saloon. It was, from all
appearances, a typical Sunday night in
the sleepy Texas border town.

But someone had no intention of letting the town rest. A group of armed
men—perhaps ten, perhaps as many as
twenty—had quietly gathered in Cowen
Alley, near a low fence that separated
Fort Brown from the town.

Suddenly the silence was shattered as
the men began moving rapidly up the
alley toward the center of town, firing at
windows as they ran. As bullets pep-
pered the houses, startled residents
dropped to the floors next to their beds.
Downtown, police lieutenant M.Y. Dominguez ran out of a saloon and mounted
his horse to investigate the disturbance.
When he suddenly rode into range of the
shadowy figures firing weapons, Dominguez wheeled his horse to escape, but
he was shot just as he made the turn. (His

arm would later be amputated.) Minutes
later the men loosed a volley into the
Ruby Saloon, killing barkeeper Frank
Natus, who was reaching out to close the
alley door.

After the shooting at the saloon, the
killers melted back into the night, leaving chaos in their wake. Mayor Combe
ran out of his house to investigate the
explosion of gunfire and was told that
"the Negroes are shooting up the town."

The firing in Brownsville ended after
just ten minutes, but repercussions from
the incident were destined to continue for
many years afterward. Because of the
racial implications involved, such emi-
nent leaders as then-Secretary of War
William Howard Taft, U.S. Senator Joseph B. Foraker, black leader Booker T.
Washington, and President Theodore
Roosevelt would become ensnared in a
mystery that has never really been solved
and in a controversy that has never fully
been laid to rest.

IT HAD ALL STARTED WHEN THE GOVERN-
ment announced that the all-white
Twenty-sixth Infantry Regiment at Fort
Brown would be replaced by three companies of the all-black Twenty-fifth Infantry Regiment, then stationed at Fort
Niobara, Nebraska. The black troopers
had compiled a long and honorable tradition of service in the Indian wars, in the
Spanish-American War, and in the Philippines. To the citizens of Brownsville,
however, the service record of the men

of the Twenty-fifth meant far less than
the color of their skin.

The news of the transfer of the
Twenty-fifth to Fort Brown was met immediately with angry talk and threats.
First Sergeant Nelson Huron of the departing Twenty-sixth overheard a resident say, "The people of Brownsville
don't want them damned niggers here
and they won't have them." Victorio
Fernandez, one of Brownsville's Mexican police officers, reportedly said, "I
want to kill a couple of them when they
get here." At a rail station in San Antonio, a man heard some Brownsville
residents say they would "shoot over the
barracks" of the Negro troops to frighten
them.

The black soldiers arrived by rail on
Saturday, July 28, and marched to Fort
Brown past sullen townspeople. Situated
at the mouth of the Rio Grande near the
Gulf of Mexico, Brownsville had seen its
heyday around the time of the Civil War,
when it had been one of the principal
seaports of the Confederacy. The end of
the war and the coming of the railroad
had spelled the end for Brownsville as a
center of commerce. In 1906, Brownsville was a small town awash with racial
hatred. Some businesses and drinking
establishments refused to serve the black
soldiers. Certain saloons opened up segregated back rooms for the blacks, Jim-
Crow fashion.

In the most serious of several incidents
that took place following the arrival of
the black soldiers, Privates James W.

From *American History Illustrated*, October 1986, pp. 10-17. Reprinted through the courtesy of Cowles Magazines,
publishers of *American History Illustrated*.

The black soldiers of the Twenty-fifth Infantry Regiment (above) had fought in Cuba during the Spanish-American War and later in the Philippines, and a number of them had been decorated for bravery in action.

Newton and Frank J. Lipscomb were taking a Sunday evening stroll through Brownsville on August 5. As they walked down Elizabeth Street they approached a group of whites on the sidewalk—among them U.S. customs inspector Fred Tate and his wife, who were conversing with a half-dozen women. Tate later claimed that the two black soldiers had continued walking straight down the sidewalk, plowing right through the ladies congregated there. The soldiers claimed that they had stepped aside into the street and that Tate had come after them. In any case, what followed was not in dispute. Tate pulled out a .45-caliber Colt six-shooter and shouted, "I will learn you how to get off the sidewalk when you see a party of white ladies standing there." He proceeded to pistol-whip Newton.

The soldiers were paid on Saturday, August 11, and passed what many in town considered the most peaceful soldiers' payday ever seen in Brownsville. Not one soldier was arrested, and there were no cases of excessive drunkenness. But later that weekend, a Mrs. Lon Evans reported that a soldier tried to crawl through a window in her home. The next day, the headlines in the *Brownsville Daily Herald* trumpeted:

INFAMOUS OUTRAGE

Negro Soldiers Invaded Private Premises Last Night and Tried to Seize a White Lady

That night, a climate of rumor and hysteria gripped Brownsville. Several men from the town were ready to go to the fort with weapons to precipitate a fight. Because of the excitement, Mayor Combe rode out to talk to Major Penrose. The mayor requested that the black soldiers be confined to quarters for the evening because of "a great deal of danger in town."

Major Penrose prudently decided to order his men in, setting a curfew of 8:00 P.M. Captain Macklin sent out patrols to fetch the men still in town. Sergeant Taliafero, one of the soldiers on patrol, later reported that a townsman called out to him, "It is a good thing your C.O. has ordered you all in tonight because some of you were going to get killed."

The soldiers spent the remainder of the evening on the post, fishing in a lagoon, talking on the barracks porches, and playing cards and billiards in the dayroom. The moon was down when "Taps" sounded at 11:00 P.M., and all was quiet.

AT MIDNIGHT, MAJOR PENROSE HEARD two shots that he thought were pistol shots, then six or seven reports that he knew were from high-powered rifles. The attack had begun—and confusion reigned. Ambrose Littlefield, who was at the corner of Cowen Alley and Thirteenth Street, saw the raiders standing under a streetlamp on the corner of Washington and Thirteenth. He later identified them as black soldiers. However, George Thomas Porter, who lived at Thirteenth and Washington, looked out of his window and did not see anyone turn out of Thirteenth, nor did he see anyone under the streetlamp.

Police Lieutenant Dominguez said that from his vantage point at Washington and Fourteenth he looked toward Cowen Alley and saw eight men cross Fourteenth in the dark. Another policeman, Officer Padron, said he met Dominguez in a different place at that time.

Paulino Preciado, who was drinking in the Ruby Saloon when the shots killed the barman, said that he saw soldiers in the alley. But he later recanted, saying that "I could not see anybody in the alley, as it was dark out there, and I was in the light."

At Fort Brown, according to the testimony of Captain Macklin, the chain of sentinels stationed along the wall were unable to see men just ten to fifteen feet away in the dark because "everything was a blank." Major Penrose assumed that someone was firing on the fort and ordered his men into emergency formation.

According to the noncommissioned officers, all the men were in formation and accounted for—*while* the firing could still be heard in town. Later that night, Penrose sent a patrol to town under the command of Captain Samuel Lyon. Lyon reported back, to the surprise of Penrose, that the townspeople thought the soldiers had done the firing. The next morning, Penrose ordered a check of the weapons and ammunition. All rifles were clean and all ammunition accounted for.

Blackson recommended that innocent "be made to suffer with others more guilty" because of their "conspiracy of silence."

ON AUGUST 13, THAT SAME MONDAY morning, the town began an investigation. The major himself retraced the line of attack and found fifty to sixty expended Army shells along the way. He appointed an investigating committee composed of leading citizens of the town. They heard the testimony of twenty-two witnesses, eight of whom implicated black soldiers as the raiders. Five of those witnesses said they actually saw blacks; three others said they recognized that the men were black from the sound of their voices. The tenor of the investigation can be surmised from one typical question:

Q. "We know that this outrage was committed by Negro soldiers. We want any information that will lead to a discovery of who did it."

On August 15, after two days of investigation, the citizens' committee sent a telegraph message to President Theodore Roosevelt in Washington, in which they informed him that the town was terrorized and under constant alarm. They asked "to have the troops at once removed and replaced by white soldiers." The War Department complied, sending the Twenty-fifth Infantry from Fort Brown to Fort Reno, Oklahoma.

Meanwhile, Texas authorities were conducting their own investigation: on August 23, warrants were issued for the arrest of twelve members of the black battalion for murder and conspiracy to commit murder. The twelve were selected by Texas Rangers after questioning. Although the investigation uncovered no solid allegations against the twelve and no witnesses could conclusively put them at the scene of the crime, they were removed to Fort Sam Houston in San Antonio.

Army General William S. McCaskey, Commanding General of the Department of Texas, said that the "manner by which

President Theodore Roosevelt approved the dismissal without honor of 167 black soldiers from the Twenty-fifth Infantry, although no evidence existed to specifically convict any individuals in the group for the Brownsville killing, and no conspiracy by the men was proven.

CULVER PICTURES, NEW YORK CITY

"The secretive nature of the race, where crimes charged to members of their color are made, is well known."

their names were procured is a mystery. As far as is known there is no evidence that the majority of them were in any way directly connected with the affair."

The Army's investigation of the incident hit a brick wall. President Roosevelt sent Major August P. Blackson, Inspector General of the Southwest Division, to check into the matter. Blackson reported that the involvement of the men of the Twenty-fifth "cannot be doubted" but that the men of the battalion would not testify against their comrades.

Blackson contended that those who refused to "peach" or "squeal" on their comrades should "be made to suffer with the others more guilty, as far as the law will permit" because of their "conspiracy of silence." He recommended that "all of the enlisted men of the three companies present on the night of August 13 be discharged from service and be debarred from reenlistment." It appears that almost no one involved in the official Army investigation seriously addressed the notion that the men might actually be innocent and that they were saying nothing because they had nothing to say.

President Roosevelt ordered General Ernest A. Garlington to get information from the twelve soldiers incarcerated at Fort Sam Houston and from the rest of the men of the Twenty-fifth at Fort Reno. Garlington reported that each man "assumed a wooden, stolid look [and] denied any knowledge of the affair," which confirmed his belief that "the secretive nature of the race, where crimes charged to members of their color are made, is well known." Garlington wrote that he knew that many men without direct knowledge would suffer, but that they had stood together during the investigation and so should "stand together when the penalty falls."

On November 5, Roosevelt instructed Secretary of War William H. Taft to

To Secretary of War William H. Taft fell the onerous task of carrying out the punishment approved by Roosevelt. The process of dismissing the men of the Twenty-fifth Infantry was subsequently completed without benefit of either hearing or trial.

Thirteen of the dismissed soldiers had been decorated for bravery. Six were Medal of Honor recipients.

carry out the recommendation. Taft waited until after the November 9 congressional elections, then began discharge proceedings against all of the men of the three companies. The process was completed within ten days—without a court-martial or a hearing. Many of the men wept as they turned in their weapons and equipment. In all, 167 men, including many who had served with honor on the frontier, in Cuba, and in the Philippines were released, making this the largest mass punishment in U.S. Army history. One of the discharged men was a twenty-six-year veteran, and thirteen of the soldiers had been decorated for bravery in the Spanish-American War. Six men were Medal of Honor recipients.*

THE PRO-ROOSEVELT *OUTLOOK* EDITORialized that there was "no doubt" that some of the soldiers of the Twenty-fifth Regiment were guilty of murder in the first degree, and that the president's decision had been "both wise and just, notwithstanding the fact that some who are innocent suffer with the guilty." The *Outlook* concluded that there was "no reason whatever for regarding this action as having any relation to the race issue.

But blacks throughout the land saw it differently. Many felt betrayed by Roosevelt, whom they had perceived to be a friend of the black people. He was, after all, the leader of the party of Lincoln—and most black people still voted for the Republicans in 1906. Beyond that, during the Spanish-American War Roosevelt had fought with black troopers on his flank, and they had rescued him on more than one occasion. He had always spoken highly of their courage and ability as soldiers, which made it particularly galling when he contended that this case should convince black people not to

Black leader Booker T. Washington lost credibility with other blacks as a result of the Brownsville incident when he failed to speak out in defense of the soldiers and was perceived as supporting President Roosevelt's dismissal action.

BROWN BROTHERS, STERLING, PENNSYLVANIA

"They had no right to eliminate me without trying me and finding me guilty, but they did. . . ."

"band together to shelter their own criminals."

Debate in the black community grew so heated that the nation's foremost black leader, Booker T. Washington, urged his people to tone down their attacks on the president. Because Washington had never spoken in defense of the soldiers, his stand was perceived to be justification of Roosevelt's action at the expense of the Negro movement. Other black leaders, most notably W.E.B. DuBois, were quick to capitalize on the issue—and they gained power in their community as Washington fell from favor.

The Constitutional League (a civil rights organization and precursor to the National Association for the Advancement of Colored People) lodged an official protest over the dismissal of the black soldiers on December 10, 1906. More importantly, the U.S. Senate began its own investigation. The hearings lasted from February 4 through June 14, 1907, and were resumed on November 18, 1907, and continued through March 10, 1908.

The Senate listened to the testimony of more than one hundred and sixty witnesses. The Majority Report concluded that the shooting had been done by some eight to twenty soldiers, who were never identified. The guns used had been 1903 Springfield rifles, according to the report, and the ammunition had been government issue. Of the witnesses, fifteen said they saw the attackers clad in soldiers' uniforms.

During the hearings the black soldiers acquired a powerful champion, Senator Joseph B. Foraker of Ohio, a politician from within Roosevelt's own Republican party and a long-time foe of the president. Senator Foraker and three other senators wrote the minority opinion. They pointed out that there had been no indictments, despite the administration's desperate measures to secure them. This was no small matter, as the *New York Evening Post* pointed out in an editorial: "When a Texas grand jury cannot find an indictment against a hated 'nigger' it looks as if the President of the United States had a pretty poor case when he discharged those men."

The dissenters also wrote that if anyone had a motive to shoot up the town of Brownsville, it was the white gambling-house owners, not the black soldiers. Their reason was financial: the houses were segregated, and the owners were losing most of the revenue they would have been taking in if Fort Brown had been manned by white soldiers. It was the contention of Foraker and the other dissenters that the owners had probably staged the incident in order to effect the removal of the black troops.

Foraker and the others charged that the black soldiers had been punished without access to their right to a fair public trial. They further stated that the soldiers had been loyal for years and that even if some were guilty, all should not have been discharged. Furthermore, no conspiracy had been proven, and much of the testimony had been contradictory and unreliable.

THESE NEW INVESTIGATIONS BROUGHT prior assumptions into question and raised new questions that would never be satisfactorily answered. An editorial in the March 19, 1908, *Independent* stated: "The investigation by the Senate leaves it somewhat doubtful whether the shooting was actually done by the soldiers."

Many of the witnesses claimed to have identified the attackers as black soldiers from a distance of thirty to one hundred feet, but in a firing conducted at night by the Army under conditions similar to those of the night of August 13, witnesses as close as fifty feet could see only the flash of weapons and nothing of the person firing. At a distance of just two paces on such a night, it was not possible to distinguish the race of men standing quietly in a line.

The forty Government-Issue shells found immediately outside the fort wall had been piled neatly in a circle approximately ten inches in diameter. Because a Springfield rifle ejects expended cartridges a distance of ten feet, it would have been necessary for the men firing the rifles to find and retrieve the spent shells in the dark and neatly pile them, an action that would have been not only bizarre but nearly impossible on a moonless night. The piles of cartridges suggest that they were left there as "evidence"—scattered by someone who wanted to make it look as if the soldiers had fired them.

According to the dissenters, the rounds *had* been fired by the men of the Twenty-fifth—but on the range at Fort Niobara, sometime prior to their transfer to Fort Brown. A microscopic study conducted at the Springfield Armory proved that all of the expended cartridges had been fired by the same four rifles, all of which belonged to members of Company B. In the check of weapons ordered by Major Penrose on Monday morning, three of the four rifles were found to be clean and covered with cosmoline, a thick lubricant that would have rendered it nearly impossible to fire them. It is possible that these three rifles could have been fired and then cleaned and oiled during the night, but it is almost certain that the fourth rifle was not fired on the night of August 13. It was found buried deep in a footlocker in the locked supply room. In order to retrieve the weapon, the investigators had to remove bunks and baggage that had been piled on the locker after the move from Fort Niobara.

The dissenters theorized that the empty shells were policed up at Fort Niobara and put into boxes, and then were transported along with other equipment to Fort Brown. The boxes containing the empty shells were left unguarded on the porches of the barracks there. It would have been easy for a civilian who worked on post to pocket these rounds without anyone noticing.

The live military rounds fired into the houses could be explained by the fact that the departing Twenty-sixth infantry had often bartered with civilians, trading ammunition for whiskey and other items. The Twenty-sixth had also left a great deal of used equipment, including old uniforms, in the barracks when they left camp. Scavengers from town were frequent visitors to the post in the time between the departure of the Twenty-sixth and the arrival of the Twenty-fifth. It was not uncommon to see townspeople

"We in government have a duty to demonstrate that we can admit an error and can correct a terrible wrong."

wearing articles of military clothing, and it certainly would not have been difficult to put together "uniforms" for the raiders.

All of these possible contradictions to the official version of the incident came to light after the men had been discharged. The mystery was never solved. No one was ever tried for the murder of Frank Natus. But the Roosevelt administration remained adamant in insisting that it had followed the right course in dismissing the men, and neither Theodore Roosevelt nor his successor, William Howard Taft, wanted anything to do with reopening the investigation.

An Army Court of Inquiry did convene to hear evidence on the issue of reinstatement of the 167 men, but the hearings were not public. On May 4, 1909, for reasons never disclosed, the Court of Inquiry reinstated fourteen of the soldiers to full honors and rank. The other 153 accused men remained pariahs, discharged without honor or chance of redemption. They had never been convicted of a crime, nor was any evidence produced against them—yet they remained outcasts.

SIXTY-SIX YEARS AFTER THE BROWNSVILLE incident, in 1972, U.S. Representative Augustus Hawkins initiated legislation to restore honor to the men of the Twenty-fifth Infantry. Senator Hubert H. Humphrey backed the motion in the Senate, saying, "We in government have a duty to demonstrate that we can admit an error and can correct a terrible wrong." Eventually, Secretary of the Army Robert F. Kroehlke issued an executive

Senator Joseph B. Foraker of Ohio was one of a small number of congressmen who defended the dismissed infantrymen, citing their decorations for bravery and years of loyal service, pointing out that even if some were to be found guilty all should not be punished, and condemning much of the testimony as contradictory and unreliable.

"None of us said anything because we didn't have anything to say. It was a frame-up through and through."

order that gave the 153 men honorable discharges, albeit without back pay or allowances. Congress in turn authorized a twenty-five-thousand-dollar pension for any of the discharged men still living and ten thousand dollars to any surviving spouse.

Only one of the men, eighty-six-year-old Dorsey Willis, lived to collect the money. Willis claimed that the dishonorable discharge had ruined his life, saying, "To take a person's rights from them is bad, you know. They had no right to eliminate me without trying me and finding me guilty, but they did. . . . None of us said anything because we didn't have anything to say. It was a frame-up through and through."

Recommended additional reading: The Brownsville Raid *by John D. Weaver (Norton, 1970).*

*Since the article was written, the statement that six Medal of Honor recipients were among those discharged has been found to be incorrect.

George Washington Carver: Creative Scientist

In the early twentieth century, this prolific and charismatic scientist played a key role in spreading the benefits of scientific agriculture throughout the southern United States.

Vivian E. Hilburn

Vivian E. Hilburn is a guidance counselor and instructor of Spanish at Paul Quinn College in Waco, Texas. She has been the director of the Black Studies Club on campus for many years.

Few scientists—and particularly few specialists in botany or chemistry—have a monument erected in their memory, and still fewer can boast of having a foundation or museum carrying their name. All of these and numerous other honors have come to George Washington Carver, a man of humble birth who, until his death in the middle of this century, etched indelible marks on the history and lives of his people and his nation.

Carver, the son of a female slave in the home of Moses and Susan Carver, was born near Diamond Grove, Missouri, circa 1864. His childhood was tumultuous because of the unstable conditions of the times. Southwest Missouri, a frontier area, was bordered by the slaveholding, secession-oriented Arkansas, "Free Kansas," and the Oklahoma Indian Territory. Moses Carver, a slaveholding Unionist, was caught in the middle of the issues dividing the nation. Linda McMurry writes in *George Washington Carver: Scientist and Symbol*, "Throughout the war, area residents were prey to looting and killing by Confederate bushwackers, Union raiders, and ordinary outlaws taking advantage of the unsettled conditions." Moses Carver's homestead was raided by Confederate bushwackers several times, and on one of those raids,

George and his mother were kidnapped and taken to Arkansas.

The Carvers were fond of Mary and her two sons—their only slaves—and wanted to find them. A neighbor, who was familiar with the guerrilla bands in the area, said he knew their whereabouts and agreed to hunt for them. His search uncovered George, who was returned to the Carvers, but Mary was never found. George and his brother Jim had always lived with their mother in a smaller cabin on the Carver property, but with the disappearance of Mary, the Carvers moved the boys into the main cabin with them and they lived as a family.

George was a frail and sickly child due to an earlier bout with whooping cough. He stuttered because of a speech impediment and had a falsetto voice about which he was often teased. The heavier chores on the farm were allotted to Jim, who was older, healthier, and stronger. George helped Susan around the house, and learned cooking, sewing, laundering, and needle work.

The young George was untiringly inquisitive and could often be seen in the woods, scraping earth, gathering bark from trees, and coddling weeds and flowers. He gathered cans and gourds in which he grew sprouts. He became so adept at cultivating plants that neighbors called him the Plant Doctor. His desire "to know" and "to do" became a lifelong obsession. Until his death Carver enjoyed making things, and his rapport with nature was nurtured by early morning walks in the woods.

From a very early age Carver was recognized as having exceptional intel-

ligence. His desire to learn, however, was thwarted for a while. Although the Missouri Constitution of 1865 made free schooling mandatory for black youngsters from age five, George could not attend school at that time because there were not enough blacks of a qualifying age in his township to warrant a school. There was, however, a school for blacks in the county seat of Neosho, and around age twelve, George left the Carvers to attend school there. In Neosho, only eight miles from Diamond Grove, George lived with his first set of black parents, Mariah and Andrew Watkins. Mariah was a midwife and she, like Susan, cultivated his homemaking skills. He also attended worship services with her at the African Methodist Episcopal Church, where religion became a central focus of his life.

Carver turned down an offer of a permanent position at Iowa State to "be of the greatest good" to his fellow blacks.

Neosho had a large black population and there George felt a sense of belonging. By now, he had learned that he was black, and being so, he could not dream of fame, affluence, or lofty achievements. But his drive "to know" and "to do" spurred him on. What was rain?—the question constantly nagged him. What was creation, order and design?

From *The World & I*, July 1987, pp. 189-197. *The World & I*, a publication of The Washington Times Corporation. Copyright © 1987.

What gives soil different colors? These questions echoed through his mind and strengthened his determination to discover truth.

But his excitement about the schooling in Neosho was short-lived. Carver soon learned that the teacher knew little more than he did. Carver's disillusionment with the Neosho school and his desire for knowledge started him on a long trek through several towns in Kansas in search of an education. Eventually, he became an art major at Simpson College in Indianola, Iowa. His cooking and laundering skills provided a livelihood wherever he went.

At Simpson, despite his talent and interest in painting, his art teacher advised him to enroll in the state agricultural college at Ames, where her father was a horticulture professor. She was convinced that his botanical skills offered him more financial security than would a career as a black artist. Despite his desire to cease his wandering, he took her advice and enrolled at Ames.

He quickly overcame the initial reservation of the other students to him as the only black on campus, and he became an active and popular member of the student body. Carver graduated in 1894 with a bachelor of science degree from Iowa State College, and took a position at the Ames Experiment Station as an assistant to Louis Pammell, a noted botanist and mycologist. He also taught freshman biology while pursuing graduate work. By the time he earned a masters degree in 1896, his abilities in mycology and plant hybridization were already remarkable.

EMPLOYMENT AT TUSKEGEE

That same year he was asked by Booker T. Washington, then widely known as an educator, author, lecturer, and reformer, to head the newly established Department of Agriculture at Tuskegee Institute in Alabama. Washington advocated industrial and agricultural education as the key to black advancement. He understood the plight of the farmers, white and black. The one-crop system that had consisted principally of cotton production had drained them of energy and incentive. Most of these farmers were tenants and sharecroppers who eked out a bare existence by borrowing money for planting in the spring and paying it back after harvest in the fall.

Washington sought to free farmers from the burden of debt, and he found an ally in George Washington Carver. Carver turned down an offer of a permanent position at Iowa State to "be of the greatest good" to his fellow blacks. He arrived in Alabama wearing a too-tight gray suit, the top button of his jacket fastened, and a pert pink rose in his lapel. He presented a striking figure with a handlebar moustache, pointed nose, and deep, burning eyes. Thin [and] stooped, he resembled a question mark. While waiting at the Chehaw railroad station for someone to take him to the campus, he immediately began plucking plants and surveying the red clay hills in the distance. "Red! Yellow! Oh! the handiwork of God!" he thought. He saw the undeveloped natural resources that could improve the lives of all Southerners.

As a trained researcher, the first item on Carver's agenda was setting up a proper laboratory. Although Tuskegee was the second best-endowed black school in the nation, it was still poor in comparison to similar white schools. With exceedingly limited funds, Washington sought to elevate an entire people. Thus Carver made his own equipment with retrievals from junk piles. His lamp served as a heater for his hands when they became stiff from the cold, as a Bunsen burner for his scientific experiments, and as a reflector for his microscope. For graders, he punched holes in pieces of tin. He used reeds as pipettes, cut broken bottles clean-edged with string, and pulverized his material using a cracked china bowl as a mortar. And since zinc sulphate was costly, he picked up discarded zinc tops from fruit jars.

It was a far cry from the equipment he had used at Iowa State. One consolation was that soon after he arrived in Tuskegee, the Institute was granted $1,500 annually by the state legislature to establish and run an agricultural experiment station. It became the only all-black-manned station, and not coincidentally the lowest-funded one. Carver's station never received more than $1,500 a year, while a nearby white station got between $60,000 and $100,000 for its annual budget.

Over the years his desire for a better and more adequate laboratory and more time to do research, free from teaching responsibilities, became the main source of a growing rift between him and Booker T. Washington. He clashed with Washington largely because Carver was a gifted teacher and researcher, but not much of an administrator. His assistant,

George Bridgeforth, eventually became the head of the Department of Agriculture and Carver was named the director of agricultural research. Although this move freed Carver from the administrative details he hated, it did not sit well with him to have anyone over him. These basic conflicts were never resolved and only ameliorated with Washington's death in 1915.

ROLE AS AN EDUCATOR

In Carver's laboratory, which he called "God's Little Workshop," the students learned the techniques of analyzing soils to determine which elements were lacking. They tested fertilizers and feeds to find out what ingredients increased tissue, fat, or milk. He taught the "trinity of relationship" between the soil, the plants growing on it, and the human beings or animals consuming the plants. He insisted that only by knowing the components of the soil could one determine the proper quantities of minerals needed to nourish each particular crop. He argued that a mastery of the economics of plant life can improve human existence. And above all, Carver preached the unity of the universe and the interrelatedness of all its parts.

Farming was unpopular at the Alabama school because blacks had been the major victims of farming's failures. Carver had to make the vocation attractive. He possessed two essential qualities of a good teacher—a thorough knowledge of his subject and an intuitive sense of how to transmit and instill it while he was able to convey his own motivating compulsion—"I don't know, but I'll find out"—he also knew "you can't teach people anything, you can only draw out what is in them." He was extraordinarily effective. Even when Washington was deeply exasperated with Carver, he admitted that the professor was "a great teacher, a great lecturer, a great inspirer of young men and old men."

Most of his students had only average intelligence, but he brought out the best points in each. He made each of them feel proud of his own ability and fostered a desire to extend it. He moved them to action with scoldings. "Get the drones off you! Remember, the more ignorant we are the less use God has for us." Carver was able to instill the "Tuskegee Ideal"—that the benefits of a student's education were to be shared with his community. Most of his students returned to their homes and spread the gospel of scientific agriculture.

He also promoted a philosophy of thrift and conservation. He thought that saving was not enough; there must be order also. To demonstrate this he showed his students a box of string, saved but snarled and entangled. "This is ignorance," he said. "And this"—he held up another box in which each piece was neatly tied or rolled into balls—"is intelligence."

In 1903 a boy's dormitory, Rockefeller Hall, was erected on the Tuskegee campus and Carver moved into two ground-floor rooms which he was to occupy for 35 years. Initially controversy arose over this special treatment. Many of the other teachers felt it unfair that he be given more space than they and that he was arrogant to expect such treatment. Carver prevailed though, and weathered quite a bit of resentment over a bachelor's occupying so much space on a crowded campus. At the same time, the students loved having him near, and for many of them he played the role of teacher, father, and spiritual adviser.

Carver graduated in 1896 with a master's degree in botany from Iowa State College. Recruited by Booker T. Washington, he then accepted a position at the fledgling Tuskegee Institute. He arrived in Alabama wearing a flower in his lapel, which became an enduring symbol.

DEMONSTRATION AS TEACHING

Carver had come South to help farmers, and the Experiment Station at Tuskegee was the nucleus of this effort. Tuskegee had long engaged in extension activities such as an annual Farmers' Conference. Carver improved and expanded such efforts. He added farmers' institutes, an annual colored fair, and easy-to-read agricultural bulletins.

Throughout the years, he did not limit his scientific demonstrations to the classroom. Believing that demonstration is the purest form of teaching, Carver went into the community to give hands-on illustrations of his theories. He would not rely on publications to relay the results of experiments because many farmers could not read. Since there were no home and farm demonstration agents, he developed the "Jesup Wagon"—a wagon equipped with demonstration materials—to communicate his ideas. Money for the project was donated by Morris K. Jesup. The Jesup Wagon, "a farmers' college on wheels," started its career in May 1906. It was operated by Thomas M. Campbell, a former student of Carver's. In November of that year, the U.S. Department of Agriculture (USDA) employed Campbell as the first "Negro Demonstration Agent." He took the wagon to surrounding communities for regularly scheduled demonstrations of plowing and planting, usually at a house where neighbors had gathered. He returned later at the appropriate time to give instructions on cultivation and harvesting.

Tuskegee was a leader in the development of movable schools. In the United States, Iowa State College was the first to experiment with a "Seed Corn Gospel Train." But the success of Tuskegee's later version was the prime reason for the idea's success. It has since helped to shape educational policies with respect to disadvantaged groups and underdeveloped countries throughout the world. Similar projects were adopted in China, India, Macedonia, and Southern Rhodesia. In regions where road systems could not accommodate motor vehicles, donkeys were used to transport educational materials as "a gift of knowledge" to farmers.

Encouraged by Washington, Carver also published numerous agricultural bulletins. By 1908 he had published fourteen bulletins and devoted many hours to his column, "Professor Carver's Advice." Here he warned farmers of impending dangers such as hog cholera, and he cautioned stockmen against poisonous weeds that their livestock might eat. One bulletin, *Some Cercosporae of Macon County, Alabama,* reflected Carver's favorite field of research, which was largely denied to him by his circumstances. He did not have the equipment or time needed for the proper identification of the many species of fungus. Nevertheless, he continued to collect fungi, and he was the first to identify several species, one of which was named *Taphrina carveri.* In 1935 the USDA made him a "collaborator," and his specimens are still preserved in the USDA herbarium in Beltsville, Maryland.

RESEARCH IN CROPS AND NATURAL RESOURCES

In 1904 the boll weevil invaded American cotton fields. By 1910 it was a full-grown menace. Spraying each plant with

A Man of Faith

I came to know George Washington Carver during the time we were together at Tuskegee Institute, where I was a student and he an instructor. At least three times a day, over a period of eight years, I observed the posture and mood of his daily life. Since both of us were housed on the east end of campus, he at Rockefeller Hall and I at Thrasher Hall, this gave me a splendid opportunity to see him as he went to and from his quarters. We also ate in the same main dining hall—he with the members of the faculty and I with the other students.

Often on long evenings, he would leave the dining room and walk toward the agriculture building. Sometimes, he took a similar route in the early morning, but frequently in the morning hours he could be found examining the roots, plants, shrubbery, and soil around campus. The area of campus where the science building, the Hollis Burke Frissell Library and Logan Hall now stand was then an open field and Dr. Carver spent a lot of time there also. During these excursions, he communed with God and nature.

I believe his intellectual resources profited from his spiritual life. He was able to accomplish so much because he prayed so much. The more difficult the task he confronted, the more time he spent preparing through prayer and meditation. Even though he kept a busy schedule, he took time for reflection and always took stock of his spiritual condition. He labored to be right with God and

he often expressed that he did not want to come to the edge of the grave before manifesting a concern about eternity. He advised that every young person should find a little time to be alone with God each day.

Many mornings I would hear a low-sounding voice under my window, only to look out and observe Dr. Carver examining a lump of dirt or a root or a growth of some kind, asking God to reveal its secrets. He knew the truth of William Cullen Bryant's words: "To him who in the love of Nature holds Communion with her visible forms, she speaks a various language."

He was not only a great scientist, but a great man of faith. Every Sunday, many students and faculty at Tuskegee Institute attended chapel services at 11:00 A.M. Later Dr. Carver would lead a Bible class of about 200 students. He told the same stories I had heard so many times before, but he made the characters in the Bible come alive. Once, while he was discussing a Bible figure, he characterized him in relation to the people with whom he associated. He pointed out his virtues and vices as he walked from one side of the room to the other. Suddenly, he astounded the entire assembly by saying that the character under consideration suffered from hemorrhoids. This is only one example of his uncanny insights into the human character.

The themes of his Bible classes, as well as chance conversations with him on

campus, were pure and uplifting. He was guileless and gentle. For a while, because of his modest and peaceful nature, I had a feeling that he didn't know how to be stern, but that opinion was changed upon several occasions when I heard him strongly scold a student for misbehaving.

His life has had a quiet influence on my own. He was so dedicated to his area of expertise that he had a great deal to do with the deepening and confirming of my own dedication to lifelong goals.

—*Rev. Andrew Fowler*
Capitol View Baptist, Washington, D.C.

TUSKEGEE UNIVERSITY ARCHIVES

Carver knew the truth of William Cullen Bryant's words: "To him who in the love of Nature holds Communion with her visible forms, she speaks a various language."

---

calcium arsenate would be financially prohibitive. Only by planting, cultivating, and harvesting early might the damage be minimized. Carver advised farmers to obtain cotton of the greatest vitality—the fastest-growing and the earliest ripening. He developed his own hybrid and distributed its seeds at the Farmers' Conference. At the same time, he urged farmers to plant less cotton and to replace this cash crop with sweet potatoes, cowpeas, and peanuts.

Cowpeas, or black-eyed peas as they were commonly called, had proved to be "the poor man's bank" as a soil health builder and excellent livestock food. At that time few people in the United States had heard of the soybean, another le-

guminous nitrogen fixer. Only much later did the USDA experiment with imported soybeans and adapt them to American soils and climatic conditions. Carver had successfully experimented

---

He made the results of his and others' research available and understandable to thousands whose lives were thereby enriched.

---

with them, and they eventually became a major crop in the region.

But Carver's most important studies revolved around the peanut. Farmers already knew about the peanut. Indigenous to South America, it had been relished by conquistadors who carried it to Spain. It found its way to Africa in the seventeenth century, and came back again to the New World with slave traders as their chief bill-of-fare for their human cargo. The African word *goober* for peanut is today an active part of the Southern vocabulary. The peanut is leguminous, and easy to plant, grow, and harvest.

The peanut is equal to sirloin beef in protein content and to potatoes in carbohydrates. Before 1913, Carver published recipes for cooking peanuts in one of his bulletins. By 1916, this bulletin was in its sixth edition, carrying directions for growing peanuts and 105 ways to prepare and eat them. Carver taught a class of senior girls who were studying dietetics the varied usages of the peanut. They served a tasty five-course lunch to Booker T. Washington and nine guests—soup, mock-chicken, vegetable, salad, bread, candy, cookies, ice cream, and coffee—all made from peanuts!

The peanut, soybean and sweet potato had not only helped enrich the soil, but they had provided bumper crops. Yet the market place was still not profitable for farmers due to the lack of viable products from these commodities. Carver's research turned to developing new uses for them in three distinct stages: finding, adapting, and creating. First he used the raw materials nature had provided. Second he rearranged these materials—wood, stones, ores, fibers, skins, metals—targeting their potential industrial use. Third he transformed these materials into new ones for the benefit of people and society.

He knew that a large portion of any farm crop was inedible and was therefore wasted. Carver abhorred waste. His solution was simple and direct: Find uses for a product's waste and thus enlarge its usefulness. He had a vision of farms as not merely food factories but as sources of raw materials for industry. In the meantime, he sought to produce cheap substitutes for the expensive goods whose purchase helped to keep share-croppers in debt.

From soybeans he had made flour, starch, meal, stains, dyes, ink, breakfast food, oil, milk, and wood fillers. But he knew that soybeans could not be promoted for industrial purposes because of Southern unfamiliarity with them. Instead, Carver concentrated on the peanut. From his research on peanuts emerged such products as beverages, pickles, sauces, meal, coffee, salve, bleach, wood filler, washing powder, metal polish, paper, ink, plastics, shaving cream, rubbing oil, linoleum, shampoo, axle grease, and synthetic rubber.

Carver's interest in the dormant mineral wealth of Alabama became more pressing. In the clay hills near Tuskegee, he discovered marble, limestone, malleable copper, azurite, iron, manganese, sugar quartz, bentonite (a de-inker for newspapers), and heat-resisting and non-conducting micas for the electrical indus-

try. He also discovered and developed various fertilizers and dyes. He was most enthusiastic about the use of native dyes for paints. In one bulletin he told farmers how to make and use such paints for their homes, fences, and barns. Later, he got two patents on processes for paint production and an unsuccessful company was formed to market them.

With World War I the danger of a food shortage came to the United States. Because Carver had always believed that a weed was merely a plant out of place, he began teaching the virtues of eating wild vegetables, both fresh and dehydrated. In January 1918, Carver was summoned to Washington to demonstrate products made from the sweet potato and to exhibit how it could be used to make bread. He demonstrated before Army bakers, chemists, dieticians, technicians, and transportation authorities. This last group was invited because of Carver's work on a method of food dehydration that not only preserved foods indefinitely, but greatly decreased their weight and bulk.

In a press conference at this meeting he said, "I do not like the word *substitute* applied to my products. I prefer to let each stand on its own merits." He defined *synthetic* as a "fourth kingdom of nature," in man's control and in which incompatible elements could unite. He predicted "a new world coming—The Synthetic World."

AWARDS AND LEGACY

George Washington Carver died on January 5, 1943, and was buried on the Tuskegee campus next to Booker T. Washington. His outstanding service to humanity had been recognized in the many awards given to him during his lifetime and has been preserved in his legacy.

International recognition was given Carver as a botanist and chemurgist. He was elected a fellow of the Royal Society of Arts of Great Britain in 1918 and awarded the Spingarn Medal in 1923. Carver received an honorary Doctor of Science degree from Simpson College in 1928 and was appointed collaborator for the USDA Mycology and Plant Disease Survey Bureau of Plant Industry. The George Washington Carver Museum was established on the Tuskegee campus in 1935.

Carver was awarded the Franklin Delano Roosevelt Medal in 1939, and re-

ceived an honorary doctorate from the University of Rochester in 1941. Carver also received many medals, scrolls, citations, and honorary degrees for his achievements in creative and scientific research and for his contributions to the improvement of health and living conditions of the Southern farmer. The United States honored him with a three-cent postage stamp in 1948, and Congress authorized the establishment of the George Washington Carver National Monument near the site of his birth in 1953.

CARVER AS SYMBOL

Few scientists have become as well known and widely acclaimed as Carver, which raises intriguing questions. He made no great theoretical breakthroughs and did not develop a single new commercially successful product. Many scientists, both white and black, have accomplished more through their research. Why then did Carver become so famous? The answers are found in the nature of his personality and the symbolic value of his work and life story.

Carver's fame was also enhanced by his adoption as a symbol by a myriad of causes.

Carver was both a complex and compelling person with many interests and activities. His prize-winning art, his mastery of the piano and several other musical instruments, and his creativity in such crafts as knitting and weaving bespeak his versatility. Some of his paintings were exhibited at the World's Fair in Chicago in 1893. One of them, *Three Peaches,* done with his fingers and with pigments he developed from the clays of Alabama, was requested by the Luxembourg Gallery.

Considered by many to be an introvert and mystic, Carver was little understood during his lifetime. He was often described by those who knew him as modest, unassuming, yet profound. At the same time, he courted and relished publicity. Deeply religious, he attributed his success in developing new products to divine guidance. He found little pleasure in material goods and frequently refused to accept payment for his services to peanut processors and others. He never asked for an increase in his starting salary of $1,200 during his four decades at Tuskegee Institute. Some of his monthly salary checks were still in his desk drawer when the banks crashed during the Depression. He had just not bothered to deposit them. However, since he rarely spent anything on himself—he continued to wear a suit given to him by his Iowa teachers and fellow students until his death—he did accumulate a sizeable savings.

In 1940, when Carver realized that he would not be able to continue his work much longer, he contributed these savings, more than $60,000 in all, to the establishment of the George Washington Carver Research Foundation, "dedicated to the progress of humanity through the application of science to the problems of agriculture and industry." During his remaining three years, Carver continued to work in the foundation with the aid of his young assistant, Austin W. Curtis.

During the next thirty years the foundation grew from a one-man operation on a meager budget to its current status as a multifaceted research organization with over 100 faculty and staff investigators and an annual operational budget in excess of $5 mlllion. These projects include pure research, training and demonstration, and outreach projects, all proper extensions of such a creative life.

His appeal was and is based on more than his idiosyncrasies or physical legacies, however. After hearing Carver speak, one person wrote, "You are the most seductive person I have ever met." His was not a surface charisma—he had a talent for making people feel special. Most acquaintances became intimate friends, and dozens of people, black and white, believed themselves to be Carver's "closest friend." The force of his personality captivated many, including journalists who wrote scores of articles about him.

Carver's fame was also enhanced by his adoption as a symbol by a myriad of causes. The romance of his rise from slavery to success was used to motivate youth to work hard and to prove the fairness of the economic system. Race relations improvement groups, such as the Commission on Interracial Cooperation, publicized his achievements and sponsored talks by him at white colleges to demonstrate the capabilities of blacks. Ironically, at the same time supporters of segregation used his story and unassuming manner to deny the crippling effects of legalized separation. Because of his publicly proclaimed reliance on divine inspiration, a number of religious groups made him a patron saint in the battle against secularism and materialism. Also, the United Peanut Association and "New South" advocates of crop diversification and industrialism saw obvious value in publicizing his work.

In the end, Carver became famous for inventing hundreds of products and saving the South from cotton dependency. This assessment both exaggerates and distorts the nature of his work. His original goal was not to produce commercially feasible commodities, but to provide impoverished sharecroppers with a way out by the use of available resources to improve their circumstances. What he advocated would later be called "appropriate technology." A lot of what he taught was not original, but he was without equal as a popularizer of scientific agriculture. He made the results of both his and others' research available and understandable to thousands whose lives were thereby enriched.

From Progressivism to the 1920s

The Populist "revolt" of the 1890s had been based largely on agrarian discontent. After the turn of the century, a new reform movement developed that drew its strength from the cities. Progressivism, as it came to be called, was far from monolithic and cut across party lines. Generally, however, the men and women drawn to the movement were disturbed by corporate power and excesses. Some wished to break up the large combinations, others to control them. Progressives usually sought to extend democratic participation in the political process through such devices as referenda, judicial recall, and extending the list of elective offices. Above all, they wanted government at all levels to be more responsive to the needs of those without power. Most were not radicals; they merely sought to make the system function more effectively and compassionately.

Despite an impressive list of legislative accomplishments, the Progressive movement ameliorated but did not cure social and political inequities. Whether more would have been accomplished had the United States remained aloof from World War I cannot be known. American entry into that conflict stifled the reform impulse as national energies were turned to winning the war. For the duration, criticism of the system often was condemned as unpatriotic and damaging to the boys "over there." Intolerance continued after the Armistice as the "Red Scare" (fear of communism) replaced the hatred directed toward all things German.

The 1920s provided an odd mixture of conformity and innovation. President Woodrow Wilson's attempt to lead the United States into the League of Nations was narrowly defeated, but in the years that followed, a sour mood of political isolationism developed. This "nativism" was expressed domestically with the rise of organizations directed against "alien" influences. Presidents Warren G. Harding and Calvin Coolidge were uninspiring leaders, although, in fairness, it must be pointed out that the times were inhospitable to political activism. Herbert Hoover was a far more able man, but his administration was swamped by the onset of the Great Depression. Socially, however, what was dubbed "The Jazz Age" was marked by increasing dissatisfaction with traditional morality and conventions. The era also produced literary and artistic achievements unmatched in any decade before or since.

President Woodrow Wilson is most often remembered as the tragic figure who failed to secure American membership in the League of Nations, and who was struck down by illness at the peak of the fight. "Woodrow Wilson, Politician" recalls the man's very considerable political gifts, and grants him high marks for presiding over one of the more fruitful periods of domestic reform legislation during his first administration. "Angel Island: The Half-Closed Door" shows that the Progressive Era brought no change in attitudes toward prospective Chinese immigrants, who were forced to endure numerous indignities and frequent rejection.

Nations at war tend to equate dissent at home with disloyalty, and the United States has been no exception. "America's Black Press, 1914–18" reveals how the government tried to influence black newspapers and journals after the United States joined the conflict. "What We Lost in the Great War" points out that the terrible physical losses were accompanied by a shattering of old beliefs and assumptions about the values of Western culture.

During the 1920s some, mostly young people, rebelled against conventional morality and beliefs. Conservative Americans were appalled by this, and by what they regarded as "foreign" influences that were undermining the society. "When White Hoods Were in Flower" describes the reemergence of the Ku Klux Klan that had first arisen during Reconstruction. This time the organization was anti-Semitic, anti-Catholic, and anti all things foreign. "Media and Morality in the Twenties" depicts the efforts of rural America to preserve traditional values against the "sinful" cities.

"Citizen Ford" traces the "rags to riches" rise of a man who once boasted that "I invented the modern age." Henry Ford revolutionized the automobile industry and helped make cars available to the ordinary citizen. Politically conservative, personally eccentric, Ford's domination of the auto industry reached a high mark during the early 1920s. After that, his resistance to change and bizarre management practices worked against him.

Looking Ahead: Challenge Questions

Analyze the reform measures passed during Woodrow Wilson's first administration. What were they supposed to accomplish? How well did they work?

World War I was an appalling carnage. Why did this catastrophe have such effects on prevailing assumptions?

What made conservative Americans so fearful of change and new ideas during the 1920s? How did they attempt to preserve traditional values and beliefs?

Woodrow Wilson, Politician

The idealistic architect of a postwar world order that never came into being: such is the popular image of President Woodrow Wilson. What it omits is the savvy, sometimes ruthless politician whose achievements in the domestic sphere were equalled by only two other 20th-century presidents, Franklin Delano Roosevelt and Lyndon Baines Johnson. Robert Dallek here restores the whole man.

Robert Dallek

Robert Dallek is professor of history at the University of California, Los Angeles. He is the author of several books on political and diplomatic history, including Franklin D. Roosevelt and American Foreign Policy, 1932–1945 *(1979), which won a Bancroft Prize, and, most recently,* Lone Star Rising: Lyndon Johnson and His Times, 1908–1960 *(1991).*

Few presidents in American history elicit more mixed feelings than Woodrow Wilson. And why not? His life and career were full of contradictions that have puzzled historians for 70 years. A victim of childhood dyslexia, he became an avid reader, a skilled academic, and a popular writer and lecturer. A deeply religious man, who some described as "a Presbyterian priest" with a dour view of man's imperfectability, he devoted himself to secular designs promising the triumph of reason and harmony in domestic and world affairs. A rigid, self-exacting personality, whose uncompromising adherence to principles barred agreement on some of his most important political goals, he was a brilliant opportunist who won stunning electoral victories and led controversial laws through the New Jersey state legislature and the U.S. Congress. A southern conservative and elitist with a profound distrust of radical ideas and such populists as William Jennings Bryan, he became the Democratic Party's most effective advocate of advanced progressivism. A leading proponent of congressional influence, or what he called "Congressional Government," he ranks

with Theodore Roosevelt, Franklin D. Roosevelt, Harry S. Truman, and Lyndon B. Johnson as the century's most aggressive chief executives. An avowed pacifist who declared himself "too proud to fight" and gained reelection in 1916 partly by reminding voters that he had "kept us out of war," he made military interventions in Latin America and Europe hallmarks of his two presidential terms.

There is no greater paradox in Wilson's life and career, however, than the fact that his worst failure has become the principal source of his historical reputation as a great American president. Administrative and legislative triumphs marked Wilson's service as president of Princeton, governor of New Jersey, and president of the United States. But most Americans who would concede Wilson a place in the front ranks of U.S. chief executives would be hard pressed to name many, if any, of these achievements. To them, he is best remembered as the president who preached self-determination and a new world order. (And not only to Americans: An upcoming Wilson biography by Dutch historian J. W. Schulte Nordholt is subtitled *A Life for World Peace.*) In the 1920s and '30s, when America rejected participation in the League of Nations and a political or military role in a world hellbent on another total war, Wilson's reputation reached a low point. He was a good man whom bankers and munitions makers had duped into entering World War I. He had also led America into the fighting out of the hopelessly naive belief that he could make the world safe for democracy and end all wars.

American involvement in World War II reversed Wilson's historical standing. Now feeling guilty about their isolationism and their rejection of his vision of a world at peace, Americans celebrated him as a spurned prophet whose wisdom and idealism deserved renewed acceptance in the 1940s. A new world league of self-governing nations practicing collective security for the sake of global stability and peace became the great American hope during World War II. When the fighting's outcome proved to be the Soviet–American Cold War, Americans saw it as another setback for Wilson's grand design. Nevertheless, they did not lose faith in his ultimate wisdom, believing that democracy and the international rule of law would eventually have to replace tyranny and lawless aggression if the world were ever to achieve lasting peace.

Now, with America's triumph in the Cold War and the Soviet-American confrontation all but over, the country has renewed faith in a world order akin to what Woodrow Wilson proposed in 1918. The idea took on fresh meaning when President Bush led a coalition of U.N.-backed forces against Iraq's attack upon and absorption of Kuwait. The triumph of coalition arms seemed to vindicate Wilson's belief that collective action through a world body could reduce the likelihood and effectiveness of attacks by strong states against weaker ones and thus make international acts of aggression obsolete.

Yet present hopes for a new world order can plummet overnight—and with them Wilson's standing. If Wilson's rep-

From *The Wilson Quarterly*, Autumn 1991, pp. 106-114. Copyright © 1991 by The Woodrow Wilson International Center for Scholars.

utation as a great president rests upon his vision of a new era in world affairs and the fulfillment of some part of that design in our lifetimes, his place in the forefront of U.S. presidents seems less than secure.

Will the ghost of Wilson be plagued forever by the vagaries of world politics? Only if we fail to give scrutiny to his full record. A careful reassessment of Wilson's political career, especially in domestic affairs, would go far to secure his place as a great American president who has much to tell us about the effective workings of democratic political systems everywhere.

FOR ALL HIS IDEALISM AND ELITISM, Wilson's greatest triumphs throughout his career rested on his brilliance as a democratic politician. He was the "great communicator" of his day—a professor who abandoned academic language and spoke in catch phrases that inspired mass support. He was also a master practitioner of the art of the possible, a leader with an impressive talent for reading the public mood and adjusting to it in order to advance his personal ambition and larger public goals. This is not to suggest that his career was an uninterrupted success. He had his share of spectacular failures. But some of these he converted into opportunities for further advance. And even his unmitigated failures had more to do with circumstances beyond his control than with flaws in his political judgment.

Wilson's early life gave little indication of a master politician in the making. Born in 1856 in Staunton, Virginia, the third of four children, he was the offspring of devout Scotch Presbyterian divines. Thomas Woodrow, his maternal grandfather, came from Scotland to the United States, where he ministered to congregations in small Ohio towns. Jesse Woodrow Wilson, Wilson's mother, was an intensely religious, austere Victorian lady with no sense of humor and a long history of psychosomatic ailments. Joseph Ruggles Wilson, Woodrow's father, was a brilliant theologian and leading light in the southern Presbyterian church, holding pulpits in Staunton, Virginia; Augusta, Georgia; Columbia, South Carolina; and Wilmington, North Carolina. Joseph Wilson enjoyed a reputation as an eloquent and powerful speaker whose "arresting rhetoric and cogent thought" made him one of the leading southern preachers and religious teachers of his time. Woodrow Wilson described

his father as the "greatest teacher" he ever knew. Yet theological disputes and clashes with other strong-willed church leaders drove Joseph, who advocated various reforms, from one pulpit to another and left him with a sense of failure that clouded his life. One Wilson biographer notes that "by mid-career, Joseph Wilson was in some ways a broken man, struggling to overcome feelings of inferiority, trying to reconcile a God of love with the frustration of his ambition for success and prominence within the church." To compensate for his sense of defeat, Joseph invested his vaunting ambition in his son Woodrow, whom he hoped would become the "very great man" Joseph himself had wished to be.

Although Joseph imparted a love of literature and politics to his son, Bible readings, daily prayers, and Sunday worship services were centerpieces of Woodrow's early years. His father also taught him the transient character of human affairs and the superiority of religious to secular concerns. Joseph left little doubt in the boy's mind that he foresaw for him a career in the ministry as "one of the Church's rarest scholars . . . one of her most illustrious reformers . . . or one of her grandest orators." But Joseph's defeats in church politics in Woodrow's formative adolescent years soured father and son on Woodrow's entrance into the ministry.

Instead, Woodrow, with his father's blessing, invested his ambitions in a political career. As Richard Hofstadter wrote, "When young Tommy Wilson sat in the pew and heard his father bring the Word to the people, he was watching the model upon which his career was to be fashioned." Before college, he hung a portrait of British Prime Minister William Gladstone above his desk and declared: "That is Gladstone, the greatest statesman that ever lived. I intend to be a statesman, too." During his years as a Princeton undergraduate (1875–79), he rationalized his determination to enter politics by describing it as a divine vocation. A career as a statesman was an expression of Christian service, he believed, a use of power for the sake of principles or moral goals. Wilson saw the "key to success in politics" as "the pursuit of perfection through hard work and the fulfillment of ideals." Politics would allow him to spread spiritual enlightenment to the yearning masses.

Yet Wilson, as one of his later political associates said, was a man of high ideals

and no principles, which was another way of saying that Wilson's ambition for self-serving political ends outran his commitment to any particular philosophy or set of goals. Like every great American politician since the rise of mass democracy in the 19th century, Wilson allowed the ends to justify the means. But Wilson never thought of himself as an opportunist. Rather, he considered himself a democrat responsive to the national mood and the country's most compelling needs. It is possible to scoff at Wilson's rationalization of his willingness to bend to current demands, but we do well to remember that the country's greatest presidents have all been men of high ideals and no principles, self-serving altruists or selfish pragmatists with a talent for evoking the vision of America as the world's last best hope.

Wilson's path to high political office, like so much else in his life, ran an erratic course. Legal studies at the University of Virginia, self-instruction, and a brief law practice in Atlanta were meant to be a prelude to a political career. But being an attorney had little appeal to Wilson, and he decided to become a professor of politics instead. Consequently, in 1883, at the age of 27, he entered the Johns Hopkins University Graduate School, where he earned a Ph.D. for *Congressional Government* (1885). His book was an argument for a Congress more like the British Parliament, a deliberative body in which debate rather than contending interests shaped legislation. For 17 years, from 1885 to 1902, he taught at Bryn Mawr, Wesleyan, and Princeton, beginning at the last in 1890. By 1898 he had grown weary of what he derisively called his "talking profession," and during the next four years he shrewdly positioned himself to become the unanimous, first-ballot choice of Princeton's trustees as the university's president.

WILSON'S EIGHT YEARS AS PRESIDENT OF Princeton (1902–1910) were a prelude to his later political triumphs and defeats. During the first three years of his Princeton term, Wilson carried off a series of dazzling reforms. Offended by the shallowness of much instruction at Princeton and animated by a desire to make it a special university like Oxford and Cambridge, where undergraduate education emphasized critical thinking rather than "the ideal of making a living," Wilson introduced a preceptorial system. It aimed at transforming Princeton "from a place where there are youngsters doing tasks to a place where there are men doing thinking, men who are conversing about the things of thought. . . ." As a prerequisite to the preceptorial system, Wilson persuaded the faculty to reorganize the University's curriculum and its structure, creating 11 departments corresponding to subjects and requiring upperclassmen to concentrate their studies in one of them. Wilson's reforms, biographer Arthur S. Unk asserts, "mark him as an educational statesman of originality and breadth and strength." His achievement was also a demonstration of Wilson's political mastery—a case study in how to lead strong-minded, independent academics to accept a sea change in the life of a conservative university.

The fierce struggles and bitter defeats of Wilson's next five years are a measure of how difficult fundamental changes in higher education can be without the sort of astute political management Wilson initially used. Between 1906 and 1910 Wilson fought unsuccessfully to reorganize the social life of undergraduates and to determine the location and nature of a graduate college. In the first instance, Wilson tried to deemphasize the importance of campus eating clubs, which had become the focus of undergraduate life, and replace them with residential colleges, or quadrangles, where students would live under the supervision of unmarried faculty members residing in the colleges. Wilson viewed the clubs as undemocratic, anti-intellectual, and divisive, and the quadrangle plan as a sensible alternative that would advance the university's educational goals and national standing. Wilson assumed that he could put across his plan without the sort of consultation and preparation he had relied on to win approval for the preceptorial system. But his failure to consult alumni, faculty, and trustees was a major political error that led to his defeat. Likewise, he did not effectively marshal the support he needed to win backing for his graduate-school plan, and again it made his proposal vulnerable to criticism from opponents.

Physical and emotional problems caused by strokes in 1906 and 1907 may partly account for Wilson's defeats in the quadrangle and graduate-school fights. But whatever the explanation for his poor performance in these academic struggles, they were by no means without

political benefit to Wilson. In fact, what seems most striking about these conflicts is the way Wilson converted them to his larger purposes of running first for governor of New Jersey and then for president of the United States.

Colonel George Harvey, a conservative Democrat who owned a publishing empire that included the *New York World* and *Harper's Weekly,* proposed Wilson for the presidency as early as 1906. Although Wilson made appropriate disclaimers of any interest in seeking the White House, the suggestion aroused in him the longing for high political station that he had held for some 30 years. In response to Harvey's efforts, Wilson, who was already known nationally as a speaker on issues of higher education, began speaking out on economic and political questions before non-university audiences. His initial pronouncements were essentially conservative verities calculated to identify him with the anti-Bryan, anti-Populist wing of the Democratic Party. "The nomination of Mr. Wilson," one conservative editor wrote in 1906, "would be a good thing for the country as betokening a return of his party to historic party ideals and first principles, and a sobering up after the radical 'crazes.' " In 1907 Wilson prepared a "Credo" of his views, which, Arthur Unk says, could hardly have failed to please reactionaries, "for it was conservative to the core." It justified the necessity of great trusts and combinations as efficient instruments of modern business and celebrated individualism. In 1908 Wilson refused to support Bryan for president and rejected suggestions that he become his vice-presidential running mate.

During the next two years, however, Wilson shifted decidedly to the left. Mindful of the mounting progressive temper in the country—of the growing affinity of middle-class Americans for reforms that would limit the power of corporations and political machines— Wilson identified himself with what he called the "new morality," the need to eliminate fraud and corruption from, and to restore democracy and equality of opportunity to, the nation's economic and political life. His academic fights over the quadrangles and graduate school became struggles between special privilege and democracy. In a speech to Princeton's Pittsburgh alumni in the spring of 1910, Wilson attacked the nation's universities, churches, and politi-

cal parties as serving the "classes" and neglecting the "masses." He declared his determination to democratize the colleges of the country and called for moral and spiritual regeneration. Incensed at his conservative Princeton opponents, who seemed the embodiment of the privileged interests, and eager to make himself a gubernatorial and then national candidate, Wilson invested idealism in the progressive crusade, leaving no doubt that he was ready to lead a movement that might redeem America.

New Jersey Democratic boss James Smith, Jr., seeing Wilson as a conservative opportunist whose rhetoric would appease progressives and whose actions would favor the corporations and the bosses, arranged Wilson's nomination for governor. Wilson seemed to play his part perfectly during the campaign, quietly accepting Smith's help even as he declared his independence from the party machine and espoused the progressive agenda—the direct primary, a corrupt-practices law, workmen's compensation, and a regulatory commission policing the railroads and public utilities. On election day Wilson swept to victory by a 50,000-vote margin, 233,933 to 184,573, and the Democrats gained control of the normally Republican Assembly. Once in the governor's chair, Wilson made clear that he would be his own man. He defeated Smith's bid for election to the U.S. Senate by the state legislature and skillfully assured the enactment of the four principal progressive measures. As he told a friend, "I kept the pressure of opinion constantly on the legislature, and the programme was carried out to its last detail. This with the senatorial business seems, in the minds of the people looking on, little less than a miracle in the light of what has been the history of reform hitherto in the State." As Wilson himself recognized, it was less a miracle than the product of constant pressure on the legislature at a time when "opinion was ripe on all these matters." Wilson's break with the machine and drive for reform reflected a genuine commitment to improving the lot of New Jersey's citizens. Most of all, they were a demonstration of how an ambitious politician in a democracy bends to the popular will for the sake of personal gain and simultaneously serves legitimate public needs.

WILSON'S NOMINATION FOR PRESIDENT BY a deeply divided Democratic convention in the summer of 1912 was an extraordinary event in the history of the party and the nation. Wilson himself called it "a sort of political miracle." Although Wilson was the frontrunner in 1911 after speaking trips to every part of the nation, by May 1912 aggressive campaigns by Missouri's Champ Clark, speaker of the House of Representatives, and Alabama Representative Oscar W. Underwood made Wilson a decided underdog. When Clark won a majority of the delegates on the 10th ballot, it seemed certain that he would eventually get the two-thirds vote needed for the nomination. In every Democratic convention since 1844, a majority vote for a candidate had translated into the required two-thirds. But 1912 was different. Wilson won the nomination on the 46th ballot after his managers struck a bargain, which kept Underwood's 100-plus delegates from going to Clark. William Jennings Bryan gave Wilson essential progressive support, and the party's most powerful political bosses—the men who, in the words of one historian, had been Wilson's "bitterest antagonists and who represented the forces against which he had been struggling"—decided to back him.

Wilson's campaign for the presidency was another milestone in his evolution as a brilliant democratic politician. He entered the election without a clear-cut campaign theme. The tariff, which he initially focused on, inspired little popular response. In late August, however, after conferring with Louis D. Brandeis, Wilson found a constructive and highly popular campaign theme. Persuading Wilson that political democracy could only follow from economic democracy or diminished control by the country's giant business trusts, Brandeis sold him on the New Freedom—the idea that regulated competition would lead to the liberation of economic enterprise in the United States. This in turn would restore grassroots political power and control. Wilson accurately sensed that the country's mood was overwhelmingly favorable to progressive reform, especially the reduction of the economic power of the trusts. He also saw correctly that Theodore Roosevelt's plea for a New Nationalism—regulated monopoly and an expanded role for federal authority in the economic and social life of the nation—impressed most voters as too paternalistic and more a threat to than an expansion of freedom. As a result, Wilson won a plurality of the popular vote in the four-

way contest of 1912, 42 percent to a combined 58 percent for William Howard Taft, TR, and socialist Eugene V. Debs. Wilson's victory in the electoral column was far more one-sided, 435 to 99 for TR and Taft. His victory was also a demonstration of his talents as a speaker who could satisfy the mass yearning for a new era in national affairs.

Wilson's election represented a triumph of democratic hopes. After nearly five decades of conservative rule by the country's business interests, the nation gave its backing to a reform leader promising an end to special privilege and the economic and political democratization of American life. "Nobody owns me," Wilson declared at the end of his campaign, signaling his readiness to act in behalf of the country's working and middle classes. Despite his own largely conservative background, his political agility and sensitivity to popular demands made it likely that he would not disappoint progressive goals.

HIS FIRST PRESIDENTIAL TERM REPRESENTS one of the three notable periods of domestic reform in 20th-century America. What makes it particularly remarkable, notes historian John Milton Cooper, is that Wilson won his reforms without the national emergencies over the economy and civil rights that respectively confronted the country during the 1930s and the 1960s. Wilson, in other words, lacked "the peculiarly favorable political conditions" aiding Franklin Roosevelt and Lyndon Johnson.

Wilson's successful leadership rested on his effective management of his party and Congress. Following the advice of Texas Representative Albert S. Burleson, a superb politician who became postmaster general, Wilson filled his cabinet with "deserving" Democrats and allowed Burleson to use patronage "ruthlessly to compel adoption of administration measures." Despite Bryan's ignorance of foreign affairs, for example, his prominence persuaded Wilson to make him secretary of state. Wilson's readiness to set a bold legislative agenda found support from both a 73-member Democratic majority in the House and a decisive majority of Democratic and Republican progressives in the Senate. The 28th president quickly proved himself to be an able manipulator of Congress. Eager to create a sense of urgency about his legislative program and to establish a mood of cooperation

Among Wilson's progressive measures was the Underwood Tariff of 1914, the first downward revision of the tariff since the Civil War.

between the two branches of government, Wilson called a special congressional session at the start of his term and then spoke to a joint meeting of both houses. Indeed, he was the first president to appear in person before Congress since John Adams. Presenting himself as a colleague rather than "a mere department of the Government hailing Congress from some isolated island of jealous power," Wilson returned repeatedly to Capitol Hill for conferences to advance his reform program.

In the 18 months between the spring of 1913 and the fall of 1914, Wilson pushed four key laws through the Congress. The Underwood Tariff of October 1914 was the first downward revision of the tariff since the Civil War; it was inspired more by a desire to reduce the cost of living for lower- and middle-class Americans than by any obligation to serve the interests of industrial giants. Wilson drove the bill through the upper house by exposing the lobbyists representing businesses that sought "to overcome the interests of the public for their private profit." Making the tariff law all the more remarkable was the inclusion of the first graduated income tax in U.S. history. Shortly thereafter, Wilson won passage of the most enduring domestic measure of his presidency, the reform of the country's banking and money system. Insisting on public, centralized control of banks and the money supply rather than a private, decentralized system, Wilson once again came before Congress to influence the outcome of this debate. The Federal Reserve Act of December 1913 combined elements of both plans, providing for a mix of private and public control. Although further reforms would occur later to make the Federal Reserve system a more effective instrument for dealing with national economic problems, the Wilson law of 1913 created the basic elements of the banking system that has existed for almost 80 years. During the next nine months, by keeping Congress in continuous session for an unprecedented year and a half, Wilson won passage of the Clayton Antitrust and Federal Trade Commission acts, contributing to the more effective regulation of big business and greater power for organized labor.

In November 1914, Wilson announced that his New Freedom program had been achieved and that the progressive movement was at an end. A man of fundamentally conservative impulses (which he believed reflected those of the nation at large), Wilson did not wish to overreach himself. His announcement bewildered advanced progressives, who had been unsuccessfully advocating a variety of social-justice measures Wilson considered too radical to support. Herbert Croly, the editor of the *New Republic,* charged that "any man of President Wilson's intellectual equipment who seriously asserts that the fundamental wrongs of a modern society can be easily and quickly righted as a consequence of a few laws . . . casts suspicion either upon his own sincerity or upon his grasp of the realities of modern social and industrial life." Similarly, Wilson's refusal to establish a National Race Commission and his active commitment to racial segregation in the federal government incensed African-American leaders who had viewed him as a likely supporter of progressive measures for blacks.

Though he did little to reverse course on helping blacks, Wilson stood ready to return to the progressive position for the sake of reelection in 1916. "I am sorry for any President of the United States who does not recognize every great movement in the Nation," Wilson declared in July 1916. "The minute he stops recognizing it, he has become a back number." The results of the congressional elections in 1914 convinced Wilson that the key to success in two years was a campaign attracting TR's Progressive backers to his standard. Consequently, in 1916, he elevated Louis D. Brandeis to the Supreme Court and signed seven additional reform bills into

law. Among other things, these laws brought relief to farmers and workers and raised income and inheritance taxes on wealthy Americans. The election results in November vindicated his strategy. Wilson gained almost three million popular votes over his 1912 total and bested Charles Evans Hughes, who headed a reunited Republican party, by 23 electoral votes. On this count alone, Wilson's two consecutive victories as the head of a minority party mark him as one of the century's exceptional American politicians.

WHY DID WILSON'S POLITICAL ASTUTEness desert him during his second term in his handling of the Versailles Treaty and the League of Nations? The answer is not naiveté about world politics, though Wilson himself believed "it would be the irony of fate if my administration had to deal chiefly with foreign affairs." In fact, the same mastery of Congress he displayed in converting so many significant reform bills into law between 1913 and 1916 was reflected in his creation of a national consensus in 1917 for American participation in the Great War.

At the start of the fighting in 1914, Wilson declared America neutral in thought and deed. And though Wilson himself had a decidedly pro-British bias, he understood that the country then was only mildly pro-Allied and wanted no part in the war. His policies initially reflected these feelings. Only as national sentiment changed in response to events in Europe and on the high seas, where German submarine violations of U.S. neutral rights drove Americans more decisively into the Allied camp, did Wilson see fit to prepare the country for and then lead it into the war. His prewar leadership became something of a model for Franklin Roosevelt in 1939–41 as he maneuvered to maintain a national majority behind his responses to World War II.

Wilson's failure in 1919–20, or, more precisely, the collapse of his political influence in dealing with the peacemaking at the end of the war, consisted of a number of things—most of them beyond his control. His Fourteen Points, his formula for making the world safe for democracy and ending all wars, was beyond the capacity of any political leader to achieve, then and now. Yet there is every reason to believe that Wilson enunciated his peace aims assuming that he would have to accept compromise

agreements on many of his goals, as indeed he did in the Versailles negotiations. A number of these compromises on the Fourteen Points went beyond what he hoped to concede, but he recognized that the conclusion of the fighting had stripped him of much of his hold over America's allies and limited his capacity to bend the strong-minded French, British, and Italian leaders to his will or to influence the radical revolutionary regime in Russia. Events were moving too fast in Europe and all over the globe for him to make the world approximate the postwar peace arrangements he had enunciated in 1918.

Faced by such circumstances, Wilson accepted the proposition that a League of Nations, including the United States, would be the world's best hope for a stable peace. Wilson's prime objective after the Versailles conference was to assure American participation in the new world body. But the political cards were stacked against him. After six years of Democratic rule and a growing conviction in Republican Party circles that the Democrats would be vulnerable in 1920, Senate Republicans made approval of the Versailles Treaty and American participation in the League partisan issues which could redound to their benefit. Moreover, between 1918 and 1920, Wilson's deteriorating health, particularly a major stroke in the fall of 1919, intensified a propensity for self-righteousness and made him uncharacteristically rigid in dealing with a political issue that cried out for flexibility and accommodation. As Edwin A. Weinstein has persuasively argued in his medical and psychological biography of Wilson, "the cerebral dysfunction which resulted from Wilson's devastating strokes prevented the ratification of the Treaty. It is almost certain that had Wilson not been so afflicted, his political skills and facility with language would have bridged the gap between [opposing Senate] resolutions, much as he had reconciled opposing views of the Federal Reserve bill . . . or had accepted the modifications of the Treaty suggested in February, 1919."

WILSON'S POLITICAL FAILURE IN 1919–20 was a striking exception in a career marked by a substantial number of political victories. His defeat and its consequences were so stunning that they have eclipsed the record of prior achievements and partly obscured Wilson's contributions to American history.

But it is not only the disaster of 1919–20 that is responsible. Mainstream academia today dismisses political history and particularly the study of powerful leaders as distinctly secondary in importance to impersonal social forces in explaining historical change. What seems lost from view nowadays is just how essential strong and skillful political leadership remains in bringing a democracy to accept major reforms. Wilson is an excellent case in point. For all the public's receptivity to progressivism in the first two decades of the century, it took a leader of exceptional political skill to bring warring reform factions together in a coalition that could enact a liberal agenda. By contrast, Wilson's physical incapacity in 1919 assured the defeat of American participation in a world league for 25 years. This is not to say that an American presence in an international body would have dramatically altered the course of world affairs after 1920, but it might have made a difference, and the collapse of Wilson's leadership was the single most important factor in keeping the United States on the sidelines.

Did social and economic and a host of other factors influence the course of U.S. history during Wilson's time? Without a doubt. But a leader of vision and varied abilities—not all of them purely admirable—was needed to seize the opportunities provided by history and make them realities. To forget the boldness of Wilson's leadership, and the importance of political leaders generally, is to embrace a narrow vision of this nation's past—and of its future.

Angel Island:
The Half-Closed Door

Brian McGinty

Brian McGinty is a frequent contributor to American History Illustrated. *His history of earthquakes in California appeared in the March/April 1990 issue.*

From 1910 to 1940, the principal immigration station on the West Coast of the United States occupied a remote site on the northern shore of Angel Island in San Francisco Bay. Facing the blue waters of one of the world's most renowned natural harbors, the Angel Island Immigration Station was the point of entry—or of deportation—for tens of thousands of Chinese and other Asian immigrants. Located only six miles from downtown San Francisco, the processing center was isolated from the mainland by deep water, imposing gray walls, and barbed-wire fences. Immigrants detained there were within easy sight of the "Promised Land," yet still a world away from it—separated from their goal by treacherous straits, discriminatory immigration laws, and bureaucratic obstacles that at times seemed insurmountable.

The history of Asian immigration to the United States is long and painful, fraught with the prejudice of the Western world. During the early years of California settlement, Oriental immigrants (mostly Chinese) were welcomed with civility if not enthusiasm. The Chinese were hard workers, and their labor was badly needed to build the burgeoning frontier's cities, bridges, and railroads. They were good businessmen, too, with rigorously frugal habits and a seemingly natural sense for the give-and-take of commerce.

So successful were the Chinese in the economic life of the West that within a few years demagogic politicians began to

blame the newcomers for the economic slowdowns that periodically beset the region. Adopting "The Chinese must go!" as their slogan, these politicians proposed a series of stern laws that would make it difficult for Chinese to live in the United States—and harder yet for new Chinese immigrants to enter the country.

American hostility toward alien cultures ultimately resulted in the Chinese Exclusion Act, passed by Congress in 1882. A series of increasingly restrictive laws that followed were designed to cut the flow of Chinese immigrants to a trickle. The laws worked as planned; in California alone, the number of Chinese declined from almost 9 percent of the total population in 1880 to less than 1 percent in 1940.

But the new legislation did not totally bar Chinese immigration. A small class of "exempts" (officials, merchants, teachers, students, and tourists) were still permitted to enter the country, as were individuals who could prove a claim to U.S. citizenship by birth or by descent from an American citizen.

Beginning in the 1880s, a stream of Chinese claiming the right to enter the country as children of native-born Chinese-Americans arrived in San Francisco. Many of these would-be immigrants were known as "paper sons and daughters," for their claims were frankly based on fraudulent documents. The destruction in the great 1906 earthquake and fire of records that verified citizenship made it easier for many new arrivals in California to fabricate claims to citizenship by right of inheritance. Driven by the poverty and privation that gripped their native land, and desperate to penetrate the legal wall Americans had erected

against them, the Chinese were willing to risk their fortunes, their freedom, and even their lives to make new homes in the country they called "The Land of the Flowery Flag."

Before 1910, Chinese arrivals in San Francisco were detained in a dismal wooden shed on the waterfront while their papers were reviewed or, if they had no papers, while witnesses were questioned to prove or disprove their claims. But conditions in the detention shed were so appalling that in 1903, under pressure from Chinatown's community leaders, the Bureau of Immigration announced its intention to build a new immigration station—on the shore of Angel Island.

The largest island in San Francisco Bay, Angel Island covers 740 acres and measures about a mile and a quarter from shore to shore at its widest point. Rising to 781 feet above sea level, the steep and hilly chunk of land lies due north of San Francisco's downtown financial district. Separated from Marin County's Tiburon Peninsula by Raccoon Strait—one of the deepest and most treacherous channels in the bay—the island, first sighted in 1769 by Gaspar de Portolá's overland expedition to Monterey, was named *Isla de Nuestra Señora de Los Angeles* by Spanish explorers under the command of Juan Manuel de Ayala, who anchored there in 1775 while charting San Francisco Bay. When Americans took control of California in the 1840s, they anglicized the name to Angel Island.

During the nineteenth century, the island served many purposes. For nearly twenty-five years, Russian settlers from Fort Ross on the nearby coast used it as a camp from which to hunt sea otters. The

 From *American History Illustrated*, September/October 1990, pp. 50-51, 71. Reprinted through the courtesy of Cowles Magazines, publishers of *American History Illustrated*.

island was a Mexican cattle ranch during the 1840s, and a decade later a quarry on its rugged eastern shore supplied stone for San Francisco buildings. During the Civil War, the U.S. Army fortified the island against possible Confederate attacks on San Francisco Bay. Over the years, the Army expanded its presence there until the island contained three main camps with officers' quarters, hospitals, parade grounds, and barracks for several thousand troops.

Taking advantage of Angel Island's isolation, the government in 1892 opened the San Francisco Quarantine Station on the northwest shore of the island. There it built housing for surgeons, pharmacists, and attendants, and dormitories and bathhouses for detainees. Passengers arriving in San Francisco were checked for signs of communicable diseases and, if infected, held at the station until they were either certified healthy or returned to their ports of origin. Although the quarantine station's activities slowed after 1915, it continued to operate well into the 1930s.

But it was as Ellis Island's Pacific counterpart that Angel Island became best-known. The new immigration station was designed to alleviate the unsafe and unsanitary conditions that had long prevailed in San Francisco's waterfront detention shed; to prevent newly arriving immigrants from communicating with friends or relatives in the city while they awaited processing; and to establish an escape-proof facility. Although construction was completed in 1908, the processing center did not officially open until January 21, 1910. The following morning, more than four hundred would-be Americans were moved into the two-story barracks serving as the station's main detention center.

Upon arrival at Angel Island, immigrants were ordered to leave their luggage in a warehouse on the wharf while they climbed the hill to the barracks. Separated by race and sex, they were led into drafty dormitories furnished with long rows of steel bunks in tiers of three. As soon as the doctors were ready to receive them, groups of newcomers were led to the hospital and examined for signs of disease. The detainees ate their meager and often scarcely palatable meals in a dining hall in the administration building. Lights went out in the station at about 9:00 P.M., at which time the massive doors to the dormitories were closed and securely locked.

Between two hundred and five hundred immigrants were housed at the Angel Island facility at any one time. Nearly all of the detainees were Asians, and the bulk of these were Chinese.

Immigrants with convincing "papers" were normally detained for only a few days. Others, who had either suspicious documents or no documents at all, had to wait until immigration officers scheduled hearings to examine the newcomers' claims. Witnesses were ferried from San Francisco. To prevent collusion between witnesses and interpreters, the interpreters were rotated on a random basis.

If a young Chinese immigrant claimed to be the son of an American citizen, immigration examiners questioned him closely What was his mother's name? In what village was his father born? How many houses were there in the village? Did he have any brothers or sisters? What were their names? Did they have a dog in the family house? Where was the rice bin kept? The witnesses, always questioned separately, were asked the same questions. Discrepancies in the testimony often resulted in rejection and swift repatriation to China. Reflecting the overwhelmingly hostile American policy toward admitting Chinese, immigration regulations specified that "in every doubtful case the benefit of the doubt shall be given to the United States government." As many as 30 percent of those examined were ultimately rejected and deported.

Depending on the circumstances of the case and the attitudes of the examiner, hearings could end in an hour or drag on as long as a week. Decisions in the applicant's favor were announced immediately; unfavorable decisions were withheld until all testimony had been transcribed and the examiner's report was completed. If an applicant decided to appeal to immigration authorities in Washington, D.C., the case could continue for months—or sometimes even years. All the while, the detainees languished in their barracks, reading the newspapers they managed to obtain from San Francisco, playing Mah-Jongg, and listening to Chinese opera on a scratchy, hand-wound Victrola.

During the long, dreadful wait, some of the detainees inscribed poetry on the walls of the barracks with knives or brushes. Composed in the classical Tan dynasty style, the poems provided a moving record of the immigrants' fears and hopes and served as a link between succeeding boatloads of detainees. One poet wrote:

This place is called an island of immortals,
When, in fact, this mountain wilderness is
*   a prison.*
Once you see the open net, why throw
*   yourself in?*
It is only because of empty pockets I can
*   do nothing else.*

And another:

Lin, upon arriving in America,
Was arrested, put in a wooden building,
And made a prisoner.
I was here for one autumn.
The Americans did not allow me to land.
I was ordered to be deported.
When the news was told,
I was frightened and troubled about re-
*   turning to my country.*
We Chinese of a weak nation
Can only sigh at the lack of freedom.

Even before the Angel Island Immigration Station was completed, proposals were made to move it back to the mainland where the detainees would be less isolated and witnesses more accessible. The government resisted all of these suggestions until a fire broke out in the administration building on August 12, 1940, reducing the structure to rubble. Less than three months later, the island's last immigrants—about two hundred in all—were transferred to a new station in San Francisco.

During World War II, the former immigrant center housed federal convicts and even some prisoners of war. In 1954—by which time immigrants were screened overseas by American consular officials prior to emigrating—the State of California took over the old quarantine station on the northwest side of the island, creating Angel Island State Park. The park was expanded in 1962 to include the immigration station and other parts of the island, excepting a seven-acre Coast Guard facility.

After a park ranger drew attention to the poems on the walls of the old barracks in 1970, a systematic effort was made to photograph, transcribe, translate, and catalog the inscriptions. In 1976 the State of California appropriated funds for preservation of the barracks building, which was converted into the Angel Island Museum. A thirty-minute walk from the island's visitor center at Ayala Cove, the museum is now one of the best-known sites on the island. There, docents offer tours of the old building. Although the last detainees left fifty years ago, the poem-covered walls still bear silent testimony to their suffering and despair.

Today Angel Island is easily accessible via ferries that regularly ply the waters between Fisherman's Wharf in San Francisco, the town of Tiburon in Marin County, and Ayala Cove. The island boasts picnic grounds, campsites, and miles of well-maintained hiking trails. But the remains of the old immigration station speak most eloquently of the history made there—and of the indelible memories that refuse to be forgotten.

Recommended additional reading: Island: Poetry and History of Chinese Immigrants on Angel Island, 1910-1940 *by Him Mark Lai, Genny Lim, and Judy Yung (Hoc Doi, 1980) contains a representative collection of the poems inscribed by immigration station detainees on their barracks walls, together with interviews and a well-researched history of the station.*

America's Black Press, 1914–18

Our boys over there? Mark Ellis *looks at how America's black newspapers and population reacted to U.S. involvement in the First War—and at the steps the government took to try and ensure a favourable press.*

Mark Ellis

Mark Ellis is Lecturer in American History at the University of Strathclyde and is completing a book on the surveillance of black Americans by the federal government, 1917–1921.

When the United States entered the First World War in April 1917, several groups of Americans refused to support the abandonment of neutrality. They included the Socialist Party, pacifist organisations such as the American Union Against Militarism, Irish Americans, who rejected the idea of an alliance with Britain, and German Americans, many of whom were of divided loyalties. However, no section of the American people had a more complex outlook on the war and the call to arms than the black population.

Since the end of Reconstruction in the 1870s, blacks had steadily been denied the vote in the southern states where most of them lived. By 1910, racial segregation, legally in the South and by custom in the North, was firmly established, and after 1913 Woodrow Wilson's Democratic administration extended segregation of federal employees in the workplace. White supremacy was maintained partly by exemplary violence: black people were hunted down by white rioters in Atlanta, Georgia, and Springfield, Illinois, in 1906 and 1908, and an average of sixty-five blacks were lynched annually between 1910 and 1919.

When Wilson announced that America had declared war 'to make the world safe for Democracy', therefore, many black spokesmen warned that they could not give him unreserved support without an assurance that steps would be taken to correct the failings of American democracy. When these reservations implying that the United States was unfit to lead an international crusade for democracy, were repeated in the black press, the government was swift to respond. It could not afford to allow 10 million Americans to be indifferent, still less hostile, to the war effort.

With the aid of civilian vigilance groups, the government attempted to suppress all forms of dissent during the war. Under the Espionage and Sedition Acts, courts could impose $10,000 fines and twenty years imprisonment on anyone who said, wrote or did anything that could be shown to interfere in any way with the prosecution of the war. This included 'disloyal, profane, scurrilous, or abusive' statements about the government, Constitution or forces of the United States. Thus, when a German spy scare in the summer of 1917 produced alarming reports that enemy agitators had begun to subvert the loyalty of the black population, federal agents began to scrutinise black newspapers for the evidence.

By the end of 1917, the Justice Department's Bureau of Investigation and the War Department's Military Intelligence Branch were making special efforts to track down 'Pro-Germanism Among the Negroes'. They were convinced that outspoken elements within the black press were causing civilian unrest, making their readership susceptible to the blandishments of the Kaiser's agents. Since most white officials regarded the advocacy of black equality as inherently seditious in peacetime, let alone war, they embarked on a campaign to change black expression.

The black press consisted of over 200 weekly newspapers and half-a-dozen monthly magazines and its very existence reflected the separateness of black and white lives in America. It catered to a wide range of opinion: conservative and religious journals, like the New *York Age* and the *Southern Workman* clung to the gradualist philosophy of the late principal of Tuskegee Institute, Booker T. Washington. They did not regard breaking down the barriers of segregation as a priority. The more radical papers, like the *Cleveland Gazette* and *The Crisis,* advocated an aggressive immediatist push for equal rights. They represented the views of the Niagara Movement—younger blacks who had helped form the National Association for the Advancement of Colored People (NAACP) in 1910.

Although editors like Harry C. Smith of the *Cleveland Gazette* pledged support to the war effort, they did so because they saw in it 'splendid strategic opportunities for the race'. They were unwilling to abandon their political objectives and stressed the moral connection between American participation in the war and the campaign to achieve equal rights at home. They were dismayed, therefore, when the government refused to investigate the mass murder of at least thirty-nine black people, mostly migrants from the South, in July 1917, at East St. Louis, Illinois. This outrage came at the height of the mobilisation of American society—a mobilisation that relied on the portrayal of the enemy as bestial and tyrannical. The response of the Norfolk, Virginia, *Journal and Guide* summed up black press comment:

. . . the United States government should renounce its purposes for entering the world war and stand convicted among the nations of the earth as the greatest hypocrite of all times.

By Mark Ellis. First published in *History Today,* September 1991, pp. 20-27. Reproduced by kind permission of History Today, Ltd., 83-84 Berwick Street, London W1V 3PJ, England.

This was the kind of thing the government was determined to eradicate. It adopted three separate approaches to this task. The first was the use of government propaganda, fed directly or indirectly to the black press, in the hope that it would be carried. The second was a form of flattery, in which black editors were taken into the special confidence of the government and told what important service they could perform. The third was the use of threats and intimidation, by unsubtle reference to, and use of, repressive emergency legislation enacted in 1917 and 1918.

The go-between chosen to relay government propaganda to blacks and monitor black opinion was Emmett Jay Scott, a former journalist who was Booker T. Washington's secretary from 1897 until the latter's death in 1915. Scott was in a difficult position. He was moving away from the conservative Tuskegee point of view, but he was still regarded as an opportunist 'Uncle Tom' by black radicals like W. E. B. Du Bois, editor of the NAACP journal, *The Crisis,* and William Monroe Trotter, editor of the *Boston Guardian.* Scott realised, however, that if he took a firm stand on discrimination in the army he would be dispensed with by the War Department, so he confined his representation of black protest to only the most glaring injustices, such as lynching. He sometimes got a sympathetic hearing from Secretary of War, Newton D. Baker, but no important changes in government policy resulted.

Emmett Scott's role as the government's spokesman thus became more significant than his role as a black representative. He was frequently mentioned in the black press, partly for what he said and partly because he was a black man holding a uniquely prominent position within the machinery of federal government. Much of his time was taken up with denying rumours about the treatment and fate of black troops. In all, 367,000 black Americans served during the war, in segregated regiments. Before they sailed for France, a rumour circulated that the War Department intended to use blacks as 'shock troops', to soak up the first waves of German attacks and draw enemy fire during Allied advances. This falsehood was followed in 1918 by stories that the government was concealing the true extent of black casualties and that secret hospital wards in New York and Washington, DC, contained horribly mutilated black soldiers, with limbs missing and their eyes, tongues and ears torn out. Federal investigators regarded these rumours as a form of German propaganda. Military Intelligence organised hospital tours for black editors, to disprove the horror stories, while Scott issued press releases stating official casualty figures and denying allegations that black prisoners of war were treated more harshly by the Germans than white prisoners. He also insisted that racial discrimination in the United States army had been stamped out.

The only black agent in Military Intelligence was former bandmaster Walter H. Loving. He conducted his own propaganda campaign in January 1918, by harnessing the eloquence of a black Republican vote-catcher, Roscoe Conkling Simmons. A nephew of Booker T. Washington, Simmons could give a rousing oration on any subject at the drop of a hat. With the approval of the secretary of war and the chief of the Military Intelligence Branch, Loving provided Simmons with outlines of what he should say at forthcoming engagements. Military Intelligence paid his expenses when Loving set up a nationwide tour of speeches, each on the subject 'My Country and My Flag', starting at Marshall, Texas, on New Year's Day, 1918. Simmons was the kind of black Republican whom historian and journalist Garry Wills has called 'half a preacher . . . half minstrel'. Loving wrote that Simmons could move ill-tempered crowds to tears with uplifting flights of this kind:

When the war is over and the smoke is cleared away, we shall see a new nation, baptized with the fire of suffering; one people with their faces set toward the future; one law for all and all for the law; honor on the throne; kings gone down; the harp of peace in the musician's hand; Ethiopia leading the hymn of a newer and grander republic: 'My Lord is Riding All the Time.'

According to Loving's reports, the tour was a massive success. However, judging by the slight coverage it received in the black newspapers of most of the cities they visited together, its real impact was minimal.

The Committee on Public Information (CPI) was more adept at implanting the government's message in the black press. Run by George Creel, a crusading journalist from Denver, the CPI was set up to bolster domestic support for the war by presenting news to Americans in palatable form—'expression, not repression', was Creel's motto. By the end of the war, however, it had become the major source of anti-Germanism and '100-percent American' super-patriotism that was to fuel the xenophobic excesses of the postwar Red Scare. It built up a network of 75,000 high-energy patriotic speakers, the 'Four Minute Men', each prepared to give an invigorating pitch to audiences of anything between a dozen and a thousand. The CPI also produced two newsreels to persuade blacks to join up.

In March 1918, Creel warned the chief of Military Intelligence that 'a very definite drive is being made to disorganize and disaffect the colored population'. A month later, when Creel was attacked by the National Committee of Patriotic Societies for publishing material that was too 'highbrow' for ordinary Americans and for reacting slowly to alleged racial subversion by Germans in the South, he promised to take steps to 'enlighten the Negroes'. Output of CPI news stories warning of the dangers posed by enemy agitation among, blacks was increased. 'Four Minute Men Bulletin No. 33' was produced specifically for black audiences, who were told that their participation in the defeat of Germany would lead to 'a wonderful amalgamation of the races in America'. Taken literally, this was sheer nonsense, but the black press *did* carry the message of this bulletin to its readers, when reporting occasions on which it was delivered.

The government's second ploy was to placate and sway the black press by flattery, at which both Emmett Scott and George Creel were skilled. In June 1918, at the suggestion of Military Intelligence, Scott persuaded Creel to stage a three-day conference of leading black editors and spokesmen in Washington, so that, as Scott put it, 'Negro public opinion should be led along helpful lines, rather than along lines that make for discontentment and unrest'. The forty-five participants included educators, churchmen and public office-holders, but the great majority were newspaper and magazine editors, the most prominent of whom were W. E. B. Du Bois of *The Crisis,* Fred R. Moore of the *New York Age,* Robert S. Abbott of the *Chicago Defender,* Robert L. Vann of the *Pittsburgh Courier,* J. H. Murphy of the *Baltimore Afro-American,* and Ed Warren of the *Amsterdam News.* Scott opened the proceedings by reminding the participants why they had been brought together by the government:

This is not the time to discuss race problems. Our first duty is to fight, and to continue to fight until the war is won. Then we can adjust the problems that remain in the life of the colored man. This is the doctrine we are preaching to the Negroes of the country.

The conference speakers included George Creel, Secretary of War, Newton D. Baker and Assistant Secretary of the Navy, Franklin D. Roosevelt. The Surgeon General's office sent a Medical Corps officer to give a lecture on venereal diseases. Thereafter, Scott allowed the black editors to air their grievances about racial discrimination, before getting them to consider concrete proposals by which black morale might be improved. They produced two documents: a 'Bill of Particulars' and an 'Address to the Committee on Public Information'. The former, modelled on Wilson's Fourteen Points, listed various ways in which the administration could gain the approval of black people. These included the passage of federal anti-lynching legislation, the ending of Jim Crow railroad cars and improvements in the treatment of black soldiers. Not one of these demands was met.

The 'Address to the Committee on Public Information', which Creel forwarded to Woodrow Wilson, was signed by all who attended, but was actually written by Du Bois. It stressed that the editors asked for reforms only in order to make the black soldier a better fighter. They were not putting a price on black loyalty; indeed, they promised, 'as students and guides of public opinion among our people', to do everything they could to keep black Americans, 'at the highest pitch, not simply of passive loyalty, but of active, enthusiastic and self-sacrificing participation in the war'. This was the kind of commitment that the organisers had hoped for and the fact that it came from the pen of Du Bois, the most influential of the radical black editors, was all the more gratifying.

Military Intelligence reported that 'the conference conformed throughout to our original plan' and noted that the editors 'were pleased at having been taken into the confidence of the Government and asked for advice and cooperation'. Newton D. Baker advised President Wilson that henceforth 'the influence of the negro press is going to be sounder' and George Creel wrote to inform Wilson that the conference had been 'all that we

could have wished for in the way of support and understanding'.

As well as trying to influence the black press through the official propaganda network and through a disingenuous form of consultation, the government was exercising a third form of more direct inducement. This was the threat of the closure of selected publications and the prosecution of their editors. Under the Espionage and Sedition Acts, the postmaster general, Albert Sidney Burleson, of Texas, could exclude from the mails any journals which criticised American involvement in the war or the Allies.

He invited Post Office employees to hold up anything that might be illegal, until the Post Office solicitor had pronounced on its mailability. Since qualification for second-class mailing permits depended on a journal being 'regularly issued at stated intervals', any journal deemed unmailable, even for one issue, could be denied second-class mailing thereafter. For periodicals, this was tantamount to suppression. By the middle of 1918, most of the socialist journals in the United States had closed.

The Post Office solicitor, William H. Lamar, thought it 'not only sensible but fair . . . to take into consideration the known attitude of the writers when searching for the "intent" behind the comment'. He derided those in the National Civil Liberties Bureau who clung to 'an exaggerated sentimentalism, a misapplied reverence for legal axioms'; he preferred 'the old adage of reading between the lines'. Hence, his exclusion of a journal for having quoted Thomas Jefferson's century-old opinion that Ireland ought to be a republic. He told the editor of another journal, 'You know, I am not working in the dark on this censorship thing. I know exactly what I am after. I am after three things and only three things—pro-Germanism, pacifism, and "high-browism" '.

In this situation, an editor had to be aware that though his words might not *in themselves* contravene the new laws, their legality depended on what Post Office officials *thought* he meant by them. The legislation thus gave white supremacists new opportunities to attack the radical black press. This Texan postmaster's condemnation of the *Chicago Defender* was typical:

. . . it is a species of rank race hatred which shows the signs of German conspiracy, and also demonstrates the malicious

tendencies of anti-Americanism at a time when we need to be a harmonious and united people. It is precisely this form of public print that stirs in the negro's revolutionary mind not only the seditious thought but the seditious act.

The *Defender* infuriated white southerners with its lurid accounts of lynchings and its encouragement of black migration to the North. Its owner, Robert Abbott, was the first black editor to be harassed by federal agents. In April 1917, following complaints by a senator from Louisiana, the Bureau of Investigation interrogated Abbott and extracted promises of loyalty from him. His finances were secretly investigated. Thereafter, he performed a skillful balancing act, in which he attacked injustice toward blacks, but avoided overt criticism of the government or the war. He was kept under surveillance and interviewed on two further occasions, but escaped prosecution each time. Abbott was also threatened by Military Intelligence. In May 1918, Walter Loving told him that 'the eye of the government [was] centered upon his paper, and caution should be his guide'.

The intimidation of the *Baltimore Afro-American* by the Justice Department followed a similar pattern. The editor, J. H. Murphy, described thirteen black soldiers of the 24th Infantry, executed in December 1917 for rioting in Houston, Texas, as 'martyrs'. In response to complaints by the army about the effects of this on black troops, the Justice Department decided that a warning might be more effective than a prosecution. The Baltimore district attorney called Murphy in: 'I told him what to expect if he continued to publish such articles, and he expressed great contrition and most elaborate promises to eliminate such stuff hereafter from his paper'.

J. E. Mitchell, editor of the *St. Louis Argus,* had told readers in May 1918:

Now is the time to protest. Now is the time to complain. Now is time to contend for legal rights that are being denied us, and now is the time to let the world know that we are not satisfied.

Mitchell's assistant was summoned by Military Intelligence in St. Louis to be lectured, whilst Walter Loving warned Mitchell that his editorials might 'invite action on the part of the government to suppress [the *Argus*] or hold [it] up in the mails'. He added some advice: 'it is not always what you say that offends, but it is the way you say it'.

Meanwhile, in New York, the government moved against the *Amsterdam News*. A junior editor, Cyril Briggs, a native of the Dutch West Indies (who later joined the Communist Party and clashed frequently with Marcus Garvey), took advantage of being left in charge for one issue to get several things off his chest. One was the idea of black self-determination and the creation of a separate black American state, and the other was that tackling American racial injustice was more important than fighting Germans. Postal censors intercepted a copy of the paper addressed to a reader in Cuba, whereupon it was declared non-mailable by Lamar.

The NAACP was frequently identified by Southern agents and informants as a probable disseminator of German propaganda. Its journal was the most influential organ of the growing radicalism of black American political thought. Between 1917 and 1918, monthly circulation of *The Crisis* rose from 41,000 to 74,000. After the association's legal adviser was called in to be rebuked by the assistant US Attorney in New York City, the NAACP agreed to censor *The Crisis* and to publish only 'facts and constructive criticism'. Anything that might 'create a feeling of dissatisfaction among colored people' would be excluded. The NAACP avoided prosecution chiefly because of its political links in Washington, the legal weakness of the Bureau of Investigation's reports, which relied heavily on racially prejudiced opinion, and its own undertakings of loyalty.

The one notable black socialist journal, *The Messenger*, edited by A. Philip Randolph and Chandler Owen, put out three issues during the war, each containing large sections criticising American belligerency. Randolph and Owen suggested that blacks who supported the war should 'volunteer to go to France, if they are so eager to make the world safe for democracy. We would rather make Georgia safe for the Negro'. They defined a 'New Patriotism'—'The new patriotism is consistent. It does not condemn massacres and lynchings in Germany and condone them in its own country'.

In August 1918, while on a speaking tour, they were jailed for three days by the Bureau of Investigation in Cleveland, interrogated and charged with inciting resistance to the United States and promotion of the cause of its enemies. They

were eventually released on bail and never tried, partly because the court wrongly assumed they were the tools of white socialists, and partly because the case against them was weak. After being kept under surveillance during the rest of the tour, Owen was drafted on his return to New York. *The Messenger* did not appear again until 1919.

Ultimately, only one black editor was convicted under the wartime legislation and the newspaper concerned was a minor one, in terms both of readership and influence. During the court-martial in San Antonio, Texas, of the 24th Infantry rioters, G. W. Bouldin of the *San Antonio Inquirer* printed an article attacking the court proceedings and applauding the mutineers. The writer suggested that death by firing squad was preferable to being 'forced to go to Europe to fight for a liberty you cannot enjoy'. This was found to be 'an unlawful attempt to cause insubordination' among black troops and hence in breach of Title I, Section 3, of the Espionage Act. Bouldin was given a two-year prison sentence in Fort Leavenworth federal penitentiary, confirmed by the Court of Appeals in December 1919.

How successful were propaganda, flattery and threat as methods of curbing the outspokenness of the black press? The propaganda approach was the least effective, partly because Emmett Scott was not universally trusted, and partly because blacks expected few favours from a Southern dominated government. As J. M. Winter notes in *The Experience of World War I* (Macmillan, 1988), 'the success or failure of propaganda is primarily a function of the willingness of people to listen to it and to believe what it has to say'. Scott's insistence that discrimination in the army did not exist was poorly received, especially since white commanders of black troops were known to be ordering them to avoid places of entertainment 'where their presence will be resented'.

Flattery of the editors, at the Washington conference, was more rewarding. The *Washington Bee* regarded the gathering as 'epoch-making'. J. E. Mitchell of the *St. Louis Argus* returned home convinced of the vital role of the black press, not just in fighting injustice, but 'in keeping morale high'. The local intelligence officer noted that the conference 'had a salutary effect' on Mitchell. However, it also produced some dissent. William Monroe Trotter of the *Boston Guardian*,

who did not attend, attacked Emmett Scott as 'a Jim Crow Negro', while a supporter of Trotter accused Scott of luring 'a number of colored editors to come to Washington to be wined and dined at the Government's expense for the sole purpose of muzzling them'.

The best results, from the government's point of view, were obtained by threatening legal action. This tactic contributed to a decline in the level of dissent in the black press in the second half of 1918. Immediately after Loving's warning Robert Abbott inserted an editorial in the *Chicago Defender,* recommending that blacks leave the fight for their rights until 'the greater task of winning this war is over'. The *Baltimore Afro-American* took similar pains not to antagonise the Justice Department after Murphy's encounter with the Baltimore district attorney. By November 1918, it was carrying pro-government stories attacking left-wing unions. The sacking of Cyril Briggs by the *Amsterdam News* for incurring the wrath of the Post Office removed a genuinely original and revolutionary voice from black discourse, until he created *The Crusader* after the war.

The most dramatic modification which the efforts of government officials produced was in the editorial position of W. E. B. Du Bois, who was subjected to a combination of threat and flattery. During the winter and spring of 1918, he wrote powerful attacks on the government. After the warning from the Justice Department, however, he began to reject similar material from other writers. In May, he was given a prominent role in the Washington editors' conference; in June, he was offered a commission in Military Intelligence to work on racial matters. In the July *Crisis,* in order to prove his loyalty to Military Intelligence, he abruptly changed his tone:

Let us, while this war lasts, forget our special grievances and close ranks shoulder to shoulder with our own white fellow citizens and allied nations that are fighting for democracy. We make no ordinary sacrifice, but we make it gladly and willingly and with our eyes lifted to the hills.

The denunciation of Du Bois by astounded fellow radicals and the strife which ensued within the NAACP suited the government's purposes. The offer of the commission was withdrawn soon afterwards.

In the short term, then, the government's efforts to change the tenor of the most influential black journals were effective. The black press in America continued to call for equal rights, but the power and bitterness of its language was greatly reduced. The Justice and War Departments had their way, without having to engage in large-scale court proceedings against representatives of the black minority. But only for a while. At the end of the war, the black press resumed its fight with even greater force. As Du Bois put it in *The Crisis'* May 1919 issue:

We return.
We return from fighting
We return fighting

The size and scope of the black press grew sharply after the war and the new titles included such radical papers as Cyril Briggs' *Crusader* and Marcus Garvey's *Negro World*. The *Messenger* reappeared, stronger than ever. The government had been able to subdue the language of black protest during 1918,

but it could not change the new clarity with which black Americans saw and understood the causes and injustice of their plight. The wartime experience of blacks, in and out of uniform, hastened the development of a radical race consciousness, which took both integrationist and black nationalist forms. The horrific level of racial violence in 1919, entailing nationwide race riots and over seventy lynchings, further intensified black protest and debate.

It is all too often overlooked that the organisational and ideological steps taken by black Americans during and immediately after the First World War set the pattern for the civil rights movement of the 1950s and 1960s. Significantly, in both 1917–21 and 1954–68, black leaders pointedly contrasted the domestic shortcomings of American democracy with its international proclamation by the government and in each period they were the targets of open and

covert retaliation in which they were accused of disloyalty to the United States.

FOR FURTHER READING:

J. L. Scheiber & H. N. Scheiber, 'The Wilson Administration and the Wartime Mobilization of Black Americans, 1917–1918,' *Labor History,* X, no 3 (Summer, 1969); Manning Marable, *W. E. B. Du Bois: Black Radical Democrat* (Boston: Twayne, 1986); Christopher N. May, *In the Name of War* (Cambridge, Mass: Harvard University Press, 1989); Herbert Shapiro, *White Violence and Black Response* (Amherst: University of Massachusetts Press, 1988); Stephen Vaughn, *Holding Fast the Inner Lines: Democracy, Nationalism, and the Committee on Public Information* (Chapel Hill: University of North Carolina Press, 1980); Neil A. Wynn, *From Progressivism to Prosperity: World War I and American Society* (New York: Holmes & Meier, 1986).

What We Lost in the Great War

Seventy-five years ago this spring a very different America waded into the seminal catastrophe of the twentieth century. World War I did more than kill millions of people; it destroyed the West's faith in the very institutions that had made it the hope and envy of the world.

John Steele Gordon

John Steele Gordon's article on the origins of the health-care crisis appeared in the May/June 1992 issue of American Heritage.

A few years ago I wrote a book called *The Scarlet Woman of Wall Street* about a place and a people that flourished in the nineteenth century: the New York City of the 1860s and 1870s. We might call it Edith Wharton's New York. Mrs. Wharton herself wrote late in her life, in the 1930s, that the metropolis of her youth had been destined to become "as much a vanished city as Atlantis or the lowest level of Schliemann's Troy." To those of us who know the modern metropolis—what we might call Tom Wolfe's New York—that city of only a century ago seems today as far away and nearly as exotic as Marco Polo's Cathay.

What happened to Edith Wharton's world? Why does the society our grandparents and great-grandparents lived in seem so very much a foreign country to us today?

To be sure, Edith Wharton's New York was a still-provincial city of horses and gas lamps, Knickerbockers and Irishmen, brownstones and church steeples. Its population was characterized by a few people in top hats and a great many people in rags, for in the 1860s grinding poverty was still thought the fate of the majority of the human race.

In contrast, Tom Wolfe's New York—far and away the most cosmopolitan place on earth—is a city of subways and neon, Korean grocers and Pakistani news

dealers, apartments and skyscrapers. If poverty has hardly been expunged, the percentage of the city's population living in want has greatly diminished even while society's idea of what constitutes the basic minimums of a decent life has greatly expanded.

It was constant, incremental change that brought about these differences, a phenomenon found in most societies and all industrial ones. Indeed, one of the pleasures of growing old in such a society, perhaps, is that we come to remember personally—just as Edith Wharton did—a world that has slipped out of existence.

But this sort of change comes slowly and is recognized only in retrospect. As the novelist Andrew Holleran explained, "No one grows old in a single day." Rather, something far more profound than incremental change separates us from Edith Wharton's world, and we look at that world now across what a mathematician might call a discontinuity in the stream of time.

ONLY RARELY IN THE COURSE OF HISTORY does such a discontinuity occur and turn a world upside down overnight. When it does happen, it is usually as the result of some unforeseeable cataclysm, such as the volcanic explosion that destroyed Minoan civilization on the island of Crete about 1500 B.C., or the sudden arrival of the conquistadors in the New World three thousand years later.

Edith Wharton's world suffered just such a calamity. The diplomat and his-

torian George Kennan called it "the seminal catastrophe of the twentieth century": the First World War.

Certainly that war's influence on subsequent world events could hardly have been more pervasive. Had there been no First World War, there would, of course, have been no Second, and that is not just playing with numbers, for in geopolitical terms the two wars were really one with a twenty-year truce in the middle.

But for the First World War, the sun might still shine brightly on the British Empire. But for the war, there would have been no Bolshevik coup and thus no Soviet state. But for the war, there would have been no Nazis and thus no genocide of the Jews. And, of course, most of us never would have been born.

Far more important, however, than its effect upon the fate of great nations, and on our own individual existence, was the First World War's influence on the way that we heirs of Edith Wharton came to question, and for a while even to dismiss, many of the basic values of the culture she lived in. Because of the war, the word *Victorian* became a term of opprobrium that extended far beyond the ebb and flow of fashion.

The reason for this is simply that the First World War, more than any other in history, was psychologically debilitating, both for the vanquished and for the victors. indeed, there really was no victory. No premeditated policy of conquest or revenge brought the war about—although both those aims had clouded the politics of Europe for years. Therefore, no aims, beyond national survival, were achieved.

Indeed, relations among the Great Powers of Europe were better in the early summer of 1914 than they had been for some time. The British and Germans had recently agreed about the Berlin to Baghdad railway and a future division between them of Portugal's colonies. Even the French, still bitter over their ignominious defeat at the hands of Prussia in 1871, were moving to improve relations with Germany, a move that Germany welcomed.

Rather, the war came about because a lunatic murdered a man of feathers and uniforms who had no real importance whatsoever. The politicians, seeking to take advantage of circumstances—as politicians are paid to do—had then miscalculated in their blustering and posturing.

The mobilization of an army when railroads were the only means of mass transportation was a very complex undertaking, one that had to be planned in advance down to the smallest detail. Once a mobilization plan was implemented, it could not be stopped without throwing a country's military into chaos, rendering it largely defenseless. Russia, seeking only to threaten Austria and thus prevent its using the assassination of Archduke Ferdinand to stir up trouble in the Balkans, discovered that it could not move just against Austria. It was general mobilization or nothing. Russia chose to mobilize.

At that point the statesmen realized that the war they had threatened so freely—but which no one, in fact, had wanted at all—had now, suddenly, become inescapable. A fearful, inexorable logic had taken decisions out of human hands.

Once it began, the generals found they had no tactical concepts to deal with the new military realities that confronted them. It had been forty-three years since Great Powers had fought each other in Europe. In those four decades the instruments of war had undergone an unparalleled evolution, and their destructive power had increased by several orders of magnitude.

Railroads, machine guns, and barbed wire made an entrenched defense invulnerable. Stalemate—bloody, endless, gloryless stalemate—resulted. For lack of any better ideas, the generals flung greater and greater numbers of men into the mouths of these machine guns and gained at best mere yards of territory thereby.

In the first day—day!—of the Battle of the Somme in 1916, Great Britain suffered twenty thousand men killed. That was the bloodiest day in the British army's long history. Altogether there were more than a million casualties in this one battle alone. An entire generation was lost in the slaughter of the Somme and other similar battles.

This almost unimaginable destruction of human life, to no purpose whatsoever, struck at the very vitals of Western society. For this reason alone, among the casualties of the First World War were not only the millions of soldiers who had died for nothing, most of the royalty of Europe, and treasure beyond reckoning but nearly all the fundamental philosophical and cultural assumptions of the civilization that had suffered this self-induced catastrophe.

For there was one thing that was immediately clear to all about the Great War—as the generation who fought it called it—and that was that this awful tragedy was a human and wholly local phenomenon. There was no volcano, no wrathful God, no horde of barbarians out of the East. Western culture had done this to itself. Because of the war, it seemed to many a matter of inescapable logic that Western culture must be deeply, inherently flawed.

In four years of blood and smoke and flame, the world of Edith Wharton became the world of W. H. Auden; the Age of Innocence, the Age of Anxiety.

For us, who can see the tragedy that was looming up in what was for them the future, and thus, for them, impenetrable, many of the cultural assumptions of Edith Wharton's world smack of the hubris that is the inevitable progenitor of tragedy. But hubris, like the winner in a horse race, can be much more easily discerned in retrospect. And people cannot live—or, for that matter, bet on horses—in retrospect.

Given their vantage point in history, the inhabitants of Edith Wharton's world had every good reason for their attitudes. Their civilization had, after all, entirely remade the world in the preceding two hundred years.

Consider the facts:

In the year 1700 there had been little to distinguish European culture in terms of power, wealth, and creativity from the other great civilizations on earth. The Ottoman Turks had conquered most of the Muslim world and much of Europe itself in the previous two centuries. The Turkish army had besieged Vienna as recently as 1683.

The Mogul emperor of India, whose father had built the incomparable Taj Mahal, sat on the Peacock Throne, ruling over an empire of a million square miles, and lived in a splendor unmatched even by the Versailles of Louis XIV.

The Chinese Empire was the largest and perhaps the most cultured on earth. It was also the most industrially advanced, running a strong trade surplus with Europe.

But by the year 1700 Europe had already invented a cultural tool of transcendent power called the scientific method. In the eighteenth century this tool was applied to an ever-widening area of inquiry with beneficial results in fields as diverse as agriculture, cloth manufacture, and metalworking. By the close of that century, Europe was clearly the dominant power center of the world and was projecting that power commercially, militarily, and politically over a wider and wider area.

And in 1782 James Watt perfected the rotary steam engine. The Industrial Revolution was under way.

A hundred years later still, at the end of the nineteenth century, any comparison between the West and other cultures bordered on the meaningless, so great had the gap in power and wealth grown. Westerners had projected that power over the entire globe and created the modern world, a world they utterly dominated. The Western people of that world took for granted what seemed to them the manifest superiority of Western technology, governance, and even religion over all others.

To better understand the predominant attitudes of the West before the First World War, consider what it accomplished in the nineteenth century as a result of the Industrial Revolution. Quite simply, the quality of life was miraculously transformed. Indoor plumbing, central heating, brilliant interior lighting, abundant clothing, and myriad inexpensive industrial products from wallpaper to iceboxes gave the middle and upper classes a standard of living undreamed of a century earlier by even the richest members of society.

In 1800 it had required a month to cross the Atlantic in a damp, crowded, and pitching ship. In 1900 vast and luxurious liners made the crossing in a week. Information that once had been limited to the speed of human travel could now circle the entire globe in minutes by telephone, telegraph, and undersea cable.

In the 1830s the lights and shadows of an instant were captured by photography. In the 1870s Edison's phonograph imprisoned sound. To the Victorians it was as though time itself had been tamed.

Newspapers, books, and magazines proliferated by the thousands so that information and entertainment could be quickly and cheaply obtained. Free public libraries spread to nearly every city in the Western world. Andrew Carnegie alone paid for nearly five thousand of them in the United States and Britain.

Physics, chemistry, geology, and biology penetrated farther into the fathomless heart of nature than anyone had thought possible a hundred years earlier. Even the mighty Newton's model of the universe was found to be less than wholly universal when Einstein published his Special Theory of Relativity in 1905.

As the new century began engineers showed the world with the Crystal Palace in London how to enclose vast spaces, with the Brooklyn Bridge in New York how to span great distances, with the Eiffel Tower in Paris how to scale great heights. The automobile, the airplane, the movies, and wireless communication promised still more wonders.

Ever more important than the technological and scientific advances of the age, however, were the economic and political ones.

The nineteenth century is usually perceived as one in which great industrial and commercial fortunes were created in the midst—even because of—the grinding poverty of the masses. This is largely a misperception. To be sure, the absolute number of people living in poverty in the Western world greatly increased in the nineteenth century, but only because the population as a whole greatly increased. Moreover, the movement of workers from agriculture to industry concentrated the poor in highly visible urban areas. But their forebears had been no less poor. The ancestors of those who lived in the unspeakable urban hovels of Dickens's England had inhabited the equally unspeakable rural hovels of Fielding's England. Meanwhile, the percentage of the population living in poverty declined.

In 1800 perhaps 85 percent of the population of Britain—then the richest and most advanced of Western nations—lived in or very near poverty, where 85 percent of the human population had always lived. These people had to work as hard as they could just to get enough to eat and obtain shelter and clothes. They stored up a little in good years, perhaps, in order to survive the bad ones. But luxuries, and even a formal education for their children, were out of the question. For millions, only rum, gin, and other spirits in staggering quantities—often quite literally in staggering quantities—made life endurable.

But by 1900 less than 30 percent of the British population was still at that economic level, and most of the children were receiving at least the rudiments of an education and therefore the hope of a better life. Meanwhile, the per capita consumption of alcohol had fallen sharply. While no one in 1900 thought that 30 percent of the population living in poverty was acceptable, parents and grandparents were there to tell them how far they had come.

In 1800 less than five percent of the British population was allowed to vote for those who represented them in Parliament, and real political power resided in fewer than two thousand families. By 1900 universal male suffrage was taken for granted and women were on the march for equal rights. Democracy, beginning to develop only in the new United States in 1800, was by 1900 the birthright of millions in both the old and new worlds.

IN TWO HUNDRED YEARS WESTERN CIVILIzation had made itself rich and powerful and learned while the rest of mankind remained poor, and therefore weak and ignorant. Political and economic power in the West had ceased to be the exclusive possession of a narrow upper class and had spread widely to other levels of society, promoting social stability by giving everyone both a stake in society's institutions and the power to affect those institutions.

It was this dispersal of economic and political power that guaranteed that no one person or segment of society could become too powerful and threaten the rights or the prosperity of others. When heavy industry, in pursuit of economies of scale, conglomerated in the late nineteenth century into huge concerns of unprecedented financial and economic power, many Americans believed they threatened a plutocracy. So society moved to check the potential abuse of power with antimonopoly legislation, such as the Sherman Antitrust Act, and to channel that power into productive, not hegemonic, purposes. This may have been a violent and wrenching process; nevertheless, it happened.

Who can blame the people who accomplished all this for feeling good about themselves? Would we, or anyone, have been any wiser or more humble?

Because of this fantastic record of progress, the people of Edith Wharton's world believed in the inevitability of further progress and the certainty that science would triumph. They believed in the ever-widening spread of democracy and the rule of law. They believed in the adequacy of the present and the bright promise of the future. To be sure, they fought ferociously over the details of how to proceed, but they had no doubt whatever that the basic principles that guided their society were correct.

Then, all at once, the shots rang out in Sarajevo, the politicians bungled, the armies marched, the poppies began to blow between the crosses row on row. The faith of the Western world in the soundness of its civilization died in the trenches of the western front.

Seventy-five years later, richer and more learned than ever, the West still struggles to find the self-confidence it had once taken for granted.

Seventy-five years later, richer, more powerful, more learned than ever, the West still struggles to pick up the psychological pieces, to regain its poise, to find again the self-confidence that in the nineteenth century it took entirely for granted.

IF THE GREAT WAR WAS THE RESULT NOT of deliberate policy but of ghastly accident, we now know it was an accident waiting to happen. Still, like most accidents, it resulted from the concatenation of separate chances, each unlikely. Indeed, it can be reasonably argued that the calamity might well never have come to pass at all if only the imperial throne of Germany had been occupied by someone other than that supreme jerk Kaiser Wilhelm II.

Although highly intelligent, he had been burdened from the start with a withered left arm caused by a difficult and medically mishandled birth. Far worse, Wilhelm had been largely raised by pedantic tutors and sycophantic military aides, for his mother was more interested in Prussian politics than in her children's upbringing.

The result was that an undisciplined, impulsive, deeply insecure neurotic inherited the throne of the greatest military power in Europe. Worse, the constitution of the German Empire gave him a very large measure of control over foreign and military policy.

The consequence was disaster for Germany and the world. And in complex societies, just as in simple ones, when disaster strikes, "the king must die." And not just Wilhelm (who spent the last twenty years of his life in exile). The entire pre-war establishment was everywhere blamed for this purposeless, victorless war. The mainstream politicians who had failed to prevent it, the businessmen who had profited from it, the scientists and engineers who had created its lethal technology—all those, in fact who had constituted the nexus of power in Edith Wharton's world suffered a grievous loss of prestige.

Those who had been only on the margins of power and influence in the nineteenth century—the Cassandras who are present in all societies, the philosophers, the artists (in short, the intellectuals)—saw their opportunities and seized them. To use Theodore Roosevelt's famous metaphor, power began to move from the players in the arena to the observers in the seats.

In the relatively peaceful 1880s, Gilbert and Sullivan in *The Mikado* had put on the Lord High Executioner's little list of social expendables "the idiot who praises, with enthusiastic tone,/ All centuries but this, and every country but his own." After the First World War people listened eagerly to just such philosophers, many of whom thought that only a radical restructuring of Western society and its economic system could prevent a recurrence of the calamity. Not sur-

prisingly, the philosophers had no lack of prescriptions for how to accomplish this and no doubt whatever as to just who should be put in charge of the project. Although many of these ideas turned out to be in Winston Churchill's phrase, so stupid that only an intellectual could have conceived" them, people were ready to give them a try.

WE MUST NOW LOOK, BRIEFLY, AT THE philosophical baby that so many intellectuals were ready to toss out with the bath water of war.

At the core of Western thought lies the concept of the importance of the individual human being. It is a uniquely Western idea, with its origins in ancient Israel and Greece (a civilization where the gods themselves were made of all-too-human clay). Later the concept was continued and elaborated on by such Christian philosophers as Augustine, Jerome, and Thomas Aquinas.

In medieval England, safe from foreign invasion behind its watery walls, the emphasis on the importance of the individual resulted in the flowering of the concept of liberty, both political and economic. Individuals, thought the English, were born with rights no one, not even kings, could take away, for the king, like his subjects, was bound by the law. This idea—that the majesty of the law was separate and distinct from the king's own majesty—is today encapsulated in the phrase *the rule of law*. It is one of the most important of Western concepts, for without it the Western achievements of the nineteenth century would not have been possible.

THE AMERICAN REVOLUTION AND THE economic dominance of Britain in the nineteenth century caused liberty's children—capitalism and democracy—to spread widely through the Western world. The increasing acceptance during the nineteenth century of the individual's right, within an ordered society, to pursue his own concept of happiness—in other words, his self-interest—had, to be sure, many consequences, some of them unpleasant. The Victorians, however, were prepared to accept these consequences. They reasoned that because human beings are social creatures, the betterment of society was, in fact, in almost everyone's self-interest. The people of Edith Wharton's world likewise believed that most of

the attributes of their society resulted from the interaction of history with human nature, and that human nature, with all its faults, was a given.

The Victorians certainly thought that mankind could get ever better and ever wiser, and in support of this idea they pointed to their own century as Exhibit A. But they equally believed that the perfection of mankind could come only with the arrival of what Christians call the Kingdom of Heaven on Earth. Until then, they thought, they would just have to make do with what they had.

But Karl Marx reversed this equation. He maintained that human nature was only a result of the society in which people lived. Change society, thought Marx, and you change human nature. Perfect society, and you perfect mankind. To Marx and the "social engineers" who followed him, the intellectual, not the grace of God, would be the redeemer of the human race.

Marx was the quintessential intellectual, remarkably detached from the real world. Although he dedicated his formidable mind to the betterment of the new industrial working class, he knew of that class only what he read in the library of the British Museum. Not once in his life did Marx ever set foot in a factory. Consequently, at the time of his death, in 1883, his grand vision stood no more chance of adoption by the real world than had Sir Thomas More's Utopia three hundred and fifty years earlier.

Further, Marx, deeply influenced by Thomas Malthus's and David Ricardo's gloomy (and erroneous) ideas, made a classic intellectual mistake. He looked at the social and economic universe around him—the early stages of the Industrial Revolution—and assumed that the conditions he saw were permanent and the trends of that era would continue indefinitely. But, of course, trends hardly ever continue indefinitely.

In fact they were rapidly evolving, as they continue to do today. But the followers of Marx regarded his theories about society and economics as the equal of Newton's theory in physics: the universal explainer of all observed phenomena.

And while Marx was only an intellectual, his greatest intellectual successor, Lenin, was much more. Lenin was a political genius. Thanks to the opportunities arising out of the First World War, he was able to seize control of a great nation and proclaim a Marxist day in which the perfecting of society was the only goal and in which the individual pursuit of happiness, or even the right to hold a contrary opinion, had no place whatever. In the first two years of Lenin's rule, fifty thousand of his political opponents were executed.

In shattered Germany, meanwhile, an already neurotic society slid toward psychosis. United only in 1871, Germany had been a latecomer to the world of Great Power politics and was "born encircled" by the other Great Powers. Lacking a vast colonial empire and a long national history, Germany depended on its economic and military might for its prestige, until its one unquestioned superiority—its incomparable army—was nonetheless defeated.

THE DRACONIAN, SCORE-SETTLING PEACE imposed on Germany at the Versailles Conference worsened matters considerably. So did the hyperinflation of the early 1920s, which wiped out whatever economic security middle-class Germans had managed to hang on to. In their humiliation the German people felt a desperate need for scapegoats, and Hitler stood ready to supply Jews, homosexuals, Gypsies, and others to fill that need—in exchange, of course, for total power. Many other countries, including Spain and Italy, also adopted fascism, as these disparate movements were collectively called. Even countries with firm democratic foundations felt the effects of this intellectual assault upon the nineteenth-century world view. Britain and France elected their first socialist governments in 1924, and both had active fascist movements.

The Second World War destroyed fascism as a political doctrine but greatly strengthened the Soviet Union, which sought to export its system to areas occupied by the Red Army and to countries in the so-called Third World. Meanwhile, the democratic left, especially in Western Europe and Britain, but increasingly in the United States as well, sought to replace the old economic and social order with systems of their devising that they genuinely believed would be fairer and more peaceful and more prosperous. In pursuit of these worthy goals, these systems tended to concentrate power, rather than disperse it as the nineteenth century had done. And democratically elected leaders—just like their totalitarian counterparts—often assumed that

human nature was only clay to be molded in a noble cause.

But human nature has proved recalcitrant. The nineteenth century, it turns out, had it right to start with. The evidence has been piling up through most of the twentieth century, and it is now overwhelming that people act not as Karl Marx and Lenin thought they would but as Adam Smith and John Stuart Mill predicted.

People pursue their self-interests, perceiving those interests to be bound up with themselves, their families—especially their children—and their society as a whole. Class divisions within a society, by which Marxists seek to explain the human universe, are an intellectual construct, with no real-world analogue. Many of the programs advocated by the social engineers, therefore, failed altogether or had vast, wicked, and entirely unanticipated consequences.

Of all the inventions of the nineteenth century, capitalism and representative democracy turned out to be the greatest. To be sure, they are intellectually untidy—often very untidy indeed: just ask Charles Keating, the Reverend Al Sharpton, or the latest congressman under indictment. Nonetheless, they work, for they are consonant with human nature. As Churchill explained, "Democracy is the worst form of government except all those other forms that have been tried from time to time." He could have made the same point about capitalism.

Capitalism made the West rich in the nineteenth century, and that wealth was spread ever more widely through society as the century went on. All the alternatives pursued in the twentieth have led only to poverty.

Democracy increasingly empowered the ordinary people in the nineteenth century as literacy, newspapers, and the franchise spread to every level. All the modern alternatives have resulted only in tyrannies far worse than any known to the world of Edith Wharton.

After decades of experiments brought on by the First World War, it is clear that what maximizes human happiness is ordered liberty—the idea that individuals should be free to pursue their political and economic self-interests under the rule of law and within the limits set by a democratic society. During the last decade, as the promises of systems that concentrated power rather than dispersed it collapsed, country after country has moved toward economic and political

liberty. Today even the citadel of totalitarianism, the Kremlin itself, has fallen to the essential force of these nineteenth-century ideas.

The nineteenth century even knew the reason why these ideas were so forceful, and indeed, one of the century's greatest political philosophers expressed it as dictum. "Power tends to corrupt," Lord Acton wrote in 1887, "and absolute power corrupts absolutely." Perhaps the cruelest legacy of the First World War is that we have required seventy-five years and untold human pain to learn this truth all over again.

All this is not to say that there was nothing to be learned from the First World War and its terrible consequences, that it was all just a ghastly aberration. I think that we heirs of Edith Wharton have learned at least four vital lessons from the catastrophe.

Before the war Westerners believed not only in the superiority of Western culture but in the innate superiority of the white race over what many, twisting Kipling's meaning, referred to as those "lesser breeds without the Law." Today no one but the hopeless bigot believes that those who could inflict the Battle of Verdun upon themselves are a special creation or the sole repository of human genius. The Great War taught us that all human beings are equally human: equally frail and equally sublime.

THE SECOND LESSON OF THE FIRST WORLD War was to hammer home forever the truth first uttered by William Tecumseh Sherman thirty-five years earlier. "I am tired and sick of war," the great general said in 1879. "Its glory is all moonshine. . . . War is hell." At 11:00 A.M., on November 11, 1918, as the guns fell silent after fifty-one months and 8,538,315 military deaths, there was hardly a soul on earth who would have disagreed with him. Nor are there many today. If wars have been fought since, they have been fought by people who suffered few illusions about war's glory.

The third lesson is that in a technological age, war between the Great Powers cannot be won in anything but a Pyrrhic sense. In the stark phraseology of the accountant, war is no longer even remotely cost-effective.

The final lesson is that it is very easy in a technological age for war to become inevitable. The speed with which war is fought has increased many fold since the

Industrial Revolution began. In 1914 the Austrians, the Russians, and the German kaiser rattled one too many sabers, and suddenly, much to their surprise, the lights began to go out all over Europe. This all too vividly demonstrated fact has induced considerable caution in the world's statesmen ever since—if not, alas, in its madmen.

Bearing this in mind, there is one aspect of the First World War for which we might be grateful: If it had to be fought, it was well that it was fought when it was. We learned the lessons of total war in a technological age less than forty years before we developed the capacity to destroy ourselves utterly with

---

There has been joy. There will be joy again.

—Alfred Bester

---

this technology. Had the political situation that led to the Great War coincided with the technological possibilities that produced the hydrogen bomb, it is improbable that there would have been a Tom Wolfe's New York—or even any New Yorkers to look back and wonder what happened to Edith Wharton's.

Rather, the great metropolis, a city humming with human life and human genius, would instead be but one more pile of rubble on a vast and desolate plain, poisoned for centuries. If we have truly learned this final lesson, and we must pray that we have, then those millions who lie today in Flanders fields did not die in vain.

When White Hoods Were in Flower

Bernard A. Weisberger

This month's historical reflections are inspired by the presidential candidacy of David Duke, a former Imperial Wizard of the Ku Klux Klan, whose elevation to at least marginal respectability reminds me uncomfortably of a time when the Klan was functioning openly and above-ground and was a very palpable force in American politics.

The "original" Knights of the Ku Klux Klan, the "invisible empire" of hooded nightriders immortalized in *The Birth of a Nation* and *Gone with the Wind,* got its start in 1866 in the defeated former Confederacy. Whatever its exact origins, its purpose soon became to drive freed blacks and their Northern allies away from the polling places and back into a state of economic and political subservience. It "persuaded" by fires, floggings, and lynchings. Forget the romantic mush; it was an outlawed terrorist organization, designed to undo Reconstruction. And with its help, Reconstruction was undone. But so, by 1872, was the Klan. However, in 1915 it underwent a second ten- to fifteen-year incarnation, of which more in a moment. That is the main story here.

During the 1950s a third, "new" Klan—or perhaps several successive new Klans—emerged, in reaction to the legal dismantling of Jim Crow, sometimes called the Second Reconstruction. Like the original KKK, the groups functioned in the South, and they were responsible for bombings and the gunshot murders of at least five civil rights workers. Post-1970 Klans have had a large, changing, Cold War-influenced list of enemies, allies, and strategies. All have led a furtive existence under legal surveillance and almost universal repudiation.

But it wasn't so with that "middle" Klan that lived in the atmosphere of World War I and the 1920s. That one targeted Catholics, Jews, and foreigners as well as blacks. In so doing, it expanded its base beyond Dixie and had more national influence than is pleasant to think about.

The evidence? How about a parade of forty thousand robed and proud-of-it Klansmen down Pennsylvania Avenue in Washington, D.C.? Or a state—Indiana—whose KKK "Grand Dragon" held a political IOU—one of many—from the mayor of Indianapolis promising to appoint no person to the Board of Public Works without his endorsement? Or a Democratic National Convention of 1924 that split down the middle of a vote to condemn the Klan by name, with just over half the delegates refusing?

This new Klan was the creation of Alabama-born "Colonel" William J. Simmons, who resuscitated fading memories of the original Knights in a Thanksgiving Day cross-burning ceremony atop Stone Mountain, Georgia, in 1915. Its credo not only pledged members to be "true to the faithful maintenance of White Supremacy" but restricted the membership to "native born American citizens who believe in the tenets of the Christian religion and owe no allegiance . . . to any foreign Government, nation, political institution, sect, people or person." The "person" was the Pope, and the new KKK tapped into a long-standing tradition of nativism that went back at least as far as the American or Know-Nothing party of the 1850s, which flared transiently in the cloudy political skies just before the Civil War.

Simmons kept and improved on the primal Klan's ritual mumbo jumbo, including secret initiations and an array of

officeholders with titles like Imperial Wizard, Exalted Cyclopes, and Grand Goblin. He struck an alliance with a publicist named Edward Clarke who helped devise a deft recruiting scheme. Recruiters called Kleagles signed up members for local chapters (Klaverns) at ten dollars a head. The Kleagle kept four dollars; one dollar went to the state's King Kleagle, fifty cents to the Grand Goblin, and so on up the chain of command, with two dollars to Simmons himself.

For many native-born, white, Gentile Americans, joiners by nature, the new Klan became a special lodge, like the Elks, the Rotarians, or Woodmen of the World, for which Simmons had been a field organizer. There were four million Klansmen by 1924, according to some estimates, in a population that turned out only about thirty million voters in that year's presidential election. So it became prudent for some politicians, President Harding included, to join the KKK or at least seek its support. According to Wyn C. Wade, author of *The Fiery Cross,* one of the latest books on the Klan, the number of municipal officials elected nationwide by Klan votes has yet to be counted. The organization likewise had input in the choice of more than a dozen senators and eleven governors.

The Klan's greatest victories were in Indiana, whose Grand Dragon, purple-robed David C. Stephenson, was a gifted publicist who organized a women's auxiliary and staged barbecues and picnics, which he visited by dropping from the sky in an airplane with gilded wings. He made enough on the regalia and literature concessions to live in princely style, with lots of clandestine booze and women available. And he endorsed a slate of state candidates that swept Indiana's Republican Convention in 1924 and followed Calvin Coolidge to victory in the fall. Stephenson's dreams of the future for himself included a Senate seat and perhaps even the White House.

What made these astonishing successes possible? Was the whole country gripped by a fever of hatred? Yes and no. Racism and xenophobia actually were enjoying a favorable climate. The KKK's rebirth in 1915 coincided with the success of *The Birth of a Nation,* which depicted the original Klan as a necessity to save Southern civilization from barbaric blacks egged on by Radical Republican plunderers. This was not much of an exaggeration of the "official" version of Reconstruction then embalmed in scholarly histories, but D. W. Griffith's cinematic skills burned it into the popular mind.

At the same time, a wave of immigration from Southern and Eastern Europe troubled "old stock" Americans. In 1924 the immigration laws were rewritten specifically to keep out such indigestible Catholic and Jewish hordes, as they were considered.

THEN THERE WAS THE EXPERIENCE OF World War I, in which "100 percent Americanism" was enforced by vigilante groups and by the government, armed with Espionage and Sedition acts. Following that, the Bolshevik Revolution inaugurated a Red scare that brought a frantic search for "agitators" to arrest or deport.

All these forces predisposed potential Klan members to accept its exclusionary message without much analysis—and to overlook incidents of violence. But there was more. Thousands of fundamentalist Christians, beleaguered and bewildered by the Progressive Era victories of evolution and the social gospel—not to mention jazz, gin, and short skirts—saw the Klan as the savior of oldtime religion.

The KKK played to their anxiety by supporting Prohibition and the teaching of religion in the schools. Had the Moral Majority then been in existence, it might have absorbed some who instead became Klan followers.

It was the onrush of change, the shakeups brought by radio and film and the auto, that spooked so many Americans. My friend David Chalmers, author of *Hooded Americanism,* put it neatly to me by phone. "They couldn't blame Henry Ford or Charles Steinmetz [the socialist engineering genius of the General Electric Company], but happily they found 'the dago on the Tiber' " instead.

In the 1920s the KKK expanded its base beyond Dixie and had far more national influence than is pleasant to think about.

But change could not be held back for long. In the mid-twenties the Klan's strength dropped off dramatically, to forty-five thousand by 1930. There were many reasons. One was internal feuding among Klan leaders over control of the organization's assets. Another was the exposure of Klan-led bombings, beatings, threats, and atrocities by courageous newspapers like the Indianapolis *Times,* the Memphis *Commercial Appeal,* and the Columbus (Georgia) *Enquirer-Sun.* They resisted boycotts and other forms of pressure in the heart of the enemy's country and told the truth. So did many courageous politicians who repudiated the votes of bigotry. Revelations that some Klan officials were given to liquor, loot, and lechery also defaced the "knightly" image. The biggest scan-

dal of all sent Grand Dragon Stephenson to jail for the brutal rape of Madge Oberholtzer, a young state employee, who afterward committed suicide. Stephenson, outraged that the Indiana authorities did not set him above the law, avenged himself by squealing on his political puppets and ruining their subsequent careers.

AND OVER TIME THE SECOND KLAN WAS repudiated because it collided with the fundamental American values of inclusiveness and pluralism. The trouble is that it also expressed equally durable American attitudes: the ongoing quest for an unalloyed "Americanism," the perverse pressure to conform to a single majority standard, and the tendency to substitute mob "justice" for the unsatisfying ambiguities of legal verdicts.

It seems that current historians, unencumbered by having lived through the period's hostilities, are more inclined to explain than to condemn the Klan of the twenties. Most of its members, they suggest, were tradition-bound outsiders to the emerging new urban money culture, more frightened than vicious. I am unpersuaded, even while acknowledging that "good" people can join "bad" associations out of understandable frustrations. But the Klan could not be separated from its hateful implications then, and the Klan spirit cannot be so separated now, however prettified, sanitized, and shorn of wacky costumes and titles. Scapegoating of "the other," assurances that "we" must safeguard our system, our heritage, and our values from "them"—these notions inevitably carry implications of violence and repression.

Yet under certain conditions they can become widespread, unless watched and guarded against. As the evidence presented shows, it has happened. Here. And not so long ago.

Citizen Ford

He invented modern mass production. He gave the world the first people's car, and his countrymen loved him for it. But at the moment of his greatest triumph, he turned on the empire he had built—and on the son who would inherit it.

David Halberstam

Part One
THE CREATOR

Late in the life of the first Henry Ford, a boy named John Dahlinger, who more than likely was Ford's illegitimate son,* had a discussion with the old man about education and found himself frustrated by Ford's very narrow view of what schooling should be. "But, sir," Dahlinger told Ford, "these are different times, this is the modern age and—" Ford cut him off. "Young man," he said, "I invented the modern age."

The American century had indeed begun in Detroit, created by a man of simple agrarian principles. He had started with scarcely a dollar in his pocket. When he died, in 1947, his worth was placed at $600 million. Of his most famous car, the Model T, he sold 15,456,868. Mass production, he once said, was the "new messiah," and indeed it was almost God to him. When he began producing the Model T, it took twelve and a half hours to make one car. His dream was to make one car every minute. It took him only twelve years to achieve that goal, and five years after that, in 1925, he was making one every ten sec-

---

*Dahlinger, who died in 1984, was baptized in the Ford christening gown and slept as an infant in the crib Henry had used as a baby. His mother was a secretary at the Ford company. —Ed.

onds. His name was attached not just to cars but to a way of life, and it became a verb—to *fordize* meant to standardize a product and manufacture it by mass means at a price so low that the common man could afford to buy it.

When Ford entered the scene, automobiles were for the rich. But he wanted none of that; he was interested in transportation for men like himself, especially for farmers. The secret lay in mass production. "Every time I reduce the charge for our car by one dollar," he said early in the production of the T, "I get a thousand new buyers," and he ruthlessly brought the price down, seeking—as the Japanese would some sixty years later—size of market rather than maximum profit per piece. He also knew in a shrewd, intuitive way what few others did in that era, that as a manufacturer and employer he was part of a critical cycle that expanded the buying power of the common man. One year his advertising people brought him a new slogan that said, "Buy a Ford—save the difference," and he quickly changed it to "Buy a Ford—SPEND the difference," for though he was innately thrifty himself, he believed that the key to prosperity lay not in saving but in spending and turning money over. When one of the children of his friend Harvey Firestone boasted that he had some savings, Ford lectured the child. Money in banks was idle money. What he should do, Ford said, was spend it on tools. "Make

something," he admonished, "create something."

For better or worse Ford's values were absolutely the values of the common man of his day. Yet, though he shared the principles, yearnings, and prejudices of his countrymen, he vastly altered their world. What he wrought reconstituted the nature of work and began a profound change in the relationship of man to his job. Near the end of this century it was clear that he had played a major part in creating a new kind of society in which man thought as much about leisure time as about his work. Ironically, the idea of leisure itself, or even worse, a leisure culture, was anathema to him. He was never entirely comfortable with the fruits of his success, even though he lived in a magnificent fifty-six-room house. "I still like boiled potatoes with the skins on," he said, "and I do not want a man standing back of my chair at table laughing up his sleeve at me while I am taking the potatoes' jackets off." Of pleasure and material things he was wary: "I have never known what to do with money after my expenses were paid," he said, "I can't squander it on myself without hurting myself, and nobody wants to do that."

Only work gave purpose: "Thinking men know that work is the salvation of the race, morally, physically, socially. Work does more than get us our living; it gets us our life."

As a good farm boy should, he hated alcohol and tobacco, and he once said that alcohol was the real cause of World War I—the beer-drinking German taking after the wine-drinking Frenchman. His strength, in his early years—which were also his good years—was in the purity of his technical instincts. "We go forward without facts, and we learn the facts as we go along," he once said. Having helped create an urbanized world where millions of God-fearing young men left the farm and went to the cities, he was profoundly uneasy with his own handiwork, preferring the simpler, slower America he had aided in diminishing. For all his romanticizing of farm life, however, the truth was that he had always been bored by farm work and could not wait to leave the farm and play with machines. They were his real love.

When Ford was born, in 1863, on a farm in Dearborn, Michigan, the Civil War was still on. His mother died at the age of thirty-seven delivering her eighth child. Henry was almost thirteen at the time. He had idolized her, and her death was a bitter blow. "I thought a great wrong had been done to me," he said. Later in his life he not only moved the house in which he grew up to Greenfield Village, and tracked down the Ford family's very own stove, whose serial number he had memorized, he also had a cousin who resembled his mother dress up in an exact imitation of the way she had and wear her hair in just the same style.

His father's people were new Americans. When the great potato blight had struck Ireland in 1846, ruining the nation's most important crop, that country had been devastated. Of a population of eight million, one million had died, and one million had emigrated to America. Among the migrants was William Ford, who had set off to the magic land with two borrowed pounds and his set of tools. He was a skilled carpenter, and when he arrived, he moved quickly to Michigan, where some of his uncles had already settled, and found work laying railroad track. With his savings he bought some land and built a house, in awe of an America that had so readily allowed him to do so. To William Ford, Ireland was a place where a man was a tenant on the land, and America was a place where he owned it.

Henry Ford started school when he was seven. The basic books were the McGuffey Reader; they stressed moral

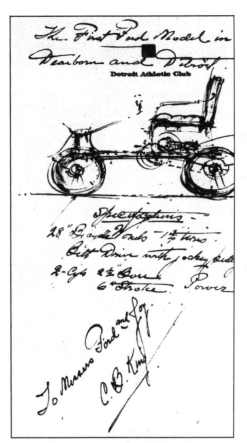

On the fiftieth anniversary of Ford's first car, in 1946, his adviser Charles Brady King made this sketch of it.

values but included sections from Dickens, Washington Irving, and other major writers, which enticed many children into a genuine appreciation of literature. Although Ford loved McGuffey, he did not like books or the alien ideas they sometimes transmitted. "We read to escape thinking. Reading can become a dope habit. . . . Book-sickness is a modern ailment." By that he meant reading that was neither technical nor functional, reading as an end in itself, as a pleasure without a practical purpose. But he was wary even of practical volumes. "If it is in a book, it is at least four years old, and I don't have any use for it," he told one of his designers.

What he truly loved was machinery. From the start, he had a gift for looking at a machine and quickly understanding it, not only to repair it but to make it work better. "My toys were all tools," he wrote years later. "They still are!" In his early teens he designed a machine that allowed his father to close the farm gate without leaving his wagon. Watches fascinated him. When he was given a watch at thirteen, he immediately took it

apart and put it back together. He soon started repairing watches for his friends. His father complained that he should get paid for this, but he never listened, for it was a labor of love.

His father wanted him to become a farmer, but it was a vain hope. Henry Ford hated the drudgery of the farm. In 1879 he entered his seventeenth year, which in those days was considered maturity. On the first day of December of that year, he left for Detroit, a most consequential departure. He walked to the city, half a day's journey.

DETROIT WAS A TOWN OF 116,000, A PLACE of foundries and machine shops and carriage makers. There were some nine hundred manufacturing and mechanical businesses, many of them one-room operations but some of them large. It was an industrial city in the making. Ten railroads ran through it. As New York City, in the next century, would be a mecca for young Americans interested in the arts, Detroit was just becoming a city with a pull for young men who wanted to work with machines. The surge in small industries was beginning, and a young man who was good with his hands could always find a job.

Ford went to work at James Flower & Brothers, a machine shop with an exceptional reputation for quality and diversity of product. As an apprentice there, Ford was immersed in the world of machinery, working among men who, like himself, thought only of the future applications of machines. He made $2.50 a week, boarded at a house that charged him $3.50 a week, and walked to work. His salary left him a dollar a week short, and as a good, enterprising young man, he set out to make up the difference. Hearing that the McGill Jewelry Store had just gotten a large supply of clocks from another store, Ford offered to clean and check them. That job added another two dollars to his weekly salary, so he was now a dollar a week ahead.

His fascination with watches led him to what he was sure was a brilliant idea. He would invent a watch so elementary in design that it could be mass-produced. Two thousand of them a day would cost only thirty cents apiece to make. He was absolutely certain he could design and produce the watch; the only problem, he decided, was in marketing 600,000 watches a year. It was not a challenge that appealed to him, so he dropped the

Ford at Detroit Edison in 1893.

By 1896, at the age of thirty-three, Ford finally had his first car on the street. He couldn't sleep for forty-eight hours before driving it.

project. The basic idea, however, of simplifying the product in order to mass-produce it, stayed with him.

He went from Flower & Brothers to a company called Detroit Dry Dock, which specialized in building steam-boats, barges, tugs, and ferries. His job was to work on the engines, and he gloried in it, staying there two years. There was, he later said, nothing to do every day but learn. In 1882, however, at the age of nineteen, he returned to the farm, and his father offered him eighty acres of land to stay there. William Ford did that to rescue his wayward son from the city and his damnable machines; Henry Ford took it because he momentarily needed security—he was about to marry Clara Bryant. Nothing convinced him more of his love of machines than the drudgery of the farm. Again he spent

every spare minute tinkering and trying to invent and reading every technical magazine he could. He experimented with the sawmill on the farm; he tried to invent a steam engine for a plow. Crude stationary gasoline engines had been developed, and Ford was sure a new world of efficient gasoline-powered machines was about to arrive. He wanted to be part of it. In 1891, with all the timber on the farm cut, he asked Clara to go back to Detroit with him. "He just doesn't seem to settle down," his father said to friends. "I don't know what will become of him."

The last thing Henry Ford was interested in was settling down. He intended, he told his wife, to invent a horseless carriage. But first he needed to know a good deal more about electricity. So he took a job with Detroit Edison at forty-five dollars a month. The city had grown dramatically in the few years since he had first arrived; its population was now more than 205,000. The railroads had begun to open up the country, and, except for Chicago, no town in America had grown as quickly. Detroit now had streetlights. There were more machine shops than ever before. In this city the age of coal and steam was about to end.

By 1896, at the age of thirty-two, Ford finally had his first car on the street. He was so excited by the prospect of his inaugural ride that he barely slept for the forty-eight hours before it. He had been so obsessed and preoccupied during the creation of the car that not until it was time for the test drive did he find that the door of the garage was too small for it to exit. So he simply took an ax and knocked down some of the brick wall to let the automobile out. A friend rode ahead on a bike to warn off traffic. A spring in the car broke during the ride, but they fixed it quickly. Then Henry Ford went home so he could sleep for a few hours before going to work. Later he drove the car out to his father's farm, but William Ford refused to ride in it. Why, he asked, should he risk his life for a brief thrill?

Henry Ford sold that first car for $200 and used the money to start work immediately on his next. It was considerably heavier than the first, and he persuaded a lumber merchant named William Murphy to invest in the project by giving him a ride. "Well," said Murphy when he reached home safely, "now we will organize a company." In August 1899 Murphy brought together a consortium

of men who put up $15,000 to finance Ford's Detroit Automobile Company. Ford thereupon left Detroit Edison to work full time on his car.

In February 1900, at the threshold of the twentieth century, Ford was ready to take a reporter from the Detroit *News Tribune* for a ride. The car, he said, would go twenty-five miles an hour. The reporter sensed that he was witness to the dawn of a new era. Steam, he later wrote, had been the "compelling power of civilization," but now the shriek of the steam whistle was about to yield to a new noise, the noise of the auto. "What kind of a noise is it?" the reporter asked. "That is difficult to set down on paper. It is not like any other sound ever heard in this world. It was not like the puff! puff! of the exhaust of gasoline in a river launch; neither is it like the cry! cry! of a working steam engine; but a long, quick, mellow gurgling sound, not harsh, not unmusical, not distressing; a note that falls with pleasure on the ear. It must be heard to be appreciated. And the sooner you hear its newest chuck! chuck! the sooner you will be in touch with civilization's latest lisp, its newest voice." On the trip, Ford and the reporter passed a harness shop. "His trade is doomed," Ford said.

Ford, however, was not satisfied. The cars he was making at the Detroit Automobile Company were not far behind the quality of the cars being made by Duryea or Olds, but they remained too expensive for his vision. Ford desperately wanted to make a cheaper car. His stockholders were unenthusiastic. By November 1900 the company had died. But Ford was as determined as ever to make his basic car, and he decided that the way to call attention to himself and pull ahead of the more than fifty competing auto makers was to go into racing. In 1901 he entered a race to be held in Grosse Pointe. He won and became, in that small, new mechanical world, something of a celebrity. That propelled him ahead of his competitors.

Two years later, in 1903, he set out to start the Ford Motor Company. He was forty years old and had, he felt, been apprenticing long enough. There were 800 cars in the city at that time, and some owners even had what were called motor houses to keep them in. Ford soon worked up his plan for his ideal, inexpensive new car, but he needed money—$3,000, he thought, for the supplies for the prototype (the actual cost was $4,000).

He got the financing from a coal dealer named Alexander Malcomson. Ford and Malcomson capitalized their original company for $150,000, with 15,000 shares. Some of the early investors were not very confident. John Gray, Malcomson's uncle, made a 500 percent return on his early investment but went around saying that he could not really ask his friends to buy into the company. "This business cannot last," he said. James Couzens, Malcomson's assistant, debated at great length with his sister, a schoolteacher, on how much of her savings of $250 she should risk in this fledgling operation. They decided on $100. From that she made roughly $355,000. Couzens himself managed to put together $2,400 to invest, and from that, when he finally sold out to Ford in 1919, he made $29 million.

This time Ford was ready. He was experienced, he hired good men, and he knew the car he would build. "The way to make automobiles," he told one of his backers in 1903, "is to make one automobile like another automobile . . . just as one pin is like another pin when it comes from a pin factory, or one match is like another match when it comes from a match factory." He wanted to make many cars at a low price. "Better and cheaper," he would say. "We'll build more of them, and cheaper." That was his complete vision of manufacturing. "Shoemakers," he once said, "ought to settle on one shoe, stove makers on one stove. Me, I like specialists."

But he and Malcomson soon split over the direction of the company: Malcomson, like Ford's prior backers, argued that fancy cars costing $2,275 to $4,775 were what would sell. At the time, nearly half the cars being sold in America fell into this category; a decade later, largely because of Ford, those cars would represent only 2 percent of the market. Malcomson wanted a car for the rich; Ford, one for the multitude. Though the early models were successful—the company sold an amazing total of 1,700 cars in its first 15 months—it was the coming of the Model T in 1908 that sent Ford's career rocketing.

It was the car that Henry Ford had always wanted to build because it was the car that he had always wanted to drive— simple, durable, absolutely without frills, one that the farmer could use and, more important, afford. He was an agrarian populist, and his own people were farmers, simple people; if he could make their

lives easier, it would give him pleasure. He planned to have a car whose engine was detachable so the farmer could also use it to saw wood, pump water, and run farm machinery.

THE MODEL T WAS TOUGH, COMPACT, AND light, and in its creation Ford was helped by breakthroughs in steel technology. The first vanadium steel, a lighter, stronger form developed in Britain, had been poured in the United States a year before the planning of the Model T. It had a tensile strength nearly three times that of the steel then available in America, yet it weighed less and could be machined more readily. Ford instantly understood what the new steel signified. He told one of his top men, Charles Sorensen, that it permitted them to have a lighter, cheaper car.

The T was a brilliantly simple machine: when something went wrong, the average owner could get out and fix it. Unimproved dirt tracks built for horses, which made up most of the nation's roads and which defeated fancier cars, posed no problem for it. Its chassis was high, and it could ride right over serious bumps. It was, wrote Keith Sward, a biographer of Ford, all bone and muscle with no fat. Soon the Ford company's biggest difficulty was in keeping up with orders.

Because the Model T was so successful, Ford's attention now turned to manufacturing. The factory and, even more, the process of manufacturing, became his real passions. Even before the T, he had been concerned about the production process. In 1906 he had hired an industrial efficiency expert named Walter Flanders and offered him a whopping bonus of $20,000 if he could make the plant produce 10,000 cars in 12 months. Flanders completely reorganized the factory and beat the deadline by two days. He also helped convince Ford that they needed a larger space. Flanders understood that the increasing mechanization meant that the days of the garage-shop car maker were over. There was a process now, a *line,* and the process was going to demand more and more money and employees. Flanders understood that every small success on the line, each increment that permitted greater speed of production (and cut the cost of the car), mandated as well an inevitable increase in the size of the company. "Henceforth the history of the industry will be the

Ford at the turn of the century.

The way to make cars, Ford said in 1903, is to make one like another, "just as one pin is like another pin, or one match like another match."

history of the conflict of giants," he told a Detroit reporter.

FORD THEREUPON BOUGHT HIS HIGHLAND Park grounds. Here he intended to employ the most modern ideas about production, particularly those of Frederick Winslow Taylor, the first authority on scientific industrial management. Taylor had promised to bring an absolute rationality to the industrial process. The idea was to break each function down into much smaller units so that each could be mechanized and speeded up and eventually flow into a straight-line production of little pieces becoming steadily larger. Continuity above all. What Ford wanted, and what he soon got, was a mechanized process that, in the words of Keith Sward, was "like a river and its tributaries," with the subassembly tributaries

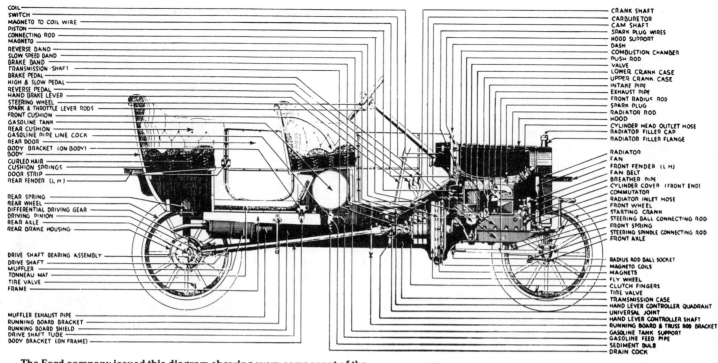

COIL
SWITCH
MAGNETO TO COIL WIRE
PISTON
CONNECTING ROD
MAGNETO
REVERSE BAND
SLOW SPEED BAND
BRAKE BAND
TRANSMISSION SHAFT
BRAKE PEDAL
HIGH & SLOW PEDAL
REVERSE PEDAL
HAND BRAKE LEVER
STEERING WHEEL
SPARK & THROTTLE LEVER RODS
FRONT CUSHION
GASOLINE TANK
REAR CUSHION
GASOLINE PIPE LINE COCK
REAR DOOR
BODY BRACKET (ON BODY)
BODY
CURLED HAIR
CUSHION SPRINGS
DOOR STRIP
REAR FENDER (L H)
REAR SPRING
REAR WHEEL
DIFFERENTIAL DRIVING GEAR
DRIVING PINION
REAR AXLE
REAR BRAKE HOUSING
DRIVE SHAFT BEARING ASSEMBLY
DRIVE SHAFT
MUFFLER
TONNEAU MAT
TIRE VALVE
FRAME
MUFFLER EXHAUST PIPE
RUNNING BOARD BRACKET
RUNNING BOARD SHIELD
DRIVE SHAFT TUBE
BODY BRACKET (ON FRAME)

CRANK SHAFT
CARBURETOR
CAM SHAFT
SPARK PLUG WIRES
HOOD SUPPORT
DASH
COMBUSTION CHAMBER
PUSH ROD
VALVE
LOWER CRANK CASE
UPPER CRANK CASE
INTAKE PIPE
EXHAUST PIPE
FRONT RADIUS ROD
SPARK PLUG
RADIATOR ROD
HOOD
CYLINDER HEAD OUTLET HOSE
RADIATOR FILLER CAP
RADIATOR FILLER FLANGE
RADIATOR
FAN
FRONT FENDER (L H)
FAN BELT
BREATHER PIPE
CYLINDER COVER (FRONT END)
COMMUTATOR
RADIATOR INLET HOSE
FRONT WHEEL
STARTING CRANK
STEERING BALL CONNECTING ROD
FRONT SPRING
STEERING SPINDLE CONNECTING ROD
FRONT AXLE
RADIUS ROD BALL SOCKET
MAGNETO COILS
MAGNETS
FLY WHEEL
CLUTCH FINGERS
TIRE VALVE
TRANSMISSION CASE
HAND LEVER CONTROLLER QUADRANT
UNIVERSAL JOINT
HAND LEVER CONTROLLER SHAFT
RUNNING BOARD & TRUSS ROD BRACKET
GASOLINE TANK SUPPORT
GASOLINE FEED PIPE
SEDIMENT BULB
DRAIN COCK

The Ford company issued this diagram showing every component of the Model T in 1913, five years after the car's birth. It was accompanied by the explanation, "The better you know your car the better will you enjoy it."

merging to produce an ever-more-assembled car.

The process began to change in the spring of 1913. The first piece created on the modern assembly line was the magneto coil. In the past a worker—and he had to be skilled—had made a fly-wheel magneto from start to finish. An employee could make 35 or 40 a day. Now, however, there was an assembly line for magnetos. It was divided into 29 different operations performed by 29 different men. In the old system it took twenty minutes to make a magneto; now it took thirteen.

Ford and his men quickly imposed a comparable system on the assembly of engines and transmissions. Then, in the summer of 1913, they took on the final assembly, which, as the rest of the process had speeded up, had become the great bottleneck. Until then the workers had moved quickly around a stationary metal object, the car they were putting together. Now the men were to remain stationary as the semifinished car moved up the line through them.

One day in the summer of 1913, Charles Sorensen, who had become one of Ford's top production people, had a Model T chassis pulled slowly by a windlass across 250 feet of factory floor,

timing the process all the while. Behind him walked six workers, picking up parts from carefully spaced piles on the floor and fitting them to the chassis. It was an experiment, but the possibilities for the future were self-evident. This was the birth of the assembly line, the very essence of what would become America's industrial revolution. Before, it had taken some thirteen hours to make a car chassis; now they had cut the time of

An oddly wistful 1912 portrait.

assembly in half, to five hours and fifty minutes. Not satisfied, they pushed even harder, lengthening the line and bringing in more specialized workers for the final assembly. Within weeks they could complete a chassis in only two hours and thirty-eight minutes.

Now the breakthroughs came even more rapidly. In January of 1914 Ford installed his first automatic conveyor belt. It was, he said, the first moving line ever used in an industrial plant, and it was inspired by the overhead trolley that the Chicago meat-packers employed to move beef. Within two months of that innovation, Ford could assemble a chassis in an hour and a half. It was a stunning accomplishment, but it merely whetted his zeal. Everything now had to be timed, rationalized, broken down into smaller pieces, and speeded up. Just a few years before, in the days of stationary chassis assembly, the best record for putting a car together had been 728 minutes of one man's work; with the new moving line it required only 93 minutes. Ford's top executives celebrated their victory with a dinner at Detroit's Pontchartrain Hotel. Fittingly, they rigged a simple conveyor belt to a five-horsepower engine with a bicycle chain and used the conveyor to serve the food

When Ford began making the Model T, the company's cash balance was $2 million; when production ceased, it was $673 million.

around the table. It typified the spirit, camaraderie, and confidence of the early days.

Henry Ford could now mass-produce his cars, and as he did so, he cut prices dramatically. In 1909 the average profit on a car had been $220.11; by 1913, with the coming of the new, speeded-up line, it was only $99.34. But the total profits to the company were ascending rapidly because he was selling so many more cars. When the company began making the Model T, its cash balance was slightly greater than $2 million. Nineteen years and more than 15 million cars later, when Ford reluctantly came to the conclusion that he had to stop making the T, the company balance was $673 million. But this was not the kind of success that merely made a company richer; it was the beginning of a social revolution.

Ford himself knew exactly what he had achieved—a breakthrough for the common man. "Mass production," he wrote later, "precedes mass consumption, and makes it possible by reducing costs and thus permitting both greater use-convenience and price-convenience." The price of the Model T touring car continued to come down, from $780 in the fiscal year 1910-11 to $690 the following year, to $600, to $550, to, on the eve of World War 1, $360. At that price he sold 730,041 cars. He was outproducing everyone in the world.

IN 1913 THE FORD MOTOR COMPANY, WITH 13,000 employees, produced 260,720 cars; the other 299 American auto companies, with 66,350 employees, produced only 286,770. Cutting his price as his production soared, he saw his share of the market surge—9.4 percent in 1908, 20.3 in 1911, 39.6 in 1913, and with the full benefits of his mechanization, 48 percent in 1914. By 1915 the

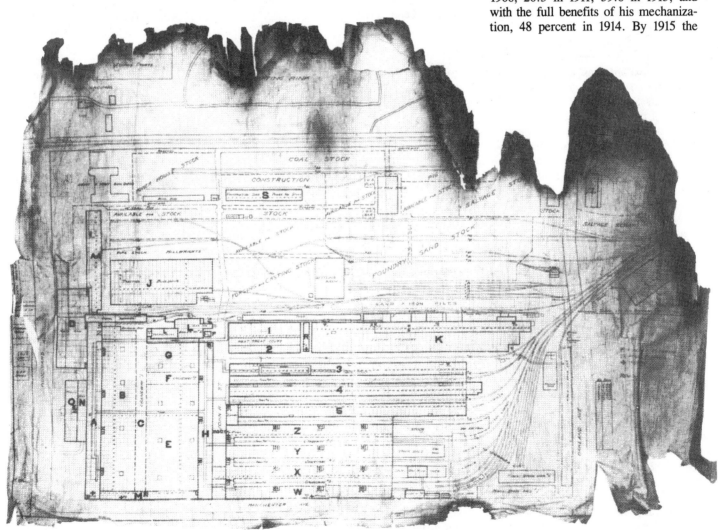

The only surviving plan of the production line that changed the world and made Ford a billionaire is this badly charred 1918 blueprint of the Highland Park plant.

company was making $100 million in annual sales; by 1920 the average monthly earning after taxes was $6 million. The world had never seen anything remotely like it. The cars simply poured off the line. An early illuminated sign in Cadillac Square said, "Watch the Fords Go By." Ford's dreams, in a startlingly brief time, had all come true. He had lived his own prophecy.

There was a moment, however, in 1909 when Ford almost sold the entire company. William C. Durant, the entrepreneur who put General Motors together from several fledgling companies, felt him out about selling the company. An earlier offer of $3 million had fallen through because Ford wanted cash. This time, his company more successful, Ford demanded $8 million. But again he wanted what he called "gold on the table."

Durant couldn't get the financing.

Ford's timing in holding on to his company, it turned out, had been exquisite. There was no point in designing an Everyman's Car unless the average man could buy fuel cheaply as well. The coming of Ford was almost perfectly synchronized with the discovery in the American Southwest of vast new reserves of oil.

If, as has been said, the American century and the oil century were one and the same thing, then that century began on January 10, 1901, in a field just outside of Beaumont, Texas. The name of the field was Spindletop, so called because of the spindly pines that grew there. For years local children had tossed lighted matches into the field; as the flames hit the strong petroleum vapors seeping up through the soil, there would be a satisfying bang. But anyone who believed that there was real oil beneath the ground was thought an eccentric. Oil was not found in Texas; it was found in places like Pennsylvania, West Virginia, and Ohio. Those states were all Standard Oil territory, and the Rockefeller people had no interest in the Southwest. "I will drink any drop of oil west of the Mississippi," boasted John D. Archbold of Standard.

It was Patillo Higgins, a Beaumont man, who had insisted that there was oil underneath Spindletop, and he had been trying to tap it for several years. It had cost him $30,000 of his own money, and he owed friends an additional $17,000. As each attempt had failed and he had been forced to go to others for financial help in order to continue drilling, his

The Model T and its creator, 1921.

As he became one of the most popular men in America, the forces he had set in motion began to summon the darkness in his character.

own share of the operation shrank. Higgins's faith had never flagged, but he had become more and more a figure of ridicule in his hometown. "Millionaire," his neighbors nicknamed him. The drilling had gotten harder and harder; just before New Year's Day they had gone through 140 feet of solid rock. That had taken them to a level of 1,020 feet. On January 10 it happened. A geyser of oil roared out of the ground and shot a hundred feet above the derrick. No one had ever seen anything like it before; with it, the word *gusher* came into use.

At first no one could figure out how much oil the field was producing. Some said 30,000 barrels a day, some said

40,000. Capt. Anthony Lucas, who had become a partner of Higgins, said 6,000, because he had never heard of a larger hole in America. In fact, that one gusher was producing 100,000 barrels a day, roughly 60 percent of the total American production. One new well at Spindletop produced as much as the total from all the 37,000 wells back East in the Rockefeller territory. Within a short time there were five more hits. Eventually analysts found that the oil from the first six holes, some 136 million barrels annually, more than twice surpassed what Russia, then the world's leading petroleum producer, could generate.

Spindletop changed the nature of the American economy and, indeed, the American future. Before the strike, oil was used for illumination, not for energy. (Until 1911 the sales of kerosene were greater than the sales of gasoline.) Spindletop inaugurated the liquid-fuel age in America. The energy of the new age was to be oil, and America suddenly was rich in it.

Texas was providing the gas; Henry Ford was providing the cars. The only limits on him were those imposed by production, and he continued to be obsessed by it. He wanted to put as much of his money as he could back into the factory. He hated bankers and financial people anyway, and he did not want to waste the company's money on stockholders. They were, to his mind, parasites, men who lived off other men's labor. In 1917 the Dodge brothers, who had manufactured many of the early components for Ford and who had been rewarded with sizable amounts of stock, sued him for withholding stock dividends. Some $75 million was at stake. During the trial, Ford testified that putting money back into the plant was the real fun he got from being in business. Fun, the opposing attorney retorted, "at Ford Motor Company expense." Retorted Ford, "There wouldn't be any fun if we didn't try things people said we can't do."

That was the trial in which he referred to the profits he was making as "awful," and when questioned about that by attorneys for the other side, he replied, with absolute sincerity, "We don't seem to be able to keep the profits down." Ford lost the suit, and the court ordered him to pay $19 million in dividends, $11 million of which went to him. The decision probably persuaded him to take as complete control of the company's stock as he

The major production problems had been solved, but labor problems lay ahead when this picture of workers in the Highland Park plant was taken in the 1920s.

could, so that as little money would be wasted as possible. Money to stockholders was a waste, money gone idle; money for the factory was not.

Out of that suit came both the means and the determination to build the River Rouge plant, his great industrial masterpiece, a totally independent industrial city-state. Nothing in the period that followed was too good for the Rouge: it had the best blast furnaces, the best machine tools, the best metal labs, the best electrical systems, the most efficient efficiency experts. Dissatisfied with the supply and quality of the steel he was getting, Ford decided to find out how much it would cost to build a steel plant within the Rouge. About $35 million, Sorensen told him. ''What are you waiting for?'' asked Ford. Equally dissatisfied with both the availability and the quality of glass, he

built a glass factory at the Rouge as well. The price of glass had been roughly thirty cents a square foot early in the life of the T; soon it had soared to $1.50 a foot. With the glass plant at the Rouge, the price came down to twenty cents a foot.

At the Rouge, barges carrying iron ore would steam into the inland docks, and even as they were tying up, huge cranes would be swinging out to start the unloading. Some sixty years later Toyota would be credited for its just-in-time theory of manufacturing, in which parts arrived from suppliers just in time to be part of the final assembly. But in any real sense that process had begun at the Rouge. As Eiji Toyoda, of the Toyota family said in toasting Philip Caldwell, the head of Ford, who in 1982 was visiting Japan: ''There is no secret to

how we learned to do what we do, Mr. Caldwell. We learned it at the Rouge.''

All of this, the creation of the Rouge as the ultimate modern plant, speeded up production even more. Before the opening of the Rouge as an auto plant in 1920 (it had produced submarine chasers for World War I in 1918), it had taken 21 days from the receipt of raw material to the production of the finished car. The Rouge cut that time to 14 days. With the opening of the Rouge steel plant in 1925, it took only 4 days.

The Rouge was Henry Ford's greatest triumph, and with its completion he stood alone as the dominant figure in America and the entire developed world. He had brought the process of manufacture to its ultimate moment; he had given the world the first people's car and by dint of his inventive genius had become

105

America's first billionaire. He was an immensely popular man as well, the man who had lived the American dream. But even then, forces he had helped set in motion would begin to summon forth the darkness in his character.

Part Two
THE DESTROYER

Henry Ford's strengths eventually became his weaknesses. One notorious example was staying with his basic car far too long, ignoring technological change in the cars themselves while obsessively pursuing technological change in their manufacture. From the very start he fought off every attempt to perfect the Model T. In 1912, while he was off on a trip to Europe, his top engineers made some changes intended to improve the car. Their version of the T was lower and some twelve inches longer. It was a better, smoother-riding vehicle, and his associates hoped to surprise and please him. When he returned, they showed it to him. He walked around it several times, finally approaching the left-hand door and ripping it off. Then he ripped off the other door. Then he smashed the windshield and bashed in the roof of the car with his shoe. During all this he said nothing. There was no doubt whose car the T was and no doubt who was the only man permitted to change it. For years anyone wanting to improve a Ford car ran into a stone wall.

What had been another Ford strength, his use of manpower, also turned sour. The early workers at Ford had been skilled artisans, tinkering with designs as they worked. A job at Ford's, as it was known, had been desirable because Henry Ford was at the cutting edge of technology, always trying to do things better, and men who cared about quality wanted to be a part of his operation. In the early days he had his pick of the best men in Detroit. But the mechanized line changed the workplace. These new jobs demanded much less skill and offered much less satisfaction. The pressure to maximize production was relentless. Men who had prided themselves on their skills and had loved working with machines found themselves slaves to those machines, their skills unsummoned. The machines, they discovered to their rage, were more important than they were. The more the plant was mechanized, the more the work force began to unravel.

At the peak of his power, about 1914.

Every year on his birthday, Ford said, he put on one old shoe to remind himself that he had once been poor and might be poor again.

Men began walking out of the Ford plant.

The turnover in the labor force in 1913, the year of the great mechanization, was 380 percent. It soon became even worse. In order to keep one hundred men working, Ford had to hire nearly a thousand. Ford and his principal business partner, James Couzens, realized they had to stabilize the work force. So they came up with the idea of the five-dollar day—that is, of doubling the existing pay. There were some who thought it was Couzens's idea, though Ford later took credit for it. Perceived by many observers as an act of generosity, it was

also an act of desperation. Ford calculated that a five-dollar day would attract the best workers, diminish labor unrest, and thus bring him even greater profits. Besides, he believed, it was a mistake to spend money on the finest machinery and then put those precious machines into the hands of disgruntled, unreliable, perhaps incompetent men.

Ford's instincts were right. Not only did the decision solidify the work force; it was so successful a public relations gesture that it allowed Ford to cut back sharply on his advertising. He liked to refer to it as one of the finest cost-cutting moves he had ever made and insisted that he had no philanthropic intent. This denial of altruism, a young Detroit theologian named Reinhold Niebuhr said later, was "like the assurance of an old spinster that her reputation as a flirt has been grossly exaggerated." Indeed in 1914, 1915, and 1916, the first three years of the five-dollar wage, the Ford Motor Company's profits after taxes were $30 million, $20 million, and $60 million.

To workingmen, the five-dollar day was electrifying. Ford had also instituted an eight-hour workday and with it a third shift, and the day after his announcement of the new wage, 10,000 men turned up at the gates of the plant looking for work. Ford had wanted the pick of workers; the pick he now had. For days the crowds grew, and policemen were needed to keep them under control. It was probably the first time that the fruits of the oil-fueled industrial age had reached down to the average worker. A worker had a grim and thankless job that rarely let him get ahead. He would end his life as he began it, and his children were doomed to the same existence. Now, however, with cheap oil and mass production, the industrial cycle was different. It was more dynamic; it generated much more profit and many more goods, which required customers with money to buy them. The worker became the consumer in an ever-widening circle of affluence.

Ford became perhaps the greatest celebrity of his time. Reporters hung out at his office, and his every word was quoted. That both helped and hurt him, because although he was a certifiable genius in manufacturing and perhaps a semi-genius for a long time in business, much of what he said was nonsense, albeit highly quotable nonsense. On cigarettes: "Study the history of almost any criminal, and you will find an inveterate cigarette smoker." On Jews: "When there is something wrong in this country, you'll find Jews.'' The Jews, he thought, were particularly unproductive people, and he once vowed to pay a thousand dollars to anyone who would bring him a Jewish farmer, dead or alive. He hated the diet of Americans of his generation—''Most people dig their graves with their teeth,'' he once said. He was prophetic about the nutritional uses of the soybean and intuitive about the value of whole wheat bread, and he wanted his friends to eat no bread but whole wheat. He felt that people who wore glasses were making a serious mistake; they should throw away their glasses and exercise their eyes. For almost all his adult life, he used unadulterated kerosene as a hair cream. He did this because he had observed, he said, that men who worked in the oil fields always had good heads of hair. ''They get their hands filled with the oil, and they are always rubbing their hands through their hair,'' he said, ''and that is the reason they have good hair.'' One of the jobs of E. G. Liebold, his private secretary, was to keep a gallon of No. 10 light kerosene on hand for Ford's hair and constantly to watch that it did not turn rancid.

On one occasion someone noticed that his shoes did not match; he replied that every year on his birthday he put on one old shoe to remind himself that he had once been poor and might be poor again.

He was in some ways a shy man. In the old Ford factory his office had a window through which he used to crawl in order to escape visitors. Nonetheless he was acutely aware that his name was the company name and that his personal publicity generally helped the company. All news from the Ford Motor Company was about him. He was also a hard man, and he became harder as he became older. He distrusted friendship and thought it made him vulnerable: friends might want something from him. He used a company group called the Sociological Department—allegedly started to help workers with personal problems in finances or health—to check up on employees and find out whether they drank at home or had union sympathies. If they were guilty of either, they were fired. For all his populism, he always took a dim view of the average employee. Men worked for two reasons, he said. ''One is for wages, and one is for fear of losing their jobs.'' He thought of labor in the simplest terms—discipline. He once told a journalist named William Richards, ''I

Edsel and Henry Ford stand with the ten millionth Model T—and the original quadricycle, Ford's first car—shortly after the T made a transcontinental trip in 1924.

have a thousand men who, if I say, 'Be at the northeast corner of the building at 4:00 A.M.,' will be there at 4:00 A.M. That's what we want—obedience.''

Even in the days before he became isolated and eccentric, he liked playing cruel tricks on his top people. He loved pitting them against one another. A favorite ploy was to give the identical title to two men without telling either about the other. He enjoyed watching the ensuing struggle. The weaker man, he said, would always back down. He liked the idea of keeping even his highest aides anxious about their jobs. It was good for them, he said. His idea of harmony, his colleague Charles Sorensen wrote, ''was constant turmoil.'' The same sort of thing was going on in the factories. The foremen, the men who ruled the factory floor, were once chosen for their ability; now, increasingly, they were chosen for physical strength. If a worker seemed to be loitering, a foreman simply knocked him down. The rules against workers talking to each other on the job were strict. Making a worker insecure was of the essence. ''A great business is really too big to be human,'' Ford himself once told the historian Allan Nevins.

Slowly, steadily, in the twenties, Henry Ford began to lose touch. He had played a critical role in breeding new attitudes in both workers and customers. But as they changed, he did not, and he became more and more a caricature of himself. ''The isolation of Henry Ford's mind is about as near perfect as it is

possible to make it,'' said Samuel Marquis, a Detroit minister who had headed the Sociological Department when its purpose had been to help the employees and who later became its harshest critic.

The Ford Motor Company was no longer a creative operation focused on an exciting new idea and headed by an ingenious leader. For its engineers and designers, the company, only a decade earlier the most exciting place to work in America, was professionally a backwater. Sycophants rose, and men of integrity were harassed. Rival companies were pushing ahead with technological developments, and Ford was standing pat with the Tin Lizzie. His own best people became restless under his narrow, frequently arbitrary, even ignorant, policies. He cut off anyone who disagreed with him. Anyone who might be a threat within the company because of superior leadership ability was scorned as often and as publicly as possible.

EVENTUALLY HE DROVE OUT BIG BILL Knudsen, the Danish immigrant who was largely responsible for gearing up the Ford plants during World War I and was widely considered the ablest man in the company. Knudsen was a formidable production man who had been in charge of organizing and outfitting the Model T assembly plants; he had set up fourteen of them in two years. But his prodigious work during World War I made him a target of perverse attacks by Henry Ford. Knudsen was a big, burly man, six foot three and 230 pounds, and he drank, smoked, and cursed, all of which annoyed the puritanical Ford. Worse, Knudsen was clearly becoming something of an independent figure within the company. He was also drawing closer to Ford's son, Edsel, believing him a young man of talent, vision, and, most remarkable of all, sanity. Together they talked of trying to improve the Model T. All of this merely infuriated the senior Ford and convinced him that Knudsen was an intriguer and becoming too big for his place. Ford took his revenge by making a great show of constantly countermanding Knudsen's production decisions. Knudsen became frustrated with these public humiliations and with the company's failure to move ahead technologically. He finally told his wife that he did not think he could work there any longer. He was sure he was going to have a major confrontation with Henry Ford.

"I can't avoid it if I stay," he said, "and I can't stay and keep my self-respect. I just can't stand the jealousy of the place any more."

"Then get out," she said.

"But I'm making $50,000 a year. That's more money than we can make anywhere else."

"We'll get along," she said. "We did before you went to work there."

In 1921 he quit, virtually forced out. "I let him go not because he wasn't good, but because he was too good—for me," Ford later said.

Knudsen went to General Motors for a starting salary of $30,000, but GM soon put him in charge of its sluggish Chevrolet division. It was the perfect time to join GM. Alfred P. Sloan, Jr., was putting together a modern automotive giant, building on Ford's advances in simplifying the means of production and bringing to that manufacturing success the best of modern business practices. Within three years of Knudsen's arrival, GM became a serious challenger to Ford.

By the early twenties the rumblings from Ford's dealers were mounting. They begged him to make changes in the Model T, but he had become so egocentric that criticism of his car struck him as criticism of himself. Ford defiantly stayed with the Model T. Perhaps 1922 can be considered the high-water mark of Ford's domination of the market. The company's sales were never higher, and with an average profit of $50 a car, it netted more than $100 million. From then on it was downhill. As Chevy made

In 1927, last year of the Model T.

After he built his fifteen millionth Model T, Ford's domination over a market that he himself had created came to an end.

its challenge, the traditional Ford response—simply cutting back on the price—no longer worked. The success of that maneuver had been based on volume sales, and the volume was peaking. From 1920 to 1924 Ford cut its price eight times, but the thinner margins were beginning to undermine Ford's success. The signs got worse and worse. For the calendar year ending February 1924, the Ford company's net profit was $82 million; of that only $41 million came from new cars, and $29 million came from the sales of spare parts. If anything reflected the stagnation of the company, it was that figure.

In 1926 Ford's sales dropped from

1.87 million to 1.67. At the same time, Chevy nearly doubled its sales, from 280,000 to 400,000. America's roads were getting better, and people wanted speed and comfort. In the face of GM's continuing challenge, Henry Ford's only response was once again to cut prices—twice in that year. The Model T was beginning to die. Finally, in May of 1927, on the eve of the manufacture of the fifteenth million Model T, Henry Ford announced that his company would build a new car. The T was dead. His domination over a market that he himself had created was over. With that he closed his factories for retooling, laying off his workers (many of them permanently).

The new car was the Model A. It had shock absorbers, a standard gearshift, a gas gauge, and a speedometer, all things that Chevy had been moving ahead on and that Ford himself had resisted installing. In all ways it seemed better than its predecessor, more comfortable, twice as powerful, and faster. When it was finally ready to be revealed, huge crowds thronged every showplace. In Detroit one hundred thousand people turned up at the dealerships to see the unveiling. In order to accommodate the mob in New York City, the manager moved the car to Madison Square Garden. Editorials ranked the arrival of the Model A along with Lindbergh's solo transatlantic flight as the top news story of the decade. The car was an immense success. Even before it was available, there were 727,000 orders on hand. Yet its success was relatively short-lived, for once again Henry Ford froze his technology. Even the brief triumph of the Model A did not halt the downward spiral of the company. Henry Ford remained locked into the past. The twenties and thirties and early forties at Ford were years of ignorance and ruffianism. Henry Ford grew more erratic and finally senile. At the end of his life he believed that World War II did not exist, that it was simply a ploy made up by the newspapers to help the munitions industry. No one could reach the old man any more. His became a performance of spectacular self-destructiveness, one that would never again be matched in a giant American corporation. It was as if the old man, having made the company, felt he had a right to destroy it.

With Knudsen's departure, the burden of trying to deal with Ford fell on his son, Edsel. Gentle and intelligent, Edsel Ford reflected the contradictions in his

The trim little Model A appeared in 1927: "Excitement could hardly have been greater," said the New York *World* of the crowd shown here, "had Pah-Wah, the sacred white elephant of Burma, elected to sit for seven days on the flagpole of the Woolworth Building."

father's life. He had been born while the Fords were still poor. (As a little boy, Edsel had written Santa Claus a letter complaining: "I haven't had a Christmas tree in four years and I have broken all my trimmings and I want some more.") By the time he entered manhood, his father was the richest man in the country, unsettled by the material part of his success and ambivalent about the more privileged life to which his son was being introduced. Henry Ford wanted to bestow on his son all possible advantages and to spare him all hardship, but, having done that, he became convinced that Edsel was too soft to deal with the harsh, brutal world of industry, symbolized by nothing better than the Ford Motor Company.

Edsel was not a mechanical tinkerer himself, but he had spent his life in the auto business, and he knew who in the company was good and who was not; he was comfortable with the engineers and the designers. Edsel knew times were changing and that the Ford Motor Company was dying. During his father's worst years, Edsel became a magnet for the most talented men in the company, who came to regard his defeats as their defeats. He was a capable executive, and an exceptionally well-trained one: his apprenticeship was full and thorough—and it lasted thirty years. Absolutely confident in his own judgment about both people and cars, Edsel Ford was beloved by his friends and yet respected in the automobile business for his obvious good judgment. "Henry," John Dodge, Henry Ford's early partner and later his rival, once said, "I don't envy you a damn thing except that boy of yours."

Edsel was the first scion of the automotive world. He married Eleanor Clay, a member of the Hudson family that ran Detroit's most famous department store. They were society, and the marriage was a great event, the two worlds of Detroit merging, the old and the new, a Ford and a Clay. Henry Ford hated the fact that Edsel had married into the Detroit elite and had moved to Grosse Pointe. He knew that Edsel went to parties and on occasion took a drink with his friends, not all of whom were manufacturing people and some of whom were upper class—worse, upper-class citified people—and was sure all this had corrupted him. It was as if Edsel, by marrying Eleanor, had confuted one of Henry Ford's favorite sayings: "A Ford will take you anywhere except into society."

ON TOP OF ALL HIS OTHER BURDENS, IT was Edsel's unfortunate duty to represent the future to a father now absolutely locked in a dying past. Genuinely loyal to his father, Edsel patiently and lovingly tried to talk Henry Ford into modernizing the company, but the old man re-

Reluctant author of the Model A, 1928.

By the 1930s the business community had begun to turn against Ford: Fortune called him "the world's worst salesman."

garded his son's loyalty as weakness and spurned him and his advice.

When everyone else in the company agreed that a particular issue had to be brought before the old man, Edsel became the designated spokesman. With Knudsen now gone, he usually stood alone. He was probably the only person who told the truth to his father. Others, such as Sorensen, were supposed to come to Edsel's defense during meetings with Henry, but they never did. Sorensen, brutal with everyone else in the company but the complete toady with the founder, always turned tail in the face of Henry Ford's opposition.

All the while the competition was getting better faster. Chevy had hydraulic brakes in 1924; Ford added them fourteen years later. Because Chevy had already gone to a six-cylinder car, Edsel pleaded even more passionately with his father to modernize the Ford engine. A six, his father retorted, could never be a balanced car. "I've no use for an engine," he said, "that has more spark plugs than a cow has teats." After all, he had built one back in 1909, and he had not liked it.

The six-cylinder engine, more than any other issue, stood between the two Fords. The quintessential story about Henry Ford and the six-cylinder engine—for it reflects not just his hatred of the new but his contempt for his son as well—concerns a project that Edsel and Laurence Sheldrick, the company's chief engineer, had been working on. It was a new engine, a six, and Edsel believed he had gotten paternal permission to start experimenting with it. He and Sheldrick labored for about six months and they were delighted with the prototype. One day when they were just about ready to test it, Sheldrick got a call from Henry Ford.

"Sheldrick," he said, "I've got a new scrap conveyor that I'm very proud of. It goes right to the cupola at the top of the plant. I'd like you to come and take a look at it. I'm really proud of it."

Sheldrick joined Ford for the demonstration at the top of the cupola, where they could watch the conveyor work. To Sheldrick's surprise, Edsel was there too. Soon the conveyor started. The first thing riding up in it, on its way to becoming junk, was Edsel Ford's and Larry Sheldrick's engine.

"Now," said the old man, "don't you try anything like that again. Don't you ever, do you hear?"

In 1936, his company under mounting pressure, Henry Ford reluctantly built a six-cylinder engine. It went into production a year later. But moves like this were too late. By 1933, *Fortune,* reflecting the growing scorn and indeed the contempt of the business community that Henry Ford had once dazzled, called him "the world's worst salesman."

He became more and more distant from the reality of his own company. As he became more senile and more threatened by growing pressure from a restive labor force, he began to cut back on the power of Charlie Sorensen and grant it instead to Harry Bennett, who was head of the company's security forces. Sorensen had been a savage man, hated by many, capable of great cruelty, eager to settle most disputes with his fists, but at least he knew something about production. Bennett was worse. An ex-seaman who had boxed professionally under the name of Sailor Reese, he had come to power in the post-World War I days, when his assignment was to hire bullies and ex-cons and wrestlers and boxers to help control the plant and keep the union out. Bennett was well suited for that role. His was an empire within an empire, and that inner empire was built on fear. He padded his pockets with Ford money— the finances of the company were in chaos. He built at least four houses with his appropriated wealth. His rise exactly paralleled the decline of the old man, and he played on all the fears the old man had, especially fear of labor and fear of kidnapping. Ford was convinced that Bennett, with his connections in the underworld, could stop any attempt to kidnap his son or grandchildren. Ford loved the fact that Bennett used force to intimidate people. "Harry gets things done in a hurry," he liked to say.

To the distress of Ford's family, Bennett's power over Henry grew almost without check in the 1930s, when the founder was in his seventies. Board meetings were a travesty. Often Ford did not show up. Or he would walk in at the last minute with Bennett and after a few minutes say, "Come on, Harry, let's get the hell out of here. We'll probably change everything they do anyway." Once a magazine writer was in a car with Ford and Bennett, and he asked Ford who was the greatest man he had ever known—after all, in so rich and varied a career he had known quite a few exceptional people. Ford simply pointed at Bennett.

At the very end he used Bennett as his principal weapon against his son. The last years were truly ugly. Sure that he was protected by Ford, Bennett harassed Edsel mercilessly. The old man took obvious pleasure in Edsel's humiliations. Already emotionally beaten down by his father, Edsel had become a sick man. He had remained loyal to his father and endured his humiliations while healthy. Now, battling stomach cancer, he had less and less to fight back with. Edsel's last years were very difficult, as he struggled to expedite the war-production work his father hated while at the same time resisting his illnesses. In 1942 Edsel got undulant fever from drinking milk from his father's dairy; Ford disapproved of pasteurization. The old man blamed it on Edsel's bad habits. In 1943 Edsel died. He was only forty-nine. Almost everyone who knew both Henry and Edsel Ford thought the son had really died of a broken heart.

This was the final, malevolent chapter in Henry Ford's own life. Not only had he destroyed his son, he had all but ruined a once-great industrial empire. By the middle of the war, the Ford Motor Company was in such poor shape that high government officials pondered whether to take it over, for the government had to keep the giant going. Without the stimulus of the war and the work it eventually brought the company, it is possible that Ford might have failed completely. As the government debated, two women stepped forward. Clara Bryant Ford and Eleanor Clay Ford, one Henry Ford's wife and the other Edsel's widow, had watched it all with dismay— the old man's senility, the crushing of Edsel, the rise of Bennett—but with a certain helplessness. "Who is this man Bennett who has such power over my husband and my son?" Clara Ford once asked. She had hated the fact that Bennett and Sorensen had both taken it upon themselves to speak for Henry against Edsel and had participated in and encouraged his destruction. Now both women feared that the same forces might prevent young Henry, Edsel's son, from ascending and assuming power.

Henry Ford II had been serving in the Navy during the war, enjoying a taste of personal freedom. But in August 1943, thanks to intervention by his mother and grandmother, he got orders sending him back to Detroit; the nation's highest officials feared that, after Edsel's death, Harry Bennett might actually take over the company. Young Henry returned reluctantly, but he was the firstborn of Edsel Ford, and familial obligation demanded it. He had no illusions about the challenge ahead. He was well aware that, except for a very few men, the Ford Motor Company was a corrupt and corrupting place.

BENNETT AND SORENSEN IMMEDIATELY began belittling him, Bennett by undoing what Henry was attempting to do each day and Sorensen by demeaning him in front of other people and by always calling him "young man." "He might just as well have called me Sonny," Henry later told friends. Henry Ford II might have titular power—he was named vice president in December 1943—and the power of blood, but unless his grandfather moved aside and Bennett left the company, he would never be able to take control. Even Sorensen was in the process of being destroyed by Bennett, and young Henry seemed very vulnerable. Again Eleanor Clay Ford put her foot down and forced an issue. Widowhood had stirred in her the kind of indignation her husband had always lacked. He had been too loyal to challenge his father, but now Edsel's company stock was hers to vote. She threatened to sell it unless old Henry moved aside in favor of his grandson. Her son would not be destroyed as her husband had been. Clara Bryant Ford backed her completely. They fought off the old man's excuses and his delaying ploys. With that threat, and a sense that these women were intensely serious, Henry Ford finally, furiously, gave up, and Henry Ford II took control.

The young man—he was just twenty-eight—had not served the long apprenticeship his father had, and he had only the scantest knowledge of the vast and complicated world he inherited. But it soon became clear that he was shrewd and tough. Through the most unsparing work he mastered the business; and he got rid of Harry Bennett. "You're taking over a billion-dollar organization here that you haven't contributed a thing to!" Bennett yelled. But, having no other recourse, he left.

In the end Henry Ford II broke all of Bennett's cronies and put an end to the bad old era. But there was no way to escape the complex legacy of the founder.

Once a popular figure with the average man, Henry Ford had become known as one of the nation's leading labor baiters. He had helped usher in a new age of economic dignity for the common man, but he could not deal with the consequences. His public statements during the Depression were perhaps the most pitiless ever uttered by any capitalist. He repeatedly said that the Depression was good for the country and the only problem was that it might not last long enough, in which case people might not learn enough from it. "If there is unemployment in America," he said, "it is because the unemployed do not want to work." His workers, embittered by his labor policies, marched against him and were put down by Bennett's truncheons and guns. His security people were so vicious that when Ford's workers marched against the company, the workers wore masks over their faces to hide their identities—something rare in America. Nothing could have spoken more eloquently of tyrannical employment practices.

IN BUSINESS HENRY FORD WAS OVERTAKEN by General Motors, which relentlessly modernized its design, its production, and its marketing. GM fed the appetites Ford had helped create. In addition, GM inaugurated a dynamic that haunted the Ford company for the next fifty years; buyers started out driving Fords when they were young and had little money, but slowly, as their earnings rose, they graduated to more expensive GM cars. As a workingman's hero, Ford was replaced by FDR. What had once been charming about his eccentricity now became contemptible.

Nothing reflected his failures more tellingly than the fate of the River Rouge manufacturing complex. It was an industrial masterpiece, and it should have stood long after his death as a beacon to the genius of its founder. But the treatment of human beings there had been so mean and violent, the reputation of the Rouge so scurrilous, that in the postwar era it stood as an embarrassment to the new men running Ford, a reputation that had to be undone.

The bequeathment had other unfortunate aspects. By fighting the unions so unalterably for so long, Ford and the other Detroit industrialists had ensured that, when the unions finally won power, they would be as strong as the companies themselves, and that there would be a carry-over of distrust and hatred. There were other, more concrete, burdens as well. Because he had been locked in the past and had frozen his technology, the company was on the verge of bankruptcy.

Probably no major industrial company in America's history was ever run so poorly for so long. By the beginning of 1946, it was estimated, Ford was losing $10 million a month. The chaos was remarkable, but some of it, at least, was deliberate. The old Henry Ford hated the government and in particular the federal income tax, and by creating utter clerical confusion he hoped to baffle the IRS. He also hated bookkeepers and accountants; as far as he was concerned, they were parasitical. When Arjay Miller, who later became president of the company, joined Ford in 1946, he was told to get the profit forecast for the next month.

Miller went down to the Rotunda, where the financial operations were centralized, or at least supposed to be. There he found a long table with a lot of older men, who looked to him like stereotypes of the old-fashioned bookkeeper. These men were confronted by bills, thousands of bills, and they were dividing them into categories—A, B, C, D. The piles were immense, some several feet high. To Miller's amazement the bookkeepers were actually estimating how many million dollars there were per foot of paper. That was the system.

Miller asked what the estimates for the following month's profits were. One of the men working there looked at him and asked, ''What do you want them to be?''

''What?'' asked Miller.

''I can make them anything you want.''

He meant it, Miller decided. It was truly a never-never land.

It was not surprising, then, that the young Henry Ford, seeking to bring sense to the madness he found all around him, turned to an entirely new breed of executive—the professional managers, the bright, young financial experts who knew, if not automobiles and manufacturing plants, then systems and bottom lines. To them Henry Ford II gave nearly unlimited power. And they, in turn, would in the years to come visit their own kind of devastation on the company. The legacy of what the old man had done in his last thirty years left a strain of tragic unreason in the inner workings of the company. So, once again did the past influence the future. For the past was always present.

TO FIND OUT MORE There has been a great deal written about Henry Ford—in fact two large new biographies have come out this year—but one older book that David Halberstam found particularly readable was Keith Sward's ''irreverent'' *The Legend of Henry Ford,* originally published in 1948 and reissued as a paperback by Atheneum in 1968. There is also, he said, a ''very good small book'' by Anne Jardim, *The First Henry Ford,* published by the MIT Press in 1970. Allan Nevins's trilogy, *Ford,* much praised by scholars, is no longer in print but is still available in libraries. For a vivid sense of the man's life, readers can visit Henry Ford's Greenfield Village in Dearborn, Michigan, which is open year-round. Writing about this ''stupendous'' museum in the December 1980 issue of American Heritage, Walter Karp said that the collection reflects Ford's mind so intimately that it becomes almost a three-dimensional autobiography.

Media and Morality in the Twenties

'I want to be naughty and yet be nice'—John D. Stevens *recounts how small-town America fought a losing battle against the louche temptations offered by magazines, tabloids and the movies.*

John D. Stevens

John D. Stevens is Professor of Communication at the University of Michigan; Fellow of Gannett Center for Media Studies, Columbia University and co-author of Mass Media Between the Wars: Perspectives of Cultural Tensions, 1918–1941 *(Syracuse University Press, 1984).*

American society was racked in the 1920s by clashes in moral standards. The rural and small-town population was fighting a series of rearguard actions to retain control and to enforce its standards on the rising cities. Each ten yearly census recorded the steady march toward urbanity. Many things about the city alarmed the ruralists, but nothing so much as its low morals. The most visible struggle was against gambling, jazz music, stage nudity and Sunday entertainment and shopping.

There also was a vigorous struggle against allegedly immoral and salacious magazines, books and films, almost none of which took place in courtrooms. The citizens of the midwest villages and towns instead used moral persuasion on local newsstands. By keeping the snappy joke books, confessions magazines and modern novels under the counter, everybody could pretend they did not exist.

In his famous essay of 1931, F. Scott Fitzgerald denounced this smug hypocrisy:

Meanwhile their granddaughters pass the well-thumbed copy of *Lady Chatterly's Lover* around the boarding school and, if they get about at all, know the taste of gin or corn [liquor] at sixteen. But the gener-

ation who reached maturity between 1875 and 1895 continue to believe what they want to believe.

Similarly, the owner of the Bijoux kept a wary eye on the films sent to him by distributors, who were mixing in more features emphasising crime and immoral behaviour with the traditional shoot-'em-up Westerns and custard-pie comedies. Some weekly newspapers worried that even the most innocuous films gave sanctions to vicious acts. Certainly in their sociological study of 'Middletown' (Muncie, Indiana), the Lynds chronicled the considerable impact of cinema on community values and ideas.

Films—and especially the titles—did get much franker. The cinema of the 1920s began with *Broken Blossoms* and *Pollyanna* and ended with The *Redeeming Sin* and *Companionate Marriage*. It was a long step from Mary Pickford and Dorothy Gish to Theda Bara and Clara Bow—too long for the taste of many.

In the few prosecutions that were brought, neither the purveyor of print nor celluloid sex had much hope of winning. The accepted legal definition of obscenity was the hoary Hicklin Rule, handed down by a British judge in 1868. Under it, material was obscene if there was any chance it might fall into the hands of someone it might deprave or corrupt—in short, a child or the village idiot. American courts interpreted the law to mean that a single word or phrase, completely out of context, could make an entire work legally obscene. To make matters worse, the Supreme Court had ruled in 1915 that motion pictures were

simply spectacles and had no constitutional protection as expression.

Postal inspectors kept a look-out for alleged pornography. In the most celebrated ease of the decade, Mary Ware Dennett, a Brooklyn mother who had put together a short compilation of sex information for adolescents, was convicted of postal obscenity. Her pamphlet had been praised in the press and from pulpits, and distributed by doctors and the YMCA. Even after she lost her mailing permit, she continued to send the pamphlet at the full first-class rate. In 1928, the Post Office charged her under the Comstock Law. Although she was convicted, the national outcry signalled a changing public attitude.

Although the *Police Gazette* and even bolder stuff sometimes was passed around at the barber shop, like the occasional 'stag movie' at the lodge hall and the town brothel, those were silently condoned as 'men's business'. An article in *Scientific American* in 1878 praised photography as a new way to see. Nowhere did photography find faster acceptance than in the United States.

Almost everyone was more worried about the pernicious effects of illustration than of words. Magazines and newspapers shifted in the early years of the century from drawings to photographs. Pictures could corrupt even those too young to read.

Explicit depictions were easier to oppose than suggestiveness. As Susan Sontag has pointed out, the history of photography has been a struggle between beautification and truth-telling. The first tradition was borrowed from fine art, the

By John D. Stevens. First published in *History Today,* November 1989, pp. 25-29. Reproduced by kind permission of History Today, Ltd., 83-84 Berwick Street, London W1V 3PJ, England.

second from science. Photographs record 'what is there' but the moral guardians feared even more their power to suggest much more.

And then, along came motion pictures, which from their beginning had a tremendous appeal for youngsters. Social scientists documented how often children, at least city children, were attending the cinema. One study found 71 per cent of boys and 64 per cent of girls attended at least once a week. They bought nearly half the tickets and overwhelmingly preferred crime films.

A judge was quoted in the *New York Times* in 1920 as saying 'At the movies the young see things they never should be allowed even to hear or think about. Under such conditions the downfall of young girls is not remote.' Films 'have directly stimulated juvenile delinquency and crime' charged *Christian Century,* a leading Protestant magazine.

In the wake of a series of Hollywood scandals in 1921 and 1922, eight states and dozens of communities established censorship boards. To stem the spread of such boards and to blunt the demands for federal censorship of films, the Hollywood producers hired as 'czar', Will Hays, Harding's eminently respectable Postmaster General and a deacon in his own church. Although critics soon charged that Hays was more interested in cleaning up the image of the cinema than the films themselves, he took his assignment seriously (Hays was a man who took *everything* seriously). From 1922 until 1925, censorship referenda went down to defeat in all thirty-seven places that considered them. Producers went on cashing in on glimpses of lingerie, legs and bosoms.

The Hays Office reviewed both scripts and finished prints to eliminate any material which might give offence. Without its seal, distributors and exhibitors would not touch a film. Once it had done that, the feature had to run the gauntlet of all the local censorship boards, which were even higher and much more capricious. Of 578 releases in 1928, only forty-two survived unscathed the scrutiny of all state boards. They required nearly 2,000 changes, of which less than one-third had anything to do with sex. Most related to the depiction of crime. Many city boards were even tougher. For example, the Chicago board insisted on nearly 7,000 changes in one year.

Moralists were as outraged by the off-screen as by the on-screen immorality in Hollywood. Seldom has the public reacted so strongly against a public figure as it did against Roscoe (Fatty) Arbuckle. The funny-man was accused of the death of an actress during a wild party in his hotel suite. Many cities adopted laws against playing any of his films. Even after three juries failed to convict Arbuckle, his films were withdrawn and he was barred from Hollywood. Hays stirred a hornet's nest when he proposed his reinstatement.

It may be an exaggeration to say that within fifteen minutes of learning to use a camera, men were making sex films, but they were among the first films produced. However, one kind of 'educational' film was approved. Building on the war-induced concern about venereal disease, some producers existing on the fringe of Hollywood respectability made a lot of money with sex hygiene films. Usually there were separate showings and separate reels for men and for women and, almost always, screenings were accompanied by a lecturer with some sort of medical credential. In the name of education and with the blessing of community leaders, the crowds flocked to look at genitals, diseased though they were. Titles (which were changed frequently) included the *The Naked Truth, Is Your Daughter Safe? The Road to Ruin,* and *Are You Fit to Marry?*

A crackdown on distributors in 1928 by the Hays Office effectively ended bookings in big cities, but the VD films were shown in small towns for years.

Although in many towns, there were showings of out-and-out stag films (often in an American Legion post or fraternal hall), they drew little criticism; to criticise would have been to acknowledge their existence. While attendance was by invitation only, few males grew to manhood without viewing at least one. Some towns ended the showings only with the advent of pornographic videotapes.

Variety reported in 1929 a flood of such films, calling most of them 'plenty raw'. Although the bulk of those films were not preserved, there are nine stag films from the 1920s in the Kinsey Institute's collection at Indiana University, all brief (less than ten minutes), silent, and in black-and-white, and depicting one white couple engaged in heterosexual sex. Titles include: The *Casting Couch, The Passionate Farm Hand* and *She Couldn't Say 'No'*.

Captain Billy's Whiz Bang was the pacesetter amongst joke books. It was published by some veterans, upon returning from France. Its circulation reached 250,000 a month, each copy undoubtedly passing through many sweaty hands. Like its numerous imitators, *Captain Billy* was—quite literally—kids' stuff. It was the youngsters (presumably, nearly all boys) who plunked down their quarters. Naturally parents assumed they must be awful. In fact, each sixty-four page issue was crammed with innocent he-she jokes, a few girlie and outhouse cartoons, bowderised verse and very short stories. Dashes were used for even the mildest profanity (for example 'd - - n'). No issue was ever banned from the post. A representative 1921 cover features a cartoon of a girl skier, head-first in a snow bank, her shapely legs protruding, while men ogled rather than went to her rescue. Especially in small towns, this was pretty hot stuff.

A typical wisecrack appeared in the issue of August, 1929: 'I call my girl rheumatism—she gets stiff in the joints.' The last lines of a poem about a flapper, from the same issue summarised the magazine itself:

I want the lights that brightly shine;
I want the men—I want the wine.
I want the fun without the price.
I want to be naughty and yet be nice.

It published no photographs and carried no advertising but at its peak in 1923 was turning a monthly profit of $35,000. Those profits provided the seed money for the Fawcett Publications empire, of which *True Confessions* became the bellweather.

Captain Billy copy-cats included *Hot Dog, Red Peppers* and *Hi-Jinks*. These magazines offended others besides small town prudes. Oswald Villard, one of the nation's most respected editors, denounced them as 'out and out vulgar'.

If moralists fretted about the effects of such magazines on boys, what must they have thought about the damage of the new breed of confession magazines on young girls? Bobbed-haired girls peeked out from every cover, boasting story titles like 'Harem Girl' 'When a Girl Trifles' and 'My Mistake'.

King of that field was Bernard MacFadden, the eccentric millionaire who championed physical fitness and free love. Seven years after he launched *True Story* in May 1919, it had a circulation of 2 million and annual advertising revenues of $3 million. Soon, he added such monthlies as *True Romance* and *True*

Experiences. For 15 to 25 cents, they all served up features on fashion, beauty tips and contests, but the emphasis was on the sentimental stories, all illustrated with both sketches and studio-posed photographs. The confession magazines spread the gospel of sexual freedom to millions, who had never read Freud. In text and photographs, these magazines presented sex far more frankly than did the newspapers.

A 1926 advertisement for *True Story* showed a couple hovering in the darkness with this headline: 'Soul-Maddening Despair Follows a Midnight Adventure'. In fact, the magazines usually delivered less than they promised, the height of their eroticism being a kiss in the closing paragraph. A typical story ended this way: the scene is the deck of a steamer on a star-filled night in the Caribbean. He tells his love that a sailor's tradition says that the gods demand a very definite return for such beauty, and that the price is a kiss for every star. As she tilts her face upward, she murmurs 'I've always heard that it's the woman who pays—and pays'.

A Methodist minister in a small Michigan town thought these 'salacious magazines' were worse than films. He warned that if the town's young people kept reading such filth, 'it will not be long before Alpena will have the same revolting sex crimes, the same unspeakable

conditions among high school students' that were plaguing larger cities. Not everyone agreed, of course. For example, a reader wrote to Street and Smith's weekly, *Illustrated Love Story Magazine* to say her mother believed the stories useful in teaching a girl 'a whole lot of this world'.

MacFadden had several brushes with the law for stories and pictures he published in his garish tabloid, the *New York Graphic,* during the 1920s. The New York vice society often reported the paper for alleged obscenity, and newsstands in several nearby cities refused to carry the paper, or at least especially lurid issues, such as the ones carrying many pages on the titilating 'Peaches and Daddy' Browning separation hearing of 1927.

Much of that outcry was aimed at the faked pictures. Models would pose for photographs to illustrate stories in the news, and then the photo editor would paste on the faces of the real participants. In one infamous case, the *Graphic* published a photograph of the recently deceased film star, Rudolph Valentino, being welcomed to Heaven by Enrico Caruso; in another it published a photograph of Charles Lindberg alone in his plane over the Atlantic. Such shenanigans only made the newspaper photograph more suspect.

Although a New York daily carried a news photograph in 1880, it was another

seventeen years before the *New York Tribune* published the first photograph on a high-speed rotary press. By 1890, technology made the publication of photographs practical, but newspaper editors were reluctant to shift from the familiar woodcuts. Newspaper photography won its spurs at the turn of the century as the servant of yellow journalism, a connection it would never quite live down.

Since MacFadden's sunbathing and art magazines featured photographs of unclothed frolickers (usually engaged in activities no more provocative than playing volleyball), MacFadden shipped those copies by train to avoid postal scrutiny. If small-town retailers sold them at all, it was from under the counter.

In the decade following the First World War Americans struggled to find new moral standards. Their mass media not only recorded that ambivalence, but was, itself, part of the debate.

FOR FURTHER READING

David Burner, *The Politics of Provincialism* (Alfred A. Knopf, 1968); Catherine Covert and John Stevens, *Mass Media Between the Wars* (Syracuse University Press, 1984); F. Scott Fitzgerald, 'Echoes of the Jazz Age' *Scribner's,* November 1931; Robert S. and Helen M. Lynd, *Middletown* (Harcourt Brace, 1929); Geoffrey Perrett, *America in the Twenties* (Simon and Schuster, 1982).

From the Great Depression to World War II

Republicans had proclaimed a "New Era" of continuous economic growth during the 1920s. With the exception of some groups such as farmers, Americans had enjoyed an unprecedented prosperity during the decade. Scholars still debate whether there was a direct connection between the stock market crash of October 1929 and what followed, but the Great Depression was the worst in the nation's history. President Herbert Hoover denied responsibility for the economic disaster and repeatedly assured the nation that recovery was just around the corner. He did support more legislation to deal with the problem than had any of his predecessors, but in 1932 the voters opted for change when conditions failed to improve.

Franklin D. Roosevelt won more because he was not Hoover than because of any coherent program he offered the public. He won in a landslide. Immediately after his inauguration he launched what became known as the "first 100 days," an almost frenzied period during which the administration sent to Congress an avalanche of bills to halt and reverse the downslide. Critics pointed out that some of the proposals contradicted one another, but this had little effect in an atmosphere of crisis. Roosevelt deflected such criticism by likening himself to a football quarterback: he would try different plays, then retain those that worked while discarding others.

Many historians have made distinctions between what they refer to as the "early" or "first" and the "late" or "second" New Deal. Emphasis during the early period was on recovery. Agencies were created, for instance, to provide public employment only until the economy became self-sustaining, at which time they would be phased out. The "second" New Deal focused more on permanent reforms designed to prevent future downturns or to mitigate their consequences. Overall, the New Deal helped cushion the effects of the Depression, but did not cure it. This was shown in 1937 when cutbacks in a number of programs caused economic indicators to plunge once again. By 1938 a coalition of Republicans and conservative Democrats blocked further experimentation. Only the onset of war in Europe in 1939 and the American preparedness program began to get the economy moving.

Adolf Hitler's rise to power in Germany and Japan's aggression in the 1930s once more raised the specter of war. Most Americans, disillusioned by the results of the Great War, were determined to stay out. Roosevelt himself, preoccupied with domestic affairs, was uncertain about what, if anything, could be done. Toward the end of the decade, he took a more active role in trying to support nations threatened by aggression. He had to move cautiously because of a deeply divided public. Critics claimed then, and some do now, that his economic policies toward Japan forced its leaders to conclude that war was the only solution. The attack on Pearl Harbor, however, effectively united the public in behalf of the war effort.

Japan's early campaign's against woefully unprepared American and British possessions succeeded beyond expectations. The tide began turning as early as the battle of Coral Sea in May 1942, however, and the battle of Midway in June inflicted a stunning defeat on Japan. Many months of savage fighting lay in store as the Japanese tenaciously resisted the Allied advance across the Pacific. Whether an invasion of the Japanese home island would have been necessary to compel surrender can never be known. Atomic bombs dropped on Hiroshima and Nagasaki caused Japan to surrender in mid-August of 1945.

Campaigns against Germany and Italy began in North Africa in the autumn of 1942, then in Sicily and Italy in 1943. Finally, in June 1944, the long-awaited invasion of the European continent began. Italy pulled out of the war early; the Germans continued fighting until they were crushed between Allied forces advancing from the west and the mighty Soviet juggernaut that had borne the brunt of fighting for years. Hitler committed suicide in his Berlin bunker, and German forces surrendered three months before the Japanese did.

As president, Franklin D. Roosevelt supported legislation that benefited organized labor. His reelection in 1936 by an unprecedented margin came in part from working class support. " 'Give Us Roosevelt': Workers and the New Deal Coalition" reveals how this relationship ran into trouble within a few years, and also describes the gulfs that developed between unions and nonwhite workers who were largely unorganized. "Things to Come: The 1939 New York World's Fair" tells how the fair dazzled Depression-weary Americans with exhibits promising a world of future delights that technology would make possible. "1941" offers a survey of conditions at home and abroad during that fateful year.

"Freedom" and "democracy" were words many Americans associated with the Allied cause during World War II, as opposed to the Nazi and Japanese tyranny and repression. "Racism and Relocation: Telling the Japanese-American Experience" recounts how one group of people, solely because of their race, were denied basic rights. " 'Since You Went Away': The War Letters of America's

Women" is based on thousands of letters written by women from all walks of life. Among other things, they show that the experiences many women went through raised their self-confidence and sense of worth.

Even though the United States suffered no physical destruction through invasion or bombing, World War II ushered in profound changes in the economic structure, race relations, and attitudes toward young people. "The Face of Victory" evaluates the war's impact and shows how many of the changes are still with us.

Looking Ahead: Challenge Questions

What did organized labor achieve during the New Deal? Why, in view of this, did some union leaders begin to criticize Franklin Roosevelt after 1936?

How could those who wished to "relocate" Japanese-Americans justify their views?

What changes in American society brought about during World War II have had lasting impact?

How did the experiences of women heighten their sense of independence?

'GIVE US ROOSEVELT' WORKERS AND THE NEW DEAL COALITION

Bruce Nelson traces how the magic of FDR and his practical social programmes welded American labour to the Democratic Party, and discusses the tensions that eventually weakened that union.

Happy days are here again – clothing workers at a 'Re-elect FDR' rally in Baltimore, 1936.

Bruce Nelson

Bruce Nelson is Assistant Professor of History at Dartmouth College, New Hampshire, and the author of Workers on the Waterfront *(University of Illinois Press, 1988).*

Nearly forty-five years after his death, Franklin D. Roosevelt's reputation as one the greatest vote-getters in the history of American politics remains intact. His smashing victory over Alf Landon in 1936 marked not only the zenith of his own popularity and power but a decisive step in the major political realignment that made the Democrats the nation's majority party after nearly forty years of Republican dominance. Although FDR attracted support from many sectors of the population, workers constituted the heart of the Roosevelt coalition.

Before the 1930s American workers had seldom if ever voted as a bloc at the national level. Cultural, ethnic, and racial divisions had driven them into different electoral camps. However, an erratic but increasingly persistent trend toward a more unified labour vote had begun developing early in the twentieth century. By 1928, the votes of urban, foreign-stock, and largely working-class voters for the Democrat Al Smith had provided a clear harbinger of the realignment that would become evident with Roosevelt's defeat of Herbert Hoover in 1932 and would solidify during his presidency.

In 1936 FDR won a then unprecedented 60.8 per cent of the popular vote and outpolled Landon by 523 to 8 in the electoral college. His landslide victory reflected the apparent willingness of the New Deal to 'deliver the goods' to the working class and to millions of other Americans who had suffered unprecedented losses during the depths of the Great Depression. The administration's commitment to relief payments and public works projects for the unemployed and hungry, along with the passage of the Social Security and National Labor Relation Acts, convinced working people that the president was on their side. Critics on the left could point out that even at its peak the principal federal relief agency provided jobs for only about a quarter of those counted as unemployed. But working people revered the president not only for what he had done, but for the things he wanted to do that remained undone, for the contrast between a compassionate FDR and an apparently uncaring and immobile predecessor, for the hatred he generated among the wealthy and others who were identified as oppressors of the 'forgotten man'. As major sectors of corporate capital went all out to defeat Roosevelt in 1936, he deftly sharpened the lines of division to his advantage with a series of verbal assaults on 'organised money' and the 'economic royalists'. Desperately, Republican nominee Alf Landon protested that the president was violating sacred American norms by injecting class conflict into the realm of politics. But Roosevelt's strategy worked brilliantly. In the aftermath of the election, the anonymous interviewee who stated that 'Mr. Roosevelt is the only man we ever had in the White House who would understand that my boss is a son-of-a-bitch' apparently spoke for millions of his fellow workers.

However, the euphoria of 1936 quickly gave way to unanticipated stumbling blocks that would bedevil the president's second administration and cast a long shadow on the 1940 election. Bitter class conflict—generated by virulent employer resistance to the aggressive organising campaigns of the Committee for Industrial Organization, or CIO—threatened to shatter the new and fragile Roosevelt coalition; another sharp economic downturn, dubbed the 'Roosevelt recession', rapidly eroded the president's aura of invincibility. By the end of 1938, attempts to implement the New Deal's increasingly social-democratic intellectual premises had run up against the impenetrable political reality of an effective congressional bloc of Republicans and conservative Democrats who were determined to thwart any new social welfare initiatives. In addition, the coming of war in Europe turned Roosevelt's priorities away from domestic reform and towards a new politics of national unity, which meant the embrace of prominent individuals in the business community who were ambivalent at best about the New Deal but shared the president's

determination to mobilise the nation to resist the expansion of German power.

Moreover, by 1940, in sharp contrast to 1936, a number of organised labour's most influential spokesmen bitterly condemned Roosevelt's course and outspokenly opposed his re-election. The outstanding example is John L. Lewis, the charismatic leader of the United Mine Workers and the CIO, who believed that the president had betrayed his working-class supporters by remaining aloof from the bloody class warfare in the steel industry during the spring and summer of 1937. Lewis' disenchantment only increased as the second Roosevelt administration unfolded, and in October 1940 he went on nationwide radio and called upon the CIO faithful to join him in voting for the Republican candidate, Wendell Willkie. The Communists and their sympathisers, who held leadership positions in a number of important CIO unions could not bring themselves to swallow Willkie and the Republicans, but by 1940 they had turned against the president and were calling upon their followers to sit out the election.

Roosevelt broke the third term taboo and won a comfortable 55 per cent of the popular vote, in an election where the 'index of class polarisation' reached its highest point in American history. Compared to 1936, there was a decline in the level of support for FDR among virtually every segment of the population. The president lost from a quarter to a third of the votes of white-collar workers and the middle classes generally. But the erosion of working-class support was much smaller. Overall, in 1940 as in 1936, blue-collar workers voted overwhelmingly for FDR and were a critical factor in his continued success. Moreover, in spite of the stance of Lewis and a number of popular left-wing unionists, the CIO rank and file, which included the most militant and radicalised sectors of the American working class, were among Roosevelt's strongest supporters. According to a Gallup poll taken shortly after the election, 79 per cent of CIO members voted for the president, along with 71 per cent of the membership of the more conservative American Federation of Labor and 64 per cent of non-union workers. After taking the pulse of the electorate, journalist Samuel Lubell declared that 1940 signified 'a class-conscious vote for the first time in American history . . . The New Deal appears to have accomplished what the Socialists,

the IWW, and the Communists never could approach. It has drawn a class line across the face of American politics'.

Although it needs to be placed in a larger context, Lubell's interpretation of the 1940 presidential election makes a good deal of sense. Workers' enthusiastic identification with Franklin Roosevelt was, in many instances, entirely compatible with a class-conscious view of American society and politics. At a time when a lively and combative sense of 'us' versus 'them' prevailed among millions of American workers, the overwhelming majority regarded the patrician FDR as one of 'us'. This was true not only of the allegedly conservative immigrant groups in the ethnic enclaves around Detroit and Pittsburgh, but of militant miners in the coalfields and radicalised maritime workers on the Pacific coast. At the local and state levels, electoral politics sometimes continued to fragment the working-class vote; it seemed to accentuate the heterogeneity of American workers and the unevenness of their consciousness. Roosevelt was the one political figure who was consistently able to transcend these tendencies. In the electoral arena, at least, he galvanised and unified working-class sentiment in a way that the leadership of organised labour could only dream of.

An examination of the Amalgamated Clothing Workers (ACW), one of the most important CIO affiliates, will demonstrate, first, the depth and character of working-class attachment to FDR; second, the way in which a fiercely independent union, with a strong tradition of left-wing political commitment, became wedded not only to Roosevelt but to the Democratic Party; and third, how the New Deal served to hasten the integration of major sections of the working class into the mainstream of American society. Integration into the American mainstream had, to some degree, been the goal of CIO unions like the Amalgamated Clothing Workers all along. But as an insurgent movement that successfully challenged some of the world's most powerful corporations, and an industrial union federation that included a leadership cadre of deeply committed left-wingers and a mass base of millions, the CIO also contained within itself the seeds of an American social democracy. The fact that those seeds failed to take root and grow is well known. The reason for that failure continues to divide historians and other students of American society.

On strike; neckwear workers in Pennsylvania, October 1936 – an echo of the class-conscious activism that characterised politics in the 30s.

In the course of the 1930s, Sidney Hillman, the dynamic and influential president of the Amalgamated, developed especially close ties to the Roosevelt administration, and by 1940 the entire ACW leadership was passionately committed to FDR's re-election. Without it, they argued, not only the continued economic well-being of American workers, but the survival of organised labour, and even of democratic institutions in general, would be placed in serious jeopardy.

This unashamed allegiance to a representative of one of the mainstream political parties was relatively new in the Amalgamated. Forged out of the struggles of twenty-six nationality groups against sweatshop conditions in the men's clothing industry, and led from the outset by Hillman, who had twice been imprisoned for revolutionary activity in Tsarist Russia, the Amalgamated had long been proud of its reputation for independence and innovation. Reflecting the cultural traditions of its Jewish members, the union had a longstanding commitment to socialism and labour-party politics. But while paying lip-service to such sentiments, Hillman had endeav-

oured for many years to build a cross-class alliance in which the independent initiative of labour would be augmented by the enlightened self-interest of liberal employers and the expertise and influence of progressive reformers.

The Depression had sorely tested the mettle of the ACW and its needle-trades constituency. However, with the coming of the Roosevelt presidency the Amalgamated prospered, adding 50,000 new members in 1933 alone and significantly expanding the union's geographical reach. During FDR's first term, the key indicators in the men's clothing industry improved dramatically, and Hillman himself flourished as a presidentially-appointed member of various New Deal agencies. From this position of bureaucratic responsibility, he lost all patience with left-wing and liberal critics of the Roosevelt administration, whom he dismissed as 'dreamers' who would 'destroy' what labour had built up over the years while they waited for the 'revolution'.

In April 1936 Hillman met the members of the Amalgamated's General Executive Board and tried to bring them into line with the new realities of American politics as he perceived them. Since

its founding in 1914, the ACW had never formally endorsed a candidate for the presidency of the United States. Now, however, in the face of what Hillman would characterise as 'the most important presidential campaign of this century', there could be no clinging to the union's socialist past. Since the coming of the Roosevelt administration, he declared, something new had happened. 'We have participated in making the labour policy of this administration.' To Hillman, it was obvious that '[our gains] would have been totally impossible' without the New Deal and FDR. With Roosevelt in the White House, 'and with this group of people in the CIO', he said, 'we could really get somewhere'.

Hillman's argument called the day. A month later, at the ACW's convention, the General Executive Board and the Committee on Political Action recommended that the union actively support efforts to promote 'independent political action for labour'. But, in a major break with tradition, they also recommended that the Amalgamated officially endorse FDR's bid for re-election. 'This endorsement is limited to the support of President Roosevelt', the resolution declared, 'and does not apply to any other candidates on the Democratic ticket'. When some of the union's 'doctrinaires' objected to supporting a representative of a 'capitalist' political party, one delegate after another rose to announce that the accomplishments of the Roosevelt presidency, and the threat of fascism, required a new direction. 'It was through Roosevelt that we organized in Connecticut and got better conditions', said Stella Gedja. Today, said August Bellanca of New York City, 'the question is not Franklin Roosevelt or the Socialist Party; the question is concentration camps or liberty'.

Others argued that whatever the convention delegates decided, the ACW's greatly expanded membership would vote for Roosevelt anyway. 'The membership', Hillman had reminded the executive board earlier, 'is just a cross section of the country . . . We could vote to support the Socialist Party, but our members would still vote Tammany'. As painful as this realisation was, Hillman did not shrink from its implications. 'The membership', he said, 'is closer to realities.' As Abraham Chatman, a member of the General Executive Board from upstate New York, warned, 'nine thousand organized clothing workers in the City of Rochester, whether you decide for or against this resolution, are going to vote for Franklin D. Roosevelt'; and the same would be true 'in Buffalo, in Utica, in Syracuse, and everywhere'.

Although a New York City delegate counselled that it was time to 'lay our traditions aside' and 'be realistic in these matters', many speakers expressed the belief that endorsing Roosevelt was not incompatible with the union's longstanding goal of building a labour party. Sarah Borinsky of Baltimore, who had 'always voted the Socialist ticket since the time when I was eligible to vote', argued that now it was necessary to support Roosevelt, because he would help enact the social legislation that workers desired. But after the election, she said, 'we hope for a labour party that will enable us to legislate these things for ourselves'.

As FDR's second term evolved and ultimately hedged on its commitment to social reform—even as Roosevelt found it politically necessary to distance himself from the CIO—Hillman swallowed hard and declared unequivocally that the President 'has kept faith with the people'. In January 1940 he announced that the Amalgamated would gladly support

Roosevelt again should he decide to run for a third term. In the face of clear evidence to the contrary, he declared: 'Has there been any retreat from the policies and programs of . . . the New Deal? There has been none'.

The Amalgamated Convention in May 1940 became an emotional demonstration of support for Roosevelt's re-election. When the Committee on Political Action recommended the drafting of the president for a third term, bedlam broke out on the convention floor. The delegates paraded around Madison Square Garden, stamped their feet, and chanted 'We Want Roosevelt', for more than an hour. In the subsequent discussion of the committee's recommendation, the attitude expressed toward FDR was one of awe and even worship. Nicholas Firello, of Minersville, Pennsylvania, declared that 'mere words cannot be used in eulogizing this great humanitarian', but many of his fellow delegates were willing to try. For Ida Warhof, of Cincinnati, 'God ha[s] blessed America with Franklin Delano Roosevelt'. For others, he was not only 'our beloved President', but 'that great leader of humanity', 'the greatest spokesman for democracy the world over', and even 'that great humanitarian Messiah'. Almost overcome by the euphoric demonstration on the president's behalf, Sam Smith of Chicago told his fellow delegates:

I heard you yell and holler and stamp, 'We Want Roosevelt.' And in my very ears there echoes the sound of the words, and the valleys and mountains, the lakes and the oceans, and the very earth and the high heavens echo it. They seem to cry out to me, 'Give Us Roosevelt.'

The contrast between the 1936 and 1940 conventions is instructive. In 1936, the delegates had enthusiastically supported FDR, and had expressed respect and affection for him and his record. For the great majority the clear priority had been Roosevelt's re-election. But the tone of the discussion had been much less worshipful, and many delegates had also argued that endorsing FDR was entirely compatible with the union's historic commitment to independent political action. In 1940, however, there was little if any mention of a labour party. The final convention resolution on political action called only for 'vigorous participation by organized labour in the political life of the nation'.

Len De Caux, a left-winger and Lewis partisan, was at the 1940 convention in

his capacity as editor of the *CIO News*. At every chance, he recalled:

' . . . with or without pretext, the band struck up 'God Bless America,' and all joined in singing it. The delegates . . . sang fervently, and with relish, sucking in deeply the sweetness of the repeated 'God Bless America, my home sweet home!'

De Caux found it 'too emotional for my taste'. But in retrospect at least, he understood the source of the delegates' fervour. Like Hillman, 'these were mostly long-Americanized Jewish immigrants. They had come from countries of anti-Semitism, feudal backwardness, political despotism'. With the Amalgamated as their weapon, and Roosevelt as their patron on high, they had fought despotic American employers and won a better life for themselves. Now Hitler was conquering the countries of their birth and annihilating their kinsfolk and co-religionists. It was a grim moment, but they could take comfort from the fact that 'their America was defended by Roosevelt in the White House, with Hillman at his side. Their emotions overflowed in this song'.

De Caux's recollection touches on a point of fundamental importance. Hillman and his executive board could shape the convention resolutions to their specifications, but they couldn't supply the emotional fervour that flowed from the delegates. In the minds of these immigrants and children of immigrants, the CIO, the New Deal, and above all Roosevelt, had made it possible for them to enter the mainstream of American life. As a woman from Georgia put it, 'This little union book gave me the right to citizenship in my industry, and this little union book also demonstrates that I am in partnership with the President of the United States'. In the face of that kind of sentiment, any talk of repudiating Roosevelt, from the Left or the Right, was bound to come up against a stone wall.

Even though Roosevelt and the New Deal were instruments of cultural integration, the process was one that involved bitter contention between and within social classes. What is striking about the thirties, in industry after industry, is that beyond questions of wages, hours, and union recognition, the very meaning of America and Americanism was at stake. People who had lived on the margins of American society, who had been victimised for generations by nativism and anti-Semitism and class prejudice, were finally standing up and saying to the self-appointed keepers of the national seal, 'We are Americans, too'. More than that, they were implying that their industrial and political adversaries were downright Un-American'. In Thomas Bell's novel *Out of This Furnace,* set in the steel towns of western Pennsylvania, steelworker Dobie Dobrejcak suddenly realised that even though he and his fellow CIO organisers were not Protestant, middle-class, and Anglo-Saxon, they were 'thinking and talking like Americans'. 'Maybe not the kind of American that came over on the Mayflower', he reflected, but 'Made in U.S.A.' nonetheless.

I'm almost as much a product of that mill down there as any rail or ingot they ever turned out . . . If I'm anything at all, I'm an American, only not the kind you read about in history hooks or that they make speeches about on the Fourth of July; anyway, not yet.

To seize the mantle of Americanism, then, was not incompatible with a continuing consciousness of social and political division rooted in the class experience of workers, from the New York City garment district to the steel mills of western Pennsylvania. But having chosen to justify themselves and their struggles in these terms, workers and their unions would soon run up against an enormous obstacle when the international conflict between the United States and the Soviet Union, and the domestic ravages engendered by McCarthyism, recast the debate over Americanism in ways that were sharply disadvantageous to the forces of working-class insurgency. Indeed, the Cold War and McCarthyism would change the meaning of the struggle between 'us' and 'them' in basic ways. As Walter Dean Burnham has reminded us, the results of the Second World War, and of the national liberation struggles in the Third World thereafter, 'were to create a kind of worldwide sectionalism', meaning that domestic 'vertical conflict' over the allocation of the fruits of American society was increasingly superseded by 'horizontal conflict' between the people of the United States on the one hand and the Soviet Union and the emerging nation states of the Third World on the other. Insofar as this conflict was pitched in terms of a Manichean struggle between good and evil, says Burnham, its 're-stricting effects on the development of political alternatives at home were, and remain, enormous'.

For organised labour, this development would indeed have enormous consequences several years before Joseph McCarthy seized the centre stage of domestic hysteria in February 1950. As early as 1946, 'Red-baiting' was used to devastating effect in heading off 'Operation Dixie', an aggressive CIO campaign designed to organise the South and thereby undercut the regional and racial inequality that had haunted the labour movement and would continue to do so for years to come. Soon thereafter, in 1949-50, the CIO expelled eleven of its own unions—comprising about 20 per cent of the industrial union federation's total membership—because the leaders of those unions were allegedly 'dominated' by the Communist party. At the same time, in the United Auto Workers, the largest and most important union in the CIO, a decade of vibrant and often chaotic multi-party democracy came to an end with the triumph of Walter Reuther and the subsequent purge of the union's sizable left wing. 'Americanism', once again, had become a weapon of exclusion and an instrument for the imposition of narrow ideological conformity. Although the experience of class would continue to be distinctive, more than ever before the articulation of the political and social aspirations of workers would be confined within the strait-jacketing framework of Cold War dogma.

This narrow framework would have an especially significant impact in the realm of electoral politics. In regard to the possibility of independent labour politics in the 1930s and beyond, the issue must be addressed not only in terms of the role of the trade union leadership in shortcircuiting such a development but also from the standpoint of the electoral behaviour of workers, especially in those instances where there seemed to be a possibility of translating working-class insurgency at the 'point of production' into political power. Here the record of the thirties—in industrial cities and towns such as Detroit, Akron, and Aliquippa (Pennsylvania)—reveals the unevenness of workers' consciousness and the continuing fragmentation of the labour vote at the local level. Perhaps a more unified, patient, and ideologically independent trade union leadership could have changed this pattern. But there always seemed to be a crisis at hand propelling labour into the arms of the Democrats. (Often, the crisis was the prospect of a Republican electoral vic-

tory.) For nearly a decade after 1940, progressive unionists would recommend 'consideration of the possible need of a new labour party later on', as three CIO officials put it in 1943. But when the moment of truth came, the 'new labour party' was always a project for the future. And by 1950 'later on' had apparently become 'never'.

The role of Hillman and his ACW lieutenants in this regard is crystal clear and somewhat ironic. As recently as 1934 it had been commonplace for delegates to the Amalgamated's biennial convention to call for the formation of 'a Labour party completely divorced from the old political parties'. But by 1936 there was a growing sense that the union's objectives—in the economic and electoral arenas—should be essentially defensive, and that only Roosevelt could serve as labour's sword and shield in the struggle to ward off capitalist reaction. At the 1936 convention, when a delegate from New York City declared that the Amalagamated should support FDR in order to 'save our bread and butter and try to avoid fascist rule in America', he received a standing ovation. By 1940 Dorothy Bellanca, an ACW vice-president, was arguing that 'Roosevelt does not need us; it is we who need Roosevelt'. And, according to his premier biographer, Hillman himself was more willing than ever 'to trust the fate of labour to Roosevelt, to in effect become the President's campaign manager within the CIO, precisely because both the CIO and the New Deal had lost the initiative'.

This trend was by no means limited to the Amalgamated. As the President's second term unfolded, there was an increasingly clear tendency within labour's ranks to argue that working people owed far more to Roosevelt than he owed them, and a belief that labour's gains were more the result of FDR's benevolence than of the workers' own initiative through their unions. Clearly, Franklin Roosevelt was the one figure who could transcend the fault-lines of division within local and state Democratic parties and an increasingly contentious labour movement. His magnetism reinforced the legitimacy of the existing political system and deepened the electoral habits and practical ties that bound workers and their unions more closely to the Democratic Party.

But there must have been more than FDR's unifying presence at work, because the upset victory of Harry Truman on a populistic platform in 1948 indicates that the working-class vote was holding solid for the Democrats, even in the absence of his charismatic predecessor. By 1948, Roosevelt had been dead for three years; the Republicans were determined to recapture the White House after sixteen years in the political wilderness; and virtually no one gave the seemingly inept Truman a chance of defeating GOP nominee Thomas E. Dewey. But he did, mainly by casting himself as the defender of the New Deal and the rights of labour. And once again the overwhelming support of workers played a vital role in the Democrats' success. Much of Truman's strength was in the cities, among the urban working classes. This was especially true of union members, who were both much more likely to vote and much stronger supporters of Truman than were nonunion workers.

Truman's victory in 1948 played a major role in undermining the recurring dream of independent labour politics. After Roosevelt's death and Truman's accession, elements of organised labour had seriously contemplated the formation of a third party. But while labour hesitated, other forces—including the Communists—formed the Progressive Party. The tarring of the progressives and their presidential candidate, Henry Wallace, with the red brush, at a time when Cold War hysteria was approaching a fever pitch, served further to 'delegitimise' third-party politics. Had Truman lost the election, at least the Progressives could have claimed the power to punish their anti-communist liberal tormentors. Instead, they became a symbol of fuzzy-minded idealism, left-wing isolation, and ignominious failure. With Truman's victory, and the Progressives' defeat, the marriage of labour to the Democratic party would become an apparently permanent feature of American political life.

Was the marriage 'barren' (as some historians have claimed)? To place this question in historical perspective, let us look once again at the sentiments of rank-and-file clothing workers on the eve of the 1940 presidential election. As the day of decision drew near, the Amalgamated sponsored a 'Write-a-Letter-to-Roosevelt' campaign among its members, and published the ones it judged best in a pamphlet entitled *The People Speak: Letters from Clothing Workers*. Almost entirely, the letters focused on immediate but vital concerns such as income, physi-

cal health, and old-age pensions. Mrs C. Londen, of Cincinnati, declared: 'I am a factory worker's wife and am voting for President Roosevelt's re-election because we are free of debts for the first time in twenty-three years of married life. I have purchased my first ready-made coat, and attended my first big-league ball game since his election.' O. H. Schneider, also of Cincinnati, wrote that 'I thought a vacation was only for the rich before Roosevelt'. Now 'I take a vacation every year . . . [and] do not have to worry about old age. I feel secure'. Thanks to the ACW and the Roosevelt administration, it seemed to Harry Wolfe of Philadelphia that 'a miracle happened to me and my family'. He reported working fewer hours, making 'a fine living', and enjoying better health. 'Roosevelt . . . made possible our dream come true'.

What these statements reveal, of course, is that the New Deal created a new relationship between the federal government and the American people. It not only built the foundations of the welfare state; it also asserted that government had an important role to play in the management of the economy and in safeguarding the economic well-being of the majority of Americans. The Democratic Party became the 'party of government' and, in circumstances of unprecedented post-war prosperity, government delivered an expanding package of benefits—pensions and medical insurance for the elderly, home loans and educational assistance for veterans, compensatory payments for unemployed workers and so on. Together, the trade unions, the Democratic Party, and the New Deal welfare state helped to soften the edges of inequality in an expanding economy, and to integrate workers into the mainstream of a consumer capitalist culture.

But the post-war consensus on the role of government in managing the economy and providing for the public welfare emerged only after sharp contention in which a number of alternatives on the left and the right were defeated. The clearest Left alternative, which historians have characterised as labour-liberal, or social-democratic, or social-Keynesian, envisaged a much more aggressive and systematic role for the state in mitigating the inequality rooted in the operation of the capitalist market. Important CIO leaders like Hillman (who died in 1946) and his youthful counterpart, Walter Reuther of the UAW, believed that, in order to

achieve a more just and equitable social order, the management of the economy must become a tripartite venture involving the leaders of labour, capital, and 'the public'. The potential political base of this social-democratic vision was the unionised workforce in the basic industries of the North and the hitherto unorganised labour force, white and black, of the South.

This policy orientation had been implicit in the intellectual premises of the New Deal by 1938, but for many reasons it was to suffer a crushing defeat in the aftermath of the Second World War. The leadership of capital, with few exceptions, rejected it as a dangerous infringement of management's 'right to manage'. The rulers of the South thwarted Operation Dixie. The federal government, especially at the Congressional level, turned sharply to the right and punished labour with the Taft-Hartley Act which imposed restrictions on the political activities of unions. And important sections of the trade-union leadership spurned this tripartite vision of industrial governance and opted instead for collective bargaining free—as much as possible—from state interference. Even among many New Deal liberals the 'statism' of the late 1930s had given way to a renewed faith in the benevolence of a corporate-dominated 'economy of abundance'. Meanwhile, in elections at the local and state level, the working-class political constituency upon whose behalf the bold new programme was to have been implemented continued to divide along ethnic and, increasingly, racial lines.

With the collapse of the tripartite vision, the most innovative sectors of labour and capital chose to create instead a kind of private welfare state through the operation of carefully controlled collective bargaining. After a pioneering agreement between General Motors and the United Auto Workers in 1948, the great breakthrough came with the so-called 'Treaty of Detroit' in 1950. In exchange for a five-year contract, and a no-strike pledge for its duration, GM gave the UAW automatic cost-of-living increases, additional wage guarantees pegged to annual increases in productivity, vacations, pensions, and generous medical insurance plans. For the Auto Workers and the unions that followed their lead, it was a dazzling achievement. Walter Reuther exulted that collective bargaining was creating a 'whole new middle class'. What he apparently failed

Banner carried in the 1938 Labour Day parade in Toledo, Ohio, depicting John L. Lewis, leader of the United Mine Workers and the CIO, who became so disenchanted with Roosevelt that he called upon workers to vote Republican in the 1940 election.

to anticipate was that an ideologically straitjacketed labour movement, basing itself upon a more affluent and secure blue-collar 'middle class', would be less and less likely to function as a mass social force nurturing within itself an alternative vision of the future. As Steve Fraser has noted, the emergence of the new social contract embodied in the Treaty of Detroit meant that 'the struggle over Nelson, power and property . . . was superseded by the universal quest for more—goulash capitalism'.

Gradually, perhaps inevitably, this quest for more within a privatised domain reduced the commitment of organised labour to an expanded welfare state, exacerbated the reality of material inequality within an increasingly segmented labour market, and served to diminish the sense of solidarity between relatively secure and well-paid sectors of the working class and their less privileged, often non-white brothers and sisters. This inequality, and declining

commitment to social solidarity, would become painfully obvious in the 1960s, when the black freedom movement turned northward and began to make demands that challenged the precarious status and security of white working-class Americans—many of them second-generation members of the CIO unions— in the realms of employment, education, and housing. It was in the mid-1960s, when their hardwon 'turf' was threatened, that these blue-collar workers and many other so-called 'middle Americans' helped make the politics of racial backlash an enduring feature of American life. Insofar as the Democratic Party embraced and supported the struggle for black equality, its relationship to the white majority of organised labour's rank-and-file constituency became more and more tenuous; while government, and the 'party of government', were increasingly perceived as part of the problem rather than part of the solution to society's ills. Ironically, the day would

come when the fading memory of Roosevelt would be invoked more effectively by a Republican president who challenged the New Deal order than by those members of FDR's own party who claimed to be his rightful heirs.

FOR FURTHER READING:

Robert S. McElvaine. ed., *Down & Out in the Great Depression: Letters from the Forgotten Man* (University of North Carolina Press, 1983), and *The Great Depression: America, 1929-1941* (Times Books, 1984); Arthur M. Schlesinger, Jr., et al, *History of American Presidential Elections, 1789-1968*, vol. IV (Chelsea House, 1971); Len De Caux, *Labour Radical—From the Wobblies to CIO: A Personal History* (Beacon Press, 1970); Melvyn Dubofsksy and Warren Van Tine, eds., *Labour Leaders in America* (University of Illinois Press, 1987); Walter Dean Burnham, *The Current Crisis in American Politics* (New York: Oxford University Press, 1982); Steve Fraser and Gary Gerstle, eds., *The Rise and Fall of the New Deal Order, 1930-1980* (Princeton University Press, 1989).

Things to Come: The 1939 New York World's Fair

For a brief moment between a Great Depression and a global war, Americans reveled in the vision of a brighter future to be achieved through science and social progress.

Bill McIlvaine

Bill McIlvaine is managing editor of Managing Automation *and a freelance writer specializing in history, technology, and business topics.*

America in 1939 was poised uneasily between a Great Depression and a global war. The thirties had been a painful and frustrating decade, and saying goodbye to them was a psychological lift the country needed. Under the circumstances, the idea that the future was sure to be a better time had never been more appealing.

On April 30, 1939, at 3:12 in the afternoon, that brighter, happier future arrived. The New York World's Fair opened in Flushing Meadow, Queens, with the flourish of a dozen Broadway spectaculars. Americans had eagerly awaited the exposition for years; this wasn't going to be just another fair, but an event of magnificent vision and proportions. It was going to be "the World of Tomorrow," with the look, sounds, sensations, and colors of a very real and attainable future. Even as the lights were beginning to go out across Europe, other lights—lots of them—were being turned on in Flushing Meadow.

Few among the tens of millions of Americans who experienced the New York World's Fair of 1939–40 have been able to forget it. Fifty years later the exposition remains unsurpassed for the imaginative vision it projected of a future shaped and perfected by science and social progress. But the fair was also a huge party. The serious, hopeful view of a new American century was wrapped up in a carnival-like atmosphere, like some weird collaboration between Buckminster Fuller and P.T. Barnum.

"It was the new age," recalls Robert Malone, who as a boy in Queens visited the fair at least a dozen times during its two-year run. "We had heard about the possibilities for the future. All these things were available and we were very definitely aware of that."

In 1930s terms, the exposition truly was a "World of Tomorrow." General Motors presented the "Futurama," a gigantic animated diorama depicting the ideal American landscape of 1960. Industrial designer Henry Dreyfuss created "Democracity," a prophetic vision of a perfectly planned metropolis of the year 2039 A.D. Westinghouse buried a time capsule to be opened by a future civilization in the year 6939. General Electric thrilled fairgoers with awesome ten-million-volt bolts of manmade lightning.

The Radio Corporation of America unveiled an electronic marvel that had rarely been seen outside of laboratories: television. The Carrier Corporation demonstrated the wonders of modern air conditioning. Du Pont and other manufacturers displayed such soon-to-be household items as nylon, Lucite, and Fiberglas, heralding the age of synthetic fibers and plastics. And hundreds of other commercial, regional, and international exhibitors called attention to a dawning era of scientific progress and enterprise.

In creating a tangible image of "The World of Tomorrow," the 1939 New York fair captured a mood of typical American optimism and a belief in the liberating powers of technology. Its futuristic streamlined architecture—typified by the sweeping incline and graceful curves of the General Motors building and such baroque Moderne touches as the Du Pont pavilion—was Art Deco's high point. Many of the fair's most spectacular exhibits, created by graphic and architectural innovators like Raymond Loewy and Norman Bel Geddes, represented the flowering of the young field of industrial design. And the exposition created at least one indelible image—the famous Trylon and Perisphere, theme center and focal point for the fairgrounds.

DEMOCRACITY. FUTURAMA. THE BRIDGE of Tomorrow. The Plaza of Light. The Lagoon of Nations. The Hall of Color. The Court of Communications. These names, suggesting optimism and expansiveness, say a lot about the fair's vision. The New York World's Fair, in the words of its charter, was a "people's fair designed for mass appeal, easy access, varied and unusual spectacles, and an overriding theme of an industrial utopia in which the little man could share."

In many ways, America was ready for this encouraging view of a better new world. By the time the fair opened in 1939 the worst of the Depression had passed, but in 1935 when Grover A. Whalen and other New York civic and business leaders began planning the exposition, the country was just bottoming out. Hollywood provided one of the few bright spots for Americans during these difficult years, making millions by producing splashy, escapist entertainments typified by Busby Berkeley's bathing-beauty revues and the inspired nonsense of the Marx Brothers.

From *American History Illustrated*, Summer 1989, pp. 32-47. Reprinted through the courtesy of Cowles Magazines, publishers of *American History Illustrated*.

And to many, the idea of a predictable, perfectible future wasn't an idle dream. Amid the economic depression of the 1930s, much had happened to make the public more comfortable with the fruits of scientific progress. By 1939 national electrification projects were making appliance- and radio-equipped homes a reality for most American families. Streamlined express trains, modern highways, and commercial airlines were shrinking distances. Newsreels and popular magazines touted the latest technological wonders. The most up-to-date designs for automobiles and many other consumer products suggested speed, and speed implied progress. Modern science, so an advertisement claimed, even made Chesterfield a better-tasting cigarette.

Chicago's 1933 Century of Progress Exposition had clearly demonstrated the public's fascination with modern technology, attracting thirty-eight million visitors by showcasing America's industrial might. Steam locomotives, giant steelmaking furnaces, metal-forming machinery, and the latest developments in electricity and electronics had proved to be immensely popular. Surprisingly for these hard times, the Chicago fair even earned a modest profit for its investors.

THE HISTORICAL RECORD SUGGESTS THAT the idea for a New York World's fair originated with a man named Joseph Shagden, but another New Yorker, Grover Whalen, has received most of the credit for providing the inspiration and drive needed to transform the huge exposition from concept into reality. Whalen was a showman every bit the equal of New York's flamboyant mayor, Fiorello La Guardia. With his dapper Clark Gable mustache and a penchant for pinstriped suits and silk top hats, Whalen was the epitome of 1930s chic. He had numerous paramours about town and held several nebulous city government posts. But he was best recognized as a promoter and public greeter known as "Mr. New York." And he saw his moment.

Impressed with the Century of Progress's success, Whalen helped to recruit 120 prominent businessmen to back a world's fair for New York. It should be a privately financed venture, he insisted, unlike European fairs, which traditionally were publicly funded. Business leaders responded enthusiastically, and the World's Fair Corporation was incorporated in September 1935 with Whalen as president. To finance the fair, the corporation issued debentures totaling $28 million at 4.5 percent interest, due in 1941.

For the fair site, the planners selected a three-and-one-half-mile-long expanse of marshes and ash dumps in the borough of Queens, about seven miles east of Manhattan. In addition to encompassing the necessary acreage, the Corona Dumps, as they were then known, promised easy access to millions of fairgoers via the Long Island railroad, New York subways, and a network of modern new highways that would become part of the urban vision of the fair itself.

Robert Moses, New York's city parks commissioner and master builder, was placed in charge of the huge reclamation project. Groundbreaking began on June 29, 1936. Thirty thousand laborers graded a 1,216.5-acre site for the fair, creating two lakes, hauling in eight hundred thousand cubic yards of topsoil, and transplanting ten thousand trees from throughout New York and neighboring states. Removal of the ash heaps alone cost more than $2 million. The fair's promoters envisioned that when the exposition was over and its structures torn down, Flushing Meadow would be one of the great municipal parks in the world, rivaling Manhattan's Central Park in size and attractiveness.

WHALEN, MEANWHILE, ENERGETICALLY set about obtaining the endorsement of the Bureau of International Expositions and enlisting business firms, state and federal agencies, and foreign governments to sponsor exhibits and pavilions. In 1938 he sent a fleet of cars across the country to deliver a personal message to each governor and the president, urging their support. He succeeded in signing up thirteen hundred commercial firms, as well as thirty-three states and territories and sixty foreign governments and international organizations. When completed, the fair site included more than three hundred structures, with one hundred major exhibit buildings, eighty restaurants, and about seventy amusement concessions.

"Careful estimates indicate the entire project involves the expenditure of between $150 million and $160 million," Whalen noted in his introduction to the fair's official guidebook. "Of this, the federal government contributed $3 million. . . . The World's Fair Corporation

spent $42 million, and foreign governments $30 million on their own exhibits."

Early in the design process, factions developed between "traditionalists" and "functionalists." Most previous world's fairs, the planners found, tended to celebrate past technical achievements and a certain cultural status quo. But the 1930s were different: despite the Depression, a concept of the future based on enlightened technological progress, coupled with social and international cooperation, was in the spirit of the times. The functionalists—who included social historian Lewis Mumford, urban planner Henry Wright, and industrial designer Walter Dorwin Teague—won out and convinced the exposition's board of directors to build the "Fair of the Future," one that would "examine the social consequences of those new processes and products."

"Mere mechanical progress is no longer an adequate or practical theme for a World's Fair," noted the fair's prospectus. "We must demonstrate that supercivilization is based on the swift work of machines, not on the arduous toil of men."

The fair's theme may have been "The World of Tomorrow," but the exposition officially recognized the 150th anniversary of George Washington's inauguration as first president of the United States. (Opening day coincided with the sesquicentennial of Washington's oath-taking at New York City's Federal Hall.) The planners turned this backward glance into an opportunity to assess the nation's progress during the intervening century-and-a-half and to acknowledge the continuing efforts to perfect its political system.

"The American experiment in democratic government has long ago ceased to be an experiment. . . . The Fair exalts and glorifies Democracy," said the proposal, adding that "the future, pregnant with high destiny, seemed more meaningful than the past with all its fateful achievements."

Unfortunately, labor problems undermined the fair's public message of unity and cooperation. During construction the electricians' union was accused of shaking down exhibitors, and a general strike loomed. Some exhibitors threatened to withdraw, and a few buildings and exhibits remained unfinished on opening day because of union slowdowns.

Despite such setbacks, the fair opened on schedule. "The only limit to our realization of tomorrow will be our doubts of today," said President Franklin D. Roosevelt in his dedicatory speech (the first such event ever broadcast on television): "Let us move forward with a strong and active faith." As dusk settled on the opening-day crowd of 198,791, physicist Albert Einstein threw a switch to collect "cosmic rays" and activate the fairground's spectacular lighting system.

The *New York Times* reported that opening-day fairgoers were overwhelmed by the size and scale of the exposition, dazzled by the light reflected from the sleek off-white buildings, and confused by the maps. Flushing Meadow soon took on a life of its own as children became lost and were found, some visitors gave birth and others died, and the *Times* began a gossip column on the daily happenings in "The World of Tomorrow."

WORLD'S FAIR HISTORIANS PARTICULARLY admire the 1939 exposition for the architecture that so effectively harmonized with its scientific vision. Henry Dreyfuss, Teague, Loewy, Geddes, and others achieved some of the finest work of their careers. "They conjured up an optimistic preview of a future America where the advances of science, the capability of technology, and the wisdom of good design would shape an orderly, healthy and content society," recalls Donald J. Bush in *The Streamlined Decade.*

The very temporality of the exposition buildings, freeing the architects from the engineering demands of permanent structures, allowed their imaginations free reign. The fair's design board, which exercised power over all construction, specified a slab-like and stark architectural style; sculpture, murals, landscaping, and lighting were to provide most of the decoration. The designers deliberately omitted windows in most buildings, both to conserve exhibition space and to exploit the possibilities of electric lighting. There were to be no Crystal Palaces—except, ironically, a small replica of the 1851 London original.

Planners strove to make fair themes comprehensible to the average fairgoer, who likely had far less education than they did. Graphics and art were big, bold, and relatively simple. Salvador Dali, Willem de Kooning, and Rockwell Kent were just three of hundreds of artists commissioned to create murals and sculptures reflecting the socially rel-

evant themes of the exposition. Murals were to be a "reflection of our own day in [their] complete lack of period style as it has prevailed in other ages."

More than sixty commissioned works of sculpture adorned the fairgrounds. These included such heroic monuments as James Earle Fraser's fifty-foot-tall statue of George Washington; "Golden Sprays" by Leo Lentelli, depicting a pair of decorous, undraped female athletes; and "Speed" by Joseph Renier, which resembled a racy radiator ornament. Once again, the temporariness of the fair was evident: most of the figures were modeled in plaster.

Although the design board issued guidelines and rules to insure a degree of uniformity in fair architecture, many interesting variations resulted. In some instances, exhibit designers followed the idea that a structure's form should literally indicate its function: the Marine Transportation building, for example, sported twin "ocean liner prows," while the Aviation building was blimp-shaped. Commercial exhibits blatantly advertised products: The Radio Corporation of America pavilion was shaped like a radio tube, the Carrier (air conditioning) exhibit resembled an igloo, the Electrical Utilities building imitated a hydroelectric dam and spillway, and pylons on the Gas Industries building simulated enormous gas burners. Fair officials considered National Cash Register's bright-red, forty-foot-tall register at such variance with guidelines that it was banished to the Amusement Zone.

THE DOMINANT ARCHITECTURAL FEATURE of the New York fair was its trademark symbol, the Trylon and Perisphere. Early concepts for the exhibition's theme center had envisioned a pair of 250-foot towers overlooking a semicircular exhibit hall. But the corporation's design board, unimpressed, rejected these. The final design, approved in March 1937 and created by architects Wallace K. Harrison and J. Andre Fouilhous, was a triumph of conceptual design. The Perisphere, an enormous snow-white globe, hovered alongside the Trylon, a slender triangular obelisk that soared 610 feet above the fairgrounds. One of these structures symbolized "the world about us," explained fair literature, "the other, aspiration." A third element—a 950-foot-long pedestrian ramp dubbed the Helicline—spiraled gracefully down to earth from the Perisphere.

In its simplicity and purity of form the theme center was eminently consistent with the design principles of the utopian future the fair's sponsors envisioned. "We feel," noted Whalen, "that simplicity must be the keynote of a perfectly ordered mechanical civilization."

Even essayist E.B. White, who was otherwise skeptical of the fair, was awestruck: "Suddenly you see the first intimation of the future, of man's dream—the white ball and spire—and the ramp and the banners flying from the pavilions and the brave hope of a glimpsed destination."

Building the Trylon and Perisphere consumed nearly seven thousand tons of structural steel and concrete, along with 150,000 square feet of gypsum board sheathing. Measuring 180 feet in diameter, the Perisphere was the largest globe built up to that time. Despite the sphere's great size and weight, mirrors and fountains around its eight supporting piers created the illusion that the huge ball was floating weightlessly just above its reflecting pool.

The Perisphere also housed the fair's theme exhibit. "Democracity," created by Henry Dreyfuss, was a spectacular model depicting a utopian metropolis of the future. Eight thousand visitors per hour ascended to the Perisphere via the world's largest escalators, then slowly circled above the enormous diorama on one of two rotating balconies. A six-minute program, narrated by popular radio commentator H.V. Kaltenborn, described the pollution- and slum-free society of the year 2039, populating the hub-city of Centerton and satellite residential and business communities. The presentation ended in a stirring musical and visual climax as legions of singing workers (projected on the interior of the dome) marched triumphantly forward.

CONSTITUTION MALL, A MILE-LONG TREE-and sculpture-lined avenue, formed the axis of the fairgrounds. Its broad walkways extended from the Trylon and Perisphere to the Lagoon of Nations and Court of Peace, where the foreign pavilions were grouped. Virtually every major industrial nation save Germany was represented here. The most spectacular of the foreign exhibits was the Union of Soviet Socialist Republics pavilion, dominated by a 190-foot Karelian marble pillar topped by a 79-foot stainless steel figure of a Soviet worker holding aloft a lighted red star. Other popular foreign attractions included the Italian pavilion, with a waterfall and a heroic rooftop statue of the goddess Roma, and the British pavilion, where replicas of the crown jewels and Magna Carta were displayed.

Each evening the Lagoon of Nations provided the setting for a sensational display of colored fountains, blazing gas jets, and fireworks with musical accompaniment. Along the mall, concealed mercury-vapor lighting caused leaves on the trees of fluoresce with unusual effect, while batteries of projectors playing on the Perisphere created the illusion that the globe was revolving on its axis. Futuristic fluorescent outdoor lighting (introduced in quantity for the first time at the fair) provided most other night illumination.

Hundreds of commercial exhibits, grouped by topic into seven zones (chief among these were Transportation, Communications, and Production and Distribution), radiated outward from the Trylon and Perisphere. In addition to commercial buildings, each zone featured a focal exhibit provided by the fair to dramatize the major themes in that area.

Gilbert Rhodes's Community Zone presentation was one of the most ambitious of the focal exhibits, showing how technology and science had transformed colonial America into modern America. New social forces had come into being, new interrelationships, and new economic realities. More leisure time meant new social concerns. Egmont Arens's Production and Distribution exhibit, complex and studded with statistical displays, asked such questions as, "Can we improve the spiritual side of life as we did the physical apparatus?"

Dioramas and models dramatizing present and future scientific wonders abounded. Consolidated Edison presented Walter Dorwin Teague's "City of Light," a block-long animated scale replica of the New York skyline that illustrated electricity's vital role in the daily functioning of America's largest city. Raymond Loewy's focal exhibit for the Transportation Zone featured a spectacular model rocketport of the future, from which passenger ships were launched on suborbital flights between New York and London.

General Motors' "Futurama," created by Norman Bel Geddes to dramatize the continuing role of transportation in the march of civilization, was universally praised as the fair's most memorable

presentation. It was just one attraction inside GM's huge pavilion, which was actually a complex of four exhibit areas devoted to the theme "Highways and Horizons." These included a theater and educational displays on transportation of all kinds, and a four-thousand-horsepower diesel locomotive.

But most visitors came solely for the Futurama, and willingly stood in line as long as two hours for the sixteen-minute tour of the America of 1960.

The Futurama began with a moving sidewalk inside the huge inclined wing of the building. This transported the visitor to one of 552 upholstered chairs mounted on a one-third-mile-long conveyer system. A narrator, whose recorded voice emanated from speakers in each chair in synchronization with 150 points of interest along the route, welcomed fairgoers to a "magic, Aladdin-like flight through time and space" and explained that the Futurama was "to demonstrate in dramatic fashion that the world, far from being finished, is hardly begun; that the job of building the future is one which will demand our best energies, our most fruitful imagination; and that with it will come greater opportunities for all."

Bob Malone was one of millions of visitors captivated by the Futurama. "One of the things that was impressive was the interactiveness," he recalls. "It's quite common now, but to sit in a moving seat and watch an exhibit go by while a recorded narration played in your ear through a speaker—all that started right there."

As they watched and listened, the riders slowly moved along the circumference of the world's largest animated model—a miniature landscape covering 35,738 square feet with a million trees and half a million buildings. (Someone pointed out that there were scandalously few churches in the cities of 1960, and artists later added more.) Fifty thousand cars and trucks streamed along pristine elevated highways. The countryside was an orderly vision of agribusiness, with hygienic farms and domed fruit trees. In some respects, it was surprisingly close to the reality that would come after the war, when Long Island's farms were bulldozed for neat rows of suburban houses, and Robert Moses's highways, interchanges, and bridges made intercity travel easy and delightful—for a while.

At ride's end, having descended toward a miniature street intersection in the "World of Tomorrow," visitors stepped

out to find themselves at that actual intersection, now life-sized, where the latest General Motors cars were on display.

THE WESTINGHOUSE CORPORATION sponsored several of the fair's most imaginative exhibits, including its famous time capsule. Machined from Copaloy (a durable alloy of copper, chrome, and silver), the torpedo-shaped container was designed to endure for five thousand years. On September 23, 1938, fair officials ceremoniously lowered the eight-foot-capsule and its contents into the "Immortal Well," a fifty-foot-deep crypt just outside the Westinghouse pavilion, where it still waits removal in the year 6939. (To alert future civilizations of the capsule's existence and location, Westinghouse deposited a "Book of Records" in two thousand libraries around the world.)

Objects in the capsule included "small articles of common use" such as an alarm clock, can opener, Mickey Mouse plastic cup, electric wall switch, fountain pen, dollar bill, and a Lilly Dache woman's hat. Newsreels documented the world of the 1930s for future viewers, and 22,000 pages of microfilmed text showing "how we lived and worked" included the Fall-Winter 1938 Sears, Roebuck catalog, copies of *Good Housekeeping, True Confessions,* and *Amazing Stories* magazines, front pages of New York newspapers, and the Lord's Prayer in three hundred languages.

Inside its pavilion, Westinghouse provided a glimpse of the home of the near-future by pitting "Mrs. Modern," who used marvelous new conveniences like an electric dishwasher, against "Mrs. Drudge," who still scrubbed by hand. (One day the dishwasher broke down, and in a remarkable show of fair play, Mrs. Drudge slowed her scrubbing as the machine was repaired, allowing Mrs. Modern to win the "Battle of the Centuries" as she always did.)

Westinghouse also had a tremendous hit with Elektro the Moto-Man. The seven-foot-tall, 260-pound robot, whose body was filled with motors, gears, photoelectric cells, and enough wire to circle the earth at the equator, performed twenty-six functions including walking, saluting, talking, and smoking a cigarette. "You could ask him questions from a prepared list," says Malone, who was one of those who stood in line to converse with Elektro. "One of the questions was, 'When will we run out of oil?' I think the answer was 1955.''

Fairgoers were equally impressed with the Hammond Company's 144-tube Novachord, said to be the first practical musical synthesizer, and American Telephone and Telegraph's VODER (Voice Operation Demonstrator). Played by skilled operators using a keyboard and foot pedals, VODER was capable of reproducing fifty phonemes to produce speech and even song.

AT&T also drew record crowds in its Demonstration Call Room, where fairgoers drew lots for a free call to "any one of the sixteen million telephones of the Bell system." As the lucky winner placed his call from a glass booth, a huge illuminated map displayed the route followed by the telephonic circuits between caller and recipient.

And so Yankee ingenuity was on full display. Crowds couldn't get enough of watching Elsie the Cow and her sisters being milked on the Walter-Gordon rotating mechanical platform in Borden's all-electric "Dairy World of Tomorrow." The Glass Center, a million-dollar exhibit put together by Corning Glass, Owens-Illinois, and Pittsburgh Plate Glass (erstwhile competitors) showed Fiberglas being spun from a heated marble. Equally wondrous were the flickering black-and-white images that illuminated seven- by nine-inch television screens in the RCA pavilion. (America's first scheduled television programming—two hours of broadcasting per week—began the day the fair opened.)

Clearly, the world of tomorrow was meant to be a consumer paradise. The fair's theme brazenly portrayed the American family as a consuming unit, and the public, which had had enough of privation anyway, was happy to go along. Inevitably, however, some decried the commercialism of even the Futurama, which could be seen as a pitch to buy more GM cars to pay for the roads of the future. And E.B. White was being sarcastic when he wrote, "In the world of tomorrow, rugs don't slip." He added, prophetically, that the future "looks expensive."

In retrospect, some visions of progress were just muddled. In 1966 one commentator observed that some exhibitors' minds were apparently blank when confronting the possibility of technological change and "seemed to take refuge in sheer size as the way of the future." National Cash Register's seven-story

cash register, for instance, rang up the daily attendance, but there was no glimmer of a computer among the exhibits. The closest that International Business Machines came was with "radio-typewriter," a kind of telex.

BUT NOT EVERYTHING WAS SO SERIOUS. Amid all the social relevance and lofty aims, the exposition featured an abundance of just plain fun. The 280-acre Amusement Zone itself was larger than many previous world's fairs. It had carnival rides, arcades, an animal freak show, and something called "We Humans" that the fair guidebook claimed was so strange and terrifying it couldn't be described. Perhaps more startling—in view of its location in the Amusement Zone—was the "Baby Incubators" building, which displayed newborn human infants.

A hit with many visitors was George Jessel's Old New York, a recreation of Gay Nineties Gotham with burlesque shows, prize fights, and re-enactments of Steve Brodie's famous leap off the Brooklyn Bridge. Fairgoers could also visit Midget Town (a Lilliputian village peopled by real midgets), Merrie England (a semiauthentic recreation of an Elizabethan street scene), and the Seminole Village.

Billy Rose's Aquacade was the Amusement Zone's answer to the Futurama. Stars of the five-hundred-member swimming extravaganza were former Olympic swimmer Eleanor Holm (who became Billy Rose's wife) and Johnny "Aquadonis" Weismuller, the movies' Tarzan. The ten-thousand-seat amphitheater was seldom less than sold out and during the course of two seasons grossed more than $4 million. From a profit–motive standpoint the Aquacade was unquestionably the most successful attraction at the fair.

Predictably, showgirls were popular in the Amusement Zone. Norman Bel Geddes adapted his industrial design skills to create an illusion called "Crystal Lassies," in which a scantily clad dancer was multiplied into a chorus line through the use of mirrors. Other educational shows of this nature included the "Arctic Girl's Tomb of Ice," "Twenty Thousand Legs Under the Sea," and "Living Magazine Covers"—all featuring curvaceous beauties in bathing suits or less.

Theatric concessionaires presented Broadway reviews such as the "Hot Mikado" with dancer Bill "Bojangles" Robinson and the "Streets of Paris" with

Gypsy Rose Lee. Nightclub shows included the Cuban Village (once raided for nude dancing) and the Savoy, which featured "the world's greatest colored dancers." Visitors to the Museum of Natural History's Theatre of Time and Space were treated to an imaginary voyage to distant planets and galaxies. John Ringling North brought in cowboys and Indians for his Frontier Village; Frank Buck exhibited wild animals in his Jungle land; and Penguin Island displayed specimens captured in the Antarctic by Admiral Richard Byrd.

Ranking second to the Aquacade in popularity was the spectacular Parachute Jump sponsored by Life Savers. Two million fairgoers paid forty cents each to experience the breathtaking drop from the top of the 250-foot tower, the world's largest amusement ride. Later the structure was dismantled and moved to Coney Island for a long, successful second career there.

THE FAIR'S FIRST SEASON ENDED IN October 1939. When it reopened the following May, the bloom was definitely off. War had erupted in Europe, shattering the hope for a geopolitical utopia that had been so promising when President Roosevelt declared the fair's opening "a symbol of peace." Whalen spent most of the off-season scrambling to prevent European countries from canceling their participation. Nevertheless, many did, most notably the Soviet Union, which razed its magnificent $4 million red marble pavilion.

There were other ominous signs: A gale ripped a section of gypsum sheathing from the Trylon, and the French pavilion, which had been damaged by a fire in 1939, was accidentally flooded. (The French chefs, stranded in America by the European war, enterprisingly opened the Pavilion in Manhattan, credited with being the first authentic French restaurant in New York.)

Attendance during the first year had fallen far below expectations. Many blamed the low figures on the admission price of seventy-five cents for adults (twenty-five cents for children), considered high for the times. There had been calls during the first weeks of the fair to cut the gate fee to fifty cents, but Whalen balked.

For the second season, however, worried fair directors lowered the entrance fee to fifty cents and added rides and concessions catering to more general tastes. Whalen, ever optimistic, continued to trumpet the fun and value of the fair, predicting that it would eventually generate $1 billion in revenue for New York. But inconsistent weather and a general loss of spirit made the 1940 season a letdown. A concessionaire told a reporter in 1940, "If I thought I'd make a decent-looking corpse, I'd go and drown myself in that Lagoon of Nations right now."

With investors facing a loss, Whalen sent brass bands with pom-pom girls and banners into the streets of New York to drum up business and instill the idea that every citizen had a civic and patriotic duty to attend the exposition. Mayor La Guardia got into the act, too, by urging Saturdays off for city employees so they could visit the fair, and he toured the Midwest personally to boost the event.

Despite these efforts, the fair failed to repay its costs. Whalen had predicted a total attendance of sixty million. While there were crowds, the final tally came to around forty-five million (still more than any previous world's fair). The fair corporation sustained a $19 million deficit.

But financial losses, naiveté, commercialism, and miscalculations aside, the 1939–40 New York World's Fair remains the example by which all other fairs are judged and fall short. Coming at a moment in America when almost nothing seemed impossible, Whalen's "miracle in the marsh" remains an inspired feat of industrious planning and sheer fantasy.

Writing in *Newsday,* Rhoda Amon notes that whenever she sees memorabilia from the fair, "I still feel that glow of effusive innocence that was ours in the spring of '39." After a half-century we are still trying to reconcile the present with the promise of that 1939 extravaganza in Flushing.

1941

For Americans, it was a time to wait. A time to gaze, transfixed, at a world at war. A time to wonder what part they would play in it all. A time to debate. A time to decide. And a time, at last—on a bright December morning— for fate to intervene.

Edward Oxford

New York writer Edward Oxford is a frequent contributor to this publication.

As midnight approached on Tuesday, December 31, 1940, more than half a million celebrants crowded into New York City's Times Square to mark the passing of the old year and coming of the new.

Lights blazed from the marquees of the theaters, hotels, and clip joints lining the Great White Way. Nightclubs charged fifteen dollars a head for a square foot of eating room and a square inch of dance floor. Champagne flowed freely at twenty dollars a bottle—double the previous year's price.

Amid the blaring of party horns, the music of dance bands, and the popping of champagne corks, New York's revelers, like tens of millions of others in cities and towns and villages across America, sought the play of lights and laughter. For this fleeting hour, at least, they would have what they could of fun and fantasy. As the clock hands clicked toward midnight and the luminous ball atop the Times Tower inched down its sixty-foot pole, the partygoers found a measure of peace and happiness in simply forgetting what time it really was across the rest of the world.

Somewhere—in lands far from the intersection of Broadway and 42nd Street—war raged. London, Rome, and Berlin were blacked out; German armies occupied the once-free nations of western Europe; and death stalked tens of thousands of men, women, and children there and in Asia. But this was still New York, USA. And this was New Year's Eve, American style.

At the stroke of midnight, a great shout rose from the crowd. It was as if the revelers were announcing to the heavens their gratitude for being safe and sound in an enduring America—and expressing their deeply-felt hope that somehow tomorrow would set things right.

In that starless American night, a new year and a new era began.

FOR THE WORLD AT LARGE, THE YEAR 1941 began much like the final act in a Shakespearean tragedy. Intrigue, hatred, revenge, bloodshed, and death piled upon death had gone before. Now onlookers could only wonder if the denouement might be even more devastating.

War dominated the world stage. There was war in Asia—an onslaught by the Japanese against China that had been in progress since 1937. There was war in Europe—Adolf Hitler's armies had swept virtually unchecked across much of the western half of the continent and now seemed poised to strike across the English Channel. And in America, there was the foreboding of war.

The battlefronts in Asia and in Europe, by the scale of miles on the global map, were far away. But the feelings of Americans defied measurement by miles on a map.

World headlines as far back as 1937 spelled out nightmares Americans hoped would not come to pass—but come to pass they had: "Today Germany, Tomorrow The World" . . . "Japanese Rout Chinese" . . . "Adolf Hitler Hailed As Nazis Take Austria" . . . "Nazis Invade Poland" . . . "Britain And France Declare War On Germany" . . . "Germans Launch Blitzkrieg" . . . "British Evacuated From Dunkirk" . . . "German Troops Parade Through Paris" . . . "Battle Of Britain Rages". . . "Japan Joins Axis Pact."

Americans had heard news reporter Edward R. Murrow broadcasting by short wave from London rooftops during German air attacks on the city. "This is London," he would begin, and they would listen. In one broadcast there came an intermission in the bombing. "You know the sound will return," the faraway voice said. "You wait and then it starts again. That waiting is bad. It gives you a chance to imagine things." The folks on Main Street USA in that somber new year were waiting. And, quite likely, they were imagining things.

One gasoline station attendant in Missouri handed customers small cards he'd had printed that seemed to reflect the sentiment of the times. The inscription read, in part: "I am 36 years old. I smoke a pack of cigarettes a day. I shoot a 12-gauge shotgun. I wouldn't have anything against Hitler if he stayed in his own backyard. I don't know any Japs, but I've made up my mind to argue with the next one I see about leaving the Chinese alone. I'm in favor of the AAA, the CCC, the IOU, and the USA. Hurry back."

For more and more people the notion deepened that, whether they lived in Bangor or San Antonio or Milwaukee or Los Angeles, the war might somehow reach them and their loved ones.

As 1941 BEGAN, AMERICA'S 130 MILLION people faced their own problems. The Depression's imprint still lingered, and ten percent of the nation's work force— 5.5 million-remained unemployed. A factory worker made about $30 a week,

From *American History Illustrated*, January/February 1991, pp. 25-36, 70-71. Reprinted through the courtesy of Cowles Magazines, publishers of *American History Illustrated*.

or little more than $1,500 annually. It took about $1,000 a year for a family of four to simply make ends meet—with plain food, meager clothing, rough-and-ready housing, no car, and no telephone. As a future president would later say of the era, "Poverty was so ordinary that folks did not know it had a name."

Americans wanted to see Hitler defeated, but they hoped that England could somehow survive without U.S. troops marching off to war.

Their dilemma had roots deep in the past. Sheltered behind two oceans, the nation had been a place set apart ever since its founding. Well into the twentieth century, Americans still heeded a dictum uttered by their first president. In his Farewell Address, George Washington had urged future Americans to be wary of "entangling Alliances."

But if many Americans had doubts about becoming "entangled" in the war in Europe, their president did not. In his annual message to Congress on January 6, 1941, Franklin D. Roosevelt called for all-out aid to the democracies besieged by dictatorships. And he urged America to help the nations of the world obtain the "Four Freedoms"—Freedom of Speech, Freedom of Worship, Freedom from Want, and Freedom from Fear. Roosevelt envisioned a world with no place for dictators.

Barely forty-eight hours after delivering his message to Congress, Roosevelt challenged that body to help the Allies finish the fight against the Axis powers. He asked the lawmakers for a then-stupendous budget of $18 billion—more than half of it earmarked for defense.

FDR—jaunty, shrewd, iron-willed—had helped America find its way out of the Depression. And now he was determined to help America find its way in a world torn by war. Already he had stripped the nation's armories of old rifles, cartridges, grenades, and field-pieces, rushing them to Britain. He had called on Congress to give America a two-ocean navy, fifty thousand war planes, and a strong army. He had effected a peacetime draft. He had swapped fifty over-age destroyers to Britain in return for eight strategic sea- and air-base sites. With a watchful eye on Japan, he had instituted a policy of "no retreat" in the Pacific. Now in 1941 he would seek to prepare the nation for the worst.

At eleven minutes past noon on Monday, January 10, Roosevelt, standing on a platform outside the east portico of the Capitol, raised his right hand, placed his left on the family Bible, and took his oath as the first president in United States history to serve a third term. He called upon America to defend mankind's faith in democracy, which, even as he spoke, was under attack by Adolph Hitler and Benito Mussolini. An unsettling atmosphere, the most ominous since Abraham Lincoln's 1861 inaugural ceremony, marked the day. The *Baltimore Sun* reported that the inaugural parade consisted mainly of armed forces units: " . . . soldiers, sailors, Marines, Coast Guardsmen, big guns, little guns, bayonets, tanks, trucks . . ." And above the German embassy, a swastika flag flew.

SHOULD AMERICA HELP ENGLAND? ASKED Americans—or should America stay clear of the European war?

The issue of intervention versus isolation centered on the Lend-Lease Bill. Introduced in Congress January 10, just four days after Roosevelt's "Four Freedoms" speech, Lend-Lease embodied FDR's determination to help the Allies. Bearing the fortuitous title H.R. 1776, it would, if adopted, empower the president to supply any threatened nation with arms, food, and other essential materials—when, as, and how he deemed it to be in America's national interest. To preserve the legal appearance of U.S. neutrality, the assisted governments would carry the war supplies away in their own ships and return or replace the materials at war's end.

The Lend-Lease Bill spawned long and bitter debate, not only in Congress but in homes and barrooms and workplaces across the nation. Assigning such broad authority to the president would almost certainly put America just one step short of war.

"Suppose my neighbor's house catches fire, and I have a length of garden hose," went Roosevelt's argument. "If he can take my garden hose and connect it up with his hydrant, I may help him to put out the fire. Now what do I do? I don't say to him before that operation, 'Neighbor, my garden hose cost me fifteen dollars; you have to pay me fifteen dollars for it. I want my garden hose back after the fire is out.' "

Senator Robert Taft glumly countered that lending arms was like lending chewing gum: "You didn't *want* it back."

Senator Burton Wheeler of Montana called Lend-Lease the "New Deal's 'triple A' foreign policy"—a plan to "plow under every fourth American boy." Roosevelt branded that remark "the most untruthful, the most dastardly, unpatriotic thing that has been said in public in my generation."

The thought of "American boys" fighting in a war thousands of miles from home gave many citizens pause. "We went over there once and pulled England's chestnuts out of the fire," one woman said. "This time let them stew in their own juices."

"Be hard. Be without mercy. The citizens of Europe must quiver in horror."

But few Americans reading of the rampages of the *Wehrmacht* could set aside the harrowing portrait of Hitler and Nazism that Roosevelt painted for them. "Never before, since Jamestown and Plymouth Rock, has our American civilization been in such danger," he warned in one speech. "The Nazi masters of Germany have made it clear that they intend to enslave the whole of Europe, and then to use the resources of Europe to dominate the rest of the world." Urging the nation to provide almost unlimited arms for the British, FDR said, "We must be the great arsenal of democracy."

SPEAKING FROM FARAWAY BERLIN, WILliam L. Shirer, a radio correspondent, described for the folks back home a Europe beset by "the Nazi blight and the hatred and the political gangsterism and the murder and the massacre and the incredible intolerance and all the suffering and the starving and the cold and the threat of a bomb blowing the people in a house to pieces, the thud of all the bombs blasting man's hope and decency."

Newsreels of Hitler's ranting speeches gave Americans the sense of a spellbinding but maniacal leader. A reporter described the effects of a Hitler speech on *Reichstag* loyalists: " . . . their faces, now contorted with hysteria, their mouths wide open, shouting, their eyes burning with fanaticism, glued on the new God, the Messiah."

Mussolini, the bombastic, size forty-eight *Il Duce* of Italy, struck many as a pompous *poseur*. But Hitler was quite another matter. The stern-eyed former corporal who had won the Iron Cross loomed as a world conqueror.

During the six remarkable years between his accession to power and the outbreak of World War II, Hitler had made himself dictator and made Germany the strongest military power in Europe. World War I's victors—the nations that thought they had vanquished Germany—looked on with awe and growing fear.

Stricken by its harsh defeat in the Great War, deep in economic depression, and stirred by a hypnotic leader, Germany had sought new hope, pride, and prosperity through National Socialism. Enthralled by a mystical vision of "a new Germany," the people seemed, in an almost nationwide hysteria, willing to follow the Führer wherever and however he chose to lead them. In 1939 Hitler had told his generals, "Be hard. Be without mercy. The citizens of Western Europe must quiver in horror."

Hitler particularly hated Jews, partly because he blamed them for Germany's defeat in World War I. He also felt that the "pure" Aryan race, as personified by the German people, was innately superior. In his book, *Mein Kampf* ("My Struggle"), he stated his belief "that today I am acting in the sense of the Almighty Creator. By warding off the Jews, I am fighting for the Lord's work."

At first, non-Jewish Germans merely despised the Jews. In time, however, this persecuted group would be rounded up—first by the hundreds, later by the hundreds of thousands—and sent to concentration camps to face death, or worse.

Here and there across occupied Europe in 1941, scrawled on walls and sidewalks, the letter "V" appeared as a new symbol for victory against the Axis powers. "Let the enemy see this sign so often," the underground radio urged, "that he will feel surrounded."

But Hitler was far from surrounded. On January 30, he shouted to twenty thousand admirers in Berlin: "Whoever imagines he can aid England must, in all circumstances, know one thing. Every ship, whether with or without escort, that comes before our torpedo tubes will be torpedoed!"

England braced for invasion. Civilians joined the Home Guard, ready with pistols and pitchforks to face the enemy.

Seeking to strangle Britain's life lines, the Germans ranged the North Sea and the Western Approaches with aircraft, prowled the Atlantic Ocean with U-boats,

and cruised the South Atlantic and the Indian Ocean with surface raiders. The British lost ships at the rate of thirty a week.

The besieged country stood alone. Bloodied, nearly beaten, the British people took the blows but remained unbowed. They had, along with their indomitable leader, made up their minds. If need be, they would die alone. But yield they would not. Not to a Hitler.

Churchill knew that Britain's salvation rested in America's hands. With America's help, the British Isles might hold on. Without it, they would go down. The prime minister repeatedly pressed Roosevelt for arms, food, and supplies. "Give us the tools," he pleaded, "and we will do the job!"

As the clock of 1941 ticked on in the U.S., Americans still clung wistfully to the notion of peace. Katherine Hepburn appeared in *The Philadelphia Story* . . . The United Service Organization (USO) brightened the off-hours of the armed forces . . . Theater-goers laughed at *Arsenic and Old Lace* . . . The Boston Bruins won their third straight hockey title . . . And shiploads of children arrived from Britain to wait out the war.

THE QUESTION OF LEND-LEASE—AND OF peace or war—quickly became a matter of moral choice. Down deep, many Americans grew convinced that there was a "right" side and a "wrong" side in the widening conflict.

Isolationists spoke out against "that man in the White House." Roosevelt, charged one Congressman, would plunge the nation "into the hell of war . . . in order that he may go down in history as America's first dictator." Groups such as the America First Committee railed at the country to "stay out of it." They contended that Hitler posed no real threat to America's security. England, they said, was fighting not for democracy but to save its empire.

The featured isolationist speaker in 1941 was famed "Lone Eagle" Charles Lindbergh. He argued that the war was not America's business. Lindbergh, along with former U.S. ambassador to England Joseph Kennedy, historian Charles Beard, and socialist leader Norman Thomas, testified against the Lend-Lease Bill.

Pacifists marched with signs that read "All Men Are Brothers." Educator Robert Hutchins warned that the "American people are about to commit suicide" by

drifting into war. Philosopher John Dewey exhorted: "No matter what happens, stay out."

Those who favored Lend-Lease saw bedrock values at stake. Author Stephen Vincent Benét felt that the world faced "a new theory of the state of man," of "master and helot, lord and serf . . ." Theologian Reinhold Neibuhr had been a committed pacifist until, while in London, he experienced an air raid. He then lashed out at intellectuals "who equated American neutrality with the Sermon on the Mount." Wendell Willkie, the presidential aspirant who had opposed Roosevelt in 1940, returned from a tour of war-torn England to exhort the Senate: "The powers asked for are extraordinary. But this is an extraordinary situation."

Finally, on March 11, the debate ended, and Congress made its decision. The momentous Lend-Lease Bill passed. Roosevelt signed it within ten minutes after it reached his desk. Five minutes later he approved a long list of bombers, artillery, and machine guns for immediate shipment to Britain. Congress, handing FDR the key to democracy's arsenal, quickly appropriated $7 billion to pay for this—and for shipments to come.

A grateful Churchill called Lend-Lease "a second Magna Carta." Britons flew American flags on London's streets.

Like the characters in James Hilton's *Lost Horizon,* Americans had sought the isolation of a "Shangri-La" where they could escape the problems of a disturbing world—but they had found that they could not stay there. The era of isolation was over. Now America and its people were neutral in name only.

In Berlin, Hitler appeared unconcerned about Britain's new "lease" on life. During a ceremony honoring the German war dead of World War I, he declared that "no support coming from any part of the world can change the outcome of this battle in any respect. England will fall."

And the war continued with unabated fury. Sweeping across Europe like a force of nature, German armies smashed into Yugoslavia, Greece, and Crete. U-boat "wolf-packs" sank British merchant ships twice as fast as they could be replaced. Erwin Rommel's Afrika Korps prowled North Africa. On April 9-10, British bombers hit Berlin. On the night of April 16, six hundred German planes bombed London.

In a radio address on May 3, Churchill affirmed: "No prudent and far-seeing man can doubt that the eventual and total defeat of Hitler is certain." In a speech the next evening, the Führer called Churchill's remarks the ravings of a drunkard. On May 10, from eleven o'clock at night until four in the morning, thousands of bombs rained down on London. The Houses of Parliament, Westminster Abbey, and the British Museum were among the landmarks hit.

"We will give it back to them," Churchill promised.

Churchill, invincible, walked the streets of London to inspect bomb damage and give a boost to British morale. In his dapper homberg, smoking his cigar, he seemed the British bulldog personified, the very embodiment of the will to win. "We will give it back to them," he promised.

And Roosevelt continued to find new ways to help his ally. Despite the fact that the United States remained technically neutral, the president seized Axis ships in sixteen U.S. ports, opened American ports to British naval vessels for repairs, and placed the U.S. Navy on patrol throughout a defense zone ranging well out into the Atlantic.

Meanwhile, the tempo of daily life continued for Americans despite the overhanging war clouds. For the ninth time in nine years, Roosevelt stood in the presidential box at Washington's Griffith Stadium and threw out the baseball season's first ball . . . *For Whom the Bell Tolls* sold, in author Ernest Hemingway's words, "like frozen daiquiris in hell" . . . German actress Marlene Dietrich became a U.S. citizen; asked by the Nazi government to return to Germany and make motion pictures there, she declined . . . In San Francisco, an American sailor climbed a fire escape to the ninth floor of the German consulate and tore a large swastika flag from its staff as hundreds of spectators cheered . . . An ad for the brewing industry declared, "In a world of strife, there's peace in beer."

WAR IN THE FAR EAST—WHERE A BITTER conflict raged between Japan and China—seemed far away to most Americans. They knew little about either nation and found it difficult to understand their seemingly alien cultures. But most peo-

ple, recalling news accounts and photographs of Japanese aggression, such as a well-publicized shot of a wounded and crying baby in the war-devastated ruins of Shanghai, sympathized with the poverty-stricken Chinese as they fought to stave off their predators.

Americans tended to view the Japanese as strange if not sinister war-makers from a mystery-shrouded island-nation. To his subjects, Japan's Emperor Hirohito was not a man but a god. Photographs showed him in regal uniform, astride his white stallion *Shirayuki* ("Snow White").

Proud, warlike, and determined, the Japanese struck some as the Oriental counterparts of Germans. Both peoples sought resources and territory; both believed that the gods had ordained that they rule their portion of the globe.

As Germany sought *Lebensraum*— "living space"—so Japan espoused "Asia for the Asians." The Japanese envisioned a "new order" on the continent— a "Greater East Asia Co-Prosperity Sphere." Roughly translated, this meant that distant powers such as America, Great Britain, France, and Holland, which represented the "white race," must leave Asia to whom it belonged by right of birth, geography, and history.

However altruistic such aspirations might have sounded, Japan's main allegiance was to its own aggrandizement. Asia's vastness held the resources upon which the small island empire depended— not merely for its well-being but for its very survival. Axis victories in Europe now offered Japan a golden opportunity to take by force the resources it coveted—Indochina's rice paddies, the Dutch East Indies' oil fields, and British Malaya's rubber plantations. Pacific Oceania, Japan's foreign minister observed, "has sufficient resources to support from 600 to 800 million people. I believe we have a natural right to migrate there."

Glory glinted in the great adventure. Hard times in Japan gave rise to the new samurai—warriors loyal to their heritage and intent on asserting their nation's honor by making conquests abroad. The Japanese soldier's field service code instructed him to "never give up a position, but rather die."

Only one nation, Japanese military leaders believed, had the strength to stay their hand—America. Throughout the 1930s, friction between the United States and Japan had steadily intensified. In

Japan, that decade would later be called *kuraitanima,* the "dark valley." These were years of economic plots, abortive coups, and assassinations—a period during which the Japanese Imperial Army drew up ambitious plans for conquest. By mid-1937, those plans had become reality, as Japanese forces strove to bomb, shoot, and terrorize China into submission. They attacked with a savagery that stunned the world.

The Japanese Imperial Army attacked China with a savagery that stunned the world.

The U.S. gave China enough aid for that country to continue fighting back. And at any time America—by cutting off its oil exports to Japan—could put tremendous pressure on the island nation to relent.

In the summer of 1940 President Roosevelt quietly took a strategic step against Japan by shifting the U.S. Pacific Fleet from its base at San Diego to Pearl Harbor, on the Hawaiian island of Oahu, where it could better serve as a mid-Pacific sentinel. The Japanese came to think of the fleet as "a dagger pointed at our throat."

In August 1940, American crypto-analysts scored an intelligence coup when they succeeded in cracking the Japanese diplomatic code. Thenceforth, the code breakers, whose operation assumed the code name "Magic," could decipher intercepted messages between Japan and its consulates abroad. Only Roosevelt's closest advisors knew of the breakthrough.

Admiral Isoroku Yamamoto, commander of the Combined Imperial Fleet, had served as a naval attaché in Washington and was wary of America's vast natural resources and industrial might. "We cannot defeat America," he warned. "Therefore, Japan should not fight America." But the anti-American clique in the war cabinet remained unconvinced.

Japan did, however, respect America's fighting power enough to take measures to guard herself against it. In September 1940, Hirohito joined Hitler and Mussolini in signing the Tripartite Pact, a formal Axis alliance aimed at keeping the United States in check. The three Axis powers agreed to help each other should the United States enter the war.

In April 1941, Japan signed a nonaggression pact with Russia, effectively protecting it from the Russian bear as well.

As the threat posed by Japan grew more apparent, anti-Japanese sentiment in the United States grew. Cartoons depicted Japanese as aggressive schemers with thick eyeglasses and deceitful smiles. Newspaper editors denounced the shipping of American scrap iron and steel to Japan. The *New York Daily News,* for example, warned that pieces of that city's dismantled Third Avenue Elevated train system, which had been sold and shipped to Japan, might "come back to us as bullets." FDR heeded such editorials and halted further shipments.

Although Japanese envoys spoke of keeping the peace, the "Magic" readings of intercepted Japanese diplomatic messages revealed Japan's designs on Southeast Asia. "It seems clear," Secretary of State Cordell Hull told President Roosevelt, "that Japan's military leaders are bent on conquest—just as are Germany's." Roosevelt desired peace, but not at the price of appeasement. He demanded that Tokyo abandon its plan to drive into Southeast Asia—and that Japan withdraw from China.

During mid-1941 Americans took their minds off war by reading the "funnies"—*Dick Tracy, Superman, Little Orphan Annie, Terry and the Pirates,* and *Joe Palooka,* among others . . . The gorilla "Gargantua" drew circus crowds . . . Workers put their dollars into defense bonds and their coins into defense stamps. . . "Dollar-a-year men" [federal consultants who received token salaries for patriotic service] moved into Washington, D.C., to run scores of new bureaus . . . Heavyweight champion Joe Louis, in his eighteenth title defense, defeated Billy Conn . . . Every Sunday evening at seven o'clock, millions of listeners tuned their radios in to "The Jack Benny Show" . . . Women swept their hair up and off their faces . . . Movie critics called Orson Welles's *Citizen Kane* an American masterwork.

WAR—OR, MORE ACCURATELY, PREPARATION for war—turned the gears of the American economy even faster. Boeing built bombers. Chrysler produced tanks. Willys-Overland cranked out Jeeps. The vaunted "Arsenal of Democracy" dramatically increased its production of rifles, machine guns, mortars, antitank guns, and field artillery pieces. Aircraft engines, fighters, and bombers rolled off assembly lines. Cruisers, destroyers, aircraft carriers, battleships, and merchant vessels slid down the ways and splashed into the waters of the Atlantic, the Pacific, and the Gulf of Mexico. Steel, aluminum, oil, machine tools, magnesium, and munitions issued forth. The machines of war demanded more steel, more coal, more everything.

America's industrial production soared—but not without problems. The year 1941 witnessed 4,500 work stoppages—nearly twice 1940's total, and far beyond those of any prior year in the nation's history. From Labor's point of view, the strikes were understandable; badly battered by the Depression, workers fought to get their fair share of what appeared to be a new but elusive prosperity.

Seventy-eight-year-old Henry Ford, calling labor unions "the worst things that ever struck this earth," tried—through strong words, mass firings, and goon squads—to keep unions out of his automobile plant. His chief enforcer, Harry Bennett, labeled the emerging union of automobile workers as "irresponsible, un-American, and no . . . good." Voting under the aegis of the National Labor Relations Board, the workers got their union. Said an embittered Ford to his negotiators: "Give 'em anything—it won't work."

DURING THE SPRING AND SUMMER OF 1941 the Atlantic Ocean became a vast panorama of danger and sudden death. American warships patrolled great stretches of the ocean to protect convoys transporting cargoes of arms and supplies to Britain. Nazi *Unterseeboots* prowled the same waters. Under such circumstances, the Atlantic seemed a likely setting for a decisive event; grim memories of a German submarine sinking the *Lusitania* during World War I came to the minds of older Americans.

In April U.S. troops established an outpost in Greenland.

On May 21, a U-boat sank an unarmed U.S. freighter, the *Robin Moor,* in the South Atlantic. Although no one died, an infuriated Roosevelt froze all German and Italian assets and closed all German consulates in the United States.

On May 22 the forty-thousand-ton German battleship *Bismarck* slipped into the North Atlantic. The following day, off Greenland, the *Bismarck* unexpectedly encountered the British battleship *Hood* and in a brief action sank her. Roosevelt directed American aircraft to assist in searching for the German warship; a British crew flying an American-made patrol plane located her. British battleships finally sank the *Bismarck* on May 27—dealing the Germans their worst naval loss of the war.

In July, U.S. Marines landed in Iceland to hold that position against Germany.

Viewing the ever-darkening scene in the Atlantic Ocean, Roosevelt proclaimed an unlimited national emergency in the U.S. The aim of the Nazis, he warned, was to rule the world. "The war is approaching the brink of the Western Hemisphere itself," he said. "It is coming very close to home."

On September 4, a U-boat off Greenland fired torpedoes at the destroyer USS *Greer*—and missed. The *Greer* had been provocatively trailing the submarine and had even dropped depth-charges. A week later, the president ordered the Navy to "shoot on sight" these "rattlesnakes of the Atlantic."

On October 17, a German torpedo crashed into the destroyer *Kearney,* killing eleven American sailors. Ten days later, in a Navy Day address to the nation, Roosevelt declared: "We have wished to avoid shooting. But the shooting has started. And history has recorded the first shot." After a dramatic pause, he continued: "In the long run, however, all that will matter is who fired the last shot."

The nation came still closer to a war-making event on October 30. While escorting a convoy bound from Newfoundland to Britain, the destroyer USS *Reuben James* was sunk by a U-boat off Iceland. Two-thirds of the destroyer's crew—115 men—perished. For the first time in World War II, a German submarine had sunk a United States warship. In Berlin, a German government spokesman archly commented that "anybody walking along the railroad tracks at night should not be surprised if he gets run over by an express train." In Washington, an outraged Congress authorized U.S. merchant ships to arm and to enter combat zones.

One of Roosevelt's aides noticed that the president's face bore "that gray fatigue which comes from long hours of close work." Still America waited, preparing for the seeming inevitability of war in the Atlantic.

Amid the tension on the homefront Bing Crosby crooned "Blue of the Night" . . . Frank Sinatra offered "I'll Be Seeing You" . . . Whirlaway, ridden by Eddie Arcaro, won the Kentucky Derby . . . "Yankee Clipper" Joe DiMaggio hit in fifty-six consecutive baseball games—setting a seemingly unbreakable major league record . . . The cryptic half-face and scrawled "Kilroy was here" appeared on walls and signboards . . . A Camel cigarettes ad declared "The *Smoke's* the Thing!" . . . The shapely Rosemary LaPlanche became 1941's "Miss America" . . . A woman asked a librarian for a copy of a book called *Mein Kampf.* The librarian asked her who wrote it. Replied the would-be reader: "I can't keep up with all these newcomers."

BY THE SUMMER OF 1941 GERMANY's *Blitzkreig* had reduced much of Europe to a smoking ruin. England steeled herself for the vengeful attack that would surely follow. But Hitler momentarily had other plans. In the summer of 1941, the German dictator did the unthinkable—despite a 1939 nonaggression pact with Russia, he invaded the gargantuan republic in an apparent effort to secure his Eastern frontier before tackling Britain.

At 3:00 A.M. on Sunday, June 22, the usual changing of the border guards on this, the year's shortest night, became a bloodbath. The German sentries, instead of saluting their Russian counterparts, gunned them down.

Thus began the most wide-sweeping attack in military history, which the Germans dubbed Operation *Barbarossa.* The vanguard of a mighty force that ultimately comprised three million troops, more than thirty-five hundred tanks, seven thousand artillery pieces, six hundred thousand vehicles, and eighteen hundred airplanes—moved deep into an astounded Russia. The tremendous armies stretched nearly two thousand miles, from the Arctic Region to the Black Sea.

Confident of victory, the Führer assured his aides that his all-conquering armies would subdue the "Mongol half-wits" of Russia within a few weeks.

Premier Joseph Stalin called upon the Russian people to make every sacrifice to save Mother Russia—lest Hitler turn them into "the slaves" of the Germans.

President Roosevelt began shipping thousands of tons of food and arms to a new ally—Russia. Most Americans had little sympathy with Communism, but their hearts went out to the Russian people as victims of the Nazis. Americans hoped for a Russian victory. They were willing to help Russia—an enemy of their enemy.

For a time, the Germans advanced faster into Russia than had Napoleon a century before. But, as the Russians held on week after week, German commanders began to experience a sense of bewilderment; Hitler's soldiers killed Russians by the tens of thousands, only to have tens of thousands more materialize from the heartland. "In the beginning," said one German general, "we reckoned with some two hundred enemy divisions. So far we have already identified three hundred and sixty divisions. When a dozen of them are destroyed, the Russians throw in another dozen."

The Eastern Front metamorphosed into a horrorscape of blood as the irresistible force of German strength met the immovable object of Russian defiance.

As they had done before against Napoleon, the retreating Russians scorched the earth. No crop, no factory, no house remained behind.

The Eastern Front metamorphosed into a horrorscape of blood as the irresistible force of German strength met the immovable object of Russian defiance. By the end of August, German troops had ripped eight hundred miles into the Soviet Union. They seized Kiev, only to find that Russian troops had seeded the city with ten thousand delayed action mines, setting off explosions for five days.

In September the German army struck Leningrad, trapping three million people in the rubble. In the frigid weather that followed, thousands of Russians died daily of exposure. Hitler forbade a direct attack, instead commanding his troops to starve the city to death. By November Leningrad residents were eating cats and crows.

In October, the *Wehrmacht* launched Operation Typhoon—a power-stroke of massed infantry, panzer, and motorized forces driving straight for Moscow. At first, the staggering Soviet losses roused Hitler's hopes for victory.

Meanwhile, upon Hitler's command, bureaucrats labored to perfect plans for *endlosung*—"the final solution"—of the "Jewish question." As mass deportation of German Jews began, the death rate of Jews trapped in the Warsaw ghetto steadily rose. Jews were executed by the thousands in conquered Russian territories. At Auschwitz concentration camp, officials experimented with exterminating groups of prisoners with poison gas, using captured Russian soldiers as test victims.

The Battle of Moscow began on October 7. The air in the city was filled with "black snow"—ashes from documents burned by Russian authorities. The Red Army, which had already lost three million men, absorbed savage attacks on the outskirts of the capital.

A besieged Stalin on November 9 sounded a call for war without mercy: "Well, if the Germans wish this to be a war of extermination, they will get it! No mercy for the German invaders!"

The Germans had their *Gotterdammerung.* As Napoleon had learned, winter in Russia held despair, desperation, and death for the invader. Here courage was not enough. The closer the *Wehrmacht* advanced toward Moscow, the more disheartening became the omens. A correspondent wrote of the bodies of German soldiers "frozen in strange positions, many with arms bent uplifted as though to ward off the inevitable."

The winter of 1941, the worst in a century, seized the *Wehrmacht.* German casualties passed the seven-hundred-and-fifty-thousand mark. Ice encased the German tanks. Soldiers in tattered summer uniforms stripped jackets and boots from captured Russian troops.

The German advance guard could see the Kremlin through binoculars. But to see it was not to reach it. On December 1, with the temperature at ten degrees below zero, the men of the *Wehrmacht*—as hard-fighting and cruel an army as the world had ever seen—reached the limit of their endurance. After driving toward Moscow for 167 days, the spectacular German invasion of the Soviet Union ground to a frozen halt. For the first time, to the disbelief of their own fierce field commanders, Hitler's once-invincible troops—now gaunt, frostbitten, and starving—had failed.

The Russians, in iron-hearted defense of their homeland, had held the line.

Within a few months after opening their Eastern Front, the battle-wise German armies had conquered more territory in less time than any other fighting force in history—only to go down in the mud, rain, and snow of an inhospitable land that would not endure their presence. Those troops of the *Wehrmacht* who could still march turned their backs on Moscow and headed back toward Germany.

Many would not make it to the fatherland. Siberian troops, moving on skis and clad in white, tore into the retreating columns. Artillery shells blew the German soldiers to bits. On December 5, the full Russian armies—their tanks in wide-sweeping array—launched a massive counterattack along the Eastern Front.

In waging the Battle of Britain, the Royal Air Force had bought time not only for England but for America. Likewise the Russian Army, in the fire and smoke of the Eastern Front, bought more time.

Back on the American homefront, Gary Cooper starred in *Sergeant York* . . . Bud Abbott and Lou Costello shared the billing in *Buck Privates* . . . Women working in defense plants earned the sobriquet "Rosie the Riveter" . . . Civilian defense officials tested air-raid sirens in mock air attacks . . . "Sad Sack" appeared in newspapers . . . "King of Swing" Benny Goodman rode high, as did Glenn Miller's "Chattanooga-Choo-Choo," Jimmy Dorsey's "Green Eyes," and Harry James's "You Made Me Love You."

As AMERICA SLIPPED NEARER TO THE EDGE of war, Roosevelt decided to meet for the first time with British Prime Minister Winston Churchill. In August, aboard a warship in a Newfoundland harbor, the two "naval persons" drew up an eight-point declaration called the Atlantic Charter, proclaiming their vision of a world built on the principles of democracy.

The meeting marked the beginning of an enduring friendship. Roosevelt afterward cabled Churchill: "It is fun to be in the same decade with you." And Churchill later recalled: "I felt I was in contact with a very great man."

The prime minister, with wry eloquence, thus described the special friendship of their respective nations: " . . . two great organizations of the English-speaking democracies, the British Empire and the United States, will have to be somewhat mixed up together in some of their affairs for mutual and general advantage."

"Give us the tools," Churchill pleaded, "and we will do the job."

Events far across the Pacific, meanwhile, were bringing the United States one step closer to joining Britain as an active war partner. On July 2, Japan sent fifty thousand troops into Indochina. President Roosevelt retaliated, freezing all Japanese assets in the United States, halting trade between the two countries, and, in a crucial move, finally cutting off oil shipments to Japan. Almost ninety percent of Japan's oil sources vanished in an instant—with Japan's military reach just short of oil fields in Borneo, Java, and Sumatra.

The Japanese Imperial armies had two choices. They could watch their last oil supplies dwindle, be forced to withdraw from Southeast Asia, and in so doing lose face; or, trusting to fate and defying America's will, they could storm onward and seize the oil riches they needed.

In the event of war with the United States, Japan's survival depended on keeping the Far East free of U.S. naval forces. By striking a sudden blow against the U.S. Pacific Fleet, the military leaders calculated that Japan had a good chance of carrying out its Far East occupation.

Should the United States decide to wage all-out war in response, Japan could fight a war of attrition, island by island, territory by territory, against this mighty opponent—and perhaps, in time, wear it down. Or—as some optimistically hoped—the United States, having suffered a devastating attack, might well sue for peace, stay put on its placid mainland, turn its eyes away from the Western Pacific, and leave Asia to the Japanese.

As early as the beginning of 1941, Japanese military leaders had begun shaping plans for a seaborne air attack against the United States. Such a strike, they felt, would "decide the fate of the war in the very first day." U.S. Ambassador Joseph Grew, stationed in Tokyo, got wind of the scheme. In January he warned Washington of a rumor "going around town" that the Japanese, in case of a break with the United States, were "planning to go all-out in a surprise mass attack on Pearl Harbor."

At the time, Roosevelt and his chief advisors presumably viewed this scenario as far-fetched. These national decision-makers had unique insights into the Pacific situation; not even America's Pacific commanders knew that America had broken the Japanese code. Day by day, unknown to the Japanese, Roosevelt's top advisors scanned messages intercepted by "Magic."

Roosevelt's inner circle believed that a Japanese attack against the British and Dutch possessions in Southeast Asia—and perhaps the Philippine Islands—was a far more likely possibility than an attack against so distant a target as Hawaii. Even today, however, controversy surrounds the matter of precisely how much Roosevelt and his key advisors knew of Japan's plans concerning an attack on Hawaii.

The Philippine Islands straddled the patch between Japan and the Southwestern Pacific. During the late 1930s, General Douglas MacArthur was assigned to the Philippines to organize a defense for the Commonwealth against Japanese incursion. In July 1941, Roosevelt named MacArthur Commander of U.S. Army Forces in the Far East. The general set up headquarters in Manila. By fall, he had under his command twelve thousand troops, thirty-five bombers, and seventy-two fighter planes.

"I make no concession concerning a withdrawal [from Southeast Asia]," declared war-minded General Hideki Tojo on October 14. "It means defeat of Japan by the United States—a stain on the history of the Japanese Empire!" A few days later Tojo became prime minister.

For eight years, Cordell Hull, the venerable U.S. secretary of state, had engaged in talks with one Japanese emissary after another. He tried patience and peaceful persuasion. But the more that Hull and the Japanese diplomats offered and counter-offered, the clearer it became that they could not find common ground.

Hull concluded that "Japan is attuned to conquest. Japan envisages war with the United States sooner or later. The Japanese Army, after almost a decade of war, has not had enough. The Japanese

Navy thinks in terms of an eventual war with this country. The Japanese still think in terms of an eventual Axis victory."

Japan's leaders urged America to cease aiding China, to let oil flow freely again to Japan, to restore normal trade with Japan, and not to strengthen American military and naval forces in the Pacific. The clipped, unwavering, fateful U.S. answer was "No."

By fall, Japan and the United States had reached an impasse—and both knew it. As Japan would not step back from its plans to conquer Southeast Asia, neither would the United States stand aside to let it proceed. Thus did the American Eagle stand poised against the Rising Sun.

CLOSE OBSERVERS HAD LONG SAID THAT IF Japan ever found itself in a hopeless corner it was capable of committing national *hara-kiri*—flinging itself at its mightiest enemy and gambling on victory over suicide.

While Japanese diplomats parried for time, the nation's militarists readied bayonets and bombs. By October, a Japanese design for a death strike against America took shape.

Throughout that somber autumn, the Japanese war-makers marked their battle arrows on the Asian map. One army would move down the Malay Peninsula toward Singapore. Another was to invade the Philippines. Another would head toward Burma. Another would seize the oil-rich Dutch East Indies. The Japanese assaults would be so fast and furious that the Allies could not stop them. Then, fighting from behind its ring of bases, Japan might be able to outlast the United States—and claim Asia for itself.

On November 3, the chief of the Japanese naval general staff gave final approval of the plan to begin war against the United States with an attack on Pearl Harbor. The mechanism for one of the most momentous events in modern history slowly swung into motion.

On November 5, U.S. Army chief of staff General George Marshall and Admiral Harold Stark, chief of Naval Operations, advised Roosevelt that "war between the United States and Japan should be avoided while building up defensive forces in the Far East."

On November 20, Tojo rendered an ultimatum to the United States. Japan would occupy no more of Asia—if the United States would cut off aid to China

and unfreeze Japan's assets in America. Such an agreement would leave Japan free to subjugate China. The Japanese government did not expect America to accept its overture.

On November 25, American code-listeners intercepted a Japanese message setting November 29 as the deadline for negotiations.

On November 26, Hull met with Japanese emissaries and again set forth the demands that America had reiterated throughout recent months: to get out of Indochina and give up its gains in China.

A *Time* magazine article, in an issue predated December 8, wrote: "One nervous twitch of a Japanese trigger finger, one jump in any direction, one overt act, might be enough. A vast array of armies, of navies, of air fleets were stretched now in the position of track runners, in the tensions of the moment before the gun."

Meanwhile, in America the clock of 1941 ticked steadily on. Brooklyn Dodgers' manager Leo Durocher knocked down an Associated Press reporter in a street fight after being asked a "tactless" question . . . Using prefabricated sections, a shipyard built the Liberty Ship SS *Robert Peary* from the keel up in five days . . . Silk stockings grew ever-scarcer . . . Walt Disney released *Fantasia* . . . Red Sox slugger Ted Williams, the "Splendid Splinter," finished the baseball season with a .406 batting average . . . Humphrey Bogart portrayed Sam Spade in *The Maltese Falcon* . . . And Greta Garbo, at age thirty-six, turned her back on Hollywood.

AMERICA STEADILY ASSUMED THE APPEARance of an armed camp. "Get in line, you stupid bastards!" sounded across training fields as drill sergeants berated draftees. By fall, the U.S. Army numbered almost a million and a half troops. Barracks sprouted by the thousands. *Saturday Evening Post* covers featured Norman Rockwell's plain-folks soldier—a rosy-cheeked young man named Private Willie Gillis, Jr.

Many an American mother gave her son a Bible to take with him when he entered military training. The army provided each recruit with a book of its own: *The Soldier's Handbook*. It matter-of-factly advised the new soldier: "Do not drink liquor. If you take a drink sometimes anyway, don't guzzle . . . Select for your female companions decent

girls or women and keep away from whore houses . . ."

The *New York Times* described draftees: "Tall, short, slim and fat, the new men will jostle one another like tired cattle. They will be bowed under the weight of new barracks bags and their uniforms will bag at the knees."

Soldiers. Sailors. Airmen. Marines. Coast Guardsmen. Not long before, they populated colleges, high schools, even elementary schools. Now they studied war.

It was a crisp, clear autumn. In New England, as always, the leaves turned russet. In cities and towns across the country, as always, high school and college youth played football, and families enjoyed Thanksgiving turkey dinners. Although the people did not realize it, America reveled in its last peaceful autumn for some time.

Newspaper columnist Raymond Clapper, as though bidding farewell to an era, wrote: "It's been a grand life in America . . ."

BEFORE DAWN ON THE MORNING OF November 26, under strict secrecy, Vice Admiral Chuichi Nagumo's *Kido Butai* (Carrier Striking Force) slipped away from the Kurile Islands off northeastern Japan. For twelve days, the strike force—six aircraft carriers, two battleships, three cruisers, nine destroyers, eight oil tankers, and sixteen submarines—moved undetected toward its attack-release point 230 miles north of the U.S. naval base at Pearl Harbor.

The waiting ended at last.

In the golden morning light of Sunday, December 7, as though in a surreal dream, flights of Japanese aircraft appeared over the island of Oahu. Vacationers on the beach at Waikiki idly watched a formation sweep in over Diamond Head. No American patrol planes ranged out on the watch over the waters around the Hawaiian Islands that morning.

A U.S. Army enlisted man, watching the screen of a mobile radar unit, noticed a sudden array of blips. The images indicated a large flight of aircraft 130 miles distant, approaching Oahu from the north. He notified an officer, who advised him not to be concerned about the blips; they were echoes from a flight of U.S. Army bombers due to arrive that morning from the mainland, the officer opined. The blips, however, were signs of another presence.

The Japanese pilots clearly saw the hundred or so ships of the United States Pacific Fleet, moored in restful order at Pearl Harbor. Among them, seven battleships stood in two neat rows; an eighth lay nearby in a drydock.

The planes overhead—red rising suns emblazoned on their wings—swept down on the fleet.

It was 7:55 A.M. on Oahu. Wave after wave of Japanese bombers, torpedo planes, dive-bombers, and fighter planes smashed in upon the ships. Fire and smoke rose from once-placid harbor.

At 7:58 A.M., a Navy radio message flashed to Washington, D.C.: "AIR RAID, PEARL HARBOR. THIS IS NOT DRILL."

At 8:55, a second attack hit Pearl Harbor. By mid-morning, the more than 350 Japanese attack planes had vanished, their grim work well done.

The battleships *Arizona, California,* and *Oklahoma* had been sunk; the *West Virginia* badly hit; and the *Maryland, Tennessee, Nevada,* and *Pennsylvania* damaged. Three light cruisers and three destroyers were sunk. More than 340 American planes lay destroyed or damaged beyond repair. Casualty figures included more than 2,400 American sailors, soldiers, and civilians dead, and some 1,200 wounded. The Japanese lost twenty-nine planes.

"Yesterday, December 7, 1941—a date which will live in infamy . . ."

Winston Churchill, learning the news on British radio, called Roosevelt.

"Mr. President, what's this about Japan?"

"It's quite true," Roosevelt replied. "They have attacked us at Pearl Harbor. We are all in the same boat now."

"That certainly simplifies things," Churchill said. "God be with you."

In Germany, a messenger read Hitler a telegram announcing the Japanese attack. "We cannot lose the war!" the delighted Fuhrer shouted. "Now we have a partner who has not been defeated in three thousand years."

The attack on Pearl Harbor represented a triumph of Japanese guile and strength. Ironically, it also guaranteed the devastation of the island nation.

Shortly after noon on Monday, December 8, Roosevelt addressed Congress: "Yesterday, December 7, 1941—a date which will live in infamy—the United States of America was suddenly and deliberately attacked by naval and air forces of the Empire of Japan . . ." Roosevelt continued speaking for six minutes, closing with the exhortation: "We will gain the inevitable triumph—so help us God. I ask that the Congress declare that since the unprovoked and dastardly attack by Japan on Sunday, December 7, a state of war has existed between the United States and the Japanese Empire."

Within the hour, Congress so declared. That night, the lights of the White House were darkened—as they remained every night for the war's duration.

Roosevelt did not ask Congress to declare war against Germany. Nevertheless, on December 11, Hitler saved him the trouble; Germany and Italy declared war on the United States. Nazi foreign minister Joachim von Ribbentrop summoned the American representative to his office and told him, "Your president has wanted this war, now he has it."

In the Philippines, the U.S. Army found itself fighting with its back to the wall for the first time since Belleau Wood. At Wake Island, Major James Deveraux, commander of the four-hundred-man U.S. Marine detachment, challenged the Japanese to "Come and get us." They did. Throughout Southeast Asia, Japanese armies followed the arrows marked on their battle maps.

U.S. ships arrived in San Francisco Bay bearing women and children bombed out of their Honolulu homes, and sailors wounded at Pearl Harbor. For four years Americans had viewed newspaper accounts and photographs of war wreckage, and of broken British, German, Polish, Russian, and Chinese bodies. Now they read news stories of their own battles and stared at images of their own dead and wounded.

Life on the home front went on much as before, but now it bore inescapable traces of the war raging overseas. Actor James Stewart donned an army private's uniform; his pay plummeted from six thousand to twenty-one dollars a month . . . Shoppers bought the elixir "Serutan—It's Natures, spelled backwards" . . . "Victory Socks" cost thirty-nine cents a pair . . . Multimillionairess Doris Duke Cromwell, photographed in a Manhattan nightclub, offered the lens-

man a thumb-of-the-nose . . . The Chicago Bears defeated the New York Giants for the National Football League championship . . . A book titled *You Can't Do Business With Hitler* hit the best-seller list . . . Popular radio shows included "Guiding Light," "Road of Life," and "Right to Happiness" . . . Albert Einstein played a violin at a benefit for refugee children.

AMERICA—AND THE REST OF THE WORLD—faced a bleak Christmas season. Tojo warned the Japanese people that the war would be long. In Berlin, propaganda minister Joseph Goebbels broadcast appeals to the German people to donate warm clothing for their soldiers on the Eastern Front.

A bitterly cold Christmas Eve chilled Washington, D.C. Soldiers with fixed bayonets guarded the White House. Nevertheless, Roosevelt admitted thousands of people onto the grounds to watch him light the national Christmas tree. After the president offered his hopes for a better year to come, the crowd listened to Churchill, who had come for a Christmas visit. He made a brief speech: "Let the children have their night of fun and laughter . . . and let us be resolved that, by our sacrifice and daring, these same children shall not be robbed of their inheritance or denied the right to live in a free and decent world." Roosevelt and Churchill stood side by side as the Marine band played "God Save the King" and the "Star-Spangled Banner."

A week later, the momentous year drew to a close.

Despite all its terrible and tangled events, 1941 was a decisive year. Hitler had declared, at year's opening, that 1941 was destined to be a time of stupendous world triumph for his people. He was wrong.

The battle lines had spread terror, bloodshed, and devastation over ever-widening reaches of the earth until they encompassed the globe. The warriors of the Axis not only killed; they died—from the waters off America's Eastern seaboard clear around the world through North Africa, Russia, China, and Southeast Asia, and across the Pacific Ocean. Colossal, costly battles raged. But, to their consternation, victory eluded the Axis powers.

At the beginning of the year the fight seemed nearly over. By December, it was just beginning. That was the significance of 1941.

America had gazed out at the world. Now the world's eyes turned toward America. It was our turn.

Why We Fight, a film series for American military forces, defined the nation's reason for entering the war: "We would fight for the country—and for an idea bigger than the country. The idea of liberty. The right of free-born people to rule themselves."

No other explanation was needed. There was, after all, a right and a wrong in the world. America had to—and did— fight for what she believed was right.

For Americans of 1941, destiny brought a time of trial. Most had lived through the Great Depression; many were now called upon to fight a global war. In a sense, that made their generation unique in American history. They inherited neither prosperity nor peace but hard times and war.

Once again, as throughout history, the common man fought the war and paid the price. American mothers hung the first gold stars in their windows—stars signifying a lost son—gone, but always remembered. As time passed, hundreds of thousands of gold stars appeared in windows throughout the land.

The New Year's Eve celebration in Times Square in 1941 outdinned the clamor of the preceding year. The traditional merry-makers—numbering more than a million—brandished more horns, bells, and noisemakers than ever before.

Officials granted permission to two thousand bars in the New York City metropolitan area to remain open until 8 A.M. In the Persian Room at the Plaza Hotel, an electric "V" sign shone. Twelve orchestras played all night at the Waldorf-Astoria. Seven thousand celebrated at the Hotel Astor. Many a toast was made for better days—and to the end of "the Japs, the Nazis, and the Fascists."

Sixteen hundred air raid wardens kept patient vigil along the Great White Way. Warning signs of a kind never before seen in these streets instructed celebrants: "In case of alarm, leave Times Square. Walk. Do not run." Sirens atop buildings stood prepared to sound warnings. That Times Square might be under the threat of an air raid—however remote a possibility—bothered the revelers not at all. Declared red and blue letters on a huge white billboard at the northern edge of Times Square: "Remember Pearl Harbor. Buy Defense Bonds."

As the lighted ball atop the Times Tower descended at midnight, Lucy Monroe sang "The Star-Spangled Banner" over a loudspeaker. The crowd joined in, and Times Square echoed and re-echoed to the national anthem as hundreds of thousands in the streets sang. At the stroke of midnight, many in the crowd hoisted men in uniform to their shoulders.

Even as the celebrants exulted, a news bulletin flashed in a moving ribbon of light around the base of Times Tower: "Manila Force In Last Stand."

The year 1942, freighted with battle and privation and sacrifice, made its way into Times Square.

Racism and Relocation: Telling the Japanese-American Experience

James A. Mackey and William E. Huntzicker

The late James A. Mackey was professor of curriculum and instruction at the University of Minnesota in Minneapolis. William E. Huntzicker is a free-lance writer and lecturer in journalism at the University of Minnesota in Minneapolis.

Gladys Ishida remembers riding with her father in their Chevrolet stake truck filled with fifty-pound lugs (wooden boxes) of apricots and peaches to the cannery at Modesto, California, five miles from their family's orchard. There they sold their dried fruit to the federal government to feed soldiers.

By the standards of the Depression, the Ishida family lived comfortably in the 1930s. They hired Mexican migrant farm workers to help harvest their fruit each year. Gladys's father, Raiji, built his farm with hard work; he came to the United States before World War I. Gladys's mother, Suye, came to the United States in 1922. Like many U.S. farm families, the entire Ishida family worked on the farm along with the hired hands.[1]

Although the Ishidas had built a successful farm, the 1913 Alien Land Law prevented Raiji and Suye from owning their own land. They were *issei,* the first generation of Japanese to emigrate to the United States, and they were not allowed to become U.S. citizens. Since alien land laws kept noncitizens from owning land, a friend of the family, a lawyer, put his name on their property.

As *nisei,* the Japanese-American generation born in the United States, Gladys and her brothers could one day own the farm, but they were not yet old enough to own land when their father was stricken with colon cancer. He died in November 1940.

A year later, the Japanese attack on Pearl Harbor and the approaching war worried Suye, but 18-year-old Gladys remained optimistic. "At least we have the orchard and we can grow vegetables," she said. But the lawyer, who had dragged his feet on transferring the land to a corporation in Gladys's name, now threatened her mother. He told her not to press the issue or he would burn all records of their transactions. In reality, he said, he owned their farm.

By the spring of 1942, the Ishidas saw notices ordering Japanese Americans to report to an assembly center at Merced, California. From there Gladys and her family were sent to the Amache Relocation Center in southeastern Colorado. "You could only take one suitcase per person," she said. "Everything else was left behind or presumably sold." They would never return to the farm.

Rumors reached them in the internment camp that their well-developed 180-acre orchard sold for $2,500 an acre in 1943. But the lawyer sent the Ishidas only $16,500.

The Ishidas were among 110,000 Japanese Americans forced from their homes, farms, and businesses in the largest deprivation of civil rights in the United States since the abolition of slavery (Weglyn 1976; Thomas and Nishimoto 1969; Irons 1983). Merced was among a dozen California assembly centers. Washington, Oregon, and Arizona each contained one. After processing, Japanese Americans were sent to relocation centers or internment camps in eleven states. No one was excluded except the critically ill, who could be left in institutions.

The experience of Japanese Americans provides an often overlooked case study of racism in U.S. culture. Its legacy emerges in current attitudes toward Asian Americans who have emigrated since the wars in Indochina.

The symbolic environment in which Californians lived in the 1920s and 1930s carried many stereotypes of Japanese Americans. Of course, Gladys Ishida knew the history of the "yellow peril" in which Californians persecuted Asians because they feared cheap labor would steal jobs from white working people. She also knew that many Asian Americans faced racial discrimination. From a relatively prosperous background, however, she never faced racism herself until the family's lawyer threatened their property and she read evacuation notices.

Californians had been racist toward Japanese long before Pearl Harbor. Although few Japanese had moved to the United States before 1890, westerners drew on a legacy of anti-Chinese sentiment in their attitudes toward Japan. Then in 1900 the annexation of Hawaii freed many Japanese contract laborers on sugar plantations to move to the United States. Japanese immigration increased. Nativist groups warned that the West would be "Japanized" as the South had become "Negroized." Japanese Americans posed an even greater threat, they said, because Japan was rising as a world power and a major Pacific naval power. Like racist southerners, some westerners worried about mixed marriages and the purity of white women (Limerick 1987, 269–273).

From *Social Education,* Vol. 55, No. 7, November/December 1991, pp. 415-418. Copyright © 1991, National Council for the Social Studies. Reprinted by permission.

Propaganda concerning the Axis powers increased as German aggression spread through Europe and Japanese aggression subdued much of Asia. But a major contrast emerged between attitudes toward the two enemies. German aggression and German enemies were often portrayed in the person of Adolph Hitler. Japanese, on the other hand, were often depicted in ugly caricatures that could be interpreted as any Japanese person. In the case of Germany, the enemy was Hitler; in the case of Japan, the enemy was the Japanese people.

When Japan attacked Pearl Harbor, about 127,000 Americans were of Japanese ancestry and, of them, about 113,000 lived in California, Washington, Oregon, and Arizona. They represented less than 0.01 percent of the U.S. population and less than 2 percent of California's population, where they lived in the heaviest concentration (Thomas and Nishimoto 1969, 1).

Despite their small numbers, the legacy of stereotypes and racism combined with wartime hysteria made the most bizarre charges against Japanese Americans seem plausible. The government declared all Japanese Americans potential spies and subversives; pressure groups, including farm organizations, expressed alarm that Japanese-American farmers threatened the U.S. food supply and that their income could be sent to the enemy in Japan. These claims defied logic, since Japanese Americans constituted a fiercely loyal ethnic group.

Soon after the attack on Pearl Harbor, General J. L. DeWitt, head of the West Defense Command, said that "any proposal for mass evacuation [of Japanese Americans] was 'damned nonsense!' " (Murphy 1972, 233). Restrictions on aliens around military bases were adequate protection, he said. After sensing that the general public disagreed, however, DeWitt advocated the removal of Japanese Americans. "They are a dangerous element," he said. "There is no way to determine their loyalty" (Grodzins 1949, 282). Executive Order No. 9066 issued February 19, 1942, required the evacuation. Two-thirds of evacuees were U.S. citizens and more of them, like Raiji Ishida, would have been if the laws had allowed. Any persons of Japanese ancestry, whether American or not, became inherently suspect. "A Jap's a Jap," DeWitt said (Grodzins 1949, 297).

Eventually, the U.S. Supreme Court held that a national emergency could justify the suspension of civil liberties for a time. Justice Frank Murphy dissented from what he called this "legalization of racism. Racial discrimination in any form and in any degree has no justifiable part whatever in our democratic way of life," he wrote (Murphy 1972, 291). Military discretion should be limited, he said, especially when it lacked substance.

Within the relocation and internment camps, many Japanese Americans faced questions of loyalty. The *issei* were ineligible for U.S. citizenship, but they were asked to "foreswear any form of allegiance or obedience to the Japanese emperor" (Weglyn 1976, 136). This statement forced the *issei* to become stateless. Those who refused the loyalty statement were sent to Tule Lake, which became a high security relocation camp. A few younger *nisei* refused the loyalty pledge on the grounds that it was a civil rights violation. Some *issei*, left penniless by the evacuation, their dreams shattered, returned to Japan with their *nisei* children.

College and military service were the only way out of the camps. Gladys Ishida tried to get out from the moment she arrived at Merced in May 1942. By late August, she and her brother, Calvin, with help from a National Student Relocation Council, attended Washington University in Saint Louis. Financially, their father's insurance money, part-time work, and scholarships enabled the three Ishida children to attend college while their mother remained at the Amache Relocation Center. Julius, the youngest, completed two years of high school in the camp and then attended Wooster College in Ohio.

The National Student Relocation Council helped students get accustomed to their new homes, where few members of their ethnic groups lived. (Gladys recalls being mistaken for an American Indian in Saint Louis.) The government imposed some restrictions, she said. For example, no Japanese-American student could enroll in a university within twenty-five miles of a railroad terminal. "I guess they thought we were all going to bomb or do something with railroad terminals to impede the war effort," she said.

Within a year, she completed her degree at Washington University and enrolled as a graduate student in international relations at the University of Chicago. There she was visited by an FBI agent, who seemed suspicious that a Japanese American would be interested in international relations. The agent was polite, she said, but he showed up on her first day of work and refused to wait until after her working day for the interview. "He insisted that I be available for the interview immediately and he got my boss to provide us a room in which he could interview me," she recalled. "He was polite, but I was embarrassed in my first day on the job. I felt like I was a spy or something." Gladys eventually received a master's degree at Chicago and a doctorate at the University of Michigan.

Other Japanese Americans left the camps for military service. Some served in language training at special camps such as the one at Fort Snelling, Minnesota, where they trained Japanese Americans to speak Japanese so they could either serve in the Pacific War or work to break codes.

Others joined active service, including the segregated 442d Japanese-American combat unit. Dan Inouye, an 18-year-old volunteer, was among the ten thousand Hawaiian *nisei* to join the war. Nine days before the end of the European war, Inouye stood to throw a grenade forty yards into a German machine gun nest in Italy. A rifle grenade severed Inouye's right arm; he picked up a second grenade with his left hand to kill the firing German. He continued directing an assault on the German position, suffering bullet wounds in his abdomen and his right leg. He received a Distinguished Service Cross and a Bronze Star. Although Inouye, now a United States Senator, returned to San Francisco with an empty sleeve, when he walked into a barber shop for a haircut, he was told: "We don't serve Japs here" (Hosokawa 1969, 416–417).

U.S. images of Japan fluctuate. After the war, Japan was seen again as a charming Oriental country represented by silk pillows and James A. Michener's *Sayonara;* and the Japanese were seen as a quaint but benign people. Japanese imports, seen as harmless, cheap toys, began to flood U.S. markets; Japanese cars became the butt of jokes.

In recent years, however, the image has swung back to that of relentless competitor. The tone in the United States continues to be ambivalent: Japan-bashing exists alongside admiration and a flood of imitation and jealousy. The United States demands high tariffs on Japanese goods and equitable trade with Japan, and complains about unfair governmental subsidies of Japanese businesses. At the same time, educators and entrepreneurs in the United States want to imitate Japanese methods. Through it all, Japanese Americans continue to suffer discrimination related to the prevailing view of Japan. White Americans who resent Japanese successes continue to use Japanese Americans as scapegoats, especially in the auto industry where U.S. workers often blame the Japanese for the failures of this country's industry.

The legacy of racism continues against other Asian Americans, even as they become the nation's fastest growing ethnic minority in the wake of the Indochina wars. Asian students excel on student aptitude and college admissions tests while the overall scores of white students have declined. As a result, Asian Americans have been selected to attend the best U.S. universities in larger proportions than their populations. They now find, like Jewish students of the 1940s and 1950s, that major campuses may be limiting their enrollment. A national television report on this issue in 1989 used as its title the old racist assumption about Japanese Americans: They were victims of their own success (ABC News 1989). Racial and ethnic minorities, it seems, are allowed to succeed only within limits. The beat goes on.

Some Japanese Americans have sought governmental review of the decision to evacuate them to relocation camps. In August 1988, the U.S. Congress passed a redress bill to pay $20,000 to each of the Japanese Americans interned in camps during World War II. Suye Ishida never lived to see the money. She died in November 1989 and her heirs received her payment in January 1991. The $20,000 was a pittance compared to the value of the farm she lost. Her children received their own redress payments in October 1991.

Despite progress on redress, Japanese Americans have again become scapegoats. Japan has become increasingly competitive in the automobile, electronics, steel, and other basic industries. At the same time, other Asians have, since the Indochina War, become the fastest growing ethnic groups in the United States. Their immigration has coincided with economic recession. While it is natural, understandable, and realistic to be anxious about relentless competition, it is just as unfair and undemocratic to attribute blame on the basis of race. It is also unjust to blame Japanese Americans for the actions of a nation their families left generations ago.

The three Ishida children, of course, have grown. They have retired from their careers: Calvin Ishida was a mechanical engineer in Northbrook, Illinois; Julius Ishida was an economist and accountant in Chicago; and Gladys Ishida Stone was a professor of sociology at the University of Wisconsin-River Falls. Suye Ishida's ashes are interred in Kitsuki, Japan, with her husband's, which were interred there after World War II when the family was allowed to return with them.

The Ishidas never returned to their family farm. Friends reported that the land became a housing development during the war. All the trees were removed. Gladys Stone returned to the site in September 1991, but development had changed the land so much that she could not even locate where her farm had been.

NOTE

1. Gladys Ishida Stone told her story to the authors in a series of interviews in April and May 1991 in Saint Paul, Minnesota. The authors are grateful for the time and assistance she has given them.

REFERENCES

ABC Television News. "Victims of their Own Success?" "20/20," 5 May 1989.

Grodzins, Morton. *Americans Betrayed: Politics and the Japan Evacuation.* Chicago: University of Chicago Press, 1949.

Hosokawa, Bill. *Nisei: The Quiet Americans.* New York: William Morrow and Co., 1969.

Irons, Peter. *Justice at War: The Story of the Japanese American Internment Cases.* New York: Oxford University Press, 1983.

Limerick, Patricia Nelson. *The Legacy of Conquest.* New York: W. W. Norton, 1987.

Murphy, Paul L. *The Constitution in Crisis Times.* New York: Harper and Row, 1972.

Thomas, Dorothy S., and Richard Nishimoto. *The Spoilage: Japanese-American Evacuation and Resettlement During World War II.* Berkeley: University of California Press, 1969.

Weglyn, Michi. *Years of Infamy: The Untold Story of America's Concentration Camps.* New York: William Morrow and Co., 1976.

'Since You Went Away'

The War Letters of America's Women

'Everyone in town is talking war, war, war'—Judy Litoff and David C. Smith sift through the hopes and fears of America's home front in this selection and commentary of letters they have assembled from wives, mothers and sweethearts during the Second World War.

Judy Litoff and David C. Smith

Judy Barrett Litoff is Professor of History at Bryant College in Smithfield, Rhode Island. David C. Smith is Bird and Bird Professor of History at the University of Maine, Orono. Persons interested in participating in the Women and Letter Writing During World War II Project are encouraged to write to Judy Barrett Litoff/David C. Smith, Women and Letter Writing During World War II Project, Bryant College, Smithfield, RI 02917.

Early in 1943, Max Lerner, the well-known author and journalist, writing for the New York newspaper *PM*, predicted that 'when the classic work on the history of women comes to be written, the biggest force for change in their lives will turn out to have been war. Curiously, war produces more dislocation in the lives of women who stay at home than of men who go off to fight'.

With the renewed interest in American women's history which has occurred over the last quarter of a century, most historians interested in women and the Second World War have addressed the implication of Lerner's statement by either explicitly or implicitly asking the question: Did the War serve as a major force for change in the lives of American women? Our reading of approximately 25,000 letters written by 400 women has

led us to conclude that the events of the War had a dramatic and far-reaching effect upon the mothers, step-mothers, grandmothers, aunts, sisters, wives, sweethearts, daughters, and female friends of the sixteen million Americans who served in the military during the Second World War.

For the past three years, we have been engaged in a major effort to locate, collect, and analyse the wartime correspondence of American women. Our search for these letters began in the spring of 1988 as we were making the final revisions on a book, *Miss You: The World War II Letters of Barbara Wooddall Taylor and Charles E. Taylor* (University of Georgia Press, 1990), which was based on thousands of pages of wartime correspondence between a young war bride and her soldier husband. We found the letters of Barbara Wooddall Taylor to be extremely powerful documents, chronicling a grand story of romance, making do, learning to cope with life, and 'growing up' during wartime. We became convinced that Barbara Taylor's story was similar to those of other women during the War. But how could we be sure? What had happened to the more than six billion letters which were sent overseas during this period?

While conducting the research for *Miss You,* we learned that the letters written by men in combat had often been carefully preserved by loved ones at home, donated to military and university

archives, and made into dozens of books. However, after conducting exhaustive searches, we came to realise that very few efforts had been made to locate and utilise women's wartime correspondence. Whenever we asked about the letters that women wrote, the response most often heard was, 'There aren't any letters from women. They were all destroyed. The men in combat were under orders not to keep personal materials'. Yet the historian in each of us could not quite believe that this was true.

Intrigued by the challenge presented to us, we began to consider possible ways to locate letters written by American women during the Second World War and sent a request for information from anyone who had knowledge of such letters to every daily newspaper in the United States and to 400 popular and professional periodicals, including publications for veterans, minorities, and women. Subsequently, we sent letters of enquiry to every state historical society and archive as well as to many other important archives throughout the United States. In total, we sent out 2,500 enquiries.

Three-and-a-half years later, our lives have been dramatically altered by our search. We have heard from 600 individuals from all fifty states, and we have collected 25,000 letters written by 400 American women. No one, including ourselves, had any idea that so many

written for everyone to read. They were directed to a small audience, usually a single reader. They were hurriedly written—sometimes during 'lunch' breaks on the midnight shift—but with an intensity that makes them read like great literature. They allow us to peer into the private thoughts, hopes, and dreams of the writers and enable us to gain a clearer understanding of how women, themselves, perceived one of the most tumultuous eras of the twentieth century.

We had expected the mark of the censor to be prominent in many of the letters. To our surprise, there is almost no evidence of official censorship. Because of the important role which mail played in building morale, we had also anticipated that many of the letters would have an artificial, upbeat quality to them. In actuality, many collections contain a surprising number of letters in which the writers 'let go' of their feelings and frankly discuss their fears and frustrations.

One of the most significant themes expressed in the letters is the new sense of self experienced by wartime women. Whether the writer was a young war bride forced to 'grow up' very quickly or a dying step-mother urging her step-son to remain at his duty station, the exigencies of war necessitated that women develop a new sense of who they were and of their capabilities.

The letters in our collection capture both the most intimate details in a woman's life and the great transformations that society at large was undergoing. They provide abundant evidence that women were actively engaged in the war effort, and they vividly depict women's growing social and political consciousness. As we read and re-read women's wartime letters, we become more convinced each day that Max Lerner was right.

The following letters, excerpted from our book, *Since You Went Away: World War II Letters from American Women on the Home Front* (Oxford University Press, 1991), demonstrate how the lives of American women were disrupted and changed by the events of the Second World War. Because wartime letters were often hurriedly composed, the writers sometimes omitted words such as 'it,' 'is,' and 'the'. We have supplied these missing words to ease readability. For the same reason, we have also added commas and apostrophes, and, occasionally, we have corrected spelling errors. Wartime letter-writers often

Women at war; this poster produced by the War Production Co-ordinating Committee to encourage women workers exemplifies the new 'can do' sense of independence and achievement that writers like Polly Crowe reflected.

letters had survived the vicissitudes of war and the post-war years.

The letter-writers range in age from six to ninety-six and represent a geographic and socio-economic cross-section of American life. Secretaries, clerks, teachers, librarians, factory workers, tenant farmers, ranch owners, migratory workers, women in uniform, housewives, and volunteer war workers have all written letters which have been donated to us. Most of this correspondence was posted to enlisted personnel or junior grade officers. In short, the letters we have collected were written by 'ordinary' Americans to other 'ordinary' Americans.

The letters themselves are wonderfully compelling. And, increasingly, it has become clear that they are compelling because they were not originally penned very long letters, in fact, ten-page letters were not uncommon. In order to include a wider sample of letters, we have provided abridged versions of many of them. We have indicated this by the use of ellipses.

Although the Second World War began in Europe in September 1939, the United States avoided direct involvement in the conflict until the Japanese attack on Pearl Harbor on December 7th, 1941. The following letter, written by Ruby Seago of Lawrenceville, Virginia to her future husband, Richard Long, who was in basic training at Camp Wheeler, Georgia, recounts the travail and uncertainty brought about by the events of that significant day.

Lawrenceville, Virginia
Sunday Nite—December 7, 1941
My Darling,

I know you feel exactly like I do right now. I've just been listening to the radio. I've never been so blue or heartsick as I am right this minute. Oh, my darling,—if it were possible I'd charter a plane—do anything—just to see you for a few minutes. . . .

Honestly, Dick, if I don't get to see you I'm going to lose my mind. Isn't there *any* thing you can do? 'Cause if you don't do it now, do you realize we may never see each other again? Of course, you do—you realize how serious the situation is, even more than I. Darling, they *can't* take you,—the finest, sweetest boy that ever lived and send you away—it just tears my heart out to think of it.

Everyone in town is talking war, war, war! Everyone is sure it will be declared tomorrow. There are some sad hearts over this world tonite. And none sadder than mine. And your poor mother.

There isn't any use of me pretending to feel other than the way I do. It's too serious now. And you'd know I was pretending, if I tried to write a cheerful letter.

Pete [a lodger in the Seago home] is in the bathroom crying her eyes out. I think she'd marry Jack tonite. I don't blame her. She'd have that much. It's better than not having anything—to remember. This is awful—I know I'm hurting you. And I can't help it. Every word is coming from my heart.

I love you Dick, more than anybody in the world. You know it already, but I want to tell you again. And I'll always love you to the end of my life. I love you because you're fine and good and just the kind of man I always wanted to meet and love. You meet all the requirements, Darling.

I'd give everything I own, or ever hope to have, to see you right now. Isn't there anything we can do?

Please don't let anything happen without letting me know.
Wire me or call me or something. If it's possible.
Forever yours,
Ruby

Isabel Kidder and her two young children lived in Durham, New Hampshire, during the three years that her husband, Maurice, a chaplain in the Army, was stationed in Europe. She wrote a very compassionate letter to him as he was awaiting shipment to England.

Durham, New Hampshire
October [?], 1942
The First Day,

My darling, I call this the first day, for it is the first day in which I do not know where you are. If your ship slipped out into the wideness of ocean last night, tonight, or tomorrow I shall not know until after the war probably. Maybe there will be many details which I shall never know, and that seems hard to bear. It must seem equally hard to you to feel that there are things which are going to happen to "we three" which you cannot know. But I shall attempt to write as many of them down as possible.

If you could see me now, pleased as punch because down in the cellar the fire is burning and it is of my creating. I am determined to master that imperturbable monster. Otherwise, it just isn't decent to have it there. But I say burning with a good deal of relief. For I was afraid it was roaring. My coal came this afternoon and I got a fire built . . . But it got away from me. The house got so hot I shut all the radiators and opened the front door, and I felt as if I'd let the genie out of the bottle . . .

This was one of October's perfect afternoons. We put our lunch in a bag—two peanut butter sandwiches apiece, an apple, two cookies, and a napkin full of those little bittersweet chocolate drops they put in cookies and took to the road. We sat on yellow leaves in a group of little trees and watched the water spreading into pools below the dam. It made a rippling sound coming over the rocks around the bend, but right in front of us it was clear and still enough to reflect the trees . . . Even the off-red of a glowing tree colored the water like the reflection of a fire. Everywhere the water-spiders glanced along over the surface and as we sat there thistledown was forever passing us and skimming out over the water. Joel (their six year old son) thought it was exactly like the milkweed fairies in *Fantasia*.

I could have stayed forever in a spellbound world where I was young and you were there . . . Good night you nut.
Isabel

California dreaming . . . a 77th Infantry Division private from San Bernadino reading a letter from home during a lull in the fighting in Okinawa.

Official exhortations to keep up morale by mail employed other media than merely a poster campaign – as this November 1943 cover of the magazine *House Beautiful*, with its Joan Crawford look-alike in the act of composition, illustrates. On the receiving end was the cheery GI – as shown in the V-Mail poster (below).

He's *Sure* to get
V···–MAIL
Safest Overseas Mail

The mobilisation of the American economy for war created an unprecedented demand for new workers. In response to this need, some 6.5 million women entered the work force. The proportion of women who were employed increased from 25 per cent at the beginning of the war to 36 per cent at the war's end—an increase greater than that of the previous four decades. The woman war worker was highly lauded and 'Rosie the Riveter' became a national heroine. Women worked in shipyards, aircraft plants, and other assembly lines. They were nurses and nurses' aides, served with the Red Cross, were employed in day care centres, and held a variety of other jobs. In their letters to loved ones, women war workers expressed pride in their jobs and often commented, with enthusiasm, about the new sense of responsibility and independence they were achieving.

Polly Crowe, shortly after taking a job as a comptometer at Jefferson Boat and Machine Company in Anderson, Indiana, wrote an enthusiastic letter about her new job to her Army husband, William, who was fighting with the Allied Forces in Europe.

Louisville, Kentucky
June 12, 1944
Darlin',
You are now the husband of a career woman—just call me your little Ship Yard Babe! Yeh! I made up my mind that I wanted to work from 4:00 p.m. 'till midnight so's I could have my cake and eat it too. I wanted to work but didn't want to leave Bill all day—in the first place it would be too much for Mother altho' she was perfectly willing and then Bill needs me . . .
Opened my little checking account too and it's a grand and a glorious feeling to write a check all your own and not have to ask for one. Any hoo, I don't want it said I charged things to 'em and didn't pay it so we don't owe anybody anything and I'm gonna start sockin' it in the savings and checking too so's we'll have something when our Sweet little Daddy comes home. Good nite, Darlin'
I love you, Polly

Edith Sokol and Victor Speert met while students at Ohio State University. They were married on June 14th, 1942, and the following month, Victor was drafted. The newlywed couple experienced a 'marriage on the move', moving fourteen times over the course of the next two years. In September 1944, Victor was sent to Europe, and Edith returned to her childhood home in Cleveland, Ohio, to live with her parents 'for the duration'. She secured a job at a federally-sponsored day care centre and was eventually appointed director of Cleveland's True Sisters Day Care Center. During the eighteen months the Speerts were separated, Edith wrote detailed letters to Victor in which she described her work as a day care director, balancing their budget, car repairs, wartime shortages, and her hopes and dreams for the post-war world. At the conclusion of the War, she took the opportunity to tell Victor that she had received a great deal of satisfaction from her war work.

Cleveland, Ohio
October 21, 1945
Darling,

Lately I just haven't had the time to sit down and write you all of what I think and feel, but I think I've given you a smattering of my moods in all my letters . . .

In a way I'm disgusted with everybody and everything—all I want is for you to come home so that I can really live! . . . Last night Mel and I were talking about some of the adjustments we'll have to make to our husbands' return. I must admit I'm not exactly the same girl you left—I'm twice as independent as I used to be and to top it off, I sometimes think I've become 'hard as nails'—hardly anyone can evoke any sympathy from me. No one wants to hear my troubles and I don't want to hear theirs. Also—more and more I've been living exactly as *I* want to and I don't see people I don't care about—I do as I damn please. As a whole, I don't think my changes will effect our relationship, but I do think you'll have to remember that there are some slight alterations in me. I'm pretty sure that holds true for you too—am I correct? . . .
I love you.
Edith

Cleveland, Ohio
November 9, 1945
Darling,

. . . Sweetie, I want to make sure I make myself clear about how I've changed. I want you to know now that you are not married to a girl that's interested solely in a home—I shall definitely have to work all my life—I get emotional satisfaction out of working; and I don't doubt that many a night you will cook the supper while I'm at a meeting. Also, dearest—I shall never wash and iron—there are laundries for that! Do you think you'll be able to bear living with me? . . .
I love you,
Edith

Patricia Aiken wrote a powerful and angry letter to her husband, A.S. Aiken, stationed in Alaska with Army Air Corps, shortly after learning that the husbands of two of her close friends had been killed in action.

Greenbelt, Maryland
April 24, 1943
Hi, Joe,

I've about reached my low point so according to the Dorothy Dix's, I shouldn't be writing to you and lowering your morale—but as I always say, what the hell's a husband for . . . On thinking the whole thing over—I wish some kind soul would blow the whole damn world to hell—and I'd be glad to be among the missing.

I think it would be better to be in Poland or Greece where they kill all the family instead of just one person and leave the others grubbing around trying to make a life out of nothing, like those two kids will have to do. I can't even feel good about us—if we do get out of it, we'll probably be fat, frightened and always running around trying to save our own necks . . .

You ought to be here where I could weep on your silly shoulder instead of so far away I can't even remember what you look like. Anyway, stall as long as you like and I hope you have a helluva good time.
Pat

Women's wartime letters also provide evidence that the political sensitivities of many women were heightened by the events of the War. In their correspondence, letter writers referred to reading newspapers and magazines, listening to the news on the radio, and hearing radio commentators debate politics and strategy. They wrote that they hung maps on the walls of their homes in order to remain close to world affairs. They offered comments on state and national politics, expressed horror at the Nazi atrocities, discussed the progress of military campaigns, praised the Soviet troops for their bravery, called for the establishment of a United Nations, and contemplated how the post-war world might differ from their own world. Indeed they thought deeply about the meaning of the struggle in which they were involved.

For American citizens of Japanese descent, the politics of this war were extremely complex. In 1942, the 120,000 Japanese-Americans living along the west coast of the United States were evacuated to camps located in remote areas of the country. This relocation process sometimes resulted in very painful separations. The following letter was written by Sonoko U. Iwata to US Attorney General Francis Biddle in Washington, DC, urging him to allow her husband, Shigezo Iwata, interned at Lordsburg, New Mexico, to be reunited with his family at the Colorado River Relocation Camp near Poston, Arizona.

Poston, Arizona
July 21, 1942
Sir:

I am taking this means to appeal to you for a reconsideration of the decision against Shigezo Iwata, my husband, who was taken into custody on March 11 from Thermal, California; given a hearing on May 15 at Santa Fe, New Mexico, where he was detained; and transferred to Lordsburg, New Mexico, on June 19 as an internee of war and now identified as ISN-25-4J-1110-C1 and located at Barrack 4, Camp 3, Company 9, Lordsburg Internment Camp.

I am an American citizen of Japanese descent and I believe in the government of the United States. I am grateful for the privileges I have been able to enjoy and share as a part of democratic America.

The decision you have recently rendered against Shigezo Iwata, my husband, must have been reached after a careful consideration, but I am making this appeal to you in the hope that there might be room for reconsideration.

I solemnly affirm that Shigezo Iwata, my husband, has at all time been loyal to America and has always cooperated with our government, observing all regulations and trying his best to add constructively to the welfare of the nation. In the almost five years of our married life, I have always known him to practice simple honesty. He has been open-hearted, too, though markedly reserved. Our life has been a struggle on a small income but always there was hope and ambition for a high living and we were slowly but surely attaining it. If Shigezo Iwata is returned to his family now settled at the Poston War Relocation Camp, I can assure you that he will cooperate and unite in efforts to build-up this city of Poston which we know is a part of democratic America.

This appeal, I make, not because of our three small children who undoubtedly will receive more adequate care if their father could be with them nor for my own desire of keeping our family together since I know that countless numbers of homes are being permanently broken because of this conflict, but because I firmly believe Shigezo Iwata, my husband, is a loyal resident and has never been or never will be dangerous to the security of the United States. Moreover, to be considered as such is a dishonor we cannot bear to face.

Whatever your final decision, I shall still have faith in God and in our government, but I keep praying that you will be able to give Shigezo Iwata a favorable decision.

Any word from you will be greatly appreciated. Respectfully yours,
Sonoko U. Iwata (Mrs. Shigezo Iwata)

Lucille Wilson, a school teacher from

Everett, Washington, wrote regularly to her only child, Private Herrett S. Wilson, who was stationed in the Pacific throughout much of the War. In a letter written in June 1944, she provided a provocative response to the question, 'Is it all for naught?'

Everett, Washington
June 27, 1944
Dearest Son,
. . . I can see why you ask the question, 'I fought and killed so that the enemy might not invade our land and I ask is it all for naught when red, white, and blue fascists drive Nisei about like coyotes and plague the fathers, mothers, and relatives of our colored comrades that fight by our side.' There are many things that will make you ask yourself this question, 'Is it all for naught?' from time to time. I've asked myself this question for you many times. I'm sure every mother has done the same . . . Millions of veterans and home folks intelligently asking this question may bring great post war changes. That is the hope of the *future*.

Jefferson gave us a goal in the Declaration of Independence and the American Bill of Rights. In the 150 years past we have made strides and have widened the base of Democracy. At first only property owners could vote and in some sections of New England only church members and property owners. So we can see visible changes in our scope of Democracy, but you are right, we have great strides to make here in our own country . . .

I will be anxiously awaiting further news of your condition, homecoming, or what have you?
Much, much love,
Mom

As the War drew to a close in the late summer of 1945, the question of the larger meaning of the conflict weighed heavily on the minds of many letter-writers. Marjorie Haselton of Athol, Massachusetts, wrote a powerful 'victory' letter to her Navy husband, Richard, who spent the last months of the war behind Japanese lines engaged in espionage and other 'hazardous' duties.

Athol, Massachusetts
V-J Day—August 15, 1945
My Darling,
I'm listening to the radio and I have a feeling that somewhere, right now, you are listening, too. Bing [Crosby] is talking to our hearts, as only he can do it, and the top talent of the USA is contributing its bit. The songs they are singing have me alternating between laughter and tears . . .

You and I were brought up to think cynically of patriotism—not by our par-

ents, but the books, plays, movies and magazine features written by the bitter, realistic writers of the twenties and thirties. They called patriotism a tool of the demagogues, a spell binder to blind our eyes to the "real" truth. We thought they were right—at least, I know, I did. I hated everything in music, books, movies, etc. that stressed love of country. That was for the yokels. The uninitiated, but not for anyone who was really in the know. Maybe I was right—I don't know. One thing I *AM* sure of—a thing this war has taught me—I love my country and I'm not ashamed to admit it anymore. Perhaps I am only thinking along the lines the nation's propagandists want me to think. But I know I am proud of the men of my generation. Brought up like you and I, in false prosperity and degrading depression, they have overcome these handicaps. And shown the world that America has something the world can never take away from us—a determination to keep our way of life . . . You boys proved that you had a fighting spirit and team work that couldn't be beaten. Call it Yankee ingenuity or whatever you will, it still is the one force that won the war—the thing the enemy never believed we had. That is why, tonight, I am proud to be an American, and married to one of its fighting men. None of you fellows wanted the deal life handed you—but just about every one of you gritted your teeth and hung on . . . I think the President sounded tonight as if he felt that way, too. Proud enough to bust. And, Gee, what other country in this world would let an insignificant *Private* introduce over the air, the head man of the country? Thank God for letting us live and bring up our family in a country like this. It's not perfect, I know, but it's the best there is—and away ahead of the rest! . . .

I've been hoping your special assignment is one that the surrender will make unnecessary. Wouldn't it be grand if you were heading home right now! I know that's too much to expect, but I hope I get a letter Tuesday with real news cause I want my chance to show you in person how much.
I love you.
Me

In her 'victory' letter to her future husband, Donald C. Swartzbaugh, who was in the Army Air Corps and stationed in India at an RAF base, Constance Hope Jones of Kirkwood, Missouri, perceptively remarked that perhaps 'the biggest job is yet ahead'.

Kirkwood, Missouri
August 18, 1945
Donnie,
Here I am again. How'd you celebrate

the great news of the Japanese surrender? I'll never forget how things happened around here. Pop got out his 45 and 38 and blasted away his long saved shells. He was just like a kid playing with a new toy! (They tell me that *men* are always little boys, anyway, and I believe it.) In addition to that the church bells rang, whistles blasted loud and long, kids got out drums, pots and pans, flags, etc. and paraded the streets, people let loose of their tires and gas and paraded thru the streets until well into the night. Thousands crowded the streets in St. Louis. At Memorial plaza, 40,000 kissed and danced their way on the streets all night long. The next day everything closed up tight. Today most of the war plants are closed up and people are wondering about jobs . . .

I think our family has been lucky in that both of our 'warriors' are safe and sound. There are thousands of families not quite so lucky . . .

Now, I suppose President Truman and Congress really have a big job of getting things and people adjusted to peace time ways of hiring and doing! Perhaps the biggest job is yet ahead.

Over the radio yesterday, I heard the starting of another war! All about how the US was developing new and secret weapons and how we should keep our secrets from the Russians! . . . Talk like that is a betrayal of those who died or were wounded in this war and of those who are working to make it possible for nations to live in peace with each other! . . .
Till later,
Connie

FOR FURTHER READING:

Judy Barrett Utoff and David C. Smith have written three books based on the wartime correspondence of American women: *Since You Went Away: World War II Letters from American Women on the Home Front* (New York: Oxford University Press, 1991); *Dear Boys: World War II Letters from a Woman Back Home* (Jackson: University Press of Mississippi, 1991); and, *Miss You: The World War II Letters of Barbara Wooddall Taylor and Charles E. Taylor* (Athens: University of Georgia Press, 1990). They are preparing a fourth book, *We're In This War Too: World War II Letters from American Women in Uniform,* to be published by Oxford University Press. They are also co-editors of a forthcoming seventy reel microfilm edition, *The World War II Letters of American Women,* to be published by Scholarly Resources, Inc. A recent anthology of World War II letters from American servicemen is Annette Tapert, ed., *Lines of Battle: Letters from American Servicemen, 1941-1945* (New York: Times Books, 1987).

The Face of Victory

The bombs that fell on Pearl Harbor were the seeds of today's America

Gerald Parshall

As it molders on the bottom of Pearl Harbor, charred and crumpled by Japanese bombs, the battleship Arizona is both a memorial and a graveyard for most of the 1,177 crewmen who died on its pitching decks and within its heaving hull. Every few minutes, a dollop of oil the size of a macadamia nut escapes from the rusting tanks deep within the ruin, threads its way upward through the twisted wreckage and flattens into a small slick on the water's surface. The bubbles, which have come without surcease for 50 years, are the last faint ripples of an event that lashed the landscape of the 20th century like a tsunami.

World War II made the United States the leading power on the globe, blocking forevermore all avenues of retreat to isolationism. It took from the British lion much of its roar. It freed Japan from militarism and restored democracy to Western Europe. It set the scene for the cold war, widening the sweep of Moscow's imperialism in the East, signing the death warrant of Western colonialism in Africa and Asia, summoning the Third World into existence. It built the bomb.

But the conflict's international repercussions, as profound as they were, did not leave as deep an imprint on American lives as the tides of social and economic change sent coursing across the then 48 states, tides that flowed far longer than the 44 months between Pearl Harbor and V-J Day, tides that in many respects flow to this day. As Americans liberated fascism's captives, they were themselves liberated from an array of domestic constraints. A gathering silent revolution at home made the U.S. populace richer, more mobile (15 million people moved out of their home counties during WWII alone) and—for blacks and whites alike—more equal. The cataclysm transformed life more drastically than any event since the Civil War.

THE PROFITS OF DOOM

We are the only nation in this war which has raised its standard of living.
—CBS BROADCASTER
EDWARD R. MURROW

Shortly after dusk on the day after Pearl Harbor, the scream of sirens—one short blast, one long, one short, one long—pierced the night in San Francisco. Radio stations went silent. Fifteen huge searchlights scoured the heavens as an Army general breathlessly informed reporters that 50 planes from an enemy aircraft carrier had been spotted 100 miles due west of the Golden Gate. Power workers fanned out downtown, cutting off streetlights. Bar patrons, climbing off their stools and growing boisterous, promoted a like result with bricks or baseball bats. With traffic already gridlocked on the city's narrow, hilly lanes, police ordered motorists not to use their headlights. For thousands, the drive home became a demolition derby beneath the waning moon. Horns blared. Tires squealed. Things went bump in the night. But not one citizen fell to enemy action. For the number of Zeros in the sky was . . . 0.

Fiorello's gloom. The scare was the first in a string of false alerts that rattled "the home front" early in the war. The government swiftly printed 57 million pamphlets on "What to Do in an Air Raid." "Never underestimate the strength, the cruelty of the enemy," exhorted New York's voluble mayor, Fiorello La Guardia, doubling as the country's civil defense chief. "The war will come right to our cities."

Of course, it never did. No war in history wreaked more havoc than this one on civilians—in London, in Dresden, in Leningrad, in Hiroshima and countless cities and hamlets in between. Yet geography—those gloriously wide shining seas—spared the United States of America. More than spared. U.S. civilians were soon basking in the serendipitous revival of good times (with the exception of Japanese-Americans on the West Coast, who were herded into internment camps on the theory that they were potential saboteurs, a group libel born of palpable racism). The war not only defeated Japan and Germany, it defeated the Great Depression when Franklin Roosevelt's brain trust, after nine years, had become all but brain dead. The American war machine deployed 15 million men and cranked out 296,000 planes, 12,000 ships, 64,000 landing craft, 86,000 tanks, 15 million guns and 40 billion bullets. The cost came close to $300 billion. In peacetime, the New Dealers would have had to puff on an exceptionally potent brand of cheroot to so much as dream of so vast a public works program (FDR's answer to the 1938 recession had been an extra $3 billion in public works).

The massive pump priming produced the most dramatic economic renaissance the country has ever known. Unemployment, still a hefty 17 percent at the time of Pearl Harbor, melted away. Corporate profits surged. Union ranks swelled from 8.7 million to 14.3 million in five years. The average worker's income more than doubled (but the top 5 percent saw their *share* of personal income slip from a quarter of the national total to a fifth as lower-paid people gained relatively more). Some 42 million tax eaters became income-tax payers, up from a mere 4 million taxpayers in 1940. Tires, gasoline and such foods as meat, sugar and coffee were rationed; makers of autos and appliances shifted their assembly lines entirely to lucrative "cost plus" defense contracts (the last car, a Ford, had rolled out in February 1942). Yet consumers increased their spending by fully 50 percent. And not just on necessities. Nightclubs jumped with the jitterbug and clinking glasses. A record number of dollars rode the ponies—$2.2 million a day at New York racetracks alone.

It's only money. Despite the sharp rebound, the public remained obstinately bearish. From laborers muttering over their lunch boxes to bank presidents declaiming at their country clubs, the prediction was the same: When the war ended and military spending was slashed, the country would again be on its uppers. Polls showed 7 out of 10 expected to be worse off. The trauma of the 1930s was deeply etched in their psyches. Besides, hadn't wars always been followed by slumps? Nearly everyone overlooked the vast reservoir of consumer demand built up over 16 years and the $146 billion in savings (triple the 1940 total) people had at the ready. When peace came, they reached for their bankbooks. By the fall of 1945, merchants were dancing to the bells on their cash registers—nylon stockings, fur coats, diamond jewelry, refrigerators, washers—we've got 'em, folks, come and get 'em.

Nine months after V-J Day, baby buggies, cribs and playpens were the ticket, as was the newly published "Pocket Book of Baby and Child Care," which became the bible of postwar parents, delivered by a mild-mannered Moses called Dr. Benjamin Spock. The buyers were the founding fathers and founding mothers of the baby boom, a national bout of fecundity that would last for two decades.

Business finally managed to cast off the dunce cap it had worn since the crash of 1929. The restoration of its confidence and prestige began with the "dollar-a-year men," who left corporate eagles' nests to superintend wartime production feats from temporary government roosts on the Potomac. The comeback of prosperity did the rest. In the 1950s, business showered an enticing array of goods on "the affluent society" (the title of John Kenneth Galbraith's book became platitudinous), a world of charcoal grills for cooking red meat and gas-guzzling cars with monstrous tail fins for keeping up with the Joneses. The quarter century after 1945, in the words of economist Robert Heilbroner, was "the longest and

most successful period of expansion in American history." The buying power of average weekly pay increased by 61 percent from 1948 to 1973 (at which point it began to shrink, stagflation becoming the skunk at the garden party).

ALPHABET CITY

Washington's a funny town. It's got scores of hotels, and you can't get a room. It's got 5,000 restaurants, and you can't get a meal. It's got 50,000 politicians, and nobody will do anything for you.

<small>A SMALL-BUSINESS MAN VISITING THE CAPITAL IN 1944</small>
From the WPB (War Production Board) and the OWI (Office of War Information) to the PWPGSJSISIACWPB (which had something to do with plumbers), Washington was a city of newborn acronyms. It was also a city of newborn bureaucrats. Lawyers in off-the-rack pinstripes, statisticians in eyeshades, sundry technical wizards packing slide rules in tiny holsters, wide-eyed young typists from Kalamazoo in smart skirts for the big city—all helped balloon the federal bureaucracy by 300 percent (critics of the New Deal had groused about a peacetime expansion of 60 percent). Temporary offices ("tempos"), gray asbestos hulks a block long, squatted in rows on prime parkland beside burnished monuments of marble. The world's largest office building, designed by 300 architects and hurriedly built by 13,000 men, emerged from a cloud of red dust. With only four stories above ground, the Pentagon provided three times the desk space of the Empire State Building, enough for 40,000 defense workers. Washington never regained the torpor of a Southern town after the war. The alphabet soup was thinned and substantial trims made in the federal work force, but some 2 million workers remained on the U.S. payroll in 1948, twice as many as in 1940. And, soon, the regulatory apparatus was growing again.

The war had demonstrated that the government *could* spend the country out of hard times—an idea seen in the 1930s as ruinous nonsense. At President Truman's behest, Congress passed the Employment Act of 1946, which called for use of tax and budget policies to promote "maximum" employment. That signaled a historic acceptance of government as the unabashed manager of prosperity.

Never again would Washington view the business cycle as an unalterable mystery. Federal spending swelled to more than 20 percent of gross national product by 1970 (up from less than 2.5 percent in 1929, 10 percent in 1940), stabilizing demand. Expanded welfare programs furnished other control mechanisms, as did a bigger tax base. In the fat years of the 1950s and 1960s, Adam Smith's "invisible hand" was very much at work. But so was the highly visible hand of Uncle Sam.

SHOCK TROOPS

Rose (brrrr—rrrr) the riveter
Rosie's got a boyfriend Charlie:
Charlie, he's a marine,
Rosie is protecting Charlie
Working overtime on a riveting machine.
<small>FROM A SONG RECORDED BY THE FOUR VAGABONDS IN 1943</small>
Their hair could be close cropped and stashed beneath a cap or bandanna. Their faces could be hidden by goggles, their figures obscured by loose-fitting coveralls. Sweaters might be banned—and shorts made a capital offense. Yet there was only so much that could be done to cushion the culture shock. "Women in the yard!" "Women in the yard!" The sneering, astonished cry was heard in shipyards, aircraft factories and other defense plants across America when the new workers arrived early in the war—workers so bold, so patriotic (or so eager for higher wages) as to think that they could master such manly arts as riveting and welding without a single Y chromosome among them.

Some male workers advertised their resentment by resorting to what a later generation would call "sexual harassment." They sent "Rosie" and her sisters on quests for a "left-handed monkey wrench" or played other pranks. They told dirty jokes and swore. They hooted and whistled. They pinched and grabbed. "You'd think at least some of these ten thousand guys would have seen women before," Josephine von Miklos wrote of her experience in an East Coast shipyard. "But that's where we evidently were wrong." Another assembly-line ingenue reported: "The first thing I noticed was that all the men were instructors."

Press clippings. Away from the plant, "the girls behind the guys behind the guns" won plenty of plaudits. Feature writers churned out profile after profile of women who were able to slap wings onto B-17s by day and still be sweet and feminine by night. By war's end, the public accepted that the weapons that defeated Hitler and Tojo, although manned by men, were built to a large extent by women (40 percent of workers or more at many defense plants)—*well* built by women. At which point, the Rosies were summarily relieved of their security badges and tools and cast out of their jobs to make room for returning GIs. Yes, they had proved they could do an array of jobs previously regarded as suitable only for men. But, no, most Americans were not yet ready to surrender the traditional belief (as one writer explained in the *Atlantic Monthly*) that "women's manifest destiny [is] to cook and breed."

The legend is that women promptly retreated en masse to home and hearth and stayed there until "women's lib" swung the kitchen doors open again in the 1960s. In fact, large numbers of cashiered defense workers found other (if usually lower-paying) jobs. World War II may not have exploded the mind-set that Betty Friedan would later call "the feminine mystique," but it planted explosives around its foundations. Rosie had gained confidence in herself and in her sex, a confidence she would impart to her daughters. Even more important, the prosperity and higher educational levels brought by the war steadily opened more and more jobs to females. Between 1947 and 1958, the proportion of married women working outside the home rose from 20 percent to 30 percent—a rate of increase just as brisk as that achieved in the ferment of the 1960s.

The war also spawned new opportunities and a new outlook among black Americans. They suddenly had fresh incentives to shake the red clay off their shoes and say goodbye to the South's poorest counties (an exodus that spurred the mechanization of Southern agriculture). Day after day, families could be seen gathered on station platforms, their belongings stuffed in ancient Gladstone bags or in cardboard suitcases tied around with rope, waiting for the Illinois Central to Chicago or clutching bus tickets to "Deetroit" or points east or west. As migrants of both races poured into war-industry towns, one scholar counted 242 racial incidents in 47 cities in the summer of 1943 alone. The worst of these erupted one steamy June night in Detroit, "the arsenal of democracy." Thirty-four people died, including 25

blacks, 17 of them by police bullets. More than 20 riots or mutinies broke out at military bases, many started by black GIs resisting the indignities of segregation. It was all a jolting reminder that while the nation warred against Hitler's "master race" megalomania, its moral armor bore a stain: "the plight of the Negro," the great "American dilemma," as Swedish sociologist Gunnar Myrdal termed it in 1944.

Blacks had been cheated of lasting gains in World War I, that earlier crusade in the name of democracy. They said: never again. A. Philip Randolph, leader of the Brotherhood of Sleeping Car Porters, threatened to bring 50,000 protesters to Washington on July 1, 1941, if blacks were not guaranteed their share of defense jobs. He canceled the march when Franklin Roosevelt agreed to set up the Fair Employment Practices Committee. The FEPC was largely toothless, but by late 1944, blacks had pushed their way into 8.3 percent of the jobs in the war plants, up from 3 percent in 1942.

Military gothic. As angry as many blacks were (one sharecropper taunted his landlord: "By the way, Captain, I hear the Japs done declared war on you white folks"), few refused to fight. More often they had to fight for the *right* to fight. Attitudes in the military had changed little since an Army War College study in 1925 that pronounced blacks a lower form of life with a "smaller cranium, lighter brain [and] cowardly and immoral character." At the start of the war, the Navy accepted blacks only as lowly mess attendants. One such, Dorris Miller, took over a machine gun at Pearl Harbor in the face of serious fire, winning the Navy Cross. By war's end, blacks had proved themselves reliable in combat, and many of the most demeaning restrictions had been eased (Harry Truman finally desegregated the armed forces in 1948).

World War II transformed the status of blacks more drastically than any event since the Civil War. In just six years, their income rose from 40 percent of white income to 53 percent. Their numbers on the federal payroll quadrupled. The GI Bill of Rights lifted their educational levels, training a new generation of leaders. The masses began mobilizing, encouraged by a pugnacious African-American press. The size of the Urban League tripled. The NAACP grew from 355 branches to 1,000, from 50,000 members to 450,000.

White consciences were pricked. Interracial committees multiplied. The American Bar Association dropped its color bar. The Supreme Court banned whites-only primaries, poll taxes and restrictive covenants. The Truman-appointed Commission on Civil Rights urged "the elimination of segregation based on color, creed or national origin, from American life." Although the revolution would take decades to unfold, the civil-rights movement had stirred to life in the shadow of the cannons.

THE PEACEMAKER

My God, what have we done?
A JOURNAL NOTATION MADE BY ROBERT LEWIS, CO-PILOT OF THE ENOLA GAY JUST AFTER THE EXPLOSION OF THE A-BOMB AT HIROSHIMA

It began like the creation of the universe in Genesis—with an unimaginable burst of light—and for a moment, a distant observer might well have mistaken it for something equally divine. Then came the rolling, rising fireball, the heat like a blast from hell, the thick, billowing dust sucked from the living earth into a lethal cloud 8 miles high. No, this was the latest work of man. *De*creation of Hiroshima. Harry Truman called the atomic bomb "the greatest achievement of organized science in history." Fully 85 percent of Americans polled said its use was justified, but the *Saturday Review* reflected the chill felt by many. Its editorial was entitled "Modern Man Is Obsolete." Those B movies in which a crazed genius manipulates basic forces of nature with disastrous effect had seemed like mere Hollywood hokum in the 1930s. Yet now science had built a Frankenstein's monster that would have done the most fertile screenwriter proud.

In a flash, "science became too important to be left to scientists," historian Geoffrey Perrett wrote, recasting the truism about generals and war. Before World War II, the United States had been a poor country cousin to urbane European science, which supplied the building blocks of such wartime wonders as radar and the proximity fuse (Britain), jet fighters (Britain and Germany) and advanced rockets (Germany). In America, the war put big government and big science permanently in bed together for a multibillion-dollar marriage to which the cold war added heat.

More bucks from a bang. In the 1950s and 1960s, scientists worried that the vast sums going to research and development projects on campus would give the government too much control over universities. They fretted about the military corrupting priorities with its big slice of the research pie. Yet they took the money and they prospered. Scientists gained key positions and unprecedented influence in the federal establishment; the United States breezed past Europe in the Nobel sweepstakes.

And the megamonster revealed socially redeeming qualities in later reels. In 1943, Niels Bohr had asked about the A-bomb in the making: "Is it really big enough?"—big enough, that is, to put a stop to world war. Forty-eight years later, with the superpower struggle at last at an end, the question put by the great Danish physicist could be answered yes.

TEENAGER AMERICANUS

If lonesome, he reminds you of the guy away from your arms. If waiting for a Dream Prince, his thrilling voice sings for you alone.

RITA STEARNS, 17, IN A PRIZE-WINNING 1943 ESSAY

On Columbus Day, Oct. 12, 1944, friendly forces laid siege to the Dream Prince, marching on Manhattan at first light, an army dressed to kill—in sweaters, skirts, saddle shoes and bobby socks. Their purses stuffed with sandwiches and bananas to avert starvation, they overran Times Square, 30,000 of them, ankling along, giggling, smashing against shop windows, jiving with New York's finest. Some 3,600 made it into the Paramount Theater and let loose a merciless fusillade of screams, shrieks, squeals and "Oh, Frankies!" that ricocheted off the ceiling and descended like a buzz-bomb attack while Raymond Paige and his orchestra assaulted a no man's land of sharps and flats.

On stage, a blue-eyed young man caressed the microphone, his suit hanging on his bony frame as loosely as on a coat hanger. Blinking under the spotlight, his Adam's apple bulging, Francis Albert Sinatra crooned: "All . . . or noth-ing at all!

"Yeeeeeeeeeeeeeeeeeeeeeeeeeee . . ."
went the bobby-soxer echelons.

"Half a love never appealed to me . . ."

"Yeeeeeeeeeeeeeeeeeeeeeeeeeee . . ."

"If your heart nev-er could yield to me . . . then I'd rath-er have noth-ing at all!"

"Yeeeeeeeeeeeeeeeeeeeeeeeeeee . . ."

Girls swayed, collapsed onto each other, swooned in the aisles and fainted as ushers deployed with smelling salts and stretchers like medics on a battlefield.

Help Wanted. The tableau at the Paramount was a hormonal testament to the coming of age of an ebullient new species of primate. It had no Latin name, but the noun *teenager* was just entering the English language. Economic recovery and wartime exigencies brought unprecedented wealth and freedom to adolescents. It was partly a case of indulging youth with Daddy's dollars. But beyond that, many teenagers now had their *own* dollars. Girls could easily get work as sales clerks and waitresses (fully two thirds of America's waitresses having taken defense plant jobs). With employers forced to replace lost manpower with "boy power," many a young male went through a rapid metamorphosis from a footloose drugstore cowboy bumming Lucky Strikes off his pals to a scrubbed-up working stiff with cash in his jeans. Money bred a heady new sense of independent identity for both sexes.

The bobby-soxers introduced the teenager as shamelessly pumped up fan, foreshadowing the even zanier upheavals to come with rock-and-roll. The "Victory Girls" gave the country a look at another stereotype that would prove equally lasting—the neglected, delinquent teenager, tarted up and running wild in the streets. These working-class Lolitas, some as young as 12, were typically the offspring of an "old man" gone to the service and an "old lady" gone to the swing shift at a munitions plant ("latchkey children" was a WWII coinage). They sashayed around juke joints and train stations picking up GIs, trading sex (and often VD) for a hamburger, a Coke or a Nehi orange. Some called them "Cuddle Bunnies." But "V-Girls" was just as apt, for they were wont to profess a "patriotic duty to comfort the poor boys who may go overseas and get killed." Psychologists pronounced them sincere in this sentiment, scant comfort to people fretting about the 130 percent rise in female delinquency from 1941 to 1943. The increase was more modest among boys, who scholars surmised were less likely to feel "left out" of the war experience.

Higher on the socioeconomic ladder, the teenager as coddled consumer was being born. The midwife was *Seventeen,* the first issue of which hit newsstands in September 1944, announcing "*Seventeen*

is your magazine, High School Girls of America—all yours!" All for them—and for the advertisers wooing them. One ad proclaimed: "Carolteen—the clothes that put hi-jinks into hi-school."

The youth market became vast in the long period of postwar prosperity, embracing music, television, the movies, fashion and more. Sales reached billions of dollars annually, and by the late 1950s, highbrow high priests such as Dwight Macdonald were writing that commercial courtship of the "new American caste—the teenagers" was debasing popular culture. When *Seventeen* itself turned 17, it remembered that in 1944 adolescents had lived in a world overwhelmingly attuned to grown-ups. It found in 1961 that "the needs, the wants, even the whims of teenagers are catered to by almost every industry . . . When a girl celebrates her 13th birthday today, she knows who she is. She's a teenager—and proud of it."

THE D.A.R. INVASION

Why go to Podunk College, when the government will send you to Yale?

TIME MAGAZINE, MARCH 18, 1946

When the veterans of World War I were mustered out, they got $60 and a rail ticket home. Veterans of World War II did better. They got a ticket to the middle class. All it took to punch it were brains and determination.

The GI Bill of Rights gave veterans a free college education—tuition plus a modest living allowance. Student populations swiftly doubled at many colleges. To house married vets, a warren of ivy-less hovels was thrown up amid the elegant old halls at Harvard University. Trailer camps, which swam in mud after a rain, appeared on many campuses, as did rows of Quonset huts with wash lines full of diapers. Alabama Polytechnic bunked veterans on tugboats, another school floated them on surplus LSTs (landing vessels). Had Robert Maynard Hutchins been correct? The University of Chicago president had warned that the GI Bill would bring a flood of "educational hobos," unmotivated men who would be standing in a bread line if they were not reclining in the groves of academe.

"Damn Average Raisers." As it happened, Joe Veteran *was* a different breed from Joe College. He disdained dinky caps, hazing and the like as "kids' stuff."

He was such a grind that professors were soon praising the postwar classes as the most serious, hardest working ever (non-veteran students at Stanford called vets D.A.R.'s for "Damn Average Raisers"). Joe Veteran was often from a family that had never before seen the inside of so much as a cow college. He often spoke in a class or regional accent that diluted the prep school honk at Harvard, Yale and Princeton. He was a drinker of beer, not a sipper of sherry.

The GI Bill and revived prosperity inaugurated higher education's egalitarian age. Access and enrollment would continue to grow in the decades ahead. Fully 2.2 million GIs went to college, and more than 5 million others went to trade schools. Veterans led an explosion in the professions: 450,000 became engineers, 360,000 became schoolteachers, 243,000 became accountants, 180,000 were trained as doctors or nurses, 150,000 as scientists, 107,000 as lawyers.

Because they remembered the insecurities of the years before the war, few wanted to be entrepreneurs (unlike many of their offspring, who would enjoy snugly secure 1950s childhoods). As *Fortune* reported of the class of 1949, most were eager "to work for somebody else—preferably somebody big" whether it be government, business, a school or foundation. William Whyte would dub them "organization men" in the 1950s. Others would label them "the new class," defined by one writer as consisting of "number crunchers, word wielders and symbol jugglers." They were intellectual worker bees, the technocratic core of an emerging post-industrial society.

AND BABY MAKES THREE

A man's health requires as many acres of meadow to his prospect as his farm does loads of muck.

HENRY DAVID THOREAU, 1862

First, potato plants stood, row upon row, as far as the eye could see. Then, the 4,000 acres on Long Island, 25 miles east of Manhattan, became a field of dreams 1947 style: Tract houses rose, row upon row, as far as the eye could see. They named it Levittown.

The all but identical boxes, completed at the rate of 30 per day, typically had two bedrooms, one bath, a fireplace, a Bendix washer, an 8-inch television and a picture window before which you could stand and be master of all you surveyed—the back yard. Priced at $7,990 for a Cape Cod, $9,500 for a ranch, with no down payment, Levittown was Shangri-La. Or so it seemed to the ex-GIs (addressed as "Mister Kilroy" in Levitt ads) who came in wave after wave, spouses and squalling tots in tow, sometimes lining up for days, sleeping in their cars, for a chance to put down roots in the potato patch.

Quality of life. Many builders, like William Levitt, had perfected assembly line methods while building wartime housing for Uncle Sam. In the spring of 1946, bulldozers were chewing the earth on the edge of nearly every city in the land to answer housing demands pent up since the crash of 1929. New, conspicuously less affluent subdivisions shot up just down the highway from the old "railroad suburbs," enclaves of the well-to-do. Low interest rates, the GI Bill and other federal policies smoothed the way for veterans and nonveterans to buy homes, speeding 9 million people into suburbia by 1954. Cars helped. Between 1945 and 1955, the number of them on the road doubled, from 26 million to 52 million.

Suburban houses were not only lower in price—they were also lower in quality (a 9-year-old boy threw a baseball right through the wall of one Sacramento abode, an investigator told Congress). But the debate more often had to do with quality of life, not the quality of gypsum board. It reached a fever pitch in the 1950s and 1960s as a flying wedge of intellectuals attacked the suburbs as an empty promise—too sprawling, too conformist. Cookie-cutter wastelands with neither the culture of the city nor the beauty of the country. Statistics tell how Middle America replied to the indictment: In 1950, 1 in 4 persons lived in suburbia; 40 years later, 1 in 2 lived there.

PACIFIC CENTURY

We have sniffed our destiny.

EARL WARREN, GOVERNOR OF
CALIFORNIA, APRIL 14, 1944

Amid the delirium of V-J Day, two sun-gilded young women popped out of a taxi at City Hall in San Francisco, clad only in their smiles. They scampered to a public fountain and within seconds were chest deep, playing peek-a-boo among the waterlilies as onlookers whooped and whistled. Postwar California could not have made a more prophetic debut. For now, more than ever, the state would be America's golden girl, a siren calling from her Pacific perch, an earth mother nurturing (as John Gunther wrote in his 1947 bestseller "Inside U.S.A.") "a bursting cornucopia of fruit, glaciers, sunshine, crackpots and petroleum."

The new gold rush. California had fancied itself El Dorado ever since the gold rush of 1849. Yet, nearly a century later, people back East still saw it as a colonial outpost, a colorful sideshow over the horizon from the true heartland. World War II torpedoed such patronizing notions. The federal government, seeking a prudent dispersal of defense production, built a vast munitions industry in California and gave it fully 12 percent of the country's war contracts. New factories—to make airplanes, electronic equipment, aluminum, steel, synthetic rubber and much else—sprouted among the yuccas; cranes flew in the shipyards; research labs spread like amoebas. The boom set off a new gold rush. Millions came to prospect, this time, for jobs. The population surged 53 percent to 10.5 million, making the state the second most populous in the union by 1950 (it passed New York in 1964).

The trek continued after the war as the state's defense industries swiftly converted to peacetime, hundreds of thousands of GIs introduced to the charms of the Coast while in uniform returned as civilians and a progressive GOP governor, Earl Warren, sank surplus revenues left over from taxes on arms production into schools, colleges, hospitals and water projects. *Kiplinger Magazine* in 1948 proclaimed the West Coast "a new citadel of power." The *New York Times* declared: "California can no longer be thought of merely as the Land of Sunshine. Politically and economically, she tips the national balance westward." In matters as diverse as freeways (1940) and Frisbees (1957), the Golden State emerged as America's great social laboratory. "So leap with joy, be blithe and gay, or weep my friends with sorrow," teased Richard Armour's verse. "What California is today, the rest will be tomorrow."

Smog was already stinging eyes in the Los Angeles basin in the 1940s. But few could have guessed the extent of the strains to come—runaway development, $300,000 tract houses, gridlock, tax revolts, teenage gangs et al. Five decades after the wartime influx began, those storied sunsets had been dulled by more than dirty air. And yet new suitors of the golden girl still came—not as many from Iowa and Kansas, perhaps, but more than ever from Latin America and Asia.

Cry 'Havoc!' and let slip the dogs of war; That this foul deed shall smell above the earth; With carrion men, groaning for burial.

WILLIAM SHAKESPEARE'S
"JULIUS CAESAR"

In the brightness of the postwar dawn, it was almost possible to forget the darkness: the global carnage that left 50 million corpses "groaning for burial"—men, women and children killed by bombings, shootings, bayonetings, gas-ings, garrotings, hangings, drownings, beatings, starvation, suffocation, radiation, fire and disease. Good and Evil have coexisted throughout history, of course, in a kind of dynamic tandem, each sparking off the other. But that so much positive change could spring from the most destructive war ever fought may be the strongest proof yet that, in the modern as in the ancient world, the appetite of the Fates for irony knows no bounds.

From the Cold War to the 1990s

The Grand Alliance of World War II began to come apart even before the conflict ended. Disputes with the Soviet Union over Poland and the treatment of Germany were just a few of the issues that began to poison the relationship. Harry S. Truman, who became president upon Roosevelt's death, vowed to continue his predecessor's effort to preserve the partnership, but he increasingly came to believe the Soviets were untrustworthy and intent upon achieving their goals regardless of consequences. Soviet rejection of an American plan to control nuclear development through the United Nations (the United States would retain its monopoly until assured safeguards were in place) resulted in an arms race that lasted until only recently.

After 1948, what became known as the "cold war" escalated to new levels. That year the Soviets staged a coup in Czechoslovakia, replacing a compliant government with an utterly subservient one, and they instituted a blockade of the land routes to Berlin deep inside eastern Germany. In 1949 they exploded their first atomic bomb, and Chinese Communists (widely believed to be controlled by Moscow) seized control of all China. In June 1950 North Korea invaded South Korea (see "The Forgotten War"—an example of a cold war confrontation), and the United States found itself at war only five years after defeat of the Axis powers had promised an era of peace.

What had gone wrong and who was to blame? A number of individuals and groups—Senator Joseph R. McCarthy was only the most famous—hurried forward to provide answers to confused and frustrated Americans. Dangerous as the Soviet Union was, according to McCarthy and others, it could be dealt with by loyal and determined Americans. The real threat, according to this view, was that disloyal government officials and others had conspired to undermine American institutions and policies. Only a thorough cleansing of such people could get the United States on track. If a few innocent people were hurt, that was the price that had to be paid.

In 1952 both parties sought the immensely popular General Dwight D. Eisenhower as their candidate for president. He would have defeated anyone the Democrats could put against him, as anger over the Korean War, corruption within the Truman administration, and charges that the Democrats had "coddled" Communists for years guaranteed a landslide. "The Ike Age," deals with the years of Dwight D. Eisenhower's presidency. A view commonly held at the time was that Eisenhower was a passive executive who spent most of his time playing golf and bridge while subordinates ran the store. The article surveys the revisionist view of Eisenhower as a far more effective president.

John F. Kennedy's election in 1960 heralded no radical departures. He was relatively young, vigorous, and promised to get the country "moving" again, whatever that meant. Actually, his legislative achievements were slight by the time of his assassination, and he had embarrassed himself by the U.S.–sponsored invasion of Cuba that ended in disaster at the Bay of Pigs. The Cuban missile crises in 1962, once trumpeted as a Kennedy victory, has recently been revealed as a jumble of misunderstandings on both sides that almost resulted in all-out nuclear war.

Lyndon B. Johnson tried to fight the Vietnam War and create a "Great Society" at the same time. Many of his social programs had some effect, but they were overtaken by events. Smoldering resentments over social injustices and the Vietnam War erupted into upheaval and violence. Riots in cities, demonstrations on campuses, and widespread disillusionment undermined Johnson's presidency. His successor, Richard M. Nixon, eventually ended the war, and the "counterculture" spawned in the sixties lost its vitality, but things would never be the same. The struggle for civil rights and liberties for blacks inspired other groups—Native Americans, Hispanics, and women, to name a few—to end repression and discrimination.

By the end of the 1970s, after uninspiring performances by presidents Gerald Ford and Jimmy Carter, the nation was ready to move to the right. Reform movements had made real strides, but backlash was setting in. Ronald Reagan appealed to many with his promises to have the nation "standing tall" again in foreign affairs and rid society of government interference in various areas. He did instill a new sense of pride in many, but disadvantaged groups suffered from cutbacks, while at the same time the national debt increased manyfold, leaving a burden for future generations. Observers differ as to how much he should share in the credit, but the cold war also drew to an end during Reagan's watch.

George Bush lacked Reagan's charisma and inherited many of the problems that Reagan had glossed over with a quip. A stagnating economy led many Americans to despair of the notion that each succeeding generation would have it better than the one before. Operation Desert Storm, which produced a stunning victory at small cost to the victors, engendered feelings of great pride in some, dismay in others. Bush's popularity skyrocketed, but faded almost as quickly. His administration's failure to do more than offer inspirational rhetoric in the face of mounting economic and social woes produced widespread apathy. Bill Clinton's victory in the 1992 presidential election was more a vote of no-confidence against Bush than a ringing endorsement of Democratic promises to repair the damage.

"If I'd Stood Up Earlier . . ." provides a personal account by one who was involved during the 1950s in the malevolent practice of "blacklisting" members of the entertainment industry for suspected disloyalty. In December 1955, Montgomery, Alabama, blacks mounted a boycott of the city's segregated transportation system and chose the Reverend Martin Luther King, Jr., as their spokesman. "Trumpet of Conscience: A Portrait of Martin Luther King, Jr.," chronicles the subsequent triumphs and failures of this inspirational leader through the turbulent sixties until his tragic death in 1968.

"Watergate Redux" deals with the sequence of events that led from a "simple burglary" to the downfall of President Richard Nixon. "Lessons From a Lost War" attempts to evaluate the false assumptions that led to the prolongation of the Vietnam War. "The New Indian Politics" provides a history of Indian political tactics before and after their occupation of Wounded Knee in 1973. "How the Seventies Changed America" offers an overview of that critical decade, the problems of which are still with us.

The Bush administration very carefully stage-managed coverage of Operation Desert Storm so that it appeared to be a brilliant victory attained at little cost to American forces. In many respect it was, but "Hollow Victory" concludes that "never before in the history of warfare have so many watched so much and seen so little."

Looking Ahead: Challenge Questions

What pressures were brought to bear on the entertainment industry during the 1950s to blacklist individuals?

Examine the philosophy and tactics Martin Luther King, Jr., used in the struggle for civil rights.

Was the war in Vietnam unwinnable? Or was it lost merely because of faulty strategy?

Discuss those troublesome issues of the 1970s that remain with us. Can they be solved? How?

THE FORGOTTEN WAR

Still unsung after 40 years, the Korean conflict left an enormous legacy that has changed the very course of the world

It was both postscript to the last war and prologue to the next, a brutal struggle that began on a monsoon-drenched morning 40 years ago this week and raged up and down a remote, ravaged Asian peninsula for 37 months. It was the cold war suddenly turned hot, Communism's boldest "war of national liberation" and the United Nations' first—and probably last—"police action." When it finally ended in stalemate, at a bleak "truce village" in a no man's land called Panmunjom, it had involved 22 nations, claimed 5 million lives and set off political and economic tremors that reverberate still.

Yet four decades after it began, the Korean War remains as hazy in America's memory as the mist-shrouded mountains that were its killing fields. Where, for example, is a memorial worthy of those who fell at Pork Chop Hill and Heartbreak Ridge, or during the retreat from the Chosin Reservoir? What colleges tutor the young about "The Korean War: Its Origins and Objectives"? And why is the war's best-known work of art a television sitcom called "M*A*S*H," which was really an allegory about Vietnam?

Slowly, those who have inherited this forgotten war are beginning to realize the size of its lien on posterity. It encouraged seven American Presidents to draw lines against Communist subversion from Vietnam to El Salvador, drew an Atlantic America irreversibly into Asia and helped catapult what had been a declining military establishment to the forefront of American foreign policy. If the Berlin Wall was the symbol of the division of Europe, the border between the two Koreas is its Asian counterpart. When they met two weeks ago in San Francisco, Mikhail Gorbachev and South Korean President Roh Tae Woo may have started a thaw that could someday eliminate the most visible remaining vestige of the cold war: The division of Korea.

Moreover, in this spring of reconciliation in Asia, both Beijing and Moscow are taking new steps toward diplomatic rapprochement with Seoul, a government that Communism's twin giants had tried to destroy in 1950 and in the 40 years since have ignored, denounced and sought to subvert. Even the relentless enmity between the U.S. and Kim Il Sung's Stalinist regime has begun to soften. American diplomats and Pyongyang's representatives have quietly been holding a series of getting-to-know-you meetings that last month resulted in the North Koreans' turning over the remains of five American servicemen who had died in Pyongyang's nightmarish prison camps. "For the first time in four decades," exults South Korea's Lee Hongku, a special assistant to Roh and a former Minister of Unification, "we can look forward with great expectations."

That it has taken almost four decades for such expectations to materialize is a measure of the epic changes wrought by the Korean conflict. The struggle not only saved the southern half of the Korean peninsula from Communist despotism (though not from anti-Communist authoritarianism), but set it on the road toward prosperity and a still precarious democracy. It also helped transform Japan into a technological superpower that is America's most formidable economic competitor. It so chilled relations between the U.S. and the new People's Republic of China that Chinese children born during the war are instantly recognized by such given names as "Resist America" and "Aid Korea."

The war's effects were felt far from its battlefields. Worried that Korea was only a diversion in advance of a Soviet attack on Berlin, the Truman administration sent four U.S. divisions to Europe to bolster the two already on occupation duty and began pressing to transform occupied West Germany into a rearmed anti-Communist bastion.

A model war

At the same time, Korea wrenched a Eurocentric America's attention back to the Pacific, where some of it has remained, uneasily, ever since. After World War II, the U.S. had begun losing interest in the Orient; the Truman administration was even creeping toward a modus vivendi with "Red China." "Asia is outside the reach of the military power, the economic control, and the ideological influence of the Western World," columnist Walter Lippmann wrote.

While there now is evidence that the conflict opened a rift that later became a chasm between China and the Soviet

Union, at the time it reinforced the image of monolithic Communism on the march, a perception that dogged American policymakers for years. It raised a protective U.S. umbrella over Taiwan, enabling it to survive as an unloved but thriving diplomatic orphan, and it focused America's attention on other likely targets of Communist aggression. One stood out: French Indochina.

More than any other event, the Korean War transformed the cold war from a political and ideological struggle into a military one. In so doing, it was a catalyst not only for the postwar policy of containment, but also for the creation of what Dwight D. Eisenhower dubbed "the military-industrial complex." Defense outlays soared from a planned $14 billion in fiscal 1951 to $54 billion in fiscal 1953.

Even more striking was the militarization of America's foreign-aid program: In fiscal 1950, military aid accounted for only 12 percent of America's aid budget; by 1960, the military's share of foreign aid was 41 percent. In *The Making of America's Soviet Policy,* Ernest R. May put it this way: " . . . before mid-1950, containment seemed to involve primarily an effort to create economic, social and political conditions assumed to be inhospitable to Communism, whereas from mid-1950 on, the policy seemed primarily one of preserving military frontiers behind which conditions unsuited to subversion could gradually evolve." With mixed results, later administrations tried to do in South Vietnam, Iran, El Salvador, the Philippines and elsewhere what Truman had done in South Korea—to hold off the Communists and hope democracy could develop.

At the same time, as historian Arthur M. Schlesinger has argued, in dispatching troops to Korea without first asking Congress to declare war, Truman continued to expand the powers of the Presidency and set the White House on a collision course with Congress and with critics of administration policies. An internal White House paper from 1951 eerily presaged Vietnam and later Oliver North's Iran-Contra defense. "The circumstances of the present crisis," the paper said, "make any debate over prerogatives and power essentially sterile, if not dangerous to the success of our foreign policy."

Korea also introduced a fundamental contradiction that was to plague American foreign policy throughout the cold war. On one hand, played out as it was against a backdrop of virulent anti-Communism at home, the war encouraged a succession of American politicians to vow to defeat Communist aggression wherever it appeared. On Sept. 30, 1950, three months after the North Korean attack, Truman enshrined containment as policy by sign-

Washington's missing memorial

Let us now praise forgotten men . . .

And some there be, which have no memorial; Who are perished, as though they had never been.
—Ecclesiasticus

About 1.5 million Americans served in Korea, 54,000 died there and more than 100,000 were wounded or reported missing. They are the forgotten warriors, neglected by a nation that only eight years before showered their brothers with ticker tape after World War II.

Not until 1986 did Congress decree that the soldiers of Korea should have a monument in Washington. The Korean War Memorial will sit on the Mall just across the Reflecting Pool from the Vietnam Veterans' Memorial. But it will not have the cathartic healing power of the black granite wall across the way. Vietnam's veterans were caught in the cross fire over whether their war was just, and their wall corrects that injustice. Korea's veterans have simply been ignored. Forty years later, the new memorial will honor them. But can it force us to remember them?

Words born in action—a Korean War glossary

Bug-out: Unauthorized retreat.
Chicoms: Chinese Communists.
Chopper: Helicopter.
Gook: Derisive slang for Koreans; a corruption of the Korean *han'guk saram,* which means "Korean."
Hooch: Small house or hut.
MASH: Mobile Army Surgical Hospital.

NAPALM: (Naphthene plus Palmitate) Jellied-gasoline bombs.
R and R: Rest and Recreation. Time away from the front; in-country for GI's, Tokyo for officers.
ROK's: Republic of Korea troops.
KATUSA's: Korean soldiers attached to U.S. Army units.

ing National Security Council paper 68 which, in language foreshadowing John Kennedy's inaugural address a decade later, declared that given the rise of Soviet power, "the nation must be determined, at whatever cost or sacrifice," to defend democracy "at home and abroad." But defending the autocratic Syngman Rhee could hardly be considered serving the cause of democracy.

Fire on the right

On another level, though, the stalemate in Korea was a reminder that in the Atomic Age (the U.S.S.R. announced its first successful nuclear test less than three months before the war began), there were compelling reasons not to let wars escalate. This new concept of "limited war," however, did not suit Gen. Douglas MacArthur, who pushed to end the war by carrying it to China with nuclear weapons. In March, 1951, an increasingly emotional MacArthur openly challenged Truman's concept of limited war in a letter to Representative Joseph Martin, a leading member of the China lobby: "Here in Asia is where the Communist conspirators have elected to make their play for global conquest," he wrote. "If we lose the war to Communism in Asia the fall of Europe is inevitable . . . We must win. There is no substitute for victory."

There also was no substitute for obeying orders. Truman finally fired MacAr-

thur for insubordination, but that did not end the debate about how vigorously Communism should be "rolled back." The ouster of the outspoken anti-Communist general encouraged demagogues like Wisconsin's Senator Joseph McCarthy to bluster that Communist sympathizers were at work in the highest ranks of the Truman administration. Thirteen years later, after the fiasco at the Bay of Pigs and with the U.S. heading into another "limited war" in Asia, Senator Barry Goldwater echoed MacArthur, telling the 1964 Republican convention that "extremism in the defense of liberty is no vice." The man who introduced Goldwater, Ronald Reagan, finally carried the conservative torch into the White House.

By demonstrating that it was easier for the U.S. to contain naked aggression than subversion, that wars of national liberation were best fought with stealth, obfuscation and patience, Korea also hastened the onset of a new kind of cold warfare. The frustrating struggle divided Americans and as the foreign policy consensus eroded, a succession of Presidents tried to cloak some of their efforts to contain Communism—in Guatemala, Iran, Cuba and Nicaragua, for example—in secrecy.

Given this far-reaching legacy, what is most surprising about the Korean War is that it has been so completely forgotten. Almost as many Americans fell in Korea (54,000) as would die in Vietnam a generation later (58,000), but the Korean

5. COLD WAR TO THE 1990s

Key events in the Korean War

1950

Jan. 12 Acheson excludes South Korea from U.S. defense perimeter in Asia
June 25 North Korea attacks
June 28 Seoul is overrun
July 1 U.S. troops arrive in Pusan, move north to engage the enemy
July–August The "bugout": U.S. forces retreat steadily southward
Sept. 10 North Korean offensive is halted at the "Pusan perimeter"
Sept. 15 Inchon landing begins
Sept. 26–29 Seoul recaptured, Syngman Rhee's government returns
Oct. 8 Advancing U.S. forces push across the 38th parallel
Oct. 15 Truman and MacArthur meet at Wake Island
Oct. 19 Chinese troops cross Yalu River into North Korea
Nov. 24–27 Chinese attack Chosin, U.S. forces start retreat to South Korea

1951

Jan. 15 Chinese resistance melts as new S. Korean–U.S. offensive begins
April 11 Truman fires MacArthur
Late May S. Korean–U.S. forces near Pyongyang, Kim Il Sung's capital. Large numbers of Chinese surrender
July 10 Truce talks begin at Kaesong, soon move to Panmunjom

1952

May–October Stalemate, but heavy fighting continues along 38th parallel
Oct. 24 Eisenhower's "I shall go to Korea" speech boosts peace hopes

1953

July 27 Truce signed, fighting stops
Aug. 5 POW exchanges begin

War never gained the same hammerlock on the nation's emotions. To those who had won unconditional surrenders from Germany and Japan, battling to a draw with North Korea and China was anything but memorable. "Korea," says retired U.S. Army Col. David Hackworth, who fought both there and in Vietnam, "was like the 49ers tying Stanford two weeks after winning the Super Bowl."

At first, though, the Americans were fortunate to fight the North Koreans to a tie, finally halting the invasion outside the port city of Pusan. "We sent in troops who'd had almost no training," recalls former Secretary of State Dean Rusk, then assistant secretary for Far Eastern affairs. "Had the North Koreans kept coming," says Rusk, "they could have overrun the entire peninsula."

MacArthur rebounded brilliantly, staging an amphibious landing at Inchon, just west of Seoul, and sending the North Koreans reeling back across the 38th parallel. Triumphant, MacArthur flew off to Wake Island in the mid-Pacific to meet with Truman.

In a hut near the airfield runway, the imperious five-star general assured the homespun former World War I artillery captain that the war would be over by Christmas. If the Chinese were foolish enough to intervene, MacArthur arrogantly predicted, the U.S. Air Force would embark on "the greatest slaughter in military history." Instead, the Chinese routed the United Nations forces so completely that a despairing MacArthur told Washington that unless the U.S. attacked China, it would risk an Asian Dunkirk. "In one cable," Rusk recalls, "he talked about the loss of morale of his troops, when he was talking about his own morale. He was clearly in a state of depression."

Without a word

But led by Lt. Gen. Matthew B. Ridgway, 56, a paratroop hero, the U.S. Eighth Army began moving northward again, inflicting huge casualties on the overextended Chinese. There was little sentiment for crossing the 38th parallel a second time, however. Truce negotiations began on July 10, 1951, but went nowhere fast. On one occasion, both delegations sat staring at each other for 2 hours and 11 minutes without uttering a word. The seesaw war of trenches and numbered hills finally came to a silent, coldly formal conclusion on the morning of July 27, 1953, almost exactly where it had begun three years before.

For all its ups and downs, Korea engaged only a small fraction of the nation. Truman extended the draft, raised taxes and imposed wage-and-price controls, but compared with World War II five years before, the domestic sacrifices were modest. Compared to Vietnam, which was nightly theater in living color, Korea was a map in the morning paper and the black-and-white photographs of David Douglas Duncan and others. As Ohio's Senator John Glenn, who as a Marine combat pilot in Korea shot down three MiG's, explains: "Korea didn't come into every American life the way Vietnam did because you didn't have blood flowing out of your TV set every night."

There is another reason why Korea never had the same mesmerizing effect as Vietnam: It did not set off what in essence was a domestic civil war. Perhaps that is because the generation that fought in Korea, the generation of Levittown and William H. Whyte, Jr.'s *The Organization Man,* had grown up amid a crusade against foreign evils—not, as its rebellious children did, during a civil-rights crusade against evils at home.

Forty years later, as the scars of Vietnam heal and the cold war recedes, there is a discernible connection between the sacrifices at Pork Chop Hill and the birth of fragile democracies in Prague, Warsaw, Budapest and in Seoul itself. Containment worked. America and its allies paid a heavy price to stop Communist aggression in Korea. But given the final outcome, history no doubt will conclude it was a price worth paying.

'If I'd Stood Up Earlier . . .'

In the dark days of television blacklisting, careers and even lives were ruined. A producer questions his courage in confronting the Communist-hunters.

Mark Goodson

Mark Goodson is a television producer whose shows have included "What's My Line," "To Tell the Truth," "I've Got a Secret," "Password" and "Family Feud."

The dark terror if the television blacklisting days (1950–1955) now seems far off, and most of us who were caught in the middle of the storm have developed fuzzy memories—perhaps deliberately. And we dig into our consciences to examine the part we played in that shameful era. Like the French after the liberation, we all claim to have been part of the Resistance. None of us were collaborators. Or were we? Was I?

My first contact with blacklisting came in June 1950, just about the same time that Red Channels: The Report of Communist Influence in Radio and Television came off the presses. Published in New York City by a newsletter called Counterattack, which was founded in 1947 by former F.B.I. men, Red Channels quickly became the bible of television, subscribed to by networks, sponsors and their ad agencies. Its underlying thesis, that Communists were infiltrating television, became the accepted doctrine of the day.

"What's My Line," my first major television production, had been on the air four months. On that early panel were Dorothy Kilgallen, Arlene Francis, Hal Block, a comedy writer, and the poet Louis Untermeyer. Our sponsor was Stopette, a deodorant. We had no sooner booked Untermeyer than CBS and the sponsor began to receive letters of protest. Untermeyer was in Red Channels. Apparently, he had, among other sins, permitted his name to be affiliated with the Joint Anti-Fascist Refugee Committee and been a sponsor of the 1948 May

Day Parade. As we soon found out, the reason for the listing was of minor importance. What counted was simply being named. The protest mail turned into a deluge, all obviously organized. Members of the Catholic War Veterans began putting stickers on drugstore windows warning "Stop Stopette Until Stopette Stops Untermeyer."

Untermeyer and I were summoned to the office of Ralph Colin, the principal CBS attorney at the time. Colin was active in the art and literary world and seemed well acquainted with Untermeyer. Nonetheless, he was harsh in his pronouncement. "Louis," he admonished, "how could you be so naïve? Don't you understand what's going on in the world today? The pressures we're under?" Untermeyer, at that time in his mid-60's was crestfallen. "I'm sorry, Ralph," he apologized. But the decision was made. Untermeyer was out, replaced by Bennett Cerf. While Bennett became a great friend of mine and was superb on the show, it's difficult to forget my feeling of helplessness and embarrassment at this strange trial that permitted no witnesses, no cross-examination, and where the prosecutor was also the judge. I confess that I did not try to fight that decision. I complained to my lawyer, a trusted friend and a liberal. He advised caution: "Be careful. Don't buy a headache." And I didn't, at least at that time.

It was many months before I found the guts to offer any kind of resistance to the hysteria.

Red Channels was not the only source that identified "subversives" by implication and association. The weekly Counterattack published additional lists; Firing Line, issued by the American Legion's Commission on Americanism, also had an array of "dupes" and "Communist fronters." Major advertising agencies

hired their own security officers and developed their own lists. So did each network. At CBS, the man in charge of "clearances" in 1950 was Joseph H. Ream, a vice president. He soon turned the task over to a dedicated full-time security man, Daniel T. O'Shea. There were lists on top of lists, and networks, ad agencies and sponsors exchanged information on a regular basis. If a performer, writer, musician, producer or director was on one list, he immediately found himself on every other list.

Every employee at CBS was required to sign a loyalty oath. So far as I know, none refused. The procedure for clearing performers was standard and mandatory. Thus, on "What's My Line," before booking a panelist or a mystery guest, a production assistant would call O'Shea's office and indicate the proposed booking. If the performer's name was on any list the word would come back: "not cleared." I remember that Leonard Bernstein, Judy Holliday, Harry Belafonte, Abe Burrows, Gypsy Rose Lee, Jack Gilford, Uta Hagen and Hazel Scott were declared off limits. It was made very clear that producers were, under no circumstances, to let performers know they were being blacklisted.

The sort of scene with Untermeyer stopped taking place. Performers were no longer confronted with the reasons that they were removed from shows or not booked in the first place. Essential to the blacklisting was a conspiracy of silence. Explanations were never given. "Not cleared" was the only communication, or—in some cases—the code phrase "a bad actor." The victim of the blacklisting seldom knew what hit him. He simply became unemployable.

In the 1950's, television programs were generally underwritten by a single advertiser. Some sponsors were more sensitive than others to charges of "un-American" leanings, and their ad agencies reflected the principals' anxiety in spades.

In 1952, our panel show "I've Got a Secret" acquired a new sponsor, the R. J. Reynolds Tobacco Company, with its advertising agency, William Esty. Garry Moore was the host of the panel, which included Henry Morgan, Bill Cullen, Jayne Meadows and Faye Emerson.

Morgan was named in Red Channels, but for such a frivolous reason that no one—not even CBS—took it seriously. Morgan was essentially an apolitical curmudgeon who shot darts at any pompous balloon he saw floating by. Certainly he was no "Communist dupe." The closest he came to being duped was by his wife, who, Morgan told me, was a leftist sympathizer, and it was understood that one reason Morgan was getting a divorce was his aversion to Mrs. Morgan's politics. Thus he was listed in Red Channels as a result of a marital connection he was trying to terminate.

But R. J. Reynolds took the listing seriously. At least the William Esty agency did, and I was informed that Morgan would have to go. I'd done previous business with the two men in charge of the account—reasonable, decent guys—and paid them a visit. They agreed completely that the charge in Red channels was nonsensical. But as they put it: "Camel cigarettes don't want to know from reasons. They're in the business of selling tobacco, and hostile mail will make Winston-Salem edgy." The account could be at risk. And for what? For one man? I left that meeting with an ultimatum: dump Morgan pronto or Reynolds would cancel.

This was about two years into the blacklisting period, and for the first time I decided, with some trepidation, to try to buck the storm. But I needed a linebacker. I went to see Garry Moore. I knew very little about Moore's politics except that he voted Republican. I proposed a deal: "If you'll refuse to perform if Henry is cut from the show, I'll refuse to deliver the program. I'll take the gamble of cancellation if you will." Garry didn't blink. "I'm with you all the way," he said.

My friends at the ad agency were flabbergasted. It seems like nothing today, but in 1952 it was virtually unheard of to have this kind of a confrontation. The executives said they would have to kick this thing around. "I've Got a Se-cret" was enormously popular, and Garry Moore, an established comedian, had agreed to do the commercials live. "We'll get back to you," they said.

Morgan was kept on. The show was not canceled, and some weeks later his name somehow simply vanished from Red Channels. We never really understood how this happened, and we didn't press our luck by trying to find out.

At roughly the same time, over at ABC, I had another show called "The Name's the Same." For whatever reason, no doubt budgetary, ABC did not maintain an elaborate monitoring department, and it soon became clear that here was a venue where I could use otherwise blacklisted performers. I remember booking Judy Holliday, Jack Gilford and others who were not permitted appearances elsewhere. And I put Abe Burrows on as a regular.

Burrows was a brilliant comedy writer known for "Duffy's Tavern" on radio, and he was a co-author of "Guys and Dolls," the 1950 Broadway hit. But he still couldn't be used in television. During the war years Burrows had apparently taken part in cultural activities sponsored by Communists in California. To clear his name, he appeared twice before the House Un-American Activities Committee. The committee, after extensive hearings, released Burrows, apparently cleared, from further questioning. But the mere story of his appearance before the committee made headlines in the tabloid press, and Aware Inc., a group formed "to combat the Communist conspiracy in entertainment-communication," and the American Legion were not so forgiving. So when we booked Burrows on "The Name's the Same," it wasn't long before organized mail began to roll in. A sponsor of that program was a privately held Midwestern company, C. A. Swanson & Sons, makers of Swanson frozen TV dinners.

The mail demanding Burrows's expulsion continued to escalate. We were receiving upward of a thousand letters a week. I quietly dropped them in wastebaskets hoping that protest groups would tire of the battle. No such luck. The mail increased. In addition, the Catholic War Veterans began to picket the theater in New York where the show was broadcast. I kept waiting for a call from the sponsor, and it finally came from Omaha. From W. Clarke Swanson.

"Are you getting mail about Abe Burrows?" he asked. I conceded that we were. "We're getting a lot of it back here," he said, worried. "Is Burrows a Communist?" I replied that to my best knowledge he was not. "In that case, what's the shooting about?" he asked. I filled him in on Abe's story. "If that's what it's all about," he said, "forget it. If you feel like it, keep on using him."

Explanations weren't given. The victim of the blacklisting seldom knew what hit him. He simply became unemployable.

Another little victory. But from what a bizarre source! First Garry Moore, now Clarke Swanson. Both Republicans. Where were my liberal friends? As the executive director of The Commonweal, John Cogley, pointed out in his Fund for the Republic Inc. Report on Blacklisting in 1956: "The operation was carried out, for the most part, by people who were personally and privately opposed to it." In 1951 the Authors' League of America indicated that it had "positive proof" of blacklisting. Yet the majority of writers who "knew for sure" that blacklisting was rife declined to testify before the Federal Communications Commission. As Cogley said: "The dangers of reprisal are too great."

In any case, a few months later even Swanson had to raise the white flag. It came face to face with Laurence A. Johnson and the phenomenon of the "Syracuse Crusade." Johnson was proof of how a small man with a tiny base but a strident voice could wield tremendous power. Johnson owned just four supermarkets in and around Syracuse. Whenever it came to his attention that a "controversial" performer was appearing on television, he would threaten to hang signs over the offending company's goods warning that the manufacturer employed "subversives" on television. He also phoned and wrote to other supermarket owners throughout the country. Many major corporations played ball. In 1952, a vice president of Kraft Foods Company wrote Johnson: "It is indeed heartening to know that you are continuing your crusade. . . . Keep up the good work." The president of the General Ice Cream Corporation wrote: "I think it is wonderful that you have taken this interest in ferreting Communists out of our entertainment industry. I wish there were more people like you."

Now it was Swanson's turn to get it. Johnson passed out ballots in his supermarkets that read as follows:

Do you want any part of your purchase price of Swanson Foods to be used to hire Communist fronters?

Yes ☐ No ☐
Indicate your choice by x in the appropriate box.

Overwhelmingly, of course, the customers voted no. Johnson sent copies of these ballots to other stores. Many of them also removed Swanson products. Clarke Swanson phoned me apologetically. "I'm sorry, friend," he said, "but we've got to let Abe go. He's a good guy, but we can't risk our business for one man." By that time ABC had also started to lean on us. So Abe was axed. When I informed Burrows of the bad news, he understood. He'd been aware of the situation and thanked us for keeping him on as long as we had. Luckily, Abe was not really damaged since he had a major hit on Broadway. The New York theater, by the way, ignored all the listings during the McCarthy era, continuing to cast such performers as Jack Gilford and Uta Hagen, who were blocked from television.

It was at about this time that I was confronted with the *reductio ad absur-* *dum* of blacklisting. We were doing a show on CBS called "It's News to Me," hosted by John Daly and later Walter Cronkite. One of the panelists was an English actress, Anna Lee. The sponsor was Sanka Coffee, a product of General Foods. The advertising agency was Young & Rubicam. One day, I received a call from the agency requesting that we drop Anna Lee at once. I had long become inured to off-the-wall blacklistings—but this one was simply too wild. "Anna Lee? Impossible. She's never been touched by any list. What's going on?" The caller was guarded: "You know we don't talk about these things. I'm sure you can find a good reason to unbook her." I then did something that in those days was *verboten*. I had lunch with Anna Lee. I probed tentatively about her politics. She seemed nonplused but told me that she was not political, except that she voted Conservative in England. "What about your husband?" "He's a Texas Republican," she responded. "Why do you ask?" I said that there was some sort of mix-up and finished the lunch.

I went right to Young & Rubicam. There were four or five executives waiting in the conference room. "Gentlemen," I opened, "this one is crazy. Anna Lee is about as leftist as Herbert Hoover." The men looked at each other and one replied. "Yes, we know. We did a little more checking, and it turned out that there is a different Anna Lee who some-times writes for The Daily Worker." "Well," I said, "I'm glad we both checked, and that takes care of that." Then came the zinger: "We're sorry, but we're going to have to drop Anna Lee anyway. We're already starting to get mail, and we can't let the sponsor be involved with protests." At that point I lost it. I said the demand was outrageous and that they were free to cancel the show if they wanted to, but I was not about to kill Anna Lee because she was guilty of having the same name as someone else.

When I got back to my office, there was a call waiting from a member of the agency—a longtime friend—with a warning: "Don't lose your temper like that in front of men who don't know you. When you stormed out of the office they asked, 'Is he a pinko?'" Subtitle of that little episode: "How I Almost Made the List Myself."

Anna Lee stayed on. The show stayed on. But so did the blacklisting, for at least three more years. Broadway stars weren't that damaged, but lesser names were exiled and made unemployable often with tragic consequences. Philip Loeb, forced off "The Goldbergs," died from an overdose of sleeping pills.

I can't help the feeling that if I'd shown more courage, if I'd stood up earlier, if more of us had been willing to take the heat, we could have brought that disgraceful era to a more rapid close. But that's hindsight.

The revisionist view of Eisenhower.

The Ike Age

Stephen E. Ambrose

Stephen E. Ambrose is professor of history at the University of New Orleans. He is the author of *The Supreme Commander* (Doubleday), *Rise to Globalism* (Penguin), and 10 other books on recent American history. He is currently at work on a full-scale biography of Eisenhower.

> For all the jokes about golf playing, he did a far, far better job of handling that office than anyone realized.
> —Ronald Reagan on Dwight D. Eisenhower

Since Andrew Jackson left the White House in 1837, 33 men have served as president of the United States. Of that number, only four have managed to serve eight consecutive years in the office—Ulysses Grant, Woodrow Wilson, Franklin Roosevelt, and Dwight Eisenhower. Of these four, only two were also world figures in a field outside politics—Grant and Eisenhower—and only two had a higher reputation and broader popularity when they left office than when they entered—Roosevelt and Eisenhower.

Given this record of success, and the relative failure of Ike's successors, it is no wonder that there is an Eisenhower revival going on, or that President Reagan and his staff are attempting to present themselves as the Eisenhower administration resurrected. Another major reason for the current Eisenhower boom is nostalgia for the 1950s —a decade of peace with prosperity, a 1.5 percent annual inflation rate, self-sufficiency in oil and other precious goods, balanced budgets, and domestic tranquility. Eisenhower "revisionism," now proceeding at full speed, gives Ike himself much of the credit for these accomplishments.

The reassessment of Eisenhower is based on a multitude of new sources, as well as new perspectives, which have become available only in the past few years. The most important of these is Ike's private diary, which he kept on a haphazard basis from the late 1930s to his death in 1969. Other sources include his extensive private correspondence with his old military and new big business friends, his telephone conversations (which he had taped or summarized by his secretary, who listened in surreptitiously), minutes of meetings of the cabinet and of the National Security Council, and the extensive diary of his press secretary, the late James Hagerty. Study of these documents has changed the predominant scholarly view of Eisenhower from, in the words of the leading revisionist, political scientist Fred Greenstein of Princeton, one of "an aging hero who reigned more than he ruled and who lacked the energy, motivation, and political skill to have a significant impact on events," to a view of Ike as "politically astute and informed, actively engaged in putting his personal stamp on public policy, [who] applied a carefully thought-out conception of leadership to the conduct of his presidency."

The revisionist portrait of Ike contains many new features. Far from being a "part-time" president who preferred the golf course to the Oval Office, he worked an exhausting schedule, reading more and carrying on a wider correspondence than appeared at the time. Instead of the "captive hero" who was a tool of the millionaires in his cabinet, Ike made a major effort to convince the Republican right wing to accept the New Deal reforms, an internationalist foreign policy, and the need to modernize and liberalize the Republican party. Rather than ducking the controversial issue of Joseph McCarthy, Eisenhower strove to discredit the senator. Ike's failure to issue a public endorsement of *Brown v. Topeka* was not based on any fundamental disagreement with the Warren Court's ruling, but rather on his understanding of the separation, the balance, of powers in the US government—he agreed with the decision, it turns out, and was a Warren supporter. Nor was Ike a tongue-tied general of terrible syntax; he was a careful speaker and an excellent writer who confused his audiences only when he wanted to do so.

Most of all, the revisionists give Eisenhower high marks for ending the Korean War, staying out of Vietnam, and keeping the peace elsewhere. They argue that these achievements were neither accidental nor lucky, but rather the result of carefully conceived policies and firm leadership at the top. The revisionists also praise Ike for holding down defense costs, a key factor in restraining inflation while maintaining prosperity.

Altogether, the "new" Ike is an appealing figure, not only for his famous grin and winning personality, but also because he wisely guided us through perilous times.

"THE BLAND leading the bland." So the nightclub comics characterized the Eisenhower administration. Much of the blandness came from Ike's refusal to say, in public, anything negative about his fellow politicians. His lifelong rule was to refuse to discuss personalities. But in the privacy of his diary, parts of which have just been published with an excellent introduction by Robert H. Ferrell (*The Eisenhower Diaries*, W. W. Norton), he could be sarcastic, slashing, and bitter.

In 1953, when Ike was president and his old colleague from the war, Winston Churchill, was prime minister, the two met in Bermuda. Churchill, according to Ike,

> has developed an almost childlike faith that all of the answers to world problems are to be found merely in British-American partnership. . . . He is trying to relive the days of World War II. In those days he had the enjoyable feeling that he and our president were sitting on some rather Olympian platform . . . and directing world affairs. Even if this picture were an accurate one of those days, it would have no application to the present. But it was only partially true, even then, as many of us who . . . had to work out the solutions for nasty local problems are well aware.

That realistic sense of the importance of any one individual, even a Churchill or a Roosevelt, was basic to Eisenhower's thought. Back in 1942, with reference to MacArthur, Ike scribbled in his diary that in modern war, "no one person can be a Napoleon or a Caesar." What was required was teamwork and cooperation.

Although Lyndon Johnson, John F. Kennedy, Hubert Humphrey, and other Democratic senators of the 1950s catch hell from time to time in Ike's diary, he reserved his most heartfelt blasts for the Republicans (he never expected much from the Democrats anyway). Thus, Ike wrote of Senator William Knowland of California, "In his case there seems to be no final answer to the question 'How stupid can you get?'" In *Eisenhower the President* (Prentice-Hall), William Bragg Ewald Jr., a former Eisenhower speechwriter, records that when Republicans urged Ike to convince Nelson Rockefeller to take the second place on a 1960 ticket with Richard Nixon, Ike did so, rather half-heartedly, and then reported on Rockefeller: "He is no philosophical genius. It is pretty hard to get him in and tell him something of his duty. He has a personal ambition that is overwhelming." Eisenhower told Nixon that the only way to persuade Rockefeller to run for the vice presidency was for Nixon to promise to step aside in Rockefeller's favor in 1964.

IKE DIDN'T like "politics," and he positively disliked "politicians." The behind-the-scenes compromises, the swapping of votes for pork-barrel purposes, the willingness to abandon conviction in order to be on the popular side all nearly drove him to distraction. His favorite constitutional reform was to limit congressional terms to two for the Senate and three or four for the House, in order to eliminate the professional politician from American life.

Nor did Ike much like the press. "The members of this group," he wrote in his diary, "are far from being as important as they themselves consider," but he did recognize that "they have a sufficient importance . . . in the eyes of the average Washington officeholder to insure that much government time is consumed in courting favor with them and in dressing up ideas and programs so that they look as saleable as possible." Reporters, Ike wrote, "have little sense of humor and, because of this, they deal in negative criticism rather than in any attempt toward constructive helpfulness." (Murray Kempton, in some ways the first Eisenhower revisionist, recalled how journalists had ridiculed Ike's amiability in the 1950s, while the president actually had intelligently confused and hoodwinked them. Kempton decided that Eisenhower was a cunning politician whose purpose was "never to be seen in what he did.")

The people Ike did like, aside from his millionaire friends, were those men who in his view rose above politics, including Milton Eisenhower, Robert Anderson, and Earl Warren. Of Milton, Ike wrote in 1953, "I believe him to be the most knowledgeable and widely informed of all the people with whom I deal. . . . So far as I am concerned, he is at this moment the most highly qualified man in the United States to be president. This most emphatically makes no exception of me. . . ." Had he not shrunk from exposing Milton to a charge of benefiting from nepotism, Ike would have made his younger brother a member of his cabinet.

In 1966, during an interview in Eisenhower's Gettysburg office, I asked him who was the most intelligent man he had ever met, expecting a long pause while he ran such names as Marshall, Roosevelt, de Gaulle, Churchill, Truman, or Khrushchev through his mind. But Ike never hesitated: "Robert Anderson," he said emphatically. Anderson, a Texan and a Democrat, served Ike in various capacities, including secretary of the navy and secretary of the treasury. Now Ewald reveals for the first time that Eisenhower offered Anderson the second spot on the Republican ticket for 1956 and wanted Anderson to be his successor. Anderson turned down the president because he thought the offer was politically unrealistic.

Which inevitably brings up the subject of Richard Nixon. Eisenhower's relations with Nixon have long been a puzzle. Ike tried to get Nixon to resign during the 1952 campaign, but Nixon saved himself with the Checkers speech. In 1956 Ike attempted to maneuver Nixon off the ticket by offering him a high-level cabinet post, but Nixon dug in his heels and used his connections with the right wing of the party to stay in place. And in 1960, Ike's campaign speeches for Nixon were distinctly unenthusiastic. Still, Eisenhower and Nixon never severed their ties. Ike stuck with Nixon throughout his life. He often remarked that Nixon's defeat by Kennedy was one of his greatest disappointments. And, of course, his grandson married one of Nixon's daughters. Sad to say, neither the diary nor the private correspondence offers any insights into Eisenhower's gut feelings toward Nixon. The relationship between the two men remains a puzzle.

SOME WRITERS used to say the same about the Eisenhower-Earl Warren relationship, but thanks to Ike's diary, Ewald's book, and the correspondence, we now have a better understanding of Eisenhower's feelings toward Warren personally, and toward his Court. In December 1955, Jim Hagerty suggested that if Ike could not run for a second term for reasons of health, Warren might make a good nominee. "Not a chance," Ike snapped back, "and I'll tell you why. I know that the Chief Justice is very happy right where he is. He wants to go down in history as a great Chief Justice, and he certainly is becoming one. He is dedicated to the Court and is getting the Court back on its feet and back in respectable standing again."

Eisenhower and Warren were never friends; as Ewald writes, "For more than seven years they sat, each on his eminence, at opposite ends of Pennsylvania Avenue, by far the two most towering figures in Washington, each playing out a noble role, in tragic inevitable estrangement." And he quotes Attorney General Herbert Brownell as saying, "Both Eisenhower and Warren were very reserved men. If you'd try to put your arm around either of them, he'd remember it for sixty days."

Ike had a great deal of difficulty with *Brown v. Topeka*, but more because of his temperament than for any racist reasons. He was always an evolutionist who wanted to move forward through agreement and compromise, not command and force. Ike much preferred consensus to conflict. Yet Ewald argues that he privately recognized the necessity and justice of *Brown v. Topeka*. Even had that not been so, he would have supported the Court, because—as he carefully explained to one of his oldest and closest friends, Sweed Hazlett, in a private letter—"I hold to the basic purpose. There must be respect for the Constitution—which means the Supreme Court's interpretation of the Constitution—or we shall have chaos. This I believe with all my heart—and shall always act accordingly."

Precisely because of that feeling, Eisenhower never made a public declaration of support for the *Brown v. Topeka* decision, despite the pleas of liberals, intellectuals, and many members of the White House staff that he do so. He felt that once the Supreme Court had spoken, the president had no right to second guess nor any duty to support the decision. The law was the law. That Ike was always ready to uphold the law, he demonstrated decisively when he sent the US Army into Little Rock in 1957 to enforce court-ordered desegregation.

Despite his respect for Warren and the Court, when I asked Eisenhower in 1965 what was his biggest mistake, he replied heatedly, "The appointment of that S.O.B. Earl Warren." Shocked, I replied, "General, I always thought that was your best appointment." "Let's not talk about it," he responded, and we did not. Now that I have seen the flattering and thoughtful references to Warren in the diary, I can only conclude that Eisenhower's anger at Warren was the result of the criminal rights cases of the early 1960s, not the desegregation decisions of the 1950s.

As everyone knows, Ike also refused publically to condemn Senator McCarthy, again despite the pleas of many of his own people, including his most trusted adviser, Milton. Ike told Milton, "I will not get into a pissing contest with that skunk."

The revisionists now tell us that the president was working behind the scenes, using the "hidden hand" to encourage peaceful desegregation and to censure McCarthy. He helped Attorney General Brownell prepare a brief from the Justice Department for the Court on *Brown v. Topeka* that attacked the constitutionality of segregation in the schools. As for McCarthy, Greenstein writes that Eisenhower,

> working most closely with Press Secretary Hagerty, conducted a virtual day-to-day campaign via the media and congressional allies to end McCarthy's political effectiveness. The overall strategy was to avoid *direct mention* of McCarthy in the president's public statements, lest McCarthy win sympathy as a spunky David battling against the presidential Goliath. Instead Eisenhower systematically condemned the *types* of actions in which McCarthy engaged.

Eisenhower revisionism is full of nostalgia for the 1950s, and it is certainly true that if you were white, male, and middle class or better, it was the best decade of the century. The 1950s saw peace and prosperity, no riots, relatively high employment, a growing GNP, virtually no inflation, no arms race, no great reforms, no great changes, low taxes, little government regulation of industry or commerce, and a president who was trusted and admired. Politics were middle-of-the-road—Eisenhower

was the least partisan president of the century. In an essay entitled "Good-By to the 'Fifties—and Good Riddance," historian Eric Goldman called the Eisenhower years possibly "the dullest and dreariest in all our history." After the turmoil of the 1960s and 1970s—war, inflation, riots, higher taxes, an arms race, all accompanied by a startling growth in the size, cost, and scope of the federal government—many Americans may find the dullness and dreariness of the 1950s appealing.

Next to peace, the most appealing fact was the 1.5 percent inflation rate. The revisionists claim that Ike deserved much of the credit for that accomplishment because of his insistence on a balanced budget (which he actually achieved only twice, but he did hold down the deficits). Ike kept down the costs by refusing to expand the New Deal welfare services—to the disgruntlement of the Republican right wing, he was equally firm about refusing to dismantle the New Deal programs—and, far more important, by holding down defense spending.

This was, indeed, Ike's special triumph. He feared that an arms race with the Soviet Union would lead to uncontrollable inflation and eventually bankrupt the United States, without providing any additional security. In Ike's view, the more bombs and missiles we built, the less secure we would be, not just because of the economic impact, but because the more bombs we built, the more the Soviets would build. In short, Ike's fundamental strategy was based on his recognition that in nuclear warfare, there is no defense and can be no winner. In that situation, one did not need to be superior to the enemy in order to deter him.

The Democrats, led by Senator John F. Kennedy, criticized Ike for putting a balanced budget ahead of national defense. They accused him of allowing a "bomber gap" and, later, a "missile gap" to develop, and spoke of the need to "get America moving again." Nelson Rockefeller and Richard Nixon added to the hue and cry during the 1960 campaign, when they promised to expand defense spending. But as long as Eisenhower was president, there was no arms race. Neither the politicians nor the military-industrial complex could persuade Eisenhower to spend more money on the military. Inheriting a $50 billion defense budget from Truman, he reduced it to $40 billion and held it there for the eight years of his tenure.

Holding down defense costs was a longstanding theme of Ike's. As early as December 1945, just after he replaced George Marshall as army chief of staff, he jotted in his diary, "I'm astounded and appalled at the size and scope of plans the staff sees as necessary to maintain our security position now and in the future." And in 1951, before he became a candidate, he wrote in his diary that if the Congress and military could not be restrained about "this armament business, we will go broke and still have inefficient defenses."

President Eisenhower was unassailable on the subject. As one senator complained, "How in hell can I argue with Ike Eisenhower on a military matter?" But as Ike wrote in 1956 to his friend Hazlett, "Some day there is going to be a man sitting in my present chair who has not been raised in the military services and who will have little understanding of where slashes in their estimates can be made with little or no damage. If that should happen while we still have the state of tension that now exists in the world, I shudder to think of what could happen in this country."

One reason why Ike was able to reduce the military in a time of great tension was his intimate knowledge of the Soviet military situation. From 1956 on, he directed a series of flights by the U-2 spy plane over the Soviet Union. He had personally taken the lead in getting the U-2 program started, and he kept a tight personal control over the flights— he gave his approval to the individual flights only after a thorough briefing on where in the USSR the planes were going and what the CIA wanted to discover. Here too the revisionists have shown that the contemporary feeling, especially after Francis Gary Powers was shot down in 1960, that Ike was not in charge and hardly knew what was going on inside his own government is altogether wrong. He was absolutely in charge, not only of broad policy on the use of the U-2, but of implementing details as well.

The major factor in Eisenhower's ability to restrain defense spending was keeping the peace. His record here is clear and impressive—he signed an armistice in Korea less than half a year after taking office, stayed out of Vietnam, and managed to avoid war despite such crisis situations as Hungary and the Suez, Quemoy and Matsu, Berlin and Cuba. The revisionists insist that

the credit must go to Ike, and they equally insist that Eisenhower, not Secretary of State John Foster Dulles, was in command of American foreign policy in the 1950s. Dulles, says Greenstein, "was assigned the 'get tough' side of foreign-policy enunciation, thus placating the fervently anti-Communist wing of the Republican party." Ike, meanwhile, appeared to be above the battle, while actually directing it on a day-to-day basis.

"In essence, Eisenhower used Dulles." So writes Robert Divine, one of America's leading diplomatic historians, in his provocative new book, *Eisenhower and the Cold War* (Oxford University Press). Divine concludes that "far from being the do-nothing President of legend, Ike was skillful and active in directing American foreign policy." All the revisionists agree that the contemporary idea that Dulles led Ike by the nose was a myth that Eisenhower himself did the most to encourage. Nevertheless, Eisenhower did have a high opinion of his secretary of state. Divine quotes Ike's comment to Emmet Hughes on Dulles: "There's only one man I know who has seen *more* of the world and talked with more people and *knows* more than he does—and that's me."

The quotation illustrates another often overlooked Eisenhower characteristic—his immense self-confidence. He had worked with some of the great men of the century—Churchill, Roosevelt, Stalin, de Gaulle, Montgomery, and many others—long before he became president. His diary entry for the day after his inauguration speaks to the point: "My first day at the president's desk. Plenty of worries and difficult problems. But such has been my portion for a long time—the result is that this just seems (today) like a continuation of all I've been doing since July 1941—even before that."

Ike's vast experience in war and peace made him confident in crises. People naturally looked to him for leadership. No matter how serious the crisis seemed to be, Ike rarely got flustered. During a war scare in the Formosa Straits in 1955, he wrote in his diary, "I have so often been through these periods of strain that I have become accustomed to the fact that most of the calamities that we anticipate really never occur."

IKE'S self-confidence was so great that, Greenstein writes, he had "neither a need nor a desire" to capture

headlines. "He employed his skills to achieve his ends by inconspicuous means." In foreign policy, this meant he did not issue strident warnings, did not—in public—threaten Russia or China with specific reprisals for specific actions. Instead, he retained his room for maneuver by deliberately spreading confusion. He did not care if editorial writers criticized him for jumbled syntax; he wanted to keep possible opponents guessing, and he did. For example, when asked at a March 1955 press conference if he would use atomic bombs to defend Quemoy and Matsu, he replied:

> Every war is going to astonish you in the way it occurred, and in the way it is carried out. So that for a man to predict, particularly if he has the responsibility for making the decision, to predict what he is going to use, how he is going to do it, would I think exhibit his ignorance of war; that is what I believe.

As he intended, the Chinese found such statements inscrutable, as they had in Korea two years earlier. When truce talks in Korea reached an impasse in mid-May 1953, Ike put the pressure on the Chinese, hinting to them that the United States might use atomic weapons if a truce could not be arranged, and backing this up by transferring atomic warheads to American bases in Okinawa. The Chinese then accepted a truce. As Divine writes, "Perhaps the best testimony to the shrewdness of the President's policy is the impossibility of telling even now whether or not he was bluffing."

Nearly all observers agree that one of Ike's greatest accomplishments was staying out of Vietnam in the face of intense pressure from his closest advisers to save the French position there or, after July 1954, to go in alone to defeat Ho Chi Minh. Ike was never tempted. As early as March 1951 he wrote in his diary, "I'm convinced that no military victory is possible in that kind of theater." And in a first draft of his memoirs, written in 1963 but not published until 1981 by Ewald, Ike wrote:

> The jungles of Indochina would have swallowed up division after division of United States troops, who, unaccustomed to this kind of warfare, would have sustained heavy casualties until they had learned to live in a new environment. Furthermore, the presence of ever more numbers of white men in uniform probably would have aggravated

rather than assuaged Asiatic resentments.

That was hardheaded military reasoning by General Eisenhower. But President Eisenhower stayed out of Vietnam as much for moral as for military reasons. When the Joint Chiefs suggested to him in 1954 that the United States use an atomic bomb against the Vietminh around Dien Bien Phu, the president said he would not be a party to using that "terrible thing" against Asians for the second time in less than a decade. And in another previously unpublished draft of his memoirs, he wrote:

> The strongest reason of all for the United States refusal to [intervene] is that fact that among all the powerful nations of the world the United States is the only one with a tradition of anti-colonialism. . . . The standing of the United States as the most powerful of the anti-colonial powers is an asset of incalculable value to the Free World. . . . Thus it is that the moral position of the United States was more to be guarded than the Tonkin Delta, indeed than all of Indochina.

Ike's international outlook, already well known, is highlighted by the new documents. He believed that the bonds that tied Western Europe and the United States together were so tight that the fate of one was the fate of the other. In May 1947, one year before the Marshall Plan, he wrote in his diary, in reference to Western Europe:

> I personally believe that the best thing we could now do would be to post 5 billion to the credit of the secretary of state and tell him to use it to support democratic movements wherever our vital interests indicate. Money should be used to promote possibilities of self-sustaining economies, not merely to prevent immediate starvation.

Ike also anticipated Kennedy's Alliance for Progress. Historian Burton Kaufman, in the narrowest but perhaps most important study reviewed here, *Trade and Aid: Eisenhower's Foreign Economic Policy* (Johns Hopkins University Press), concludes: "Not only did Eisenhower reorient the mutual security program away from military and toward economic assistance, he was also the first president to alter the geographical direction of American foreign aid toward the developing world." After an exhaustive examination, Kaufman also gives Ike high marks for resisting Nel-

son Rockefeller and others who wanted the president to enourage private investment overseas through tax breaks, while reducing or eliminating all forms of public foreign aid. Kaufman's basic theme is "the transition of a foreign economic program based on the concept of 'trade not aid' when Eisenhower took office to one predicated on the principle of 'trade and aid,' with the emphasis clearly on the flow of public capital abroad, by the time he left the White House."

That Ike himself was in charge of this transition, Kaufman leaves no doubt. That Kaufman likes Ike is equally clear: the foreign aid and trade program, Kaufman writes, "demonstrates the quality and character of Eisenhower's intellect and the cogency and forcefulness of his arguments in defense of administration policy. Finally, it emphasizes Eisenhower's flexibility as president and his capacity to alter his views in response to changing world conditions."

Kaufman, however, is critical of Ike on a number of points. Eisenhower himself, it turns out, could be as hypocritical as the "politicians" he scorned. In his speeches, Ike espoused the principles of free trade with sincerity and conviction; in his actions, he supported a protectionist agricultural policy and made broad concessions to the protectionist forces in Congress. Kaufman reaches the conclusion that "he often retreated on trade and tariff matters; he gave up the struggle with hardly a whimper."

And, as Blanche Wiesen Cook, another of the new Eisenhower scholars (but no revisionist), points out in *The Declassified Eisenhower* (Doubleday), Ike's vision of a peaceful world was based on a sophisticated version of Henry Luce's "American Century." Cook argues that Eisenhower's "blueprint . . . involved a determination to pursue political warfare, psychological warfare, and economic warfare everywhere and at all times." Under Ike's direction, she writes, the CIA and other branches of the government "ended all pretentions about territorial integrity, national sovereignty and international law. Covert operatives were everywhere, and they were active. From bribery to assassination, no activity was unacceptable short of nuclear war."

Cook does stress the importance of Eisenhower's stance against general war and his opposition to an arms race,

but insists that these positions have to be placed in context, a context that includes the CIA-inspired and -led governmental overthrows in Iran and Guatemala, covert operations of all types in Vietnam and Eastern Europe, and assassination attempts against political leaders in the Congo and Cuba. Returning to an earlier view of Ike, Cook regards him as a "captive hero," the "chosen instrument" of the leaders of the great multinational corporations "to fight for the world they wanted."

ONE DOES NOT have to accept Cook's "captive hero" view to realize that it may indeed be time, as Kaufman indicates, to blow the whistle on Eisenhower revisionism. Ike had his shortcomings and he suffered serious setbacks. For all his openness to new ideas, he was rigid and dogmatic in his anti-communism. The darker side of Eisenhower's refusal to condemn McCarthy was that Ike himself agreed with the senator on the nature, if not the extent, of the problem, and he shared the senator's goals, if not his methods. After his first year in office, Ike made a list of his major accomplishments to date. Peace in Korea was first, the new defense policy second. Third on the list: "The highest security standards are being insisted upon for those employed in government service," a bland way of saying that under his direction, the Civil Service Commission had fired 2,611 "security risks" and reported that 4,315 other government workers had resigned when they learned they were under investigation. That was the true "hidden hand" at work, and the true difference between Ike and McCarthy—Ike got rid of Communists and fellow travelers (and many liberals) quietly and effectively, while McCarthy, for all his noise, accomplished nothing.

Thus, no matter how thoroughly the revisionists document Ike's opposition to McCarthy personally or his support for Warren, it remains true that his failure to speak out directly on McCarthy encouraged the witch hunters, just as his failure to speak out directly on the *Brown v. Topeka* decision encouraged the segregationists. The old general never admitted that it was impossible for him to be truly above the battle, never seemed to understand that the president is inevitably a part of the battle, so much so that his inaction can have as great an impact as his action.

With McCarthy and *Brown v. Topeka* in

mind, there is a sad quality to the following Eisenhower diary passage, written in January 1954, about a number of Republican senators whom Ike was criticizing for being more inclined to trade votes than to provide clear leadership:

> They do not seem to realize when there arrives that moment at which soft speaking should be abandoned and a fight to the end undertaken. Any man who hopes to exercise leadership must be ready to meet this requirement face to face when it arises; unless he is ready to fight when necessary, people will finally begin to ignore him.

One of Ike's greatest disappointments was his failure to liberalize and modernize the Republican party, in order to make it the majority party in the United States. "The Republican party must be known as a progressive organization or it is sunk," he wrote in his diary in November 1954. "I believe this so emphatically that far from appeasing or reasoning with the dyed-in-the-wool reactionary fringe, we should completely ignore it and when necessary, repudiate it." Responding to cries of "impeach Earl Warren," Ike wrote in his diary, "If the Republicans as a body should try to repudiate him, I shall leave the Republican Party and try to organize an intelligent group of independents, however small." He was always threatening to break with the Republican party, or at least rename it; in March 1954, he told Hagerty, "You know, what we ought to do is get a word to put ahead of Republican—something like 'new' or 'modern' or something. We just can't work with fellows like McCarthy, Bricker, Jenner and that bunch."

A favorite revisionist quotation, which is used to show Ike's political astuteness, comes from a 1954 letter to his brother Edgar:

> Should any political party attempt to abolish social security and eliminate labor laws and farm programs, you would not hear of that party again in our political history. There is a tiny splinter group, of course, that believes that you can do these things. Among them are H. L. Hunt, a few other Texas oil millionaires, and an occasional politician and businessman from other areas. Their number is negligible and they are stupid.

Good enough, but a critic would be quick to point out that Ike's "tiny splinter group" managed to play a large role in the nominations of Barry Goldwater, Richard Nixon, and Ronald Reagan. In short, although Ike saw great dangers to the right in the Republican party, he did little to counter the reactionary influence in his own organization. Franklin Roosevelt did a far better job of curbing the left wing in the Democratic party, and generally in building his party, than anything Ike did for the Republicans.

THE EISENHOWER legacy for the Reagan administration, in brief, is mixed. Reagan can choose to emphasize the darker side of Ike's foreign policy, with its emphasis on CIA activities and reflexive opposition to communism, or he can follow Ike's lead and reject any thought of general war while searching for a genuine peace. Similarly, on the domestic front he can ignore the poor and the minorities in an attempt to balance the budget and curb inflation, or he can again emulate Ike and insist on retaining a strong Social Security system backed by the federal government. He could also recall that Ike presided over the largest public works program in the history of mankind, the Interstate Highway System.

What Reagan cannot do, and still remain faithful to Eisenhower's legacy, is spend increasing sums on the military. From the end of World War II to his last day in the White House, Eisenhower resisted swollen military budgets. In January 1952 he noted in his diary his fear of "the danger of internal deterioration through the annual expenditure of unconscionable sums on a program of indefinite duration, extending far into the future." Or, as he told some members of Congress, "It is perfectly clear that you can't provide security just with a check book. You've got to be prepared to live with a series of [crises] for the next 40 years. If these people decide to put another $3 billion into the budget every time Russia tries to push, they might as well go all the way to a garrison state." The style and rhetoric of the Reagan administration might well be those of the Eisenhower administration—the quick and easy smile, low-key cabinet government on the Whig model, practical businessmen in charge, balanced budgets and lower taxes, stern opposition to communism—but so long as the Reagan people insist on expanded military expenditures the reality can never be the same. Ike's legacy means more than presidential style; he also bequeathed us a record of achievement.

Shortly after Ike left office, a group of leading American historians was asked to rate the presidents. Ike came in near the bottom of the poll. That result was primarily a reflection of how enamored the professors were with FDR and Harry Truman. Today, those same historians would compare Ike with his successors rather than his predecessors and place him in the top 10, if not the top five, of all our presidents. No matter how much one qualifies that record by pointing to this or that shortcoming or failure of the Eisenhower administration, it remains an enviable record. No wonder the people like Ike.

Trumpet of Conscience
A Portrait of Martin Luther King, Jr.

A noted biographer examines the life and legacy of the civil rights leader who may have been the most-loved and most-hated man in America during the turbulent 1960s.

Stephen B. Oates

Biographer and historian Stephen B. Oates is Paul Murray Kendall Professor of Biography and Professor of History at the University of Massachusetts, Amherst. He is the author of twelve books, including award-winning biographies of John Brown, Nat Turner, Abraham Lincoln, and Martin Luther King, Jr. His newest biography, William Faulkner: The Man and the Artist, *was published by Harper & Row in 1987. "This article on Martin Luther King," writes Oates, "is dedicated to the memory of James Baldwin, who had a powerful influence on me in the 1960s, when I was a young writer trying to understand the complexities of American race relations."*

He was M.L. to his parents, Martin to his wife and friends, Doc to his aides, Reverend to his male parishioners, Little Lord Jesus to adoring churchwomen, De Lawd to his young critics in the Student Nonviolent Coordinating Committee, and Martin Luther King, Jr., to the world. At his pulpit or a public rostrum, he seemed too small for his incomparable oratory and international fame as a civil rights leader and spokesman for world peace. He stood only five feet seven, and had round cheeks, a trim mustache, and sad, glistening eyes—eyes that revealed both his inner strength and his vulnerability.

He was born in Atlanta on January 15, 1929, and grew up in the relative comfort of the black middle class. Thus he never suffered the want and privation that plagued the majority of American blacks of his time. His father, a gruff, self-made man, was pastor of Ebenezer Baptist Church and an outspoken member of Atlanta's black leadership. M.L. joined his father's church when he was five and

came to regard it as his second home. The church defined his world, gave it order and balance, taught him how to "get along with people." Here M.L. knew who he was—"Reverend King's boy," somebody special.

At home, his parents and maternal grandmother reinforced his self-esteem, praising him for his precocious ways, telling him repeatedly that he was *somebody.* By age five, he spoke like an adult and had such a prodigious memory that he could recite whole Biblical passages and entire hymns without a mistake. He was acutely sensitive, too, so much so that he worried about all the blacks he saw in Atlanta's breadlines during the Depression, fearful that their children did not have enough to eat. When his maternal grandmother died, twelve-year-old M.L. thought it was his fault. Without telling anyone, he had slipped away from home to watch a parade, only to find out when he returned that she had died. He was terrified that God had taken her away as punishment for his "sin." Guilt-stricken, he tried to kill himself by leaping out of his second-story window.

He had a great deal of anger in him. Growing up a black in segregated Atlanta, he felt the full range of southern racial discrimination. He discovered that he had to attend separate, inferior schools, which he sailed through with a modicum of effort, skipping grades as he went. He found out that he—a preacher's boy— could not sit at lunch counters in Atlanta's downtown stores. He had to drink from a "colored" water fountain, relieve himself in a rancid "colored" restroom, and ride a rickety "colored" elevator. If he rode a city bus, he had to sit in the back as though he were contaminated. If he wanted to see a movie in a downtown theater, he had to enter through a side

door and sit in the "colored" section in the balcony. He discovered that whites referred to blacks as "boys" and "girls" regardless of age. He saw "WHITES ONLY" signs staring back at him in the windows of barber shops and all the good restaurants and hotels, at the YMCA, the city parks, golf courses, swimming pools, and in the waiting rooms of the train and bus stations. He learned that there were even white and black sections of the city and that he resided in "nigger town."

Segregation caused a tension in the boy, a tension between his parents' injunction ("Remember, you are *somebody*") and a system that constantly demeaned and insulted him. He struggled with the pain and rage he felt when a white woman in a downtown store slapped him and called him "a little nigger" . . . when a bus driver called him "a black son-of-a-bitch" and made him surrender his seat to a white . . . when he stood on the very spot in Atlanta where whites had lynched a black man . . . when he witnessed nightriding Klansmen beating blacks in the streets. How, he asked defiantly, could he heed the Christian injunction and love a race of people who hated him? In retaliation, he determined "to hate every white person."

Yes, he was angry. In sandlot games, he competed so fiercely that friends could not tell whether he was playing or fighting. He had his share of playground combat, too, and could outwrestle any of his peers. He even rebelled against his father, vowing never to become a preacher like him. Yet he liked the way Daddy King stood up to whites: he told them never to call him a boy and vowed to fight this system until he died.

From *American History Illustrated,* April 1988, pp. 19-27, 52. Reprinted through the courtesy of Cowles Magazines, publishers of *American History Illustrated.*

Still, there was another side to M.L., a calmer, sensuous side. He played the violin, enjoyed opera, and relished soul food—fried chicken, cornbread, and collard greens with ham hocks and bacon drippings. By his mid-teens, his voice was the most memorable thing about him. It had changed into a rich and resonant baritone that commanded attention whenever he held forth. A natty dresser, nicknamed "Tweed" because of his fondness for tweed suits, he became a connoisseur of lovely young women. His little brother A.D. remembered how Martin "kept flitting from chick to chick" and was "just about the best jitterbug in town."

AT AGE FIFTEEN, HE ENTERED MOREHOUSE College in Atlanta, wanting somehow to help his people. He thought about becoming a lawyer and even practiced giving trial speeches before a mirror in his room. But thanks largely to Morehouse President Benjamin Mays, who showed him that the ministry could be a respectable forum for ideas, even for social protest, King decided to become a Baptist preacher after all. By the time he was ordained in 1947, his resentment toward whites had softened some, thanks to positive contact with white students on an intercollegiate council. But he hated his segregated world more than ever.

Once he had his bachelor's degree, he went north to study at Crozer Seminary near Philadelphia. In this mostly white school, with its polished corridors and quiet solemnity, King continued to ponder the plight of blacks in America. How, by what method and means, were blacks to improve their lot in a white-dominated country? His study of history, especially of Nat Turner's slave insurrection, convinced him that it was suicidal for a minority to strike back against a heavily armed majority. For him, voluntary segregation was equally unacceptable, as was accommodation to the status quo. King shuddered at such negative approaches to the race problem. How indeed were blacks to combat discrimination in a country ruled by the white majority?

As some other blacks had done, he found his answer in the teachings of Mohandas Gandhi—for young King, the discovery had the force of a conversion experience. Nonviolent resistance, Gandhi taught, meant noncooperation with evil, an idea he got from Henry David Thoreau's essay "On Civil Disobedience." In India, Gandhi gave Thoreau's theory practical application in the form of strikes, boycotts, and protest marches, all conducted nonviolently and all predicated on love for the oppressor and a belief in divine justice. In gaining Indian independence, Gandhi sought not to defeat the British, but to redeem them through love, so as to avoid a legacy of bitterness. Gandhi's term for this—Satyagraha—reconciled love and force in a single, powerful concept.

As King discovered from his studies, Gandhi had embraced nonviolence in part to subdue his own violent nature. This was a profound revelation for King, who had felt much hatred in his life, especially toward whites. Now Gandhi showed him a means of harnessing his anger and channeling it into a positive and creative force for social change.

AT THIS JUNCTURE, KING FOUND MOSTLY theoretical satisfaction in Gandhian nonviolence; he had no plans to become a radical activist in the segregated South. Indeed, he seemed destined to a life of the mind, not of social protest. In 1951, he graduated from Crozer and went on to earn a Ph.D. in theology from Boston University, where his adviser pronounced him "a scholar's scholar" of great intellectual potential. By 1955, a year after the school desegregation decision, King had married comely Coretta Scott and assumed the pastorship of Dexter Avenue Baptist Church in Montgomery, Alabama. Immensely happy in the world of ideas, he hoped eventually to teach theology at a major university or seminary.

But, as King liked to say, the Zeitgeist, or spirit of the age, had other plans for him. In December 1955, Montgomery blacks launched a boycott of the city's segregated buses and chose the articulate twenty-six-year-old minister as their spokesman.* As it turned out, he was unusually well prepared to assume the kind of leadership thrust on him. Drawing on Gandhi's teachings and example, plus the tenets of his own Christian faith, King directed a nonviolent boycott designed both to end an injustice and redeem his white adversaries through love. When he exhorted blacks to love their enemies, King did not mean to love them

*See "The Father His Children Forgot" in the December 1985 issue of American History Illustrated.

as friends or intimates. No, he said, he meant a disinterested love in all humankind, a love that saw the neighbor in everyone it met, a love that sought to restore the beloved community. Such love not only avoided the internal violence of the spirit, but severed the external chain of hatred that only produced more hatred in an endless spiral. If American blacks could break the chain of hatred, King said, true brotherhood could begin. Then posterity would have to say that there had lived a race of people, of black people, who "injected a new meaning into the veins of history and civilization."

During the boycott King imparted his philosophy at twice-weekly mass meetings in the black churches, where overflow crowds clapped and cried as his mellifluous voice swept over them. In these mass meetings King discovered his extraordinary power as an orator. His rich religious imagery reached deep into the black psyche, for religion had been the black people's main source of strength and survival since slavery days. His delivery was "like a narrative poem," said a woman journalist who heard him. His voice had such depths of sincerity and empathy that it could "charm your heart right out of your body." Because he appealed to the best in his people, articulating their deepest hurts and aspirations, black folk began to idolize him; he was their Gandhi.

Under his leadership, they stood up to white Montgomery in a remarkable display of solidarity. Pitted against an obdurate city government that blamed the boycott on Communist agitation and resorted to psychological and legal warfare to break it, the blacks stayed off the buses month after month, and walked or rode in a black-operated carpool. When an elderly woman refused the offer of a ride, King asked her, "But don't your feet hurt?" "Yes," she replied, "my feet is tired but my soul is rested." For King, her irrepressible spirit was proof that "a new Negro" was emerging in the South, a Negro with "a new sense of dignity and destiny."

That "new Negro" menaced white supremacists, especially the Ku Klux Klan, and they persecuted King with a vengeance. They made obscene phone calls to his home, sent him abusive, sickening letters, and once even dynamited the front of his house. Nobody was hurt, but King, fearing a race war, had to dissuade angry blacks from violent retaliation. Finally, on November 13, 1956, the U.S. Supreme Court nullified the Alabama laws that enforced segregated buses, and handed King and his boycotters a resounding moral victory. Their protest had captured the imagination of progressive people all over the world and marked the beginning of a southern black movement that would shake the segregated South to its foundations. At the forefront of that movement was a new organization, the Southern Christian Leadership Conference (SCLC), which King and other black ministers formed in 1957, with King serving as its president and guiding spirit. Operating through the southern black church, SCLC sought to enlist the black masses in the freedom struggle by expanding "the Montgomery way" across the South.

The "Miracle of Montgomery" changed King's life, catapulting him into international prominence as an inspiring new moral voice for civil rights. Across the country, blacks and whites alike wrote him letters of encouragement; *Time* magazine pictured him on its cover; the National Association for the Advancement of Colored People (NAACP) and scores of church and civic organizations vied for his services as a speaker. "I am really disturbed how fast all this has happened to me," King told his wife. "People will expect me to perform miracles for the rest of my life."

But fame had its evil side, too. When King visited New York in 1958, a deranged black woman stabbed him in the chest with a letter opener. The weapon was lodged so close to King's aorta, the main artery from the heart, that he would have died had he sneezed. To extract the blade, an interracial surgical team had to remove a rib and part of his breastbone; in a burst of inspiration, the lead surgeon made the incision over King's heart in the shape of a cross.

THAT HE HAD NOT DIED CONVINCED KING that God was preparing him for some larger work in the segregated South. To gain perspective on what was happening there, he made a pilgrimage to India to visit Gandhi's shrine and the sites of his "War for Independence." He returned home with an even deeper commitment to nonviolence and a vow to be more humble and ascetic like Gandhi. Yet he was a man of manifold contradictions, this American Gandhi. While renouncing material things and giving nearly all

of his extensive honorariums to SCLC, he liked posh hotels and zesty meals with wine, and he was always immaculately dressed in a gray or black suit, white shirt, and tie. While caring passionately for the poor, the downtrodden, and the disinherited, he had a fascination with men of affluence and enjoyed the company of wealthy SCLC benefactors. While trumpeting the glories of nonviolence and redemptive love, he could feel the most terrible anger when whites murdered a black or bombed a black church; he could contemplate giving up, turning America over to the haters of both races, only to dedicate himself anew to his nonviolent faith and his determination to redeem his country.

In 1960, he moved his family to Atlanta so that he could devote himself fulltime to SCLC, which was trying to register black voters for the upcoming federal elections. That same year, southern black students launched the sit-in movement against segregated lunch counters, and King not only helped them form the Student Nonviolent Coordinating Committee (SNCC) but raised money on their behalf. In October he even joined a sit-in protest at an Atlanta department store and went to jail with several students on a trespassing charge. Like Thoreau, King considered jail "a badge of honor." To redeem the nation and arouse the conscience of the opponent, King explained, you go to jail and stay there. "You have broken a law which is out of line with the moral law and you are willing to suffer the consequences by serving the time."

He did not reckon, however, on the tyranny of racist officials, who clamped him in a malevolent state penitentiary, in a cell for hardened criminals. But state authorities released him when Democratic presidential nominee John F. Kennedy and his brother Robert interceded on King's behalf. According to many analysts, the episode won critical black votes for Kennedy and gave him the election in November. For King, the election demonstrated what he had long said: that one of the most significant steps a black could take was the short walk to the voting booth.

The trouble was that most blacks in Dixie, especially in the Deep South, could not vote even if they so desired. For decades, state and local authorities had kept the mass of black folk off the voting rolls by a welter of devious obstacles and outright intimidation. Through

1961 and 1962, King exhorted President Kennedy to sponsor tough new civil rights legislation that would enfranchise southern blacks and end segregated public accommodations as well. When Kennedy shied away from a strong civil rights commitment, King and his lieutenants took matters into their own hands, orchestrating a series of southern demonstrations to show the world the brutality of segregation. At the same time, King stumped the country, drawing on all his powers of oratory to enlist the black masses and win white opinion to his cause.

Everywhere he went his message was the same. The *civil rights issue,* he said, *is an eternal moral issue that will determine the destiny of our nation and our world. As we seek our full rights, we hope to redeem the soul of our country. For it is our country, too, and we will win our freedom because the sacred heritage of America and the eternal will of God are embodied in our echoing demands. We do not intend to humiliate the white man, but to win him over through the strength of our love. Ultimately, we are trying to free all of us in America— Negroes from the bonds of segregation and shame, whites from the bonds of bigotry and fear.*

We stand today between two worlds— the dying old order and the emerging new. With men of ill-will greeting this change with cries of violence, of interposition and nullification, some of us may get beaten. Some of us may even get killed. But if you are cut down in a movement designed to save the soul of a nation, no other death could be more redemptive. We must realize that change does not roll in "on the wheels of inevitability," but comes through struggle. So "let us be those creative dissenters who will call our beloved nation to a higher destiny, to a new plateau of compassion, to a more noble expression of humaneness."

That message worked like magic among America's long-suffering blacks. Across the South, across America, they rose in unprecedented numbers to march and demonstrate with Martin Luther King. His singular achievement was that he brought the black masses into the freedom struggle for the first time. He rallied the strength of broken men and women, helping them overcome a lifetime of fear and feelings of inferiority. After segregation had taught them all their lives that they were *nobody,* King taught them that they were *somebody.* Because he made them believe in themselves and in the beauty of chosen suffering, he taught them how to straighten their backs ("a man can't ride you unless your back is bent") and confront those who oppressed them. Through the technique of nonviolent resistance, he furnished them something no previous black leader had been able to provide. He showed them a way of controlling their pent-up anger, as he had controlled his own, and using it to bring about constructive change.

THE MASS DEMONSTRATIONS KING AND SCLC choreographed in the South produced the strongest civil rights legislation in American history. This was the goal of King's major southern campaigns from 1963 to 1965. He would single out some notoriously segregated city with white officials prone to violence, mobilize the local blacks with songs, scripture readings, and rousing oratory in black churches, and then lead them on protest marches conspicuous for their grace and moral purpose. Then he and his aides would escalate the marches, increase their demands, even fill up the jails, until they brought about a moment of "creative tension," when whites would either agree to negotiate or resort to violence. If they did the latter, King would thus expose the brutality inherent in segregation and so stab the national conscience so that the federal government would be forced to intervene with corrective measures.

The technique succeeded brilliantly in Birmingham, Alabama, in 1963. Here Police Commissioner Eugene "Bull" Connor, in full view of reporters and television cameras, turned firehoses and police dogs on the marching protestors. Revolted by such ghastly scenes, stricken by King's own searching eloquence and the bravery of his unarmed followers, Washington eventually produced the 1964 Civil Rights Act, which desegregated public facilities—the thing King had demanded all along from Birmingham. Across the South, the "WHITES ONLY" signs that had hurt and enraged him since boyhood now came down.

Although SNCC and others complained that King had a Messiah complex and was trying to monopolize the civil rights movement, his technique worked with equal success in Selma, Alabama, in 1965. Building on a local movement

there, King and his staff launched a drive to gain southern blacks the unobstructed right to vote. The violence he exposed in Selma—the beating of black marchers by state troopers and deputized possemen, the killing of a young black deacon and a white Unitarian minister—horrified the country. When King called for support, thousands of ministers, rabbis, priests, nuns, students, lay leaders, and ordinary people—black and white alike—rushed to Selma from all over the country and stood with King in the name of human liberty. Never in the history of the movement had so many people of all faiths and classes come to the southern battleground. The Selma campaign culminated in a dramatic march over the Jefferson Davis Highway to the state capital of Montgomery. Along the way, impoverished local blacks stared incredulously at the marching, singing, flag-waving spectacle moving by. When the column reached one dusty crossroads, an elderly black woman ran out from a group of old folk, kissed King breathlessly, and ran back crying, "I done kissed him! The Martin Luther King! I done kissed the Martin Luther King!"

In Montgomery, first capital and much-heralded "cradle" of the Confederacy, King led an interracial throng of 25,000—the largest civil rights demonstration the South had ever witnessed—up Dexter Avenue with banners waving overhead. The pageant was as ironic as it was extraordinary, for it was up Dexter Avenue that Jefferson Davis's first inaugural parade had marched, and in the portico of the capitol Davis had taken his oath of office as president of the slave-based Confederacy. Now, in the spring of 1965, Alabama blacks—most of them descendants of slaves—stood massed at the same statehouse, singing a new rendition of "We Shall Overcome," the anthem of the civil rights movement. They sang, "Deep in my heart, I do believe, We have overcome—*today.*"

Then, within view of the statue of Jefferson Davis, and watched by cordons of state troopers and television cameras, King mounted a trailer. His vast audience listened, transfixed, as his words rolled and thundered over the loudspeaker: "My people, my people listen. The battle is in our hands. . . . We must come to see that the end we seek is a society at peace with itself, a society that can live with its conscience. That day will be a day not of the white man, not of the black man. That will be the day of

man as man." And that day was not long in coming, King said, whereupon he launched into the immortal refrains of "The Battle Hymn of the Republic," crying out, "Our God is marching on! Glory, glory hallelujah!"

Aroused by the events in Alabama, Washington produced the 1965 Voting Rights Act, which outlawed impediments to black voting and empowered the attorney general to supervise federal elections in seven southern states where blacks were kept off the rolls. At the time, political analysts almost unanimously attributed the act to King's Selma campaign. Once federal examiners were supervising voter registration in all troublesome southern areas, blacks were able to get on the rolls and vote by the hundreds of thousands, permanently altering the pattern of southern and national politics.

In the end, the powerful civil rights legislation generated by King and his tramping legions wiped out statutory racism in America and realized at least the social and political promise of emancipation a century before. But King was under no illusion that legislation alone could bring on the brave new America he so ardently championed. Yes, he said, laws and their vigorous enforcement were necessary to regulate destructive habits and actions, and to protect blacks and their rights. But laws could not eliminate the "fears, prejudice, pride, and irrationality" that were barriers to a truly integrated society, to peaceful intergroup and interpersonal living. Such a society could be achieved only when people accepted that inner, invisible law that etched on their hearts the conviction "that all men are brothers and that love is mankind's most potent weapon for personal and social transformation. True integration will be achieved by true neighbors who are willingly obedient to unenforceable obligations."

Even so, the Selma campaign was the movement's finest hour, and the Voting Rights Act the high point of a broad civil rights coalition that included the federal government, various white groups, and all the other civil rights organizations in addition to SCLC. King himself had best expressed the spirit and aspirations of that coalition when, on August 28, 1963, standing before the Lincoln Memorial, he electrified an interracial crowd of 250,000 with perhaps his greatest speech, "I Have A Dream," in which he described in rhythmic, hypnotic cadences his vision of an integrated America. Because of his achievements and moral vision, he won the 1964 Nobel Peace Prize, at thirty-four the youngest recipient in Nobel history.

STILL, KING PAID A HIGH PRICE FOR HIS fame and his cause. He suffered from stomachaches and insomnia, and even felt guilty about all the tributes he received, all the popularity he enjoyed. Born in relative material comfort and given a superior education, he did not think he had earned the right to lead the impoverished black masses. He complained, too, that he no longer had a personal self and that sometimes he did not recognize the Martin Luther King people talked about. Lonely, away from home for protracted periods, beset with temptation, he slept with other women, for some of whom he had real feeling. His sexual transgressions only added to his guilt, for he knew he was imperiling his cause and hurting himself and those he loved.

Alas for King, FBI Director J. Edgar Hoover found out about the black leader's infidelities. The director already abhorred King, certain that Communist spies influenced him and masterminded his demonstrations. Hoover did not think blacks capable of organizing such things, so Communists had to be behind them and King as well. As it turned out, a lawyer in King's inner circle and a man in SCLC's New York office did have Communist backgrounds, a fact that only reinforced Hoover's suspicions about King. Under Hoover's orders, FBI agents conducted a ruthless crusade to destroy King's reputation and drive him broken and humiliated from public life. Hoover's men tapped King's phones and bugged his hotel rooms; they compiled a prurient monograph about his private life and showed it to various editors, public officials, and religious and civic leaders; they spread the word, Hoover's word, that King was not only a reprobate but a dangerous subversive with Communist associations.

King was scandalized and frightened by the FBI's revelations of his extramarital affairs. Luckily for him, no editor, not even a racist one in the South, would touch the FBI's salacious materials. Public officials such as Robert Kennedy were shocked, but argued that King's personal life did not affect his probity as a civil rights leader. Many blacks, too, declared that what he did in private was his own business. Even so, King vowed to refrain from further affairs—only to succumb again to his own human frailties.

As for the Communist charge, King retorted that he did not need any Russians to tell him when someone was standing on his neck; he could figure that out by himself. To mollify his political friends, however, King did banish from SCLC the two men with Communist backgrounds (later he resumed his ties with the lawyer, a loyal friend, and let Hoover be damned). He also denounced Communism in no uncertain terms. It was, he believed, profoundly and fundamentally evil, an atheistic doctrine no true Christian could ever embrace. He hated the dictatorial Soviet state, too, whose "crippling totalitarianism" subordinated everything—religion, art, music, science, and the individual—to its terrible yoke. True, Communism started with men like Karl Marx who were "aflame with a passion for social justice." Yet King faulted Marx for rejecting God and the spiritual in human life. "The great weakness in Karl Marx is right here," King once told his staff, and he went on to describe his ideal Christian commonwealth in Hegelian terms: "Capitalism fails to realize that life is social. Marxism fails to realize that life is individual. Truth is found neither in the rugged individualism of capitalism nor in the impersonal collectivism of Communism. The kingdom of God is found in a synthesis that combines the truths of these two opposites. Now there is where I leave brother Marx and move on toward the kingdom."

BUT HOW TO MOVE ON AFTER SELMA WAS a perplexing question King never successfully answered. After the devastating Watts riot in August 1965, he took his movement into the racially troubled urban North, seeking to help the suffering black poor in the ghettos. In 1966, over the fierce opposition of some of his own staff, he launched a campaign to end the black slums in Chicago and forestall rioting there. But the campaign foundered because King seemed unable to devise a coherent anti-slum strategy, because Mayor Richard Daley and his black acolytes opposed him bitterly, and because white America did not seem to care. King did lead open-housing marches into segregated neighborhoods in Chicago, only to encounter furious mobs who waved Nazi banners, threw bottles and bricks, and screamed, "We hate niggers!" "Kill the niggers!" "We want Martin Luther Coon!" King was shocked. "I've been in many demonstrations all across the South," he told reporters, "but I can say that I have never seen—even in Mississippi and Alabama—mobs as hostile and as hate-filled as I've seen in Chicago." Although King prevented a major riot there and wrung important concessions from City Hall, the slums remained, as wretched and seemingly unsolvable as ever.

That same year, angry young militants in SNCC and the Congress of Racial Equality (CORE) renounced King's teachings—they were sick and tired of "De Lawd" telling them to love white people and work for integration. Now they advocated "Black Power," black separatism, even violent resistance to liberate blacks in America. SNCC even banished whites from its ranks and went on to drop "nonviolent" from its name and to lobby against civil rights legislation.

Black Power repelled the older, more conservative black organizations such as the NAACP and the Urban League, and fragmented the civil rights movement beyond repair. King, too, argued that black separatism was chimerical, even suicidal, and that nonviolence remained the only workable way for black people. "Darkness cannot drive out darkness," he reasoned: "only light can do that. Hate cannot drive out hate: only love can do that." If every other black in America turned to violence, King warned, then he would still remain the lone voice preaching that it was wrong. Nor was SCLC going to reject whites as SNCC had done. "There have been too many hymns of hope," King said, "too many anthems of expectation, too many deaths, too many dark days of standing over graves of those who fought for integration for us to turn back now. We must still sing 'Black and White Together, We Shall Overcome.'"

In 1967, King himself broke with the older black organizations over the ever-widening war in Vietnam. He had first objected to American escalation in the summer of 1965, arguing that the Nobel Peace Prize and his role as a Christian minister compelled him to speak out for peace. Two years later, with almost a half-million Americans—a disproportionate number of them poor blacks—fighting in Vietnam, King devoted whole speeches to America's "immoral" war against a tiny country on the other side of the globe. His stance provoked a fusillade of criticism from all directions—from the NAACP, the Urban League, white and black political leaders, *Newsweek, Life, Time,* and the *New York Times,* all telling him to stick to civil rights. Such criticism hurt him deeply. When he read the *Times*'s editorial against him, he broke down and cried. But he did not back down. "I've fought too long and too hard now against segregated accommodations to end up segregating my moral concerns," he told his critics. "Injustice anywhere is a threat to justice everywhere."

That summer, with the ghettos ablaze with riots, King warned that American cities would explode if funds used for war purposes were not diverted to emergency antipoverty programs. By then, the Johnson administration, determined to gain a military victory in Vietnam, had written King off as an antiwar agitator, and was now cooperating with the FBI in its efforts to defame him.

The fall of 1967 was a terrible time for King, the lowest ebb in his civil rights career. Everybody seemed to be attacking him—young black militants for his stubborn adherence to nonviolence, moderate and conservative blacks, labor leaders, liberal white politicians, the White House, and the FBI for his stand on Vietnam. Two years had passed since King had produced a nonviolent victory, and contributions to SCLC had fallen off sharply. Black spokesman Adam Clayton Powell, who had once called King the greatest Negro in America, now derided him as Martin Loser King. The incessant attacks began to irritate him, creating such anxiety and depression that his friends worried about his emotional health.

Worse still, the country seemed dangerously polarized. On one side, backlashing whites argued that the ghetto explosions had "cremated" nonviolence and that white people had better arm themselves against black rioters. On the other side, angry blacks urged their peo-

ple to "kill the Honkies" and burn the cities down. All around King, the country was coming apart in a cacophony of hate and reaction. Had America lost the will and moral power to save itself? he wondered. There was such rage in the ghetto and such bigotry among whites that he feared a race war was about to break out. He felt he had to do something to pull America back from the brink. He and his staff had to mount a new campaign that would halt the drift to violence in the black world and combat stiffening white resistance, a nonviolent action that would "transmute the deep rage of the ghetto into a constructive and creative force."

OUT OF HIS DELIBERATIONS SPRANG A BOLD and daring project called the poor people's campaign. The master plan, worked out by February 1968, called for SCLC to bring an interracial army of poor people to Washington, D.C., to dramatize poverty before the federal government. For King, just turned thirty-nine, the time had come to employ civil disobedience against the national government itself. Ultimately, he was projecting a genuine class movement that he hoped would bring about meaningful changes in American society—changes that would redistribute economic and political power and end poverty, racism, "the madness of militarism," and war.

In the midst of his preparations, King went to Memphis, Tennessee, to help black sanitation workers there who were striking for the right to unionize. On the night of April 3, with a storm thundering outside, he told a black audience that he had been to the mountaintop and had seen what lay ahead. "I may not get there with you. But I want you to know tonight that we as a people *will* get to the promised land."

The next afternoon, when King stepped out on the balcony of the Lorraine Motel, an escaped white convict named James

Earl Ray, stationed in a nearby building, took aim with a high-powered rifle and blasted King into eternity. Subsequent evidence linked Ray to white men in the St. Louis area who had offered "hit" money for King's life.

For weeks after the shooting, King's stricken country convulsed in grief, contrition, and rage. While there were those who cheered his death, the *New York Times* called it a disaster to the nation, the *London Times* an enormous loss to the world. In Tanzania, Reverend Trevor Huddleston, expelled from South Africa for standing against apartheid, declared King's death the greatest single tragedy since the assassination of Gandhi in 1948, and said it challenged the complacency of the Christian Church all over the globe.

On April 9, with 120 million Americans watching on television, thousands of mourners—black and white alike—gathered in Atlanta for the funeral of a man who had never given up his dream of creating a symphony of brotherhood on these shores. As a black man born and raised in segregation, he had had every reason to hate America and to grow up preaching cynicism and retaliation. Instead, he had loved the country passionately and had sung of her promise and glory more eloquently than anyone of his generation.

They buried him in Atlanta's South View Cemetery, then blooming with dogwood and fresh green boughs of spring. On his crypt, hewn into the marble, were the words of an old Negro spiritual he had often quoted: "Free at Last, Free at Last, Thank God Almighty I'm Free at Last."

Recommended additional reading: Let the Trumpet Sound: The Life of Martin Luther King, Jr. *by Stephen B. Oates (Harper & Row, 1982), and* A Testament of Hope: The Essential Writings of Martin Luther King, Jr. *edited by James M. Washington (Harper & Row, 1986).*

Watergate Redux

Even after 20 years, the story is still unfolding

Karlyn Barker
and Walter Pincus

Washington Post Staff Writers

Sgt. Paul Leeper and officers Carl Shoffler and John Barrett were headed toward Georgetown in their unmarked police car and had just passed under the Whitehurst Freeway at 1:52 a.m. when a dispatcher alerted them to "doors open" and a possible burglary underway at the posh Watergate complex.

A quick U-turn and a minute or two later, the three "casual clothes" District of Columbia policemen pulled up in front of the hotel/office building near the Kennedy Center and walked into the lobby to look for the security guard who had reported trouble.

"We didn't jump out of the car and go running up there," Leeper says, recalling their initial ho-hum response in those early morning hours of June 17, 1972. "You get so many calls like that—burglary in progress—and 90 to 95 percent of them aren't anything."

But they saw the tape-covered door latches in the parking garage, the same kind of tampering on doors leading to the sixth-floor headquarters of the Democratic National Committee, the disheveled files inside. Maybe something was going on after all. Then Barrett, gun drawn, spotted a moving figure and got the shock of his young life: "Five middle-aged guys stand up . . . wearing suits and ties and surgical gloves. And

they've got a walkie-talkie . . . and tools and all this electrical stuff."

Thus began the scandal that became known by a single word: Watergate. From a routine police summons and bungled burglary and bugging to the unprecedented resignation two years later of a discredited president facing almost certain impeachment, it mesmerized the nation's capital and ultimately the whole country.

Month by month, an appalled public confronted accounts of secret slush funds, hush money for the burglars, forged cables, wiretapping and illegal entries by a secret "Plumbers" squad, enemies' lists, a secret tape-recording system in the White House and the flagrant and greedy abuse of presidential power.

By the time Richard M. Nixon waved goodbye to a red-eyed White House staff and boarded a helicopter for California exile on Aug. 9, 1974, his administration had disintegrated into disgrace. What seemed impossible, even unthinkable, had occurred: The president, sworn to uphold the Constitution and laws of the United States, had been implicated with his top aides in an elaborate conspiracy to cover up criminal behavior and political sabotage.

Today, 20 years later, Watergate is contested history, constantly reexamined in books, on talk shows and in high school classrooms filled with students who were not yet born when the burglars got caught. What were they really doing

there that night? Was it a scandal or merely politics as usual? Who was "Deep Throat" and will Washington Post reporter Bob Woodward ever tell?

Watergate even changed the language of politics. It seems a scandal isn't a scandal unless it ends in a "gate."

This is a retelling of the central story using publicly released FBI investigative files, oral histories, private memos, handwritten notes and other documents, most of them gleaned from the National Archives and not available when President Nixon resigned 18 years ago. This account includes voices from both well-known and little-known participants in the extraordinary crisis.

There are the two FBI agents first assigned to the case, the bookkeeper at the Committee for the Reelection of the President who risked her job to tell what she knew, the law clerk who holed up in a windowless jury room and listened aghast to the tapes of the president's conversations. There are the prosecutors, lawmakers and reporters who ferreted out a president's ugly secrets.

Nixon, the law-and-order president who promised to "Bring Us Together" and then clung to his second term insisting, "I'm not a crook," has spent the years since his resignation trying to rehabilitate himself. Now a 79-year-old author and global counselor, he wants to be remembered as the president who went to China, not the unindicted co-conspirator who might have gone to prison.

THE TRAGIC IRONY, ESPECIALLY FOR NIXON, is that Watergate's criminal and riskiest operations were not born of any great threat to his presidency. On the eve of the break-in, the polls showed him leading all likely election rivals by 19 percentage points. "All we had to do was sit back and wait for the Democrats to nominate George McGovern," the eventual nominee in 1972, a top Nixon reelection aide said later. "Unfortunately, we were doing a good deal more."

After some of the participants had reluctantly told their stories, in the courts and in televised congressional hearings that riveted the nation, more than 30 Nixon administration officials, campaign officers and financial contributors pleaded or were found guilty of breaking the law. Of these, 19 of the president's aides and hirelings went to jail, serving sentences of one to 52 months. Nixon received an unconditional presidential pardon a month after leaving office.

For historian Stanley Kutler, the lessons of Watergate have nothing to do with what he calls the "trivia" surrounding the break-in. That event merely "parted the veil" on Nixon's illegal activities, says Kutler, a University of Wisconsin professor and author of "The Wars of Watergate." The government survived a constitutional crisis, he says, "because people did their jobs."

For Judy Hoback, the bookkeeper who exposed a small piece of the scandal's puzzle to the FBI and later to reporters, it never seemed that easy. She was newly widowed with a baby daughter. She remembers how small she felt, how big the White House seemed. Now her daughter teaches history and has urged Hoback to talk publicly about her role after all these years.

"A lot of people might say it was no big deal, that they're all crooks," says Hoback, who now lives in Florida. "But it was a BIG DEAL, and it did have some meaning. I feel it was good justice was done."

Frank Wills, an $80-a-week security guard, saw the masking tape on the door latches in the Watergate parking garage while making his rounds about 12:30 a.m. He wasn't concerned. The 24-year-old Wills figured the maintenance crew had done it to keep the doors ajar and had forgotten to remove the tape. He stripped it off and went across the street to the Howard Johnson's Motor Lodge restaurant for some takeout food.

About an hour later, Willis saw that the doors had been taped again. Rattled, he called the police.

A very nervous Wills escorted Leeper, Shoffler and Barrett to the taped doors. They shut off the elevators and moved up the stairwell to investigate.

Barrett bounded ahead, checking stairwell doors as he ran up the stairs and shouting back to his partners. He found more tape on the sixth and eighth floors. The three men searched the eighth floor, found nothing and entered the sixth floor offices occupied by the Democratic National Committee.

A room to the right looked ransacked, with file drawers open and papers strewn about. A second room was in the same condition. Proceeding cautiously, they discovered a chair propping open a door to a large terrace overlooking Virginia Avenue.

Warily, Leeper and Shoffler went outside. Gun in hand, Shoffler crawled along an adjoining ledge to see if anyone was hiding. He noticed a man watching him intently from a balcony across the street at the Howard Johnson's.

Inside the DNC offices, Barrett moved carefully from room to room, flipping on lights as he went. Near the conference room, he crouched behind a glass and wood partition. "I was afraid to make a turn," he says, recalling his hesitation 20 years later. "It's dark, and Carl and Paul aren't here."

Suddenly, "I saw an arm hit the glass right next to my face. It scared the shit out of me."

Barrett remembers yelling something like "Back here!" to summon his partners and then shouted, "Police! Come out with your hands up!"

Not one, but five men stood up. In the tense moments that followed, Leeper jumped up on a desk to cover the group. Barrett eyed one man who had a black overnight bag in one hand and a trench coat draped over an arm, obscuring his other hand. Barrett yelled at him to drop the bag and coat and raise his hands. The man didn't react. Barrett pointed his pistol directly at the man's chest. Another intruder said something in Spanish, and the man's hands flew up.

"I almost shot him," Barrett recalls.

The size of the group made Leeper edgy too. Were there others, perhaps hiding under desks? He was also worried because they had only two pairs of handcuffs. Shoffler had left his in the car.

They ordered the five men to face the wall, hands up. They advised the suspects of their rights and patted them down, finding penlights, tiny tear-gas canisters and keys to Room 214 at the Watergate Hotel.

One of the suspects had a spiral notebook with a key taped to the outside cover. Twice, he tried to sneak his hand into his coat pocket to hide the key. Shoffler slammed him against the wall, then seized the notebook. The key fit the desk of Ida "Maxie" Wells, secretary to R. Spencer Oliver, executive director of the Association of State Democratic Chairmen.

At 2nd District police headquarters, the suspects declined to contact lawyers, noting cryptically that the "appropriate people" had already been notified. And they stuck to false, prearranged identities, giving police the names they had used to register at the hotel.

Except that two of them got mixed up.

"They gave me the same alias," says Barrett. "I said, 'Wait a minute, fellas, you've got to get your stories straight.' And they both giggled."

It took a few more hours to pierce through the phony names and establish their true identities: Bernard I. Barker, 53; Virgilio R. Gonzalez, 46; Eugenio Martinez, 50; Frank A. Sturgis, 47; and James W. McCord Jr., also 47.

BUT THE NAMES DID NOT EXPLAIN WHAT the suspects were doing or why they were carrying an astonishing array of electronic and photographic equipment. Barker had a walkie-talkie and keys to a rental car. Gonzalez had lock-picking tools. McCord carried a wire cutter and screwdrivers and had pocketed four documents, including a letter to DNC Chairman Lawrence F. O'Brien and application forms for college press credentials to cover the upcoming Democratic National Convention in Miami. All but McCord were carrying crisp, new $100 bills.

Later that day, as the police sought frantically to find out more about the uncooperative suspects, a shocked 2nd District officer recognized the man calling himself Edward Martin: "That's Jim McCord," he told his stunned colleagues. "He's the security chief at the Committee to Reelect the President."

That first morning, a Saturday, Special Agent Angelo J. Lano was awakened at 8 by a call from FBI headquarters. There was a report that five international jewel thieves had been caught at the Watergate, where Lano had investigated previous burglaries.

By the time Lano arrived at the 2nd District police station, however, officers wanted him to look at what appeared to be the makings of a bomb. Lano rummaged around in the bag police had seized. "I grabbed a piece of tissue paper and pulled it out," he says now, "and this little black device with wires fell into my hand. And I set it aside and I reached in and pulled out tissue paper and another black device fell out."

This was no bomb. The devices were something "you would use to monitor a conversation. Either intercept a conversation in a room, or a telephone bugging device." The FBI laboratory confirmed Lano's suspicions within 15 minutes.

A burglary, even at the DNC, was something the local cops could handle. But electronic eavesdropping put the crime squarely into federal jurisdiction. And so began the case that would absorb Lano, then 33 and a relatively junior agent, for the next five years, first with the office of the U.S. Attorney for the District of Columbia and later for the special prosecutors appointed to take over the mushrooming probe.

Lano and his then-29-year-old partner, Daniel C. Mahan, have never discussed their Watergate work publicly. They consented to interviews now because the FBI made their investigation—all 16,000 pages—public several years ago under the Freedom of Information Act.

It also grates on them that the public seems to believe that The Washington Post and reporters Bob Woodward and Carl Bernstein solved the Watergate case. Woodward and Bernstein's book on their reportage, "All the President's Men," later was made into a popular Hollywood film starring Robert Redford and Dustin Hoffman.

ACCORDING TO LANO, MUCH OF WOODward and Bernstein's work reflected what the FBI already knew. "I resent that they have been perceived as the individuals who responded and solved the investigation," Lano says. "I feel the bureau . . . solved it, even though the public doesn't know that."

The FBI investigation and The Post's early reporting seemed to feed one another. The Post did publish information first turned up by the FBI, but the continuation of the investigation almost certainly depended on the political pressure

resulting from the reporting of The Post and others.

Lano and his fellow FBI agents knew on that first Saturday, of course, that they had a bugging case on their hands. Apart from the electronic devices, the crime scene made that clear: The air conditioner panel was ajar in the DNC's conference room, the screws on a telephone jack had been loosened and some ceiling tiles had been removed.

What they learned about the suspects that day added to the mystery. Barker, Gonzalez and Martinez were Cuban Americans who lived in Miami, as did Sturgis, and all had been involved in anti-Castro activities tied to the CIA. Barker and McCord were former CIA agents. Lano wondered if they had stumbled upon a CIA operation.

That afternoon, D.C. police came across the first big break. A search of the men's Watergate hotel room turned up $3,500 in sequentially numbered $100 bills in a dresser drawer. Martinez's attache case contained his pop-up address lister, Barker's small black address book, and a sealed, stamped envelope with a $6.36 check made out to the Lakewood Country Club in Rockville. The check was drawn on the account of an E. Howard Hunt Jr.

Barker's book contained the initials "HH" above the notation "WH" and a telephone number. Martinez's address book listed the same number next to "Howard Hunt (W-House)."

A quick trace showed that the phone number rang at a White House office. Suddenly, the stakes had become a lot higher.

THE FBI WAS MOVING FAST, BUT SO WERE the president's men. Though they would deny it for months, top White House and campaign officials knew that first day that the "Cubans" caught at the Watergate were working for them. The news about McCord was a jolt, though. No one who worked for the Committee for the Reelection of the President (CRP) was supposed to go along on the actual break-in.

The president was enjoying a long weekend at the Florida White House in Key Biscayne. His major campaign aides were in Los Angeles, attending several political functions in advance of the Republican National Convention in August.

On Sunday, June 18, Nixon's chief of

staff, H. R. (Bob) Haldeman, spoke to deputy campaign director Jeb Stuart Magruder in California. Hurriedly, the two former advertising executives went over plans for containing the crisis.

The immediate problem was an Associated Press report that morning linking McCord to the reelection committee. They went over a press release that the CRP planned to release deploring the break-in. As they talked, Haldeman jotted down the intent of this message: "to get it as confused as poss.—& keep up idea of McCord's other emplmt."

In the first of the many bold lies that would characterize the scandal, the statement described McCord as a private consultant who had worked for the committee months ago.

"This man and the other people were not operating on our behalf or our consent," said the statement, issued under the name of CRP chairman John N. Mitchell, the former U.S. attorney general. "There is no place in our campaign or in the electoral process for this type of activity."

The evening after the break-in, Alexander P. Butterfield, an obscure White House aide, innocently mentioned to one FBI agent that Hunt had worked on "highly sensitive, confidential matters" at the White House several months earlier.

As Haldeman now knew, Hunt had been a $100-a-day consultant for Charles W. Colson, White House special counsel, and still had a desk and files in the Executive Office Building. Since April, Hunt had worked for the reelection committee.

But Haldeman and Magruder were most worried that the FBI might link the break-in to G. Gordon Liddy, the CRP finance counsel. Liddy, a swaggering former county prosecutor, had conceived of the break-in and recruited people to do it. And Liddy knew far too much about the administration's earlier illegal activities.

Over Labor Day weekend in 1971, using some of the same Cubans and a spy camera and fake ID's obtained from the CIA, Liddy and Hunt had supervised a break-in at the Los Angeles office of Lewis J. Fielding, psychiatrist to Daniel Ellsberg, leaker of the now-famous "Pentagon papers" to the New York Times. The June 13, 1971, publication of this secret history of U.S. involvement in the Vietnam War infuriated Nixon, even more so because it shared the front page with news of his daughter Tricia's White House wedding.

ELLSBERG'S EMBARRASSING LEAK LED TO the birth of the "Plumbers," a special unit charged with stopping disclosures of politically sensitive information. Operating from Room 16 at the Executive Office Building, the unit soon focused attention on getting dirt on Ellsberg, who was facing trial on espionage and conspiracy charges.

Haldeman was determined to keep the Fielding break-in secret. John D. Ehrlichman, Nixon's domestic affairs adviser, was even more determined: He had authorized it and arranged the CIA assistance to Hunt and Liddy.

But that wasn't all they had to hide.

Nixon's lieutenants, determined to control and manipulate the political process, had ordered the wiretapping, tailing and infiltrating of prominent antiwar leaders, news reporters, even government officials, all in the name of national security. They also had set up an elaborate operation to spy on and undermine the primary election campaigns of Democratic candidates.

Worse, plans for these illegal activities—including the Watergate break-in itself—had been approved by Mitchell while he was attorney general.

The prospect of any or all of this becoming public, especially during an election year, was terrifying to Nixon's men. Could the Watergate burglars be trusted to keep quiet? Liddy, while admitting that he had goofed by using McCord for the DNC job, assured Magruder that the burglars would never say anything to implicate him or others. He even offered to stand on a designated street corner and let someone shoot him if it would help matters.

On June 20, Nixon, Haldeman and Erlichman met to plot a Watergate public relations offensive. Later that day, Nixon and Mitchell discussed the probe on the telephone. There could be no more slip-ups. The president's counsel, John W. Dean III, was ordered to keep track of the FBI.

Later that day, an upbeat Haldeman told Mitchell not to worry, according to Haldeman's notes of their phone conversation. The White House, he said, "may be able to keep [the investigation] under control."

At the Florida White House, Ron Ziegler, Nixon's press secretary, dismissed the break-in as "a third-rate burglary attempt." In Washington, the FBI and the newly assigned prosecution team weren't scoffing.

Prosecutors Earl J. Silbert, the principal assistant U.S. attorney in the D.C. office, fraud chief Seymour Glanzer and wiretap expert Donald Campbell knew they had an open-and-shut case against the five burglars. But they still did not know who had sent them there. McCord and the Cubans weren't talking—just as Liddy had promised. Neither was the mysterious Hunt.

But the FBI already knew that the Nixon campaign was more involved than it was admitting. On that first Saturday, the investigators managed to fill in some pieces of Hunt's background: He was a former White House consultant and, like Barker and McCord, an ex-CIA agent.

On Sunday, a desk clerk at the Howard Johnson's recognized McCord's picture in the newspaper and told the FBI he had rented a room at the motel. Tracing phone calls, the FBI found the lookout Shoffler had noticed on the balcony that night. His name was Alfred C. Baldwin III. Who had hired him?

By Thursday, June 22, agents had tracked most of the confiscated $100 bills to Barker's account at a Miami bank. They learned that Barker had deposited five large checks in April: a $25,000 cashier's check from Kenneth H. Dahlberg, a wealthy Minneapolis industrialist and a top Nixon campaign fund-raiser, and four checks totalling $89,000 from Manuel Ogarrio, a Mexican attorney. Barker had then withdrawn $10,000 in $100 bills from this account.

Agents also learned that Barker had dropped off film at a Miami photo shop just a week before the break-in, ordering a "rush job" on large prints that included, as best a shop employee could recall, copies of documents on DNC letterhead, including some signed by DNC Chairman O'Brien.

The FBI was also hot on the trail of Donald H. Segretti, who had turned up in Hunt's telephone records. Segretti was mixed up in some kind of political dirty tricks that, at first blush, didn't appear illegal.

But as the agents got to the source of the burglars' money the White House laid plans to throw the investigators off by encouraging the notion that the break-in was part of some mysterious CIA caper. The White House knew the FBI was theorizing possible CIA involvement in the break-in because acting FBI Director L. Patrick Gray was regularly briefing White House counsel John Dean about the investigation.

Nixon, in a June 23 tape-recorded conservation with Haldeman that was termed the "smoking gun" tape when it became public, approved a plan to have the CIA block the investigation by telling the FBI that tracing the money could jeopardize a national security operation.

Specifically, the White House wanted to stop the bureau from interviewing Dahlberg and Ogarrio, whose checks had turned up in Barker's bank account. Both men had collected money from people who wanted to make secret contributions to Nixon's campaign and then hid the donations by writing their own checks to the CRP. Those checks—and here is where the Nixon people had knots in their stomachs—had been given to Liddy, who converted them to cash from Barker's account and returned the money to the CRP's safe.

At the White House's request, Gray told his agents to hold off on interviews with Ogarrio and Dahlberg. But the idea of using the CIA to delay the inquiry failed when the CIA balked.

MEANWHILE, THE INVESTIGATION WAS GOing in another direction anyway—back toward the White House. On June 28, following up on the seized address books, investigators located "George," a name listed in both. George turned out to be George Gordon Liddy. But Liddy too wouldn't talk.

Liddy, Hunt, McCord—all had ties to the Nixon campaign or the White House. Did it stop there? If not, how high did it go? Lano, Mahan and other FBI agents interviewed dozens of aides at the White House and at the Nixon campaign; no one seemed to know much of anything.

Then on July 1, a woman in McCord's office at the CRP asked to see FBI agents. She wanted to see the agents alone, away from the prying eyes of the CRP attorneys who had sat in on her previous interview.

Did the FBI know, she asked during a rambling, seven-hour conversation in a Holiday Inn hotel room, that committee records had been destroyed on the day the burglars were caught?

When the prosecutors and the FBI finally tracked down lookout Alfred Baldwin in Connecticut, he had one hell of a story to tell, including an account of how he had accompanied Hunt on a reconnaissance visit to McGovern headquarters on Capitol Hill for a break-in attempt that never came off.

But the most astonishing information he gave them—the shocker that made so many other clues fit—was that the McCord/Miami crew had broken into the Democrats' Watergate offices on Memorial Day weekend. The group placed listening devices on O'Brien's and Oliver's phones and photographed DNC documents. Since then, Baldwin had lived in Room 723 of the Howard Johnson's, acting as chief eavesdropper. But the O'Brien "bug" never worked right. Replacing it was one objective of the return visit in June.

The day after the break-in, Baldwin fled to Connecticut and consulted with his lawyers. One was a well-connected Democrat named John Casidento. According to Baldwin, Casidento said the following day that he had been "in touch with very specific individuals on the Democratic side who are aware of what's happening, aware that you're a key player."

On June 20, three days after the break-in, the Democrats filed a $1 million lawsuit and dropped hints publicly about how Watergate was much bigger than a bungled burglary. Few believed them.

Baldwin told the prosecutors that Nixon was obsessed with O'Brien, so much so that even after the break-in, Nixon ordered the IRS to audit O'Brien's taxes.

O'Brien felt that way too. "There were two targets throughout 1971, 1972: Larry O'Brien and the front-runner of the Democratic Party," O'Brien, now deceased, said in a 1987 oral history interview. "The objective was to destroy."

SPENCER OLIVER WAS A DIFFERENT MATter. The Republicans wanted political intelligence on Oliver's efforts to encourage a stop-McGovern movement. The Nixon crowd saw McGovern as a weak opponent and had been using dirty tricks to undermine McGovern's rivals. Baldwin told prosecutors that the bug on Oliver's phone had worked well.

The night of the break-in, he saw three men drive up to the Watergate in a beat-up blue Ford, but they were not dressed like cops. Even when he spotted two men, one holding a gun, on the DNC terrace, he was not too concerned—until he spoke to Hunt.

"Are our people dressed casually or are they in suits?" he asked over his walkie-talkie. "Suits," replied Hunt tersely, who was holed up with Liddy in Room 214 at the Watergate Hotel. "Then we've got a problem," Baldwin warned.

Rushing into the room, Hunt ordered Baldwin to wipe it clean of fingerprints, take all the electronic equipment to McCord's home in suburban Maryland, then get out of town.

"I'm living here for weeks and there's no way I know what all I touched," Baldwin remembers thinking. But all he said to Hunt was, "Does this mean we're not going to Miami?" Hunt, already at the door, just stared at him.

Baldwin's testimony gave prosecutors enough evidence to indict Hunt, Liddy, McCord and the four Miamians on Sept. 15, 1972. But when prosecutor Silbert and the others tried to push the investigation further, they hit a stone wall.

There were plenty of hints that people as high up in the campaign as Mitchell and Haldeman controlled the funds used to pay the burglars. Hugh W. Sloan Jr., the CRP treasurer who had resigned a month after the break-in once he saw a coverup forming, told prosecutors that Mitchell and others had approved almost $200,000 in payments to Liddy. Sloan also told them that Magruder had urged him to lie about how much money Liddy got.

Magruder denied it and said the money to Liddy was to set up an intelligence-gathering system to infiltrate and monitor radical groups that might try to disrupt the GOP's convention. Other White House and campaign officials, including Mitchell, corroborated Magruder's story.

Mitchell, in particular, made a convincing witness.

"Mitchell's public image was cold and severe," Silbert recalls. "But in front of the grand jury he was warm and charming and seemed to be very cooperative."

At his subsequent trial, Mitchell was convicted of lying to the grand jury. In all, prosecutors later calculated, at least 20 witnesses either lied or withheld information from the grand jury.

Prosecutors did not know their job was being made tougher by their supervisor at the Justice Department, Henry E. Petersen. They were regularly briefing Petersen, who was passing along information to John Dean at the White House. Dean also was getting FBI interview reports from acting Director Gray and was briefing Magruder, Mitchell, Ehrlichman and Haldeman, enabling the coverup participants to keep abreast of the investigation.

Ehrlichman and Dean had even persuaded Gray to destroy political sabotage files from Hunt's Executive Office Building safe. They told him the material was not related to Watergate, a shame-faced Gray later revealed before announcing his resignation. The documents, which Gray burned in his fireplace, included a dossier Hunt had assembled on Democratic Sen. Edward M. Kennedy of Massachusetts and a State Department cable Hunt had doctored to make it appear that President John F. Kennedy was involved in the 1963 assassination of South Vietnamese President Ngo Dinh Diem.

WHILE DEAN WAS DOING HIS BEST TO blunt the investigation, some witnesses felt the prosecutors were not pushing hard enough. One was Hoback, the CRP's bookkeeper.

She had made one brief appearance before the grand jury and was concerned that nobody asked her anything of consequence. "I was surprised at how fast I was in and out," Hoback says. "I waited out in the hallway longer than I was in there testifying."

Hoback, then 35, contacted the FBI even before her boss, Sloan, had. In repeated interviews, she told investigators about the money disbursed to Liddy and others and about the destruction of CRP ledgers. A CRP attorney later upbraided her for talking privately to the prosecutors.

"I remember getting about as red as an apple, I was so nervous," Hoback recalls.

When the first set of indictments went no higher than Hunt and Liddy, Hoback says she grew concerned and finally started talking to the persistent Woodward and Bernstein.

Hoback, never political, stayed on through the 1972 election. She never became a public figure, not even when the Watergate movie came out and she found herself portrayed by actress Jane Alexander—but never named.

Based on information from Hoback, Sloan and other sources, The Post published articles in the fall of 1972 alleging that the break-in was part of a coordinated campaign of political espionage carried out by top Nixon aides, and that a coverup was underway.

U.S. District Court Chief Judge John J. Sirica, the blunt-spoken, crusty jurist who assigned himself the Watergate case and was known for his tough sentencing, was interested in the higher-ups too.

While Silbert, Campbell and Glanzer built their case around what they could prove—the break-in—"Maximum John" Sirica, then 68, showed little patience with this narrow focus. The jury, he said in December, a month before the trial began, "is going to want to know what did those men go into that headquarters for? Was their sole purpose political espionage? . . . Who hired them? Who started this?"

Silbert says he wanted those answers too, and that he thought the American people should have them before the November elections. Twenty years later, he is still uncomfortable discussing the "special pitch" made to McCord's lawyers about 10 days before the election.

"We offered him this great deal—the chance to plead to one count of conspiracy—if you come forward RIGHT NOW and tell us what you know," Silbert says.

Not then, not now, does he think this was proper for a criminal investigator.

"Do you ever as a prosecutor do anything because of an election?" he asks. "My answer is you don't and, frankly, we deviated from that."

Nothing came of the offer. There is a dispute about whether McCord's lawyers ever told him of the offer.

Nixon, whose personal lawyer Herbert W. Kalmbach had already started raising about $250,000 in "hush money" for the defendants, won reelection over McGovern in a landslide.

When the trial began in January 1973, Hunt pleaded guilty. Five days later, the Miami quartet did the same. All professed ignorance about anyone else's involvement. McCord and Liddy went to trial and were found guilty on all counts.

The wall of silence was intact. Try as he did, Sirica had not broken through.

While the defendants awaited sentencing, the Senate, prodded by media accounts of a possible coverup, prepared to hold full-blown investigative hearings. Then, out of nowhere, the first major crack appeared in the nine-month-long coverup.

It came on March 23, in Sirica's courtroom. The judge, reading from a letter McCord had sent in hopes of avoiding jail, delivered a bombshell. "There was political pressure applied to the defendants to plead guilty and remain silent," McCord had written. "Perjury occurred during the trial [and] others involved in the Watergate operation were not identi-

fied." The stonewall was over. Now, the real investigation could begin.

IF MARCH WAS BAD FOR NIXON, APRIL was worse. With McCord crumbling, with intensified pressure on the Nixon administration to appoint a special prosecutor, a "third-rate burglary" was now a first-rate political threat to the president.

Senate Watergate committee Chairman Sam Ervin of North Carolina was threatening to subpoena just about everyone, including CIA officials.

The word went out that McCord was "naming names," and two prominent ones soon surfaced: Magruder, which was no surprise, and Dean, which was. First Dean, then Magruder, approached prosecutors about a deal. They offered evidence against Haldeman, Ehrlichman and Mitchell. Magruder pleaded guilty to one felony count. Dean wanted immunity from prosecution, but Silbert was having none of it, not even when Dean gave prosecutors another motive for the coverup: the break-in by the "Plumbers" at Ellsberg's psychiatrist's office.

"Dean's the White House counsel, he's the orchestrator [of the coverup], the one who makes it work," Silbert says now, explaining his hard line. "No way does that guy deserve a pass."

Having protected Nixon at his own peril, Dean finally laid his last card on the table. The president, he told the prosecutors, had actually discussed raising $1 million to pay the Watergate defendants to keep quiet and he had approved $250,000 in "hush money" for them in the months since the break-in.

The newspapers were coming out with one story after another, a revelation a day. On April 27, 1973, came the worst news of all: the judge in the Ellsberg espionage case disclosed the secret that Nixon and his men had tried so hard to protect: the Ellsberg break-in, involving Hunt and Liddy.

On April 30, with Dean bargaining with investigators, Nixon moved to preserve his presidency. Dean, Haldeman and Ehrlichman—all forced out. Also gone: Richard G. Kleindienst, who had replaced Mitchell as attorney general and had recently insisted on telling the judge in the Ellsberg case about the break-in by the "Plumbers."

Increasingly isolated, his political position eroding, Nixon sought to regain his credibility. On the second day of the Senate hearings, Attorney General-designate Elliot L. Richardson announced

the selection of former U.S. solicitor general Archibald Cox to be special prosecutor.

Dean's congressional testimony a month later "electrified the public," says Samuel Dash, the Senate committee's chief counsel. "He was the first eyewitness to the president's involvement in the coverup and payment of hush money, a man who sat in the Oval Office and talked to the president about those things."

Dean told a nation watching on television of a "cancer on the presidency." But it was still Dean's word against Haldeman, Ehrlichman and Nixon. At one point, Dash sent some students from Georgetown law school over to the National Archives.

"These kids came back with their eyes bulging," Dash recalls. It seems that Magruder, at the end of the 1972 campaign, had packed up a bunch of his "Eyes Only" memos from Haldeman and Ehrlichman and sent them to the archives for storage.

But the most incriminating evidence of all were the president's own words.

DEAN HAD TOLD INVESTIGATORS THAT NIXon seemed to be whispering into a bookcase during one of their Watergate conversations, almost as if he were afraid the room was bugged. Committee staffers suspected a secret taping system and began methodically interviewing White House aides.

They had gone through about 50 before getting to Alexander Butterfield, the man who first confirmed Hunt's White House employment to the FBI.

Butterfield, a former Air Force pilot, says now that he had made up his mind "that if the question is direct I'll have to give a direct answer."

On July 13, a Friday, more than four hours into an interview with Senate investigators, Don Sanders, a Republican committee staff member, asked the right question. "I was wondering when you would get around to asking me that," Butterfield replied.

In the 20 years he has had to think about it, Butterfield, now 66 and a San Diego businessman, wonders whether "maybe, deep down, I wanted to say it."

Butterfield's revelation set in motion a bitter constitutional fight. Cox and the Senate committee both wanted the tapes. Nixon refused, citing executive privilege as protecting presidential material. On July 23, 1973, for the first time in 166 years, a president of the United States was subpoenaed. Nixon refused that request too.

On Oct. 20, in a desperate exercise of presidential power quickly dubbed the "Saturday Night Massacre," Nixon ordered Richardson to fire Cox, who had rejected a compromise on the tapes. He refused and quit. Nixon ordered Richardson's deputy, William D. Ruckelshaus, to fire Cox. He refused and was fired.

Reaching down one more level, Nixon ordered Solicitor General Robert H. Bork to oust Cox. Bork did.

Nixon finally won—and lost. Twenty years later, it seems so much more inevitable than it did then. The House Judiciary Committee immediately began impeachment proceedings. A new special prosecutor took Cox's place. Nixon gave up the tapes, under court order. Many included profanities. One was missing 18 1/2 minutes. But what the rest showed was damning enough. Impeachment loomed. The later release of other tapes made it virtually certain.

Todd Christofferson, then Sirica's 26-year-old law clerk, remembers the day the tapes arrived. No one had a machine that could handle reel-to-reel tapes, so Sirica's office borrowed one from the White House.

Christofferson and Sirica went to a windowless jury room, put a specially rigged set of headphones on, and listened, hoping to hear the words that would exonerate the president. Christofferson recalled how he felt as Nixon participated in hush money and coverup conversations. He felt that Nixon had another choice.

"He could have said, 'No, it goes no further. Let the chips fall where they may.' And he didn't, and it mushroomed. That one failing brought the whole house down."

Washington Post staff writer Lawrence Meyer and staff researchers Lucy Shackelford and Mary Stapp contributed to this report.

Lessons from a Lost War

What has Viet Nam taught about when to use power—and when not to?

The customary reward of defeat, if one can survive it, is in the lessons thereby learned, which may yield victory in the next war. But the circumstances of our defeat in Vietnam were sufficiently ambiguous to deny the nation [that] benefit.
—Edward N. Luttwak
The Pentagon and the Art of War

Ten years after the fall of Saigon, the debacle in Southeast Asia remains a subject many Americans would rather not discuss. So the nation has been spared a searing, divisive inquest—"Who lost Viet Nam?"—but at a heavy price. The old divisions have been buried rather than resolved. They seem ready to break open again whenever anyone asks what lessons the U.S. should draw from its longest war, and the only one to end in an undisguisable defeat.

Was that loss inevitable, or could the war have been won with different strategy and tactics? Was the war fought for the right reasons? Did its aftermath prove or explode the domino theory? The questions are not in the least academic. They bear on the all-important problem of whether, when and how the U.S. should again send its troops to fight abroad.

Pondering these questions, Secretary of Defense Caspar Weinberger argues, citing Viet Nam, that "before the U.S. commits combat forces abroad, there must be some reasonable assurance that we will have the support of the American people and . . . Congress." Secretary of State George Shultz replies that "there is no such thing as guaranteed public support in advance." The lesson Shultz draws from Viet Nam is that "public support can be frittered away if we do not act wisely and effectively." And this open dispute between two senior members of the Reagan Cabinet is mild compared with the arguments among policy

"I want to rail against wind and tide, kill the whales in the ocean, sweep the whole country to save people from slavery."
—TRIEU AU, VIET NAM'S "JOAN OF ARC" A.D. 248

"France has had the country for nearly 100 years, and the people are worse off than at the beginning."
—FRANKLIN D. ROOSEVELT 1944

"Kill ten of our men and we will kill one of yours. In the end, it is you who will tire."
—HO CHI MINH 1946

analysts, Viet Nam veterans and the public about what kinds of wars can be won or even deserve public support in the first place.

A number of experts doubt that the U.S. can evolve any common view of Viet Nam and its lessons for many years to come. Says Graham Martin, the last U.S. Ambassador to South Viet Nam: "I estimated at the end of the war that it probably would be at least two decades before any rational, objective discussion of the war and its causes and effects could be undertaken by scholars who were not so deeply, emotionally engaged at the time that their later perceptions were colored by biases and prejudices." William Hyland, editor of *Foreign Affairs* magazine, thinks an even longer perspective may be required: "We always want to make historical judgments two days after the fact. Historians need 100 years."

But the U.S. is unlikely to have anywhere near that much time to decide what lessons to draw from Viet Nam and how to apply them. The initial impulse after the American withdrawal was to avoid any foreign involvement that might conceivably lead to a commitment of U.S. troops. Scholars differ on how seriously this so-called Viet Nam syndrome inhibited an activist U.S. foreign policy, but in any case it is fading—witness the enthusiastic approval of the Grenada invasion in late 1983 (to be sure, that was a rare case in which the U.S. was able to apply such overwhelming force that it could not have failed to win quickly). Says Maine's Republican Senator William Cohen: "The legacy of Viet Nam does not mean that we will not send our sons anywhere. It does mean that we will not send them everywhere." Even some fervent doves agree that memories of Viet Nam should not keep the U.S. from ever fighting anywhere. Sam Brown, onetime antiwar leader who now de-

U.S. AIR FORCE

POWER

*B-52 dropping bombs on guerrillas, 1966: Was it a
matter of too much force, or not enough?*

velops low-cost housing in Colorado, remains convinced that if it were not for the protests against U.S. involvement in Viet Nam that he helped organize, "we would have three or four other wars now." Even so, concedes Brown, some "wrong lessons" might be drawn, among them "the risk that we won't be prepared if our national interest is genuinely threatened."

But if the specter of Viet Nam no longer inhibits all thought of projecting U.S. military power overseas, it still haunts every specific decision. In the Middle East, Weinberger's fears of entrapment in a drawn-out conflict fought without public support caused him at first to oppose sending Marines to Lebanon and then to insist on their withdrawal after terrorist attacks left 266 U.S. servicemen dead. Shultz objected that the pullout would undercut U.S. diplomacy in the area, and still regards it as a mistake. But Ronald Reagan ordered the withdrawal anyway and won the approval of voters, even though critics portrayed the pullout as a national humiliation. The reason, suggests Democratic Political Analyst William Schneider, is that the President sensed the persistence of a popular attitude toward foreign military commitments that is summarized by the Viet Nam-era slogan "Win or Get Out." Says Schneider: "In Grenada we won. In Lebanon we got out. So much for the Viet Nam syndrome."

The Viet Nam experience colors al-

"Master fear and pain, overcome obstacles, unite your efforts, fight to the very end, annihilate the enemy."
—GENERAL GIAP
1954

"I could conceive of no greater tragedy than for the U.S. to [fight] an all-out war in Indochina."
—DWIGHT D. EISENHOWER
1954

"You have a row of dominoes set up, you knock over the first one and [the last one] will go over very quickly."
—EISENHOWER
1954

"We do commit the U.S. to preventing the fall of South Viet Nam to Communism."
—ROBERT MCNAMARA
1961

most every discussion of Central American policy. Nebraska Governor Bob Kerrey, who won a Congressional Medal of Honor and lost part of a leg fighting with the Navy SEAL commandos in Viet Nam, maintains that if memories of the ordeal in Southeast Asia were not still so strong, "we'd be in Nicaragua now." In Congress, Kerrey's fellow Democrats fret that the Administration's commitment to resist the spread of Marxist revolution throughout the isthmus could eventually bog down American troops in another endless jungle guerrilla war.

Reaganites retort, correctly, that while Viet Nam is halfway around the world and of debatable strategic importance to Washington, Central America is virtually next door, an area where U.S. interests are obvious. Moreover, the amounts Washington is spending to help the government of El Salvador defeat leftist guerrillas and to assist the contra rebels fighting the Marxist Sandinista government of Nicaragua are pittances compared with the sums lavished on South Viet Nam even before the direct U.S. military intervention there. Still, the Administration every now and then feels obliged to deny that it has any plan or desire to send U.S. troops to fight in Central America. Weinberger last November coupled his remarks about the necessity of popular support for any foreign military commitment with a pledge that "the President will not allow our military forces to creep—or be drawn gradually—into a combat role in Central America."

One of the few propositions about Viet Nam that commands near unanimous assent from Americans is the obvious one that the U.S. lost—and a growing number would qualify even that. Richard Nixon, in his new book, *No More Vietnams,* argues that "we won the war" but then abandoned South Viet Nam after the Communist North began violating the 1973 Paris accords that supposedly ended the fighting. Though the former President's self-interest is obvious, parts of his analysis are supported even by the enemy. U.S. Army Colonel Harry Summers Jr., who considers Viet Nam "a tactical success and a strategic failure," was in Hanoi on a negotiating mission a few days before Saigon fell. Summers recalls telling a North Vietnamese colonel, "You know, you never defeated us on the battlefield." The foe's reply: "That may be so, but it is also irrelevant." In essence, the U.S. was outlasted by an enemy that proved able and willing to fight longer than America and its South Vietnamese allies.

Given the weakness of South Viet Nam, the determination of the North and the extent of the aid it could count on from the Soviet Union and neighboring China, even some hawks concede that Hanoi's victory might have been inevitable. Says Military Analyst Luttwak: "Some wars simply cannot be won, and Viet Nam may have been one of them." Nonetheless, the main lesson they would draw from the war is that the U.S. threw away whatever chance for victory it may have had through blunders that must not be repeated.

The most detailed exposition of this view comes from Colonel Summers, whose book, *On Strategy: A Critical Analysis of the Vietnam War,* has become must reading for young officers. Summers argues that the U.S. should have sealed off South Viet Nam with a barrier of American troops to prevent North Viet Nam from sending troops and materiel through Laos and Cambodia to wage war in the South. Instead, he says, the U.S. "wasted its strength" fighting the guerrillas in the South, a hopeless task so long as they were continually reinforced from the North and one that American troops had no business trying to carry out in the first place. The U.S., he contends, should have confined itself to protecting South Viet Nam against "external aggression" from the North and left "pacification," the job of rooting out the guerrillas, to the South Vietnamese. By in effect taking over the war, the U.S. sapped the initiative and ultimately the will of its Southern allies to carry out a job only they could do in the end.

Luttwak carries this analysis a step further by pouring scorn on the tactics used in the South: "The jet fighter bombing raids against flimsy huts that might contain a handful of guerrillas or perhaps none; the fair-sized artillery barrages that silenced lone snipers; the ceaseless firing of helicopter door gunners whereby a million dollars' worth of ammunition might be expended to sweep a patch of high grass." This "grossly disproportionate use of firepower," says Luttwak, was not just ineffective; it alienated South Vietnamese villagers whose cooperation against the guerrillas was vital. At least equally important, "Its imagery on television was by far the most powerful stimulus of antiwar sentiment" back in the U.S. Former CIA Director William

Y.R. OKAMOTO—LBJ LIBRARY

POLITICS
Defense Secretary McNamara brooding after troop call-up, 1965: Would Americans have backed a bigger war?

"But it will be just like Berlin. The troops will march in; the bands will play; the crowds will cheer; and in four days everyone will have forgotten. Then we will be told we have to send in more troops."
—JOHN F. KENNEDY
1961

"There just isn't any simple answer. We're fighting a kind of war here that I never read about at Command and Staff College. Conventional weapons just don't work here. Neither do conventional tactics."
—FROM GRAHAM GREENE'S *THE UGLY AMERICAN*

"You let a bully come into your front yard, the next day he'll be on your porch."
—LYNDON B. JOHNSON
ON SEVERAL OCCASIONS

Colby agrees that the U.S. got nowhere as long as it tried to defeat guerrillas with massed firepower and only began to make progress when it shifted to a "people's war" in which the South Vietnamese carried the main burden of the fighting. By then it was too late; American public sentiment had turned irreversibly in favor of a fast pullout.

According to Hyland, "The biggest lesson of Viet Nam is that we need to have a much better notion of what is at stake, what our interests are, before we go into a major military undertaking." Weinberger voiced essentially the same thought last fall in laying down several conditions, beyond a reasonable assurance of public support, that must be met if U.S. troops are again to be sent into battle overseas: "We should have clearly defined political and military objectives, and we should know precisely how our forces can accomplish those." Other criteria: "The commitment of U.S. forces to combat should be a last resort," undertaken only if it "is deemed vital to our national interest or that of our allies," and then "with the clear intention of winning" by using as much force as necessary.

Weinberger's speech, delivered after he had talked it over with President Reagan, is the closest thing to an official Administration reading of the lessons of Viet Nam. But some rude jeers greeted the Weinberger doctrine. Luttwak, for example, called Weinberger's views "the equivalent of a doctor saying he will treat patients only if he is assured they will recover. Columnist William Safire headlined a scathing critique ONLY THE 'FUN' WARS, and New York Democrat Stephen Solarz, who heads the House Subcommittee on Asian and Pacific Affairs, pointed out, "It is a formula for national paralysis if, before we ever use force, we need a Gallup poll showing that two-thirds of the American people are in favor of it."

More important, what is a "vital interest"? To some Americans, the only one that would justify another war is the defense of the U.S. against a threat of direct attack. Decrying "this whole practice of contracting our military out just for the survival of some other government and country," Georgia Secretary of State Max Cleland, who lost an arm and both legs in Viet Nam, insists, "There is only one thing worth dying for, and that is this country, not somebody else's."

Diplomats argue persuasively that a policy based on this view would leave the U.S. to confront Soviet expansionism all alone. No country would enter or maintain an alliance with a U.S. that specifically refused to fight in its defense. But in the real world, an outright Soviet attack against a country that the U.S. is committed by treaty to defend is quite unlikely. The decision whether or not to fight most probably would be posed by a Communist threat to a friendly nation that is not formally an ally. And then the threat might well be raised not by open aggression but by a combination of military, political and economic tactics that Moscow is often adept at orchestrating and Washington usually inept at countering: the front groups, the street demonstrations, the infiltrated unions, the guerrilla units. One reason the U.S. sent troops to Viet Nam is that it lacked other alternatives to help its allies prevail against this sort of subversion. In fact, developing a capacity to engage in such political action and shadowy paramilitary activities might help the U.S. to avert future Viet Nams.

Merely defining U.S. interests, in any event, can prove endlessly complicated. Geography alone is no guide in an age of ocean-spanning missiles. Economics may be vital in some areas like the Persian Gulf, where the flow of oil must be maintained, unimportant in others like Israel, where political and moral considerations are paramount. There may be

"In the final analysis it is their war . . . We can help them . . . but they have to win it, the people of Viet Nam."
—KENNEDY
1963

"We are not about to send American boys 10,000 miles away to do what Asian boys ought to be doing for themselves."
—JOHNSON
1964

"Hell no, we won't go!"
—ANTIWAR CHANT
1965

"I'm not going to be the first President who loses a war."
—RICHARD NIXON
1969

"Peace is at hand."
—HENRY KISSINGER
1972

times too when U.S. intervention, even if it seems justified, would be ineffective. Not much is heard these days of the once fashionable argument that in Viet Nam the U.S. was on the wrong side of history because it was fighting a nationalistic social revolution being waged by a regime that was, deep down, benign; Hanoi's brutality within Viet Nam and its swift move to establish hegemony over all of Indochina removed all doubt that the foe was and is not only totalitarian but imperialistic besides. Today, with the focus on Central America, the argument is often heard that economic and social misery have made leftist revolution inevitable. To those who maintain that revolution is the only way to progress, the counterargument is that whatever social and economic gains may be achieved by Communist takeovers usually carry an extremely high price tag: the establishment of tyranny.

About the only general rule that foreign-policy experts can suggest is not to have any general rule, at least in the sense of drawing up an advance list of where the U.S. might or might not fight. They still shudder at the memory of a 1950 definition of the U.S. "defense perimeter" in Asia that omitted South Korea—which promptly suffered an outright Communist invasion that took three years and 54,000 American lives to repel. Walt Rostow, who was Lyndon Johnson's National Security Adviser, recalls how the late Soviet Foreign Minister Andrei Vishinsky "told a group of Americans that we deceived them on Korea." Says Rostow: "I believe that's correct."

The decision on where American military intervention might be both necessary and effective can only be made case by case, based on a variety of factors that may be no easier to judge in the future than they were in Viet Nam: the nature and circumstances of war, the will and ability of the nation under attack to defend itself, the consequences of its loss. Any such debate is sure to revive another long buried but still unresolved controversy of the Viet Nam era: whether a Communist takeover of one country would cause others to topple like a row of dominoes. Hawks insist that this theory was vindicated by Communist triumphs in Laos and Cambodia after the fall of Saigon. Opponents point out that the Asian "dominoes" that most concerned the U.S.—Thailand, Burma, Malaysia, Singapore, Indonesia, the Philippines—

have all survived as non-Communist (in several cases, strongly anti-Communist) societies. Rostow, now a professor of political economy at the University of Texas, offers a counterrebuttal. Those countries might have gone under if Saigon had fallen in 1965, he contends. The U.S. intervention in Viet Nam bought them ten years to strengthen their economies and governments and, says Rostow, "bought time that was used extremely well by Asians, especially Southeast Asians."

Be that as it may, the evidence would seem to argue against any mechanical application of the domino theory. It originated in the 1950s, when world Communism was seen as a monolithic force headquartered in Moscow, with Peking a kind of branch office. Today China, never really comfortable with its Hanoi "allies," has resumed its ancient enmity toward Viet Nam; both Washington and Peking are aiding guerrillas battling against the Soviet-backed Vietnamese in Kampuchea. That does not mean that the domino theory has lost all validity everywhere, but its applicability is also subject to case-by-case application.

The most bedeviling of all the dilemmas raised by Viet Nam concerns the issue of public support. On the surface it might seem to be no issue at all: just about everybody agrees that Viet Nam proved the futility of trying to fight a war without a strong base of popular support. But just how strong exactly? Rostow argues that the only U.S. war fought with tremendous public backing was World War II. He points out that World War I "brought riots and splits," the War of 1812 was "vastly divisive" and even during the War of Independence one-third of the population was pro-revolution, one-third pro-British and one-third "out to lunch." Rostow proposes a 60-25-15 split as about the best that can be expected now in support of a controversial policy: a bipartisan 60% in favor, 25% against and 15% out to lunch.

A strong current of opinion holds that Lyndon Johnson guaranteed a disas-

trously low level of support by getting into a long, bloody war without ever admitting (perhaps even to himself) the extent of the commitment he was making. Colonel Summers, who considers Viet Nam a just war that the U.S. could and should have won, insists that any similar conflict in the future ought to be "legitimized" by a formal, congressional declaration of war. Says Summers: "All of America's previous wars were fought in the heat of passion. Viet Nam was fought in cold blood, and that was intolerable to the American people. In an immediate crisis the tendency of the American people is to rally around the flag. But God help you if it goes beyond that and you haven't built a base of support."

At the other extreme, former Secretary of State Dean Rusk defends to this day the Johnson Administration's effort "to do in cold blood at home what we were asking men to do in hot blood out in the field." Rusk points out that the war began with impressive public and congressional support. It was only in early 1968, says Rusk, that "many at the grassroots level came to the opinion that if we didn't give them some idea when this war would come to an end, we might as well chuck it." The decisive factor probably was the defection of middle-class youths and their parents, a highly articulate segment that saw an endless war as a personal threat—though in fact the burden of the draft fell most heavily on low-income youths.

Paradoxically, though, Johnson might well have been able to win public support for a bigger war than he was willing to fight. As late as February 1968, at the height of the Tet offensive, one poll found 53% favoring stronger U.S. military action, even at the risk of a clash with the Soviet Union or China, vs. only 24% opting to wind down the war. Rusk insists that the Administration was right not to capitalize on this sentiment. Says he: "We made a deliberate decision not to whip up war fever in this country. We did not have parades and movie stars selling war bonds, as we did in World

War II. We thought that in a nuclear world it is dangerous for a country to become too angry too quickly. That is something people will have to think about in the future."

It certainly is. Viet Nam veterans argue passionately that Americans must never again be sent out to die in a war that "the politicians will not let them win." And by win they clearly mean something like a World War II-style triumph ending with unconditional surrender. One lesson of Viet Nam, observes George Christian, who was L.B.J.'s press secretary, is that "it is very tough for Americans to stick in long situations. We are always looking for a quick fix." But nuclear missiles make the unconditional-surrender kind of war an anachronism. Viet Nam raised, and left unsolved for the next conflict, the question posed by Lincoln Bloomfield, an M.I.T. professor of political science who once served on Jimmy Carter's National Security Council: "How is it that you can 'win' so that when you leave two years later you do not lose the country to those forces who have committed themselves to victory at any cost?"

It is a question that cannot be suppressed much longer. Americans have a deep ambiguity toward military power: they like to feel strong, but often shy away from actually using that strength. There is a growing recognition, however, that shunning all battles less easily winnable than Grenada would mean abandoning America's role as a world power, and that, in turn, is no way to assure the nation's survival as a free society. Americans, observes Secretary of State Shultz, "will always be reluctant to use force. It is the mark of our decency." But, he adds, "a great power cannot free itself so easily from the burden of choice. It must bear responsibility for the consequences of its inaction as well as for the consequences of its action."

—By George J. Church.
Reported by David S. Jackson/Austin and Ross H. Munro/Washington, with other bureaus.

The New Indian Politics

Stephen Cornell

Stephen Cornell, 37, is associate professor of sociology at Harvard University. Born in Buffalo, New York, he received a B.A. from Mackinac College in Michigan (1970) and a Ph.D. from the University of Chicago (1980). His book, Return of the Native: American Indian Political Resurgence, *was published by Oxford University Press, 1990.*

On December 28, 1890, near the Badlands of South Dakota, a band of exhausted Sioux Indians, including perhaps 100 warriors and some 250 women and children, surrendered to the blue-clad troopers of the U.S. Seventh Cavalry and agreed to travel with them to the Indian agency at Pine Ridge. The joint party camped that night in freezing weather at Wounded Knee Creek, 20 miles from Pine Ridge. Surrounding the Indian tepees were nearly 500 soldiers and a battery of four Hotchkiss light artillery pieces.

The next morning, the Indian men were told to turn in their weapons. Few obeyed. The cavalrymen began to search the tepees. When they turned up few additional guns, the troops began to search the warriors themselves. Reports of subsequent events vary but tensions ran high.

A scuffle broke out between an Indian and some soldiers. In the struggle, the warrior, intentionally or not, fired his rifle. That did it. Instantly both Indians and soldiers began firing at each other. Within moments, the Army gunners were pouring explosive Hotchkiss shells into the Indian camp.

Most of the Sioux warriors died in the opening volleys. Others, along with a large number of women and children, were shot as they fled down adjacent ravines. By the time the firing ended, nearly 200 Indians—perhaps more, the estimates vary—had been killed.

The survivors of this slaughter were among the last Indians to come under the direct administrative control of the U.S. government. Confined to reservations, they joined 300,000 others, from coast to coast, in a state of despondent dependency, sunk in poverty, wards of a white man's government that they had learned not to trust.

Eighty-two years later, on the wintry night of February 27, 1973, a group of armed Oglala Sioux from South Dakota's Pine Ridge Reservation joined forces with activists from the American Indian Movement (AIM) and seized the reservation village of Wounded Knee, the site of the 1890 massacre. They did so to protest corruption in the tribal government at Pine Ridge as well as U.S. violations of the 1868 Fort Laramie Treaty (which recognized Sioux sovereignty over much of what is now the Dakotas, Montana, Wyoming, and Nebraska). "We want a true Indian nation," said Carter Camp, an AIM coordinator, "not one made up of Bureau of Indian Affairs puppets."

Within 24 hours, a force of 250 Federal Bureau of Investigation agents, U.S. Marshals, and Bureau of Indian Affairs (BIA) police had cordoned off the village. The much-publicized siege lasted 10 weeks, punctuated by exchanges of gunfire that left two Indians dead and several men wounded on each side. In May after lengthy negotiations, the Indians surrendered to federal authorities. The second battle of Wounded Knee was over.

The 1890 massacre brought one era to a close. The Euro-American advance across the continent was now complete. As Black Hawk, war leader of the Sauk and Fox, had said of himself a half century earlier, "He is now a prisoner to the white men; they will do with him as they wish."

86 MILLION ACRES

The 1973 occupation also represented the culmination of an era. America's roughly 790,000 Indians still lived, for the most part, in considerable misery afflicted by poverty, alcoholism, high unemployment, and inadequate education. But the days of dull Indian acquiescence were long gone. Beginning in the 1940s, Indians had not only been demanding a voice in federal Indian policy; increasingly they had appropriated such a voice for themselves, forcing the surrounding society to respond. *"We* talk, *you* listen" was the title of a 1970 book by Sioux author Vine Deloria, Jr. And as they demonstrated at Wounded Knee, Indians did more than talk.

All in all, the path from the Wounded Knee I to Wounded Knee II traced an Indian political resurgence of striking proportions. There had always been, of course, politics *about* Indians. For the most part it was non-Indian politics, carried on in Washington, among the governors of Western states and territories, and among missionaries, reformers, and bureaucrats. The situation today is dramatically different, marked by the emergence of a new and genuinely Indian politics.

In hindsight, the turning point appears to have been the Indian Reorganization Act (IRA) of 1934. Prior to its passage, two goals had guided federal Indian policy: the acquisition of Indian lands and the cultural transformation of Indians into Euro-Americans—in a word, "assimilation." Those goals were enshrined in the Dawes Act (1887), which heralded the age of "allotment." Washington broke up much of the tribal land base, withdrawing some property from Indian ownership and distributing other, often marginal, lands to individual tribal members. "Surplus" lands, more often than not the richest, were then sold off to white settlers. Between 1887, when the Dawes Act was passed, and 1934, when allotment ceased, some 86 million acres—60 percent of the remaining Indian lands—passed into the possession of non-Indians.

Allotment, which reached a peak just before World War I, was not merely a means of appropriating Indian territory. It was part of a concerted effort to break up tribal nations, of which there were—and are—several hundred, each with a distinct history, most still with a distinct culture. This effort, like everything else on the reservations, was overseen by the Bureau of Indian Affairs, established by Secretary of War John Calhoun in 1824.

"The Indians," wrote Indian Commissioner Thomas Morgan in 1889, "must conform to 'the white man's ways,' peaceably if they will, forcibly if they must." On the reservations, BIA officials put Indian children into English-language boarding schools, dispersed village settlements, moved tribal members off communal (and on to individual) tracts of land, and took control of economic resources. Indigenous religious ceremonies, such as the Sun Dance of the Plains tribes, were outlawed.

WAITING FOR FDR

By the 1920s, white America's appetite for Indian lands (the best of which had already been taken) had begun to diminish. A postwar slump in farm prices helped reduce demand. Combined with the staggering extent of poverty, disease, and other social ills now apparent on the Indian reservations, these circumstances created a climate for reform.

The reform movement can be traced in part to the ideals of Progressivism and to the growing academic interest in the notion of "cultural pluralism" as a plausible alternative to the assimilation of America's ethnic groups. In 1922, when the Harding administration backed the Bursum Bill, which threatened the land and water rights of New Mexico's Pueblo Indians, a number of liberal, non-Indian organizations—the General Federation of Women's Clubs, for example—joined the Pueblos in opposing the legislation. The thriving community of artists, writers, and intellectuals around Santa Fe and Taos supported the protest. Writing in the *New York Times,* novelist D. H. Lawrence claimed that the bill played "the Wild West scalping trick a little too brazenly." The Pueblo leaders themselves, acting in concert for the first time since the Pueblo Rebellion in 1680, declared that the bill "will rob us of everything we hold dear—our lands, our customs, our traditions." After protracted debate, the Bursum Bill was defeated in Congress.

Such protests publicized the Indians' situation. But it was not until Franklin Roosevelt's election to the presidency and his appointment of John Collier as Indian Commissioner in 1933, that a reform package won approval in Congress.

Collier, a former social worker and educator, and champion of the Pueblo cause during the 1920s, placed great faith in the power of "community." Native American communities, he was convinced, "must be given status, responsibility and power." Backed by FDR, Collier led a drive to reorient US. Indian policy. The result, in 1934, was the Indian Reorganization Act.

Indian policy did an abrupt about-face. The IRA legislation not only put an official stop to allotment; it actually allocated modest funds for *expansion* of the Indian land base. It provided money (though never enough) for economic development on Indian reservations and subsidies for Indians to set up tribal business corporations. But most important, it allowed Indians into the decision-making process by making explicit the right of any Indian tribe "to organize for its common welfare" and to adopt a constitution and bylaws for that purpose. By 1936, more than two-thirds of the tribes had endorsed the IRA in special elections (although far fewer actually organized themselves under its provisions).

The mechanisms of the IRA—representative government, for example, and the business corporation—were alien to Indian tribes. Even so, during the next few years many groups took advantage of what has been called "the Indian New Deal." The majority of today's tribal councils are one result. For some groups, such as the Papago and Apache in the Southwest or the Sioux tribes on the northern Plains, these councils represented the first comprehensive political institutions in their history. But their powers were limited. As an Apache leader from Arizona's San Carlos Reservation put it, "[BIA] Superintendent [James B.] Kitch was still the boss." Nevertheless, Indian groups enjoyed greater control over their own affairs, including a power of veto over some federal actions. For the first time in half a century, numerous Native American groups could also have federally recognized political organizations that could represent the tribal interests in Washington, state capitals, and the courts.

WORLD WAR II AS CATALYST

Another step followed. In 1944, representatives of 42 tribes founded the National Congress of American Indians (NCAI), the first major attempt to pull together Indian groups and governments in a single, supratribal organization. In the NCAI and the regional organizations that came afterwards, tribal leaders began talking to one another. The purpose of the congress, which is still active today: "to preserve Indian cultural values; to seek an equitable adjustment of tribal affairs; to secure and to preserve rights under Indian treaties with the United States; and otherwise to promote the common welfare of the American Indian." In 1948, the NCAI and other groups began a campaign designed to secure Indian voting rights—withheld at the time in both New Mexico and Arizona.*

If the IRA gave Indians the legal tools with which to organize, World War II gave many of them the motivation. In what the Interior Department described at the time as "the greatest exodus of Indians from reservations that has ever taken place," some 25,000 Indians joined the armed forces and saw action in Europe and the Pacific. Some 40,000 quit the economic desert of the reservations for jobs in war industries. For many Indians, experiences in the factory or on the battlefront constituted their first real exposure to the larger American society.

The identities of Native Americans have long been rooted in tribes, bands, villages, and the like, not in one's presumed "Indianness." The reservation system helped to preserve such identities and inhibited the emergence of a more inclusive self-consciousness. As a result, Indians, unlike American blacks, have had difficulty forming a common front. World War II brought Indians from different tribes into contact with one another, and with other Americans who thought of them indiscriminately as "In-

---

*Both U.S. citizenship and the voting franchise came to Indians in stages. Some Indians acquired citizenship through allotment, some through military service or congressional dispensation. In 1924, the Indian Citizenship Act made citizens of all Indians born in the United States, a status that some Indians, then as now, protested as imposed against their will. Until the 1950s, some jurisdictions nevertheless denied Indians the right on the grounds that Indian lands were exempt from taxation.

The Price of Isolation

The poorest county in the United States, with an annual income per capita of $2,841 (in 1982), is not in the Deep South, the Appalachians, or any of the other regions in the United States frequently associated with rural poverty. It is in South Dakota: Shannon County (pop. 11,800), site of the Pine Ridge Indian Reservation.

The poverty of Pine Ridge is shared by many Indians, especially those on the nation's 270 Indian reservations. Roughly 23 percent of all urban Indians and 33 percent of all rural Indians live below the official "poverty line"—compared with 14 percent for the entire U.S. population. In 1980, overall reservation unemployment stood at twice the national average; in some places, unemployment ranged near 80 percent.

Other statistics are even more sobering. In 1982, Indians ranked first in divorce and in deaths caused by suicide and alcohol consumption. Afflicted by poor health, family disarray, and low expectations, more than 40 percent of all Indian students entering high school drop out before graduation. No less important, note James Olson and Raymond Wilson in *Native Americans in the Twentieth Century* (1984), is the fear of many Indian parents that local public schools "alienate Native American children from tribal values." As a result, the percentage of Indians enrolled in schools is the lowest of any ethnic group in the United States.

To counter these and other difficulties, Indians on and off the reservations received roughly $2.6 billion in 1984 from federal agencies, notably the departments of Interior, Health and Human Services, Agriculture, and Education. A total that includes Social Security payments and food stamps, this amounts to $1,900 per Indian. Yet in a 1983 report, the National Tribal Chairmen's Association claimed that 70 percent of the almost $1 billion allotted to the Bureau of Indian Affairs (BIA) was spent supporting 15,000 BIA employees—or one employee for every 23 reservation Indians.

The Reagan administration has sought to reduce red tape and spur employment on Indian reservations by turning over federal programs to state, local, and tribal governments, and by encouraging private industry to invest in Indian communities. Between 1982 and 1984, Congress cut spending on Indians by 18 percent. But because almost 30 percent of all employed Indians work in public sector jobs, federal spending cuts tend to increase unemployment before they do anything else. As Peterson Zah, chairman of the Navaho, pointed out, "We don't have the people that Reagan is calling on-private sector development business people-to pick up the slack."

Those Indians who have prospered have done so primarily by leaving the reservation. Almost one-half of all Indians now reside in cities or towns, where a smaller percentage of Indians than of blacks or Hispanics live below the poverty line.

Yet few Indians adjust to urban life. Most return frequently to their reservations, where they often leave their children with relatives, and where they often choose to retire. Assimilation, the path to prosperity taken by generations of American immigrants, is an anathema to many Indians. "The pervasive fear of Indians," observes longtime Indian activist Vine Deloria, Jr., "is that they will . . . move from their plateau of small nationhood to the status of [just] another ethnic group in the American melting pot."

---

dians,'' not as Navahos or Apaches or Sioux.

It also forcefully brought home to Indians their second-class status. One Lumbee veteran told anthropologist Karen Blu: "In 1945 or '46, I applied to UNC [University of North Carolina]. I had six battle stars. They said they didn't accept Indians from Robeson County." In the Southwest, not surprisingly, it was the Indian veterans who went to court to seek voting rights. Former G.I.'s were prominent in the NCAI. In 1952, the *New York Times* reported that "a new, veteran-led sense of political power is everywhere in Indian country."

Such analyses proved premature. There had always been strong opposition to the Indian Reorganization Act, from the political Right and from politicians of all colorations in the West, partly on the grounds that it perpetuated an undesirably distinct status for Native Americans.

After the fading of the New Deal, the status of Native Americans as wards of the federal government seemed to go against the American tradition of self-reliance. Sen George Malone (R.-Nev.) complained that Indian reservations represented "natural socialist environments" —a charge echoed by Interior Secretary James Watt three decades later. Break up the tribal domains, so the argument ran, remove the protective arm of government, and cast the Indian into the melting pot and the marketplace. Everyone would benefit.

Such, in essence, was the conclusion of the so-called Hoover Commission on governmental organization, which in 1949 proposed "integration of the Indian into the rest of the population." It recommended that Indians leave the reservations and, implicitly, the tribal framework. Assimilation, the commission urged, should once again become "the dominant goal of public policy."

ENDING SEGREGATION

By the mid-1950s it was. Under "termi-nation," as this latest turn in Washington's policy came to be called, Congress set out to dismantle the reservation system, disband tribal nations, and distribute their assets among tribal members. What Sen. Arthur V. Watkins (R.-Utah), an architect of the new policy, called "the Indian freedom program" received both liberal and conservative support. Liberal opinion during the late 1940s and '50s tended to view the problems of Indians in terms derived from the black experience and the early days of the struggle to end racial exclusion. Reservations were seen as "rural ghettoes"; termination would put an end to "segregation." As historian Clayton Koppes has noted, this view reflected the liberal emphasis on "freeing the individual from supposedly invidious group identity."

This was exactly what most Indians did not want, but Washington was not in a listening mood. Commissioner of Indian Affairs Dillon S. Myer's orders to BIA employees were explicit. "I realize that it will not be possible always to

The White Man's Law

"You tell us of your claim to our land and that you have purchased it from your State," scolded Red Jacket, chief of the Seneca, in a speech delivered 160 years ago to white speculators near Lake Geneva, New York. "How has your State, which has never owned our land, sold it to you? Even the whites have a law . . ."

White law nowadays has become a key element in each tribe's survival strategy. More than 500 Indians today hold law degrees (versus fewer than a dozen 20 years ago), and virtually all of them grapple with issues of Indian jurisprudence. Those issues involve the nature of tribal government, protection of Indian lands, freedom of religion, hunting and fishing rights, rights to water from specified rivers and lakes, and other matters.

The tangled privileges and prohibitions that govern Indian life could discourage even Felix Frankfurter, who once described Indian law as "a vast hodgepodge of treaties, judicial and administrative rulings, and unrecorded practices." Because Indian law so often rests on treaties made by Indian nations

with a foreign government—the United States of America—legal actions brought by Indians often end up before the U.S. Supreme Court.

In recent years, the drive by Indians to assert their rights has been led by the Native American Rights Fund (NARF), whose 11 lawyers work out of an old college fraternity house in Denver, Colorado. NARF was founded in 1970 with help from the Ford Foundation. Now headed by John Echohawk, a Pawnee, its annual budget is roughly $3 million.

NARF has been involved in almost every significant court case concerning Indians during the past 15 years. The group's attorneys helped the Menominee of Wisconsin and the Siletz of Oregon regain their status as tribes; fought for Chippewa fishing rights in Michigan; and established a homeland for the Traditional Kickapoo in Texas. In 1983 alone NARF handled business on behalf of 75 tribes in 25 states.

Three years ago, NARF lost three important water rights cases (*Arizona v. California, Nevada v. United States,* and *Arizona v. San Carlos Apache Tribe*)

before the U.S. Supreme Court. After many successes, the judicial reverses paralleled the rise of a political backlash sparked by groups such as the Interstate Congress for Equal Rights and Responsibilities. In some states, this movement has successfully contested the Indians' "special treatment" under the law. The Supreme Court of Washington, for example, has charged that the federal government, by treaty "conferred upon tribal Indians and their descendants what amounts to titles of nobility"

Indians view their legal status not as something the white man gave them but as something the white man left them. That is why the Indian recourse to white justice will persist, seeking white support and reminding us that we are, besides much else, a nation governed by law.

—*Richard J. Margolis*

Richard J. Margolis, author of Risking Old Age in America *(1989, Westview Publishing), has written widely on Indian affairs and has been an adviser to the Rosebud Sioux and Navaho tribes.*

---

obtain Indian cooperation," he wrote in 1952. Nonetheless, "we must proceed."

During the summer of 1953, under House Concurrent Resolution 108, Congress effectively repudiated the spirit of the Indian New Deal, stipulating that Indians were to be removed from federal supervision "at the earliest possible time," with or without Indian consent. Under Public Law 280, Congress transferred to California, Minnesota, Nebraska, Oregon, and Wisconsin all civil and criminal jurisdiction over Indian reservations—previously under federal and tribal jurisdiction. Some tribal lands were broken up and sold, while many functions once performed by Washington—such as running schools and housing programs—were usually turned over to the states or other agencies.

PICKING UP THE PIECES

Meanwhile, to spur assimilation, Indians were urged to relocate to the cities. As Senator Watkins remarked: "The sooner

we get the Indians into the cities, the sooner the government can get out of the Indian business." In 1940, fewer than 30,000 Indians were city residents; almost three-quarters of a million are today. But the government is not out of the Indian business.

That is because termination did not work. Take the case of the 3,000 Menominees in Wisconsin, one of the larger groups freed from the federal embrace. When Congress passed the Menominee Termination Act in 1954, the Menominee tribe was riding high. Poverty on the more than 200,000-acre reservation was widespread, but the tribe itself had large cash reserves and a thriving forest products industry that provided jobs and income.

With termination the Menominee reservation became a county. Tribal assets came under the control of a corporation in which individual Menominees held shares, while previously untaxed lands suddenly became subject to state and local taxes. The tribal hospital once financed by Washington was shut down, and some Menominees, faced with rising

taxes and unemployment, had to sell their shares in the corporation. Before long, the corporation itself was leasing lands to non-Indians in an attempt to raise money. Soon it was selling the land in order to survive. By the mid-1960s the state and federal governments, forced to pick up the pieces, were spending more to support the Menominees than they had before termination. As more than one Menominee asked in frustration, "Why didn't they leave us alone?"

In 1969, faced with disaster, the Menominees began to fight back, organizing a major protest movement in favor of restoration of federal jurisdiction and services, preservation of the land base, and a return to tribal status. Congress acquiesced late in 1973. The Menominee Restoration Act reinstated federal services to the Menominees, and formally re-established them "as a federally recognized sovereign Indian tribe."

The assimilationist orientation of the termination policy, and Washington's complete indifference to the views of its target population, aroused Indians across the country. They saw in termination the greatest threat to tribal survival since the Indian wars of the 19th century.

Termination did not die officially until 1970, when President Richard Nixon repudiated it. As federal and state officials came to recognize that the policy was creating more problems than it solved, protests by Indian groups slowed. Nonetheless, some Indian groups had been irreparably harmed.

In retrospect, the chief accomplishment of termination ran directly counter to Congress's intention: It provided Indians of diverse backgrounds with a critical issue around which to mobilize. At the American Indian Chicago Conference in 1961, recalled Flathead anthropologist D'Arcy McNickle, the 500 Indians from 90 tribes who gathered for the event "had in common a sense of being under attack." The termination crisis persuaded many Indians of the utility—indeed, the necessity—of united action. Strength would be found in numbers. The category "Indian," invented and named by Europeans, was rapidly becoming the basis of a new wave of minority group politics.

UNCLE TOMAHAWK

The tempest over termination coincided with a second development. Just as the late 1950s and early '60s were a time of change in the black movement for civil rights, they also saw the beginnings of change in American Indian Leadership and its activity. In part, the change was one of tactics. There were glimmers of the future in actions by Wallace "Mad Bear" Anderson and other Iroquois in New York State: When the New York State Power Authority in 1958 sought to expropriate a large chunk of the Tuscarora Reservation for a new water reservoir, Anderson and 100 other Indians scuffled with state troopers and riot police, attempting to keep surveyors off the property. During that same year, several hundred armed and angry Lumbee Indians in Robeson County, North Carolina, reacted to Ku Klux Klan harassment by invading a Klan rally and driving the participants away with gunfire. The harassment stopped.

The new assertiveness reflected the emergence of a new generation of Indian leaders. During the 1950s the number of Indians enrolled in college in the United States substantially increased. According to the BIA, only 385 American Indians were attending postsecondary institutions in 1932; thanks in part to the post-World War II G.I. Bill, that number had swelled to 2,000 by 1957. On campuses, off the reservations, educated Indians from different tribes began to discover one another. That sense of discovery is apparent in Navaho activist Herbert Blatchford's description of the clubs that began to appear among Indian college students, particularly in the Southwest. "There was group thinking," he told writer Stan Steiner. "I think that surprised us the most. We had a group world view."

In 1954, Indian students began holding a series of youth conferences in the Southwest to discuss Indian issues. The largest such conference, in 1960, drew 350 Indians from 57 tribes. Some of the participants eventually turned up at the 1961 Chicago conference—and found themselves at odds with the older, more cautious tribal leaders. In *The New Indians* (1968), Steiner quotes Mel Thom, a young Paiute from Nevada who attended the conference: "We saw the 'Uncle Tomahawks' fumbling around, passing resolutions, and putting headdresses on people. But as for taking a strong stand they just weren't doing it."

Two months later, at a meeting in Gallup, New Mexico, 10 Indian activists—a Paiute, a Ponca, a Mohawk, two Navahos, a Ute, a Shoshone-Bannock, a Potawatomi, a Tuscarora, and a Crow—founded the National Indian Youth Council (NIYC). "We were concerned with direct action," recalled Thom. It was time for Indians "to raise some hell."

They began raising hell in the Pacific Northwest. The trouble started during the early 1960s, when the State of Washington arrested Indians fishing in off-reservation waters. Though in violation of state regulations, "the right of taking fish at accustomed places" had been guaranteed by the Treaty of Point No Point and other agreements made during the 19th century between various Northwestern tribes and the United States. In 1964, a new regional organization—Survival of American Indians—joined the NIYC in protests supporting Indian treaty rights. They held demonstrations at the state capital in Olympia and, more provocatively, sponsored a series of "fish-ins," deliberately setting out to fish waters forbidden to them by the state.

EQUAL RIGHTS

Growing numbers of Indian tribes became involved—the Muckleshoot, Makah, Nisqually Puyallup, Yakima, and others—and began to assert their claims in defiance of court injunctions and state actions. The protests continued into the 1970s and became more violent. In August 1970, Puyallup Indians in a fishing camp on the Puyallup River exchanged gunfire with police who had surrounded them. No one was injured, but 64 Indians were carted off to jail. A year later Hank Adams, leader of Survival of American Indians, was shot by white vigilantes as he sat in his car on the banks of the Nisqually, near Tacoma.

Adams survived, and the struggle went on. Ultimately, in 1974, a federal district court ruled in the tribes' favor on the fishing rights issue, a decision upheld by the U.S. Supreme Court five years later. But the battle is not over. In November 1984, voters in Washington approved Initiative 456, designed to undermine the Treaty of Point No Point and other similar treaties.

Jack Metcalf, a Washington state senator and author of Initiative 456, says that "the basic point is not fish—it's equal rights." But, of course, the issue *is* fish and other treaty-protected Indian resources. From the Indian point of view, it is an issue long since resolved. In the treaties they signed during the 19th century, they agreed to give to the United States most of what are now the states of Washington and Oregon as well as parts of Idaho and California. In return, the United States, among other things, recognized forever their right to fish in Northwestern waters.

Indian activism did not appear only in the countryside; it erupted in the cities as well. For many Indian migrants of the postwar period, the move from the reservation to Denver, Chicago, Seattle, and other cities merely replaced one form of poverty with another. Largely unskilled, lacking experience in the non-Indian world, victimized by discrimination in housing and jobs, Indian migrants swelled the ranks of the urban poor.

LANDING ON ALCATRAZ

They also discovered that, unlike blacks or Hispanics, they had become "invisible." In the eyes of state and local officials, urban Indians, just like reservation

Indians, were the sole responsibility of the BIA. The BIA, for its part, believed that its responsibility stopped at reservation's edge. In 1963, Indians in Oakland, San Francisco, and San Jose began protesting BIA relocation policies and the failure of the Bureau to deal with urban Indian problems. They took a cue from the tactics being employed by American blacks. Observed Vine Deloria, Jr.: "The basic fact of American political life—that without money or force there is no change—impressed itself upon Indians as they watched the civil-rights movement."

The two most militant Indian political organizations took root in the cities: the American Indian Movement, founded in 1968, and Indians of All Tribes, which materialized a year later.

AIM first made its mark in Minneapolis, organizing an Indian Patrol to combat alleged police brutality in Indian neighborhoods. It soon had chapters in cities throughout the Midwest. Indians of All Tribes was founded in San Francisco in response to a specific incident. On November 1, 1969, the San Francisco Indian Center, which served the large Bay Area population, burned to the ground. There was no ready replacement for the building or the services that it provided. On November 9, a group of Indians—perhaps a dozen—landed on Alcatraz Island in San Francisco Bay, site of an abandoned federal prison, and claimed it for a new Indian center. Authorities removed them the next day. The Indians returned on November 20, now 80 strong. By the end of the month several hundred were living on the island, calling themselves Indians of All Tribes. Wary of public reaction to the use of force, federal officials pursued negotiations for 19 months. Not until June 1971, when the number of Indians on the island had dwindled and public interest had waned, did federal marshals and the Coast Guard retake "the Rock."

Alcatraz was a watershed. It drew massive publicity providing many Indians with a dramatic symbol of self-assertion. Said occupation leader Richard Oakes, a Mohawk: "This is actually a move, not so much to liberate the island, but to liberate ourselves." During the next five years Indians occupied Mount Rushmore, Plymouth Rock, and more than 50 other sites around the country for varying lengths of time. The wave of takeovers culminated with the seizure of the BIA headquarters in Washington,

D.C., in 1972, and the Wounded Knee occupation in 1973. AIM, led by Dennis Banks and Russell Means, was a major actor in both.* All made for vivid television news stories.

The Indian activists, noted Yakima journalist Richard La Course, "blew the lid off the feeling of oppression in Indian country." They also provoked a concerted response from Washington. The FBI and the BIA began an effective infiltration campaign, directed in particular at the American Indian Movement. (AIM's chief of security it would later be revealed, was an FBI informer.) More than 150 indictments came out of the Wounded Knee incident. Making headlines and the network evening news had its price. Conceded one AIM member in 1978, "We've been so busy in court fighting these indictments, we've had neither the time nor the money to do much of anything else."

GOING TO THE COURTS

Radical Indian action has abated since the mid-1970s. But the new Indian politics has involved more than land seizures and demonstrations. Beginning in the late 1960s, the Great Society programs opened up new links between Indian leaders and the federal government. By 1970, more than 60 Community Action Agencies had been established on Indian reservations. Office of Economic Opportunity (OEO) funds were being used to promote economic development, establish legal services programs, and sustain tribal and other Indian organizations. Through agencies such as OEO and the Economic Development Administration, tribes were able for the first time to bypass systematically the BIA, pursuing their own political agendas in new ways.

---

*Charges against AIM leaders Banks and Means were dropped on account of misconduct by government prosecutors. Banks was convicted in 1974 of charges stemming from a riot at a Custer, South Dakota, courthouse in 1973. He fled to California and was given sanctuary by Gov. Jerry Brown, who refused extradition. Republican George Deukmejian, elected governor in 1982, was less sympathetic. Banks surrendered to South Dakota officials in 1984 and served one year in prison. He now works as an alcohol-prevention counselor on the Pine Ridge Indian Reservation in Oglala, South Dakota. Means is currently associated with the International Indian Treaty Council, a lobbying group registered with the United Nations.

Indian activists have also turned to the courts. The legal weapon is especially potent in the Indian situation because the relationship of Native Americans to the United States, unlike that of any other group in American life, is spelled out in a vast body of treaties, court actions, and legislation. In 1972, for example, basing their case on a law passed by Congress in 1790 governing land transactions made with Indian tribes, the Penobscot and Passamaquoddy tribes filed suit to force the federal government to protect their claims to more than half of the state of Maine. This action led eventually to the Maine Settlement Act of 1980, which deeded 300,000 acres of timberland to the two tribes.

Behind such actions lies an assortment of Indian legal organizations that sprang up during the 1970s, staffed by a growing cadre of Indian lawyers and supported by both federal and private funds (see box). Indeed, organizing activity of every stripe has marked the past two decades. By the late 1970s, there were more than 100 intertribal or supratribal Indian organizations, ranging from the National Indian Youth Council to the Association of American Indian Physicians to the Small Tribes of Western Washington, most with political agendas, many with lobbying offices in Washington.

Despite generally low Indian voter turnout, Indians have not ignored electoral politics. In 1964, two Navahos ran for seats in the New Mexico state legislature and won, becoming the first Indian representatives in the state's history. Two years later, 15 Indians were elected to the legislatures of six Western states. In 1984, 35 Indians held seats in state legislatures.

Of course the leverage Indians can exercise at the polls is limited. In only five states (Alaska, Arizona, New Mexico, Oklahoma, and South Dakota) do Indians make up more than five percent of the population. At the local level, on the other hand, Indians are occasionally dominant. (Apache County, Arizona, for example, is nearly 75 percent Indian.) Indians also can make a difference in particular situations. In 1963, after the South Dakota legislature had decided that the state should have civil and criminal jurisdiction over Indian reservations, the Sioux initiated a "Vote No" referendum on the issue, hoping to overturn the legislation. They campaigned vigorously among whites and were able to turn out their own voters in record numbers. The referendum passed. A similar Indian grassroots effort and high voter turnout in 1978 led to the defeat of Rep. Jack Cunningham (R.-Wash.), sponsor of legislation in Congress to abrogate all treaties between Indian tribes and the federal government.

THE FINEST LAWYERS

If Indians lack more than limited political clout in elections, during the 1970s they found new opportunities in the economy. The 1973–74 energy crisis and rising oil prices sent the fortunes of some tribes through the roof. Suddenly, Indian lands long thought to be worthless were discovered to be laden with valuable natural resources: one-quarter or more of U.S. strippable coal, along with large amounts of uranium, oil, and gas. Exploration quickly turned up other minerals on Indian lands. For the first time since the drop in land prices during the 1920s, Indians had substantial amounts of something everybody else wanted. In an earlier time this realization would have occasioned wholesale expropriation. In the political atmosphere of the 1970s, and in the face of militant Indians, that was no longer possible. Now the tribes began demanding higher royalties for their resources and greater control over the development process. The result, for some, was a bonanza. During the 41 years between 1937 and 1978, Native Americans received $720 million in royalties and other revenues from mineral leases; during the four years from 1978 to 1982, they received $532 million.

Most of this money went to only a few tribes, much of it to meet the needs of desperately poor populations. It also had a political payoff. Michael Rogers tells the story of an Alyeska Pipeline Company representative in Alaska, who during the mid-1970s lectured pipeline workers about the importance of maintaining good relations with local Indian and Eskimo communities. "You may wonder why they are so important," the representative told his hard-hats. "They are important because they are a people, because they were here before us, and because they have a rich heritage. They are also important because they belong to regional corporations that are able to afford the finest legal counsel in the country."

WHAT DO INDIANS WANT?

This new Indian assertiveness, in its multiple manifestations, had a major impact on U.S. policy. In 1975, responding to "the strong expression" of Indians, Congress committed itself to a policy of "self-determination," to providing "maximum Indian participation in the government and education of the Indian people." From now on, the government was saying, it not only would attempt to listen to Indian views and honor Indian agendas but would grant to Indians a central role in the implementation of policy.

But self-determination raises an awkward, chronic question. What is it the Indians want?

According to Bill Pensoneau, former president of the National Indian Youth Council and now economic planner for the Ponca Tribe in Oklahoma, what the Indians want is "survival." In his view it is not individual survival that is of primary concern. What is at stake is the survival of Indian *peoples:* the continued existence of distinct, independent, tribal communities.

Among other things, of course, that means jobs, health care, functioning economies, good schools, a federal government that keeps its promises. These have not been any easier to come by in recent years. Federal subsidies to Native Americans have been cut steadily under the Reagan administration by about $1 billion in 1981–83. Cancellation of the Comprehensive Employment and Training Act program cost the Poncas 200 jobs. The Intertribal Alcoholism Center in Montana lost half its counselors and most of its beds. The Navaho public housing program was shut down.

Aside from those with lucrative mineral rights, few tribes have been able to make up for such losses of federal subsidies. With no economic base to draw on, most have found themselves powerless in the face of rising unemployment, deteriorating health care, and a falling standard of living.

But the survival question cuts more deeply even than this and reveals substantial divisions among Native Americans themselves. There are those who believe that survival depends on how well Indians can exploit the opportunities offered by the larger (non-Indian) society. Others reject that society and its institutions; they seek to preserve or reconstruct their own culture.

There are many points of view in between. Ideological divisions mirror economic and social ones. In the ranks of any tribe these days one is likely to find blue-collar workers, service workers, professionals, and bureaucrats, along with those pursuing more traditional occupations and designs for living. Most tribes include both reservation and city populations, with contrasting modes of life. The resultant Indian agenda is consistent in its defense of Indian peoples but often contradictory in its conception of how best they can be sustained. This proliferation of Indian factions, many of them no longer tribally defined, has made Indian politics more difficult for even the most sympathetic outsiders to understand.

The Indian politics of the 1960s and '70s, both confrontational and conventional, was too fragmented, the actors were too dispersed, the goals too divergent to constitute a coherent, organized, political crusade. What it represented instead was the movement of a whole population—a huge collection of diverse, often isolated, but increasingly connected Indian communities—into more active political engagement with the larger society, seeking greater control over their lives and futures. To be sure, compared with other political and social events of the period, it was only a sideshow. It did not "solve" fundamental difficulties. But in the world of Indian affairs, it was a remarkable phenomenon, surpassing in scale and impact anything in Indian-white relations since the wars of the 19th century which finally came to an end at Wounded Knee.

How the Seventies Changed America

The "loser decade" that at first seemed nothing more than a breathing space between the high drama of the 1960s and whatever was coming next is beginning to reveal itself as a bigger time than we thought

Nicholas Lemann

Nicholas Lemann, a national correspondent for The Atlantic, *is the author of* The Promised Land: The Great Black Migration and How It Changed America, *published by Alfred A. Knopf [1991].*

"That's it," Daniel Patrick Moynihan, then U.S. ambassador to India, wrote to a colleague on the White House staff in 1973 on the subject of some issue of the moment. "Nothing will happen. But then nothing much is going to happen in the 1970s anyway."

Moynihan is a politician famous for his predictions, and this one seemed for a long time to be dead-on. The seventies, even while they were in progress, looked like an unimportant decade, a period of cooling down from the white-hot sixties. You had to go back to the teens to find another decade so lacking in crisp, epigrammatic definition. It only made matters worse for the seventies that the succeeding decade started with a bang. In 1980 the country elected the most conservative President in its history, and it was immediately clear that a new era had dawned. (In general the eighties, unlike the seventies, had a perfect dramatic arc. They peaked in the summer of 1984, with the Los Angeles Olympics and the Republican National Convention in Dallas, and began to peter out with the Iran-contra scandal in 1986 and the stock market crash in 1987.) It is nearly impossible to engage in magazine-writerly games like discovering "the day the seventies died" or "the spirit of the seventies"; and the style of the seventies—wide ties, sideburns, synthetic fabrics, white shoes, disco—is so far interesting largely as something to make fun of.

BUT SOMEHOW THE SEVENTIES SEEM TO BE creeping out of the loser-decade category. Their claim to importance is in the realm of sweeping historical trends, rather than memorable events, though there were some of those too. In the United States today a few basic propositions shape everything: The presidential electorate is conservative and Republican. Geopolitics revolves around a commodity (oil) and a religion (Islam) more than around an ideology (Marxism-Leninism). The national economy is no longer one in which practically every class, region, and industry is upwardly mobile. American culture is essentially individualistic, rather than communitarian, which means that notions like deferred gratification, sacrifice, and sustained national effort are a very tough sell. Anyone seeking to understand the roots of this situation has to go back to the seventies.

The underestimation of the seventies' importance, especially during the early years of the decade, is easy to forgive because the character of the seventies was substantially shaped at first by spillover from the sixties. Such sixties events as the killings of student protesters at Kent State and Orangeburg, the original Earth Day, the invasion of Cambodia, and a large portion of the war in Vietnam took place in the seventies. Although sixties radicals (cultural and political) spent the early seventies loudly bemoaning the end of the revolution, what was in fact going on was the working of the phenomena of the sixties into the mainstream of American life. Thus the first Nixon administration, which was decried by liberals at the time for being nightmarishly right-wing, was actually more liberal than the Johnson administration in many ways—less hawkish in Vietnam, more free-spending on social programs. The reason wasn't that Richard Nixon was a liberal but that the country as a whole had continued to move steadily to the left throughout the late sixties and early seventies; the political climate of institutions like the U.S. Congress and the boards of directors of big corporations was probably more liberal in 1972 than in any year before or since, and the Democratic party nominated its most liberal presidential candidate ever. Nixon had to go along with the tide.

IN NEW ORLEANS, MY HOMETOWN, THE hippie movement peaked in 1972 or 1973. Long hair, crash pads, head shops, psychedelic posters, underground newspapers, and other Summer of Love-inspired institutions had been unknown there during the real Summer of Love, which was in 1967. It took even longer, until the middle or late seventies, for those aspects of hippie life that have endured to catch on with the general public. All over the country the likelihood that an average citizen would wear longish hair, smoke marijuana, and openly live with a lover before marriage was probably greater in 1980 than it was in 1970. The sixties' preoccupation with self-discovery became a mass phenomenon only in the seventies, through homebrew psychological therapies like est. In politics the impact of the black enfranchisement that took place in the 1960s barely began to be felt until the mid- to late 1970s. The tremendously influential feminist and gay-liberation movements were, at the dawn of the 1970s, barely under way in Manhattan, their headquarters, and certainly hadn't begun their spread across the whole country. The sixties took a long time for America to digest; the process went on throughout the seventies and even into the eighties.

The epochal event of the seventies as an era in its own right was the Organization of Petroleum Exporting Countries' oil embargo, which lasted for six months in the fall of 1973 and the spring of 1974. Everything that happened in the sixties was predicated on the assumption of economic prosperity and growth; concerns like personal fulfillment and social justice tend to emerge in the middle class only at times when people take it for granted that they'll be able to make a living. For thirty years—ever since the effects of World War II on the economy had begun to kick in—the average American's standard of living had been rising, to a remarkable extent. As the economy grew, indices like home ownership, automobile ownership, and access to higher education got up to levels unknown anywhere else in the world, and the United States could plausibly claim to have provided a better life materially for its working class than any society ever had. That ended with the OPEC embargo.

While it was going on, the embargo didn't fully register in the national consciousness. The country was absorbed by a different story, the Watergate scandal, which was really another sixties spillover, the final series of battles in the long war between the antiwar liberals and the rough-playing anti-Communists. Richard Nixon, having engaged in dirty tricks against leftish politicians for his whole career, didn't stop doing so as President; he only found new targets, like Daniel Ellsberg and Lawrence O'Brien. This time, however, he lost the Establishment, which was now far more kindly disposed to Nixon's enemies than it had been back in the 1950s. Therefore, the big-time press, the courts, and the Congress undertook the enthralling process of cranking up the deliberate, inexorable machinery of justice, and everybody was glued to the television for a year and a half. The embargo, on the other hand, was a nonvideo-friendly economic story and hence difficult to get hooked on. It pertained to two subcultures that were completely mysterious to most Americans—the oil industry and the Arab world—and it seemed at first to be merely an episode in the ongoing hostilities between Israel and its neighbors. But in retrospect it changed everything, much more than Watergate did.

By causing the price of oil to double, the embargo enriched—and therefore increased the wealth, power, and confidence of—oil-producing areas like Texas, while helping speed the decline of the automobile-producing upper Midwest; the rise of OPEC and the rise of the Sunbelt as a center of population and political influence went together. The embargo ushered in a long period of inflation, the reaction to which dominated the economics and politics of the rest of the decade. It demonstrated that America could now be "pushed around" by countries most us had thought of as minor powers.

Most important of all, the embargo now appears to have been the pivotal moment at which the mass upward economic mobility of American society ended, perhaps forever. Average weekly earnings, adjusted for inflation, peaked in 1973. Productivity—that is, economic output per man-hour—abruptly stopped growing. The nearly universal assumption in the post–World War II United States was that children would do better than their parents. Upward mobility wasn't just a characteristic of the national culture; it was the defining characteristic. As it slowly began to sink in that everybody wasn't going to be moving forward together anymore, the country became more fragmented, more internally rivalrous, and less sure of its mythology.

Richard Nixon resigned as President in August 1974, and the country settled into what appeared to be a quiet, folksy drama of national recuperation. In the White House good old Gerald Ford was succeeded by rural, sincere Jimmy Carter, who was the only President elevated to the office by the voters during the 1970s and so was the decade's emblematic political figure. In hindsight, though, it's impossible to miss a gathering conservative stridency in the politics of the late seventies. In 1976 Ronald Reagan, the retired governor of California, challenged Ford for the Republican presidential nomination. Reagan lost the opening primaries and seemed to be about to drop out of the race when, apparently to the surprise even of his own staff, he won the North Carolina primary in late March.

It is quite clear what caused the Reagan campaign to catch on: He had begun to attack Ford from the right on foreign policy matters. The night before the primary he bought a half-hour of statewide television time to press his case. Reagan's main substantive criticism was of the policy of détente with the Soviet Union, but his two most crowd-pleasing points were his promise, if elected, to fire Henry Kissinger as Secretary of State and his lusty denunciation of the elaborately negotiated treaty to turn nominal control of the Panama Canal over to the Panamanians. Less than a year earlier Communist forces had finally captured the South Vietnamese capital city of Saigon, as the staff of the American Embassy escaped in a wild scramble into helicopters. The oil embargo had ended, but the price of gasoline had not retreated. The United States appeared to have descended from the pinnacle of power and respect it had occupied at the close of World War II to a small, hounded position, and Reagan had hit on a symbolic way of expressing rage over that change. Most journalistic and academic opinion at the time was fairly cheerful about the course of American foreign policy—we were finally out of Vietnam, and we were getting over our silly Cold War phobia about dealing with China and the Soviet Union—but in the general public obviously the rage Reagan expressed was widely shared.

A couple of years later a conservative political cause even more out of the blue than opposition to the Panama Canal Treaty appeared: the tax revolt. Howard Jarvis, a seventy-five-year-old retired businessman who had been attacking taxation in California pretty much continuously since 1962, got onto the state ballot in 1978 an initiative, Proposition 13, that would substantially cut property taxes. Despite bad press and the strong opposition of most politicians, it passed by a two to one margin.

Proposition 13 was to some extent another aftershock of the OPEC embargo. Inflation causes the value of hard assets to rise. The only substantial hard asset owned by most Americans is their home. As the prices of houses soared in the mid-seventies (causing people to dig deeper to buy housing, which sent the national savings rate plummeting and made real estate prices the great conversation starter in the social life of the middle class), so did property taxes, since they are based on the values of the houses. Hence, resentment over taxation became an issue in waiting.

The influence of Proposition 13 has been so great that it is now difficult to recall that taxes weren't a major concern in national politics before it. Conservative opposition to government focused on its activities, not on its revenue base, and this put conservatism at a disadvantage, because most government programs are popular. Even before Proposition 13, conservative economic writers like Jude Wanniski and Arthur Laffer were inventing supply-side economics based on the idea that reducing taxes would bring prosperity. With Proposition 13 it was proved—as it has been proved over and over since—that tax cutting was one of the rare voguish policy ideas that turn out to be huge political winners. In switching from arguing against programs to arguing against taxes, conservatism had found another key element of its ascension to power

The tax revolt wouldn't have worked if the middle class hadn't been receptive to the notion that it was oppressed. This was remarkable in itself, since it had been assumed for decades that the American middle class was, in a world-historical sense, almost uniquely lucky. The emergence of a self-pitying strain in the middle class was in a sense yet another sixties spillover. At the dawn of the sixties, the idea that *anybody* in the United States was oppressed might have seemed absurd. Then blacks, who really were oppressed, were able to make the country see the truth about their situation. But that opened Pandora's box. The eloquent language of group rights that the civil rights movement had invented proved to be quite adaptable, and eventually it was used by college students, feminists, Native Americans, Chicanos, urban blue-collar "white ethnics," and, finally, suburban homeowners.

Meanwhile, the social programs started by Lyndon Johnson gave rise to another new, or long-quiescent, idea, which was that the government was wasting vast sums of money on harebrained schemes. In some ways the Great Society accomplished its goal of binding the country together, by making the federal government a nationwide provider of such favors as medical care and access to higher education; but in others it contributed to the seventies trend of each group's looking to government to provide it with benefits and being unconcerned with the general good. Especially after the economy turned sour, the middle class began to define its interests in terms of a rollback of government programs aimed at helping other groups.

As the country was becoming more fragmented, so was its essential social

unit, the family. In 1965 only 14.9 percent of the population was single; by 1979 the figure had risen to 20 percent. The divorce rate went from 2.5 per thousand in 1965 to 5.3 per thousand in 1979. The percentage of births that were out of wedlock was 5.3 in 1960 and 16.3 in 1978. The likelihood that married women with young children would work doubled between the mid-sixties and the late seventies. These changes took place for a variety of reasons—feminism, improved birth control, the legalization of abortion, the spread across the country of the sixties youth culture's rejection of traditional mores—but what they added up to was that the nuclear family, consisting of a working husband and a nonworking wife, both in their first marriage, and their children, ceased to be so dominant a type of American household during the seventies. Also, people became more likely to organize themselves into communities based on their family status, so that the unmarried often lived in singles apartment complexes and retirees in senior citizens' developments. The overall effect was one of much greater personal freedom, which meant, as it always does, less social cohesion. Tom Wolfe's moniker for the seventies, the Me Decade, caught on because it was probably true that the country had placed relatively more emphasis on individual happiness and relatively less on loyalty to family and nation.

LIKE A SYMPHONY, THE SEVENTIES FINALLY built up in a crescendo that pulled together all its main themes. This occurred during the second half of 1979. First OPEC engineered the "second oil shock," in which, by holding down production, it got the price for its crude oil (and the price of gasoline at American service stations) to rise by more than 50 percent during the first six months of that year. With the onset of the summer vacation season, the automotive equivalent of the Depression's bank runs began. Everybody considered the possibility of not being able to get gas, panicked, and went off to fill the tank; the result was hours-long lines at gas stations all over the country.

It was a small inconvenience compared with what people in the Communist world and Latin America live through all the time, but the psychological effect was enormous. The summer of 1979 was the only time I can remember when, at the level of ordinary life as

opposed to public affairs, things seemed to be out of control. Inflation was well above 10 percent and rising, and suddenly what seemed like a quarter of every day was spent on getting gasoline or thinking about getting gasoline—a task that previously had been completely routine, as it is again now. Black markets sprang up; rumors flew about well-connected people who had secret sources. One day that summer, after an hour's desperate and fruitless search, I ran out of gas on the Central Expressway in Dallas. I left my car sitting primly in the right lane and walked away in the hundred-degree heat; the people driving by looked at me without surprise, no doubt thinking, "Poor bastard, it could have happened to me just as easily."

In July President Carter scheduled a speech on the gas lines, then abruptly canceled it and repaired to Camp David to think deeply for ten days, which seemed like a pale substitute for somehow setting things aright. Aides, cabinet secretaries, intellectuals, religious leaders, tycoons, and other leading citizens were summoned to Carter's aerie to discuss with him what was wrong with the country's soul. On July 15 he made a television address to the nation, which has been enshrined in memory as the "malaise speech," although it didn't use that word. (Carter did, however, talk about "a crisis of confidence . . . that strikes at the very heart and soul and spirit of our national will.")

TO REREAD THE SPEECH TODAY IS TO BE struck by its spectacular political ineptitude. Didn't Carter realize that Presidents are not supposed to express doubts publicly or to lecture the American people about their shortcomings? Why couldn't he have just temporarily imposed gas rationing, which would have ended the lines overnight, instead of outlining a vague and immediately forgotten six-point program to promote energy conservation?

His describing the country's loss of confidence did not cause the country to gain confidence, needless to say. And it didn't help matters that upon his return to Washington he demanded letters of resignation from all members of his cabinet and accepted five of them. Carter seemed to be anything but an FDR-like reassuring, ebullient presence; he communicated a sense of wild flailing about as he tried (unsuccessfully) to get the situation under control.

5. COLD WAR TO THE 1990s

I REMEMBER BEING ENORMOUSLY IM-pressed by Carter's speech at the time because it was a painfully honest and much thought-over attempt to grapple with the main problem of the decade. The American economy had ceased being an expanding pie, and by unfortunate coincidence this had happened just when an ethic of individual freedom as the highest good was spreading throughout the society, which meant people would respond to the changing economic conditions by looking out for themselves. Like most other members of the word-manipulating class whose leading figures had advised Carter at Camp David, I thought there *was* a malaise. What I didn't realize, and Carter obviously didn't either, was that there was a smarter way to play the situation politically. A President could maintain there was nothing wrong with America at all—that it hadn't become less powerful in the world, hadn't reached some kind of hard economic limit, and wasn't in crisis—and, instead of trying to reverse the powerful tide of individualism, ride along with it. At the same time, he could act more forcefully than Carter, especially against inflation, so that he didn't seem weak and ineffectual. All this is exactly what Carter's successor, Ronald Reagan, did.

Actually, Carter himself set in motion the process by which inflation was conquered a few months later, when he gave the chairmanship of the Federal Reserve Board to Paul Volcker, a man willing to put the economy into a severe recession to bring back price stability. But in November fate delivered the *coup de grâce* Carter in the form of the taking hostage of the staff of the American Embassy in Teheran, as a protest against the United States' harboring of Iran's former shah.

As with the malaise speech, what is most difficult to convey today about the hostage crisis is why Carter made what now looks like a huge, obvious error: playing up the crisis so much that it became a national obsession for more than a year. The fundamental problem with hostage taking is that the one sure remedy—refusing to negotiate and thus allowing the hostages to be killed—is politically unacceptable in the democratic media society we live in, at least when the hostages are middle-class sympathetic figures, as they were in Iran.

There isn't any good solution to this problem, but Carter's two successors in the White House demonstrated that it is possible at least to negotiate for the re-lease of hostages in a low-profile way that will cause the press to lose interest and prevent the course of the hostage negotiations from completely defining the Presidency. During the last year of the Carter administration, by contrast, the hostage story absolutely dominated the television news (recall that the ABC show *Nightline* began as a half-hour five-times-a-week update on the hostage situation), and several of the hostages and their families became temporary celebrities. In Carter's defense, even among the many voices criticizing him for appearing weak and vacillating, there was none that I remember willing to say, "Just cut off negotiations and walk away." It was a situation that everyone regarded as terrible but in which there was a strong national consensus supporting the course Carter had chosen.

So ended the seventies. There was still enough of the sixties spillover phenomenon going on so that Carter, who is now regarded (with some affection) as having been too much the good-hearted liberal to maintain a hold on the presidential electorate, could be challenged for renomination by Ted Kennedy on the grounds that he was too conservative. Inflation was raging on; the consumer price index rose by 14.4 percent between May 1979 and May 1980. We were being humiliated by fanatically bitter, pre-modern Muslims whom we had expected to regard us with gratitude because we had helped ease out their dictator even though he was reliably pro-United States. The Soviet empire appeared (probably for the last time ever) to be on the march, having invaded Afghanistan to Carter's evident surprise and disillusionment. We had lost our most recent war. We couldn't pull together as a people. The puissant, unified, prospering America of the late 1940s seemed to be just a fading memory.

I WAS A REPORTER FOR THE *WASHINGTON Post* during the 1980 presidential campaign, and even on the *Post's* national desk, that legendary nerve center of politics, the idea that the campaign might end with Reagan's being elected President seemed fantastic, right up to the weekend before the election. At first Kennedy looked like a real threat to Carter; remember that up to that point no Kennedy had ever lost a campaign. While the Carter people were disposing of Kennedy, they were rooting for Reagan to win the Republican nomination because he would be such an easy mark.

He was too old, too unserious, and, most of all, too conservative. Look what had happened to Barry Goldwater (a sitting officeholder, at least) only sixteen years earlier, and Reagan was so divisive that a moderate from his own party, John Anderson, was running for President as a third-party candidate. It was not at all clear how much the related issues of inflation and national helplessness were dominating the public's mind. Kennedy, Carter, and Anderson were all, in their own way, selling national healing, that great postsixties obsession; Reagan, and only Reagan, was selling pure strength.

IN A SENSE REAGAN'S ELECTION REPRE-sents the country's rejection of the idea of a sixties-style solution to the great problems of the seventies—economic stagnation, social fragmentation, and the need for a new world order revolving around relations between the oil-producing Arab world and the West. The idea of a scaled-back America—husbanding its resources, living more modestly, renouncing its restless mobility, withdrawing from full engagement with the politics of every spot on the globe, focusing on issues of internal comity—evidently didn't appeal. Reagan, and the country, had in effect found a satisfying pose to strike in response to the problems of the seventies, but that's different from finding a solution.

Today some of the issues that dominated the seventies have faded away. Reagan and Volcker did beat inflation. The "crisis of confidence" now seems a long-ago memory. But it is striking how early we still seem to be in the process of working out the implications of the oil embargo. We have just fought and won a war against the twin evils of Middle East despotism and interruptions in the oil supply, which began to trouble us in the seventies. We still have not really even begun to figure out how to deal with the cessation of across-the-board income gains, and as a result our domestic politics are still dominated by squabbling over the proper distribution of government's benefits and burdens. During the seventies themselves the new issues that were arising seemed nowhere near as important as those sixties legacies, minority rights and Vietnam and Watergate. But the runt of decades has wound up casting a much longer shadow than anyone imagined.

Hollow Victory

A new book by U.S News, to be published next month, tells the unreported story of Operation Desert Storm

A year ago, for the first time in history, the whole world watched in fascination as a war unfolded, live, on its television screens. Laser-guided bombs dropped by invisible Stealth fighters flew down the ventilation shafts of Iraqi buildings, and long lines of ragged Iraqi soldiers surrendered en masse to Americans, Egyptians, even television crews. Scud missiles, guided mostly by fate, landed on Tel Aviv, Riyadh and Dhahran, full of sound and fury but signifying nothing. Like Parisians and Romans before them, tearful Kuwaitis waved American flags at their liberators. After 43 days of war in the air and 100 hours of fighting on the ground, Saddam Hussein, the dictator whom George Bush had compared to Adolf Hitler, was driven from Kuwait and humiliated.

Today, a year after Operation Desert Storm began in the night skies over Baghdad, Saddam Hussein's ability to destabilize the vitally important Persian Gulf region is severely impaired. Iraq's weapons of mass destruction have largely been destroyed. Had there been no war, Iraqi scientists might well have produced a crude nuclear bomb by now, and there is no reason to think that if he had such a device, Saddam Hussein would not use it.

But America's triumph in the gulf was hardly complete. Saddam Hussein remains defiant. The U.S. president has authorized a covert CIA effort to destabilize the Iraqi leader, and the Joint Chiefs of Staff have given Bush a classified memorandum outlining his military options if it looks like any Iraqi opposition group might topple Saddam Hussein. The chances of that are slim. Despite support from Syrian President Hafez Assad, none of the opposition groups that gathered recently in Damascus to plot a strategy has much chance

of getting at Hussein. The Iraqi leader's scientists, meanwhile, openly vow to resume building nuclear weapons as quickly as possible.

In the 12 months since the beginning of Desert Storm, a team of *U.S. News* reporters has studied the causes, the prosecution and the aftermath of the war. The effort was born of a conviction that because of the difficulties inherent in covering a war that moved so quickly across so much remote territory, and because of the constraints the Pentagon imposed on reporters during the course of the conflict, the full story of the gulf war had not been told. The result of the effort, the product of more than 600 postwar interviews, is "Triumph Without Victory: The Unreported History of the Persian Gulf War," to be published next month by Times Books/Random House.

"Triumph Without Victory" reveals that the television war had very little to do with the war that was fought in the skies and on the desert floor. The adaptations from the book on the following pages tell the unreported story. Among the book's principal findings:

■ Despite the Bush administration's repeated denials that it had specifically targeted Saddam Hussein, in the final hours of the war—within hours of the ceasefire—two U.S. Air Force F-111F aircraft dropped specially designed 5,000-pound bombs on an Iraqi command bunker 15 miles northwest of Baghdad in a last-ditch effort to kill the Iraqi leader (see box).

■ The decision to seek the blessing of the United Nations for the use of force against Iraq was part of a larger, more cynical strategy of the Bush administration to bypass Congress and its constitutional authority to commit military forces to offensive operations. "In going first to

the U.N.," said a senior administration official, "we boxed the Democrats in very nicely."

■ In the very week that King Fahd was persuaded to invite American forces to Saudi Arabia to defend his monarchy, a U.S. intelligence officer who had been secretly dispatched to Kuwait City before the Iraqi invasion by the head of the U.S. Central Command, Gen. H. Norman Schwarzkopf, was reporting that Iraq's elite Republican Guard force had begun drawing back from the Saudi border to southern Iraq. The intelligence officer remained in Iraqi-occupied Kuwait for weeks as Schwarzkopf's "deep throat," reporting on the movement of the Iraqi invasion force.

■ Just weeks before American Air Force jets dropped the first bombs on Baghdad on Jan. 17, 1991, U.S. intelligence agents successfully inserted a computer virus into the large computers that control and coordinate much of Iraq's air-defense batteries. The virus was designed to disable Iraqi air defenses. It worked.

■ Critics argue that it would have been foolish for U.S. and coalition forces to drive on to Baghdad, but allied commander Gen. Norman Schwarzkopf never intended to go there. His plan called for crushing the Iraqi Republican Guard in its strongholds, and instead of heading for the Iraqi capital, his forces turned east toward the Persian Gulf. The plan called for the U.S. VII Corps and the British 1st Armored Division to pin the bulk of the Republican Guard in what was called the "Basra Pocket" north of Kuwait City and south of Basra. But the cease-fire prevented those forces from completing the maneuver and allowed the bulk of the Republican Guard forces to escape with their weapons. The Guard later proved instrumental in quashing the rebellions of Iraqi Shiites in southern

Bombs Away

The Last-Gasp Effort to Get Saddam

At 7:19 p.m. on February 27, less than 12 hours before hostilities against Saddam Hussein's Army would end, a U.S. Air Force C-141 transport plane skidded to a halt at a darkened air base deep in the Saudi Arabian desert. Inside, an Air Force weapons specialist was already scrambling toward the forward exit. On the tarmac, a vehicle waited to carry the weapons expert to a high-security hangar. In the cargo hold of the C-141 were two highly unusual bombs. These were the product of a crash Air Force program that had not begun until January 19—three days after the start of the air war. The two bombs; the first of their kind to be manufactured, had been designed expressly to penetrate the deepest, most hardened Iraqi bunkers, the ones in which Saddam Hussein and his most trusted aids were likely to be hiding. Unofficially, the new bomb was called the "bunker-buster." Its official name was the GBU-28. GBU is a standard Air Force acronym. It stands for glide-bomb unit. The GBU-27 bombs that the Air Force's F-117A Stealth pilots had dropped on Baghdad weighed 2,000 pounds. The GBU-28 weighed 5,000 pounds.

Hide and seek. U.S. intelligence officials had never known exactly where Saddam Hussein was holed up during the course of the war. But on January 16, the first night of the air war, General Schwarzkopf's air commanders had made certain that the pilots of the F-117A Stealth fighters delivered their 2,000-pound "smart" bombs to every known Iraqi command bunker. The generals of the U.S. Central Command, which planned and prosecuted Operation Desert Storm, had hoped and expected that Saddam Hussein would be inside one of the bunkers. "Now that would not have targeted Saddam Hussein," said Air Force Lt. Gen. Charles Horner, the Desert Storm air commander. "But it targeted key command-and-control facilities, and he should have been present for duty."

On the evening of February 27, the two bombs loaded in the cargo hold of the C-141 transport plane were intended to give the Central Command one final shot at the elusive Hussein. Although President Bush and his generals asserted that they did not target the Iraqi leader specifically, numerous officials familiar with the classified development and production program that had produced the GBU-28 bunker-buster say the bomb was designed with precisely that purpose in mind. A senior Central Command officer intimately involved in deciding where to drop the two new bombs said their purpose was unmistakable. "I would be lying to you," this officer said, "if I told you they weren't meant for Saddam."

Knowledgeable officials said the target chosen on the evening of February 27 represented their best guess at where the Iraqi leader might be. The hardened bunker at the al-Taji air base approximately 15 miles northwest of Baghdad had already been hit three times by 2,000-pound bombs. But U.S. Air Force and intelligence officials say that had concluded that the bunker, several stories deep and some 200 feet square, apparently had suffered little damage. Saddam Hussein, Americans believed, might well think it was his safest refuge on the final night of the war.

Mission improbable. The pilots who were to deliver the two new bombs on the evening of February 27 were given this intelligence. Minutes after landing in the C-141 with the two GBU-28s, the weapons officer from the 431st Test and Evaluation Squadron at McClellan Air Force Base in Sacramento who had accompanied the bombs to Saudi Arabia was briefing the airmen who had been chosen to carry out this last-chance mission of the gulf war. They were two F-111F pilots and their weapons officers from the 48th Tactical Fighter Wing at the Royal Air Force Base at Lakenheath, England.

The Air Force weapons expert from California explained that the GBU-28 had the same outside diameter as the GBU-27 so it could be mounted on the existing F-111F bomb rack. But while the two GBU-28s were the same diameter as the smaller GBU-27s, they were much, much longer. What they used were old hardened-steel howitzer tubes with pointed nose cones, machined into dartlike deadliness at the 175-year-old Watervliet Arsenal in Upstate New York. One machinist guessed their top-secret purpose. He wrote on one bomb: "The Saddamizer."

As rumors of an imminent cease-fire swirled around them, the two F-111F pilots and their weapons officers absorbed their instructions on how to arm, release and guide the bomb. Outside the briefing room, technicians had loaded one GBU-28 under each of the F-111F's wings and hung a 2,000-pound MK-84 unguided bomb under the other wing in order to balance the two aircraft. It would be up to the weapons officers, sitting next to the pilots, to guide the big bombs onto their targets with their laser controls.

Their briefing completed, the two F-111F crews climbed into their cockpits as their crew chiefs completed hasty preflight checks. The two big bombers roared off into the night. Several hours later over al-Taji, the first F-111F flew over the Iraqi bunker, and the weapons officer released the four lanyards that secured the long bomb to its rack. Right behind the first F-111F, the second pilot crossed the target and released his GBU-28. With their laser controls, the two weapons officers guided the bombs directly onto the target, a section of the bunker's roof around an air duct. One after the other, the 5,000-pound bombs crashed through the roof. Several seconds after that, smoke began billowing from the six entrances. The bunker, finally, was destroyed. Several hours later, U.S. officials confirmed that Saddam Hussein had not been inside.

Iraq and Iraqi Kurds in the north. Thousands were reported killed in both insurrections while U.S. forces stood by helplessly, just miles away.

■ The decision to conclude the ground war after 100 hours, rather than the 144 hours (six days) planned by General Schwarzkopf, was partly the result of

pressure from Saudi Arabia and Egypt. Schwarzkopf actually requested several more hours to prosecute the ground war because many of his advance units had run out of fuel and had not achieved the objectives set for them the previous evening. The decision to stop was also driven by growing complaints at home and abroad that American pilots had engaged in unwonted carnage on the so-called Highway of Death that led from Kuwait City to Basra—where the death toll actually was quite low. President Bush also may have been influenced by growing pressure on Soviet President Mikhail Gorbachev from Soviet military and KGB hard-liners as the ground war progressed.

■ The largest tank battle of the war, which was previously unreported in any detail, conclusively demonstrated the superiority of American tanks and fighting doctrine over that of the former Soviet Union. Some M1A1 tanks recorded confirmed kills of Iraqi T-72 tanks at over 3,200 meters, well beyond the range previously thought possible. Taken as a whole, the ground war also showed that the new post-Vietnam American military doctrine—emphasizing speed, maneuverability and deception—clearly outclassed the plodding tactics of the Iraqis, who had been taught by Soviet instructors.

■ Although the Pentagon disparaged the Iraqi forces after the war, some American commanders encountered some Iraqi units that were well led and fought hard. Several U.S. units that unexpectedly encountered Iraqi soldiers in battles never previously reported were driven back, losing equipment and men.

■ As other reports have suggested, the Iraqi Army in the Kuwait theater of operations was probably much smaller than the Pentagon claimed. Iraq's frontline forces were probably about 70 percent Shiites and 20 percent Kurds—Hussein's "throwaway divisions"—which helps explain their mass desertions and unwillingness to fight. Thus, on the eve of the war, Iraq may have had as few as 300,000 soldiers in the Kuwait theater, less than half the 632,000 claimed by General Schwarzkopf or the 540,000 estimated by the Pentagon. Ground units found they had to make their own estimates of enemy forces because the numbers compiled by the Central Command were so skewed and misleading.

■ Similarly, Iraqi casualties were probably far lower than the 100,000 estimated by the Defense Intelligence Agency. In fact, as few as 8,000 Iraqi soldiers may have been killed in the Kuwait theater of operations during the 43 days of combat, according to the book.

■ The number of American soldiers who perished on the battlefield as a result of so-called friendly fire is not fully reflected in the figures cited by the Pentagon. Of the 148 Americans killed in action, the Pentagon claimed that 35, or 24 percent, were victims of friendly fire. But another 11 American soldiers were killed by unexploded allied munitions, and accounting for those soldiers would raise the number of casualties caused by friendly fire to 31 percent. Another 18 American soldiers were killed by unexploded Iraqi ordnance, bringing the number of casualties caused by postbattle contact with unexploded ordnance to 20 percent. Many American soldiers say the thousands of unexploded mines and bomblets they encountered, especially allied ordnance, were far more dangerous than enemy fire.

If wars are truly the most honest tests of nations, the conflict with Iraq reveals an America resolute and undiminished in its historic strengths. Confronted with an act of untenable international aggression, Washington responded boldly; the diplomacy employed by President Bush and Secretary of State James Baker was, at times, breathtaking. On the battlefield, America's all-volunteer Army performed magnificently. Weapons systems functioned far better than anyone expected. Commanders commanded, soldiers fought, courageously and well. As a result, the threat of "another Vietnam" has lost much of its ability to panic and paralyze the nation.

But never in the history of warfare have so many watched so much and seen so little. Despite the thousands of hours of television footage and the millions of words in newspapers and magazines, essential elements of the conflict—the terror and the heroism, the professionalism and diligence—occurred out of sight. Entire missions, battles and areas of operations went uncovered. As a result, what the world saw and read at the time was incomplete and sometimes inaccurate. When nations wage war, the risks and the rewards are great. "Triumph Without Victory" helps us understand both more fully.

New Directions for American History

For decades the cold war intruded on virtually every foreign policy decision and played a major role in the American economic structure. Now, not only has the cold war ended, but the once-mighty Soviet Union has dissolved into its constituent parts. The ultimate consequences of these momentous developments cannot be foretold. What President Bush once heralded as a "new world order" has more nearly resembled a new world disorder, as catastrophic developments in Eastern Europe, Africa, and elsewhere rage unchecked. Neither the United States and its allies nor the United Nations have been able to do more than express dismay. Military might, once deemed imperative to effective diplomacy, now seems less relevant than economic strength. And there is growing alarm that the planet is becoming endangered by rampant environmental degradation.

"America and Russia, Americans and Russians" reviews the history of these former cold war enemies and concludes that there is no intrinsic reason why they should not live in peace and relative harmony.

The United States has contributed greatly to world pollution and, though there has been some progress, it continues to do so. Some of the more ardent environmentalists have condemned all economic growth as potentially catastrophic, while certain business groups have been equally adamant in equating regulation with economic disaster. "Cleaning Up the Environment" presents five proposals that may provide a compromise that both sides could live with. Various groups continue their struggles to end discrimination based on gender, race, or sexual preference. "Remember the Ladies" recounts the failure to attain passage of the Equal Rights Amendment.

In addition to economic stagnation, the United States has been beset by a number of domestic problems that so far have defied compromise. Bitter disputes over affirmative action, abortion, gay and lesbian rights, and multiculturalism have permeated political discourse. "The Suburban Century Begins" argues that this demographic process will have profound effects on all aspects of the American society.

Conflict over multiculturalism and "political correctness" began on college campuses, but they can now be found on state and local school boards, and elsewhere. A pair of articles in this section present two views. "The Disuniting of America" warns that the *way* multiculuralism is being presented is bound to set groups against one another and to produce a "balkanized" society. "The Painful Demise of Eurocentricism" rejects this view as characteristic of those who are unwilling to recognize challenges to orthodox versions of history. "Black and White in America" points out that, despite some progress, racial harmony in this country appears as far as ever from being realized.

Looking Ahead: Challenge Questions

Cold war considerations prompted the United States to extend itself globally and at times to resort to military intervention—as in the case of Vietnam. What, if any, circumstances would warrant future interventions? Ethnic bloodshed in Eastern Europe? Widespread famine and starvation in Africa?

The United States never was a "melting pot," as some proclaimed. Will racial and ethnic divisiveness be diminished or exacerbated by multiculturalism and "political correctness"? If one should not be discriminated against because of race, gender, or ethnic background, what excuses such treatment of those whose sexual preferences are different from the majority?

Unit 6

The Suburban Century Begins

The real meaning of the 1992 election

William Schneider

William Schneider is a contributing editor of The Atlantic *and a political analyst for Cable News Network. He is also a resident fellow at the American Enterprise Institute and is currently the Speaker Thomas P. O'Neill Jr. Visiting Professor of American Politics at Boston College.*

The United States is a nation of suburbs. The 1990 census makes it official. Nearly half the country's population now lives in suburbs, up from a quarter in 1950 and a third in 1960. This year will see the first presidential election in which a majority of the voters will in all likelihood be suburbanites—the first election of the suburban century.

That explains the obsessive focus on the middle class in the 1992 campaign. The middle class is who lives in the suburbs. The word that best describes the political identity of the middle class is "taxpayers." Democrats have been talking about "the forgotten middle class," and for good reason. For the past twenty-five years the Democrats have forgotten the middle class. And they have paid dearly.

They can't afford to do that anymore. The third century of American history is shaping up as the suburban century. Until 1920 most Americans lived in rural areas. By 1960 the country was a third urban, a third rural, and a third suburban. That balance didn't last long, however. By 1990 the urban population had slipped to 31 percent and the rural population was down to less than a quarter. We are now a suburban nation with an urban fringe and a rural fringe.

The first century of American life was dominated by the rural myth: the sturdy and self-reliant Jeffersonian farmer. By the end of the nineteenth century, however, Americans were getting off the farms as fast as they could, to escape the hardship and brutality of rural life. How could you keep them down on the farm after they'd seen Kansas City?

Most of the twentieth century has been dominated by the urban myth: the melting pot; New York, New York; the cities as the nation's great engines of prosperity and culture. All the while, however, Americans have been getting out of the cities as soon as they can afford to buy a house and a car. They want to escape the crowding and dangers of urban life. But there is more to it than escape. As Kenneth T. Jackson argues in *Crabgrass Frontier,* a history of suburbanization in the United States, the pull factors (cheap housing and the ideal of a suburban "dream house") have been as important as the push factors (population growth and racial prejudice).

The 1990 Census tells the story of the explosive growth of suburbs. That year fourteen states had a majority suburban population, including six of the ten most populous states (California, Pennsylvania, Ohio, Michigan, Florida, and New Jersey).

Five of the nation's ten fastest-growing counties were majority suburban; two others had considerable suburban development. Three were outside Atlanta. Nineteen of the nation's twenty-five fastest-growing "cities" were really suburbs. They included the Los Angeles–area suburbs of Moreno Valley, Rancho Cucamonga, and Irvine; the Phoenix suburbs of Mesa, Scottsdale, and Glendale; and the Dallas suburbs of Arlington, Mesquite, and Plano.

Suburban growth is not likely to end anytime soon. According to the polls, 43 percent of Boston residents, 48 percent of people who live in Los Angeles, and 60 percent of those who live in New York City say they would leave the city if they could. When the Gallup Poll asked Americans in 1989 what kind of place they would like to live in, only 19 percent said a city.

Is there a suburban myth? Sure there is. It has been a staple of American popular culture since the 1950s, from television shows like *The Adventures of Ozzie and Harriet* and *Leave It to Beaver* to movies like *E. T.* The suburban myth was challenged in highbrow culture as soon as it emerged, however, in books like David Reisman's *The Lonely Crowd* (which criticized suburbia's "other-directedness") and William H. Whyte Jr.'s *The Organization Man* (which called it "group-mindedness"). The debunking of the suburban myth has now reached American popular culture, where television comedies like *Roseanne* and *The Simpsons* portray the harsh realities of suburban life—unemployment, dysfunctional families, and, above all, stress.

In 1990 five of the nation's ten fastest-growing counties were majority suburban; two others had considerable suburban development. Nineteen of the twenty-five fastest-growing "cities" were really suburbs.

Suburban stress has not produced any large-scale countermovement back to the cities or out to the countryside, however. Instead, the larger suburbs have become what the author Joel Garreau calls "edge cities"—places where jobs have migrated to follow the population. These, in turn have spawned more-distant suburbs of their own—"exurbs." The prevailing life-style in all these places remains distinctively suburban, meaning home-owning, homogeneous, and largely white.

The prevailing imperative of suburban life is security—both economic and physical. When I interviewed Dan Walters, a columnist for the *Sacramento Bee* and one of the keenest observers of California politics, he explained to me how the culture and life-style of the suburbs work to undermine political consensus.

"The theory of California," Walters explained, "is, 'I bought this house. It's mine. This is my little preserve.' The first thing the homeowner would do was put up a six-foot fence around his entire house. Then the developers started putting in the fences themselves.

"The next step after that was to put a fence around the entire development and put a guard at the gate. The development became a walled community. These walled communities created their own governmental structures. They might be private structures, like homeowners' associations, that exercised government-like powers. But in some cases they actually created public entities that served as private guardians."

Walters offered the following theory: "Personal security in a time of economic and social uncertainty is a very salable commodity. Developers are not selling security but a sense of security." The result, in his view, was "the loss of a sense of common purpose" in California. "We don't have a social consensus," he said, "so we cannot achieve a political consensus. All politics does is implement the social consensus."

THE DECLINING URBAN SECTOR

In the 1890s the social consensus broke down in this country when declining rural areas rose up in rebellion against urban America. The Populists spoke for the old rural America that was being displaced economically and culturally by immigration and the rise of great cities. The countryside was driven to radical extremes by economic pressure and the loss of political influence. In the election of 1896 the Democrats fused with the Populists and nominated William Jennings Bryan, shutting themselves out of presidential politics for most of the next thirty-six years.

The social consensus is breaking down again in the 1990s. Urban America is facing extreme economic pressure and

the loss of political influence. The cities feel neglected, and with good reason: they are the declining sector of American life. Just as the Populists of the 1890s exalted the rural myth, urban leaders of the 1990s are trying to glorify the urban myth.

In 1990 the mayors of thirty-five of the nation's big cities held an "urban summit" in New York City. They published a position paper pleading the case that their urban agenda was, as the title suggested, "In the National Interest." "Urban centers are the focus of national vitality in trade, manufacturing, finance, law and communications," the mayors insisted. "American culture is profoundly affected by the artistic and intellectual communities that thrive in the compressed space of cities." Mayor Tom Bradley, of Los Angeles, warned, "If we do not save our cities, we shall not save this nation."

The mayors wanted to designate the 1990s "The Decade of the City." They called for "a public education campaign around the theme of why cities are essential." Finally, however, they gave in. They said "city" needs to be redefined "to include the entire urban region as a community." If you can't beat the suburbs, join them.

Like the Populists before them, today's urban activists react with rage and frustration to the neglect of their agenda. Jesse Jackson grumbles that the Democratic Party is turning away from its base. Last year he complained about "an unholy alliance between the two parties—leaving the electorate with two names but one party, one set of assumptions, and no options."

Jackson's mission in 1984 and 1988 was to rally the declining urban sector in a populist protest movement. But this year Jackson decided not to run—much to the relief of Democratic strategists, who dreaded the spectacle of Jackson's again extorting concessions from the party's nominee. They fear that Jackson is as out of step with suburban America today as Bryan was with urban America in the 1890s.

When the U.S. Conference of Mayors met in Washington, last January, the Democratic mayors decided not to rally around a presidential candidate. Mayor Raymond L. Flynn, of Boston, the conference president, complained that none of the major contenders performed strongly enough on the urban agenda. "I want a little fire in the belly here for

America's cities," Flynn told *The New York Times.* "There's still this hesitancy among the candidates. . . . We want somebody who's really going to have a feeling of commitment to problems like homelessness and AIDS."

Actually, one Democratic candidate did draw a positive response from the mayors—Larry Agran, the former mayor of Irvine, California. Agran was regarded, of course, as a long shot for the nomination. The mayors' conference was one of the few candidate forums that included him. What he promised was $25 billion in direct, no-strings-attached aid to cities, paid for by a gigantic cut in military spending. Delighted, the mayors said he was the only candidate who understood the needs of urban America.

The mayors and other liberal activists worry that the Democrats are moving toward a suburban agenda. They are right. The mayors know that problems like poverty, homelessness, and AIDS can't be solved with middle-class tax cuts and entitlement programs. Even robust economic growth doesn't do the cities much good, as the country discovered in the 1980s. What the cities need is targeted resources. But that's exactly what Democrats are afraid of—redistributive programs that take resources from the suburbs to pay for the problems of the cities. That sounds like the Great Society programs that got the Democrats in trouble with the suburban middle class in the 1960s. But isn't it "in the national interest" to bail out the cities? The suburbs have given their answer: walled communities.

Nowhere has the gap between city and suburb been more dramatically demonstrated than in the notorious not-guilty verdict in the trial of four Los Angeles police officers last April. The trial, which took place in Simi Valley, an overwhelmingly white suburb, produced an incomprehensible verdict. The reaction in the inner city of Los Angeles was one of incomprehensible violence.

THE REPUBLICANS' SUBURBAN EDGE

Presidential politics these days is a race between Democratic cities and Republican suburbs to see who can produce bigger margins. The suburbs are winning.

In 1960 urban areas cast 33 percent of the national vote, 20 percent Democratic and 13 percent Republican. So the Democrats came out of the cities with a seven-point lead. In 1988 the urban vote was down to 29 percent of the total. It split 18 percent for the Democrats and 11 percent for the Republicans. That's still a seven-point lead. Thus, from 1960 to 1988 two things happened to the urban vote: it became smaller, and it became more Democratic. As a result, the Democrats' lead coming out of the cities held constant.

Presidential politics these days is a race between Democratic cities and Republican suburbs. The suburbs are winning. They are growing larger faster than the cities are becoming Democratic.

Over the same period the rural vote became smaller and more Republican. So the Republican lead coming out of the countryside also stayed about the same (a two-point lead in 1960, a three-point lead in 1988).

What happened to the suburban vote from 1960 to 1988 was quite different. While the suburbs grew larger, they also became more Republican. In 1960 the suburbs generated a third of the national vote. The suburban third divided 18 percent for the Republicans and 15 percent for the Democrats. So the Republican Party came out of the suburbs that year with a three-point lead. In 1988 the suburbs accounted for 48 percent of the vote. And that vote split 28–20 for the Republicans. Thus they came out of the suburbs with an eight-point lead in 1988—enough to cancel out the Democrats' lead in the cities. The suburbs had arrived, politically.

The suburbs are growing larger faster than the cities are becoming more Democratic. That has tipped the balance to the Republicans in presidential elections in a number of key states.

Illinois is a case in point. In 1960 Chicago cast 35 percent of the Illinois presidential vote. With a little help from Richard J. Daley's machine, the city voted 63 percent Democratic that year. In 1988 Chicago's vote was down to 23

percent of the Illinois total. With no apparent help from the Daley machine, the city voted 69 percent Democratic.

At the same time, the suburban vote outside Chicago became slightly more Republican, moving from 60 percent for Nixon in 1960 to 62 percent for Bush in 1988. The number of voters in the suburbs grew enormously, however. The suburbs accounted for 26 percent of the Illinois vote in 1960—a quarter less than Chicago. They cast 38 percent of the Illinois vote in 1988—two thirds more than Chicago.

In 1960 the Democrats came out of Chicago with a 456,000-vote lead for President. The Republicans came out of the suburbs 254,000 votes ahead. Illinois went Democratic. In 1988 the Democrats came out of a smaller but more Democratic Chicago with a 420,000-vote lead. But the Republican margin was 423,000 votes in the suburbs. Illinois went Republican.

In 1960 Detroit cast 22 percent of the Michigan vote. Seventy-one percent of those votes went Democratic. Kennedy got a 312,000-vote lead out of Detroit. The Detroit suburbs also went Democratic that year, by 84,000 votes. Michigan ended up in the Democratic column.

By 1988 Detroit voted a whopping 85 percent Democratic. But the city was down to eight percent of the Michigan vote. It gave Michael S. Dukakis a 217,000-vote lead. Detroit's suburbs were now voting 60 percent Republican. And they accounted for a third of the Michigan vote. The suburbs gave Bush a 230,000-vote lead. Michigan went Republican.

In 1960 Los Angeles County had two and a half times as many voters as the five suburban counties of southern California. But the Republican lead in the suburban counties (138,000 votes) was already large enough to offset the Democratic lead in Los Angeles County (21,000 votes). By 1988 L.A. County and the southern California suburbs were casting the same number of votes. The Democrats' lead of 133,000 votes in L.A. County was dwarfed by the Republicans' lead of 717,000 votes in the suburbs. A state that had gone Republican by 36,000 votes in 1960 went Republican by 353,000 votes in 1988.

How bad has it gotten for Democrats? Bush's margin in Ohio (477,000 votes) was far larger than his total vote in Cleveland (34,000 votes). His margin in Michigan (290,000) was greater than his

total vote in Detroit (44,000). Ditto for Georgia and Atlanta. And for Louisiana and New Orleans. The same was very nearly true for Maryland and Baltimore and for California and Los Angeles. Bush's margin in Missouri (83,000 votes) was about the same as the total number of votes he got in St. Louis and Kansas City together (85,000).

In other words, Bush could have carried most of these states without getting a single vote in their largest cities. Republicans can afford to ignore the cities. But the Democrats, like many urban residents, have to worry about becoming trapped in them—exactly the way the Democrats got trapped in rural America in the 1890s.

THE SUBURBAN VIEW OF GOVERNMENT

Democrats have not done badly among suburban votes in elections below the presidential level. California, for instance, is a heavily suburban state that has voted for the Democratic ticket only once since Harry Truman (the 1964 LBJ landslide), but Democrats have won ten out of twenty-four elections for governor and senator since 1952, have held a majority of California's seats in the House of Representatives since 1958, and have controlled both houses of the state legislature since 1974.

Across the country suburban voters usually vote more Democratic in state elections than in presidential elections. The difference averages between five and eight points in nonsouthern states like California, Illinois, and Michigan. Among suburban voters in southern states like Texas and Florida, Democratic candidates for governor and senator typically do 15 to 25 points better than Democratic presidential candidates.

In 1990 a hundred and seventy congressional districts had majority suburban populations (according to data in the 1980 Census). That was substantially more than the number of majority urban (ninety-eight) or majority rural (eighty-eight) districts. (The remaining seventy-nine districts were "mixed.") Democrats represented more than 80 percent of the urban districts, almost 60 percent of the rural districts, and a bare 50 percent of the suburban districts. The Democrats' ability to sustain a majority in the House of Representatives depends on the party's continuing competitiveness in the suburbs.

And that, in turn, depends on the Democrats' ability to understand the suburban view of government. Suburbanization means the privatization of American life and culture. To move to the suburbs is to express a preference for the private over the public. The architects Andres Duany and Elizabeth Plater-Zyberk offer this disdainful characterization:

The classic suburb is less a community than an agglomeration of houses, shops, and offices connected to one another by cars, not by the fabric of human life. . . . The structure of the suburb tends to confine people to their houses and cars; it discourages strolling, walking, mingling with neighbors. The suburb is the last word in privatization, perhaps even its lethal consummation, and it spells the end of authentic civic life.

There is a reason why people want to be confined to their houses and their cars. They want a secure and controlled environment. Suburban commuters show a determined preference for private over public transportation. Automobiles may not be efficient, but they give people a sense of security and control. With a car you can go anywhere you want, anytime you want, in the comfort of your own private space.

Entertainment has also been privatized. Suburbanites watch cable television and rent videos. They can watch anything they want, anytime they want, in the comfort of their own private space. People have control over what they see—remote control. And they don't have to put up with the insecurity and disorder of public spaces. Historically, enjoying public spaces was one of the reasons people lived in cities.

Even public activities like shopping have been privatized. The difference between a mall and a downtown is that a mall is a private space, a secure environment. Young people can hang out there. Old people can "mall walk" for exercise. Those are difficult and dangerous things to do in uncontrolled public spaces. Even the streets of a suburb are not really public areas. Suburban houses have decks, which protrude into private back yards. In the great American suburb there are no front porches.

Suburbanites' preference for the private applies to government as well. Suburban voters buy "private" government—good schools and safe streets for the people who live there. They control their local government, including taxes, spending, schools, and police.

There are rich suburbs (Fairfax County, Virginia) and poor suburbs (Chelsea, Massachusetts); black suburbs (Prince Georges County, Maryland) and Hispanic suburbs (Hialeah, Florida); liberal suburbs (Marin County, California) and conservative suburbs (Orange County, California). Can suburban voters, then, be said to have a defining characteristic? Yes: suburban voters are predominantly property owners. And that makes them highly tax-sensitive.

A major reason people move out to the suburbs is simply to be able to buy their own government. These people resent it when politicians take their money and use it to solve other people's problems.

A major reason people move out to the suburbs is simply to be able to buy their own government. These people resent it when politicians take their money and use it to solve other people's problems, especially when they don't believe that government can actually solve those problems. Two streams of opinion seem to be feeding the anti-government consensus as American politics enters the suburban era. One is resistance to taxes, which is strongest among middle-class suburban voters. The other is cynicism about government, which is strongest among the urban poor and the poorly educated.

Upscale voters are the most likely to say that government has too much power and influence, that taxes should be kept low, and that people should solve their problems for themselves. That's the "elitist" suburban view. Downscale voters express doubts about what government *can* do. They are the most likely to say that public officials don't know what they are doing, that most of them are crooks, that they don't pay attention to what people think, that government is run by a few big interests, and that you can't trust the government to do what is right. That's the cynical, "populist" view. Put the two together and you have a powerful, broad-based, anti-government, anti-tax coalition.

Polls show that people want government to do more about education, the environment, the infrastructure, and health care. But they trust it less than ever. The more expansive view of what government *should* do has been canceled out by the more constricted view of what government *can* do. No one wants to give politicians more money to spend, even if the nation's problems are becoming more serious.

The last time the nation was in this kind of anti-political frenzy was during the Progressive era, in the early decades of this century. Progressives, however, were anti-political but pro-government. The reforms of that era were aimed at curbing the power of political parties by expanding what Progressives saw as the rational, managerial authority of government (for example, having cities run by professional city managers instead of politicians). They used the attack on politics to justify an essentially liberal agenda: making government more professional.

Today the attack on politics serves an essentially conservative agenda: taking government out of the hands of a professional political elite and making it more responsive to the people. How? By limiting terms, limiting pay, limiting spending, and limiting taxes. In the suburban era, unlike the Progressive era, opposition to politics and opposition to government go hand in hand.

SPEND BROADLY, TAX NARROWLY

The suburbanization of the electorate raises a big problem for the Democrats: How can they sell activist government to a constituency that is hostile to government? The answer is, they have to learn how to talk about taxes and spending in ways palatable to the middle class. There are two lessons the Democrats should have learned by now.

One is that the only social programs that are politically secure are those that benefit everybody. Medicare, for example, is the principal enduring legacy of Lyndon Johnson's Great Society. Like Social Security, Medicare helps everybody, not just those in greatest financial need. The Democrats found it impossible to sustain support for LBJ's War on Poverty, however, precisely because it was not a universal entitlement. It was targeted at the poor.

Consider two kinds of government spending. Public-works spending is salable to middle-class voters. Social-welfare spending is not. Public-works spending involves benefits that are available to everyone and that people cannot provide for themselves—things like good schools, fast highways, safe streets, and a clean environment.

Social-welfare spending is targeted by need. It helps disadvantaged people get things that others are able to provide for themselves, like housing, food, and medical care. That is fine with middle-class voters, as long as they are persuaded that the benefits are going to the "truly needy" and that no one is taking advantage of the system. But middle-class voters tend to be suspicious of programs aimed at creating social change rather than providing public services.

Entitlement programs are like public works. By definition, entitlements are not based on need. People are entitled to a benefit because they belong to a certain category, and it is a category anyone can belong to—the elderly, children, veterans, disabled persons (everyone was once a child, everyone expects to get old, and everyone can join the service or become disabled). True, entitlement programs are wasteful, expensive, and inefficient ways to bring about social change. But that is not their purpose. Entitlement programs, like Social Security, are only incidentally redistributive. In effect, middle-class voters are bribed to support them because they get benefits too.

It is worth remembering that the New Deal was not a social-welfare program. The Great Depression was a natural disaster that affected everybody, the just and the unjust alike. When the Democrats took the White House in 1933, they did not attempt a tremendous program of social change. What they came up with was an ambitious program of public works.

The other lesson for Democrats comes from the Reagan era: Don't raise taxes that hurt everybody. Democrats saw what happened to Walter Mondale in 1984 when he proposed a general tax increase. Suburban middle-class voters, however, are willing to consider specifically targeted fees and taxes. That was the principle behind the highway bill passed in 1987 over President Reagan's veto. The bill designated revenues from the highway trust fund to pay for road

and bridge construction. Congress proudly pointed to the fact that the bill did not do anything to increase the federal deficit. Of course, it did not do anything to reduce the deficit either.

An even more ingenious solution to the revenue problem is not to raise taxes or spend government money at all. Just mandate that employers pay more in benefits to their workers. Raise the minimum wage. Require employers to pay for health insurance and grant parental and medical leave. The idea is to expand "workers' rights" and "family rights"—that is, entitlements—by making business, not government, pay for them. These kinds of proposals elicit a great many complaints from business, particularly small business, which bears most of the burden. But they draw few complaints from taxpayers. According to *The New York Times,* state and local governments have been relying increasingly on special-purpose taxes, revenues frequently raised from specific groups of taxpayers and used for specific purposes. Among the examples: a $10 increase in marriage-license fees in Colorado to pay for child-abuse prevention programs. Higher real-estate taxes for downtown property owners in an eighty-block area of Philadelphia to pay for enhanced security and special street-cleaning services. A dollar a year added to automobile insurance premiums in Michigan to pay for auto-theft prevention programs. Taxes on beer in several states to pay for anti-drunk-driving and alcohol rehabilitation programs.

"The logical place for this to wind up," the criminologist Lawrence W. Sherman told the *Times,* "is that every crime will have its own tax, except for the unpopular offenses that involve the poor or that are not important to middle-class voters." Precisely. Special-purpose taxes are the suburban ideal—not just private government but private taxes.

The message to Democrats is: In order to compete for a suburban electorate, keep spending as broad as possible and make taxes as specific as possible.

That, of course, is the exact reverse of urban priorities. The urban agenda consists of broad-based taxes and targeted spending programs; tax as many people as possible in order to provide for the needs of specific disadvantaged groups. That requires means-testing. Probably the most difficult thing to do in politics these days is to sell means-tested programs to suburban voters. They know

that they will end up paying for the programs and that the benefits will go to people of more modest means. To middle-class voters, a program that helps the few and taxes the many is an outrage. A program that helps the many and taxes the few seems eminently fair.

THE COLLAPSE OF "OPERATIONAL CONSERVATISM"?

Twenty-five years ago, in *The Political Beliefs of Americans,* Lloyd A. Free and Hadley Cantril described the American public as ideologically conservative and operationally liberal. Their polls showed that Americans professed a belief in small government but at the same time supported a wide range of government subsidies and spending programs. The Democrats ruled by appealing to those operational sentiments. "President Johnson was correct," Free and Cantril concluded, "when he indicated that the argument over the welfare state had been resolved in favor of federal action to achieve it."

The Reagan era appears to have reversed that formulation. During the 1980s public opinion grew more liberal on issues of government spending and intervention. Nevertheless, the anti-tax consensus has held fast. Today's "operational conservatism" is sustained by both continued public resistance to tax increases and widespread cynicism about what government can do. That operational conservatism has enabled Republicans to control the agenda since 1978.

The operational liberalism of the Johnson era was legitimized by the Democratic Party's ability to keep the country prosperous. The New Deal and the Second World War, with their unprecedented expansion of federal power, had saved the country from the Great Depression. Americans are pragmatists. They believe that if something works, it must be right. If liberalism meant prosperity, as it did from the 1930s through the 1960s, then it was all right with most Americans.

The operational conservatism of the Reagan era also had pragmatic roots. It was legitimized by the Republican Party's ability to keep the country prosperous. The Reagan Revolution, with its tax cuts and its unprecedented attack on federal power, saved the country from the Great Inflation. As long as low taxes and limited government worked, Americans had no quarrel with Reaganomics.

But Reaganomics isn't working anymore. *The Boston Globe* has reported that after four years in office, Bush is likely to end up with the poorest record of economic growth of any President since Harry Truman. Economists estimate that the country's average annual growth rate from 1989 through 1992 will be 1.6 percent—far lower than the yearly growth rate under Ronald Reagan (3.0 percent), Jimmy Carter (3.1 percent), Richard Nixon and Gerald Ford (2.2 percent), and Lyndon Johnson (4.6 percent). No President with that kind of record is supposed to be reelected. During his 1988 campaign Bush promised to create thirty million new jobs in eight years. At the rate he is going, fewer than five million will have been created by the end of 1996.

Bush's failure gives Democrats an opportunity to woo the middle-class vote on the economic issue—but only if they understand the middle-class view of government. In 1988 Michael Dukakis went after middle-class voters the same way Democrats have always gone after constituencies. His message was: You've got a problem; we've got a program.

Dukakis had a program to provide child care to families with working parents. He had a program to help young families afford home mortgages. He had a program to help students cope with college-tuition costs. He had a program to provide health insurance to all working Americans. His programs were, for the most part, ingeniously designed to be self-financing. The Democrats could do it all without a tax increase. How? All you had to do was read the position papers.

But middle-class voters were suspicious of government programs. They figured that they would end up paying for the programs while the benefits would go to someone else. George Bush's answer to "the middle-class squeeze" was far more persuasive. What he promised middle-class voters was prosperity. "I am optimistic and I believe we can keep this long expansion going," Bush said in the second campaign debate.

That's what the middle class wanted to hear. Their message to the candidates was: Just protect our jobs, keep the paychecks coming in, and hold taxes down. We'll solve our problems for ourselves. We'll send our kids to college. You just keep the recovery going.

But Bush didn't. And now he's in danger of losing the middle class. Some

Republicans believe that if they lose middle-class votes on the economy, they can get them back with an appeal to values. A Republican strategist told *The New York Times* early this year, "If you look at the middle class as just this monolithic group driven by economic self-interest, I think that's wrong . . . that's what the Democrats are doing right now, and I think they'll get blind-sided by a whole set of values and other issues that will appeal to these voters."

The problem with that argument is that middle-class voters are well educated and tend to be moderate on social issues. Democrats, too, can appeal to their values. If the Supreme Court votes to overturn *Roe v. Wade* this year, Republicans will find themselves on the defensive on values as well as economics.

On social issues, the suburban voters of the 1990s are quite different from the silent majority of the 1970s or the Reagan Democrats of the 1980s. They are not backlash voters. Look at California, the model for the new suburban electorate. Since the passage of Proposition 13, in 1978, California has tended to be tax-averse and stingy with public funds. But it is also one of the most environmentally conscious and pro-choice states in the country.

New Jersey Senator Bill Bradley knows these voters. He is one of them, and he almost got destroyed by their tax revolt in his own state. In a deeply felt and highly personal speech delivered in the Senate last July, Bradley accused President Bush of "inflaming racial tension to perpetuate power and then using that power to reward the rich and ignore the poor." Bradley said to Bush, "You have tried to turn the Willie Horton code of 1988 into the quotas code of 1992."

Bradley's message was a simple and powerful "*J'accuse.*" He didn't accuse Bush of being a racist. He accused him of dividing the country and failing to provide moral leadership. And he came close to accusing Bush of being a hypocrite. "We measure our leader by what he says and by what he does," Bradley said. "If both what he says and what he does are destructive of racial harmony, we must conclude that he wants to destroy racial harmony."

In an interview later in his office, Bradley told me that he believes there are a lot of voters out there who feel the way he does. He described them as "independent suburban voters who are under fifty and who care about civil rights, who care about America's role in the world, who

are concerned about the budget deficit because they are starting to have kids."

He didn't think those voters could be reached by appealing to their racial or economic resentment. One had to appeal to their aspirations and ideals. "They define our national identity partly in terms of ethnic and racial harmony," Bradley explained. The Democrats can get them by exposing the Republicans as the party of divisiveness and intolerance. "They're going to turn off," Bradley said, once they know they're being asked to support "someone whose path to power has been to destroy that harmony, consciously, explicitly, and deliberately."

Bradley is on to something. The swing voters in the electorate today are young, well educated, moderate, and independent. They fill the suburbs of states like New Jersey and California. They have been voting Republican, not because of race but because they see the Democrats as either corrupt or fiscally incompetent. These voters are uncomfortable with the Republican positions on race and abortion; at least, they will be if the Republicans keep pursuing the "southern strategy"—that is, running on the same conservative social values they used in 1988 to portray Michael Dukakis as outside the national mainstream.

A SOUTHERN OR A SUBURBAN STRATEGY?

These days, democratic presidential candidates consistently do worse in the South than in any other part of the country. Even Carter could not hold the South against Reagan in 1980. Democrats can either try to win it back or pursue a suburban or "California" strategy—go for the industrial states of the West Coast, the Midwest, and the Northeast.

Which strategy seems more promising for 1992? If you rank the states by the average vote they gave Jimmy Carter in 1976 and 1980 you get the southern strategy. The two elections in which the Democrats did best in California, relative to the national average, were 1972 and 1988. Those were the years when the Democrats nominated New Politics liberals, George McGovern and Michael Dukakis. If you average the 1972 and 1988 Democratic votes and rank the states, you have the suburban strategy.

There are eleven states (plus the District of Columbia) that the Democrats would have to carry under either strategy to get an electoral-vote majority. The

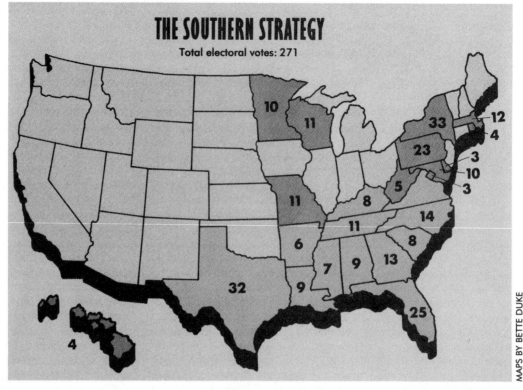

THE SOUTHERN STRATEGY
Total electoral votes: 271

MAPS BY BETTE DUKE

eleven states are West Virginia, Rhode Island, Minnesota, Maryland, Massachusetts, Delaware, New York, Hawaii, Missouri, Pennsylvania, and Wisconsin. These are the Democrats' base. Seven of them are in the North and East. The Democrats averaged 53.5 percent of the vote in these states and the District in 1988. Eight went for Dukakis, while the other four (Pennsylvania, Maryland, Missouri, and Delaware) voted for Bush.

Under the suburban strategy, the Democrats would need to carry eleven additional states, mostly on the West Coast and in the industrial Midwest. Only three of those states went Democratic in 1988. But the vote tended to be close. On average, the eleven states needed for the suburban strategy voted 48.4 percent Democratic in 1988.

The southern strategy also adds eleven new states to the Democratic base. All of them are southern. Not a single one voted for Dukakis in 1988. The Democrats averaged only 41.0 percent of the vote in these eleven states.

This means that it would take a much stronger swing to get the South to vote Democratic in 1992 than it would to build a winning coalition outside the South. Dukakis was supposed to be pursuing a suburban strategy in 1988. In fact, Dukakis did pretty well in the prototypical suburban state, California— 47.6 percent, two points better than he did in the country as a whole. In both

1976 and 1980 Carter did worse in California than he did in the country as a whole. Nevertheless, Democrats know one thing about Dukakis: he was a disaster. He got wiped out in the South, despite the presence of Texas Senator Lloyd Bentsen on the ticket.

The southern strategy is the anti-Dukakis strategy. It targets Reagan Democrats, the white, blue-collar constituency that is Democratic by heritage but has abandoned the Democratic Party in presidential elections since the civil-rights movement of the 1960s. Reagan Democrats tend to be liberal on economic issues (pro-labor, pro-"fairness") and conservative on social issues (race, religion, and foreign policy). In other words, they are populists.

The southern strategy means going after the states where Dukakis was weakest in 1988—and where the Democrats have been weakest for twenty-five years. The alternative is to build strength in the states where Dukakis did relatively well, like California. That requires a suburban strategy, which would target the so-called "new collar" Baby Boom voters. (Southern suburban voters, in contrast, are usually very conservative socially and economically, and therefore much harder for the Democrats to capture.) They are relatively affluent and well educated. They tend to be fiscally conservative and socially liberal, the antithesis of populism. They are independent by heritage

and anti-establishment by inclination. They don't like racial politics. They are pro-choice on abortion. And they feel betrayed by George Bush on the economy.

Ross Perot's prospective candidacy as an independent helps make the case for the suburban strategy. The polls show Perot running strongest in the West. Perot could take enough votes from Bush to tilt this historically Republican region to the Democrats—but only if Clinton makes a credible showing in a region where he, too, is weak.

To win back the middle class, Democrats will have to regain credibility on the issue of economic growth. They will have to persuade the voters that Democrats can manage the economy better than Republicans. The recession gives the Democrats an opportunity—but only an opportunity—to do that.

Bill Clinton, the presumptive Democratic nominee, pitches his message directly at what he calls "the forgotten middle class." He calls on Democrats to abandon the "tax and spend" policies of the past. He criticizes congressional Democrats for contributing to the mismanagement of the economy during the 1980s. He talks about restoring a sense of personal responsibility. That's a subtle way of trying to change the Democratic Party's image. More personal responsibility means less government responsibility. It's a way of saying, "We're not going to have a program for every prob-

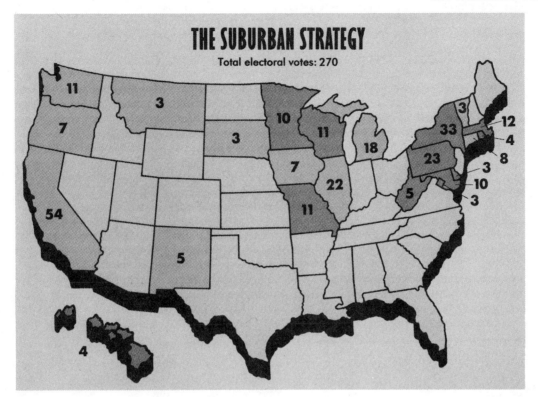

THE SUBURBAN STRATEGY
Total electoral votes: 270

lem. People are basically responsible for themselves. That's the middle-class way."

If New York Governor Mario M. Cuomo had run for President, Bill Clinton would have been Gary Hart, the candidate of new ideas. Instead, after Paul Tsongas won the New Hampshire primary, Clinton was thrust into the role of Walter Mondale, the fairness candidate.

Clinton is not an Old Politics Democrat, however. The candidate who came closest to that message in 1992 was Tom Harkin. Harkin's departure from the race in early March marked a turning point. He was the last New Dealer. None of the other Democrats defended the party's traditional message of taxing, spending, and big government, and its championing of big labor.

In fact, the three Democrats who have done best this year, Clinton, Tsongas, and Jerry Brown, share a skeptical, pragmatic view of government. Clinton, after all, chaired the Democratic Leadership Council, an organization whose objective has been to move the Democratic Party away from interest-group liberalism (and from Jesse Jackson who has referred to the DLC as "Democrats for the Leisure Class"). Clinton's message,

like that of Tsongas, is aimed squarely at the suburban middle class.

Clinton won the primaries by combining the South with the Democrats' shrinking urban base. That is not a formula for victory in November, however. The South is no longer solidly Democratic. And the urban base doesn't have enough votes anymore. The Democrats have to break into the suburbs by proving that they understand something they have never made an effort to understand in the past—namely, the values and priorities of suburban America.

Clinton may be able to do that. But he also has to do something else: overcome unusually strong personal negatives. In some ways Clinton is in the same situation that Ronald Reagan was in 1980. As unpopular as Carter was that year, the votes were afraid of Reagan. They saw him as a right-wing extremist who might start a war or throw old people out in the snow. The election remained a dead heat until the last few days of the campaign, when Reagan took advantage of the final debate to recast the election as a referendum on Carter's record ("Ask yourself,

are you better off than you were four years ago?"). Reagan also reassured the voters that he was not a monster and would not do the foolish things he often said he wanted to do. Things were so bad under Carter that the voters finally decided they had to have change. The country couldn't keep going the way it was going. So they took a chance and elected Reagan.

Bill Clinton has a harder task. He must reassure voters of his basic integrity. He may be able to do it, because he is a skillful and accomplished politician. That is his strength. It is also his weakness, because 1992 is a year when the voters do not seem to be looking for a skillful and accomplished politician—as the rise of Perot, the populist billionaire anti-politician, indicates.

Clinton is a master at having everything both ways. As he tries to straddle the South and the suburbs, the shrinking Democratic base and the swing voters of the middle class, that quality of his political persona and his personal character will be put to the test. In fact, he will face two tests. One test is whether he can do it. The other is whether the voters want someone who can do it.

The Disuniting
of America

Arthur M. Schlesinger, Jr.

The fading away of the cold war has brought an era of ideological conflict to an end. But it has not, as forecast, brought an end to history. One set of hatreds gives way to the next. Lifting the lid of ideological repression in eastern Europe releases ethnic antagonisms deeply rooted in experience and in memory. The disappearance of ideological competition in the third world removes superpower restraints on national and tribal confrontations. As the era of ideological conflict subsides, humanity enters—or, more precisely, re-enters—a possibly more dangerous era of ethnic and racial animosity.

For the mutual antipathy of tribes is one of the oldest things in the world. The history of our planet has been in great part the history of the mixing of peoples. Mass migrations produce mass antagonisms. The fear of the Other is among the most instinctive human reactions. Today, as the twentieth century draws to an end, a number of factors—not just the evaporation of the cold war but, more profoundly, the development of swifter modes of communication and transport, the acceleration of population growth, the breakdown of traditional social structures, the persistence of desperate poverty and want—converge to stimulate mass migrations across national frontiers and thereby to make the mixing of peo-

ples a major problem for the century that lies darkly ahead.

What happens when people of different ethnic origins, speaking different languages and professing different religions, settle in the same geographical locality and live under the same political sovereignty? Unless a common purpose binds them together, tribal hostilities will drive them apart. Ethnic and racial conflict, it seems evident, will now replace the conflict of ideologies as the explosive issue of our times.

On every side today ethnicity is the cause of the breaking of nations. The Soviet Union, Yugoslavia, India, South Africa are all in crisis. Ethnic tensions disturb and divide Sri Lanka, Burma, Ethiopia, Indonesia, Iraq, Lebanon, Israel, Cyprus, Somalia, Nigeria, Liberia, Angola, Sudan, Zaire, Guyana, Trinidad—you name it. Even nations as stable and civilized as Britain and France, Belgium and Spain and Czechoslovakia, face growing ethnic and racial troubles. "The virus of tribalism," says the Economist, "risks becoming the AIDS of international politics—lying dormant for years, then flaring up to destroy countries."

Take the case of our neighbor to the north. Canada has long been considered the most sensible and placid of nations. "Rich, peaceful and, by the standards of

almost anywhere else, enviably successful," the Economist observes: yet today "on the brink of bust-up." Michael Ignatieff (the English-resident son of a Russian-born Canadian diplomat and thus an example of the modern mixing of peoples) writes of Canada, "Here we have one of the five richest nations on earth, a country so uniquely blessed with space and opportunity that the world's poor are beating at the door to get in, and it is tearing itself apart. . . . If one of the top five developed nations on earth can't make a federal, multiethnic state work, who else can?"

The answer to that increasingly vital question has been, at least until recently, the United States.

Now how have Americans succeeded in pulling off this almost unprecedented trick? Other countries break up because they fail to give ethnically diverse peoples compelling reasons to see themselves as part of the same nation. The United States has worked, thus far, because it has offered such reasons. What is it then that, in the absence of a common ethnic origin, has held Americans together over two turbulent centuries? For America was a multiethnic country from the start. Hector St. John de Crèvecoeur emigrated from France to the American colonies in 1759, married an American woman, settled on a farm in Orange County, New York, and published his *Letters from an American Farmer* during the American Revolution. This eighteenth-century French American marveled at the astonishing diversity of the other settlers—"a mixture of English, Scotch, Irish, French, Dutch, Germans, and Swedes," a "strange mixture of blood" that you could find in no other country.

Ethnic and racial conflict will now replace the conflict of ideologies as the explosive issue of our times.

He recalled one family whose grandfather was English, whose wife was Dutch, whose son married a Frenchwoman, and whose present four sons had married women of different nationalities. "From this promiscuous breed," he wrote, "that race now called Americans have arisen." (The word *race* as used in the eighteenth and nineteenth centuries meant what we mean by nationality today; thus people spoke of "the English race," "the German race," and so on.) What, Crèvecoeur mused, were the characteristics of this suddenly emergent American race? *Letters from an American Farmer* propounded a famous question: "What then is the American, this new man?" (Twentieth-century readers must overlook eighteenth-century male obliviousness to the existence of women.)

Crèvecoeur gave his own question its classic answer: *"He is an American, who leaving behind him all his ancient prejudices and manners, receives new ones from the new mode of life he has embraced, the new government he obeys, and the new rank he holds. The American is a new man, who acts upon new principles. . . . Here individuals of all nations are melted into a new race of men."*

E pluribus unum. The United States had a brilliant solution for the inherent divisibility of a multiethnic society: the creation of a brand-new national identity, carried forward by individuals who, in forsaking old loyalties and joining to make new lives, melted away ethnic differences. Those intrepid Europeans who had torn up their roots to brave the wild Atlantic *wanted* to forget a horrid past

and to embrace a hopeful future. They *expected* to become Americans. Their goals were escape, deliverance, assimilation. They saw America as a transforming nation, banishing dismal yesterdays and developing a unique national character based on common political ideals and shared experiences. The point of America was not to preserve old cultures, but to forge a new *American* culture.

One reason why Canada, despite all its advantages, is so vulnerable to schism is that, as Canadians freely admit, their country lacks such a unique national identity. Attracted variously to Britain, France, and the United States, inclined for generous reasons to respect diverse ethnic inheritances, Canadians have never developed a strong sense of what it is to be a Canadian. As Sir John Macdonald, their first prime minister, put it, Canada has "too much geography and too little history."

The United States has had plenty of history. From the Revolution on, Americans have had a powerful national creed. The vigorous sense of national identity accounts for our relative success in converting Crèvecoeur's "promiscuous breed" into one people and thereby making a multiethnic society work.

This is not to say that the United States has ever fulfilled Crèvecoeur's ideal. New waves of immigration brought in people who fitted awkwardly into a society that was inescapably English in language, ideals, and institutions. For a long time the Anglo-Americans dominated American culture and politics. The pot did not melt everybody, not even all the white immigrants.

As for the nonwhite peoples—those long in America whom the European newcomers overran and massacred, or those others brought against their will from Africa and Asia—deeply bred racism put them all—red Americans, black Americans, yellow Americans, brown Americans—well outside the pale. The curse of racism was the great failure of the American experiment, the glaring contradiction of American ideals and the still crippling disease of American life.

Yet even nonwhite Americans, miserably treated as they were, contributed to the formation of the national identity. They became members, if third-class members, of American society and helped give the common culture new form and flavor. The infusion of non-Anglo stocks and the experience of the New World steadily reconfigured the British legacy

and made the United States, as we all know, a very different country today from Britain.

Crèvecoeur's vision of America prevailed through most of the two centuries of the history of the United States. But the twentieth century has brought forth a new and opposing vision. One world war destroyed the old order of things and launched Woodrow Wilson's doctrine of the self-determination of peoples. Twenty years after, a second world war dissolved the western colonial empires and intensified ethnic and racial militancy around the planet. In the United States itself new laws eased entry for immigrants from South America, Asia, and Africa and altered the composition of the American people.

In a nation marked by an even stranger mixture of blood than Crèvecoeur had known, his celebrated question is asked once more, with a new passion—and a new answer. Today many Americans turn away from the historic goal of "a new race of man." The escape from origins has given way to the search for roots. The "ancient prejudices and manners" disowned by Crèvecoeur have made a surprising comeback. A cult of ethnicity has arisen both among non-Anglo whites and among nonwhite minorities.

The eruption of ethnicity had many good consequences. The American culture began at last to give shamefully overdue recognition to the achievements of minorities subordinated and spurned during the high noon of Anglo dominance. American education began at last to acknowledge the existence and significance of the great swirling world beyond Europe. All this was to the good. Of course history should be taught from a variety of perspectives. Let our children try to imagine the arrival of Columbus from the viewpoint of those who met him as well as from those who sent him. Living on a shrinking planet, aspiring to global leadership, Americans must learn much more about other races, other cultures, other continents. As they do, they acquire a more complex and invigorating sense of the world—and of themselves.

But, pressed too far, the cult of ethnicity has had bad consequences too. The new ethnic gospel rejects Crèvecoeur's vision of individuals from all nations melted into a new race. Its underlying philosophy is that America is not a nation of individuals at all but a nation of groups, that ethnicity is the defining experience for most Americans, that ethnic

The curse of racism was the great failure of the American experiment, the glaring contradiction of American ideals and the still crippling disease of American life.

ties are permanent and indelible, and that division into ethnic groups establishes the basic structure of American society and the basic meaning of American history.

Implicit in this philosophy is the classification of all Americans according to ethnic and racial criteria. But while the ethnic interpretation of American history like the economic interpretation, is valid and illuminating up to a point, it is fatally misleading and wrong when presented as the whole picture. The ethnic interpretation, moreover, reverses the historic theory of America—the theory that has thus far managed to keep American society whole.

Instead of a transformative nation with an identity all its own, America increasingly sees itself in this new light as preservative of diverse alien identities. Instead of a nation composed of individuals making their own unhampered choices, America increasingly sees itself as composed of groups more or less ineradicable in their ethnic character. The multiethnic dogma abandons historic purposes, replacing assimilation by fragmentation, integration by separatism. It belittles *unum* and glorifies *pluribus*.

The historic idea of a transcendent and unifying American identity is now in peril in many arenas—in our politics, our voluntary organizations, our churches, our language. And in no arena is the erosion of faith in an overriding national identity more crucial than in our system of education.

The schools and colleges of the republic train the citizens of the future. Our public schools in particular have been the historic mechanisms for the transmission of the ideal of "one people." What students are taught in schools affects the way they will thereafter see and treat other Americans, the way they will thereafter conceive the purposes of the republic. The debate about the curriculum is a debate about what it means to be an American.

The militants of ethnicity now contend that a main objective of public education should be the protection, strengthening, celebration, and perpetuation of ethnic origins and identities. Separatism, however, magnifies differences and stirs antagonisms. The consequent increase in ethnic and racial conflict lies behind the hullabaloo over "multiculturalism" and "political correctness," over the iniquities of the "Eurocentric" curriculum, and over the notion that history and literature should be taught not as intellectual disciplines but as therapies whose function is to raise minority self-esteem.

One wonders. Do not the ethnic militants see any dangers in a society divided into distinct and immutable ethnic and racial groups, each taught to cherish its own apartness from the rest? What is ultimately at stake is the shape of the American future. Will the center hold? or will the melting pot give way to the Tower of Babel?

I don't want to sound apocalyptic about these developments. Education is always in ferment, and a good thing too. Schools and colleges have always been battlegrounds for debates over beliefs, philosophies, values. The situation in our universities, I am confident, will soon right itself once the great silent majority of professors cry "enough" and challenge what they know to be voguish nonsense.

The impact of ethnic and racial pressures on our public schools is more troubling. The bonds of national cohesion are sufficiently fragile already. Public education should aim to strengthen those bonds, not to weaken them. If separatist tendencies go on unchecked, the result can only be the fragmentation, resegregation, and tribalization of American life.

I remain optimistic. My impression is that the historic forces driving toward "one people" have not lost their power. For most Americans this is still what the republic is all about. They resist extremes in the argument between "unity first" and "ethnicity first." "Most Americans," Governor Mario Cuomo has well said, "can understand both the need to recognize and encourage an enriched diversity as well as the need to ensure that such a broadened multicultural perspective leads to unity and an enriched sense of what being an American is, and not to a destructive factionalism that would tear us apart."

Whatever their self-appointed spokesmen may claim, most American-born members of minority groups, white or nonwhite, while they may cherish particular heritages, still see themselves primarily as Americans and not primarily as Irish or Hungarians or Jews or Africans or Asians. A telling indicator is the rising rate of intermarriage across ethnic, religious, even (increasingly) racial lines. The belief in a unique American identity is far from dead.

But the burden to unify the country does not fall exclusively on the minorities. Assimilation and integration constitute a two-way street. Those who want to join America must be received and welcomed by those who already think they own America. Racism, as I have noted, has been the great national tragedy. In recent times white America has at last begun to confront the racism so deeply and shamefully inbred in our history. But the triumph over racism is incomplete. When old-line Americans, for example, treat people of other nationalities and races as if they were indigestible elements to be shunned and barred, they must not be surprised if minorities gather bitterly unto themselves and damn everybody else. Not only must *they* want assimilation and integration; *we* must want assimilation and integration too. The burden to make this a unified country lies as much with the complacent majority as with the sullen and resentful minorities.

The American population has unquestionably grown more heterogeneous than ever in recent times. But this very heterogeneity makes the quest for unifying ideals and common culture all the more urgent. And in a world savagely rent by ethnic and racial antagonisms, it is all the more essential that the United States continue as an example of how a highly differentiated society holds itself together.

Low self-esteem is too deep a malady to be cured by hearing nice things about one's own ethnic past. Institutionalized separatism only crystallizes racial differences and magnifies racial tensions.

THE DECOMPOSITION OF AMERICA

Low self-esteem is too deep a malady to be cured by hearing nice things about one's own ethnic past. History is not likely to succeed where psychiatry fails. Afrocentrism in particular is an escape from the hard and expensive challenges of our society—the need for safer schools, better teachers, better teaching materials, greater investment in education; the need for stable families that can nourish self-discipline and aspiration; the need for jobs and income that can nourish stable families; the need to stop the ravages of drugs and crime; the need to overcome the racism still lurking in the interstices of American society. "The need," William Raspberry observes of his own people, "is not to reach back for some culture we never knew but to lay full claim to the culture in which we exist."

I

The ethnicity rage in general and Afrocentricity in particular not only divert attention from the real needs but exacerbate the problems. The recent apotheosis of ethnicity, black, brown, red, yellow, white, has revived the dismal prospect that in happy melting-pot days Americans thought the republic was moving safely beyond—that is, a society fragmented into ethnic groups. The cult of ethnicity exaggerates differences, intensifies resentments and antagonisms, drives ever deeper the awful wedges between races and nationalities. The end game is self-pity and self-ghettoization.

Now there is a reasonable argument in the black case for a measure of regrouping and self-reliance as part of the preparation for entry into an integrated society on an equal basis. Integration on any other basis, it is contended, would mean total capitulation to white standards. Affirmation of racial and cultural pride is thus essential to true integration. One can see this as a psychological point, but as a cultural point?

For generations blacks have grown up in an American culture, on which they have had significant influence and to which they have made significant contributions. Self-Africanization after 300 years in America is playacting. Afrocentricity as expounded by ethnic ideologues implies Europhobia, separatism, emotions of alienation, victimization, paranoia. Most curious and unexpected

of all is a black demand for the return of black-white segregation.

"To separate [black children] from others of similar age and qualifications solely because of their race," Chief Justice Warren wrote in the school-integration case, "generates a feeling of inferiority as to their status in the community that may affect their hearts and minds in a way unlikely ever to be undone." In 40 years doctrine has come full circle. Now integration is held to bring feelings of inferiority, and segregation to bring the cure.

This revival of separatism will begin, if the black educator Felix Boateng has his way, in the earliest grades. "The use of standard English as the only language of instruction," Boateng argues, "aggravates the process of deculturalization." A "culturally relevant curriculum" for minority children would recognize "the home and community dialect they bring to school." (Not all black educators, it

---

The militants of ethnicity now contend that a main objective of public education should be the protection, strengthening, celebration, and perpetuation of ethnic origins and identities.

---

should be said, share this desire to handicap black children from infancy.) "One fact is clear," notes Janice Hale-Benson of Cleveland State University "Speaking standard English is a skill needed by Black children for upward mobility in American society and it should be taught in early childhood.")

If any educational institution should bring people together as individuals in friendly and civil association, it should be the university. But the fragmentation of campuses in recent years into a multitude of ethnic organizations is spectacular—and disconcerting.

One finds black dormitories, black student unions, black fraternities and sororities, black business and law societies, black homosexual and lesbian groups, black tables in dining halls. Stanford, Dinesh D'Souza reports, has "ethnic theme houses." The University of Pennsylvania gives blacks—6 percent of the

enrollment—their own yearbook. Campuses today, according to one University of Pennsylvania professor, have "the cultural diversity of Beirut. There are separate armed camps. The black kids don't mix with the white kids. The Asians are off by themselves. Oppression is the great status symbol."

Oberlin was for a century and half the model of a racially integrated college. "Increasingly," Jacob Weisberg, an editor at *The New Republic,* reports, "Oberlin students think, act, study, and live apart." Asians live in Asia House, Jews in "J" House, Latinos in Spanish House, blacks in African-Heritage House, foreign students in Third World House. Even the Lesbian, Gay, and Bisexual Union has broken up into racial and gender factions. "The result is separate worlds."

Huddling is an understandable reaction for any minority group faced with new and scary challenges. But institutionalized separatism only crystallizes racial differences and magnifies racial tensions. "Certain activities are labeled white and black," says a black student at Central Michigan University. "If you don't just participate in black activities, you are shunned." A recent study by the black anthropologist Signithia Fordham of Rutgers concludes that a big reason for black underachievement is the fear that academic success will be taken as a sellout to the white world. "What appears to have emerged in some segments of the black community," Fordham says, "is a kind of cultural orientation which defines academic learning in school as 'acting white.'"

Militants further argue that because only blacks can comprehend the black experience, only blacks should teach black history and literature, as, in the view of some feminists, only women should teach women's history and literature. "True diversity," according to the faculty's Budget Committee at the University of California at Berkeley, requires that courses match the ethnic and gender identities of the professors.

The doctrine that *only* blacks can teach and write black history leads inexorably to the doctrine that blacks can teach and write *only* black history as well as to inescapable corollaries: Chinese must be restricted to Chinese history, women to women's history, and so on. Henry Louis Gates criticizes "ghettoized programs where students and members of the faculty sit around and argue about whether a white person can think a black thought." As for the notion that there is a "mystique" about black studies that requires a person to have black skin in order to pursue them—that, John Hope Franklin observes succinctly, is "voodoo."

The voodoo principle is extended from scholarship to the arts. Thus the fine black playwright August Wilson insists on a black director for the film if his play *Fences.* "We have a different way of responding to the world," Wilson explains. "We have different ideas about religion, different manners of social intercourse. We have different ideas about style, about language. We have different esthetics [*sic*]. . . . The job requires someone who shares the specifics of the culture of black Americans. . . . Let's make a rule. Blacks don't direct Italian films. Italians don't direct Jewish films. Jews don't direct black American films." What a terrible rule that would be!

In the same restrictive spirit, Actors' Equity tried to prevent the British actor Jonathan Pryce from playing in New York the role he created in London in *Miss Saigon,* announcing that it could not condone "the casting of a Caucasian actor in the role of a Eurasian." (Pryce responded that, if this doctrine prevails, "I'd be stuck playing Welshmen for the rest of my life.") Equity did not, however, apply the same principle to the black actors Morgan Freeman and Denzel Washington who were both acting in Shakespeare at that time in New York. *The Wall Street Journal* acidly suggested that, according to the principle invoked, not only whites but the disabled should protest the casting of Denzel Washington as Richard III because Washington lacked a hunchback.

The distinguished black social psychologist Kenneth B. Clark, whose findings influenced the Supreme Court's decision in the school-integration case, rejects the argument that blacks and whites must be separated "because they represent different cultures and that cultures, like oil and water, cannot mix." This, Clark says, is what white segregationists have argued for generations. He adds, "There is absolutely no evidence to support the contention that the inherent damage to human beings of primitive exclusion on the basis of race is any less damaging when demanded or enforced by the previous victims than when imposed by the dominant group."

II

The separatist impulse is by no means confined to the black community. Another salient expression is the bilingualism movement, ostensibly conducted in the interests of all non-English speakers but particularly a Hispanic-American project.

Bilingualism is hardly a new issue in American history. Seven years after the adoption of the Constitution, a proposal to print 3,000 sets of federal laws in German as well as English was narrowly defeated in the House of Representatives. (This incident gave rise to the myth, later cherished by Nazi propagandists like Colin Ross, that German had nearly displaced English as America's official language.) In the nineteenth century, newly arrived immigrants stayed for a season with their old language, used it in their homes, churches, newspapers, and not seldom in bilingual public schools, until acculturation reduced and the First World War discouraged the use of languages other than English.

The separatist impulse is by no means confined to the black community. Another salient expression is the bilingualism movement.

In recent years the combination of the ethnicity cult with a flood of immigration from Spanish-speaking countries has given bilingualism new impetus. The presumed purpose is transitional: to move non-English-speaking children as quickly as possible from bilingual into all-English classes. The Bilingual Education Act of 1968 supplies guidelines and funding; the 1974 Supreme Court decision in *Lau v. Nichols* (a Chinese-speaking case) requires school districts to provide special programs for children who do not know English.

Alas, bilingualism has not worked out as planned: rather the contrary. Testimony is mixed, but indications are that bilingual education retards rather than expedites the movement of Hispanic children into the English-speaking world and that it promotes segregation more than it does integration. Bilingualism shuts doors. It nourishes self-ghettoization, and ghettoization nourishes racial antagonism. Bilingualism "encourages concentrations of Hispanics to stay together and not be integrated," says Alfredo

Mathew, Jr., a Hispanic civic leader, and it may well foster "a type of apartheid that will generate animosities with others, such as Blacks, in the competition for scarce resources, and further alienate the Hispanic from the larger society."

Using some language other than English dooms people to second-class citizenship in American society. "Those who have the most to lose in a bilingual America," says the Mexican-American writer Richard Rodriguez, "are the foreign-speaking poor." Rodriguez recalls his own boyhood: "It would have pleased me to hear my teachers address me in Spanish. . . . But I would have delayed . . . having to learn the language of public society. . . . Only when I was able to think of myself as an American, no longer an alien in *gringo* society, could I seek the rights and opportunities necessary for full public individuality."

Monolingual education opens doors to the larger world. "I didn't speak English until I was about 8 years of age," Governor Mario Cuomo recently recalled, "and there was a kind of traumatic entry into public school. It made an immense impression on me." Traumatic or not, public school taught Cuomo the most effective English among politicos of his generation.

Yet a professor at the University of Massachusetts told Rosalie Pedalino Porter, whose long experience in bilingual education led to her excellent book *Forked Tongue,* that teaching English to children reared in another language is a form of political oppression. Her rejoinder seems admirable: "When we succeed in helping our students use the majority language fluently . . . we are empowering our students rather than depriving them."

Panicky conservatives, fearful that the republic is over the hill, call for a constitutional amendment to make English the official language of the United States. Seventeen states already have such statutes. This is a poor idea. The English language does not need statutory reinforcement and the drive for an amendment will only increase racial discrimination and resentment.

Nonetheless, a common language is a necessary bond of national cohesion in so heterogeneous a nation as America. The bilingual campaign has created both an educational establishment with a vested interest in extending the bilingual empire and a political lobby with a vested interest in retaining a Hispanic constituency. Like Afrocentricity and the ethnicity cult, bilingualism is an elitist, not a popular, movement—"romantic ethnicity," as Myrdal called it; political ethnicity too. Still, institutionalized bilingualism remains another source of the fragmentation of America, another threat to the dream of "one people."

III

Most ominous about the separatist impulse is the meanness generated when one group is set against another. What Harold Isaacs, that acute student of racial sensitivities and resentments, called the "built-in we-they syndrome" has caused more dominating, fearing, hating, killing than any other single cause since time began.

Blacks, having suffered most grievously (at least in America) from persecution, have perhaps the greatest susceptibility to paranoia—remembering always that even paranoids may have real enemies. After all, considering what we now know about the plots against black Americans concocted by J. Edgar Hoover and executed by his FBI, who can blame blacks for being forever suspicious of white intentions?

Still, the *New York Times*—WCBS-TV poll of New Yorkers in 1990 is startling. Sixty percent of black respondents thought it true or possibly true that the government was making drugs available in black neighborhoods in order to harm black people. Twenty-nine percent thought it true or possibly true that the AIDS virus was invented by racist conspirators to kill blacks.

When Mayor Edward Koch invited the irrepressible Leonard Jeffries of CCNY to breakfast to discuss the "ice people-sun people" theory, Jeffries agreed to come "but said he would not eat because white people were trying to poison him. When he arrived," Koch reports, "I offered him coffee and danish, but he refused it. I then offered to be his food taster, but he still declined."

On another occasion, Jeffries observed that "AIDS coming out of a laboratory and finding itself localized in certain populations certainly has to be looked at as part of a conspiratorial process." After a Jeffries class, 10 black students told the *Times* reporter that AIDS and drugs were indeed part of a white conspiracy. "During the Carter administration," one said, "There was a document put out that said by the year

2000, one hundred million Africans had to be destroyed." "Because of who's being devastated the most, and growing up in the U.S. and knowing the history of slavery and racism in this country," an older black man said, "you can't be black and not feel that AIDS is some kind of experiment, some kind of plot to hit undesirable minority populations."

Nor is such speculation confined to the feverish sidewalks of New York. "Let me make a speech before a black audience," testifies William Raspberry, "and sometime during the Q & A someone is

---

A common language is a necessary bond of national cohesion in so heterogeneous a nation as America.

---

certain to ask if I believe there is a conspiracy against black Americans. It doesn't matter whether the subject is drugs or joblessness, school failure or teen pregnancy, politics or immigration. I can count on hearing some version of the conspiracy question."

The black case is only a more extreme version of the persecution complex—the feeling that someone is out to get them—to which nearly all minorities on occasion succumb. Mutual suspicion and hostility are bound to emerge in a society bent on defining itself in terms of jostling and competing groups.

IV

"The era that began with the dream of integration," Richard Rodriguez has observed, "ended up with scorn for assimilation." Instead of casting off the foreign skin, as John Quincy Adams had stipulated, never to resume it, the fashion is to resume the foreign skin as conspicuously as can be. The cult of ethnicity has reversed the movement of American history, producing a nation of minorities or at least of minority spokesmen—less interested in joining with the majority in common endeavor than in declaring their alienation from an oppressive, white, patriarchal, racist, sexist, classist society. The ethnic ideology inculcates the illusion that membership in one or another ethnic group is the basic American experience.

Most Americans, it is true, continue to see themselves primarily as individuals and only secondarily and trivially as adherents of a group. Nor is harm done when ethnic groups display pride in their historic past or in their contributions to the American present. But the division of society into fixed ethnicities nourishes a culture of victimization and a contagion of inflammable sensitivities. And when a vocal and visible minority pledges primary allegiance to their groups, whether ethnic, sexual, religious, or, in rare cases (communist, fascist), political, it presents a threat to the brittle bonds of national identity that hold this diverse and fractious society together.

A peculiarly ugly mood seems to have settled over the one arena where freedom of inquiry and expression should be most unconstrained and civility most respected—our colleges and universities. It is no fun running a university these days. Undergraduates can be wanton and cruel in their exclusion, their harassment, their heavy pranks, their wounding invective. Minority students, for the most understandable reasons, are often vulnerable and frightened. Racial cracks, slurs, insults, vilification pose difficult problems. Thus posters appear around the campus at the University of Michigan parodying the slogan of the United Negro College Fund: A MIND IS A TERRIBLE THING TO WASTE—ESPECIALLY ON A NIGGER. Decent white students join the protest against white bullies and thugs.

Presidents and deans begin to ask themselves, which is more important—protecting free speech or preventing racial persecution? The Constitution, Justice Holmes said, embodies "the principle of free thought—not free thought for those who agree with us but freedom for the thought that we hate." But suppose the thought we hate undercuts the Constitution's ideal of equal justice under law? Does not the First Amendment protect equality as well as liberty? How to draw a bright line between speech and behavior?

One has a certain sympathy for besieged administrators who, trying to do their best to help minority students, adopt regulations to restrict racist and sexist speech. More than a hundred institutions, according to the American Civil Liberties Union, had done so by February 1991. My own decided preference is to stand by the First Amendment and to fight speech by speech, not by censorship. But then, I am not there on the firing line.

The black case is only a more extreme version of the persecution complex to which nearly all minorities on occasion succumb.

One can even understand why administrators, not sure what best to do for minorities and eager to keep things quiet, accept—even subsidize—separatist remedies urged by student militants. They might, however, ponder Kenneth Clark's comment: "The white liberal . . . who concedes black separatism so hastily and benevolently must look to his own reasons, not the least of them perhaps an exquisite relief." And it is sad, though instructive, that the administrations especially disposed to encourage racial and ethnic enclaves—like Berkeley, Michigan, Oberlin, the University of Massachusetts at Amherst—are, Dinesh D'Souza (himself an Indian from India) points out, the ones experiencing the most racial tension. Troy Duster, a Berkeley sociologist, finds a correlation between group separatism and racial hostility among students.

Moderates who would prefer fending for themselves as individuals are bullied into going along with their group. Groups get committed to platforms and to we-they syndromes. Faculty members appease. A code of ideological orthodoxy emerges. The code's guiding principle is that nothing should be said that might give offense to members of minority groups (and, apparently, that anything can be said that gives offense to white males of European origin).

The Office of Student Affairs at Smith College has put out a bulletin listing types of oppression for people belatedly "realizing that they are oppressed." Some samples of the Smith litany of sins:

ABLEISM: Oppression of the differently abled by the temporarily able.

HETEROSEXISM: Oppression of those of sexual orientation other than heterosexual, such as gays, lesbians, and bisexuals; this can take place by not acknowledging their existence.

LOOKISM: The belief that appearance is an indicator of a person's value; the construction of a standard for beauty/attractiveness; and oppression through stereotypes and generalizations of both those who do not fit that standard and those who do.

Can they be kidding up there in Northampton? The code imposes standards of what is called, now rather derisively, "political correctness." What began as a means of controlling student incivility threatens to become, formally or informally, a means of controlling curricula and faculty too. Clark University asks professors proposing courses to explain how "pluralistic (minority, women, etc.) views and concerns are explored and integrated in this course." A philosopher declined to sign, doubting that the university would ask professors to explain how "patriotic and pro-family values are explored and integrated."

Two distinguished American historians at Harvard, Bernard Bailyn and Stephan Thernstrom, offered a course in population history called "The Peopling of America." Articles appeared in the *Harvard Crimson* criticizing the professors for "racial insensitivity," and black students eventually presented them with a bill of particulars. Thernstrom, an advocate of ethnic history, the editor of the *Harvard Encyclopedia* of *American Ethnic Groups,* was accused of racism. He had, it developed, used the term "Indians" instead of "Native Americans." He had also referred to "Oriental" religion—the adjective was deemed "colonial and imperialistic." Bailyn had recommended diaries of Southern planters without recommending slave narratives. And so on, for six single-spaced pages.

The episode reminds one of the right-wing students who in Joe McCarthy days used to haunt the classrooms of liberal Harvard professors (like me) hoping to catch whiffs of Marxism emanating from the podium. Thernstrom decided to hell with it and gave up the course. A signal triumph for political correctness.

Those who stand up for what they believe invite smear campaigns. A favorite target these days is Diane Ravitch of Columbia's Teachers College, a first-class historian of American education, an enlightened advocate of school reform, and a steadfast champion of cultural pluralism. She is dedicated to reasoned and temperate argument and is perseveringly conciliatory rather than polemical in her approach. Perhaps the fact that she is a woman persuades ethnic chauvinists that they can bully her. Despite nasty efforts at intimidation, she continues to expose the perils of ethnocentrism with calm lucidity.

Ravitch's unpardonable offense seems to be her concern about *unum* as well as about *pluribus*—her belief that history should help us understand how bonds of cohesion make us a nation rather than an irascible collection of unaffiliated groups. For in the end, the cult of ethnicity defines the republic not as a polity of individuals but as a congeries of distinct and inviolable cultures. When a student sent a memorandum to the "diversity education committee" at the University of Pennsylvania mentioning her "deep regard for the individual," a college administrator returned the paper with the word *individual* underlined: "This is a *red flag* phrase today, which is considered by many to be *racist*. Arguments that champion the individual over the group ultimately privileges [sic] the 'individuals' belonging to the largest or dominant group."

The contemporary sanctification of the group puts the old idea of a coherent society at stake. Multicultural zealots reject as hegemonic the notion of a shared commitment to common ideals. How far the discourse has come from Crèvecoeur's "new race" from Tocqueville's civic participation, from Emerson's "smelting pot," from Bryce's "amazing solvent," from Myrdal's "American Creed"!

Yet what has held the American people together in the absence of a common ethnic origin has been precisely a common adherence to ideals of democracy and human rights that, too often transgressed in practice, forever goad us to narrow the gap between practice and principle.

The American synthesis has an inevitable Anglo-Saxon coloration, but it is no longer an exercise in Anglo-Saxon domination. The republic embodies ideals that transcend ethnic, religious, and political lines. It is an experiment, reasonably successful for a while, in creating a common identity for people of diverse races, religions, languages, cultures. But

What has held the American people together has been precisely a common adherence to ideals of democracy and human rights that forever goad us to narrow the gap between practice and principle.

the experiment can continue to succeed only so long as Americans continue to believe in the goal. If the republic now turns away from Washington's old goal of "one people," what is its future?—disintegration of the national community, apartheid, Balkanization, tribalization?

"The one absolutely certain way of bringing this nation to ruin, of preventing all possibility of its continuing to be a nation at all," said Theodore Roosevelt, "would be to permit it to become a tangle of squabbling nationalities, an intricate knot of German-Americans, Irish-Americans, English-Americans, French-Americans, Scandinavian-Americans, or Italian-Americans, each preserving its separate nationality." Three-quarters of a century later we must add a few more nationalities to T.R.'s brew. This only strengthens his point.

The Painful Demise of Eurocentrism

Arthur Schlesinger cannot see his own Anglo-Saxon bias nor multiculturalism's nourishing contribution to America's core identity.

Molefi Kete Asante

Molefi Kete Asante is professor and chair of the Department of African American Studies at Temple University. He is the author of thirty-two books including three seminal works on the Afrocentric philosophy Afrocentricity, The Afrocentric Idea, *and* Kemet, Afrocentricity, and Knowledge.

Arthur Schlesinger, Jr., won Pulitzer prizes for his books *The Age of Jackson* (1945) and *A Thousand Days* (1965). These works and the *Age of Roosevelt, The Imperial Presidency,* and *Robert Kennedy and His Times* established him as a leading American historian. Yet Schlesinger's latest book, *The Disuniting of America,* serves to call into question his understanding of American history and his appreciation of diversity. As a designated great American historian, he is supposed to know something about what he writes. However, one of the most obvious manifestations of hegemonic thinking in cultural matters is pontification. Measuring the amount of pontification in *The Disuniting of America,* one comes away with a certain distrust of Schlesinger's writing as well as his perspective on American society. This is doubly so if one is an African American.

Schlesinger envisions an America rooted in the past, where whites, actually Anglo-Saxon whites, defined the protocols of American society, and white culture itself represented the example to which others were forced to aspire. He loves this vision because it provides a psycho-logical justification for the dominance of European culture in America over others. In his vision, there is little history of enslavement, oppression, dispossession, racism, or exploitation. In effect, there is no disunion in the Union; adjustments need to be made, for sure, but they are minor ripples in the perfect society. Fortunately, many whites as well as African Americans see this vision as corrupted by the arrogance of political, academic, and cultural dominance. How, they ask, can one have such a vision of America with what we know of our history? Yet this is Schlesinger's perspective on American society.

Alas, the vision is clouded by Afro-centrists, the bad guys in Schlesinger's book, who bring disunity to this perfect world. Trapped in his own cultural prison, Schlesinger is unable to see the present American cultural reality, and I believe he has missed the point of the past as well. The evidence suggests that he holds a nearly static view of America. Perhaps the America of his youth—its academic life, social life, business environment, and political institutions—was framed for him in some version of the white American dream.

There is, of course, a nightmarish side to Schlesinger's vision or fantasy. He peoples his vision with negations, col-ored by axioms that support no truth but that are ultimately structured to uphold the status quo of white male privilege and domination. Had Schlesinger admit-ted this as a goal of his book, it would have allowed a more honest footing for discussion and debate. Nevertheless, this mixture of fact and fiction presents itself for analytical deinvention, not national disunity.

DISUNION AND DISBELIEF

Schlesinger might have cited any number of issues as disuniting America: unequal protection under the law, taxation without representation, gender strife, economic class antagonisms, corrupt politicians, rampant anti-Africanism, growing anti-Semitism, or pollution of the environment. Instead, he focuses on the African-American challenge to the educational system, calling it a disuniting element; indeed, he believes it is a fright-ening development. Why should an Afrocentric position—that is, a position where Africans describe themselves as subjects rather than objects—create such an uproar?[1]

Are we to conclude that Schlesinger does not see the hegemonic imposition of the Eurocentric idea? Or do we conclude that he sees it and understands it and supports it? If he does not see it, then he will not understand the substance of what I am saying in this essay. Hegemonic thinking is like a person standing on the lid of a manhole. The fact that another person will rise out of that manhole means that the person standing on the lid will have to change positions.

---

1. See Molefi Kete Assante, *The Afrocentric Idea* (Philadelphia: Temple University press, 1987).

From *The World & I*, April 1992, pp. 305-317. *The World & I*, a publication of The Washington Times Corporation. Copyright © 1992.

Will the Afrocentric perspective affect the Eurocentric hegemony on information and in education? Absolutely, because our perceptions are altered by new information whether we admit it or not. A lifetime of delusion that denies Africans and Africa a place in human history creates a basic disbelief in facts that are presented in an Afrocentric framework. Indeed, *The Age of Jackson* did not indicate any real appreciation of the nature of Jackson's racism and anti-Indian sentiments. Schlesinger's glorification of Andrew Jackson, whom even Davy Crockett considered a scoundrel, is demonstrative of Schlesinger's disregard for the multiethnic, multicultural, pluralistic reality of American society.

Schlesinger envisions an America rooted in the past, where whites, actually Anglo-Saxon whites, represented the example to which others were forced to aspire.

One must be factual, and in trying to be factual I have always believed primary description is better than secondary interpretation. Thus, when Afrocentrists say that George Washington and Thomas Jefferson were slaveowners, *inter alia,* who did not believe in the equality of Africans, that is a fact descriptive of those two individuals. One can excuse the fact on the grounds of interpretation, one can claim ignorance, one can argue that their good points outweighed their bad points, and so on; but the fact is that they believed in the inferiority of Africans. Students must be introduced to this factual information in order to make proper assessments and judgments. Schlesinger would insist that we not mention the racist heritage of the "founding fathers" because that would create disunity. If that be creating disunity, I am guilty, as he claims in his book, and I will create more disunity. Nothing is more valuable than the truth in bringing about national integration.

Eurocentric control of space and time in publishing and the media has meant that legitimate intellectual and scholarly voices of African Americans are seldom heard by whites who refuse to read Afri

can-American scholarly journals. The *Journal of Black Studies,* the *Journal of Negro Education,* the *Journal of African Civilizations, Western Journal of Black Studies,* and *Imhotep* are a few of the prominent journals that are accessible to scholars. They remain relatively unread by writers such as Schlesinger, who apparently believes that there is little outside of the "white" journals worth reading. That is a serious mistake in scholarship, because reading the African-American journals would greatly increase appreciation for new findings and new ideas.

Can Schlesinger really believe that only whites or blacks who believe they are white have reasonable ideas? Afrocentrists, who got their degrees from the same institutions as white scholars, tend to have a far broader reading program that allows for more critical leverage to analysis. The fact that cyclopean stone tombs dating from 5700 B.C., among the earliest in the world, have been found in the heart of the Central African Republic may not be a part of one's knowledge base, but if it were known, it would add to any discussion of historical time lines. Yet without reading any of my books or those of other Afrocentrists in depth, as far as I can discern, Schlesinger attempts to paint Afrocentrists as some kind of wild bunch out to create disunity in American society.

What this celebrated white American historian seeks is a dismissal of historical facts related to Africans as insignificant in the American nation. He seems to operate within a closed system of thought, and such systems are prodigious in producing closed minds. Education within such a system is found to produce those who speak a certain restrictive language, use a handed-down political vocabulary, and believe in elves.

Try to make Africans and Asians copies of Europeans and women copies of men and you will force the disunity Schlesinger fears.

The danger, quite frankly, is that Schlesinger's attitude toward difference creates insiders and outsiders, those who are free to define themselves and others and those who are the defined. There is

no question in his mind about who will do the defining. Afrocentrists flatly reject this kind of thinking and insist on defining their own reality within the context of society.

To be Afrocentric is not to deny American citizenship. Just as to be a Chinese American, live in Chinatown, employ Chinese motifs in artistic expression, and worship Buddha is not anti-American, the person who believes that the African American must be recentered, relocated in terms of historical referent, is not anti-American. This is neither a destructive nor a disuniting behavior. It suggests the strengths of this country compared to other countries. The conviction that we will defend the rights of all cultural expressions, not just Greco-Roman-Hebraic-Germanic-Viking cultures, must be strongly embedded in our political psyches if the nation is to survive.

In this way we avoid what I call the Soviet problem, that is, the Russification of the empire. Respect for each other's culture must be the guiding principle for a truly remarkable society. Since the American idea is not a static but a dynamic one, we must constantly reinvent ourselves in the light of our diverse experiences. One reason this nation works the way it does is our diversity. Try to make Africans and Asians copies of Europeans and women copies of men and you will force the disunity Schlesinger fears. This does not mean, as some dishonest writers have said, that black children will be taught black information and white children will be taught white information and so forth. No Afrocentrist has articulated such a view, though it has been widely reported in the news.

UNITY IN AMERICA

The unity of America is based upon shared goals, a collective sense of mission, a common purpose, and mutual respect. It should be clear to the reader, upon reflection, that Schlesinger's view of America is too provincial; it is as if he has not outgrown the way of thinking he expressed in *The Age of Jackson.* I believe his view is planted in the narrow confines of a particular ethnic or racial identity. Thus, it cannot produce a harvest of unity. The unity of the American nation is not a unity of historical experiences or cultural backgrounds. Because each of us could give a different version of the same story, there must be an acceptance of pluralism without ethnic or cultural hegemony. Only in this manner can we build a common culture. For the present we have many cultures, occasionally interacting with each other, but we have only one society. This means that it is no longer viable for white cultures to parade as the only American culture.

I find it curious that Schlesinger, who has spent a lifetime championing an elitist educational program, is now interested in a multicultural one. This may be a result of his professorship at City University of New York, or of the controversy surrounding a number of his colleagues at the City University. I should not be mistaken. I like the idea that Schlesinger sees multiculturalism as important; it is just that he would be the last person I would consider knowledgeable of this field.[2]

There is no particularist multiculturalism or pluralist multiculturalism; there is, quite simply, multiculturalism. I pointed out in response to Diane Ravitch (a deputy assistant secretary of education) who came up with the notions of particularist and pluralist multiculturalisms, that the first is an oxymoron and the second a redundancy. Multiculturalism is not a complicated proposition; it is clear and simple. In a multicultural society, there must be a multicultural curriculum, a multicultural approach to institution building, and so forth.

Afrocentrists say that one should not be able to declare competency in music in America without having been introduced to the spirituals, Duke Ellington, or the blues. Yet every year this happens in major American universities.

AN AFROCENTRIC ORIENTATION

What Schlesinger dislikes in the Afrocentric position is the emphasis on re-centering of African Americans in a subject position vis-à-vis history, culture,

2. There are a great number of intercultural communicationists who have written intelligently on this subject. Schlesinger might have looked at two of my works in this field, *Transracial Communication* and *Handbook of Intercultural Communication*. Others such as Andrea Rich, William Gudykunst, Erika Vora, Tulsi Saral, and Thomas Kochman, have written extensively on the question of culture and cultural interactions.

and science. However, 374 years of white domination have disoriented, dislocated, and displaced many African Americans. This is the legacy of stealing us from Africa, of dehumanizing and enslaving us. So fearful of Africans were the slave masters that they sought to rob us of our heritage, memory, languages, religion, customs, traditions, and history. In the end, it is true, some of us did lose our way and *our* minds, and decentered, disoriented, and often alienated—would claim that we came to America on the *Mayflower*.

Afrocentrists do not take anything away from white history except its aggressive urge to pose as universal.

Afrocentricity seeks to understand this phenomenon by beginning all analysis from the African person as human agent. In classes, it means that the African-American child must be connected, grounded to information presented in the same way that white children are grounded, when we discuss literature, history, mathematics, and science. Teachers who do not know this information when it comes to Africans must seek it out from those who do. Afrocentrists do not take anything away from white history except its aggressive urge to pose as universal.

The meaning of this school of thought is critical for all Americans. I make a claim that we must see ourselves within American society, with points of reference in our culture and history. Our children as well as other children must know about us in the context of our own history. The Afrocentric school of thought becomes useful for the expansion of dialogue and the widening of discourse—the proper function of education. The white self-esteem curriculum now present in most school systems is imposed as universal.

We know this curriculum is not universal, of course, but rather specific social studies and humanities information centered on a particular culture. There is nothing fundamentally wrong about a Eurocentric curriculum so long as other cultures are not denied. The real question is whether Eurocentrism can exist without denial of the Other. To speak arrogantly of this model as a conquest

model is to assert a claim of right by force, not on the basis of facts nor on the ground of what is useful for this society. We ought to be able to develop a curriculum of instruction that affirms all people in their cultural heritages.

A FINISHED PARADIGM

It is bizarre to find that Schlesinger attacks my vision of a multicultural nation without having read any of my works. At the end of the twentieth century, the United States must be spared the intellectual intolerance, xenophobia, ethnic hatred, racist thinking, and hegemonic attitudes that now seem to be running rampant in Europe.

Schlesinger makes judicious use of the critical remarks of African-American scholars such as John Hope Franklin, Henry Louis Gates, and Frank Snow in order to divide African-American intellectuals into two camps. There are also women who accept the male view of history. There were Jews who accepted the German version of culture. There will always be members of the dominated group who will accept certain ideas from those dominating. We all experience our particular dislocations. But as for me, an American citizen of African descent, I shall never abandon my ancestors' history. Neither would I expect Schlesinger to abandon his, though that is his right. Whatever he does about it, I will not say he is sowing disunity.

Dividing African scholars in order to set off conflict is an old game, but it avoids raising the issue discussed by the Afrocentrists. Why should a monocultural experience and history dominate a multicultural and multiethnic nation? There is no good answer to this question, so Schlesinger believes in shoring up the old, "perfect" order as the best procedure. But it will not wash. His description is of a paradigm that is finished. It is not enough for Schlesinger to cite majority support, since popular belief and mass acceptance are not adequate for validating ideas. Description and demonstration are the principal calling cards of proof, not authoritative pronouncements, even if they come from a well-known historian. Neither hegemony nor power can determine truth.

NATIONALITY AND CULTURE

Schlesinger's book is unfortunate at this stage in national integration and development. He confuses American nationality with American culture. Whether by choice or circumstances, we are American in nationality. So one can say that my nationality and citizenship are American, but my historical and cultural origins are African. My ancestors did not arrive in this country from Europe. They did not see a mountain of possibility but a valley of despair.

It is this distinction, this historical cleavage, that cannot be resolved by some mythical idea that we all came here on the *Mayflower.* The preferred resolution of such dual experiences is a true multiculturalism, where Europeans are seen working for national purpose alongside other people, not in a hegemonic position. This takes a measure of humility that is not evident in Schlesinger's book. Without a reorientation from conquest, from dominance, from superiority, the whites in this country can never understand the discourse of unity expressed by Africans, Latinos, Asians, and Native Americans.

I agree with Franklin Roosevelt's observation that "Americanism is not a matter of race and ancestry but of adherence to the creed of liberty and democracy." This means that the litmus test for Americanism must not be how Eurocentric a person becomes but whether the person adheres to the idea of mutual individual and cultural respect. One cannot equate a Chinese American's love of Chinese motifs, food, decorations, and myths with a rejection of Americanism: It *is* Americanism. Of course, we all are free to reject our ethnic or cultural past, but that does not mean we do not possess culture.

Afrocentrism is not about sympathy or insult; it is about the proper presentation of factual information in a multicultural society.

Schlesinger writes in a very condescending manner: "Nor is there anything more natural than for generous-hearted people, black and white, to go along with Afrocentrism out of a decent sympathy for the insulted and injured of American society and of a decent concern to bind up the wounds." But Afrocentrism is not about sympathy or insult; it is about the proper presentation of factual information in a multicultural society. To frame an argument in the context of the generous hearted doing something for Africans is to miss the point. What we do by making America safe for diversity is to ensure the unity of the nation.

Schlesinger's continuation suggests that his condescension is unabated, "Still, doctrinaire ethnicity in general and the dogmatic black version in particular raise questions that deserve careful and dispassionate examination." This representation seeks to diminish the Afrocentric movement's rational arguments through hyperbole. Doctrinaire ethnicity, if it exists in America is not to be found in the African-American community. He is especially exercised by "the dogmatic black version," which he does not describe in any detail. Yet he says that the Afrocentric campaign most worries him. His problem with Afrocentric scholarship is that he cannot dismiss it. For example, he wants to question the African origin of civilization and counterposes Mesopotamia as the cradle of civilization. But this does not work, either in theory or reality.

THE AFRICAN ORIGIN OF CIVILIZATION

Cheikh Anta Diop wrote in *The African Origin of Civilization* that Africa is the cradle of human civilization. He expanded his argument in his massive work *Civilization and Barbarism,* assembling evidence from disparate sources such as linguistics, botany, osteology, history, and molecular biology. Numerous scholars have supported the arguments Diop made in those books. In fact, Theophile Obenga has shown the origin of medicine, theology, queenship, astronomy, mathematics, ethics, and philosophy in Africa. There is no comparable evidence of antiquity in any other continent.[3]

Mesopotamia does not figure in an-

---

3. Theophile Obenga, *African Philosophy in the Time of the Pharaohs* (Paris: Presence Africaine, 1991). Furthermore, the works of Maulana Karenga and Jacob Carruthers are useful documents. See *The Husia,* edited by Maulana Karenga (Los Angeles: University of San Kore Press) and Carruthers, *Essays in Ancient Kemetic Studies* (Los Angeles: University of San Kore Press, 1985).

cient civilization, either concretely *or* philosophically, at the same level as ancient Egypt. Even were one to take evidence from the ancient Egyptian, Hebrew, Greek, and Ethiopian peoples, one would find that the Nile Valley of Africa rather than the Tigris Euphrates Valley was considered the most ancient cradle of human civilization.

Plato's corpus includes twenty-eight extant dialogues; in twelve of those dialogues, he discusses Egypt, not Mesopotamia, Sumer, or Babylon. Of course, Plato himself was taught in Africa by Seknoufis and Kounoufis. He did not think of Mesopotamia as a high civilization on the level of Egypt. The Hebrew Bible mentions Egypt nearly one thousand times but refers to Mesopotamia no more than twenty times. The Ethiopians refer to Egypt, not to Mesopotamia, in their ancient sacred books, the *Kebra Nagast* and *The Book of Henok.* While I believe Mesopotamia is a significant civilization, I also believe that it is advanced as a sort of contemporary anti-African project, a kind of counterpoint to the African origin of civilization. This is why some writers claim that Mesopotamian civilization can be dated one hundred years prior to the First Egyptian Dynasty. However, dynastic Egypt was not the beginning of civilization in the Nile Valley. There had been at least sixteen kings of Upper (Southern) Egypt before Narmer (Menes), who is normally given as the first dynastic king. My point is that the ancients did not consider Mesopotamia more important than Egypt; this is preeminently a contemporary project.

Let us examine Schlesinger's assault on the Egyptian scholarship of African scholars. He admits that he is no expert on ancient Egypt and, in a broad stroke for justification, claims, "neither are the educators and psychologists who push Afrocentrism." I do not know what special criteria Schlesinger is using for expertise, but Cheikh Anta Diop, Theophile Obenga, Wade Nobles, Jacob Carruthers, Maulana Karenga, Asa Hilliard, and others have spent more than one hundred collective years in the study of ancient Africa. Their research and publications are accessible and well known to those of us who consider ourselves Afrocentrists. All of these scholars are students of ancient languages: Mdu Netr, the language of the ancient Egyptians, Ge'ez, Greek, and Latin. Although my knowledge of ancient languages is not nearly at the level of the scholars I have mentioned, my familiarity with the ancient literatures is indicated in many of the books that I have written. My book *Kemet, Afrocentricity and Knowledge* explores various aspects of the historiography of ancient Africa.

Schlesinger's attack seeks to undermine the Africanness of the ancient Egyptian. Indeed, he brings three witnesses to his case: Frank Snowden, Frank Yurco, and Miriam Lichtheim. All three of these people have deeply invested interests in the Eurocentric paradigm of history (that is, the projection of Eurocentric concepts in African people). Snowden, a retired Howard University professor, has written on the African image in Greece and Rome. He does not read Mdu Netr and certainly is no scholar of ancient Africa. Yurco, a librarian at the University of Chicago, has produced nothing of the caliber of any of the Afrocentrists. From his Regenstein Library desk at the University of Chicago, Yurco has made a career of responding to Diop, Carruthers, Bernl, Hilliard, and, lately, my book *Kemet, Afrocentricity, and Knowledge*. His ideological perspective appears to fog his analysis. His essay, cited by Schlesinger, in *Biblical Archaeology Review is* a nasty little piece written against Martin Bernl.

Afrocentrists claim that Eurocentric scholars have attempted to take Egypt out of Africa and to take Africans out of ancient Egypt in a whitening process of the earliest civilizations.

Lichtheim is by far the best-known ancient Egyptian scholar, but the comment Schlesinger chooses to use from Lichtheim is rather strange.

I do not wish to waste any of my time refuting the errant nonsense which is being propagated in the American black community about the Egyptians being Nubians and the Nubians being black. The Egyptians were not Nubians, and the original Nubians were not black. Nubia gradually became black because black peoples migrated northward out of Central Africa. The "Nile Valley School" is obviously an attempt by American blacks to provide themselves with an ancient history linked to that of the high civilization of ancient Egypt.

Neither Schlesinger nor Lichtheim names or quotes any African or African-American scholar as saying anything "about the Egyptians being Nubians." However, it is possible to say that the difference between Nubians and Egyptians was much like that of Sicilians and Italians, Icelanders and Danes, or Germans and Austrians. Lichtheim's comment and Schlesinger's use of it is meant to suggest that the ancient Egyptians and ancient Nubians were of different races. Nubians and Egyptians looked alike and came from the same general culture. In addition, both were black-skinned peoples.

Lichtheim's denial of the blackness (that is, the black-skinnedness) of the ancient Nubians borders on intellectual incompetence because it disregards the available concrete evidence in texts, sculptures, paintings, and linguistics. Lichtheim's statement that the "Egyptians were not Nubians" is correct but misleading. One can say that the French are not Spanish or the Swedes are not Norwegians, but that is not a statement about the color of skin. I can say that the Yoruba are not Ibo, but that tells me something about ethnicity and perhaps national identity, not about their complexions. So to say that the Egyptians were not Nubians is to say no more than that the two people who lived along the Nile occupied different geographical areas.

The fact is that the Egyptians saw themselves and Nubians as looking exactly alike in physical appearance as well as dress. One only needs to know the first ethnology in the world, the Biban el-Moluk bas-relief from the tomb of Sesostris I, to see that Egyptians painted themselves and Nubians as coal black and whites and Asians as lighter in complexion. There are four people on the bas-relief, representing four different cultures: Egyptian, Nehasi (Nubian), Namou (Asian), and Tamhou (Aryan). The Egyptian and the Nehasi are exactly alike, even to their clothes. They are visibly different from the Namou and the Tamhou.

But the greater nonsense is Lichtheim's statement that the "original Nubians were not black." Does Lichtheim mean to imply that they were what we would call white today? Does she mean they were lighter complexioned blacks? Or does Lichtheim mean to suggest, as some white Egyptologists suggested in the past, that the people were black-skinned whites? The problem here is racialist thinking. Since the discourse under which white academics have often operated is Eurocentric, it is difficult for them to admit that civilization started in Africa and that it was black people who started it.

As far as we know, human beings originated on the African continent and migrated outward. No scientist suggests that the people who migrated outward and who peopled the continent of Africa were white.[4] Indeed, the monogenesis thesis argues that hominids, the Grimaldi, migrated to Europe and emerged after the Ice Age as white in complexion because of environmental and climatic factors.

To apply e pluribus unum, *a term of political structure, to the American cultural reality is to miss the point of both politics and culture. A nation of more than 130 cultural groups cannot hope to have all of them Anglo-Saxonized.*

The Nubians were not only black physically but shared with the Egyptians and others of the Nile Valley the same African cultural and philosophical modalities. Present-day Egypt, like present-day America, is not a reflection of its ancient past. Arabs came from Arabia with the jihads of the seventh century A.D. Therefore, Arabic is not indigenous to Africa, as English is not indigenous to the United States.

The aim of Schlesinger's remarks and Lichtheim's quote is not the Nubian issue but the question of the complexion of the ancient Egyptians. Afrocentrists claim that Eurocentric scholars have attempted to take Egypt out of Africa and to take Africans out of ancient Egypt in a whitening process of the earliest civilizations. Children's books still exist with Egyptians looking like Scandinavians.

---

4. Martin Bernal, *Black Athena*, vols. 1 and 2 (New Brunswick: Rutgers University Press, 1987).

The evidence of the blackness of the ancient Egyptians is overwhelming. The early Greeks said that the Egyptians were black. They never wrote that the Egyptians were white. In fact, Aristotle wrote in *Physiognomonica* that both the Egyptians and the Ethiopians (Nubians) were black. Herodotus writes in *Histories* that the people of Colchis must be Egyptians because "they are black-skinned and have woolly hair."[5] One could cite Sfrabo, Pindar, and Apollonius of Rhodes as making similar attestations about how the Egyptians looked.

Thus, Lichtheim's statement is not only errant but pure nonsense. It flies in the face of all available evidence and, beyond that, it defies logic. Perhaps this style of written pontification by white scholars is the source of confusion in the minds of the American public. Lichtheim proposes what Bernal has aptly called the Aryan Model of Ancient History, which suggests, among other things, that civilization could not have started in Africa, and, if civilization is found in Africa, it had to be the results of an external movement into Africa.

E PLURIBUS UNUM

Schlesinger likes to quote Diane Ravitch. But both Schlesinger and Ravitch are wrong when they suggest that *e pluribus unum* meant out of many cultures, one. Actually, this expression was initially applied to the fact that several colonies could produce one federal government. Thus, out of many colonies, one central government. To apply this term of political structure to the American cultural reality is to miss the point of both politics and culture. A nation of more than 130 cultural groups cannot hope to have all of them Anglo-Saxonized. Such a vision is disastrous and myopic. What we can wish for and realize is a society of mutual respect, dynamism, and decency. Rather than labeling or setting cultural groups against each other, we should empower a vision that sees the American kaleidoscope of cultures as uniquely fortunate. Schlesinger sees multiculturalism as a danger. I see it as a further indication that the shift to a new, more operable paradigm in this mighty nation is well on its way.

---

5. *The Works of Aristotle,* W. D. Ross, vol. VI, *Physiognomica* (Oxford: Clarendon Press, 1913), 812.

"Remember the Ladies"

Joan Kennedy Taylor

Joan Kennedy Taylor is working on a book about feminism and individualism.

*I*n March of 1776, when sentiment in the colonies was strong for independence, Abigail Adams wrote to her husband, John Adams, asking him to use his influence in any new government to change the legal status of married women. "In the new code of laws which I suppose it will be necessary for you to make," she wrote, "I desire you to remember the ladies, and be more generous to them than your ancestors. Do not put such unlimited power in the hands of husbands. Remember, all men would be tyrants if they could." Today, 200 years after the drafting of the Constitution, the legal rights of women are still ambiguous.

When Abigail Adams wrote, women's legal status was governed by British common law, which treated them as children. Politically, they had no rights at all. Economically, many occupations were forbidden to them. Their main occupation was marriage, but under common law, as the legal authority William Blackstone put it, "the husband and wife are one person in law; that is, the very being or legal existence of the woman is suspended during the marriage."

A married woman had no right to buy, sell, or manage property. She could not legally own property that she inherited or that had been hers before marriage. She did not even have the right to keep any wages she earned; they belonged to her husband. She could not sign contracts, sue or be sued, or testify in court. She had no right to her children in case of legal separation or divorce, and divorce was almost impossible for her to obtain. She was legally obliged to obey her husband, who could keep her prisoner or physically punish her, although not with excessive force.

Up from Slavery

*T*he founding of the United States did not dismantle women's common-law status. That would take a long, painful effort that has not yet been completed—some states still restrict married women's freedom to manage property, change their residence, and start businesses. Women didn't even organize to protest their status until 1848, when a Declaration of Rights and Sentiments was read aloud by Elizabeth Cady Stanton at a Woman's Rights Convention at Seneca Falls, New York.

The declaration used the format and language of the Declaration of Independence to declare it a self-evident truth that all men and women are created equal. "The history of mankind," it asserted, "is a history of repeated injuries and usurpations on the part of man toward woman, having in direct object the establishment of an absolute tyranny over her. To prove this, let facts be submitted to a candid world."

The audience was heavily composed of abolitionists, for it was in the antislavery movement that women discovered that one political right was open to them—the First Amendment right "to petition the Government for a redress of grievances." Yet they were criticized, not just for holding unpopular opinions but for being unwomanly in trying to promote *any* opinions, and many women abolitionists became aware for the first time of their subservient position. They, and the male abolitionists who worked with them, began to think and talk of women's rights as well as Negro rights.

The Seneca Falls Convention itself was organized by two women, Lucretia Mott and Elizabeth Cady Stanton, who had met at a London antislavery convention eight years before. There, they had found that they were not only forbidden to speak but were required to observe the proceedings from behind a curtain.

At Seneca Falls, Stanton also called for women's "inalienable right to the elective franchise," a demand that seemed so excessive, even to the others who had helped her draft the declaration, that only the black abolitionist Frederick Douglass would take the floor to support it. Within two years, however, women were to take the idea of suffrage so seriously that they were initiating petition campaigns for it in eight states, as well as continuing to agitate with increasing effect for property rights and marriage reform. But with the outbreak of the Civil War, women postponed such work to assist the war effort.

After Lincoln's Emancipation Proclamation, women collected almost 400,000 signatures petitioning for an amendment to abolish slavery. Once that had been accomplished with the passage and ratification of the 13th Amendment in 1865, the Anti-Slavery Society began agitating for suffrage, and a 14th Amendment was proposed and introduced in Congress. Its original purpose was to give the vote to slaves and to take it away from southerners who had fought against the Union, but for the first time in the history of the Constitution, it was proposed that the word *male* be used to characterize voters.

Abolitionist feminists were alarmed. Many abolitionists who had championed women's right to vote in the abstract were unwilling to make it a concrete political issue. Wendell Phillips, president of the Anti-Slavery Society, refused to support votes for women, arguing that "this hour belongs to the Negro." Senator Charles Sumner, a former advocate of women's rights, called the women's campaign "most inopportune." Such sentiments prevailed. Women were unsuccessful in gaining the right to vote through either the 14th or 15th amendments.

But had the 14th Amendment *inadvertently* given women the right to vote? "All persons born or naturalized in the United States," declared the amendment, "are citizens of the United States and of the State wherein they reside. No State shall make or enforce any law which shall abridge the privileges or immunities of citizens." In 1871, two members of the House Judiciary Committee signed a minority report holding that, under the amendment, women had the right to vote. The next year, Susan B. Anthony led 16 women to vote the straight Republican ticket.

On registration day, Anthony read both the 14th Amendment and the state election law to the election inspectors, pointing out that neither one prohibited women from voting. The women were allowed to register, and on election day, to vote. Although Anthony was arrested, tried, and convicted, she did not pay her fine and was never jailed for her defiance, which made it impossible for her to bring the case to the Supreme Court.

Women's only recourse was to get voters to amend the Constitution. This they succeeded in doing in 1920, after 50 years and what Carrie Chapman Catt, president of the National Woman Suffrage Association at the time, summarized as "56 campaigns of referenda to male voters; 480 campaigns to get legislatures to submit suffrage amendments to voters; 277 campaigns to get state party conventions to include woman's suffrage planks; 30 campaigns to get presidential party conventions to adopt woman's suffrage planks; and 19 campaigns with 19 successive Congresses."

One Step Forward, Two Steps Back

*W*hile women were campaigning for the vote, another issue had crept up on them: protective labor legislation. Progressive legislators had enacted a whole network of laws singling out women—laws that women were divided about.

A prime example was protective legislation to limit hours and working conditions. Such laws had been held to be a violation of men's right to contract, but in 1908, in the case of *Muller* v. *Oregon,* the Supreme Court decided that an Oregon law limiting the working hours of *women* was constitutional.

The case was the first in which sociological data persuaded the justices to modify legal principle. The brief that was filed cited reports by state commissions to prove that women are just what the common law assumed they are—frail, and in need of special protection. The rights of men—in this case, to liberty of contract—need not be available to working women, as they had traditionally not been available to married women.

Woman has always been dependent on man, said the decision, and this is natural. "Though limitations upon personal and contractual rights may be removed by legislation, there is that in her disposition and habits of life which will operate against a full assertion of those rights....Differentiated by these matters from the other sex, she is properly put in a class by herself, and legislation designed for her protection may be sustained, even when like legislation is not necessary for men, and could not be sustained."

The issue divides the women's movement to this day. An organization called the National Woman's Party, founded in 1913 to work for suffrage, became convinced that the view of women exhibited in the *Muller* decision was a threat to the idea of equal rights they had been working for. So in 1921, the party reorganized to work for the removal of all legal distinctions based on sex. At first they undertook a state-by-state campaign but soon decided to lobby instead for constitutional reform— an equal rights amendment. The amendment was introduced in Congress in 1923, and with two exceptions, substantially the same wording was submitted every year thereafter until 1972, when the ERA was finally passed by Congress and sent to the states for ratification.

From the beginning, the main opposition to the ERA was from supporters of the trade union movement. Clearly, protective labor legislation, whatever else it did, served to curb women's competition for jobs. In 1950 and 1953, the ERA was amended with a rider, urged by Eleanor Roosevelt, that would have left protective legislation intact by providing that the amendment "shall not be construed to impair any rights, benefits, or exemptions now or hereafter conferred by law upon persons of the female sex."

But it was precisely the singling out of women that the National Woman's Party opposed. So although the amended ERA twice passed the Senate, the party helped to defeat it in the House.

When Congress held hearings on the equal rights amendment in 1970 and 1971, six of the eight statements against it were submitted by organized labor, including one from the AFL-CIO. One legal expert suggested a rider to keep protective legislation intact.

During the years in which the ERA was being unsuccessfully proposed, attempts were made—also unsuccessfully—to strike down various discriminatory laws for violating the equal-protection clause of the 14th Amendment. The rationale was well expressed by scholar Bernard Schwartz, in an observation included in the record of the 1970 House hearings on the amendment by ERA foe Senator Sam Ervin: "The case law has consistently ruled that, even though women are 'persons' within the scope of the equal-protection clause, the protection which that provision affords them must be interpreted in the light of the disabilities imposed upon women at common law. Thus, as recently as 1966, a state court ruled that, until the common-law disqualification of sex is removed, women are not eligible to serve on juries—and that regardless of the equal-protection clause."

In 1971, the Supreme Court finally held that a specific classification based on sex was not "reasonable." In the years since, the Court has considered a number of challenges to statutes that differentiate on the basis of sex. "While the Court has several times struck down such statutes," comments one legal source, "those occasions have been proportionately far fewer than in suits challenging classifications based on race."

Although the Court can reverse a previous ruling, and has done so, it does not do so with abandon and generally tries to support such reversals by appealing to the "plain language" of the Constitution or to the intent of those who framed the section being interpreted. Intent is discovered by examining the debates that took place at the time the wording was adopted—the legislative history. And the legislative history of the 14th Amendment explicitly did not include women, so it would require an extremely "creative" decision to hold that the amendment applies to women.

The Slow Death of the ERA

*T*hus, the stage is set for the sad tale of the Equal Rights Amendment. Its legislative history seemed clear at the time it passed Congress. Both its supporters and its opponents agreed that it would apply only to the actions of governments; that it would *not* address private discrimination, which could only be reached by legislation that invoked Congress's power to regulate commerce; and that it would invalidate protective labor legislation that makes women less competitive in the marketplace.

In the congressional hearings, no one, not even Sam Ervin, who voiced many of the qualms that the conservative campaign against the ERA in the '70s was to pick up, thought that the amendment would expand the power of government. It would invalidate laws, not create them. In fact, Ervin feared the ERA would bring "legal chaos" because it would "merely abolish all laws making any distinction between men and women. It would not bring into existence any new laws giving us a discrimination-free society."

And feminists agreed. "ERA will not prevent discriminations by persons or by private industry," wrote Ann Scott in the pages of the popular feminist magazine *Ms.* "It will not, directly at least, change social relations. What it will do, over the long run and on a most basic level, is to prevent the government from determining the rights of women and men on the basis of sex. And that's a hell of a lot."

Then came the conservative campaign against the amendment. Not only would the ERA change social relations by driving women out of the home and into the work force and by legalizing homosexual marriage, but it was also alleged to be "a big power grab by the Federal Government." The amendment "will eliminate all-girls' and all-boys' schools and colleges," said conservative literature. It "may compel the states to set up taxpayer-financed child-care centers for all children" and "may give the Federal Government the power to force the admission of women to seminaries equally with men, and possibly force the churches to ordain women."

In response to these attacks, feminists gradually expanded their accounts of what the ERA might do. They didn't exactly *say* that the amendment would be applied to make people economically equal, but they started wearing buttons calling attention to the statistic that women earned 59 cents to a man's dollar (a misleading figure—see Jennifer Roback's "The 59-Cent Fallacy," REASON, Sept. 1984).

The ERA was supported by a broad coalition that now included many of the union forces that still wanted to expand social legislation. They thought that they could have it all—that women could be legally equal and legally different and special, all at the same time. After all, those who made blacks their constituency had pulled off that trick by changing the interpretation of the Civil Rights Act to mean present-day affirmative action with its goals and benign quotas.

So feminists started agreeing with the conservatives that the new amendment would have broad effects. Where the conservatives called it a federal power grab, Eleanor Smeal, president of the National Organization for Women (NOW), called it "a Constitutional prohibition against sex discrimination." In a letter to supporters, she said, "Unless we fight harder and in a more organized fashion than we ever have before, women will continue to be doomed to a second rate economic status of lower pay, unequal credit and inadequate job security. After all, that's what the ERA fight is *really* all about—making the lot of women really equal to the lot of men, especially when it comes to money. That's the critical litmus test of equality."

The amendment had five years to achieve ratification, and it failed to do so. The deadline was extended until 1982, and it failed again, this time permanently. Prospects for passage of a new ERA are unlikely.

The ERA was a remnant of the classical liberalism of the early abolitionist feminists, who sought equal responsibility and laws that had neither special privileges nor special restrictions for women. It could have been used as a vehicle to enunciate that philosophy to a wide audience today, but it was not. Instead, its supporters, who began by describing it correctly, came to agree with their opponents that it would engender sweeping changes in private action. And that agreement would become a self-fulfilling prophecy should the ERA pass Congress again in the near future; it has created a climate of opinion that would provide a different and malignant legislative history, one that could make all the worst nightmares of federal power grabs come true.

So the ERA is dead, but *Muller* v. *Oregon*, the cornerstone of protective legislation, has never been overruled. And the status of women is basically what state legislatures (and majority opinion) say it is. While the ERA was wending its way through the state legislatures, it became fashionable to grant women equal treatment; several states passed state equal-rights amendments to their constitutions. But the trouble with not having the Constitution view women as fully equal and independent beings is that, if the fashion changes, there is nothing to stop the laws from changing back.

Indeed, a number of feminists are now campaigning for a new kind of protective legislation, this time aimed at helping women in the workplace with laws that mandate maternity leave and provide child-care assistance. Such legislation is a pendulum that can swing either way. In *Women and Work in America*, Robert Smuts says, "The most obvious effect of the depression of the 1930s was to throw many women out of work and intensify the feeling that working women took jobs away from male breadwinners. Many state and local governments revived old bans on the employment of married women in teaching and other public jobs, and several state legislatures considered bills to prohibit the employment of wives in public industry." It could happen again.

Black & White in America

The integration ideal of a generation ago is vanishing as intellectual and social forces pull the races apart

"With this faith we will be able to transform the jangling discords of our nation into a beautiful symphony of brotherhood."
—Martin Luther King Jr., 1963

None of King's dreams has died so hard as his hopes for racial integration. Each week brings fresh reminders that the American dilemma remains unresolved. Washington's bitter fights over civil-rights protections and the Clarence Thomas Supreme Court nomination show there's no end to the debate about the best route to black progress. Many blacks think not enough effort has been expended—and that they're in danger of losing hard-won gains. Many whites, by contrast, have come to see affirmative action itself as an unfair form of racial preference, a betrayal of King's own injunction that people should be judged on the content of their character, not on the color of their skin; they feel taxes from those who work have become transfer payments to those who don't. Ironically, advocates of virulent anti-white beliefs have played off the guilt of white administrators and developed followings on a growing number of campuses—traditionally the most tolerant institutions in the land. At the opposite pole, the commission examining the beating of Rodney King by Los Angeles police reports that racism in the department is as raw as this message from one white cop to another: "Sounds like monkey-slapping time."

Race fatigue grips America as the fight over a once-revered value has become mired in haggling over numbers and racial balances. Except in rare places like the Mount Airy neighborhood in Philadelphia, the ideal has been overwhelmed by forces that either sharply slowed integration or are resegregating the land. The integration story itself has two distinct phases: large-scale progress that lasted from the early 1940s until the mid-1970s, followed by an abrupt slowdown in the melding of the black and white worlds that continues today. Few are willing to celebrate the first period, and large numbers are embittered by the second.

The danger of the disintegration of the ideal is that its replacement strays far from what the great sociologist Gunnar Myrdal called the "American Creed"—that is, "ideals of the essential dignity of the individual human being, of the fundamental equality of all men and of certain inalienable rights to freedom, justice, and a fair opportunity." Nowadays, group identity and group grievances are supplanting that creed. As historian Arthur Schlesinger Jr. writes in his new book, "The Disuniting of America": "America increasingly sees itself as the preservative of old identities. Instead of a nation composed of individuals making their own free choices, America increasingly sees itself as composed of groups more or less indelible in their ethnic character. The national ideal had once been *e pluribus unum* [from many, one]. Are we now to belittle *unum* and glorify the *pluribus*? Will the center hold?"

Schlesinger's main target is a group of Afrocentric academics, who posit everything from the theory that white racial inferiority is related to a genetic inability to produce skin pigments to the notion that Africa is the mother of Western civilization, since Egyptians were black and heavily influenced the Greeks—contentions most scholars say are flat wrong. Variations of these ideas are now circulating in a number of public school curricula, including those of Portland, Ore., Philadelphia, Baltimore, Pittsburgh, Indianapolis, Atlanta and Milwaukee—despite criticism from reputable black scholars.

Their growing acceptance occurs against the backdrop of other disheartening trends. Several so far insurmountable forces have worked against integration. The first is that antisegregation laws simply cannot touch all the kinds of behavioral and economic realities that have driven the races apart. Attempts to desegregate the nation's schools through mandatory busing led, in many cities, to white flight to private schools or the suburbs—not always out of racism but for fear of drugs and violence in city streets and classrooms. And although many corporations have initiated ambitious affirmative action programs, other personnel policies and skill differences often have kept the races apart, placing whites in one batch of jobs and blacks in others. Economic pressures have also worked against the assimilation of young blacks, putting a premium on jobs requiring solid academic credentials. High-paying, low-skill manufacturing jobs are disappearing, replaced by far lower-paying service-sector jobs. The Bureau of Labor Statistics reports that the proportion of black male high-school dropouts ages 20 to 24 who had not worked at all during the previous year hurtled from 15.1 percent in 1974 to 39.7 percent in 1986.

The second force that has sapped the hopes of integration is the growth of a class of poor blacks whose circumstances place them completely beyond the reach of traditional integration remedies. They are the products of what Sen. Daniel Patrick Moynihan calls a "post-marital" society—an environment where the traditional two-parent family has utterly disintegrated. When Moynihan first wrote of the problems of the black family in 1965, 23.6 percent of all black chil-

 From *U.S. News & World Report*, July 22, 1991, pp. 18-21. Copyright © 1991 by U.S. News & World Report.

dren were born out of wedlock. Today, that number is a stunning 61 percent nationally—and approaches 80 percent in many cities. For black children, the likelihood of living with both parents until age 17 dropped from 52 percent in the 1950s to 6 percent in the 1980s. Their communities are saturated with crime and drugs. Schools, if the children attend at all, are dysfunctional.

No government intervention is going to give these imperiled children what they most need: functioning homes. Though the black underclass is relatively small—probably 2 million to 3 million persons—its existence is an immense drag on the entire race. Its frightful conditions have fueled white fears and driven a good number of middle-class blacks out, too. One out of 4 black men between ages 20 and 29 is in prison, on parole or on probation. Among wage-earning whites, whose real incomes have been stagnant over the past generation, the underclass has helped inspire enormous hostility toward policies that used to enjoy widespread support: Many object to paying taxes to help people whose behavior seems so at odds with the norms of the larger community.

How much have these forces undermined the once pre-eminent goal of social policy?

■ **Housing.** The latest census data reveal that more than 9 million blacks, about 30 percent of the total, still live in almost complete racial isolation, according to an analysis by the *Miami Herald*. That is only a small improvement from the "hypersegregation" of 34 percent of the black population a decade ago, reports sociologist Douglas Massey. Housing is where investigators and researchers find the most persistent open discrimination. Even statistics showing a black exodus to the suburbs can be misleading, since what often happens is that close-in areas turn increasingly black as whites move farther away—a move they think makes them more secure from crime and drug problems. University of Michigan Prof. Reynolds Farley says this means that the appreciation in value of homes owned by blacks lags far behind that of homes owned by whites. That helps account for the fact that the median wealth of black families was only one tenth that of white families.

■ **Schools.** After a spurt of progress in the late 1960s, the move toward greater integration halted. In 1968, says Gary Orfield of the University of Chicago,

76.6 percent of blacks went to predominantly minority schools. Since 1972, the proportion has hovered around 63 percent. "Intensely segregated schools"—those 90 percent or more black—educated 64 percent of blacks in 1968. The percentage dropped to 39 in 1972 and then to 33 in 1980 but has held steady since then.

■ **Workplace.** This is the arena where blacks and whites are most likely to run elbows. Once, even the wealthiest blacks were largely confined to a few professions, such as teacher (in all-black schools) or mortician (tending to black bodies). In 1939, 60 percent of black women were domestics; today, the figure is less than 6 percent. Even before the legal barriers to black progress were torn down, a thriving black middle class was beginning to emerge. Now, according to economists James Smith and Finis Welch, fully two thirds of blacks could be characterized as middle class. A recent Urban Institute study showed that equally qualified white and black job applicants were treated equally three quarters of the time. When discrimination did occur, though, it was three times more likely to be aimed at a black job applicant than a white.

■ **Politics and culture.** In the public arena, white attitudes toward blacks have improved markedly. Most striking is the growing comfort whites have in electing black officials to lead them. In the past 20 years, the number of black elected officials has soared from 1,500 to 7,370. The trend is most notable in midsize cities with lopsided white majorities that have elected black mayors—places like Denver, Seattle, Kansas City, Mo., Rockford, Ill., Dayton, Ohio and Tallahassee, Fla. Similarly, black artists have added extraordinary vibrancy to mainstream culture.

In assessing the remaining problems between the races, it is all too easy to forget the stunning progress that has occurred on other fronts in little more than two generations. The proportion of blacks who drop out of high school has tumbled from 31 percent in 1970 to 18 percent in 1988. In 1960, 281,000 African-Americans held college degrees; today more than 2 million do. The consequence for integration is that blacks are no longer confined to a few fields, though it is still true that blacks disproportionately hold low-wage jobs. Overall, blacks still earn an average of just 59 cents for every dollar earned by whites. But the greater the educational advancement, the smaller

the gap. Well-educated young blacks earn about 85 percent of what their white counterparts earn.

As much as anything, it is differing assessments of all the change that have unhinged the national debate. Democratic pollsters have found that the response of many whites—especially in the working class—to the complaints of civil-rights leaders about lack of progress has been deep and alienating anger. Focus groups and polls since the mid-1980s showed that these voters were so disillusioned that they interpreted Democratic appeals to "opportunity and fairness" as code words for helping blacks. They reject the whole government panoply of support to minorities and object to paying taxes for them. On the other hand, blacks have been turning inward. One level of their response suggests a kind of despair. A surprising 60 percent of blacks said in a 1989 ABC News–*Washington Post* poll that "if blacks would try harder, they could be just as well off as whites." Benjamin Hooks, head of the NAACP, the institution that has driven the integration idea for 50 years, argued last week that blacks cannot solve their problems by continually blaming whites. "The time for excuses is over," he said.

Despite the acrimony of this period, there are hopeful signs in Washington that there is a new consensus about how to attack some of these problems. White House and congressional figures are generally in agreement that a major expansion of preschool programs such as Head Start for underprivileged children of *all* races is essential to improving their work in school, as are financial incentives to students, teachers and schools that perform well.

The stunning success of the U.S. military in offering opportunity and training to blacks has also given leaders a model structure for integration that works beyond school. The formula is simple: Make sure everyone has an equal shot at learning the skills that are necessary to do the job, then base advancement on performance. Vast majorities of Americans of both races say they believe in a system where race imposes neither advantages nor handicaps. That is the American Creed that Martin Luther King Jr. had in mind in the first place.

BY HARRISON RAINIE WITH SCOTT MINERBROOK, MATTHEW COOPER, CONSTANCE JOHNSON, STEVEN V. ROBERTS AND TED GEST

America and Russia, Americans and Russians

The Cold War was an anomaly: more often than not the world's two greatest states have lived together in uneasy amity. And what now?

John Lukacs

John Lukacs's essay on the transatlantic duel between FDR and Hitler appeared in the last issue.

Exactly two hundred years after George Washington's inauguration as the first President of the United States and three hundred years after Peter the Great's ascent to the Russian throne, a new chapter opened in the history of the relations of the two greatest states of the world.

The United States and Russia never fought a war. Twice in the twentieth century they were allies. Their governments and the structure of their societies have been very different, yet there are similarities in the character of the two countries. The relationships of the two states and of their peoples have often been interesting, rather than dramatic—the reason for this being the great geographic distance separating them (except in the Arctic), a dominant fact even now.

For more than a century Russia's main rival was often Great Britain. The clever Czarina Catherine the Great favored the cause of American independence against Britain (she also made John Paul Jones a rear admiral in the Russian navy, where he served against the Turks—the kind of oddity that has so often punctuated American-Russian relations). The counterpart of John Paul Jones, who was a native Scotsman choosing to fight on the American side against his own countrymen, was the Connecticut-born John Ledyard, who spent the years of the American War of Independence in the service of Great Britain, indeed aboard the ships of the famous explorer James Cook. Ledyard was the first American

attracted by the prospect of crossing the icy Bering Sea narrows from Siberia to Alaska. He did not quite make it, but he came close enough to evoke the interest of Thomas Jefferson.

In any event, at that time the few settlements in Alaska and on the northwestern rim of the great Pacific Ocean, reaching down to San Francisco, were Russian, not American. The United

States (and Great Britain) were fortunate in that the rulers of Russia, in faraway St. Petersburg, seldom had a strong interest in sea power, including the making of a seaborne Russian empire in the Pacific (whose eastern rim the Russians had reached more than a century before the first Americans debouched in the West). In that great global region of the Pacific the relations between Americans

Wilson arrives at the Paris Peace Conference during the dawn of the Soviet Union in 1918.

Reprinted with permission from *American Heritage,* Vol. 43, No. 1, February/March 1992, pp. 64-73. Copyright © 1992 by American Heritage, a division of Forbes, Inc.

and Russians have almost always been friendly—even during the worst years of the so-called Cold War.

AGAINST GEORGE WASHINGTON'S WISHES, and against his exhortation to the American people in his Farewell Address, the new American ship of state was badly buffeted by the waves of the last great Atlantic world war between Britain and France, of which the "Second War of American Independence" was but a part. In 1812 John Quincy Adams was the American minister to Russia. His friend Benjamin Rush wrote to him from Philadelphia: "The year 1812 will, I hope, be immortal in the history of the world for having given the first check to the overgrown power and tyranny of Britain and France. Russia and the United States may now be hailed as the deliverers of the human race." Adams was wiser and more circumspect. Although the United States was a de facto ally of Napoleon against Britain, Adams welcomed and saw the immense significance of Napoleon's defeat in Russia (just as many Americans, 130 years later, recognized the immense significance of Hitler's defeat before Moscow). John Quincy Adams did, in 1823, interpret the Monroe Doctrine (of which he was the author) to the Russian minister in Washington to the effect that the United States "would contest the right of Russia to any territorial establishment on this continent," but Adams never thought that the destiny of the United States should be that of a "deliverer of the human race." His phrase in 1821—that we are friends of liberty everywhere "but we do not go abroad in search for monsters to destroy"—should be engraved over the mantel of the Oval Office to remind every President.

Whether this wisdom of a great American statesman evoked a deep resonance within American popular sentiment is arguable. What remains certain is that the relations of the United States and Russia during the nineteenth century were seldom hostile, and for the most part satisfactory. Americans were, at times, justifiably exercised by the Russian subjugation of Poland, by the cruelties of Russian penal practices, by forced exile to Siberia, by the mistreatment of Jews, by the very image of an autocratic and unconstitutional government ruled by a czar; but there were statesmen enough in America to understand, too,

that there were no real conflicts between the vital interests of the Russian and American states. The statesmen in St. Petersburg also thought that, but their estimation of their relationship with the United States was part of their larger calculations. While it is an interesting coincidence that Czar Alexander II's abolition of serfdom in Russia was decreed at almost the same time (1861) as was Lincoln's Emancipation Proclamation (1863), it is even more telling that during the Civil War Russia was sympathetic to the North (in 1863 a Russian fleet paid a friendship visit to New York, an occasion for riotous celebrations). It is certainly telling—and surely consequential—that St. Petersburg was willing to sell Alaska to Washington in 1867 for a pittance ($7.2 million). The Russians' reasoning was simple. They wanted to embroil the United States with Britain, which during the Civil War had been considering supporting the South and which in the 1860s seemed to be engaged in a race with the Americans toward British Columbia and the southern panhandle of Alaska.

THEODORE ROOSEVELT, TOO, WAS STATESman enough to rise above the tides of American popular sentiment. During the Russo-Japanese War in 1904 and 1905, that sentiment, including much of the press, seemed to relish the stunning Japanese triumphs, "the gallant little Jap" pummeling the Russian Bear. Yet when Roosevelt accepted the chairmanship of the peace conference at Portsmouth, the Japanese were disappointed to find that he was not inclined to give them all that they wanted. He struck a kind of balance; he understood that in view of the rising naval and colonial power of the Japanese in the western Pacific it was not in the American interest to see the Russian presence there reduced to nothing.

IN 1917, FOR THE FIRST TIME IN THEIR history, the United States and Russia became military allies, in a world war, against the prospect of a German domination of Europe. Events within Russia in March 1917 had played an important part in Woodrow Wilson's decision to go to Congress a few weeks later to request a declaration of war against Germany. A revolution in Petrograd (St. Petersburg had been renamed in 1914) had forced the czar to abdicate. Wilson (who knew very little about Russia) thought that this was

a tremendous contribution to the purity of the cause of a war waged for democracy: the Allied ranks would no longer be compromised by a czarist regime among them. Wilson thought—and said—that the democratic Russian Revolution of March 1917 was one of the greatest events in the history of mankind, comparable to 1776 in America. He was wrong. The Russian liberal regime collapsed in less than eight months. Its leaders were incompetent; chaos and disorder erupted all over Russia; discipline in the army evaporated; the war against Germany was unpopular. Lenin and the Bolsheviks were more determined. They took over the city of Petrograd (after the leaders of the government had abandoned it to them); they made peace with the Germans, for their hands were full of a developing civil war in Russia, which they eventually won, less on the battlefield than because their opponents, dependent on diminishing Allied support, gave up the fight one by one.

Like Lenin's, Wilson's view of the world was ideological rather than historical. The Progressive professor became a bitter enemy of Bolshevism.

Wilson was stunned and shocked. He attributed these catastrophic events to a giant conspiracy, abetted by the Germans. He—in this he was not alone—did not see the real meaning of these events: Russia's withdrawal from the war; Russia's withdrawal from Europe. Like Lenin's, Wilson's view of the world was ideological rather than historical and geographic. The Progressive professor-President became the bitterest opponent of the Bolsheviks. One result of this was the attempt at American military intervention in the Russian civil war. It was short-lived and marginal; there was practically no fighting between American soldiers and the Red Army; it was marked by the temporary presence of a handful of American troops in a few ports on the Arctic and the Far Eastern rim of the great Russian Empire. By late 1920 this odd episode was over. What was not over was the powerful popular attraction of anticommunism: the tendency to attribute most of the evils of the world, all of the dangers to democracy and to American national interests, to a world conspiracy organized in and emanating from Moscow.

One of its consequences was the American refusal, alone among the great powers of the world, to recognize—that is, to maintain diplomatic relations with—the new government of the Russian Empire, now called the Soviet Union. In reality this did not make much difference. Trade and other relations between the two vast countries went on in the 1920s. In 1933 President Franklin Roosevelt recognized the Soviet Union. By then few people in the United States were opposed to that. In Moscow too, Lenin, who had been a revolutionary and not a statesman, was succeeded by Stalin, who was the opposite. He was willing to sign all kinds of

---

By 1920 the odd episode of Americans fighting in Russia was over; what was not over was the powerful popular attraction of anticommunism.

---

meaningless paper declarations in the recognition treaty, especially because around that time he feared a Japanese move against the Soviet Union and saw the United States as a potential ally. That soon passed; the primary problem, for both powers, would become Germany, not Japan. But the unscrupulous and unsavory behavior of Stalin's government—even before Stalin in 1939 chose to sign a virtual alliance with that apostle of anticommunism Adolf Hitler—soured American-Russian relations. An example of this was William C. Bullitt, one of the most brilliant American diplomats in this century, whom Roosevelt appointed as the first American ambassador to the Soviet Union and who had gone off to his post with extraordinary energy and enthusiasm; two years later he wished to be posted elsewhere, so bitterly disappointed had he become with Stalin and his regime.

In the long run none of this mattered. In 1941 Hitler attacked Russia. *That* was what mattered. The United States and Russia became instant allies again. Their troublesome alliance did not survive

World War II, as it had not survived World War I, but there was a great difference now. In 1918 the Western Allies, including the United States, could win World War I even after Russia dropped out. In World War II, without Russia they could not have conquered Hitler's Third Reich. Eventually enormous amounts of American materiel were funneled to Russia during the war (by an odd coincidence lend-lease to Russia cost nearly the same—$11 billion—as the Marshall Plan, aimed to build up Western Europe after the war). Still, the fact remains that on D-day there were four German divisions struggling against the Russians in the east for each one facing the Allies in France. There was even more to that. By early 1945—at the time of the often debated Yalta Conference—the entire American military and naval establishment, including later vocal anticommunists such as General MacArthur, was praising the Red Army to the skies. One of their main reasons was to expedite an eventual Russian attack on Japan. (The Japanese had not joined the Germans in going to war with Russia in 1941; they had chosen instead to war with the United States and Britain, for reasons known only to themselves.) At Yalta Stalin promised Roosevelt that he would attack Japan three months after V-E day in Europe. He was as good as his word—for reasons of his own, of course. They were the reconquest of Russian lands and bases in the Far East that the czars had lost to Japan in 1905 (a Russian defeat that Lenin had welcomed at the time).

BY THEN—AUGUST 1945—THE FIRST SIGNS of the coming Cold War between the United States and the Soviet Union were accumulating. They had less to do with the Far East than with Europe—particularly with Eastern Europe. Entire libraries have been written about the origins and the development of the Cold War, including books by this writer. I will sum up my view as briefly as I can. In essence it conforms with the views of Winston Churchill, who—as early as 1940—saw things clearly. There were only two alternatives: either all of Europe dominated by Germany or the eastern part of Europe dominated by Russia—and half of Europe (especially the western half) was better than none. Moreover, as Churchill told de Gaulle in 1944, that division, in the long run, would not last: the Russians

would not be able to digest Eastern Europe (that is what happened). In any event, at the end of the war, when the Anglo-American presence in Europe would become very strong, a limit must be set to the Russian sphere of their interest. Very few Americans, including President Roosevelt, saw this quite in that way.

They wanted the Russian-American wartime alliance to prevail; they put undue hopes in the United Nations, that American-made international instrument that Stalin consented to join. They did not devote much attention to Eastern Europe, where they hoped that Stalin (in addition to a few, relatively minor territorial gains) would be satisfied with the establishment of pro-Russian, though not necessarily communist, governments in that Russian sphere of interest. That was not the case. Stalin thought that his sphere of interest could not be secure unless it consisted of satellite governments composed by people who were wholly subservient to him. Otherwise the Americans, who were now the greatest world power, holding the monopoly of the atom bomb, would be able to challenge and reduce his predominance in Eastern Europe, including East Germany. That was not really what the United States wanted, but Stalin's suspicions governed him.

The Cold War grew from the congealing reaction to the Soviets' repellent brutalities in Eastern Europe and East Germany, including the fear that the Russians were now making ready to advance beyond the Iron Curtain, to foment and foist communism on Western and Southern European countries. The result was the American policy of containment and the beginning of the Cold War, which was under way by 1947. The recognition that the United States was the only power on the globe that could—and should—contain a further Russian, or communist, expansion was both timely and proper. The concomitant belief that the Russians were willing, or even able, to risk a third world war with the United States for the sake of conquering more territories for communism was not. The wartime illusions about Stalin and the Soviet Union had contributed to the bitterness of the disappointment of Americans and to the rapid change from American-Russian alliance and friendship to confrontation and enmity. The no less illusory attribution to communism of most of the existing evils in the world, the inability to

Friends for an hour: American infantrymen link up with their Russian counterparts at the town of Torgau on the Elbe River, April 25, 1945.

U.S. ARMY

distinguish between communist propaganda and Russian state interests, and the elevation of anticommunism as if it were not only an ingredient but the essential element of American patriotism were no less damaging in the long run.

THE COLD WAR WAS AN ANOMALY, A forty-year chapter in the history of American-Russian relations, a consequence of the Second World War, in the shadows of which all of us were living, until very recently. It ended in 1989, with the retreat of the Russians from Eastern Europe and with the end of the division of Germany.

Yet in many ways the essential condition of the Cold War—the division of Europe between Americans and Russians—began to fade much earlier. A crucial day in the long history of Europe, of Germany, and of Russian/American relations was a Wednesday, April 25,

1945, when the triumphant advancing American and Russian armies met at Torgau on the banks of the Elbe River amid the wreckage of spring and war. Among the soldiers of the 58th Russian Guards Division there were some whose home was Vladivostok, who arrived in the center of Europe from the shores of the western Pacific. Among the soldiers of the U.S. 69th Division there were some whose home was San Francisco: they too had been sent to conquer halfway around the world. They met in the middle of Germany and in the middle of European history: Torgau on the Elbe is about midway between Wittenberg, where Luther's fire of great revolutions had started, and Leipzig, where Napoleon's course of great victories had ended. The American and Russian soldiers drank and celebrated together into the night. If that was the peak hour of American-Russian comradeship in arms, it was also

the high-water mark of the Russian-American tide flooding Europe.

IT WOULD NOT LAST. TEN YEARS LATER, IN the midst of the Cold War, the disengagement of the United States and the Soviet Union began: they agreed on their mutual evacuation of Austria. The Russians were already gone from Yugoslavia and Finland. There were crises in American-Russian relations to come, about the Russian suppression of the Hungarian uprising in 1956 or about those missiles in Cuba in 1962, for example, but it was evident (at least to some of us) that the United States was no more willing to risk a war with Russia over Hungary than were the Russians willing to risk a war with the United States over Cuba. Slowly, gradually—albeit periodically interrupted by crude reassertions of their predominance—Russian (and also communist) influence was weakening and retreating throughout Eastern Europe and the Far East, until in the late 1980s that extraordinary Russian leader Mikhail Gorbachev thought it best to write off those liabilities—principally for the sake of improving Russia's relations with the United States. Meanwhile, the American presence in Western Europe has been declining too, all superficial impressions to the contrary notwithstanding. A new chapter has opened now in Russian-American relations, and it is by no means impossible—especially in the Far East—that Russians and Americans, if threatened by certain combinations of other powers, may one day become allies again.

Americans and Russians, sent to conquer halfway around the world, met in the middle of Germany and in the middle of European history.

The problem is, however, what does "Russia" and what do "Russians" now mean. The recent coup attempt and the consequent ending of the communist period in the long history of Russia may have been dramatic and inspiring, but it amounts to little or nothing when measured against the much greater phenomenon: the retreat and dissolution of much of the traditional Russian Empire itself, of which the "Soviet Union" was but a cover name, by now as antiquated and meaningless as the Holy Roman Empire. (Keep in mind, too, that while the Holy Roman Empire lasted almost nine hundred years, the Union of Soviet Socialist Republics lasted but seventy.) It is to the credit of President Bush and his Secretary of State that they seem to recognize how the dissolution of a great empire may present new and unforeseeable problems not only to their inhabitants but to the world at large and to the United States in particular. They ought to keep in mind also what Bismarck was reputed to have said on one occasion: that Russia is never as strong, or as weak, as it might seem.

I am asking my readers to consider that all of the foregoing concerned, almost exclusively, the relations of two great states—which is apposite since, at least for the last five hundred years, the relations and the struggles of states have been the predominant factors in the history of the globe. *Predominant,* but not *exclusive*—certainly not in the history of the United States, which is the history of a people as much as that of a state, of the governed as well as of their government. So something must be said about the relations of the American and Russian peoples: of their mutual perceptions, of their reciprocal images of each other.

ONE OF THE REASONS (IF NOT THE MAIN reason) why the Cold War between America and Russia never became a real war is that their peoples have never felt a traditional hostility to each other. An element in this has been the great geographic distance between them; another that—unlike, say, animosities between Germans and Poles, Serbs and Croats, British and Irish—the masses of Americans and Russians had no historical reasons to resent each other. Indeed, there have been many episodes when Americans and Russians discovered that they, strangely or not so strangely, had many things in common. There are many phenomena that illustrate this. On the Russian side the extraordinary friendliness and attraction (uncontaminated by cultural snobbery, as sometimes is the case with Western Europeans) for the United States, their belief in the superior nature of American civilization and technology (very evident even under the rule of Lenin), their intellectuals' avid interest in certain American writers (alas, not always the best ones, manifest in the huge Russian readership of Jack London and Ernest Hemingway), and—perhaps—the old linguistic condition whereby, unlike most Europeans, Russians and Ukrainians find it easier to speak English with an American accent than with an English one. On the American side we find the extraordinary assimilation of intellectuals, scholars, and artists born in Russia, the swiftness of their contributions to American arts, ranging from first-generation immigrants of the Nabokov or Balanchine kind to second-generation artists such as a George Gershwin; the impact of Tolstoy and Dostoevsky (alas, often at the expense of other, better Russian writers) on the American intelligentsia; the generous American efforts aiding Russia at the time of incipient famine, as in 1921, the worst time of the Lenin years; and the frequent eagerness with which Americans have been willing to assist in the building of a modern Russia, as in the case of numerous American railroad planners and other industrialists throughout the nineteenth century. (I will mention but one example. Through forty years during the nineteenth century William Gilpin, the first territorial governor of Colorado, argued for *The Cosmopolitan Railway Compacting and Fusing Together All the World's Continents,* the title of his 1890 book—a railroad that would connect western America with eastern Siberia through the Bering Strait, linking up with the then still nonexistent Trans-Siberian Railway, leading westward to Europe. Gilpin argued that consequently not only would Denver be "the center of the world" but, more important, this American-Russian railroad would be "the link in the great center of progress" through which the great peoples of the globe would be connected.)

THAT WAS AMERICAN PRACTICAL IDEALISM in one of its typical forms. Political idealism, and its subsequent winter of discontent, have at times led to misinformation and to misleading images of the two peoples—as, for example, in *Life* magazine's Picture of the Week in 1942, when a full-page photograph of Lenin was printed with the caption "This Was Perhaps the Greatest Man of the Century"; ten years later the editorial pages of *Life* were preaching a crusade against communism and Russia. During the twentieth century another element complicating American-Russian relations was the increasing influence of ethnic groups advocating this or that American policy toward Russia as well as attempting to influence the perception of Russia by Americans. As early as 1905 the czar's relatively liberal foreign minister, Count Witte, felt compelled to travel to the United States in order to assuage the anti-Russian sentiments of the press and of other people, caused by their memories of the often crude mistreatment of Jews and others by the czar's government. Conversely, after the overthrow of the czar and for decades thereafter, many Americans, especially intellectuals (and not just immigrants from Russia or their descendants), nurtured and propagated false and unwarranted illusions about the humane nature of the communist regime in Russia—ideological preferences that, among other things, resulted in the limited but not inconsiderable influence of communists and their sympathizers in American intellectual commerce and at times even in a few places in Washington. Eventually, because of their realization—often lamentably slow—of the brutal (and often anti-Semitic) record of Soviet governments, some of these former sympathizers became extreme anti-communists and anti-Russians, agitating against any improvement of American-Russian relations. The decision of American administrations to include "human rights" on their diplomatic agenda has not always been productive in that regard.

Will Americans rejoice in the humiliation of the once great Russian state? I doubt it; neither American idealism nor American generosity is extinct.

As in the relations of the two states, so in the relations of the two peoples a new phase has now come about, with consequences that are incalculable. Will the American people rejoice in the humiliation of the once-great Russian state? I doubt it; neither American idealism nor American generosity is extinct—to wit, the early and almost instantaneous positive American reaction to Mikhail Gorbachev and his reforms. Will American governments feel compelled, in part because of ethnic pressures, in part because of the dubious principle of "national self-determination," to recognize the independent sovereignty of portions of the erstwhile Soviet Union's new nationalist republics that contain millions of ethnic Russians and that were never even remotely "independent" or "sovereign" in the past? To see a vast portion of the globe torn by protracted civil wars cannot be in the interest of the United States—not of its government and not of its people either.

IN THIS RESPECT IT MAY BEHOOVE US TO turn once more to the past—to the beginning of a now closed chapter of it—and contemplate its then two principal personages, Woodrow Wilson and Vladimir Ilyich Lenin. For a short time, near and after the end of World War I, they seemed not only to preside over two of the greatest powers of the globe but also to incarnate the two major ideas of the century, one standing for global democracy, the other for international communism. The two men died thirteen days apart, in 1924, but years before their deaths they were broken men, and not only physically; Wilson, for one, had been repudiated by the majority of his countrymen. Yet—for such is the irony of history—the ideas of this pale Presbyterian professor-President turned out to be more revolutionary than those of the half-Tatar Bolshevik radical from the middle Volga region. Wilson's propagation of the idea of self-determination helped bring about the destruction of entire empires in 1918, and now, seventy-odd years later, that idea is about to destroy not only some of the very states created by Wilson—Yugoslavia and perhaps even Czechoslovakia, for instance—but possibly the Russian Empire itself. That is still an open question, as indeed is Wilson's place in American history (although he has been admired not only by liberals but by Herbert Hoover, Richard Nixon, and Ronald Reagan), while Lenin's embalmed body will soon be removed from his mausoleum in Red Square, surely for good. Thus not only Wilson's reputation but his ideas seem to have triumphed over Lenin's. But that semblance is false. The ideas, indeed the personalities, of these ephemeral protagonists of the early twentieth century belonged to the nineteenth. Lenin believed that history was nothing but the warfare of classes, and that the Bolshevik revolution would soon be repeated all over Europe. It did not happen. Wilson believed that World War I was a democratic crusade culminating in a League of Nations, the war to end all wars; it led to World War II instead. Both men's views of the world were outdated, and wrong. To think that the United States could—or should—make the world safe for democracy (or, more precisely,

that American democracy could make the world safe) was—and remains—a shortsighted and self-serving idea, as was that of international communism.

ONE HUNDRED YEARS BEFORE 1917 Napoleon, at St. Helena, mused about the prospect of Russia and the United States replacing France and Britain as the greatest powers in the world. Others, seeing the expansion of the United States and Russia into vast empty spaces, inhabited, if at all, by primitive tribes, saw the same prospect. Alexis de Tocqueville, after his visit to the United States, concluded the first volume of his *Democracy in America* with a sudden speculation about America and Russia: "There are at the present time [1835] two great nations in the world, which started from different points, but seem to tend toward the same end. I allude to the Russians and the Americans. Both of them have grown up unnoticed; and while the attention of mankind was directed elsewhere, they have suddenly placed themselves in the front rank among the nations, and the world learned their existence and their greatness at almost the same time.

"All other nations seem to have nearly reached their natural limits, and they have only to maintain their power; but these are still in the acts of growth. . . . The principal instrument of [the Anglo-American] is freedom; of the [Russian], servitude. Their starting-point is different, and their courses are not the same; yet each of them seems marked out by the will of Heaven to sway the destinies of half the globe."

These words of this great visionary were not only prophetic but especially apposite during the Cold War. But they no longer are. I am not alluding only to the present movement in Russia from political servitude to democracy. That may, or may not, last. I am alluding to the fact that the territorial expansion of the American and of the Russian empires is now over. New tides of barbarian invaders, internal and/or external, as well as new kinds of servitude, imposed by technology and bureaucracy, may threaten both, but that is another story, the problem of the future, of the twenty-first century.

Cleaning Up the Environment

Helping the Planet and the Economy

Tension and suspicion have marred relations between the environmental movement and the business community for the past two decades, ever since the greening of America first pricked the nation's consciousness. Environmentalists counted economic growth and corporate dominance as a curse on the planet. Business leaders reviled environmentalists for trying to divert precious capital into pollution control and attempted to lobby the ecological issue away.

Environmental concerns haven't disappeared, of course. In fact, loving the earth has become a Main Street passion. As public demand for a greener world grows, environmentalists have come to realize that their goals are too costly not to involve the cooperation of corporate America. And after spending more than $850 billion cleaning up their pollution over the past 20 years—$72 billion in 1990 alone—business leaders realize that it's frequently less expensive to confront environmental issues before the regulators do.

In the spirit of this reconciliation, the following special report offers five recommendations that will help build a healthy planet without breaking the back of the economy. At the heart of these proposals lies the recognition that competitive, profitable companies are not an obstacle to a clean environment but its very hope.

PUT A PRICE ON POLLUTION

Nobody disputes the need for a clean environment. But the key question in the minds of many is whether we can afford to purify the planet's air and water. Economists say we can—as long as the profit motive is harnessed in pursuit of pollution control.

That old idea is rapidly gaining new acceptance in the corridors of Washington. Last week, Environmental Protection Agency chief William Reilly issued a report listing pressing ecological problems that lend themselves to market solutions. The driving principle behind this study is simple: Government sets broad limits on the amount of pollution allowed for a region or industry and allots permits to firms for their share of that total. Polluters can buy or sell these allowances, so that firms that can reduce a pollutant inexpensively will benefit by selling their allowances to dirtier neighbors. The companies that clean up most cheaply cut pollution furthest; those that find it economically prohibitive to meet pollution standards might less expensively buy up permits from cleaner companies. Already, the nation's few experiments with market environmentalism have saved the economy $1 billion to $10 billion while contributing to the nation's cleanup. Those figures will soar if Congress turns from its old regulatory ways and gives chief executives the opportunity to save money while still protecting the environment.

The bravest experiment in market environmentalism begins later this decade. The Clean Air Act amendments signed by President Bush in November lowered the maximum allowable sulfur dioxide emissions for 111 utilities but gave them the right to trade permits for sulfur dioxide emissions—the major culprit in acid rain. James Geurts, president of General Electric Environmental Systems, says utilities are now requesting his company's best scrubbers, which remove 98 percent of sulfur dioxide from their smokestacks. When those utilities scrub nearly all of their sulfur dioxide, they will have exceeded the government's requirement. With extra sulfur dioxide al-

lowances, they can sell the excess to less-well-scrubbed companies and thus help defray the cost of their newly purchased pollution control equipment.

Under earlier regulations, each utility had to reduce its pollution equally, and there were no incentives to make extra reductions. Economist Paul Portney, of the think tank Resources for the Future, estimates that while under old style regulations utilities could have spent between $7 billion and $8 billion complying with the new sulfur dioxide reductions, the tradable permits will allow them to meet the targets for $4 billion to $5 billion.

Few car drivers ever knew it, but as the EPA was phasing out lead in gasoline during the 1980s, most reaped savings from pollution trading every time they filled up at the pump. Rather than forcing all refiners to simultaneously build equipment for making low-lead gas—a costly proposition—the government instituted lead allowance trading to permit each refinery to make the switch at its own pace. Large firms such as Amoco, which had marketed some unleaded fuels for decades, could easily make the transition, but small oil companies would have struggled to re-engineer their refineries under the government's timetable. Amoco economist Jerrold Levine recalls that when his company was using less lead than federal limits allowed, he would sell millions of permits worth about a penny apiece, each allowing another refiner to add lead to a gallon of gasoline. By 1986, all refiners had changed to producing low-lead gasoline, and permit trading ended. But in that short period of time, lead permit trading had saved the economy some $200 million by trimming some 3 to 5 cents off the price of unleaded gasoline.

James River Graphics of South Hadley, Mass., saves money by trading pollution rights, too, but the commercial coater of papers and films trades with itself. Unlike most plants, which must reduce emissions equally from every smokestack and exhaust vent, James River has special regulatory approval to measure its pollutants as if a big bubble covered its factory site. As long as the total amount of pollution under the bubble is low enough, James River doesn't have to worry what is happening at each individual vent. In 1989, when Charles Quinby, the environmental safety and health manager at James River, wanted to reduce emissions of toxic solvents, he had two options. On one coating machine, he could switch from using coating solvents to a water-based solution, spending $500 for every ton of solvent emissions saved. On his other machines, Quinby could reduce pollution only by installing expensive reclamation equipment at a cost of up to $8,000 per ton of solvent removed. By inexpensively eliminating all solvent emissions from the first machine and leaving the others alone, Quinby reached his overall emissions goals and saved millions of dollars. In a sense, the first machine "traded" its extra pollution savings to the other machines with higher emissions, while average air quality under the bubble improved.

Not every environmental problem has a magic market solution. There are some chemicals so toxic that no firm should be allowed to buy permits for them. And no community wants its stream fouled by pollution rights bought from a factory on another town's river. But where corporations share common air and water, they can also learn to efficiently share the burden of keeping them clean.

MAKE GREEN TRACKS FOR GREENBACKS

As summer approaches, U.S. chemical companies will be laboring to fill out environmental compliance forms. But when these firms have detailed their progress on pollution control, they won't mail the results to federal regulators in Washington. Instead, they will send them to the Chemical Manufacturers Association, which now demands that its members not only meet Environmental Protection Agency requirements but exceed them. Chemical makers who refuse to comply can be asked to leave the association.

The CMA's bold new program exemplifies a sea change in U.S. business. A number of corporations—such as Monsanto, 3M and Du Pont—are betting that those who stay two steps ahead of environmental regulators will stay one step ahead of the competition. No chief executive pretends that pollution reductions yield fast cash. Environmental commitments demand investment upfront and stolid patience as the returns trickle in. But early indications from several companies suggest that this may be a worthy wager. In addition to the public relations value, these companies find that without regulators breathing down their necks, they have the time and flexibility to reduce pollution at the least possible cost. They are discovering that they can save money by preventing pollution early rather than trying to cope with it later. Companies are also learning that by rethinking their manufacturing processes from the ground up, they can not only reduce pollution but also save on labor and raw materials.

Minnesota Mining and Manufacturing began absorbing that lesson early. 3M's Pollution Prevention Pays strategy has saved the company over half a billion dollars since 1975 by identifying more than 2,500 environmental projects that justified themselves on economic grounds. When 3M was considering a new wastewater treatment plant for an Alabama facility, for example, the company first decided to reduce the volume of water pollution it needed to treat by recycling cooling water through the plant. With effluent flow cut in half, 3M built a much smaller treatment plant, saving $320,000 on the project. "Efficient pollution control is not just sticking something on the end of a pipe," says Stephen Harlan, a management consultant with KPMG Peat Marwick.

Companies that cut pollution may also find that they can more easily beat their competitors to market. 3M has learned from experience that manufacturing new products with solvents will always catch the eye of environmental regulators concerned about emissions. In the fast world of consumer marketing, every month spent awaiting EPA authorization to operate a new factory means lost profits. Now, the company avoids that danger by often coating products with safer, water-based solutions. Says Robert Bringer, 3M's top environmental officer, "If we want to be a more flexible company and get products to the market faster, we have to eliminate those materials that are triggering regulations."

AUTO EMISSIONS

BLOWING AWAY SMOG

PROBLEM: After decades of urban pollution-control efforts, almost 100 American cities still fail to pass the environmental protection agency's health standard for ozone. Los Angeles, for example, now has until 2010 to get its dangerous ozone levels down to the federal government's standards. Automobile emissions remain a primary culprit, despite sophisticated emissions-control systems that now add hundreds of dollars to the price of each new car and can remove 96 percent of all hydrocarbons and 76 percent of nitrogen oxides—the primary chemicals that help form ozone.

SOLUTION: Auto emissions must be controlled. But at the present time, consumers have few incentives to buy low-polluting cars. And auto makers have fewer incentives to produce them. One proposal would assess an annual inspection fee for each car based on the tailpipe emissions and the number of miles that have been driven since the last inspection. Forcing people to pay for their pollution could speed development of such alternate fuels as compressed natural gas and could encourage drivers to buy soon-to-be-available electric cars.

As the nation demands tighter controls on toxic emissions, the advantages of going beyond compliance have become even clearer. Bringer says new regulations will force many solvent users in the business of coating paper, plastic and metal to reduce their emissions 90 percent by 1995, a goal that 3M had already planned to reach by 1992. While others panic at the costs of such drastic cuts in emissions, Bringer blithely remarks, "The amendments won't affect us."

The quest to eliminate pollution often helps companies discover that they are unnecessarily squandering raw materials. Monsanto chief executive Richard Mahoney, who in 1988 committed his chemical firm to reducing all pollution by 90 percent by the end of 1992, calculates that wasted raw materials alone cost the St. Louis firm some $150 million a

SOLID WASTE

TAKING OUT THE GARBAGE

PROBLEM: No country in the world can match the United States in producing waste. The average American throws away 4 pounds of garbage a day, and the figure is rising. The refuse overload is not only an environmental problem but an economic one as well, taxing citizens and businesses alike. Of 6,000 dumps currently operating in the nation, half will close by the year 1996 and a combination of stricter environmental standards and not-in-my-back-yard activism is slowing the opening of new landfills. As a result, the cost of dumping a ton of garbage in Minneapolis, for example, has quintupled in the last five years.

SOLUTION: Most local efforts at reducing trash have lost money and bogged down in citizen apathy. But several communities have met with success by making taxpayers pay according to the amount of waste they create. Seattle, for example, charges $9 per month for each extra trash can left at the curb. With this incentive to take advantage of free recycling and to cut down on excess waste, Seattleites now put out 22 percent less trash. At the same time, 36 percent of all trash is recycled, almost triple the national average.

year. When Monsanto executives charged their chemists with reducing the volume of waste left over from the manufacture of the popular herbicide Roundup, the scientists stumbled upon a new formula that is now saving the company $75 million a year in raw materials. The new process cuts pollution by 80 percent, while reducing costs 22 percent.

Frequently, leading-edge companies find that the most effective way to reduce pollution is to spread the word. In 1987, when Joseph Cannon started Geneva Steel in Utah, his coke plant barely met the EPA requirement, which states that at least 90 percent of all coke-oven doors must seal perfectly against leaks. Cannon, concerned about the steel plant's impact on the town's air, asked all of his employees to work toward improving its

track record. The best solutions came not from the corporation's executives or environmental scientists but from blue-collar workers. With redesigned, easier-to-clean door plugs developed by Geneva union employees at the coke plant and a new dedication to carefully cleaning the oven seals, Geneva now boasts perfect seals on 97 percent of the oven doors.

Harlan of Peat Marwick says too many companies entrust their environmental mandates to corporate pollution experts rather than spreading the commitment from the executive suite to the factory floor. "All the people up and down the line have to believe in the environmental program," says Harlan. "Freeing up minds is the lowest-cost way to do it." And a new mindset in corporate America could do as much to save the planet as it does to save money.

SCRUB THE WORLD CLEAN

Often buried in the avalanche of numbers that estimate spending on the environment is the fact that on the other side of the ledger lies a vibrant new industry that manufactures pollution-control devices. A report last month by the McIlvaine Co., a Chicago-based management consulting firm, estimates that the market for desulfurization alone could reach $24 billion in the United States by the year 2002—more than the American semiconductor industry's sales of $20 billion for 1990.

Yet despite these expectations, there are troubling signs that the nation's early lead in environmental engineering may be slipping away as Japanese and European pollution-control firms expand in the global export market. Business and government leaders in the United States now realize that staying ahead in the environmental technology race may require economic incentives that will encourage far more innovation than traditional regulations do.

Regulatory stagnation slowed the U.S. pollution-control industry in the 1980s. As the Reagan administration stalled the advance of government intervention, polluters who had already complied with federal standards were left with little incentive to buy improved scrubbers, catalytic converters and other environmental technologies. For most of the 1980s, U.S. expenditures on pollution-control research and development hovered below spending levels of the late 1970s. As a result, says Jeffrey Smith,

GREENHOUSE EFFECT

COOLING OFF THE WORLD

PROBLEM: Carbon dioxide, much of it from burning oil and coal, in combination with other gases, threatens to change the global climate in the next century. While societies could adapt to gradual warming, many scientists fear the temperature will change too fast, severely disrupting agriculture. At this stage in the industrial age, it is probably too late for nations to reduce their carbon dioxide emissions sufficiently to halt climate change. But many hope it is not too late to slow the process, giving society time to adapt. To do so will require unprecedented international cooperation on environmental policy.

SOLUTION: Many economists agree that the most efficient way to address carbon dioxide emissions is to tax fuels worldwide, according to their carbon content, with coal charged the highest tax, then oil and natural gas. Nuclear and renewable energy sources would require no taxes. How to levy a tax is a more difficult problem. A recent study suggests that taxing carbon at wellheads and mines would heavily favor energy-exporting countries, which would collect the revenues, while taxing at the gas pump would favor energy importers.

executive director of the Industrial Gas Cleaning Institute, the United States lost its lead in the smokestack-scrubber market to Japan and Europe.

Meanwhile, America's international competitors have shown a fierce interest in this rapidly growing business. Japan, for example, is looking to make money because of the widespread concern over global climate change. The trade ministry in Tokyo has drawn up a 100-year plan, which looks at scientific advances that could become crucial to countering global warming. Japanese pollution-control technology has become so sophisticated that many American utilities, to comply with the recently signed Clean Air Act amendments, will find themselves buying scrubbers made by Mitsubishi and Hitachi.

WATER SHORTAGE

LOOKING FOR LIQUID

PROBLEM: California's water shortage has hit so hard that it is difficult to tell which is suffering more, the economy or the environment. One consultant believes that a continuing drought could cost Southern California $25 billion and 400,000 jobs. Los Angeles is considering curbing new construction if the drought deepens. Meanwhile, wildlife suffers as already diverted rivers slow to a trickle and wasteful irrigation practices speed agricultural chemicals into the environment. To make matters worse, costly desalination plants now under consideration threaten to consume an abundance of energy.

SOLUTION: California actually has enough water for most of its needs, but farmers, paying a tenth to a twentieth of the price that cities must pay for their water, have no incentive to conserve. Drowning in almost 85 percent of the state's water, farmers grow such climatically ill-suited crops as rice and cotton. California authorities find it hard to alter these water rights, but more-rational water use will follow if proposals encouraging farmers to sell their subsidized water to cities succeed in Sacramento and in Washington.

The American pollution-control industry has been subject to wild market swings as Washington's regulatory deadlines approach and then pass. But it doesn't have to be this way, say economists. Widespread environmental market incentives would endlessly motivate polluters to search out the most advanced and cost-effective control technologies. Provisions for permit trading in the new Clean Air Act amendments already have American scrubber manufacturers predicting a return to world dominance. Says Bob Conley, president of Pure Air, a Pennsylvania pollution-control venture: "When the system rewards overcompliance, it stimulates the best products."

Ultimately, markets beyond American borders could decide the extent to which the pollution-control industry in this country succeeds. Worldwatch Institute estimates that in Eastern Europe, for example, Poland will need to spend $20 billion, Czechoslovakia $23.7 billion and eastern Germany more than $250 billion over the next 20 years to clean up their ecological disasters. But the sooted tragedy of Eastern Europe serves as more than just a new market for pollution-control devices. It is a lesson as well: that where technology is allowed to fall behind, the environment suffers, too.

LOOK BEYOND THE CORPORATE SMOKESTACK

Even at their desks, the chief financial officers of many industrial firms in Los Angeles feel the effects of smog. Some companies pay hundreds of thousands of dollars a year in pollution taxes. But in smoggy cities like Los Angeles, industry typically contributes only 15 percent of the air pollution. Most of the smog is caused by scattered "nonpoint" sources—cars, bakeries, even barbecue grills—pollution culprits Los Angeles is only starting to confront. Since the beginning of the green revolution, the corporate smokestack has symbolized our national pollution problem. But now that major polluters are cleaning up, less visible sources of environmental contamination loom large. Farms and urban runoff, for instance, account for the major part of all water pollution. Yet the United States in 1987 spent only $779 million on nonpoint water pollution, while spending $34 billion on more-blatant sources of environmental trouble such as factories. The time has come for the nation to focus on this diffuse but dangerous problem, say economists. To do otherwise will hurt both business and the environment. Until the United States addresses these thousand points of blight, says American Enterprise Institute economist Robert Hahn, "we're going to pay a lot more than is necessary to reach our environmental goals."

The residents along the shores of Dillon Reservoir, Colo., are trying a more cost-effective approach. In 1983, they were told that their lake was on the verge of becoming eutrophic from phosphorus pollution. But the only obvious sources of phosphorus, municipal waste-water treatment plants, were already high-tech, award winning facilities. Each extra pound of phosphorus removed from their effluent would cost some $860. An equal amount of phosphorus could be elimi-

DEFORESTATION

KNOCKING ON WOOD

PROBLEM: Roughly a third of all softwood timber in America is harvested from the national forest system, and a significant portion of it is old-growth forest, clear-cut on steep slopes. This process leads to soil erosion, silted rivers and altered wildlife habitat. Besides, some timber cutting from America's forests is subsidized by the National Forest Service, mostly through road building. Though the forest service claims to earn $700 million a year from all timber cutting taken as a whole, the U.S. government consistently loses money on harvests in areas in and around the Rocky Mountains and in the state of Alaska.

SOLUTION: Subsidizing the American timber industry is as offensive to conservatives as clear-cutting the forests is to environmentalists. Though timber representatives argue that the roads create recreational opportunities and logging creates jobs, the Bush administration has advocated a limited, one-year program to eliminate below-cost timber sales in 12 of 156 national forests. More-dramatic proposals likely to be considered this year would eliminate subsidized cutting entirely or reduce the forest service's road-building budget.

nated for an average of just $119, however, by processing water from septic tanks and storm sewers that were leaking untreated into the lake. By hooking up houses to the local sewer system and running storm-sewer water through rudimentary filtration, the Dillon area is saving its reservoir and an estimated $1 million at the same time.

Frustrated with nonpoint pollution in Los Angeles, Unocal spent $6 million to prove that affordable solutions exist. Last fall, the Southern California oil company bought up and junked 8,376 pre-1971 autos—each made before the advent of emissions control—for $700 each. Since these cars, on average, belched out 60 times the pollutants of new autos, Unocal's $6 million effort saved the Los Angeles Basin from an annual 10.7 million pounds of smog-forming hydrocarbons and nitrous oxide as well as carbon monoxide. Unocal figures that to create the same pollution savings at its local refinery, which is already equipped with sophisticated controls, it would have had to virtually eliminate all emissions. And the price tag would have been not $6 million but an estimated $160 million.

STOP FEEDING THE CONSUMER GARBAGE

Hefty trash bag manufacturer Mobil Corp. had to have a twist-tie cinched around its neck before promoting a "degradable" product. But after years of insisting that biodegradable plastics would not solve the solid-waste problem, the company capitulated. In June 1989, it offered its reformulated Hefty bags, positioning the product as a friend of the earth. Within months, however, the tide turned, and environmental groups pronounced degradable plastics to be the sham they are; in dark, airless landfills, virtually nothing degrades. Mobil has returned to its old package, but now is fending off suits in six states over its environmental claim.

Just a few years after the phenomenon suddenly sprouted, green marketing shows signs of wilting. Some companies are avoiding new ecological boasts. Dow Chemical, for example, has withdrawn packaging that identified its HandiWrap as "recyclable." And environmentalists are disenchanted with a large number of the superficial claims that remain. Despite this discordance, many analysts believe that American consumers won't abandon their environmental demands. The greenbacks are enormous for companies that can market products that make a genuine difference for the planet.

But until some order is brought to the wild arena of environmental claims, economists say, both profits and the environment could suffer. The green chaos has prodded businesses to ask the government for help. Last month, the National Food Processors Association filed a petition with the Federal Trade Commission requesting guidelines for environmental claims. The codes would, for example, disallow a package claiming to be "recycled" unless it explicitly lists which elements of the product are recycled and what percentage of their materials are reused. "With no standards or definitions out there, we're wasting a lot of time and money," says Harvard Business School fellow Jeffrey Rayport.

Some companies are finding the safest route is to clear their moves in advance with environmental organizations. After an expensive effort to defuse opposition to its foam hamburger boxes by recycling them, McDonald's last November announced that it would drop the clamshell packaging. The company had come within months of taking its money-losing recycling program nationwide, but that risked spending millions without placating consumers. Now McDonald's is working closely with the Environmental Defense Fund to be assured that when its replacement wrapping, a less bulky film of paper and plastic, is introduced, it will have a green light from environmentalists—for the safety of the earth and for the safety of its profits.

BY DON L. BOROUGHS
WITH BETSY CARPENTER

Credits/ Acknowledgments

Cover design by Charles Vitelli

1. Reconstruction and the Gilded Age

Facing overview—National Archives.

2. Emergence of Modern America

Facing overview—Library of Congress. 41—United Nations
photo. 54, 55—Reproductions from the collections of Library of
Congress.

3. Progressivism to the 1920s

Facing overview—Library of Congress. 79—Reproduction from
the collection of Library of Congress. 99–110—Photographs from
the Collections of Henry Ford Museum and Greenville Village.

4. Great Depression To World War II

Facing overview—U.S. Navy photo. 118, 120—Labor-Management
Documentation Center, Cornell University. 124—The Archives of
Labor and Urban Affairs, Wayne State University. 145, 147—By
courtesy of the authors. 146—War Department, National
Archives, Washington, DC.

5. Cold War To The 1990s

Facing overview—John F. Kennedy Library.

6. New Directions for American History

Facing overview—New York Stock Exchange photo by Edward
Topple.

ANNUAL EDITIONS ARTICLE REVIEW FORM

■ NAME: _____ DATE: _____

■ TITLE AND NUMBER OF ARTICLE: _____

■ BRIEFLY STATE THE MAIN IDEA OF THIS ARTICLE: _____

_____

_____

_____

_____

■ LIST THREE IMPORTANT FACTS THAT THE AUTHOR USES TO SUPPORT THE MAIN IDEA:

_____

_____

_____

_____

_____

■ WHAT INFORMATION OR IDEAS DISCUSSED IN THIS ARTICLE ARE ALSO DISCUSSED IN YOUR TEXTBOOK OR OTHER READING YOU HAVE DONE? LIST THE TEXTBOOK CHAPTERS AND PAGE NUMBERS:

_____

_____

_____

_____

_____

_____

■ LIST ANY EXAMPLES OF BIAS OR FAULTY REASONING THAT YOU FOUND IN THE ARTICLE:

_____

_____

_____

_____

■ LIST ANY NEW TERMS/CONCEPTS THAT WERE DISCUSSED IN THE ARTICLE AND WRITE A SHORT DEFINITION:

_____

_____

_____

_____

We Want Your Advice

ANNUAL EDITIONS:
AMERICAN HISTORY, Vol. II
Reconstruction Through the Present
Article Rating Form

Here is an opportunity for you to have direct input into the next revision of this volume. We would like you to rate each of the 40 articles listed below, using the following scale:

1. **Excellent: should definitely be retained**
2. **Above average: should probably be retained**
3. **Below average: should probably be deleted**
4. **Poor: should definitely be deleted**

Your ratings will play a vital part in the next revision. So please mail this prepaid form to us just as soon as you complete it.
Thanks for your help!

Annual Editions revisions depend on two major opinion sources: one is our Advisory Board, listed in the front of this volume, which works with us in scanning the thousands of articles published in the public press each year; the other is you—the person actually using the book. Please help us and the users of the next edition by completing the prepaid article rating form on this page and returning it to us. Thank you.

Rating	Article	Rating	Article
	1. The First Chapter of Children's Rights		22. 1941
	2. "Master Fraud of the Century": The Disputed Election of 1876		23. Racism and Relocation: Telling the Japanese-American Experience
	3. *These* Are the Good Old Days		24. 'Since You Went Away': The War Letters of America's Women
	4. The Great Oklahoma Land Rush of 1889		25. The Face of Victory
	5. Geronimo		26. The Forgotten War
	6. The Cycle of Reform		27. 'If I'd Stood Up Earlier . . .'
	7. Ellis Island and the American Immigration Experience		28. The Ike Age
	8. Our First Southeast Asian War		29. Trumpet of Conscience: A Portrait of Martin Luther King, Jr.
	9. Anti-Semitism in American Caricature		30. Watergate Redux
	10. Fighting Poverty the Old-Fashioned Way		31. Lessons From a Lost War
	11. The Brownsville Affray		32. The New Indian Politics
	12. George Washington Carver: Creative Scientist		33. How the Seventies Changed America
	13. Woodrow Wilson, Politician		34. Hollow Victory
	14. Angel Island: The Half-Closed Door		35. The Suburban Century Begins
	15. America's Black Press, 1914-18		36. The Disuniting of America *and* The Painful Demise of Eurocentrism
	16. What We Lost in the Great War		37. "Remember the Ladies"
	17. When White Hoods Were in Flower		38. Black and White in America
	18. Citizen Ford		39. America and Russia, Americans and Russians
	19. Media and Morality in the Twenties		40. Cleaning Up the Environment
	20. 'Give Us Roosevelt': Workers and the New Deal Coalition		
	21. Things to Come: The 1939 New York World's Fair		

(Continued on next page)

ABOUT YOU

Name_____ Date_____

Are you a teacher? ☐   Or student? ☐

Your School Name _____

Department _____

Address _____

City _____ State _____ Zip _____

School Telephone #_____

YOUR COMMENTS ARE IMPORTANT TO US!

Please fill in the following information:

For which course did you use this book? _____

Did you use a text with this Annual Edition?   ☐ yes   ☐ no

The title of the text? _____

What are your general reactions to the Annual Editions concept?

Have you read any particular articles recently that you think should be included in the next edition?

Are there any articles you feel should be replaced in the next edition? Why?

Are there other areas that you feel would utilize an Annual Edition?

May we contact you for editorial input?

May we quote you from above?

AMERICAN HISTORY, Vol. II, Twelfth Edition
Reconstruction Through the Present

No Postage
Necessary
if Mailed
in the
United States

BUSINESS REPLY MAIL

First Class   Permit No. 84   Guilford, CT

Postage will be paid by addressee

The Dushkin Publishing Group, Inc.
Sluice Dock
DPG **Guilford, Connecticut 06437**